The rise and decline of the
British motor industry

New Studies in Economic and Social History

Edited for the Economic History Society by
Michael Sanderson
University of East Anglia, Norwich

This series, specially commissioned by the Economic History Society, provides a guide to the current interpretations of the key themes of economic and social history in which advances have recently been made or in which there has been significant debate.

In recent times economic and social history has been one of the most flourishing areas of historical study. This has mirrored the increasing relevance of the economic and social sciences both in a student's choice of career and in forming a society at large more aware of the importance of these issues in their everyday lives. Moreover specialist interests in business, agricultural and welfare history, for example, have themselves burgeoned and there has been an increased interest in the economic development of the wider world. Stimulating as these scholarly developments have been for the specialist, the rapid advance of the subject and the quantity of new publications make it difficult for the reader to gain an overview of particular topics, let alone the whole field.

New Studies in Economic and Social History is intended for students and their teachers. It is designed to introduce them to fresh topics and to enable them to keep abreast of recent writing and debates. All the books in the series are written by a recognised authority in the subject, and the arguments and issues are set out in a critical but unpartisan fashion. The aim of the series is to survey the current state of scholarship, rather than to provide a set of prepackaged conclusions.

The series has been edited since its inception in 1968 by Professors M. W. Flinn, T. C. Smout and L. A. Clarkson, and is currently edited by Dr Michael Sanderson. From 1968 it was published by Macmillan as *Studies in Economic History*, and after 1974 as *Studies in Economic and Social History*. From 1995 *New Studies in Economic and Social History* is being published on behalf of the Economic History Society by Cambridge University Press. This new series includes some of the titles previously published by Macmillan as well as new titles, and reflects the ongoing development throughout the world of this rich seam of history.

For a full list of titles in print, please see the end of the book.

The rise and decline of the British motor industry

Prepared for the Economic History Society by

Roy Church
University of East Anglia

CAMBRIDGE
UNIVERSITY PRESS

Published by the Press Syndicate of the University of Cambridge
The Pitt Building, Trumpington Street, Cambridge CB2 1RP
40 West 20th Street, New York, NY 10011-4211, USA
10 Stamford Road, Oakleigh, Melbourne 3166, Australia

The rise and decline of the British motor industry first published by
The Macmillan Press Limited 1994
First Cambridge University Press edition 1995

Printed in Great Britain at the University Press, Cambridge

A catalogue record for this book is available from the British Library

Library of Congress cataloguing in publication data applied for

ISBN 0 521 55283 4 hardback
ISBN 0 521 55770 4 paperback

CE

Contents

Themes

Among the major manufacturing countries before 1914 Britain was the last to establish a sizeable motor industry; it was also the first to witness its collapse as an independent national enterprise. Whereas until the second decade of the twentieth century the emergence of the industry was relatively slow, production overtook that of other European countries between the wars. For a time the exceptionally favourable conditions immediately following the Second World War perpetuated Britain's lead in Europe as the world's second largest motor manufacturing nation and the biggest exporter of cars and of commercial vehicles.

Even before that time the industry's capacity to generate demand for materials and intermediate inputs from other industries, thereby increasing employment, signalled its potential to become a major force in the economy. After the Second World War the industry's strategic importance to the economy was underlined by its capacity to contribute massively to Britain's balance of trade at a time when foreign, particularly dollar, earnings were vital to the economy. This phase in the industry's development proved to be transitory, for the mid 1960s saw the beginning of a precipitous decline. Britain's 10 per cent share in the car output of the major vehicle-producing countries on the Continent of Europe, in the US and Japan had fallen to half that twenty years later. The American multinational companies (MNEs), Ford and General Motors (through its Vauxhall subsidiary), produced a similar volume of output in Britain to that made by British firms, and dominated sales in the domestic market.

Concern for the adverse impact of decline of an industry

described by an influential parliamentary committee as of 'central significance' to the British economy led to *de facto* nationalization in 1975. Thirteen years later, the 'national champion', formerly British Leyland/BL, the remaining British-owned mass producer of motor vehicles (in which the Japanese firm, Honda, already held a 20 per cent share), was sold by the government. As 'Rover' the remaining skeleton of the British volume car industry became a subsidiary company of British Aerospace, a mixed defence and property conglomerate. Before the end of 1989 the three surviving British luxury car makers, Jaguar, Aston Martin and Lotus, had been sold to the American multinationals, while the car-making division of Rolls Royce was acquired by Vickers, the major military hardware manufacturer. The remnants of British commercial vehicle (CV) manufacturing were acquired by the Dutch firm, DAF, completing the demise of an independent British motor industry. The speed and scale of the industry's decline is one of the most dramatic developments in Britain's post-war economic history.

Except for war and the immediate post-war periods, the volume of goods and passenger service vehicles produced was roughly one-third the number of private cars and taxis; by value the difference was around one half (PEP, 1950, *Table 3*). During the inter-war period commercial vehicle makers were in many cases separate from car manufacturers, but the latter soon became also the largest CV makers, mainly as producers of lightweight trucks. When in 1968 a small manufacturer of specialist commercial vehicles took over the major British car producer to form British Leyland, the success of the CV branch of the industry was increasingly affected by the new company's performance also as a mass producer of motor cars. This survey, therefore, will concentrate mainly on the car industry, and primarily on British-owned manufacturers. It focuses principally on interpretation rather than narrative. We highlight historians' disagreements and assess the validity of sometimes conflicting explanations for international differences since the establishment of pre-eminence in Europe between the wars and the reasons for decline thereafter.

1
The origins of British pre-eminence in Europe

(i) The rise of the British motor industry before 1914

Among the most striking contrasts presented by the early history of the motor industry is the technical success of French metal manufacturers in exploiting German patent inventions which formed the basis of the motor industry during the 1890s. Another is the scale and rapidity with which the industry was established a few years later in the US where in 1903 production overtook that of France. The emergence of a motor industry in Britain was slow by comparison, and was heavily dependent upon developments and the flow of information, imports and components from the Continent. With a few exceptions, notably the engineer, inventor and entrepreneur, Herbert Austin, who built the first all-British four-wheeled car in 1899/1900, company promoters and speculators showed more interest in the new industry than did the major engineering companies (Saul, 1962; Church, 1979). While their rationality in this respect has been questioned (Saul, 1962), in part this is explained by the higher rates of return on capital investment which large engineering companies, possessing the financial resources and engineering capacity to make cars in volume, were achieving from other activities (notably the production of armaments (Irving, 1975). Not until a broad consensus evolved among engineers and public on what constituted dominant motor design did other British engineer-entrepreneurs, many of whom were cycle manufacturers, began to invest in the sizeable production of British-made vehicles (Saul, 1962; Harrison, 1981).

A series of successful company flotations from 1905 reflected in part the resilience of investors following the disturbing and deterrent effects of the activities of financial speculators dealing in the shares of motor and related companies. No fewer than 221 firms entered the industry between 1901 and 1905, of which 90 per cent had either discontinued motor production or ceased trading altogether by 1914 (Saul, 1962, *Table I*). Following the general liquidity crisis of 1907 business confidence returned (Michie, 1981; Lewchuck, 1985a), a recovery which the stabilization in design and the reduction in risk which that implied for investors may have assisted and strengthened (Nicholson, 1983, *3*; Harrison, 1981). The main feature of the dominant design was the basic power train, which incorporated engine, transmission, clutch, drive shaft, differential and axle; these were the mechanical components which generated power and transmitted it to the driving wheels attached to the chassis. This standard form superseded the various three- and four-wheeled vehicles which were little more than tri-cars, quadri-cycles or dog carts. Other dominant design features by this time included column (rather than tiller) steering, front-mounted engine enclosed within an embryo bonnet, seating side-by-side (rather than face-to-face), pneumatic (rather than solid) tyres, and the option of a completely enclosed saloon car. Petrol became the acknowledged preference as the power source (Caunter, 1957).

Slow off the mark, the British industry lagged behind until a sharp rise in production began to close the gap between French and British output. While French production rose by barely one-third between 1909 and 1913 British output increased threefold. In 1913 British car (including commercial vehicle) production had reached 34,000, compared with 45,000 in France, and 23,000 in Germany. The European total, however, was less than a quarter of the output in the US.

Disparity in the size of national production did not mirror precisely the extent of national markets. Ownership density in the US was one vehicle for every 77 people in 1913, a figure derived from 1.26 m in use. The comparable densities in Europe were 165 in Britain, 318 in France, and 950 in Germany (Bardou, Chanaron, Fridenson and Laux, 1982; US Bureau of Census, 1976). Britain, therefore, was the largest market in Europe, to which the French were the major exporters. Much has been made of Britain's lag behind the Americans in the speed and scale of development. Saul blamed British engineers, whose approach to the market, to product development and to production methods he described as having been 'well nigh fatal' (Saul, 1968, *224*). Saul condemned the failure to invest in plant to produce in volume a small, inexpensive car of the kind which by 1910 dominated the American market and was more common in France than in Britain (Saul, 1962). He also criticized the passion shown by British engineers for an irrational pursuit of technical perfection and individuality, the exceptions having been individuals trained abroad. Lack of attention to new production methods, he argued, led to low productivity.

The basic problem is seen to have been the inability of the industry to 'free itself from the older traditions of engineering . . . the most crucial weakness was the failure to realize that the new engineering industries called for a complete change from the old ways of mechanical engineering so as to make full use of the new techniques of production engineering' (Saul, 1968, *224*: 1962). Specifically, Saul contrasted British methods of manufacture with those based on repetitive production and the assembly of interchangeable parts. His criticism was that not only were these processes not widespread before 1914 but that British firms did not organize production in such a way as to exploit the new machinery to the full. In other words, the artisanal craft-based methods of manufacture continued to predominate until 1914 and beyond, whereas the American industry had already been transformed. Interchangeability, advanced division of labour and the assembly of standardized parts along a production line culminated in 1913 with Henry Ford's moving assembly line installed at the Highland Park factory near Detroit.

Finally, underlying these particular production weaknesses was the lack of 'commercial acumen' among those responsible for designing and selling cars (Saul, 1962, *41*). These conclusions have been echoed elsewhere, contributing to a conventional wisdom. Mathias, for example, referred to decision-makers having paid more attention to technical than to market criteria, and added the absence of cost consciousness in most firms to the list of the industry's weaknesses (Mathias, 1983), a gloss on Saul's conclusions which points in the direction of entrepreneurial failure. Are his wide-ranging criticisms valid in the light of subsequent research?

A comparison with the French industry suggests that higher levels of production in France cannot be explained by superior entrepreneurial performance or greater engineering imagination. The trend towards integrated manufacture, which has been attributed to the desire of engineers to make the entire vehicle themselves and to reject standardization, was no less characteristic of French manufacturers (Laux, 1976). Laux's detailed examination of French manufacturers' approach to markets found little evidence of low costs from large-scale production as supposed by Foreman-Peck (1979). Lewchuck argued that vertical integration did not, in any case, preclude standardization. Even by 1905 some of the larger British vehicle manufacturers were using American and British machine tools designed for repetitive manufacture and the assembly of virtually interchangeable components (Lewchuck, 1987). Typically in both countries production occurred in small batches, compared with the sequential flow production system in use in the large American factories. Small batch production involved a division of work between several gangs of workers who moved along a row of stationary assembly stands. Such a system also allowed rectification of defects by hand in product or jig design and fixtures. Whereas Saul took this as evidence of conservatism Lewchuck emphasized the British system's flexibility, suited for factories characteristically producing a variety of models for a limited and socially stratified market (Saul, 1962; Lewchuck, 1987). Lewchuck has also challenged the blanket condemnations of British compared with American productivity. His comparison of the productivity of British and American manufacturers making similar kinds of vehicles showed little difference, although the estimates which were the basis for the comparison were few and may not have been representative (Lewchuck, 1987).

As for the superiority of French-trained engineers, Laux found that barely one-fifth of the leaders of the French motor industry received a 'high-class education' in engineering. It is also evident that their approach to manufacturing methods was similar to that employed by their British counterparts. Furthermore the favourable French balance of trade in motor vehicles cannot be explained by superior marketing, for the large market for French cars in Britain was developed primarily by British agents (Laux, 1976). The larger British and French firms typically supplied a variety of models at prices which the rich, the professional and business classes could afford. An emphasis on technical design and quality, 'fit and finish', rather than price competition, was characteristic of the motor trade in both countries until shortly before the war (Church, 1981). Indeed, the absence of striking differences between the strengths and weaknesses of the supply and quality of the factors of production and the extent and characteristics of the market in the two countries suggest that the critical factor explaining the more rapid early development of the French industry may have been a chance competitive advantage. This was secured in 1888 when Gottlieb Daimler approached French metal-manufacturing firms with a view to their becoming the first to manufacture his patent petrol engine, and so initiate an industry based on the internal combustion engine (Nubel, 1987).

After the initial pioneering phase of the motor vehicle, the lag of British and French production behind that in the US and the contrasts in methods and approach cannot be explained without reference to the enormous difference in the size of internal markets. The levels and distribution of real income, and a social geography and rail density which by the automobile age had given Europe close and efficient communication systems both within and between towns and cities, were key differences. They were important factors which shaped entrepreneurs' perceptions of the market and the types of vehicles that could be sold. On the eve of the First World War the high productivity of Ford's American plant was based on economies of scale from production in large volume, interchangeable parts, special-purpose machinery and flow production, combined with a disciplined, highly-paid labour force. In 1913 Ford produced over 200,000 units, compared with some 5000 by Peugeot, the largest French manufacturer, and 3000 by the Wolseley Motor Company, the largest British car maker (Bardou *et al.*, 1982). The capital investment required to produce on an American scale, however, was justified only if it seemed possible to those in the industry, or to newcomers, that vehicles could be sold in such numbers and at a profit.

Perceptions of market possibilities began to alter both in Britain and in France shortly before the First World War, evidence of which is the repositioning by some manufacturers who began to build cars to sell within a lower price range than hitherto. In

Britain the catalyst was Henry Ford who was persuaded by Percival Perry, formerly an importing agent selling Ford cars in England, to establish a branch. Tax advantages explain why in 1911 the branch, opened in 1909, was replaced by the Ford Motor Company (England), wholly-owned by the parent company. The assembly of Model T cars from imported kits began at Trafford Park near Manchester in the same year (Wilkins and Hill, 1964). The price of the Ford Model T Runabout was £135, and the Tourer £150. Designed to suit American road conditions in rural and urban America, to travel long distances, and to be within the purchase range of farm and business users, both were regarded by the British press as unattractive 'cheap and nasty' vehicles. Built with high horsepower and a slow-speed engine, the Model T could achieve smooth running without requiring the level of technical precision in the machining of parts that was needed in constructing the typically high-speed engines used in British cars (Wilkins and Hill, 1964; Saul, 1962).

The Model T proved successful in the British market because of its low price, roughly 25 per cent cheaper than the Morris Oxford. This was the 'popularly-priced' car introduced in 1913 to compete with Ford by the British car maker, W. R. Morris, whose recently established company was later to become Britain's largest car producer (Overy, 1976). The high productivity of American parts suppliers incorporated in the knocked-down kits dispatched from Detroit gave Ford an important cost advantage derived from large-scale production for the huge American market. Combined with Ford's highly efficient assembly plant at Trafford Park, Ford virtually created and dominated the cheap market for motor cars before 1914. Estimates of the sale of cars in the price range £200 and below, regarded by contemporaries as below the luxury and semi-luxury threshold, suggest that the 7310 Ford cars sold in 1913 accounted for more than 60 per cent of the total in that price range (Church, 1982).

While a handful of well established, though small, manufacturers ventured into the lower segment of the market from 1912, the major British entrant into the popular car market was a newcomer, W. R. Morris. Like most other car makers his origins were in the cycle trade, although whereas the founders of most firms which survived into the 1930s had some knowledge of engineering,

Morris was essentially a mechanic with an innovative inclination combined with a willingness to take risks. In 1912 the newly formed W. R. M. Motors began to prepare for the low-cost volume production of cars aimed at a popular market. The starting capital for this venture was £1000, which was supplemented by financial backing from the Earl of Macclesfield. Morris moved against the trend towards vertical integration by assembling cars entirely from components built by specialist suppliers on contracts, the system widely employed in the cycle industry. This strategy enabled him to exploit the human and physical capital resources of the engineering trade, to take advantage of their economies of scale, and to expand rapidly without the need for large capital expenditure (Andrews and Brunner, 1955; Overy, 1976).

The price of the Morris 8 h.p. Oxford basic model, first sold from a blueprint at the Motor Show in October 1912, was £175, enabling it to compete with the handful of other British cars aimed at the same market made by the Singer, Standard and Hillman Motor companies. Built to conventional high European standards of materials and finish, the Oxford incorporated a multi-cylinder engine of low horsepower, high speed and high efficiency. In order to compete with Ford, however, Morris planned a second model, the Cowley, lower in horsepower than the Oxford and lower in price. To meet his requirements for supplies of low-cost components in large volumes to make possible large-scale, low-cost assembly, Morris turned to the US, but his plan to commence volume production in 1915 was checked when war intervened (Andrews and Brunner, 1955).

(ii) War and its aftermath: gains and losses

Historians disagree on the effects of the First World War on British industry. Some have stressed the stimulus which virtually compelled British firms to adopt the production methods already widespread in the United States. Others have emphasized the damage caused to the economy by postponing the transfer of resources from the production of traditional goods to the manufacture of new products, notably consumer durables, thereby delaying structural change (Richardson, 1965; Alford, 1981).

Effects on the motor industry were both positive and negative. War conditions restricted the demand for cars at a time when Morris was poised for mass production. The McKenna tariff introduced in 1915, imposing a $33\frac{1}{3}$ per cent *ad valorem* duty on cars and components, was intended to limit the import of an item 'extensively used solely for the purpose of luxury' and to save shipping space (Plowden, 1971, *110*). One effect was to eliminate Morris's potential cost advantage over other British manufacturers by cutting off high-productivity American suppliers. Another was to accelerate the substitution at the Ford factory of parts made in Britain for those hitherto imported from the parent company. When it became clear that the tariff would remain in place after the war Ford's policy from 1920 was to move towards local manufacture entirely. By 1924 Ford was countering a 'Don't buy American' campaign by publicizing that Ford cars assembled at Trafford Park were 92 per cent British built, though at that time the Ford factory at Cork was a major parts supplier (Wilkins and Hill, 1964).

Alford stressed the gains in efficiency resulting from the stimulus war production gave to the adoption of interchangeable parts (Alford, 1986). The enforced learning experience of munitions manufacture did benefit Morris, but some other larger, longer established car producers already possessed considerable experience of the use of American special purpose machinery, interchangeability, and production with fewer skilled workers. Moreover, those large manufacturers, such as Austin and Wolseley, who supplied aeroplanes, armoured vehicles, ambulances and lorries for the war effort could learn less from the limited production runs normally required for these items. They also found difficulty in applying techniques used to manufacture shells to the production of immensely more complex motor vehicles after the war (Lewchuck, 1987; Church, 1979).

Of critical importance for post-war development was the effect of using standard jigs and tools and the subdivision of processes into simple tasks. This allowed semi-skilled, usually female, labour to be employed in the place of skilled male fitters (Andrews and Brunner, 1955). While this trend was present in car plants before 1914, war accelerated the progressive dilution of labour. Facilitated by the intervention of the Board of Trade in agreement with the Engineering Employers' Federation and the trade unions, jointly represented on a committee of production, employers were free to introduce or extend dilution for the duration of the war. The learning experience of how machinery might be used to deskill large elements of the production process, at least outside the body shops, was to affect employers' approach to manufacturing methods. It also affected the nature of managerial control after the war. The Pre-war Practices Act envisaged that one year after hostilities ceased job controls hitherto exercised by the various craft unions would revert to managers. In fact the effects of dilution were to prove permanent and fundamental to production and labour management (Cole, 1923).

War contracts allowed Morris not only to more than double the size of his Cowley factory and to install modern machinery financed by government, but also to develop a circle of subcontractors and build up a larger, better-trained workforce. The stock of American parts acquired in 1915 permitted car production to continue, albeit at low levels, throughout the war, when many of the technical problems affecting both product and production were solved (Overy, 1976).

While for some firms the enforced learning experience of munitions production proved beneficial, some of the largest car manufacturers suffered adverse effects resulting from the very large expansion of premises and plant not easily converted to peacetime use. Whereas Morris's factory merely assembled parts for munitions, manufacturers such as Austin and Wolseley found themselves with large purpose-built factories which involved heavy capital expenditure and delay in resuming car production after the war. Austin's works manager declared that during the war the size of the workforce at Longbridge rose from 2000 to 22,000. He described the plant as it existed in peacetime conditions in 1918 as 'of an entirely useless character for its needs' (Church, 1979; Lewchuck, 1987). The evidence suggests, therefore, that even within a single industry war affected different firms in diverse ways.

In the longer term, however, all were affected by the protection offered by the McKenna duties which, with a brief interruption in 1924–5, were retained for nearly 50 years (pp. 13–17). War was also the catalyst which led to a reversal of Ford's dominance of the British market. When the war ended it became clear that Henry

Ford wished to operate Trafford Park as no more than a branch, leaving little scope for local initiative. Perry was in poor health following his major wartime role in the Ministry of Munitions, which he had combined with managing the Ford Motor Company (England) while he was also at odds with his pacifist employer, Henry Ford, and other senior managers in Detroit. This was the combination of circumstances which precipitated Perry's forced resignation as managing director. Henry Ford's decision to replace him with American managers was to have serious consequences both for the American company and for the development of the British industry in which in 1913, on a rapidly rising curve, Ford accounted for roughly 20 per cent of the industry's total output (Wilkins and Hill, 1964).

The immediate post-war conditions brought chaos to the vehicle market. There was a decline in private motoring during the war, due partly to the diversion of productive capacity to munitions and partly to restrictions on the importations of cars, except under licence. These, in addition to the tariff, created a pent-up demand (Church, 1979). The demonstration effects of the military use of vehicles seem to have contributed further to this demand. These influences, to which was added the removal of petrol restrictions, produced a climate of expectancy and optimism among would-be consumers and potential suppliers alike. The mood of the time can be gauged from the crusading motto, coined by the British Motor League, of 'Motoring for the Million' (Plowden, 1971). Despite the tariff, imports were sucked in mainly from the United States (Miller and Church, 1979). Soaring car prices stimulated adaptation of the plant of pre-war car-making firms and led to entry into the industry of a host of new producers (Maxcy, 1958).

Erstwhile general engineers, garage proprietors and such unexpected aspirants as the Manchester Cooperative Wholesale Society were among those in 1919 who announced plans for production on a scale reflecting little more than inflated expectations, which quickly proved to be illusory. The *Economist* referred to the many new companies, never having made a single motor vehicle, simply acquiring empty premises, issuing prospectuses illustrated with cars and containing generous profit estimates, whose expectations outran the economic realities of the trade. Between 1919 and 1920, 40 new makes of car were offered on the market (Plowden,

1971), but the principal beneficiaries of the overheated market were the high-productivity producers in the United States which, despite the tariff, were responsible for most of the 34,000 units shipped to Britain during the hectic post-war boom (Miller and Church, 1979).

Many of the new British entrants were unsuccessful and few survived. The expanded capacity and flood of imports sparked off cut-throat competition when depression in the wider economy was transmitted to car sales, bringing about the deepest depression the industry was to experience before the Second World War (Miller and Church, 1979). This was a critical period, when the industrial structure changed from one of intense competition consisting mainly of a large number of small firms possessing a high mortality rate to one dominated by a few relatively large firms with a comparatively low mortality. The number of car-producing companies fell from 88 in 1922 to 31 in 1929, by which time the industry was dominated by only three, all British, companies: Morris Motors, Austin and Singer, which together accounted for 75 per cent of car production in Britain (Maxcy and Silberston, 1959).

(iii) The framework of protection: demand at home and overseas

Critics of the industry's performance who have compared the scale of British production and density of car ownership with those in the United States have concentrated either on supply factors or those affecting demand. Later we shall consider the determinants of supply, but in sections (iii) and (iv) we shall first discuss the effects on demand of factors external to firms, followed by a consideration of the character and consequences of corporate marketing strategies, particularly the extent to which they may have restricted demand.

The principal determinant of the demand for cars, from first time purchasers, from those replacing a vehicle, and from buyers of second-hand cars, has been the level of consumers' incomes. The second most important factor has been the price of cars in relation to general price levels in the economy (Maxcy and

Silberston, 1959). The pent-up post-war demand for vehicles sucked in imports, presenting a serious threat to British manufacturers in the process of adapting plant to peacetime production. The request by the Society of Motor Manufacturers and Traders (SMMT) that the McKenna duties should be extended, at least until the end of 1920, was formally rejected by the Board of Trade, yet no move was made to remove the duties (Plowden, 1971). The onset of the industry's worst depression of the interwar period in 1920–1 seems to have been further justification for inactivity on the part of the Board of Trade (Plowden, 1971). Virtually by accident a temporary measure aimed at checking luxury consumption in wartime became a protective framework which was to have a major effect on the subsequent history of the industry.

The duties were retained, with one brief suspension in 1925, throughout the interwar period, becoming consolidated within the general tariff structure in 1938 and remaining unaltered at the $33\frac{1}{3}$ per cent level until 1956. From 1926 those duties also applied to commercial vehicles. From the standpoint of manufacturing efficiency, the importance of the tariff lies in its possible effect on the size of the market by choking off imports. In a broader context Richardson dismissed the effects on British industries of the general tariff on imports introduced in 1931 as having been insignificant (Richardson, 1961). However, Capie's calculations of effective protection rates, a concept which gives expression to the margin of protection on value added in the process of production rather than simply on the price of the product, led him to draw a different conclusion. Moreover, his estimates showed that the tariff's effect in reducing import penetration was greater in the case of motor vehicles than for any other product category (Capie, 1983). An indication of the degree of effective protection enjoyed by the car industry is the jump in the share of net imports in home sales from 15 to 28 per cent during the short-lived experiment in free trade in 1925 (Miller and Church, 1979).

Foreman-Peck emphasized a further effect of the tariff in enabling the industry to achieve lower costs and prices as a result of economies of scale by the large producers, Morris, Austin and Ford (Foreman-Peck, 1981a). This was undoubtedly true for Morris and Austin, but managerial failure during the 1920s, and later large excess capacity at the new Dagenham plant throughout the 1930s, suggests that scale economies for the American subsidiary were illusory before the Second World War (Wilkins and Hill, 1964). Between 1924 and 1934 the SMMT index of car prices dropped from 100 to 52; in 1938 the figure was 49, but this represented an absolute price which was 30 per cent above that of the average car in the US (Rhys, 1972).

The tariff contributed to the persistence of this differential, though the effects of the tariff may be interpreted differently in each of the two decades, mainly because of the transition from a stage of 'initial demand', which lasted until the late 1920s, to that of a 'mature market' which developed after the slump. By initial demand is meant the stage when consumers who could afford to buy were persuaded that motor vehicles had reached a level of development at which ownership seemed to be desirable. The stimuli to demand during this phase were product development, publicity and communications, and the widespread practice of instalment buying (Maxcy and Silberston, 1959). Elasticities of income and price (or motoring costs as a whole) were likely to have been less important in this stage than the elasticity of product improvement – the propensity to reallocate existing incomes to cars as their reliability improved (Maxcy and Silberston, 1959; Miller and Church, 1979). During this phase the tariff enabled the infant volume car industry to establish itself on a competitive basis within the home market, where manufacturers lowered costs and prices to compete with each other.

It seems doubtful whether price elasticity is central to an explanation for the rapid growth in car sales and production during the twenties. Home sales reached a peak in value in 1925 which was exceeded again only in 1936 and 1937. However, a steep fall in car prices between 1925 and 1929 saw a drop in sales to first-time buyers. This suggests that even large real price reductions failed to induce enlarged consumption in the late twenties (Miller and Church, 1979) and that from this period changes in real income became the key to the level of demand. The industry had reached the stage envisaged by W. R. Morris in which ownership would percolate down 'the pyramid of consumption' and new purchases would become less stable (Andrews and Brunner, 1955).

The contrast with growth in the 1930s is obvious; the real

Table 1 *New car registrations by horsepower 1927–38 (percentages)*

	1927	1930	1934	1938
Less than 8 h.p.	16	27	23	30
9 to 12 h.p.	34	26	51	48
13 to 16 h.p.	33	32	17	11
17 and above	16	15	9	11

Source: PEP (1950), Table 17.

average value of new cars purchased between 1932 and 1937 fell by only 8 per cent whereas new-owner sales rose more than threefold. This suggests that the minimal fall in prices was more than compensated by the rise of middle-class real incomes after the slump, when the great engine of income elasticity came into operation. At the same time, the dramatic shift in the structure of sales favouring cars of up to 10 h.p. points to consumers' sensitivity to annual running costs, which in the 1930s might be one-third of the original purchase price of a car of 8 h.p. (PEP, 1950; Bowden, 1991) (see Table 1). In the sense that new car sales came to depend primarily on replacement rather than first-time purchases, a phase of 'mature demand' was reached in the 1930s (Maxcy and Silberston, 1959; Miller and Church, 1979). Nonetheless, throughout the 1930s car ownership continued to be a middle-class phenomenon, for the price of even an average family car could be compared with semi-detached house prices in some provincial towns (Bowden, 1991).

It seems possible that by keeping prices higher than they might have been otherwise the tariff checked home demand, preventing prices from falling to levels at which elasticity affected sales to lower-income first-time buyers. For two reasons this hypothetical relationship is at least open to debate. First, the main imports in the 1920s were American cars with substantially higher running costs than British-built vehicles. Second, the tariff was not the sole measure affording protection.

The effects of taxation in protecting the industry are disputed, as are its consequences for exports and for the level of home demand. Taxation on car ownership and use in Britain was a flat rate annual tax and a duty on petrol, and it is the former which has been the subject of disagreement, both among contemporaries and historians. The horsepower tax, as it became known, took its description from the formula used for the annual tax on cars introduced in the budget of 1909 to raise revenue intended to contribute to the financing of road-building and improvement (Plowden, 1971). Based on a vehicle's piston diameter multiplied by the number of cylinders in the engine, the initial formula devised by the Royal Automobile Club (RAC) in 1906 was intended originally to guide potential buyers when comparing prices, at a time when the power of the engine was closely related to cylinder capacity. The effect of using the formula for tax purposes, with which the representatives of the motor trade and industry concurred, was to tax high-powered, high-rated cars (according to the equation) more heavily than others. This meant that cars with engines of equal cubic capacity were taxed more heavily if the piston area of their engines was larger.

On its introduction the rates charged rose with horsepower, though not proportionately. In 1920, however, the decision to adopt proportionality increased the progressiveness of the tax, which was fixed at £1 per horsepower. Comparisons between the incidence of tax on British models of different horsepower revealed relatively modest differences, for example adding 1s. 2d. per week to the running costs of a 12 h.p. compared with one of 8 h.p. (Maxcy and Silberston, 1959). By comparison with the Model T Ford, however, rated at 22.5 h.p. under the RAC formula, the weekly difference was 4s. 1d. Whereas before 1920 the Model T paid £6 6s., the new figure was £23 (the same for a Rolls Royce Phantom which was several times more expensive) adding roughly 10 per cent to its 1921 price (Plowden, 1971). In this way, apparently by historical accident, British cars received an advantage over American imports the specifications of which attracted high rating and tax (Maxcy and Silberston, 1959).

Any suggestion that the tax created the British small, high-performance light car which dominated sales and production in Britain between the wars (Wyatt, 1968) is without foundation. Not only did its origins precede the introduction of the tax, but the typical engine design in France and in Germany (where no vehicle tax was payable) was similar to that in Britain. So too was the structure of sales in those countries. European road conditions, consumer preferences and manufacturers' approach to production and the market, rather than taxation, are the factors which help to explain Anglo-European differences in vehicle design (Plowden, 1971).

It has been argued that in one respect the horsepower tax was ineffective and in two others detrimental to the industry's progress. Bowden concluded that even as a protective measure the tax was a failure. The evidence adduced in support of this view is Ford's 20 per cent share of the British market in 1937 (Bowden, 1991). This, however, consisted of cars manufactured in Britain after Perry had finally persuaded the Ford management to produce cars designed specifically for the British market and therefore avoid the discriminatory effect in the horsepower tax (Wilkins and Hill, 1964). It marked the introduction of Ford's first model containing a high-speed engine, small cylinder bore and low horsepower, manufactured in its entirety at the Dagenham plant. It was also a reassertion of British market imperatives by Sir Percival Perry, reinstated in 1928 as the managing director of Ford in England, whose dismal record in Britain since his departure in 1918 he was reappointed to reverse (Wilkins and Hill, 1964).

The short-lived rise in imports from North America following the tax reduction in 1935 suggests that the horsepower tax did add somewhat to the protection afforded by the duties. Imports remained, however, at low levels. In 1937 they represented less than 6 per cent of total car sales in Britain, higher than in previous years since the post-war boom in 1920, and mainly the result of dumping on the British market by Germany and Italy (Miller and Church, 1979). A highly protected home market was supplemented by Imperial Preference, which from 1938 gave British producers an advantage over their European competitors. In that year 97 per cent of British car output was sold in protected markets, either in Britain or in the Empire. The trade in commercial vehicles reveals a sharp reduction of imported American vehicles beginning in 1926, a consequence of the extension of the McKenna duties to commercial vehicles in that year. From 1930 both Ford and General Motors (through its Vauxhall subsidiary) manufactured CV chassis in entirety in Britain (Miller and Church, 1979). What is clear from the surge of imports that occurred when the tariff was suspended briefly in 1925 is the inadequacy of the tax alone in providing effective protection from superior American productivity.

Contemporaries criticized the tax not only because of its effect on car prices but for providing a disincentive to the production of large-engined cars of the American type which were popular in potentially important export markets, mainly within the Empire. This was also the conclusion of the National Advisory Council in its 1947 Report, which led to the replacement of the horsepower tax based on cylinder capacity only (NAC, 1947; Plowden, 1971). While accepting that the tax did impose some bias towards low-powered cars, Maxcy and Silberston concluded that it was less important as a hindrance to exports than such factors as income and the nature of terrain (Maxcy and Silberston, 1959). Manufacturers' views differed during the late 1920s. By this time the American import penetration had been checked, partly by the tax and partly by the reintroduction of the duty on petrol in 1928 which raised the running costs of American-built vehicles.

Some manufacturers conceded that their own model designs had been influenced by the tax while others denied its importance (Plowden, 1971). Engine type in British cars was not the only cause for complaint from Australia, one of Britain's best export markets at that time. Excessive prices, the lack of a standard wheel track and too little ground clearance were added to the criticisms of underpowered engines unsuitable for Australian road conditions (Plowden, 1971). These complaints strengthen the view that other factors were more important in explaining export performance.

A further criticism of the tax, reduced by 25 per cent in 1935, was that the level of tax reduced home consumption and thereby reduced the possibility for economies of scale in the industry. One calculation has shown that even after the reduction direct tax could represent 36 per cent of the total burden of car taxation, including petrol tax and insurance. The average tax per 1000 c.c. was eight times that in the US, nearly twice that in Germany and 50 per cent greater than in France (Bowden, 1991).

The rise in car sales in the home market which followed the tax cut in 1935 has been interpreted as evidence of the retardative effect of tax-inflated car prices. It is for this reason that Bowden adversely contrasts motor taxation policy in Britain with the various tax concessions introduced by the German government from 1933, which were intended to stimulate car purchase.

Bowden condemned the British government's fiscal stance as having been 'particularly unenlightened' because of the adverse effects on the demand for cars (Bowden, 1991, *258–60*). By contrast the principal aim of the German government's *Motorisierung* policy, of extensive road-building, fiscal concessions and encouragement to enrol in the National Socialist Car Corps, was to stimulate employment (Overy, 1975; Blaich, 1981; Reich, 1990). Britain, on the other hand, neither experienced comparable depths of depression nor, by European standards, low car density.

Car ownership in Germany almost doubled between 1934 and 1938, although (as was the case in Britain) cars of medium size accounted for most of the increase (Blaich, 1987), which cautions against seeing the price, including tax, of the cheapest car as the key to the level of demand. Even after the tax reduction the number of cars in use per 1000 population in Germany reached only 19, compared with 42 in Britain and 41 in France. Although the Second World War was to postpone the realization of wide car ownership in Germany, the key in the long term was the 'people's car'. This was the outcome of a fertile collaboration between the accomplished car designer Ferdinand Porsche and Adolf Hitler, who ordered the Labour Front to arrange for the design of a low-priced family car for mass production. Although Porsche, to whom it fell to achieve this objective, had long been working towards a similar end, the impetus provided by Hitler intensified the focus, hastened the process, and ensured the funding to ensure a rapid and successful outcome. This was the origin of the post-war Volkswagen 'Beetle' (Overy, 1973; Blaich, 1987).

Historians' assessments of the industry's interwar performance range from failure to qualified success. Alford compared per capita car ownership figures in 1938 for Britain with the much higher ones of the United States, implying a marketing failure by the British industry (Alford, 1972, 1981). Like others he dwelt especially on the backwardness of the industry by comparison with that of America. There, the sheer scale of standardized production enabled Ford, producing about half a million Ford V 8s in Detroit, to deliver in Europe at a price 30 per cent lower than the price of the same model manufactured at Dagenham, where fewer than

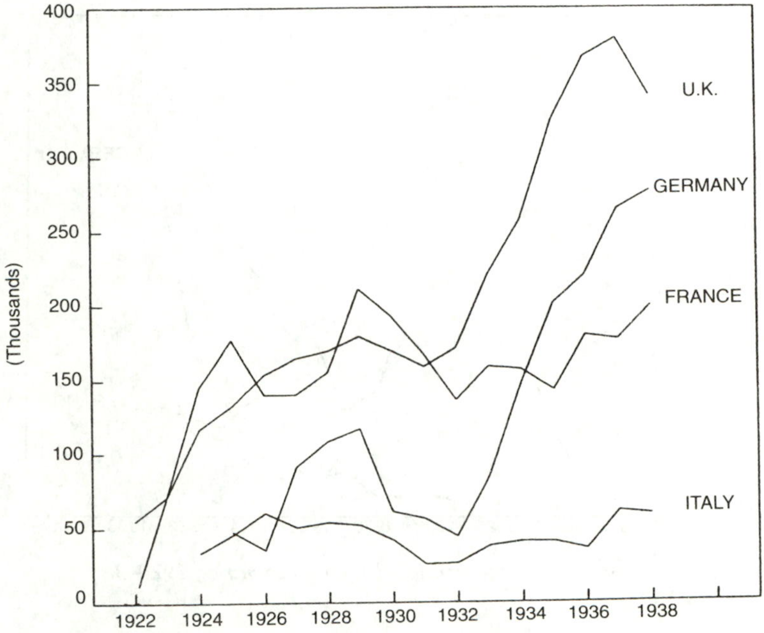

Figure 1 *Car production in Europe, 1922–38*
Source: SMMT

4000 were produced in a year (Rhys, 1972). Other historians, while not disputing the facts of Anglo-American comparisons, have questioned the usefulness of choosing the United States as a comparator. They argue that the American industry had evolved within a market of such contrasting size, in terms of population, income, geographical distances and terrain, and where fuel was abundant at low cost, that superiority offers no surprise (Church, 1981; Bowden, 1991). By virtually every criterion the British motor industry failed when compared with the United States. But by comparison with European competitors the inter-war period saw manufacturers in Britain catch up and surpass French production in 1930, retaining an overall lead in Europe until 1956 (see Figure 1).

The disparity in car ownership between European countries also narrowed, though it was not until 1963 that Britain achieved the level of 7 residents per car which was the level attained by the

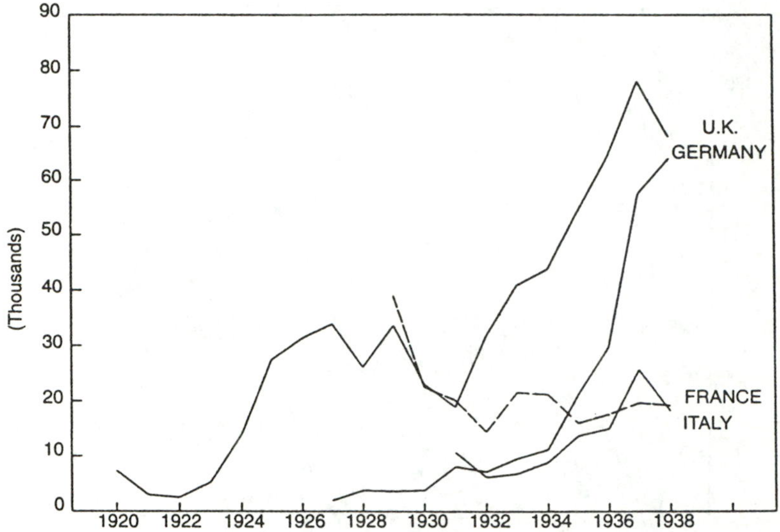

Figure 2 *Car exports, from the principal European countries, 1920–38*
Source: SMMT

United States as early as 1924. That figure was reached in France in 1962, in Germany in 1964 and in Italy in 1967. Market penetration was affected by differences in levels of private car taxation, import duties and credit terms and facilities. These meant that differences in running costs added to already existing intra-European disparities in real incomes and are fundamental in explaining international patterns of ownership density (Foreman-Peck, 1981; Bowden, 1991). Within Europe average real wages were highest in Britain, where the terms and conditions of hire purchase available from the 1920s were also as favourable as anywhere in Europe. Average car prices in Britain were marginally lower than in other European countries (Bowden, 1991).

After the slump Britain became the leading European exporter, accounting for about a half of all cars exported from Europe (including Britain) in the 1930s (see Figure 2). The markets of European car-producing countries were protected by tariffs, which were higher in France than in Britain throughout the period, as they were in the Fascist states in the late 1930s (Jones, 1981). The British industry's 'failure', therefore, was of a similar character to that identifiable in other European countries: an inability or unwillingness on the part of manufacturers to penetrate beyond the upper and middle income groups in a context of overall limited market demand constrained by levels of real income (Church, 1981; Bowden, 1991).

The extent to which this represented a failure on the part of manufacturers is disputed. Historians who have emphasized the industry's shortcomings on the supply side, especially those who have focused on Anglo-American comparisons, are critical of British manufacturers for not having followed the Fordist approach to achieve mass production for a mass market. Others who stress the similarities between European industries, at least until the late 1930s, remain sceptical of the idea that a transformation of the British market so as to resemble the market for cars in the United States was a real possibility.

(iv) Fordism and the British system of mass production: technology and labour

The most detailed exposition of the failure thesis does not, however, begin from such assumptions but instead draws heavily on the labour process literature which stresses the centrality of the institutional context of production. In a major, valuable, comparative study of the industry, and in a series of articles and essays, Lewchuck's interpretation of the dynamics of the British industry since its foundation has offered a fresh and challenging analysis. Its starting point is a model of technical change in which the 'effort bargain' between employer and worker is crucial. The outcome of interaction between employers and workers within a changing institutional context, the struggle between capital and labour is seen to determine which group controls effort norms, to what degree, and with what effects on capital investment (Lewchuck, 1987).

Even before 1914, Ford's sale of American vehicles assembled at Trafford Park achieved considerable success in tapping a hitherto latent market for low-priced vehicles designed to provide basic transport. Lewchuck argued that the consequence of the failure of British manufacturers to follow this strategy proved permanently debilitating and ultimately in the 1970s disastrous (Lewchuck, 1986, 1987). Specifically, Lewchuck was critical of a failure on the part of British manufacturers to adopt a Fordist system of mass production which he considered to be the key which could have unlocked latent mass demand before 1939 as it had in the US.

That system consisted not only of mass production of standardized units but also involved a high degree of direct control over the labour force. This was necessary in order to realize the full potential for large-scale economies by achieving continuous, closely supervised flow production. Both at the Ford plant at Dearborn in the US and at Trafford Park trade unionists were sacked and other workers dissuaded from union membership by the offer of high day wages. Between 1912 and 1932, when the Dagenham plant opened, the Manchester factory employed only non-union labour (Wilkins and Hill, 1964). Dagenham, too, was free from union influence until 1944, when the Labour Minister, Ernest Bevin compelled that company and others, to discontinue anti-union policies (Lewchuck, 1986).

Until that time, at least, Lewchuck presented the 'Fordist system' as one which gave maximum authority to the 'new managerial class'. Systematic, direct managerial control over labour involved strict supervision, which included the monitoring of workers by Ford security police, instant dismissal for trivial offences, unpaid layoffs, and the casualization of some workers. High day wages were systematically and unilaterally fixed by managers on the basis of time and motion studies (Friedman and Meredeen, 1980; Beynon, 1973; Thornhill, 1986). Lewchuck contrasted these conditions with the 'British system of mass production', in which management relied on piecework to determine the pace of work, a system which gave workers the responsibility for setting production targets by linking earnings directly to output – and effort – expended on the job (Lewchuck, 1986, 1987).

According to Lewchuck's account, beginning in 1914 British manufacturers, most of whom were members of the Engineering Employers' Federation (EEF), attempted to create the conditions for a Ford-style industrial strategy. Shop stewards in Coventry, a major centre of engineering employment where the movement was increasing in strength, campaigned against a Fordist strategy of direct control and machine pacing, ultimately forcing employers to concede a degree of control over effort norms by falling back on piecework systems, leaving the decision governing production levels to individual workers. In Lewchuck's interpretation this basic structure of labour management, in which the balance of control lay with labour, was established during negotiations between the Engineering Employers' Federation and the trade unions between 1919 and 1922. These occurred during a period when the trade unions and shop floor committees enjoyed newly gained power resulting from the overheated labour market during the war, and during the immediate post-war boom.

The labour management system adopted by employers was also interpreted as a strategy by which British vehicle makers sought to create a sense of mutual interest between employers and workers (Lewchuck, 1987). From that time, Lewchuck argued, managerial authority in British-owned car factories was less than complete, and the ability of British manufacturers to create an industry comparable in productivity and commercial penetration with their counterparts in the United States was damagingly crippled (Lewchuck, 1986, 1987).

This strong hypothesis has been criticized from several directions. Tolliday argued that when viewed in historical context piecework may be seen to have been as coercive as daywork, and that both direct control and piecework could operate as tight or slack systems, leaving considerable scope for variation in form and effect (Tolliday, 1987a, b). British manufacturers' attempts to extend piecework represented a longstanding drive on the employers' part to gain control over the terms and conditions under which new techniques and practices should be introduced. The achievement of the piecework systems imposed at the time of the major engineering lockout of 1922 was perceived by employers as a victory, winning the right to manage through payment by results (Zeitlin, 1980). A further question that needs to be pursued is whether, after the war ended, organized labour was sufficiently strong to impose and maintain a significant degree of control over work pace and productivity.

Following the national engineering stoppage in 1922 a period of feeble trade unionism allowed employers to apply semi-automatic and automatic machinery and to introduce flow production methods. Ford, which was not a member of the Engineering Employers' Federation, was blatantly anti-union, as were the two other major companies outside the EEF, Morris and Vauxhall, though both also practised a form of welfare to secure workers' compliance (Whiting, 1983; Holden, 1984; Thornhill, 1986). As a member of the EEF, Austin was required to recognize the trade unions, but organization at Longbridge was discouraged and sometimes penalized (Church, 1979). Craft workers, the most highly unionized section of the industry before 1921, were a dwindling proportion of all car workers between the wars, especially outside the body and machine shops. Clayden estimated that by the mid 1930s between 60 and 70 per cent of workers in the industry were semi-skilled, including women and boys; in the volume production factories of Austin and Morris the figure was between 70 and 80 per cent (Clayden, 1987).

Not only did the numerical strength of trade unions decline in spectacular fashion but newcomers entering the industry from outside engineering, and from rural districts around Oxford and Luton, were generally acknowledged to be willing to work hard in return for earnings almost twice the average levels of agricultural workers, and well above those in coalmining from which labour was also attracted (Chapman and Knight, 1953). The minimum weekly wage for labourers on Oxford farms varied between 28s. and 36s., compared with 70s. and 80s. for Cowley car workers, whose hours were slightly less but their employment more irregular (Whiting, 1983). During the 1930s the motor towns attracted huge numbers of migrants from the depressed areas, notably Wales and Scotland, but their militant trade union traditions do not appear to have had an immediate effect on trade unionism in the motor industry. Clayden concluded that the migrants' contribution was in providing organizational experience and leadership once local workers had taken an initiative; they did not play key roles in initiating action (Clayden, 1987).

Their opportunities, in any case, were limited, for unionization remained stunted in a period when semi-skilled and craft workers at Morris Motors were paid at rates some of which were around 30 per cent above the area levels for craft workers agreed between the Federation and the National Union of Vehicle Builders (Whiting, 1983; Thornhill, 1986). High earnings diminished the incentive to organize, as did the threat of victimization by employers, who with few exceptions maintained an anti-union stance. Moreover, those unions which possessed the greatest potential for organizing workers in the motor trades, recruiting mainly from woodworking trades, skilled heavy engineering, docks and transport, accorded the recruitment of motor workers a low priority (Clayden, 1987).

Given the weakness of trade unionism between the wars, therefore, and in spite of its recovery in the late 1930s, Lewchuck's claim that 'British labour would not tolerate a managerial strategy which stripped them of any control over shop floor decisions' (Lewchuck, 1987, *183*), does not seem convincing. The weakness of the trade unions, and the virtual absence of shop stewards from most car factories between 1922 and 1934, not only removed labour's ability to improve conditions but enabled employers to ignore those elements of joint regulation embodied in the 1922 National Agreement between the EEF and the unions. Specifically, whereas mutual agreement between management and labour was required in fixing piece rates, which should be adjusted only when production methods altered, employers proceeded to impose piece rate changes unilaterally, regardless of circumstances other than market advantage (Thornhill, 1986).

How far does Lewchuck's characterization of management–labour relations and production methods at the major motor companies present an accurate picture? And is the 'British system of mass production' a valid explanatory concept? On close scrutiny, the implied contrast between the British and the American system is an oversimplification. The claim that after General Motors took over Vauxhall in 1925 management strategy assumed Fordist characteristics has been disputed by the historian of Vauxhall (Holden, 1984). Not only was the degree of managerial supervision of workers reduced but a bonus payments system was introduced. These formed the basis of management–labour relations at Vauxhall, which were also accompanied by a 'pragmatic welfarism', which included profit sharing, life insurance schemes, sports and social clubs, works outings and social events (Clayden, 1987).

Neither do the largest British manufacturers conform closely to the model. Austin was the one which adopted a piecework incentive system conforming most closely to the model, yet an alternative to Lewchuck's interpretation of its significance is possible. The introduction of bonus incentives payments, which Lewchuck regards as a concession on the employer's part to secure workers' cooperation (Lewchuck, 1987), did elicit increased effort from labour which did contribute to higher productivity. The 'concession' of self-regulation, however, was accompanied by the payment of semi-skilled and some craft workers below district rates, and below the widely accepted notoriously low basic rates for engineering labourers contained in the EEF agreement.

As a consequence, intensive effort became necessary, rather than optional, if piece rate workers were to ensure reasonable earnings. Neither this policy of hard driving through the manipulation of piece rates, nor that of displacing craftsmen by semi-skilled labour, a process which proceeded further at Longbridge than at most other car factories, justifies the terms 'concession', 'cooperation' and 'self-regulation' in describing Austin's labour management. Between 1924 and 1928 heavy investment in mechanization and flow line assembly led to a reduction in the workforce by one-third in a period of rapidly expanding output (Thornhill, 1986). Managerial control between the wars was sustained by workers' compliance which was withdrawn temporarily when rate-cutting went too far. Hence the unusually large strikes, which involved mainly unskilled workers, in 1929, 1936 and 1938. These, together with the large stoppage at Ford in 1933, were triggered in response to rate or wage cuts and accounted for 82 per cent of all days lost through strikes in the industry (Turner, Clack and Roberts, 1967).

At the other end of the British spectrum, Lewchuck characterized the managerial approach at Morris factories as having been 'outside the mainstream of British management thought', where payment by results was combined with direct control and some machine pacing on Fordist lines. Yet at Cowley, as at Longbridge when mechanized lines for axle assembly and for the assembly of chassis were introduced in 1928, the line speeds were controlled by management (Thornhill, 1986; Engelbach, 1927–8).

The managers of British companies did differ from Ford in their use of piece rates and bonus payment, but the differences were those of degree. Furthermore, even if, as Lewchuck argued, the Morris factories were in some respects an exception to the British system of mass production, the model itself becomes more vulnerable to criticism. For throughout the interwar years those plants accounted for at least 40 per cent of the output from the four largest British-owned, volume car-making factories. In any case, within the context of the British market during the interwar years, the drastic decline in Ford's share, which only began to recover in the late 1930s, showed that Fordism was inappropriate. As an approach which was both a marketing strategy as well as a production philosophy it lacked that flexibility which enabled British manufacturers to re-establish their dominance.

(v) The dynamics and limitations of 'personal capitalism'

The failure to adopt a Fordist strategy, the obverse of the 'British system', is also seen by Lewchuck to have been in part a consequence of shareholders' preference for dividends over investment, or as Bowden presents it, 'a tendency to play it safe, for short-term profitability' (Lewchuck, 1985a, 1986, 1987; Bowden, 1991). Chandler has incorporated this version of financial short-termism into his broader model of 'the dynamics of personal capitalism', which he believed to have been the key characteristic of much of British manufacturing industry in contrast with the United States (Chandler, 1990). The motor industry is offered by Chandler as an exemplification of the baleful effects upon investment resulting from the dominance of family firms or by enterprises led by dominant personalities who inhabited owner-managerial structures, which typically distributed a high proportion of profit to the detriment of asset growth.

The financial dimension of the Chandler hypothesis rests almost entirely on Lewchuck's analysis of the profit and dividend policies of motor manufacturers, the basis for his explanation of differential rates of asset growth between British and American vehicle producers (Lewchuck, 1985a, 1986, 1987). It is true that by the 1950s Ford's assets, which in 1929 were below those of either Morris or Austin, had outstripped their combined asset value. Any explanation of the disparate rate of investment which produced such an outcome, however, must take into account the comparable rates of asset growth recorded by Morris and Ford during the 1930s despite the differences in corporate characteristics. The different effects of war on British and American companies is another factor which cannot be disregarded. Similarly, Lewchuck's concern that the capital–labour ratio fell in the 1930s overlooks the complication resulting from rearmament, which beginning in 1936 saw the transfer of motor workers to aircraft production. For this reason the Austin ratios which he used to demonstrate falling labour–capital ratios took no account of several hundred aero workers at Longbridge by 1938 (Thornhill, 1986).

Lewchuck acknowledged that the lack of data does not permit direct comparisons between the financing of British and American firms before 1919. None the less his conclusions have been incorporated in Chandler's robust interpretation of the dynamics of British industrial decline, which further justifies careful consideration of the foundations on which the model was based. Lewchuck argued that whereas British companies enjoyed access to a capital market attuned to, and enthusiastic about, public issues, American firms had to rely on private sources and retained earnings to finance investment. But access to public funds, accompanied before 1914 by risks of fraudulent promotion and financial fluctuation, was not critical to corporate growth. Neither Morris Motors nor Singer, producing nearly 60 per cent of cars in Britain in 1929, sought capital from the Stock Market before the mid 1930s (Saul, 1962; Harrison, 1981; Thoms and Donnelly, 1985; Overy, 1976).

On the basis of a sample of British motor companies' balance sheets for the period between 1919 and 1932 Lewchuck found a relatively low proportion of retained profits (Lewchuck, 1985a). The sample, however, excluded private firms, which unlike public companies were not obliged to submit financial returns to the Registrar of Companies. For that reason Morris Motors was excluded from Lewchuck's list of pre-1926 firms. This is an important omission from any analysis seeking to generalize about the dynamics of the British motor industry, because Morris Motors, which was owned entirely by W. R. Morris (Later Lord Nuffield) until 1936, was retaining an average of 80 per cent of pre-tax profits in the 1920s, partly reinvested but also used to accumulate large reserves (Overy, 1976).

For the period between 1927 and 1951 Lewchuck noted that

Morris retained only 26 per cent of earnings generated (Lewchuck, 1987). Closer scrutiny of the accounts reveals that a break in trend occurred from 1936, which coincided with Morris's first public flotation (Andrews and Brunner, 1955), and the decline of his personal holding to 18.8. per cent. This review of the profitability of Nuffield's businesses does not reveal long-term corporate behaviour which conformed to a particular structure of ownership and managerial control on the Chandler–Lewchuck model. In the context of that model the Nuffield deviance is important because the company was so central to the industry. During the 1920s Morris Motors produced some 38 per cent of all British cars; however, the sports model built by Morris's other car company, MG, added to the larger, more expensive cars produced by Wolseley Motors, acquired by Morris in 1926, increased the percentage to above 40. In 1929 the figure was 51 per cent of cars produced by the 'Big Six', at a time when the industry was virtually a duopoly (Maxcy and Silberston, 1959). Since Britain's largest motor company does not fit easily into the Chandler–Lewchuck model of corporate behaviour, any explanation of the industry's performance which relies on that model invites scepticism.

Reservations also need to be made concerning the financial history of the Austin Motor Company, the second largest British vehicle manufacturer from the late twenties, which emerged from the war crippled by debt and from 1920 heavily geared. Until 1928, therefore, the company paid no dividends on preference shares and none on ordinaries until 1929 (Church, 1979). In contrast with Morris Motors this was a period of immense financial difficulty for Austin which had threatened to bankrupt the firm in 1920/1. Yet it was during the 1920s that the company eventually paid off large debenture loans and invested heavily in re-equipment and reorganization for volume production of a successful small low-priced popular car, the 'baby' Austin Seven. In the 1930s Austin was retaining a lower proportion of profits than in the 1920s, but the company's financial difficulties and heavy investment programmes had left shareholders particularly hungry for dividends during the 1930s (Church, 1979).

A comparison between the proportion of earnings retained by British companies and the competing American subsidiaries reveals a more complex pattern than one consistent with the

Table 2 *Proportion of net earnings retained by 'Big Six' car manufacturers (%)*

	1929–33	1934–8	1947–56	1952–6
Morris	50	25	39	} 68
Austin	33	31	72	
BMC				
Standard	80	40	52	
Rootes			79	
Ford	20	23	79	
Vauxhall	72	42	74	

Source: Maxcy and Silberston (1959), Table 7 and Table 18.

Lewchuck–Chandler hypothesis. At the very least the 'pattern' is ambiguous (see Table 2). Lewchuck interpreted Rover's high-dividend policy in the 1950s as a measure intended to avoid a possible takeover (Lewchuck, 1986). This cannot, however, explain low profit retention throughout the industry in previous decades, for it was not until after the Companies Act of 1948, which required greater disclosure of companies' finances, that predatory bids began to pose threats of unwanted advances from corporate raiders (Hannah, 1983).

How valid is the distinction drawn by Chandler between, on the one hand, those enterprises managed personally or by families which typically resisted the adoption of a modern corporate structure in the pursuit of economies of scale and scope, and on the other those organizations administered by salaried, career managers? The distinction is central to Chandler's model of the dynamics of capitalism, for he argued that whereas in Britain managerial firms were more likely to adopt growth of assets as a major goal, personally managed or family-dominated firms favoured short-termism in the form of 'a steady flow of cash to owners who were also managers' (Chandler, 1990, *390*).

The largest, Morris Motors, was the company most completely under financial and ultimately managerial control of its founding entrepreneur who even after it became a public company in 1936 continued to be the major single shareholder and chairman until the BMC merger in 1952 (Andrews and Brunner, 1955; Sargant Florence, 1961). The ownership of the Austin Motor Company, too, was dominated by its founder until the 1930s. However, his 22.4 per cent holding was dispersed after Lord Austin's death in 1941 so that by 1951 no single shareholder possessed more than 1.4 per cent of the voting equity. The 20 largest shareholdings (which included directors) dropped from 12.4 to 0.1 per cent (Sargant Florence, 1961).

Throughout the entire life of the Rootes Group the company continued to conform to the founder-owning family enterprise dominated by the two Rootes brothers. Even in 1951, and indeed long after, the largest 20 shareholders, but mainly the Rootes brothers, held 55 per cent of all voting shares, of which 34.4 per cent belonged to the chairman and managing director William (Billy) Rootes (Sargant Florence, 1961).

The Standard Motor Company, the other major British motor manufacturer in the 1930s, was also led by a manager who possessed a substantial financial interest in the company. John Black was trained as a solicitor but it was his experience in the army, followed by management of the Hillman Motor Company, which brought him success as the joint managing director of that motor company. After Hillman was taken over by Rootes, Captain Black had joined Standard as the assistant of its founder, Reginald Maudsley, whom he succeeded as managing director after Maudsley's death in 1934 (Thoms and Donnelly, 1985).

In each case the management and control of the major British companies appears to have rested with the founder-owners who have been described as firmly in control of their firms until well after the Second World War (Hannah, 1976; Chandler, 1990). This is undoubtedly true of Rootes until the company ceded control to Chrysler in the 1960s, and of Standard until Maudsley's death in 1934. However, in the two much larger companies the respective managerial roles of Morris (Lord Nuffield) and Sir Herbert Austin had diminished well before the war. At Austin the change began in 1921, when to avoid bankruptcy Sir Herbert reluctantly consented to share the managerial power with two nominee directors put in place by the Creditors' Committee on the advice of the Midland Bank, one an engineering expert in production organization, the other a financial director. This left the founder to concentrate his attention on design (Church, 1979). Whereas Morris Motors conformed to the stereotype of a 'personally managed' firm until the 1930s, share ownership in Austin was more widely dispersed. In 1925 this led to Sir Herbert lobbying shareholders in opposition to his co-directors who objected to his proposal to merge the company with General Motors (Church, 1979).

W. R. Morris's autocratic managerial rule began to weaken from the late 1920s. In recognition of the company's increasing dependence on the expertise of managers, in the 1930s he helped to reorganize the company in the form of a divisional structure which combined stricter central control with a more rational system of decentralized management of the subsidiary companies. His biographer noted that Nuffield 'accepted the usurpation of his throne for the sake of the survival of the enterprise' – though this did not mark the end of his personal interventions. These were erratic and sometimes perverse, affecting the company's strategy and its managerial personnel until the merger with Austin in 1952 (Overy, 1976). The company's history from the 1930s raises doubts concerning the degree to which the multidivisional reforms of those years, or the 1947 organization chart which set down the new relationship between departmental heads, boards of directors and chairman, came into effective operation (Overy, 1976; Pagnamenta and Overy, 1984).

Although decision-making was increasingly left to boards of directors, comprised of a handful of managers whose equity ownership was minimal, founder-owners influenced business policies in the later years, despite organizational changes which at least implied limitations on their formal powers. Arguably equally important, is their continued influence on corporate strategies after their deaths through the senior figures whom they had appointed and whose roles during the critical post-war period were to be central to the industry's performance (pp. 91–6).

(vi) Fordism and the British approach to markets and marketing

One of the assumptions underlying Lewchuck's comparisons between Fordism and the British approach to mass production is that the large-scale, single, low-priced model strategy, had it been adopted by British manufacturers, would have created a market large enough to enable producers to achieve the economies of scale needed to justify investment in mass production (Lewchuck, 1986, 1987). Supply factors, in other words, are deemed to have been paramount.

Other historians have attached particular importance to the differences between the market in Britain and that in the United States. Demand in the US was sufficiently large to enable American producers to secure economies of scale at each stage in the manufacture and assembly of parts and components. This was the case at Ford after 1910 and at General Motors from the late 1920s, even though that company's strategy was to produce a range of models aimed at different socio-economic groups (Rae, 1959). Maxcy and Silberston, and Miller and Church have shown that throughout the 1920s the British market lacked social depth, a market limitation which was not overcome until the economic recovery lifted middle-class incomes, beginning in the 1930s. The extent of car ownership in Britain continued to lag far behind American levels and was overtaken by France in the late 1920s. At around 40 cars in use per 1000 people, ten years later ownership in the two countries was roughly similar (Blaich, 1987).

Whereas in the early 1920s price competition led by Morris was the key to a rapid growth in sales, during the 1930s design and model differentiation within price and horsepower bands was the principal determinant of companies' share of the market (Overy, 1976). Even at relatively low levels of car ownership, by the late 1920s replacement sales, rather than sales to first-time buyers, had become the major constituent of demand in what had become a 'mature' market. In order to deal with this development an important shift took place in British companies' market strategies, which began to pay increasing attention to the visual appeal of motor cars.

An increasing emphasis upon non-price competition was a response not only to a stagnating market but to technical innovation. Beginning in the late 1920s, the widespread adoption of closed saloon cars with roofs made of stamped steel made appreciable styling change possible (Maxcy and Silberston, 1959; Church and Miller, 1977). Price stability in the short run replaced cut-throat competition, while design and styling, influenced to a degree by streamlining, which became popular in the US, became the weapons of business rivalry. Slight modifications to body contour (the origins of streamlining in Britain), accessories and colour were intended to yield an increasing number of visibly different variants for each of the basic standardized engines and chassis (Church and Mullen, 1989).

Even Austin cars, renowned for their founder's philosophy of utilitarian design (the industry was not, he told Austin agents at the launch of the Seven in 1922, 'a fancy trade'), succumbed to the model price competition practised by Nuffield. From 1929 Austin employed an Italian designer who undertook a radical redesign of the Austin Seven saloon car, the 'Ruby'. Conceived by Sir Herbert in 1921 as the ultimate utility vehicle, the 'Ruby' was described by its original creator as a necessary but regrettable capitulation to the vagaries of public taste – especially that of women (Church and Mullen, 1989). The 1930s also saw a burgeoning of advertising, which included copy in magazines and newspapers, catchphrases and songs which drew attention less to mechanical reliability, which had been a preoccupation of the early 1920s, than to unique qualities and services. The purpose of the production of a full range of models and a profusion of variants was both to persuade buyers to retain brand (marque) loyalty among existing owners and to persuade them to switch to different makes of car. Such a policy was favoured by dealers in a market which was relatively stagnant and in which such a policy afforded greater protection to dealers' margins.

For a time, each of the major firms displayed at least one new model, or at least a 'facelift' at the annual Motor Show, a process which was costly for the volume car producers but presented even greater financial problems for the rest (Overy, 1976). The relatively high cost of closed bodies, which incorporated styling changes, was due not only to additional capital cost but also to the added work by hand required to form the compound roof curves, and to the labour-intensive assembly and welding of the body and fitting the doors and windows. In the US the increase in the rate of model obsolescence which was a consequence of the annual styling introduced during the mid 1920s, had brought about a sharp decline in the number of small producers. This forced small manufacturers out of the industry, and eventually compelled Ford to abandon his single Model T marketing strategy (Thomas, 1973). In Britain, however, the period of annual model changes was brief, ended by Morris in 1935. Thereafter the entire range of Morris cars, known as a 'series', were to remain unchanged, except for minor technical modifications, over several years until necessity required otherwise (Overy, 1976). In the United States there was a continued reduction in the number of competing firms largely as a result of the cost pressures imposed by the annual model change. In Britain a few small producers secured a growing market share, their successful design and marketing strategies fragmenting the market through product differentiation (Church and Miller, 1977; Church, 1993).

During the growth phase of the 1920s, when the Morris Cowley, followed by the 'baby' Austin Seven, pushed down 'the pyramid of consumption', Morris and Austin came to dominate the industry. Whereas in 1922 their combined output was an estimated 13 per cent of all cars produced in Britain, by 1929 the figure was 60 per cent. Meanwhile, Ford's share of car production fell from almost 30 to 10 per cent. Clearly, Fordism in the form practised at Trafford Park, directed from Detroit, was a failure and continued to be so until well after the commencement of production at the Dagenham factory in 1932 (Wilkins and Hill, 1964).

Why did Fordism fail in Britain and why did the British system of mass production and its variants succeed at Ford's expense? Ford's single-model policy in the 1920s was based on a car designed for the American market. The low-cost Model T and its successors until 1932 were designed regardless of the fiscal differences existing in the two countries. In Britain the horsepower tax had the effect of raising the price of a Ford to a level closer to that of the new models produced by British volume manufacturers. However, throughout the 1920s, and indeed after the Model T's replacement from 1928 until the war, Ford's lowest priced model was the cheapest which sold in appreciable numbers. Until 1932 the approach of most British manufacturers differed from the Fordist market strategy by taking into account British consumers' preferences regarding performance, roadholding, running costs, appearance, and a basic degree of comfort (Church, 1981). In the production of these models British manufacturers selected those elements of Fordism which seemed useful for flexible production policies. In 1925 C. R. F. Engelbach, Austin's head of production engineering at Longbridge, explained that company's manufacturing strategy in relation to the British market:

> A change has come over the spirit of our dreams of quick time floor to floor production performances, accompanied by the spectacular removal at miraculous speeds of chunks of metal to the musical ticking of stop watches . . . Rapid changes in fashion and ideas have slowed up the progress of special single operation machines. Continuous high production is too uncertain for special machines to be further developed. Designs have to be changeable at short notices . . . [and] at present there is probably no market likely to develop sufficiently that will lead to the extension of such specialized tool methods. (Engelbach, 1933–4, 7)

For this reason British manufacturers chose neither to invest in completely automatic transfer machines, which required long production runs to cover capital costs, nor to adopt machine pacing, which likewise depended on large standardized throughputs in order to be economic. Both Morris and, to a lesser extent, Austin opted for the flexibility offered by a low level of integration, purchasing a high proportion of parts and components from outside suppliers for assembly and finishing at Cowley and Longbridge. At the same time, Tayloristic subdivision of the timing and measurement of jobs and the production of standardized engines and chassis were features of volume production in British factories during the 1920s and 1930s (Tolliday, 1987b).

Whereas Lewchuck emphasized labour resistance and the 'underdevelopment of the managerial function' (Lewchuck, 1986) to explain the development and persistence of the British system of mass production, others have attempted to explain Anglo-American differences by stressing the character of the market and managers' approach to it. Khan's view was that the deployment of resources in ways which led to the proliferation of models represented a failure of the industry's marketing strategy which was not conducive to growth in the scale of production (Khan, 1946). This view was endorsed by Alford, who explained this trend in part as the result of the lack of personnel adequately trained to appraise the commercial value of technical advances regardless of their country of origin (Alford, 1972).

Bowden's econometric analysis of the interwar market for cars in Britain also dwelt on the adverse effects of British manufacturers'

Table 3 *Shares in car production in Britain 1919–38 (%)*

	1919	1921	1923	1925	1927	1929	1932	1935	1938
Morris/Nuffield	2	10	28	42	37	35	33	31	23
Austin		7	8	10	23	25	27	23	21
Ford		22	11	2	6	4	6	17	18
Rootes, Standard and Vauxhall						8	23	23	31

Source: Maxcy (1958), Table IV; Overy (1976), Table 1; Wyatt (1981), Table I; Church and Miller (1977), Table 9.2.

approach to the market. It prompted the conclusion that by failing to initiate the supply-side changes which might have enabled price reductions to take place, British manufacturers were limiting the size of their potential domestic market. Product differentiation in the form of model-price competition, producing several models each to compete with the models of other producers within a notional discrete price range, had the effect, she argued, of limiting the scope for economies of scale, lower costs and product prices which might have led to mass consumption (Bowden, 1991).

Others have argued that while this widely held view may be theoretically sound in terms of neo-classical economics, it ignores the reality of competition in the British market. In particular it overlooks Ford's post-war failure in Britain until the mid 1930s. In 1929 Ford accounted for only 4 per cent of car production in Britain, a percentage which did not rise appreciably until after the slump when new models manufactured at Dagenham and specially designed for the British market were introduced. The reduction in the price of the 8 h.p. Ford Popular by 25 per cent in 1935 reinforced this revival and a return to a 17 per cent share in car production in Britain in the same year. In 1938 Ford's 18 per cent share compared with 23 per cent for the Nuffield organization and 21 per cent for Austin (see Table 3). As percentages of car production of the Big Six, the figure for Ford was 19 per cent, for Nuffield 26 per cent and Austin 22 per cent (Maxcy and Silberston, 1959).

By that time Ford had increased the number of basic models and engines on offer to 4, which compared with 8 and 7 by Austin, and 17 and 10 by the Nuffield enterprises (Church and Miller, 1977). Contrary to the counterfactual expectations which historians have linked to Fordist single-model, low-price marketing strategy, no vast new market was created by the price cuts of the mid 1930s. Although Ford's share in production rose, the appearance of competitors' new models, beginning with the Morris Eight in 1934 and its successors, followed by the Austin Eight and Ten, the Standard Eight and the Vauxhall Ten, were accompanied by falling sales of cheaper Ford cars. They were outsold by more expensive models which offered greater comfort, performance, appearance and in some cases individuality. Sir Miles Thomas, commercial director of the Nuffield organization, remarked of his company's competitor to the £100 10 h.p. Ford Popular, the £100 Morris Minor, that 'no one wants to keep down with the Joneses' (Thomas, 1964, *168*), a reference to buyers' preferences for cars priced above that of the basic model in any given range.

That British, rather than American Fordist, marketing strategies were optimal under 1930s conditions is further suggested by the experience of those other European manufacturers who did imitate Ford. Both Berliet and Citroën in France and Fiat in Italy, 'dazzled by the Ford spectacle built capital-intensive plants designed for mass production of single models' (Tolliday, 1987b, *33*; Bardou *et al.*, 1982). They underestimated the persistent consumer demand for quality and differentiation which also characterized the British market between the wars, causing serious financial problems for the Fordist imitators in Europe, bringing them to the brink of ruin (Tolliday, 1991).

If the production strategies may be understood as rational, for the British companies achieved substantially higher profitability than Ford, was there nonetheless a failure of innovation and marketing as has been suggested? An analysis of engine and model types, advertising copy and production figures, model by model, indicates that, with the exception of the Nuffield organization, the leading companies manufactured a much narrower range of cars than has been supposed, by Khan for example (Khan, 1946; Church and Miller, 1977).

Many of the additional 'models' were made by the simple expedient of combining basic components in various ways. Nuffield was the major culprit, producing more than twenty models in the early 1930s, compared with seven from Austin and four from Ford. The contention that the industry failed to innovate, though, has been disputed. The American industry was the source of invention and design developments, but while such improvements as synchromesh gearbox, independent front suspension and unitary construction were first introduced widely in the production of Vauxhall cars in Britain they soon became available from other manufacturers (Church and Miller, 1977).

Sales methods, too, were influenced by American practices adapted to suit British dealers and car buyers. Even in the mid 1920s the larger British manufacturers were employing 'modern and intensive selling methods' of a kind which impressed a representative of the United States Bureau of Domestic and Foreign Commerce. These included hire purchase, available since 1920, extensive distribution networks, after-sales service, induction of sales personnel, and advertising, including company journals such as *The Morris Owner* and *The Austin Advocate* (Overy, 1976; Church, 1981). Such evidence on marketing and business strategy practised by firms producing about one-half of total output has been offered as support for the view that within the context of the British (and European) market before 1940 the British manufacturers were, on the whole, rational in their responses, and relatively successful financially. Within the protected British market the slow growth of new-owner sales between the mid 1920s and the mid 1930s encouraged product differentiation as the favoured competitive strategy.

Ford's rapid progress from 1932, when cars produced at Dagenham were for the first time designed specifically for the British market, might suggest that Fordism was at last transforming the market. However, the simultaneous increase in the market share of Standard and Rootes and the slow growth in the 1930s of the lowest priced, lowest powered cars, point to a more complicated segmentation of market structure. Seen from the standpoint of competing car producers, within any given range price was not the single most important factor influencing consumers.

(vii) Debilitating environment: structures and strategies

One effect of the non-price competition of the 1930s, which was to have longer term consequences for the restructuring and rationalization of the industry, was that it enabled medium-sized firms, notably Rootes, Standard and Vauxhall, General Motors' subsidiary company, not only to compete but to increase their share of production. From 8 per cent in 1929 these three companies increased their share to 31 per cent by 1938 (see Table 3). The success of these firms depended in part upon the heavy use of bought-out supplies of components parts, mainly from large specialist producers, thereby giving assemblers access to external economies of scale. A report on the industry in 1950 gave examples of companies in which bought-out components were responsible for between 63 and 74 per cent of production costs, including raw materials (PEP 1950). Variations in the degree of integration between major producers were important, but the PEP report made it clear that external economies were considerable by the mid 1930s. At the same time, by lowering fixed capital entry requirements the prevailing industrial organization helped to perpetuate the survival of the smaller manufacturers.

Foreman-Peck has drawn attention to another source of market failure, which enabled firms displaying competitive weakness, either through managerial failure or cyclical financial difficulty, to avoid the penalty of 'exit' from the industry. Adopting a similar approach to that of the Midland Bank towards the Austin Motor Company in 1920–1 (Church, 1979), in 1931–2 Lloyds Bank together with major suppliers, which included Pressed Steel and Lucas, agreed to continue financial support for the Rover Motor Company, an ailing, long-established specialist car manufacturer. The condition for rescue was the appointment of an independent accountant, subsequently elected to the Board of Directors, to investigate the company's affairs and make recommendations for improvements (Foreman-Peck, 1981a, b). At the Standard Motor Company, too, 'voice' – a say in corporate policy in return for financial support – was the condition laid down by Barclay's Bank for their support in difficult times. The bank insisted on appointing two nominees to the board (Richardson, 1972). Either out of

Table 4 *Rates of return on capital by the 'Big Six' car manufacturers 1929–38 (%)*

	1929	1930	1931	1932	1933	1934	1935	1936	1937	1938
Morris	16	17	11	12	6	8	15	19	16	12
Austin	21	25	9	14	15	18	16	15	16	11
Standard	loss	19	24	48	27	19	25	23	26	9
Humber	loss	4	loss	loss	7	22	14	14	14	8
Ford	12	11	3	loss	loss	7	4	6	5	3
Vauxhall	n/a	n/a	12	18	41	54	58	47	32	24

Source: Maxcy and Silberston (1959), Table 6.

loyalty or for fear of further losses in the event of bankruptcy, bankers contributed to companies' survival, thereby perpetuating an industrial structure which saw a decrease in the level of concentration during the 1930s.

Technical internal economies of scale, therefore, did not guarantee market dominance. What they could do, as the Dagenham plant showed from the mid 1930s, was to provide low-cost production. But Ford's sales and profit experience demonstrated that such an advantage only ensured survival with unstable sales and low profitability (Maxcy and Silberston, 1959). Between 1929 and 1938 Ford's rate of return was consistently far below that of the other Big Six vehicle manufacturers (see Table 4). The flexibility of organization in the vertically-disintegrated structure of the volume car industry enabled car assemblers to purchase supplies from parts and components manufacturers operating on a larger scale. This made the specific performance of the main competitors more a function of individual marketing strategies and management abilities than scale economies of car production.

The expansion of the industry was chiefly the result of the internal growth of firms. Morris had purchased the bankrupt Wolseley company in 1926 and acquired the little specialist car-making firm, Riley, in 1938, but only Rootes among the Big Six car-making firms between the wars was the result of mergers of several existing companies – Hillman, Humber and Commer Cars. The commercial success of Rootes, Standard and Vauxhall during the 1930s resulted in an industrial structure which under different market conditions after the Second World War would make rationalization problematical. In 1938 the big three companies, Nuffield, Austin and Ford, accounted for 62 per cent of the output of cars in Britain. This compared with 69 per cent by the largest three producers in Germany and 73 per cent in France. Once again, however, the difference between the much higher ratio of industrial concentration in the United States, where the figure was 85 per cent, is significant in underlining the greater similarities between the major car manufacturing countries in Europe before 1939 (PEP, 1950). Nonetheless, a major focus for contemporary commentators, and subsequently for historians reflecting upon the industry's prospects and performance after 1945, was the debilitating effect of the industry's structure.

On the eve of the First World War, the British motor industry, then organized in a large though diminishing number of competing firms, was under threat from the Model T Ford, assembled from kits imported from the US. Ford's output in Britain was twice that of the largest British producer while the American company took a rapidly rising share of the home market. A handful of British manufacturers had begun to make smaller, lower priced cars in quantity to compete, but to an even greater extent compared with other European producers the scale of production of the largest enterprises was counted in thousands rather than tens – and for Ford hundreds – of thousands. Under peaceful free trade conditions the output of the industry in Britain was rapidly catching up with that of France. However, the principal contributor to this process was Ford.

By the outbreak of the Second World War the industry had become the largest in Europe. Protection and, by European standards, buoyant middle-class incomes, particularly in the 1930s, had enabled the infant British industry to establish volume manufacture comparable in scale to the largest manufacturers in Europe. Critics pointed to the continuing contrasts with the much larger size of plants and firms in the United States. There the higher degree of standardization and the concentration of production on fewer models had enabled American manufacturers to achieve levels of efficiency far above those in Britain, where cars were still only affordable by a limited middle class. The National Advisory Council (NAC) initiated in Whitehall made all of these points in its 1945 Report, although it concluded that: 'The industry has shown by its past performance that it is in itself vigorous and efficient . . . and if its future environment is such as to apply the appropriate stimuli, there is every reason to expect that it will respond to them vigorously and effectively' (NAC, 1947, 9). This more optimistic note no doubt owed something to the presence on the NAC of an eight-member majority representing the Society of Motor Manufacturers and Traders.

2
The roots of decline

(i) Post-war pre-eminence: attainment and erosion

The immediate effect of war was a reduction in the output of cars to very low levels in order to facilitate the production of goods-carrying vehicles to meet military requirements. The Shadow Factory Scheme, financed and introduced by government in 1936 had already provided extra plant and equipment for aircraft manufacture by motor firms, to which was added the production of tracked carriers, tanks, tractors, and a wide range of military goods. New buildings and much of the machinery installed for these purposes expanded the industry's motor manufacturing capacity after the war (Maxcy and Silberston, 1959; Thoms and Donnelly, 1985). The strength of the trade unions and in particular that of the shop stewards' movement, was one wartime development which was to have longer lasting effects on the industry than it had following the First World War. These developments were powerfully reinforced by the 1939 Emergency Powers Act, which made it more difficult for employers to dismiss labour, and by the role given to shop stewards by the Joint Production Committees which employers were obliged to set up (Flanders, 1952). Another development of long-term and industry-wide importance was the 1941 Coventry Tool Room Agreement, reached between the Amalgamated Engineering Union and Coventry employers at a time when fierce competition for labour caused the pay of semi-skilled production workers and dilutees to exceed that of apprentice-trained toolroom craftsmen. The accord, which effectively protected skilled workers' differential rates relative to those paid to production workers, remained in operation until unilateral termination of this agreement by the Coventry and District Engineering Association in the early 1970s and was to have major repercussions throughout the industry (Thoms and Donnelly, 1985).

Home demand after the war was buoyant but constrained by government controls on the supply of steel which was channelled to firms which exported 50 per cent (raised in 1947 to 75 per cent) of their output. This policy was part of the government's strategy to counter the loss of dollar earnings resulting from the war by a systematic export drive. A sellers' market was created by the absence of competition from Europe, where productive capacity was slower to recover from the effects of defeat or occupation. This was combined with a resurgence of pent-up demand in the United States and some Commonwealth countries, notably Australia, which American producers could not satisfy. The result was a surge of British vehicle exports at unprecedented levels to which devaluation in 1949 brought a further boost (Maxcy and Silberston, 1959).

For a time Britain was the world's leading car exporter. The industry's share of world motor exports rose from 15 per cent in 1937 to 52 per cent in 1950. In that year 75 per cent of all cars and more than 60 per cent of commercial vehicles (mostly chassis and vans) were sold abroad. Yet car production was one-third greater and commercial vehicles almost twice as large in 1950 compared with 1937. This exceptional trading record lasted until the mid 1950s. By that time the American motor industry had resumed its virtual monopoly of the US market and European manufacturers had also recovered. Germany overtook French car production in 1953 and that of Britain in 1956, when Germany's long-term dominance in Europe commenced (see Figure 3).

Thereafter, Britain's share of world trade in cars averaged 24 per cent between 1957 and 1962, falling to 19 per cent in 1963–7. The comparable figures for trade in CVs were 28 and 30 per cent. British production as a proportion of output from the major manufacturing countries fell from 11.4 in 1960 to 8.5 per cent in 1970. The positive balance of trade in motor vehicles, which continued, though declining, until 1977 was increasingly attributable to buoyant commercial vehicle exports. From 1974, for the first time since 1914, the value of car imports exceeded exports (SMMT). These developments occurred within a context of the

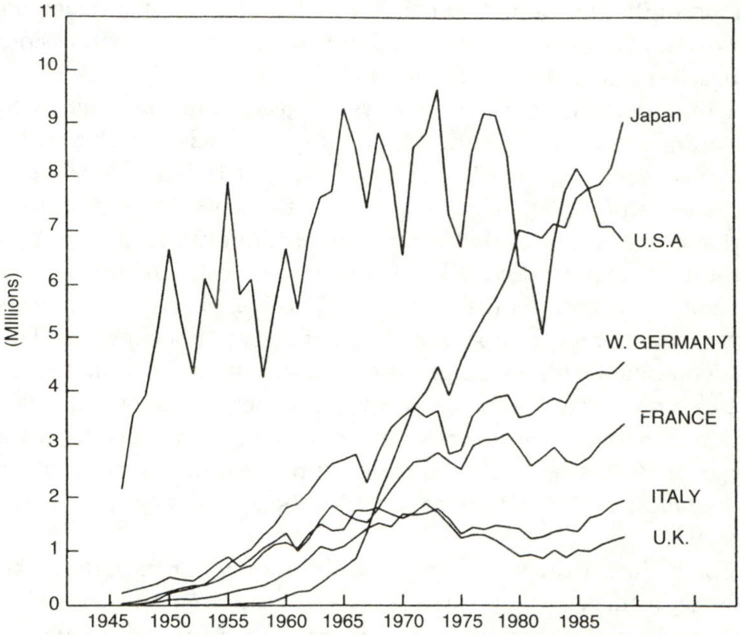

Figure 3 *Car output in the principal producing countries, 1946–89*
Source: SMMT

recovery of European production capacity and a progressive, international reduction in protection.

Market development also played a part. In 1938 the number of cars in use per thousand population was 19 in Germany, compared with 41 in France and 42 in Britain (Blaich, 1987). By 1960 the figure for West Germany was 84, compared with 119 in France and 106 in Britain, although during the 1960s car density in West Germany overtook that in both countries (SMMT). By 1970 the real GDP per capita of Germany and France was respectively 75 and 72, compared with 63 in the UK (as a percentage of US purchasing power parity), the outcome of higher rates of growth in those two economies in each quinquennium throughout the 1960s which continued in the 1970s (Jones, 1981) (see Table 5). The slackening in the rate of increase in car ownership in Britain was reflected in the falling proportion of sales to new owners, which dropped from some 72 per cent in 1960–4 to 34 per cent in 1970–4,

Table 5 *Western European growth rates of GDP and the motor industry (annual average per cent change)*

	1960–4	1964–9	1969–73	1973–8
GDP				
W. Germany	5.1	4.6	4.5	2.0
France	6.0	5.9	6.1	3.0
UK	3.1	2.5	3.0	1.4
Italy	3.5	5.6	4.1	2.1
Motor car industry output by value (at constant prices)				
W. Germany	8.1	6.5	4.8	2.5
France	5.5[b]	9.1	7.4	3.1
UK	5.6	2.2	0.4	−2.4
Italy[a]	n.a.	n.a.	3.6[d]	1.7
Motor car industry employment				
W. Germany	6.2	2.3	2.3	0.5
France	2.5	2.6	5.1	0.7[e]
UK	2.4	0.9	1.3	−1.4
Italy	4.9[c]	6.8	1.5	1.4[e]
Motor car industry output by units produced				
W. Germany	9.1	4.4	2.3	1.2
France	4.2	8.8	7.0	1.7
UK	6.5	−1.3	−0.2	−4.7
Italy	14.0	7.9	5.2	−2.9

Notes:
[a] Relates to transport equipment, not just the motor vehicle industry.
[b] 1962–4
[c] 1961–4[d] 1970–3
[e] 1973–7
Source: Jones (1981), Table 1.

leaving replacement demand once again the main determinant of sales. In Britain the rate of growth of the total stock of cars rose by more than 10 per cent between 1953 and 1963 before falling to 8 per cent in 1963–8 and 4.5 per cent in 1968–73. This compared with an annual average of 12 per cent growth in the major European markets throughout the period (HC, 14th Report, 1975).

To some extent, therefore, disparity in the rate of market development between Britain and continental competitors was merely a symptom of catching-up, made possible in part by trade creation within the EEC where incomes were growing more rapidly than in Britain. The differential stimulus to investment within the separate protected British and EEC markets were reinforced during most of the 1960s by an overvalued pound sterling. Between 1956 and 1968 the 33.3 per cent tariff on cars was reduced to 22 per cent, while under the Kennedy Round the general tariff fell to 11 per cent by 1972. Entry into the EEC in 1973 heralded the complete removal of tariffs between Britain and the major west European vehicle-producing countries in 1977.

By that time the decline in the British motor industry was well advanced, although the possibility of such a deterioration in its international competitiveness had been mooted shortly after the war ended. In 1945 a Whitehall committee had drawn attention to the industry's poor export record before the war, and commented on the division of the industry into 'too many, often small scale units, each producing too many models' (Barnett, 1986, *165*). Two years later, the National Advisory Council for the motor industry predicted that when the sellers' market of the post-war years ended, higher productivity would be a necessary condition for continued success in export markets (NAC, 1947). Both the Council and the report on the industry by the advisory body to the Ministry of Supply (PEP) drew attention to the fragmented structure, the excessive variety of models, lack of standardization of components, and the high unit costs associated with small-scale production relative to American car-makers, features which they argued must be changed if the industry was to compete internationally. This was, of course, a problem which had its origins in the particular form which non-price competition had taken during the 1930s.

Criticisms from Whitehall had prompted the SMMT to promote standardization of components and parts used in the industry, but it was left to individual manufacturers to implement agreements and they showed little interest. For a brief period the Nuffield and Austin companies participated in the scheme, but cooperation broke down when Lord Nuffield had second thoughts about pooling technical information which might prejudice his organiza-

Table 6 *'Equivalent' motor vehicles produced per employees per annum 1955–76*

	Britain	Germany	United States
1955	4.1	3.9	19.8
1965	5.8	6.4	25.0
1970	5.6	7.5	19.6
1973	5.8	7.7	25.0
1976	5.5	7.9	26.1

Source: Jones and Prais (1978), Table 4.

tion's competitive position (Overy, 1976; Jeremy, 1984–6). Ten years later two leading economists drew similar conclusions to those of PEP concerning the structure of the industry, which they described as unsuited to the economics of car production for a mass market. They maintained that the industry consisted of too many firms producing too many different models even to approach the technical optimum level of production (Maxcy and Silberston, 1959).

Comparable, and possibly marginally higher, productivity was one of the factors which explains Germany's competitive lead in production from 1957. However, calculations of international productivity differences are fraught with difficulty. For the pre-war years the lack of adequate statistical data has forced historians to use crude productivity estimates, dividing the total number of vehicles produced by the numbers employed in the industry. The flaw in this approach lies in the disparity in the typical sizes of vehicles in different countries and in the raw material inputs they embody. Pratten and Silberston devised a weighting system to take vehicle size into account, measuring productivity in terms of 'vehicle equivalents' (Pratten and Silberston, 1967).

A refinement of this weighting formula by Jones and Prais resulted in the international comparisons presented in Table 6. The figures shown for 1955 imply productivity differences of a similar order to those estimated by Rostas for 1935/6 (Rostas, 1948) and suggest that until the late 1950s the motor industry in Britain appears to have been broadly in step with that in other European countries. Ten years later the productivity of American plants in the United States remained four to five times higher than in European factories, but more worrying for those concerned with the competitiveness of the British industry was the disparity between labour productivity in the German industry (6.4) and that in the British industry (5.8), revealing a gap which increased further in the 1970s. Productivity estimates based on net output values and employment showed German productivity in 1970 to have been two-thirds greater than that of the British industry (Jones and Prais, 1978).

In 1958, when the beginning of a shift towards German superiority was barely discernible, a detailed study by Maxcy and Silberston concluded that the British industry still enjoyed a cost competitiveness though that was attributed to a considerable degree to the efficiency of large-scale component suppliers. As in other observers' earlier reports, however, they concluded that unless the scale of production of individual models was appreciably increased motor manufacturing might not continue to be 'the most progressive of British industries' (Maxcy and Silberston, 1959, *198*). They also drew attention to overmanning, as well as to weakness in vehicle design, quality, salesmanship and service, which they thought had already begun to affect exports.

These criticisms were repeated in more forceful terms during the mid 1970s in a number of major official inquiries into the ailing industry. Differing in most respects only in detail in their diagnoses, there was general agreement that the lack of international competitiveness resulted from a failure to secure economies of scale, due to a considerable extent to the continued existence of too many models, too many plants and too much capacity (HC, Ryder Report; HC, 14th Report; CPRS Report, 1975). Low productivity and a lack of investment which left the industry with obsolescent plant were other defects, although in terms of future government policy towards the industry it was the condemnation of overmanning, restrictive work practices and poor industrial relations which was regarded by government to be the key to initial improvement (pp. 105–6).

The decline of the industry falls into three stages. The first began in the 1960s with a series of mergers between British companies and the acquisition of Rootes by Chrysler to form Chrysler UK in 1967. This stage culminated in 1968 in the merger of British Motor Holdings (BMH) with Leyland Motors to form the British Leyland Motor Corporation (BLMC, later BL). From that time, with the exception of highly specialist manufacturers – Rolls Royce, Aston Martin, Lotus and Morgan – BLMC/BL comprised the whole of the British-owned motor manufacturing industry. The second phase continued until 1975, when the industry came under state control, thus marking the beginning of the third phase of decline. Historians and other commentators have differed in the emphasis which they have placed on the variables contributing to the industry's difficulties. These include the role of government, industrial relations, industrial structure, investment and marketing policies, business strategies, the quality of management, and the role of multinationals.

(ii) Private investment and public policies: government and industry

The role of government is central in some accounts of the industry's decline. Successive governments' policies towards the motor industry after 1945 had the effect, Pollard argued, of corroding enterprise. 'Thirty years of discouragement had by the 1970s accustomed manufacturers to a low-growth, low-investment economy' (Pollard, 1982, *127*; see also Dunnett, 1980, and Barnett, 1986). Those policies included the imposition and variation of purchase, and later value added, taxes, hire purchase restrictions affecting minimum deposit levels and periods for repayment, interest rates, incomes and regional policies (Dunnett, 1980). Why was the industry seen to be central to the success of government macroeconomic policies designed, at one time or another, either to promote exports and improve the balance of payments, to sustain the exchange rate, to control inflation, or to protect employment?

The resilience of the industry during the interwar period continued to impress contemporaries for more than twenty years after the Second World War, and was part of Rostow's justification for describing the industry as a 'leading sector' in the economy until the 1960s (Rostow, 1963). The value of net output rose from £300m to £639m between 1954 and 1966, an increase from 3.4 to

5.1 per cent of all industrial net output. This represented 7.5 per cent of all manufacturing production and 6 per cent of all manufacturing employment. A growth of 113 per cent during that period compared with an increase in industrial production of 41.5 per cent. It had been estimated that, between 1954 and 1966, 9 per cent of the economy's growth was attributable to motor vehicles, investment in the industry representing slightly less than 10 per cent in all manufacturing industry (Armstrong, 1967).

By the 1960s total direct employment in the industry was close to 0.5m, rising by 33 per cent between 1959 and 1973, mostly located in the West Midlands and in the South-East (Durcan, McCarthy and Redman, 1983). Figures for total employment in the industry, including other supply and component sectors (though excluding employment in sales, repair and maintenance) brought the number to 0.8m in 1973 (HC, 14th Report, 1975). Throughout the post-war period the motor industry grew faster than gross domestic product, as it was to do in France, Italy and above all in West Germany, until the early 1970s (Jones, 1981). In 1963 one estimate based on input-output analysis of the combined contribution of indirect and direct inputs to total industrial production was nearly 11 per cent, a figure accepted as plausible by an official committee investigating the industry a dozen years later (Armstrong, 1967; CPRS, 1975). Nearly one-third of industrial growth in the economy in the 1950s and 1960s has been attributed to the motor industry and its suppliers. The state of the motor industry, therefore, was a major influence through the multiplier effects of a wide range of interdependent industries (Armstrong, 1967).

In what ways, then, did government policies affect development and international competitiveness after 1945? Corelli Barnett's robust critique of government, aimed specifically at the Coalition and Labour governments of the immediate post-war years, focused on a search for a 'New Jerusalem' in the form of the welfare state which absorbed both attention and resources which should have been applied to industry. The motor industry, he argued, suffered particularly badly from a mixture of a lack of interest by the politicians or at the very least by 'tinkering' as a substitute for policy (Barnett, 1986). One very important piece of tinkering was the setting of high export targets, which in 1948 rose to 75 per cent of each company's output, as part of the national drive to earn dollar currency. In the pursuit of this objective the government imposed penalties, in the form of restricted raw material supplies, rather than extending substantive support to British car manufacturers. Short-term instrumentalism of this kind Barnett interpreted as evidence of a complete disregard for the need for a national, long-term, industrial strategy, a part of which should have been rationalization.

To some extent this is to confuse outcome with intention. The National Advisory Council (NAC) was the creation of Whitehall in 1945 and produced a report which pointed to the need for the industry to move towards standardization, for systematic analysis of export markets and improved designs to meet consumers' requirements. The lack of progress in these directions, favoured by Whitehall, is explained by the resistance of the industry to intervention which involved any measure of compulsion. That position was successfully imposed on the NAC by the SMMT representatives, who from its inception outnumbered others on the Council. It remained, therefore, no more than a channel of communication (Tiratsoo, 1992).

Dunnett maintained that the government's post-war export drive contributed much to achieving the national objective of dollar earnings. Yet the method of allocating quotas of scarce steel froze the industry's fragmented structure and organization by, in effect, protecting the least efficient. Quotas were allocated to firms regardless of size or production costs, the sole criterion being the ability to meet annually-set export targets. In an immediate post-war sellers' market and under pressure to accelerate production for exports no new models appeared on the market until the popular 8 h.p. Morris Minor in 1948.

When the war ended, the pressure of demand was greatest in non-European markets to which British pre-war models were unsuited. Nonetheless, the immediate pent-up demand for cars in short supply worldwide, coupled with the necessity to reconstruct European production capacity, enabled British producers to re-enter imperial markets. It also enabled them to establish a foothold in the US, where for a time British models filled a niche as a second car for local use (Maxcy and Silberston, 1959).

British manufacturers had long argued that the horsepower tax penalized high-powered vehicles of the kind popular in the United States and the Empire, placing them at a disadvantage in export markets. Cars with high-speed engines, narrow track, low ground clearance and limited luggage space, which were suitable for the home market, were less suited to European markets. Yet the financial risk attached to developing cars specially designed for export deterred such a strategy (Church, 1979). It seems more likely, however, that the profitability of the protected home market in the 1930s had provided insufficient inducement to manufacturers to develop overseas markets outside the Commonwealth. In any case, the outcome of Lord Nuffield's patriotic attempt to cultivate exports suggests a flawed perception of consumer preferences outside Europe. The 'Empire Oxford', which was conceived by him and built specifically for the overseas market, was returned unsold in large numbers and the project abandoned as a failure (Overy, 1976). Within ten years, however, the Volkswagen Beetle, already selling widely in Europe, with no concessions to the conventional requirements of automobiles sold in the US had established a valuable and enduring foothold in that rapidly expanding market (Nelson, 1967).

In 1946 government accepted the arguments of the motor manufacturers by replacing the horsepower tax with a flat rate tax. Nonetheless, it was the popularity of small cars in the home market which increased, though that trend went into reverse during the 1960s. This suggests that the discriminatory horsepower tax was less critical than other determinants of consumer demand, particularly income levels and running costs, in influencing the structure of car sales at home and in overseas markets. Manufacturers' allegations (implicitly accepted in the 1948 tax reform) that exporting was hampered by the horsepower tax limiting sales of larger, more powerful cars are unsupported (Rhys, 1972).

During this period the reputation of British vehicles suffered from the shipment of unsuitable and defective models by manufacturers who were short of high-quality raw materials and under pressure to meet export targets. In 1950 British commitments to the Korean War led to a sharp increase in the demand for steel for rearmament. As before, quotas were reintroduced which, in common with orders for military vehicles, were placed irrespective of allocative efficiency. Again the industry's structure was reinforced by the same Ministry of Supply that had criticized fragmentation in 1947 (Dunnett, 1980; NAC, 1947).

The contrast with West Germany is revealing. The Volkswagen plant was built at Wolfsburg immediately before the war when it was planned to produce the 'people's car', or 'Beetle' as Porsche's low-priced utility car came to be known, at an annual rate of 150,000 units (Overy, 1975). Between 1934 and 1939 Volkswagen benefited from Nazi policy which took various forms of discrimination against other firms and multinationals. The company came under the direct control of the Ministry of Munitions in 1943, a period which saw further diminution of workers' already minimal political and economic rights (Reich, 1990). After the war, a particular British (Treasury-driven) concern among the occupying powers that the export capacity of German industry should be re-established rapidly to ease the Allies' burden of feeding and clothing the population has been held to have produced an unintended effect. This was to reinforce the relationships and institutions existing prior to the occupation, ensuring a continuing discrimination by the state in favour of Volkswagen. Contrary to the commonly-held view, while the quality of the Beetle occasioned scepticism among British observers they acknowledged that the Wolfsburg plant, virtually undamaged, was probably the most modern installation in the world (Reich, 1990).

In 1948 the German administrator appointed by the British to prepare the plant for peacetime production was succeeded by Heinz Nordhoff, formerly of General Motors' German Opel division. Under his management a new system of financial control and cost accounting, and a new distributor and dealer system were introduced, as was the practice whereby senior managers gave regular reports to workers on the company's overall progress and problems. Because of the limited home market and the Allies' stringent financial requirements Volkswagen's survival was virtually dependent on exports. From the post-war beginning, therefore, high-quality reliability and service, supported by an extensive distribution network across Europe, formed a major part of Volkswagen's corporate strategy (Nelson, 1967). By 1956 two completely new large factories had been built, while a network of exclusive Volkswagen dealers on the Ford model offered service and parts. This network was well placed to exploit the fashion which developed among certain sections of the American population, notably the young, for inexpensive, small cars during the mid 1950s. Already by 1956 German cars sold overseas, almost entirely Volkswagens destined mainly within Europe but increasingly to the United States, exceeded Britain's total car exports (Nelson, 1967).

By comparison with British car manufacturers Ford emerged from the post-war period in a strong position. This was partly because of historical circumstances, in particular the construction of the new large plant at Dagenham, and partly because of Ford's access to the parent company's resources. When the new plant commenced production in 1932 its annual capacity was 200,000 units, a substantial proportion of which was planned to supply markets in Continental Europe, where, in accordance with Perry's long-held vision, the Ford subsidiaries were subordinate to the Ford Motor Company in England. The contrast between the scale and modernity of Dagenham and British car plants, most of which had developed from small factories built early in the century, was clear and remarked on in *The Times* in 1947, when Dagenham was described as a showpiece (Wilkins and Hill, 1964). Not until the post-war boom did peacetime production reach full capacity and the economies associated with it, when the state-sponsored export drive enabled Ford to exploit its international distribution network to expand overseas sales.

In 1950 Ford was the leading vehicle exporter in Britain, a dollar-earning performance which government recognized by freeing dollars to enable that company to purchase American machinery and equipment unavailable elsewhere. The parent company's assistance also took the form of help, on a contract basis, in designing two new post-war models which entered the market in 1950 (Wilkins and Hill, 1964). Novel in their symmetrical appearance and in construction, incorporating steel-welded bodies, independent front-wheel suspension and new hydraulic brakes, the Ford Consul, 20 per cent lower in price than other models of the same horsepower, and Zephyr set new standards (Adeney, 1989; Wood, 1988).

Whereas before the war both the levels and rates of growth in assets of Morris and Ford were similar, the immediate post-war years were a turning point. After 1945 investment in Ford saw a rise in net asset values which in 1956 exceeded those of the British

Motor Corporation (BMC), formed in 1952 by a merger between the constituent parts of the Nuffield organization and Austin (Maxcy and Silberston, 1959). BMC was still the largest car producer, accounting for some 39 per cent of all cars manufactured in Britain. But Ford's share was 27 per cent, having risen from 14.4 per cent (compared with Austin and Nuffield's combined proportion of 43.4 per cent) since 1946 (SMMT).

While the government may have given Ford special help to achieve relatively rapid preparation for post-war conditions Reich's view of this as an almost discriminatory treatment of the American MNE in comparison with dealings with British firms may be challenged on the basis of the immediate post-war history of the Standard Motor Company, the third largest British car manufacturer. Its forceful director's blueprint for an attack on overseas markets, based on mass production of a single model designed specifically for the export trade, met with substantial support from Whitehall. This took the form of dollars with which to buy machine tools, a low rental for a large, well-equipped shadow factory, and financial bridging arrangements to enable Standard to commence production of the Vanguard, launched in 1947. This suggests, contrary to Barnett's view that the government ignored the need for an industrial policy, that within the constraints of industrialists' implacable opposition to intervention at the industry level it was prepared, regardless of corporate nationality, to support companies which seemed likely to succeed. Standard's failure to achieve comparable success to that of Ford had more to do with internal corporate problems than to government (Tiratsoo, 1992).

Even though Ford was one of the two firms which it has been suggested received favoured treatment compared with others, the company was affected none the less by the same macroeconomic policies which several historians have identified as particularly deleterious, notably to investment and industrial relations. As the leading dollar-earner in the manufacturing sector, the motor industry was especially affected by general measures intended ultimately to protect the value of sterling by choking off home demand and restricting imports to improve the balance of payments. Hire-purchase terms, which since the mid 1920s were involved in most car sales and were an important determinant of demand, were changed seventeen times between 1952 and 1968.

Adjustments in purchase tax were made thirteen times (Rhys, 1972; Dunnett, 1980).

Both contemporary and recent commentators have argued that these alterations were the cause of a demand instability which resulted in alternating periods of investment and expansion. One consequence was the underutilization of plant capacity which adversely affected productivity; another was the intermittent laying-off of workers in an industry in which employment for semi-skilled production workers had always been seasonal. The effect of the first was to increase manufacturers' unit costs, reduce profitability and check investment. The second contributed to a deterioration in industrial relations (Dunnett, 1980).

By maintaining the value of sterling government also increased the difficulty of exporting. Competition in third markets in which no indigenous motor industry existed against vehicles sold in undervalued currencies necessitated reductions in dealers' margins to be competitive. Consequently the attraction of a British manufacturer's franchise among dealers overseas was affected both by the limited turnover by comparison with the major European producers and by low profit-margins. The devaluation of sterling in 1967 followed by the revaluation of the Deutsche Mark in 1969 tended to remedy the imbalance, but by that time the large-scale production and extensive distribution systems of the leading European manufacturers, notably Volkswagen, were already well developed (Rhys, 1972).

Critics of government policy have argued that the uncertainty which frequent changes in fiscal and monetary policies had upon demand, growth, and profitability in the home market hampered investment and checked improvements in productivity (Bhaskar, 1979; Dunnett, 1980). Estimates of productivity relative to the German industry between 1965 and 1970 show a ratio of German to British 'equivalent' motor vehicles rising from 1.1 to 1.3: the comparable American to British ratio was 3.5 (see Table 6 above). By that time the one remaining volume car manufacturer in British ownership possessed the lowest assets per man of any of its rivals in Europe and the next to lowest value added. The assets per man of Ford UK were the highest of any British car maker, but nonetheless ranked fifth after Ford (Germany), Opel and Volkswagen, and sixth in terms of value added (Rhys, 1972).

Both the Ryder Report and the Fourteenth Report of the Trade and Industry Expenditure Committee agreed that a substantial increase in investment was a necessary condition if the British motor industry was to match European levels of productivity. Comparing output per man with fixed assets per man, the Expenditure Committee found a significant correlation. However, using the same data, a statistical analysis of the relation between productivity and capital intensity in fourteen vehicle companies in various countries led Jones and Prais to conclude that the evidence on which the committee's view was based did not show that a greater capital input per unit of output was necessarily coupled with a higher output per unit of labour (Jones and Prais, 1978). They insisted that the particular emphasis placed on capital expenditure as a cause of lower productivity in Britain was mistaken, and that capital utilization, which depended on organizational and human factors, was probably a more important explanation (Jones and Prais, 1978).

Nonetheless, the difference in investment levels between major European companies was considerable. On an already different investment and technological base level, annual investment between the mid 1960s and the mid 1970s was £197.5m at Volkswagen and £117.5m at the state-owned Renault company, compared with £86m at BLMC. This discrepancy helps to explain the relative age of the British company's plant and equipment on which the Expenditure Committee commented and which, all things being equal, placed a ceiling on the productivity levels achievable. Productivity at BLMC was half that of Ford UK (Jones and Prais, 1978), a discrepancy which receives further consideration below.

To what extent can these international differences be explained by government policies affecting demand, as has been argued (Bhaskar, 1979; Dunnett, 1980; Pollard, 1982)? How far did taxation levels adversely affect home demand and production? After purchase tax was cut from 45 to 25 per cent in 1962 tax fluctuations were limited within the 20 to $33\frac{1}{3}$ range before 1970 (Dunnett, 1980). Over roughly the same period these figures compare with between 11 and 21 per cent in Germany, between 13 and 28 per cent in Italy, and between 12 and 28 per cent in France (Rhys, 1972). The differences, therefore, are those of degree, the relative impact of which the absolute levels prevailing in Britain overstate. At least equally important in affecting the overall demand for new cars was credit, which became increasingly restrictive during the late 1960s. The minimum deposit on cars was raised in 1965 from 20 to 25 per cent and the repayment period reduced from 36 to 30 months; in 1966 this dropped to 24 months plus 40 per cent deposit. Thereafter, fluctuations in minimum deposit levels between 40 and 25 per cent were accompanied by variations in repayment periods between two and three years (Dunnett, 1980).

Such alterations did, inevitably, affect sales, but international comparisons of demand fluctuations suggest that, as with respect to taxation, the British experience was not exceptional. Comparisons between instability of the demand for vehicles in the British market with those of Germany and the United States between 1955 and 1975 reveal a remarkable similarity (Jones and Prais, 1978). Evidence from various sources suggests, therefore, that whatever the destabilizing effect of the British governments' fiscal, credit, and general interest rate policy measures on the motor industry, the essential characteristic of the motor vehicle as a capital good, subject to postponable purchase or replaceable from the large second-hand market, was probably the dominant influence on demand in Britain as in other countries.

There is no doubt that the effects of these policies on the industry were adverse, but it does not necessarily follow that government policies explain all, or even most, of the relative deterioration in Britain's international ranking from the 1960s. There is little doubt that the macroeconomic policies of British governments intensified instability, perhaps to a greater degree compared with the effects of policies in Europe. In all countries the market for motor vehicles showed a sensitivity to cyclical changes in the ratio of cost of acquisition to income, although there may have been differences in the degree to which government measures intensified instability (Bardou *et al.*, 1982).

While disagreement exists over the importance of macroeconomic measures as causes of the industry's increasing lack of international competitiveness, there is no dispute over the adverse effects, as yet unquantified, on companies' activities of regional economic policy introduced by the British government in the

1960s. The objective underlying geographical dispersion was to reduce unemployment in depressed areas, in Scotland, South Wales and Merseyside, where firms in growth industries were 'encouraged' to locate expansion in new plants built in those particular regions. Through the offer of subsidies and the withholding of the industrial development certificates required for planning the construction of new plants, motor manufacturing investment in Britain was funnelled away from the Midlands and the South-East, the traditional centres of motor production. It was diverted to areas remote from the main assembly plants, away from the major component suppliers and from concentrations of skilled labour (Wilks, 1984). One effect was to deter rationalization of an already geographically fragmented industry and probably, though as yet to an unmeasurable degree, to increase production costs (Dunnett, 1980). Dunnett argued that another adverse effect was to introduce 'an unsuitable fractious labour cohort' into the industry (Dunnett, 1980, *181*). Workers influenced by experience in collieries and shipyards or by the prevailing culture of trade union militancy associated with those areas exacerbated labour relations in the motor industry (Dunnett, 1980).

The post-war years presented the industry with a secular expansion in demand favourable to investment and the development of overseas markets on an unprecedented scale. Whereas government policies reinforced the growth of exports, macroeconomic policies intended to achieve economy-wide objectives included specific measures which intensified demand instability, with adverse effects on industrial investment. How far these policies adequately explain the relative decline which began in the 1960s, however, is open to question. So too is the extent to which they contributed to poor labour relations, regarded by many contemporaries and subsequent historians of the industry as the key to a cumulative competitive failure.

(iii) Manufacturing systems, management and labour

Before the Second World War British manufacturers had been more successful than Ford in the home market in terms of production and market share. Marketing strategies have been adduced as a major part of the explanation for the British success in establishing its leading position in Europe. Lewchuck's analysis of corporate performance seemed unhelpful in the interwar context. It is possible, however, that Lewchuck's explanation for the roots of decline gains plausibility when applied to the period after 1939. The shift in the balance of power between labour and employers may have increased the importance of the difference emphasized by Lewchuck between the Fordist approach to mass production, involving a high degree of managerial control over labour, and the British system in which piece-rate payment systems contained an inherently greater potential for a high level of control by labour over the work process (Lewchuck, 1986).

Before 1940 the potential for workers in British factories to assume quasi-managerial functions, central in Lewchuck's analysis, remained unfulfilled, the explanation for which was the weakness of trade unions in the face of anti-union employers, and the growth of semi-skilled, non-unionized labour (Tolliday, 1987a). After the war a sellers' market shifted the balance in favour of organized labour at the same time that employers' introduction of automatic transfer machines to meet rapidly expanding demand required renegotiation of piece rates. This new technology so increased the minimum efficient scale of production that in order to secure scale economies it became essential to utilize plant intensively. Increased capital–labour ratios required sharply increased labour productivity through continuous production and improved working practices (Maxcy and Silberston, 1959; Rhys, 1972).

In the final assembly process, which amounted to between 15 and 20 per cent of the average car manufacturer's costs in Britain, the economies from flow production were exhausted at an output of 100,000 units per year, and the same was true of foundry operations. However, the machining of major components – cylinder blocks for example – could be carried out most efficiently at levels between 400,000 and 500,000, utilizing very expensive, model-specific equipment. The pressing of body panels, roof and doors necessitated an output of 1m units a year for optimum production in order to obtain lower unit costs by intensive utilization of hugely expensive dies. This process, therefore, set the overall technical optimum scale for car manufacture at about 1m units in the 1950s. By 1970 further technical advances in the various processes had doubled the overall optimum figure to 2m units, though only the giant American producers – General Motors, Ford and Chrysler – were operating at these levels (Rhys, 1972).

Even at the much lower levels of output of European and British manufacturers, efficient labour utilization and a greater intensity in the use of capital became imperative from the 1950s when automatic transfer machines were widely adopted in most British factories of appreciable size (Turner, Clack and Roberts, 1967). Under such conditions, Fordism, according to Lewchuck, had a major advantage. It assured management greater control over the deployment of workers and the pace of production. This was a critical determinant of unit costs. The abnegation of management under the 'British system' placed British companies at a serious disadvantage at a time when accelerating technical change required close and effective managerial control over work processes, particularly the pace of assembly lines and day wages. Piece rates placed that control largely in the hands of workers on the shop floor (Lewchuck, 1986).

British employers found themselves at a relative disadvantage in this respect. To varying degrees, they had favoured piece rate systems during the interwar years at a time when organized labour was weak. This was followed by a political context in which the wartime National Government and the subsequent trade union-dominated post-war Labour government were sympathetic to labour. War and the post-war boom created labour shortages and enabled workers, particularly at shop floor level, to assume an appreciable degree of managerial control.

The likelihood either of altering the existing payments system or of adapting working practices was not increased by managerial attitudes to labour. Addressing the National Union of Manufacturers in 1947 Leonard Lord, chairman and managing director of Austin, and soon to lead BMC, referred to the government's plea for cooperation between industrialists and workers and asked 'With whom are we going to cooperate – the shop stewards? The shop stewards are communists' (Wyatt, 1981, *239*). The superior investment, productivity and financial performance of Ford after 1945 suggests that although there may be sound reasons to reject

Lewchuck's hypothesis when applied to the British industry before 1939, such an analysis might offer a valid explanation of the decline of the motor industry under the very different circumstances prevailing after the war. Not only had the technology of car production altered dramatically, but the fragile state of trade unionism before the late 1930s was transformed by a growth in membership. After the war government ensured that trade unions gained some form of recognition from employers although, with the exception of Vauxhall, managers were grudging in making this concession (Clayden, 1987; Thornhill, 1986).

Recognition provided a climate conducive to a rapid growth in union membership at a time of booming demand for car workers. The well-established practice whereby trade union officials and the Engineering Employers' Federation negotiated formal wage agreements for the whole of the engineering sector, rather than for the car workers as a separate group, continued after the war. This was a system which took little account of the disequilibrium in the labour market in the fastest growing industry within the engineering sector. One effect was to make recruitment to car factories more difficult, another was to frustrate workers' material aspirations at a time when market conditions were favourable. Furthermore, although considerable changes occurred in car technology and working conditions after the war the EEF continued to refuse to negotiate on matters other than wages and hours (Turner, 1971; Durcan, McCarthy and Redman, 1983). In response to pressure from the shop floor, the Amalgamated Engineering Union and the Transport and General Workers' Union placed a growing reliance on shop stewards to secure effective organization (Turner, 1971). In the light of subsequent criticisms of the role of stewards in undermining industrial relations and preventing improvements in productivity it is relevant to ask how they were so successful in achieving not only substantial increases in pay but an extraordinary degree of control over the work process. Was this the main cause of the industry's deteriorating performance from the 1960s?

The consequences for factory management of these developments may be illustrated by the events at the Standard Motor Company in Coventry, which during the 1950s was the third largest British car producer. In 1949 Standard was the first company to adopt a piecework system intended to facilitate the introduction of new technology and production methods. The arrangements adopted drastically reduced the numerous grades to which piece rates applied. The complexity of the previous piece-rate structure was replaced by a system whereby production bonuses were paid to large 'gangs' of workers operating as teams. In the determination of production levels, therefore, the collective responsibility of the 'gang' largely superseded that of the individual. Part of this new arrangement was the principle of 'mutuality', embodied in the 1922 Agreement but since then largely ignored by employers. Mutuality required managers to seek shop stewards' agreement on working practices before implementing change of any kind affecting production. These included not only piece rates, but manning levels, work station mobility and the setting of performance criteria. This most extreme form of managerial abdication prevailed until 1956, during a period when the growth of trade union membership in a context of booming, if fluctuating, demand for labour enabled shop stewards to enforce mutuality and to negotiate rates at levels which seriously increased costs and threatened the firm's viability.

The structure which was introduced in 1956 also included a production bonus, but by dispersing this more widely among workers Standard's managers sought to weaken the position of shop stewards, though in the event with little success (Melman, 1958). The post-1956 agreement left the mutuality principle intact, and with it shop stewards' power to affect working practices. Stewards in other car factories pressed for similar concessions as a way of enhancing earnings and protecting conditions at work. The result was that job control became a central feature of labour relations in British car factories for more than twenty years, generating a tension (Melman, 1958) between full-time union officials constrained by agreements and procedures, and shop stewards whose resort to unofficial action embarrassed union officers (Turner *et al.*, 1967).

Piecework accompanied by less than complete managerial control also prevailed at BMC. Evidence submitted to the Royal Commission on Trade Unions in 1966 revealed that at BMC's largest plant at Longbridge shop stewards were expected not only to avoid disputes and strikes but were also called upon to coordinate production at shop floor level. Several factors have been adduced to explain why in the 1950s and 1960s a sectionally-based labour movement succeeded in filling the vacuum left at shop floor level by the weakness of managerial control. The sheer growth in the number of trade unionists working in the industry provided the basis for strength in bargaining. The marked cyclicity of demand, in part the consequence of government monetary and fiscal policies, coupled with employers' characteristic short-term hire and fire practices led to a search by the trade unions for greater security of employment and earnings (Turner *et al.*, 1967). However, the form which these campaigns took was influenced not only by union strength through large membership but by multiple unionism.

The existence of numerous unions in the industry resulted in interunion competition to establish workplace organization, another factor which complicated industrial relations. So too did overlapping jurisdiction between unions which produced rivalry in recruiting members, notably between the Amalgamated Engineering Union and the Transport and General Workers Union. Both of these unions placed a growing reliance on shop stewards, regarded as essential in securing effective organization. Clayden considered this aspect of union activity in the motor factories to be an important yet neglected factor explaining the particularly vigorous development of workshop organization in the motor industry (Clayden, 1987). He suggested that the interaction of sectional trade unionism with the employers' strategy of indirect managerial control through piece rates resulted in 'sectionalism within the work place, job control and fragmented bargaining' (Clayden, 1987, *321*). Workers tended to be loyal to organization at gang level, much less so at plant level, and hardly influenced at all by union organization outside the factory (Adeney, 1989).

Similar strictures were made on the adverse influence of shop floor power on productivity and costs in a report by BL's joint productivity committee in the 1970s, in which the working practices of the company were compared with those of its competitors. The report drew attention to the greater amount of non-productive time, frequently prolonged by go-slows and arguments about job mobility or demarcation, more relaxation time, more generous time standards, and a worse record of disputes (Marsden *et al.*, 1985). Just how important these factors were in contributing to the industry's difficulties, and identifying where responsibility for such practices lay, requires further consideration.

(iv) The role of organized labour: strikes and productivity

Compared both with other manufacturing industries, and with the motor industries of other countries, the British motor industry was highly strike-prone. The number of stoppages increased tenfold between 1948 and 1973 while average numbers of workers involved grew ninefold. Working days lost were seven times as many at the end of the period (Durcan *et al.*, 1983). The rise was appreciable from 1964, reaching a peak in the 1970s. In 1969–73 the average number of strikes was 273, resulting in the loss of 1.8m working days. In 1974–8 strikes averaged 194 and working days lost numbered 1894. Figure 4 shows the long-term trends in production, strikes and associated working days lost.

There is some evidence which suggests that the percentage of man-days lost in vehicle manufacture in the 1960s and 1970s was half as high again as in the United States and ten times greater than in Germany (Jones and Prais, 1978). As the scale of plants in both countries was considerably larger than those in Britain, and as in manufacturing industry generally larger plants tended to be more strike-prone, it has been suggested that the explanation for the difference in strike propensity is to be found in contrasts between the industrial relations systems in the respective countries (Jones and Prais, 1978).

Those differences also affected the impact of strikes on production and productivity. In contrast to the United States and Germany, where single union plants entered into contracts for a specific period, British multi-union plants enjoyed much shorter periods of strike-free intervals. Jones and Prais concluded that because productivity in volume car production depended on large plant size the failure of employers and workers to resolve disputes without stoppages was the most important single factor contributing to the industry's decline (Jones and Prais, 1978). In various forms this stress on industrial relations as the major factor appears both in contemporary commentaries and in historians' analyses (HC 14th Report, 1975; Bhaskar, 1979; Dunnett, 1980).

There is ample evidence of the weaknesses of labour relations. In 1966 the motor industry Joint Labour Council appointed Jack Scamp, a leading trade unionist outside the motor industry with a

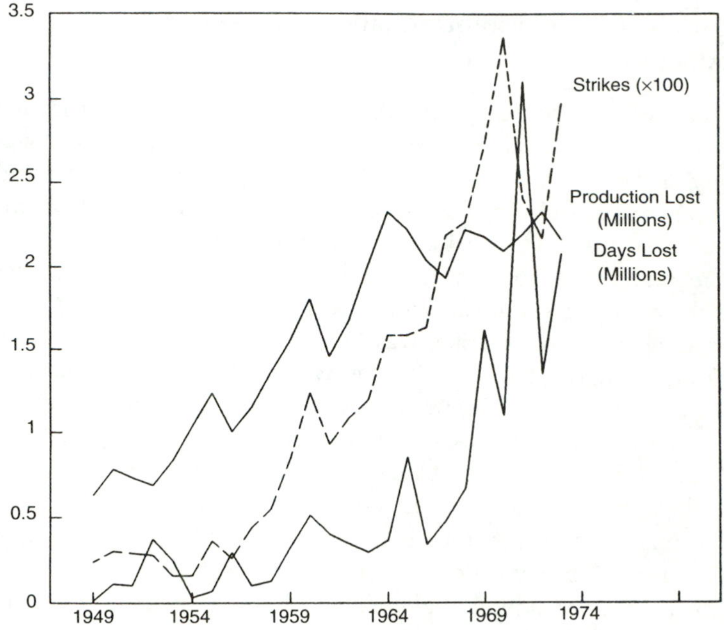

Figure 4 *Strikes, working days lost and production, 1949–74*
Sources: Turner, Clack and Roberts (1967), p. 110; Durcan, McCarthy and Redman (1983), p. 315; SMMT

reputation for skill in negotiation and conciliation, to investigate the industry's record. Three aspects received particularly critical comment. One was the irregularity of employment and the casual attitudes it engendered among both employers and employees (Durcan *et al.*, 1983); second, piece rates, though potentially productive, had an adverse effect because of the high degree of interdependence between the producers and their suppliers; third, stoppages at suppliers produced irregular earnings and differentials, both contentious issues which have led to disputes involving car workers. Yet when piecework payments halved in 1970–3 strike activity remained at high levels (Durcan *et al.*, 1983).

While noting certain specific management weaknesses, notably the continued refusal of the EEF to bargain on matters other than wages and hours, Scamp's report reserved its major criticism for the lack of internal structure of the many unions represented in the factories. To this, more than any other single factor, was attributed the failure to enforce collective agreements which lay at the heart of the industry's appalling labour relations record. It was this fundamental weakness which has been described as evidence of 'obsolescence in institutions' (Turner *et al.*, 1967, *339*). Dunnett and others have linked poor labour relations with associated stoppages and restrictive work practices to inefficient utilization of plants and low productivity (Dunnett, 1980; Bhaskar, 1979; Jones and Prais, 1978).

Others have played down the connection between strikes and productivity. Turner, Clack and Roberts, and Durcan, McCarthy and Redman explained the sharp rise in the level of strikes and working days lost between the late 1950s and early 1980s in terms of fluctuations in the demand for cars. Turner *et al.* suggested that the connection might be explained by management allowing stoppages to drag on or to widen out at times when demand fell. This strategy avoided redundancies and did not require explicit acknowledgement by negotiators on either side (Turner *et al.*, 1967). Because this hypothesis refers to motivations it remains little more than a plausible explanation. Calculation of productivity by Jones and Prais, however, suggests that the direct effect of working days lost due to labour disputes was marginal. For example the number of vehicles produced per worker per year fluctuated between 7 and 9 not only throughout the 1950s but also during the subsequent period of very high strike activity after 1964. This gave some credibility to the Turner hypothesis (Jones and Prais, 1978).

Comparisons with other European industries suggest that the British motor industry was not exceptional in experiencing labour difficulties. Introduction of the new technology into French and Italian factories, involving a shift towards higher capital–labour ratios, new job classifications and renegotiated pay, resulted in rising absenteeism, high labour turnover and major strikes (Bardou *et al.*, 1982). One important difference affecting success in achieving closer control over labour on the Fordist model on the Continent is to be found in the contrasting character of the labour supply. During the 1950s British car factories offering high earnings attracted workers from other parts of Britain and the 1960s saw location of production outside the major centres of the trade, in Scotland, Merseyside and South Wales. At the same time in Europe untrained, foreign or 'marginal workers' recruited to the motor industry required a completely new factory discipline to inculcate entirely novel working practices (Bardou *et al.*, 1982). Britain's adverse record of strike activity compared with the rest of Europe needs to be set against markedly better figures for turnover and absenteeism among British workers (Durcan *et al.*, 1983).

Industrial relations were damaging to the industry. Without more systematic quantitative comparisons, however, it remains difficult to assess the relative importance in their effect on the industry of British car workers' propensity for 'formal' conflict with employers compared with the 'informal' type which characterized industrial relations in the rest of Europe.

(v) Industrial relations: Fordism and post-Fordism

How far did Ford's post-war industrial relations system contribute to that company's superior productivity record? Willman argued that in this respect Ford possessed a 'comparative innovative advantage' (Willman, 1986), a view consistent with Lewchuck's conclusion on the superiority of Fordism as a system of management control in which high day wages were coupled with firm labour discipline (Lewchuck, 1986, 1987). Tolliday has questioned this analysis, which he regards as valid, but only to a degree, before Ford's takeover of Briggs Bodies in 1953. From that time onwards Ford began to experience similar influences to those affecting British-owned factories. Unlike workers at Dagenham, Briggs workers had been accustomed to shop floor bargaining and differential wage-grade structure. When they were moved from Southampton to man the new Dagenham Body Department a determination to perpetuate custom and practice led to a series of disputes and strikes in the face of Ford management's refusal to concede their demands (Tolliday, 1991).

The 'bell ringer' dispute of 1957, when a shop steward stopped the line to call a meeting over workers who had been disciplined by managers for leaving Dagenham to lobby a meeting of national negotiators, signalled a period of endemic conflict. The intensity of the conflict was aggravated by a group of well-organized communists, 'a union within a union', resisting managers' attempts to reimpose their right to manage (Adeney, 1989). In 1962, a year after the parent company had purchased the remaining shares held in Britain to restore complete American ownership, the managers of Ford UK effectively destroyed shop floor organization at Dagenham after a major strike precipitated by the dismissal of 17 activists (Tolliday, 1991). At Ford's Halewood plant near Liverpool, however, stewards established some control over manning levels and work pace. By the mid 1960s Ford's rigid wages structure began to change as competition for skilled labour compelled managers to extend special merit payments and allowances throughout the company. This resulted in differentials in addition to those built into Ford's rigid grading system.

These departures from the company's traditional 'industrial creed', in which workers and shop stewards were completely subordinate in return for high day wages, culminated in radical reform in the 1970s. When that occurred, however, it was in reaction to the company's failure to enforce in the courts a mutually binding employment contract with Ford's national Joint Negotiating Committee as part of the 1969 pay deal. Ford managers had expected to receive the support of the Labour government because of its declared aim nationally to find an alternative, orderly system of industrial relations in place of strife. Ford's attempt to devise their own legally enforceable contract proved unpopular with the trade unions, while the government gave no indication of approval for Ford's action. Opposition from the unions and inactivity of government combined to prompt a rethinking of management's approach to labour. A realization that legally enforceable contracts on the American model would not provide a method of orderly pay bargaining was followed by a growing recognition that neither would the traditional Ford managerial ideology of paternalism and direct control offer a solution to the problems of labour management (Tolliday, 1991).

These events finally prompted the move towards a new relationship with the shop floor representatives, accepting their legitimacy as negotiators, while retaining their own managerial prerogative intact. Shop stewards and plant conveners became part of the newly formed joint negotiating committee designed to integrate union organization into the collective bargaining process. Tolliday concluded that by the late 1960s – as in the mid 1950s – managerial control over the labour process was failing, the evidence of which included frequent labour disputes, off-standard performance, inflexible skills, loss of productive time and lack of right-first-time production. Time lost due to strikes rose (Tolliday, 1991).

Tolliday's account of industrial relations at Ford, therefore, reveals variation and, beginning in the mid 1960s, the gradual disintegration of the Fordist model system of labour management. Market pressures, together with the success of shop stewards in British factories in raising earnings, diminished the longstanding differentials between workers at Ford and those employed elsewhere, with adverse effects on Ford's labour relations. Coincidentally, following the formation of BLMC in 1968, moves were made to abandon piecework in British factories and to introduce machine pacing and measured daywork along traditional Fordist lines (Tolliday, 1991).

By such steps it was envisaged that British managers would restore 'the right to manage'. Measured daywork was introduced on a plant-by-plant basis between 1971 and 1974 in return for fixed earnings levels. However, shop stewards succeeded in negotiating bargaining rights with respect to effort norms, work methods and manning levels – the principle of 'mutuality'. In effect, while the responsibility for pacing and work effort was removed from the workers, with whom, to a considerable extent, it had lain under the piece rate system, managers now found themselves responsible. The extent to which managers succeeded under the new system depended not only on their ability to counteract shop floor concern over improving job conditions and security, but critically on managers' preparedness to shoulder their new role of maintaining continuity and quality of production, a question to be pursued below.

(vi) Fordist structure and strategy: the managerial organization

While the validity and importance of the contrasts between the classic Fordist system of management and labour relations and the so-called 'British system' have occasioned debate, little disagreement exists concerning the significant differences between the corporate structure and investment and marketing strategies of Ford and its British competitors in the volume car market. Ford's renaissance in the 1930s coincided with the replacement of American by British executive management including Sir Percival Perry, investment in new models, for the first time designed specifically for the British market, and the construction of the massive Dagenham plant equipped for mass production to supply cars throughout Europe.

For the post-war period, as for earlier periods, Lewchuck has stressed what he regarded as an important difference in the investment policies of American and British companies. Ford invested more heavily than British motor companies, a contrast which Lewchuck explained in terms of a preference in British companies for high dividends at the expense of capital retained in the business – itself a consequence of the readier availability of external finance (Lewchuck, 1985a, 1986). British companies – and Vauxhall – did raise external capital after the war, but Maxcy and Silberston stressed the relative unimportance of capital issues or bank advances as sources of funds; a similar conclusion was drawn by Rhys for the 1960s. He detected no deliberate corporate policy of high distribution, although the maintenance of dividends in the face of fluctuating profits does suggest an appreciable sensitivity of managers to stock market perceptions of equity capital. At the same time, however, and in contrast to the years between 1946 and 1962, depreciation became a much more important source of funds compared with retained earnings (Rhys, 1972).

He concluded that while equity capital and bank loans were important in financing total assets during the 1960s, gross fixed investment was largely dependent on internally generated funds (Rhys, 1972). Neither Maxcy and Silberston nor Rhys offers evidence which unambiguously supports Lewchuck's stress on British companies' preference for low profit retention, interpreted as reflecting a short-term corporate view which relegated investment and growth in their priorities. Of greater significance is the difference between the depreciation policies of Ford compared with the British companies. Between 1929 and 1938 Ford's depreciation figure was 16 per cent above that of Austin and

Morris combined, a level which rose to 24 per cent between 1947 and 1956 (Maxcy and Silberston, 1959). Although Maxcy and Silberston's analysis shows the proportion of retained earnings plus depreciation to have been greater after 1945 than before the war, the increase in Ford's net assets grew so substantially that by 1956 their value exceeded that of BMC (comprising Austin and the Nuffield organization) (Maxcy and Silberston, 1959). Ford's fixed asset per employee (a measure of capital intensity and a proxy for machinery per worker) and output–labour ratio in 1969 were roughly three times those of the major British producer, BLMC, for which the figure was the lowest in Europe. Of the five least capitalized firms in Europe, two others, the American subsidiaries Vauxhall and Chrysler UK (formerly Rootes), were in Britain. The five firms with the greatest capitalization were in Germany (Rhys, 1972).

Although highly capitalized by British standards, Ford UK compared poorly with Ford (Germany), Opel, the General Motors subsidiary, and Volkswagen, where value added per employee was also substantially higher than that of Ford UK (Rhys, 1972). These relativities persisted during the 1970s (Bhaskar, 1979). The fact that Ford UK's real assets fell between 1968 and 1973 suggests that even Fordist management was not immune from the effects of government policies and labour difficulties, regardless of whether these are considered to have been of primary or only secondary importance in explaining the industry's weakness. Unlike the British manufacturers, however, the multinationals possessed alternative options, for the reorganization of the Ford companies in Britain and Continental Europe in 1967 in the form of Ford of Europe heralded a new stage in the trend towards the globalization of motor manufacturing (pp. 112–20).

The question remains, why did Ford perform so much better than its British competitors within an environment of sluggish economic growth in an industry particularly sensitive to the effects on demand of government macroeconomic policies? Ford, like British firms, was constrained in its choice of investment location and was equally affected by taxation and credit policies, yet Ford succeeded in generating levels of profits which enabled asset ratios to increase and productivity to remain above that of British car makers.

Ford's immediate post-war success was the outcome partly of a strategy, determined in Dearborn, that the company should compete strongly in the British market. This helps to explain the considerably heavier capital investment in Britain compared with that in other European subsidiaries (Reich, 1990). Ford benefited too, however, from especially cordial relations with the British government, a consequence, it has been suggested, of Sir Percival Perry's role in the national armaments procurement policies, and of the building of the Fordson tractor plant in Cork, seen as a valuable contribution to increasing food production in the UK (Reich, 1990; Wilkins and Hill, 1964). In addition to favourable steel allocation, another advantage which strengthened Ford's position after the war was the £6.6m government-funded plant built in Manchester to produce Merlin aircraft engines. The investment in multi-purpose machinery, again financed by government, was adaptable to car production when the war ended, whereas the single-purpose machinery installed in many British factories for aircraft production was not (Wilkins and Hill, 1969; PEP, 1950).

Reich has argued that the goodwill generated by Ford's role during the war, together with the company's safety from the threats of nationalization when the Labour government was formed in 1945, enabled Ford to disregard price regulation, part of the government's anti-profiteering policy, although the company did observe limitations on dividend payments (Reich, 1990; Dunnett, 1980). As a result, Ford's post-war profits increased rapidly between 1945 and the Korean War. Another important factor peculiar to Ford in 1945 was that it possessed a factory built for the purpose of mass production. In accordance with the pre-Dagenham vision of Sir Percival Perry, Dagenham had been intended to be the major Ford plant in Europe supplying Continental markets with Ford vehicles. Such a vision helps to explain the factory's annual capacity of 200,000 units whereas the maximum number of vehicles sold in the British market in any year before 1940 had been 318,000 cars and 78,000 commercial vehicles in 1937, a level not exceeded until 1953 (SMMT).

When in 1934 the control of Ford's German subsidiary was acquired by the National Socialists, the power to determine Ford strategy in the rest of Europe was also weakened, in part the effect of rising intra-European tariffs. This left Dagenham dependent almost entirely on the home market, which limited production to levels at barely half-capacity. When after the war a decision was taken in Detroit to abandon the Perry pan-European strategy, Dagenham's large capacity became at once a spur to expansion and an advantage at the higher levels of production which were to become necessary for all successful volume car producers in Europe. The immediate post-war years also saw a reform of Ford's corporate organization in preparation for the most rapid expansion in the company's history since before the First World War.

A central policy-making committee was set up in 1948 to help shape the company's activities in Britain. The new managing director was Sir Patrick Hennessey, Irish by birth and one of the three senior managers in charge of Dagenham – regarded by contemporaries as the strongest team of any of the Ford subsidiaries (Wilkins and Hill, 1964). After taking a course in agriculture at Cork University, Hennessey had worked through the foundry, machine shops and assembly department of Ford's tractor plant, moving to sales and service at Trafford Park and on to Dagenham, where he took charge of purchasing and became general manager in 1939 (Jeremy, 1984–6). By adopting American purchasing methods, involving interactive production planning with suppliers, Hennessey held down the cost of intermediate inputs.

In 1951 Ford managers from Dearborn introduced financial control systems already in use by the parent company. This also marked the beginning of recruitment and training of financial analysts and later of engineers from the universities and the transfer of some engineering functions from Detroit to Dagenham. A new product-planning department was established in 1953, introducing a marketing strategy to develop new models which incorporated simple but effective engineering, displaying a concern first with price and second with design: designing to a price rather than pricing a design. The first fruit of this reorganization was the Anglia, introduced in 1959, the first British Ford to provide four forward gears, and sell 1m units (Adeney, 1989). Production concentrated on a small number of models to maximize economies of scale. In order to ensure the potential profitability of each model, costs were contained by redesigning those components found to exceed their target cost (Wilkins and Hill, 1964). The integration of the planning and organization of marketing, product development, and pricing with cost control and production became a central feature of the company's corporate culture.

(vii) Industrial structure, organization and corporate culture: the origins and performance of the British Motor Corporation

The contrast with Ford's British competitors after the war could hardly have been greater. Each of the four large producers, Austin, the Nuffield organization, Rootes and Standard, produced cars aimed at the popular 8 to 10 horsepower market, though each also produced a range of higher powered, more expensive models. The small specialist manufacturers which supplied only medium- and high-powered, expensive models included Rover, Triumph, Rolls Royce and Jaguar. The contrast between the single-plant, centralized operations of Ford at Dagenham and the fragmented, multi-company, multi-plant, multi-model characteristics of the British volume car industry was not lost on contemporaries. The 1950 PEP report criticized the continuing production of a variety and range of models which the volume of production could not economically support (PEP, 1950).

The report acknowledged that since 1939 the number of basic models in production had been reduced from 136 to 48, of which 17 came from the factories of the Big Six. Even so, the number was still considered much too large to enable either manufacturers or suppliers (whose components and accessories bought in from outside suppliers were estimated to be two-thirds of a car's factory value) to reap scale economies (PEP, 1950; NAC, 1947). Twenty-five years later the CPRS report also pointed to the excessive number of plants as the cause, to a large extent, of the industry's weakness (CPRS, 1975).

International comparisons made more recently by Jones and Prais revealed that the number of volume car assembly plants in Britain in the mid 1970s was 13, compared with 12 in Germany (Jones and Prais, 1978). It appears that the significant disparity lay in the size rather than in the number of plants. Census of production data suggests that by 1961 German median plants were larger than those in Britain and by the mid 1970s the output of the median German plant was estimated at between four and five times that of the British figure (Jones and Prais, 1978).

In terms of employment the contrast was less striking, mainly because of the higher productivity of German plants. In Germany the three largest car assembly plants each employed between 30,000 and 50,000 workers, not dissimilar to the workforces of the largest three American plants. The average of the biggest three in Britain was 23,000, consisting of Ford at Dagenham, 28,000, Austin (BL) at Longbridge, 22,000, and Morris (BL) at Cowley, including the nearby Pressed Steel plant, 20,000. The greatest relative divergence in plant sizes was between the vehicle assembly plants of Britain and Germany which was reflected in extreme differences in productivity. Neither in component manufacture nor in the production of bodies for commercial vehicles were significant productivity differences recorded (Jones and Prais, 1978). Because critics of the industry's performance have dwelt on the lack of scale economies in British plants it is important to know when the discrepancy originated in order to explain this weakness. The difference with US plants pre-dated the First World War, but on the basis of census figures Jones and Prais suggested that the origins of adverse comparisons with Germany were to be found not in the immediate post-war period, when the national Advisory Council and PEP were so critical of the industry, but from the early 1960s.

A degree of structural change had occurred in the British industry in the form of ownership (see Figure 5), and in the number of models and engines in production. Even within the Nuffield group of companies, basic models in production fell from 38 before the war to 10 by 1946, and engines from 21 to 5 (PEP, 1950). But these developments involved neither the construction of new plants nor rationalization and concentration of production in fewer factories. Post-war conditions sustained existing companies, their physical manufacturing capacity increased by the Shadow Factories built for war production. Any explanation why, during the twenty years after the war, German plants were so much larger must also explain why the concentration of production in fewer plants did not take place in Britain, and why the range of

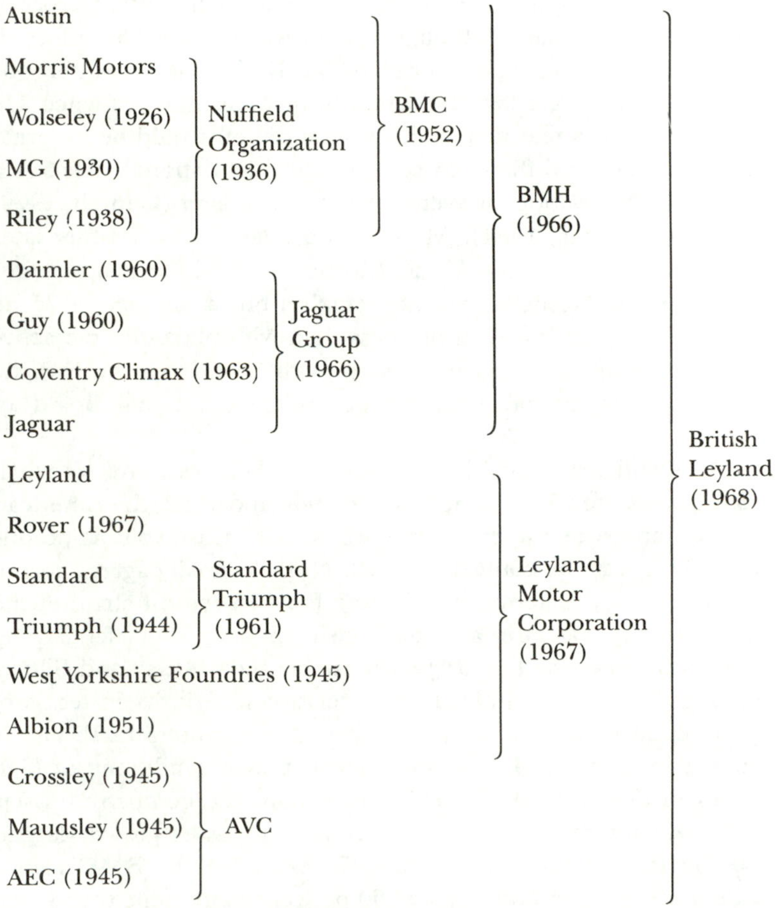

Figure 5 *Principal mergers involving British motor manufacturers before 1968 showing years of acquisition and amalgamation*

models in production was not reduced much further. This requires an examination of the origins, organization and management of the British Motor Corporation during the 1950s and 1960s.

In 1924 market forces had produced financial difficulties for Austin and pushed Wolseley, the Vickers subsidiary, towards bankruptcy. This had prompted the irrepressible Dudley Docker, acting for Vickers, always alert to money-making opportunities from once and for all financial rationalization of manufacturing companies, to try to persuade Morris and Austin of the advantages of a merger of the three companies. Although Austin was prepared in effect to concede ownership and control to W. R. Morris the latter was opposed to even the slightest compromise to his independence. He also expressed a fear that such an organization would be 'so great that it would be difficult to control and might strangle itself' – a prescient observation, as events were to show later (Church, 1979; Davenport-Hines, 1984). More than a quarter of a century later Lord Nuffield (formerly W. R. Morris) was still the major shareholder in the Nuffield corporate empire; but at the age of 75 he was preoccupied less with business than with philanthropic activities – although the decision to merge with Austin to form BMC he took, as was his practice, without reference to his Board of Directors (Overy, 1976).

Meanwhile, the combined market share of Ford and Vauxhall rose from 23 to 29 per cent between 1946 and 1952, the American proportion exceeding that of the two largest British volume producers. This was the context in which Nuffield finally agreed to sell out to Austin, thereby consolidating the 40 per cent share of the domestic car market in a single British company and safeguarding the organization he had originally established (Maxcy and Silberston, 1959; Overy, 1976). BMC's relative superiority in terms of production compared with the other manufacturers in Britain is shown in Table 7. In the short term, under conditions of high levels of demand BMC's ability to exploit the company's assets fully was impressive. While the company's asset growth lagged behind that of Ford, which in 1956 exceeded the BMC's asset value, the latter produced some 50 per cent more units than Ford. This was achieved by duplicating lines and machines in existing factories rather than by constructing a new purpose-built plant for mass production. None of the BMC's ageing factories was closed during the company's lifetime.

The formation of BMC was untypical of mergers in the industry in that hitherto few had taken place between firms which did not face serious financial difficulties (Maxcy and Silberston, 1959). Described by a former manager as 'the merger that never was' (Pagnamenta and Overy, 1984) the new organization came under the management of Leonard Lord, managing director and deputy chairman. Through a central panel Lord controlled investment

Table 7 *Shares of car production by major motor manufacturers in Britain, 1947–89 (%)*

				1947	1954	1960	1967	1974	1978	1982	1985	1989
Austin	BMC	BMH		20.9								
Morris	BMC	BMH		19.2	38.0	36.5	34.7					
Jaguar		BMH		1.6	1.5	1.7	1.4					
Standard-Triumph			British Leyland /BL /Rover Group	13.2	11.0	8.0	7.9					
Rover				2.7	1.7	1.6	2.7	48.2	50.0	43.2	44.4	36.0
Rootes-Chrysler		Chrysler	Peugeot –Talbot	10.9	11.0	10.6	11.7	10.9	16.1	6.3	6.4	8.3
Singer				2.1								
Vauxhall				11.2	9.0	10.7	12.7	8.0	6.9	12.7	14.0	16.0
Ford				15.4	27.0	30.0	28.4	25.0	26.5	34.5	30.3	29.5
Nissan												5.9

Sources: Dunnet (1980), p. 20; SMMT.

allocation to the constituent companies, and to that extent reorganization represented a move towards a multi-divisional structure. His rationalization programme was limited to rearranging the production of engines (reduced in number from nine to three), axles and gear boxes to secure greater specialization between plants. However, assembly continued to be dispersed in the factories of the merged companies. This was partly because BMC continued to produce the models associated with the formerly competing companies in an attempt to retain goodwill. Dispersed production was also the longer term solution adopted to meet the rapid expansion and scale of demand for the Mini, the company's best selling model in the 1960s, which was assembled in three different locations (Adeney, 1989).

Rationalization did not extend to marketing strategy. Until the early 1960s the Nuffield and Austin organizations retained separate entities each possessing a board of directors and a set of accounts (Turner, 1971). Such a corporate structure was not conducive to a rationalization of planning and the formulation of overall strategy. It reflected the history of managerial disarray within the Nuffield organization before 1952, which after merger was compounded by personal animosities between the managers of the merged companies. Both Leonard Lord, managing director and deputy chairman of BMC and formerly the senior figure at Longbridge, and George Harriman (who like Lord had been a senior figure first with Nuffield then with Austin), initially also deputy chairman and joint managing director of BMC, viewed the merger as a long-awaited victory for Austin (Turner, 1971).

Yet the marketing strategy continued to embrace the Nuffield philosophy of a full model range. Although the number of engines was reduced, BMC offered 14 different models, 9 from the former Nuffield factories and 5 from Longbridge. Each basic model was adapted, by variations in trim and accessories, to appeal to customer loyalties for whom the badge denoting the company of origin was regarded as an important selling advantage (Turner, 1971). 'Badge engineering', as it became known, was symptomatic of a policy of sales competition between the constituent organizations. The senior managers continued to encourage competition between Longbridge and Cowley, the former producing vehicles under the Austin name, the latter under the Morris banner, each marketing separately through Morris and Austin dealers (Turner, 1971). Hanks, formerly Morris's chief executive who later became vice-chairman of BMC, displayed a similar determination to that of Lord, his predecessor, to perpetuate this rivalry after merger (Adeney, 1989). BMC was a firm divided against itself.

Distributors and dealers were retained as separate sales outlets, reinforcing the intracompany competition between the Austin and Nuffield marques which survived the merger. The first 'corporate' BMC model, the Austin 40, was introduced in 1958, yet by comparison with Ford practice product planning continued to be as unsystematic as in the past. BMC's chairman and managing director explained the company's cautious approach to product development as a consequence of the high costs of retooling necessitated by the new technology introduced in the 1950s. In his view only the superior financial resources of Ford and Vauxhall made a regular model replacement policy economic. For that reason the company concentrated on advanced engineering so as to avoid the need for frequent model replacement. This contrasted with the incremental approach to innovation which was characteristic of Ford (Turner, 1971). Not until 1949 had Morris appointed an 'experimental engineer', and a 'standards engineer', when still the 'research director' complained that 'development thinking took place only in pubs, at dinners, and in washrooms'. Nuffield's spending on research was about 1 per cent of turnover (Overy, 1976).

Even after merger the pricing of vehicles continued to be largely an intuitive process. Lord had adopted the principle that popular Austin models should be less expensive than Morris cars competing in the same range, yet nowhere was information available on production costs specific to particular models (Adeney, 1989). Not until 1965 was a director of planning appointed with the responsibility of pricing models with reference to market criteria. The same year brought the appointment of a finance director and the establishment of a market research department. It also marked the introduction of a policy to recruit graduates, reversing Nuffield's antipathy to training other than through apprenticeship, again in contrast with the practice at Ford (Turner, 1971; Wood, 1988).

The limited effect which these belated changes had on rationalization and restructuring before BMC was taken over was revealed in an independent report on the company undertaken in 1968 on behalf of its prospective buyer, Leyland Motors. The report stressed the lack of an effective system of financial control and product planning. It also pointed to the prevailing corporate priorities which placed engineering excellence above financial control. The report also criticized low investment (Turner, 1971).

The history of the Mini exemplified these weaknesses. The price of this commercially successful model, both in the home and overseas markets, was fixed intuitively on the assumption that only if it was the lowest priced car on the market would sales of the Mini be large. In pricing the model before the prototype had been produced, no allowance was made for the full cost of innovations incorporated in the new design by (Sir) Alec Issigonis. This design for the prototype construction of the Mini, which incorporated front-wheel drive, transverse engine mounting and high-performance engineering, was carried out under the personal control of Issigonis. Allowed virtual freedom from cost limitations, Issigonis's design was highly innovative, but the cost implications were left to solution at the production stage while pricing was fixed regardless (Turner, 1971; Wood, 1988; Adeney, 1989).

The huge sales of the Mini which immediately followed the launch in 1961 led Ford's planning department to strip one down for detailed cost analysis. On each model priced at £496 the estimated loss was £30. Over a period of years, Sir Terence Beckett, Ford's manager of product planning, correlated BMC's profits with sales of Minis and the slightly larger 1100/1300 model. An inverse relationship prompted the conclusion that BMC had assets estimated at £170m locked up in the manufacture of these two models, neither of which earned the company a return (Adeney, 1989). Sir John Pears of Cooper Brothers, management accountants, concluded that the lack of cost information within BMC explained why the company had failed to devise a sensible way of pricing cars. This was symptomatic of a lack of managerial cohesion and of an autocratic managerial ethos which gave little sign of a sense of direction for the company other than the pursuit of engineering excellence (Turner, 1971; Wood, 1988). Sixteen years after the formation of BMC (enlarged in 1966 by acquiring the body builders, Pressed Steel Fisher, and by merging with Jaguar to form British Motor Holdings) the accounting system in

Britain's largest vehicle manufacturer was still not designed to supply precise information on model costs (Turner, 1971).

Between 1945 and 1968 car production in Britain fell from first to second place behind Germany. The growth in industrial concentration affected ownership rather than managerial structure, producing an underdevelopment of the strategic managerial function, one tangible manifestation of which was badge engineering, a symptom of intracompany competition, minimal central cost control and a lack of planning. Underdevelopment of the management function was also in evidence at the shop floor level, where various forms of piece rate systems enabled labour to shift the balance of advantage against managers. These continued to hamper the company during the 1960s, when the move towards freer international trade began to intensify competition in home and overseas markets. It was this development which precipitated further mergers, culminating in 1968 with the birth of British Leyland.

3
The vicissitudes and collapse of a 'national champion'

(i) Anatomy of a merger: the rise of British Leyland

When in 1968 BMH merged with the Leyland Motor Company to form the British Leyland Motor Corporation (BLMC, renamed BL in 1977), the new organization became the second largest motor manufacturer outside the United States and the fifth largest manufacturing company in the private sector in Britain. At the beginning of the second phase of decline, Britain's 'national champion' held 40 per cent of home sales and 35 per cent of the truck market (Cowling, 1980). The effects of mergers have been a subject for debate between those who stress the greater opportunities mergers offer for achieving economies of scale and scope – the prevailing conventional wisdom within government in the mid 1960s – and those who emphasize the contingent nature of these potential advantages. This raises the questions: Why did the merger occur? What were its effects on the industry's performance, and how can they be explained?

The possibility of restructuring and reorganizing the entire industry became stronger from the 1950s when Leyland Motors, the small Lancashire manufacturer of specialist commercial vehicles, acquired others of a similar kind: Albion Motors and Scammell, followed by ACV in 1962 (Turner, 1971). Leyland's success in this sector contrasted with its history of failure as a car manufacturer. For a brief period during the 1920s Leyland had produced two models, the 'Straight Eight', designed to compete with Rolls Royce, and the Trojan, a small, solid-wheeled vehicle whose tram-wide wheel span could create a hazard for urban driving. In 1961 Leyland re-entered the car trade when it took over

Standard Triumph, followed in 1967 by Rover. Both were manufacturers of specialist cars, neither of which was strong financially but each dominated market niches, Standard Triumph in the market for sports cars, Rover selling medium-quality cars in addition to the unique Land Rover for commercial use. In these limited market niches the Leyland–Standard Triumph connection proved relatively successful during the six years before the Leyland–BMH merger in 1968 (Turner, 1971; Rhys, 1972).

The ultimate decision on merger was that of the shareholders of the participating companies, among whom Prudential Insurance held a substantial interest, following lengthy negotiations which involved the respective company directors of Leyland and BMH. However, the Labour government played a key role in bringing about the regrouping. The initial suggestion that the two companies might merge came from Anthony Wedgwood Benn, the Minister of Technology in the Labour government of Harold Wilson. In preparing a national economic plan civil servants at the Department of Economic Affairs had identified the car industry as one of the economy's major problems, which led both Benn and Wilson to become personally involved in its solution through merger. Formal pressure to promote the prospective merger was applied through the Industrial Reorganization Corporation (IRC). This was the governmental body (of which Sir Donald Stokes, Leyland's managing director, was a member) charged with the responsibility for promoting mergers for the purpose of rationalizing British industry (Turner, 1971).

The IRC ensured that in the restructuring which resulted, 'cress', the codename for BMH, which was regarded as a badly-managed company, should be subordinate to 'mustard', the corresponding cipher for Leyland Motors, whose contrastingly strong financial position derived mainly from the buoyant commercial vehicle sector. The IRC assumed that Sir Donald Stokes, regarded as one of the country's leading salesman, would be able to duplicate that company's success as a producer of cars for the volume car market. The government's intervention at that time betrayed increasing concern at the growing strength of the American multinational manufacturers in the British market. The Leyland merger, described by Benn as 'a fantastic achievement' (Benn, 1988, *16*) may thus be seen at least in part to have been driven by government in response to Chrysler's acquisition in 1967 of a substantial shareholding in the ailing Rootes group, the other British volume car producer (Young and Hood, 1977).

In order to understand why the merger failed it is necessary to establish the objectives of the various parties to the negotiations. The government's aim was to bring to an end the fragmented structure of the industry in order to consolidate and rationalize an independent British industry. As the largest manufacturing exporter, the industry was important to the balance of payments, which before devaluation in 1967 had been especially critical to the government's economic policies. As a major employer, too, the industry attracted special interest from the increasingly interventionist Labour administration (Turner, 1971). Sir Donald Stokes and his co-directors expressed concern that their shareholders' interests should not suffer as a result of the merger, a fear which diminished somewhat as the relative share prices of the two companies moved in opposite directions, lowering the cost to Leyland when the takeover occurred.

The managers of BMH were initially opposed to merger. Even after personal intervention by the Prime Minister to persuade its ailing chairman to agree in the national interest, the BMH managers proceeded on a mistaken assumption that despite the company's deteriorating financial position the larger size of the volume car business would ensure the dominance of BMH in any amalgamation and the subsequent corporate reorganization (Turner, 1971; Adeney, 1989). As it turned out, the financial strength of Leyland together with the connivance of the IRC enabled Leyland to take over BMH and to control the board of the new company. Furthermore, an immediate £25m loan from the IRC for retooling was the first indication that Leyland was to be afforded special treatment as a 'national champion'. The following year Stokes became deputy chairman of the IRC, the organization responsible for monitoring the performance of British Leyland – of which he was now the head (Turner, 1971).

Outright takeover of this kind was virtually without precedent in the industry since the 1920s. Hitherto, the holding company had been the characteristic form of amalgamation. By perpetuating the constituent corporate entities, and with few exceptions retaining the owners or managers who ran them, holding companies had not been instrumental in achieving corporate and industrial integration. The formation of the British Leyland Corporation was seen as offering an opportunity to begin the long postponed transformation.

Expressed in terms of the historian's model which relates successful business strategy to structural adaptation (Chandler, 1990; Channon, 1973), a necessary, though not sufficient, precondition for effective corporate performance was a transition from a personal and entrepreneurial structure, characteristic of both BMH and Leyland, to a corporate, managerial organization – in reality as well as on paper. Ostensibly, Lord Stokes's task was to integrate eight public companies into one, but the constituent companies were themselves the products of previous mergers (Cowling, 1986). The chronological history of the precursors of British Leyland is presented in Figure 5. Lord Stokes later reflected on the overwhelming difficulty he had faced in welding together '50 or 60 different companies all trying to retain their independence even though they had been take over' (Adeney, 1989, *254*). John Barber, Leyland's new finance director, formerly of Ford and the electrical manufacturer AEI, referred to BLMC as consisting of 'a mass of unrationalized plants and unrationalized products' (Adeney, 1989, *256*). On its formation BLMC produced roughly one-half of all cars made in Britain (see Table 7).

(ii) The effects of merger

In 1974–5 three official reports offered diagnoses of the industry. The first was prepared by an independent body, the Ryder Committee, set up by the Labour government as a preliminary to deciding on a policy for the industry. The second was that of the Trade and Industry Sub-Committee which conducted its investigations, complete with extensive evidence from numerous witnesses from within the industry, in response to the Ryder Report and its recommendations. The third was produced by the government's 'think tank', the Central Policy Review Staff (CPRS).

The conclusions drawn by these three bodies differed mainly in emphasis, though they were in agreement that BLMC was in danger of terminal collapse. Ryder emphasized the handicap of the company's outdated plant and machinery, its excessively centralized corporate organization, and also criticized weaknesses in management–labour communications which contributed to a bad record of industrial relations. The Trade and Industry Sub-Committee was also critical of a debilitating bargaining structure, but attached greater importance to overmanning and excess capacity which reflected a failure to respond to consumer demand (HC, 14th Report). The CPRS levelled similar criticisms, but blamed lack of maintenance of plant and equipment and working practices which slowed workpace and restricted productivity. With various differing emphases, these several interpretations of the nature of the company's problems have been incorporated in subsequent attempts to explain decline (Bhaskar, 1979, 1983; Dunnett, 1980; Williams *et al.*, 1983, 1987; Wood, 1988; Adeney, 1989).

While the reports differed in specifics they revealed general agreement on the extent to which the government's optimism concerning the future of BLMC in 1968 had not been realized. Why not? One reason was the sheer scale of the rationalization needed. Britain's only large vehicle manufacturer now possessed 48 factories which included 23 major plants accumulated by BMH. The product range ran from low-priced volume cars, specialist, luxury and sports cars to heavy goods vehicles, buses, fire engines and dustcarts. A former assistant controller of Ford of Europe who was recruited to British Leyland described the characteristics of the new merger as a 'multiplicity of style, multiplicity of technology, multiplicity of everything . . . The organization lacked a common system, a common ethos or culture' (Wood, 1988, *247*).

The attempt to provide a coordinating multi-divisional structure to a considerable extent perpetuated historical continuities and functions, which existing geographical dispersion tended to reinforce. The Truck and Bus Division was based at Leyland; Austin–Morris, the volume car division, produced in Birmingham and Oxford; while the Specialist Car Division included the Coventry factories of Triumph and Jaguar, and the Solihull Rover plant. The remaining four divisions were those specializing in bodies, power and transmission, parts and kits for assembly and an overseas division dealing with exports and foreign subsidiaries (Salmon, 1975). The activities of these divisions, each represented by a managing director responsible for the profit centre and participating in the formulation of overall corporate policy along with senior staff directors under the chairman, were subject to control by central office organized on a basis of staff and line management. A large central staff department was responsible for monitoring and controlling the seven divisions. A greatly enlarged staff, however, was not accompanied by the delegation which was normally a feature of the managerial hierarchies of multi-divisional companies and this led to duplication. No fewer than 21 directors and managers reported directly to the chairman, in effect perpetuating the personal, hierarchical tradition of the company he had worked for since boyhood (Salmon, 1975). A former manager employed by Ford, later briefly chief executive of BLMC, described the process of decision-making at BLMC as lacking in documentation and almost intuitive. The company lacked explicit corporate objectives, which meant that neither monitoring nor analysis of corporate performance were systematically employed in the assessment and formulation of business strategy (Pagnamenta and Overy, 1984).

While a multi-divisional structure had been introduced, the strategic policy-making, coordinating, monitoring and informational advantages which restructuring was intended to achieve remained unrealized. Six years after the merger the Specialist Car Division remained largely unchanged, evidence of a continuing conflict of subcorporate philosophies compounded by a legacy of distrust rooted in the past (Salmon, 1975). This continued to be the case after the Ryder reforms of 1975. Although they were intended to reduce centralization by substituting four for seven divisions (combining Austin Morris and Specialist Cars to form BLMC's car product planning division), they left the balance of power shared between divisional managing directors and the overall corporate managing director as a matter of 'personal chemistry', and left lower level local management within the divisions with ill-defined authority (Salmon, 1975; HC, 14th Report, 1975).

Clashes of culture continued to occur. One example is that which led to the closure of a high-technology £25m plant built at Solihull to produce a new Rover model, codenamed SDI, to compete with BMW. The insistence by Leyland head office on rapid quantity production of the new car conflicted with Rover's tradition of emphasizing high-quality vehicles manufactured in relatively small volume. Difficulties over overmanning, demarcation, and over-optimistic sales forecasts culminated in BLMC's senior managers overruling the Rover factory's inspectors. The first immediate consequence was a poor reputation for the new car; the second was the plant's closure after only five years (Pagnamenta and Overy, 1984).

The evident failure of the Leyland version of multi-divisional operations did little to integrate the former corporate units and provoked suspicion and hostility towards central management. This has been interpreted as evidence of Leyland managers' lack of experience of mass production, large workforces, and extensive managerial hierarchies (Cowling, 1986). Whereas at the time of the merger Leyland was making 23,000 commercial vehicles a year, the car-making capacity of BMH exceeded a million, and employed 200,000 workers (Wood, 1988). The chairman and managing director of the new company, Sir Donald Stokes, had worked for the small, Lancashire-based heavy truck and bus-making company since he joined as an engineering apprentice in the 1930s, although it was as an effective sales manager for Leyland heavy trucks and buses that he was to make his contribution to the company's success after the war. From its formation as the Lancashire Steam Motor Company in the 1890s until 1963, three generations of the owner-founding Spurrier family had been chairman, or general manager, or both (Turner, 1971). When in 1963 terminal illness removed the ageing Henry Spurrier II from Leyland, and Stokes became deputy chairman and managing director of the Leyland Motor Corporation (the precursor of BLMC), he was the only director below the age of 70, reflecting a disregard for managerial succession characteristic of British firms (Turner, 1971).

Rootes, the second largest British car manufacturer and the greatest loss-making motor company in Britain, had been in the hands of the Rootes family since its foundation in the 1920s. Until 1967, when control was conceded to Chrysler, the firm had displayed characteristics similar to those of Leyland. It had been built up through a series of mergers. An incoming Chrysler manager described the Rootes organization as having been divided into a number of largely uncoordinated separate family empires. The autocratic rule of Lord Rootes, who died in 1964, had been followed by 'a period of less decisiveness', but most significant as evidence of the intuitive approach to managing the organization was the lack of adequate cost accounting and other financial controls and the absence of a profit plan (Young and Hood, 1977; Wood, 1988).

In an attempt to keep Rootes in British hands, in 1967 the Minister for Technology, Anthony Wedgwood Benn, had invited both BMH and Leyland to rescue Rootes, then sliding towards bankruptcy (Benn, 1988). Neither company expressed interest, perhaps because the directors of both companies recognized a lack of managerial depth in their respective organizations. BMC's graduate recruitment policy was of recent origin and had suffered high turnover. Stokes was also conscious of Leyland's own serious shortage of managers capable of transforming the British car industry (Adeney, 1989). Later he described himself and other Leyland managers as not being 'motor car people. . . . We switched off lights and saved pennies' (Wood, 1988, *163*).

Clearly the supply and quality of management was a weakness which the departure of certain senior managers of high quality, resulting from the takeover in 1968, probably made worse (Turner, 1971). In part this was because the production and market characteristics in the heavy commercial vehicle sector contrasted markedly with the mass produced car sector. New cars produced since the Second World War were of unitary body shell construction providing the rigidity to support the power train. This, together with the importance of body shape and size as the major source of product diversity, meant that body panel construction dominated the economics of car production. In the heavy commercial vehicle sector chassis and body remained separate, the special requirements of industrial consumers resulting in a high degree of product diversity (Rhys, 1972).

In the light and medium weight section of the industry, van and truck production benefited from standardization and since the 1930s had been dominated by the mass producers, Morris, Ford and Bedford (Vauxhall's CV subsidiary). Until the merger with Leyland, BMC was the largest CV manufacturer, responsible for about one-third of total CV production, although that was concentrated almost entirely on light, car-derivative models and medium vehicles. Ford and Bedford each accounted for between 20 and 25 per cent during the same period. Leyland's concentration at the opposite end of the range gave that company barely a 6 per cent share of CV production, which on merger with BMC rose to about 40 per cent. Until that time Leyland's success depended mainly on small-scale, skilled, labour-intensive manufacture of vehicles to customers' detailed specifications in a segment of the market less affected by the extreme slumps experienced by the car industry (Rhys, 1972).

The failure of the Leyland merger of 1968 was the result of both external and internal factors. International movements towards freer trade intensified the competition from manufacturers in Continental Europe. Internal weaknesses were those of an industry in which historical and personal continuities frustrated corporate reform along multi-divisional lines. A complicating factor was that the volume car division came under the management of those whose training and experience was mainly in the production and sale of specialist commercial vehicles and, briefly, medium-quality cars. Furthermore, BLMC was also constrained by the indirect effects of various governments' balance of payments, income and employment policies, which inhibited labour relations and created a climate of uncertainty unfavourable to sustained investment policy. Employment policy was the government's justification for rescuing Rootes, thereby intensifying competition within the home market and reducing Leyland's opportunity to gain volume and reduce costs. Whatever the corporate weaknesses, government policies hindered rather than helped the British motor industry.

(iii) British Leyland's productivity dilemma: markets and productivity

After 1968 car production accounted for 70 per cent of BLMC's business, though the models in production were becoming outdated. The Mini, still the top-selling model, was nine years old, and the Morris 1100/1300 six years old. Both were under competition from more recent models, particularly the Ford Cortina (replaced by the Escort in 1968) and the Vauxhall Viva (Cowling,

1986; Williams, Williams and Haslam, 1987). Yet BLMC lacked the financial resources to design and launch a completely new model. The Austin Allegro, which went into production in 1973 to replace the Morris 1100/1300, closely resembled its predecessor, while the Morris Marina, first introduced in 1971 to compete in the medium-car class, incorporated some of the parts used for the 1948 Morris Minor (Adeney, 1989).

The inability to sell models in large numbers was critical to production at competitive costs. This was Leyland's productivity dilemma. Estimates of the minimum production levels at which the scope for economies of scale existed suggest that only in the assembly process were some models produced in sufficient numbers annually (between 0.2m and 0.25m) to achieve them. The optimum levels of annual output for engine blocks of about 1m and for body panels of 2m (at which level all processes achieved scale economies) were beyond those of any model produced in Europe, with the exception of the Volkswagen 'Beetle' (Rhys, 1972). Some progress was made towards the rationalization of models, reduced from 39 to 24; however, the extent of this process was limited by the board's reluctance to concentrate production in fewer factories with a smaller workforce, regardless of the criticisms of BMH reported to the Leyland directors prior to the new merger (Cowling, 1986).

BLMC's new finance director, formerly a manager at Ford and subsequently at AEI, considered the company to be overmanned by 30,000, which Stokes attempted to reduce through exhaustive consultation with the trade unions. The recent massive redundancies which had followed the rationalization of the GEC–AEI merger had alerted the trade unions to the possibility of a similar threat, increasing the risk of further strikes should BLMC pursue a similar tactic (Wood, 1988). A disinclination on the part of management to tackle the overmanning problem at a time of difficult labour relations meant that it was not until 1978, when the factory at Speke was closed by Stokes's successor, Michael Edwardes, that plant rationalization and a reduction of manning levels began in earnest.

Not surprisingly, Cowling's estimates of efficiency gains for this period show none attributable to merger (Cowling, 1986). Furthermore, such model rationalization that did take place had damaging consequences for the company's share of the home market. Ford had reduced its dealer network in 1963 by one-third over five years, at a time before imports had gained a permanent and substantial foothold. When BLMC carried out a similar rationalization between 1968 and 1976 one-third of the 7000 dealers whose franchises were withdrawn soon took up franchises for importing European and Japanese vehicles. Even after rationalization Ford dealers sold on average double the number of cars of each outlet handling BL cars (Williams, Williams and Thomas, 1983; Adeney, 1989).

Leyland's delay in rationalization was a serious handicap during the 1970s when the state of the motor industry worldwide, damaged by the oil crises, their economic ramifications and the emergence of excess capacity in the industry, made profitable trading problematical. Until the late 1960s none of the major companies in Britain had recorded more than one or two losses since the war, though Ford's profit record was considerably superior to that of the other volume car makers. Between 1960 and 1967 the pre-tax profits of BMC-BMH amounted to £132m compared with Ford's £174m (Dunnett, 1980). Ford, moreover, produced roughly one-third fewer cars than the British manufacturer. Higher unit profits and a higher rate of return on capital were the key factors explaining Ford's financial strength and its superior cash flow which supported higher gross investment (Maxcy and Silberston, 1959; Silberston, 1965; Rhys, 1972; Dunnett, 1980). Between 1974 and 1982 Ford was the only car manufacturer in Britain which did not make a loss (after tax) in every year except one. Before tax, the comparable figures for BL show a net loss over the period of £198,000, although losses were widespread also among companies in Europe and in the US (Bhaskar, 1984a).

The origin and timing of the British company's weakness may also be highlighted by comparing estimates of the profitability of the three principal categories of motor vehicles: volume cars, specialist models (which before the Leyland merger were produced by Jaguar, Rover and Standard Triumph) and trucks and buses. Estimates suggest that during the early 1960s BMC's volume car production generated roughly three times as much profit as each of the other two categories. Between 1967 and 1972 the Austin–

Morris Division of BLMC contributed 17 per cent, the Special Cars Division 49 per cent, and trucks and buses 34 per cent (Bhaskar, 1975). Thus, well before the sharpest reductions in tariffs occurred and the globalization of international production which followed, volume car production was already the least profitable of BLMC's activities, and exercised a financial drag on investment in the other two divisions.

The difficulties which the combined effects of these developments presented to BLMC's market position intensified as a result of two further changes. One was the shift from indirect to direct full-line competition, the commencement of which Williams *et al.* (1987) identified in 1977. Ford entered the small car market for the first time with the Fiesta, followed by BL's attack on all three main market segments: small, light and medium. The other new factor was Vauxhall's successful re-emergence as a major car maker in Britain in the 1980s, when the company produced the J Series Cavalier. Financed by GM and designed by its Opel subsidiary, the model was aimed at the medium fleet car market (Williams *et al.*, 1987). Market fragmentation and direct competition led to a relatively even distribution of sales of the ten best-selling models, four from Ford, three each from Vauxhall and Rover, none of which reached 10 per cent of the share in its class. Under such circumstances, capturing 20 per cent of the market with three models became virtually impossible for any company. In effect the possibility of reaching scale economies without very substantial exports or a multinational operational basis had been removed (Williams *et al.*, 1987).

BLMC's relatively poor sales record has been attributed in part to the distinctive structure of the market for cars in Britain which Williams *et al.* (1987) have argued made the industry particularly vulnerable to aggressive importing when tariffs fell. Their analysis revealed two almost discrete submarkets, one for business users, either as purchasers of fleets or separately, and the other for individuals making private purchases. The submarket for business began to develop in the mid 1960s when employers reacted to government income policies by offering subsidized company cars as a way of circumventing pay constraints for managers. Between 1964 and 1975 cars owned by firms and subsidized by employers (who also received tax concessions on their purchases) (Ashworth,

Kay and Sharpe, 1982) rose from 17 per cent of domestic sales to 40 per cent. This meant that the segment of the market which was expanding most rapidly was that which BLMC was least well equipped to exploit, for Ford already dominated sales in this market with the medium-sized, medium-priced 1500–1600 h.p. Cortina, its capacious boot and rakish lines contrasting with those of the Maxi and the Marina (Wood, 1988). Another consequence of this structural change was that BLMC was left with an extensive distribution network suited to private consumers. Yet when it was rationalized the beneficiaries also included importers, who from the early 1970s were attacking the private car market and required established outlets through which to distribute sales (Williams *et al.*, 1987).

The context in which restructuring and rationalization were attempted became increasingly difficult from the mid 1960s. The sheer acceleration of changes affecting competition in both home and overseas markets tested entrepreneurial and managerial limits to the full. After nearly 50 years of protection the tariff was reduced to 25 per cent in 1963, to 17 per cent in 1969 and to 11 per cent by 1972 (22 per cent on CVs). From 8.3 per cent on entry to the EEC in 1973, by 1977 the tariff had disappeared altogether. These developments coincided with the worldwide recession which resulted from the threefold increase in oil prices in 1973–4, and again in 1979, intensifying competitive pressures. The nature of that competition also became more complex as the process of globalization, initiated by the American multinationals in the late 1960s, began to alter the dynamics of international trade in motor vehicles. As tariffs fell, the British industry became vulnerable to competition from Europe, particularly from the high-volume, high-productivity Volkswagen plant. In 1965 the German industry had produced 6.4 'equivalent' motor vehicles per employee per year compared with 5.8 in Britain; by 1970 the comparable figures were 7.5 and 5.6, and in 1976, 7.9 and 5.5 (Jones and Prais, 1978). Successful new designs from the French state-owned Renault company also contributed to import penetration (Rhys, 1972).

A further development requiring flexible managerial organization, additional capital expenditure and highly trained staff was the higher rate of innovation made possible by computer-assisted

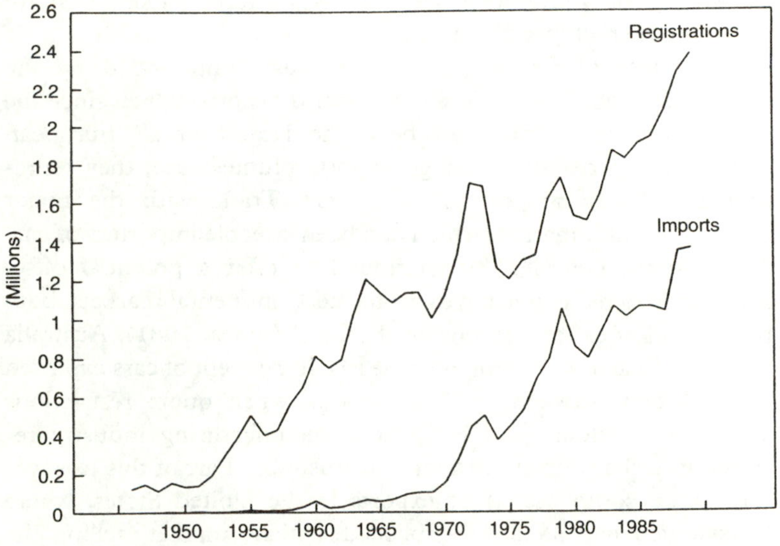

Figure 6 *New car registration and imports, 1946–89*
Source: SMMT

design, engineering and production. The demand for such technological and human resources was further increased by new safety and pollution standards required for vehicles sold in the American market, a trend which during the 1980s became both international and progressive and caused difficulties (Whipp and Clark, 1986), although by that time the British industry's strong trading position had already been severely eroded.

Freer international trade, faster productivity growth in Europe and Japan, together with the greater competitiveness of foreign cars in terms of price and design, enabled importers to penetrate the British market. When during the peak sales and production period during the summer of 1971 easier credit and lower purchase tax on cars had the effect of increasing car sales by 43 per cent, imports were sucked in to meet a demand which the domestic industry could not supply. This episode has been described as the catalyst which heralded a permanent shift in the tastes of British consumers in favour of foreign cars (Dunnett, 1980). Thereafter, regardless of the buoyancy or otherwise of the

British economy, import penetration took a rapidly rising share of the home market (see Figure 6).

The effect of import penetration was compounded by the relative decline in Britain's share of world exports, which since the 1920s until the 1950s had been the largest of all European countries. Thereafter, although export volumes rose, they represented a lower proportion of output. Trade with the major Commonwealth markets which had been sizeable importers of cars from Britain before 1939 continued to offer a potential offset against restricted exporting to protected Continental markets, both before and after the creation of the EEC (Jones, 1981). Australia and New Zealand accounted for nearly 40 per cent of cars exported from Britain between 1947 and 1956, when quota restrictions aimed at developing an indigenous manufacturing industry resulted in a sharp drop in exports to Australia. Part of this loss was for a time compensated by exports to the United States, where Volkswagen had already established a niche market, selling the small European utility vehicle as a second family car. In 1959 British cars comprised nearly 50 per cent of American car imports, but they fell sharply to 10 per cent in 1961 when American manufacturers countered with their own new range of compact cars. Among European manufacturers only Volkswagen retained a substantial hold on this market (Rhys, 1972; Nelson, 1967).

Meanwhile, the adverse implication for trade of British manufacturers' relative absence, historically, from the European market was reinforced by very marked trade expansion within the EEC. Whereas by the late 1970s France and Germany traded on average 1.25m units within Europe, the figure for British sales was below 200,000. Part of the explanation for the British lag lies in the existence of Continental tariffs, but other factors are also important. One was the pressure exerted by government for a very rapid growth in exports during the post-war dollar shortage which meant that both quality control and the building of an adequate distribution and service network took a lower priority than production for an overheated market (Rhys, 1972; Wood, 1988). The experience of the widely publicized, new 'world car', the Standard Vanguard, aimed especially at international markets, illustrates this. Since there was a lack of time to test for foreign conditions, the Vanguard proved to be too underpowered to meet American requirements, insufficiently sturdy to overcome the dust and corrugations of the roads and tracks of South America, Australasia and Africa, and inadequately sprung to give comfort on paved Continental surfaces. Accordingly it attracted a reputation for unreliability which became difficult to dispel (Turner, 1971; Pagnamenta and Overy, 1984).

Neither in France nor Germany did a dealer network selling British cars exist during the 1950s. Furthermore, when in the 1960s successful sales of the Mini offered an opportunity to develop an international distribution system (following Volkswagen's strategy) BMC had opted for a policy of local assembly, exporting kits rather than complete vehicles. Of the three assembly operations set up by BMC in Belgium, Italy and Spain in the 1970s, however, only the Belgian plant at Seneffe was owned by BMC. The licences issued to the Italian and Spanish companies for the assembly and sale of Minis and Allegros were merely temporary, however, terminable either by lessor or licensee. Only the highly innovatory Mini, with transverse engine and front-wheel drive, obtained success in Europe, where in the 1960s it accounted for 70 per cent of all of British car sales (Williams *et al.*, 1987). From the 1970s, however, these innovations had been incorporated as common features of international car design.

European manufacturers had introduced newly designed models which included the slightly larger, less Spartan varieties of super-Minis and hatchbacks to compete with the Mini and with BLMC's much less successful models, the Marina and the Allegro. Replacement of these, however, was prevented by BLMC's low profitability and insufficient cash flow in consequence of limited sales volume and underpricing. This was worsened by continued dividend payments which at least in the short term weakened the overall financial position of the merger. It is also possible that one effect of dividend payments during the recession of 1966–7, the intention of which was to shore up BMC's market value (Turner, 1971; Rhys, 1972), was to inflate Leyland shareholders' expectations after the merger. This might explain why between 1968 and 1975 out of £74m profit £70m was paid out to shareholders, evidence of that short termism which Lewchuck considered to have been a long-established feature of British motor manufacturers. However, state and industry discussions of the level of investment needed to rescue BLMC in 1975 make it clear that the scale of the company's diversion of profit was small in comparison with the volume of funds required to introduce new models and methods. It should not, therefore, be regarded as fundamental to the company's deep-seated problems (Adeney, 1989).

One of the consequences of BLMC's weakness in the market at a time when vehicle manufacturers in all countries were experiencing the effects of a contracting world demand was a dramatic rise in import penetration as vehicle producers looked to overseas markets to compensate for sharp falls in home demand. In 1975 imported cars accounted for 33 per cent of new registrations, exceeding BLMC's share of 31 per cent for the first time. BLMC's production dropped from 1.7m in 1973 to 1.26m in 1975. In the same year the company declared a loss of £76m, representing between £90 and £160 on every vehicle sold. When the banks refused to continue their financial support it was left to the government to decide whether to allow the 'national champion' to collapse, accepting the dire consequences for unemployment and the balance of trade.

(iv) The nationalized champion: policies and personalities

BLMC was not allowed to go bankrupt because the government was concerned over the effects on the balance of trade and on employment. Prime Minister Harold Wilson described the industry as 'an essential part of the United Kingdom economic base' (Wilson, 1979, *137*). The company was given a £50m guarantee, pending an investigation of its affairs by a small committee under the chairmanship of Sir Don Ryder, the head of the newly established National Enterprise Board (NEB). The outcome was a recovery plan agreed between government and BLMC which involved the acquisition of public equity and an expenditure of £2000m over eight years. Benn, minister at the Board of Trade and Industry, set out in detail the purpose of the government's strategy: 'to subsidize British motor manufacturing that would otherwise be replaced by imports from the EEC and elsewhere; and to provide long-term capital at non-commercial rates to re-equip and improve capacity and competitiveness' (Benn, 1989, *364*). After Ryder's plan had been accepted by government the body responsible for its implementation was the NEB. In effect, because of the very large volume of funds which the plan called for, the British-owned industry came under state control.

The plan adopted for the industry originated from an internal company document prepared by BLMC managers even before Ryder had conducted his own investigation, but of which he became informed in the course of his inquiry. He accepted their predictions for future sales, a critical planning assumption which in the event proved excessively optimistic. It was on that basis, however, that the Ryder plan justified the need for expanding production and no redundancies. In the light of concern expressed by a cabinet minister that if the company was not rescued 'a comprehensive motor industry' and nearly a million jobs would be lost (Castle, 1980, *374*), the two assumptions underlying Ryder's strategy were at least consistent with the government's overriding aims in nationalizing the company.

They may also have been decisive in securing cabinet approval for such massive public investment. Cabinet accepted Ryder's analysis, which persuaded members that the problems, in the words of one participant in the discussion, were those of 'poor management . . . grotty machinery and bad industrial relations' (Castle, 1980, *374–5*). Part of the formula for revitalization was a change in management. Stokes assumed an honorary role and received a peerage; John Barber was sacked. The new managing director, Alec Park, hitherto Leyland's finance director, assumed the major responsibility together with a part-time chairman (Adeney, 1989).

From the outset relations between management and the NEB caused difficulties, for while the NEB held responsibility for monitoring the company's progress, reporting back to the Secretary of State, the plan was framed in such vague terms that the point of ultimate responsibility was unclear (Jones, 1981). An intervening period ensued during which Ryder, acting almost independently of the advice from members of the NEB, not only monitored the company's activities but intervened in day-to-day decision-making. This *de facto* assumption of the role of quasi-chairman of the board was an arrangement which neither managers nor trade union leaders found satisfactory (Bhaskar, 1979; Adeney, 1989).

Equally unsatisfactory was the new system of industrial relations machinery introduced on Ryder's recommendation. On the principle of industrial democracy a joint management and trade union consultation process was established at three levels. While the principle of industrial democracy was intended to signal to the trade unions a new era, in practice the unions found the dispersion of consultation did nothing to strengthen the powers of negotiation of official trade union leaders with corporate management, consequently in 1979 they withdrew from the new Joint Management Councils (Willman and Winch, 1987). Within two years of the new regime the consequences of an inflation rate above 20 per cent, repeated stoppages, declining sales, and an import penetration which rose to 45 per cent in 1977 brought about a further managerial reconstruction.

The prevailing ambiguity of authority was replaced by the unambiguous managerial control of a single figure who was both chairman and managing director, receiving advice from two close aides (Bhaskar, 1983). Under a new Labour Prime Minister, James Callaghan, and a new Secretary of Trade and Industry, Eric Varley, Stokes's successor was a self-styled apostle of free enterprise. He was Sir Michael Edwardes, a member of the NEB, who was appointed on a five-year secondment from his position as chief executive of Chloride, the largest battery-supplier to the motor industry. Trained as a lawyer, though experienced in rationalizing the battery-making industry in southern Africa and therefore familiar with the motor trade, his particular strength was considered to be in managing organizational change. Closely monitored by government, but without intervention in the implementation of mutually agreed objectives, the Edwardes strategy of producing new models depended on continuing, substantial government finance. The 1975 formula worked out by the government guided by Ryder had made that conditional on three objectives – the ending of overmanning, a transformation of working practices, and improvements in industrial relations.

Under Ryder changes in industrial relations had been structural rather than substantive at the operational level (Willman and Winch, 1987) and made no significant contribution to achieving an improved strike record and reductions in overmanning. From 1977, under a new regime which no longer ruled out plant closures, Edwardes introduced a confrontational approach to the trade unions, particularly to shop floor activists, over pay claims, plant closures and work practices (Willman and Winch, 1987). Edwardes sacked the communist Derek Robinson, popularly known as 'Red Robbo', who led the opposition against the introduction of new working practices of any kind, particularly those which allowed the movement of workers between jobs. By this action Edwardes sought to end the buying out by managers of restrictive custom and practice (Edwardes, 1983). Cuts in the workforce of some 50,000 between 1977 and 1982, when those on the payroll numbered 83,000, were in part achieved through brinkmanship. Explaining the company's difficulties, and the need to persuade the government that the recovery strategy was working, Edwardes appealed directly and personally to meetings of shop stewards or other workers, who were asked to accept the need to reduce the numbers employed and to avoid stoppages (Willman and Winch, 1987; Adeney, 1989).

Corporate organization and structure were transformed. The car-making division, known as BL, was separated from Leyland Trucks and Leyland Buses. Unipart was the division manufacturing spare parts. With the aid of psychological testing the company undertook a systematic weeding of managerial staff at all levels, accompanied by highly selective promotion and recruitment of new senior managers, several of whom were attracted from Ford. The entire process represented a systematic attempt aimed at creating a completely new corporate culture in the boardroom, in offices and on the shop floor. These reforms proved sufficient to secure issue of £450m in government equity to enable the company to create two new models. However, the lead time for design and for the installation of new computer-aided technology left a potential two-to-three year gap between the launch of a replacement for the Mini and a new car aimed at the medium-price range.

To bridge the gap BL entered into an agreement with Honda, whose car production was similar in scale to that of the British company, and which was the third largest Japanese motor manufacturer. The first fruit of the memorandum of understanding between the companies was the appearance in 1981 of the Honda Ballade, developed in Japan, built at Canley and sold under the Triumph badge. The second product of joint Anglo-Japanese development was the Rover 800, the first of a new Rover series introduced in 1984 (Wood, 1988). The first new all-British model from BL was the Metro, conceived as the 'super Mini', which for the first two years after its launch in 1981, manufactured in a new robotized body shop at Longbridge, sold at an annual rate of over 170,000. That was followed in 1983 by the Maestro, the new medium-sized saloon car, which also exceeded 100,000 sales. The outcome of systematic research and design and of cooperation with Honda, these developments were seen by academic commentators and many other observers as symptomatic of, as well as instrumental in achieving, a turning-point in the recovery of BL (Jones, 1985; Willman and Winch, 1987).

(v) From nationalization to privatization

A detailed re-evaluation in 1987 suggested that these judgements were misplaced (Williams *et al.*, 1987). While the undoubted changes in industrial relations and more flexible working practices were achieved between 1977 and 1985 and acknowledged (Williams and Winch, 1987; Williams *et al.*, 1987), yet BL's falling market share at home and declining exports were signs that higher productivity was not enough to retrieve the company's position (see Table 8). Factories at home and overseas were closed in order to reduce fixed overhead costs, including the Belgian plant which had assembled over 50 per cent of the company's cars sold in EEC countries between 1976 and 1980. The closure in Belgium almost coincided with the drop in trade with Italy following Italia Innocenti's switch to Japanese engines and gearboxes for its rebodied Mini, which in the late 1970s accounted for between a quarter and a third of exports to the EEC (Williams *et al.*, 1989). Because the Austin cars shipped to Belgium and Italy were assembled locally they had established a status of quasi-indigenous products; without that exports to these two countries, and to Europe, collapsed after 1981. In the absence of a distribution network selling identifiably British cars, a switch to direct exports of complete vehicles

Table 8 *British Leyland production, exports and share of new car registrations, 1970–89*

of cars (000s)	Production cars (000s)	Exports of car sales (000s)	Total UK car sales (000s)	BL home share (%)	UK market
1970	788.7	368.4	1076.9	410.4	38.1
1971	868.7	385.8	1285.6	516.3	40.2
1972	916.2	347.3	1637.8	542.4	33.1
1973	875.8	348.0	1661.4	529.6	31.8
1974	738.5	322.5	1268.8	415.4	32.7
1975	605.1	256.7	1194.1	368.7	30.8
1976	687.9	320.8	1285.6	352.7	27.4
1977	651.0	293.3	1323.5	322.1	24.3
1978	611.6	247.9	1591.9	373.8	23.5
1979	503.8	200.2	1716.3	337.0	19.6
1980	395.8	157.8	1513.8	275.8	18.2
1981	413.4	126.2	1484.7	285.1	19.2
1982	405.1	133.9	1555.0	277.3	17.8
1983	473.3	118.3	1791.7	332.7	18.6
1984	383.3	78.6	1749.7	312.1	17.8
1985	465.1	112.8	1832.4	328.0	17.9
1986	404.5	123.6	1882.5	297.5	15.8
1987	471.5	165.7	2013.7	301.8	14.9
1988	474.7	137.0	2215.6	332.6	15.0
1989	466.6	138.5	2300.9	312.3	13.6

Source: Williams, Williams and Haslam (1987), Table B2, p. 126; SMMT.

required investment, successful models, and time for development. Meanwhile the high and rising value of sterling both undermined competitiveness and squeezed profit margins.

Williams, Williams and Haslam argued that BL's trading weakness was due mainly to a flawed business strategy, which resulted in a 'market-led failure' (1987, *67*). The new cars, the Metro and Maestro, were not sold in sufficient numbers, consequently between 1980 and 1985 capacity utilization averaged 56 per cent – well below the estimated 70–80 per cent needed to enable the Longbridge and Cowley factories to break even after covering depreciation, let alone secure economies of scale. Indirectly this drag on productivity was attributable, they maintained, to a failure to recognize the changing character of competition in the market, particularly within Britain. BL's strategy was the same which had led to Ford's strength in the British market since the late 1930s, the production of a narrow range of four basic models. However, because of the high capital costs of changeover each of the BL models was planned to have a long production life (Williams *et al.*, 1987). This was in the BMC tradition and in contrast to Ford. However, even as BL's new model strategy began to be implemented, Ford introduced the small Fiesta car in 1977, while Volkswagen replaced the 'Beetle' with the more conventionally designed and extremely successful Polo. Together they heralded a new phase of competition which in certain respects resembled the full-line model price competition of the 1930s, when manufacturers divided the market into niches. This made BL's lack of new models in the medium range at once a serious handicap, for the new competitive conditions reduced the likelihood of Metro sales reaching the predicted levels on which the Metro's planned production, costing, pricing and profitability were based.

Williams *et al.* (1987) argued that BL's difficulty not only stemmed from an inability to reach production levels which would bring scale economies, but that the particular capital-intensive technology employed on the Metro line at Longbridge was disadvantageous. While it offered flexibility in producing variants of models the technology did not allow variation in the number of basic models, small and light/medium cars which could be produced on the lines. The Dagenham plant both facilitated the production of variants and allowed flexibility in product mix. The new technology did increase BL's labour productivity, but capital productivity fell. So did the profits shown in the company's balance sheets (but which actually concealed losses) (Williams *et al.*, 1987). By 1987 the car division of BL (by that time renamed Rover Group) held only 15 per cent of the home market; imports had risen from roughly one-third at the time of nationalization to one-half (Table 8).

In the commercial vehicle branch, too, the British company was being squeezed. Both the American multinationals and some European manufacturers were competing effectively in the market not only for light- and middle-weight trucks but for heavy commercial vehicles, the demand for which grew in response to increasing transcontinental road transport. This was a sector in which until the 1960s Leyland, and later BLMC, had performed strongly both at home and overseas (Rhys, 1972). The penetration by European manufacturers into a market hitherto insulated from foreign competition was the result partly of the virtual stagnation in Leyland's commercial vehicle production capacity at a time when the demand, particularly for heavy vehicles, was growing, and partly to freer trade, culminating in entry to the EEC (Rhys, 1972). Arguably the merger of Leyland with BMH into which £3bn had been injected by government between 1975 and 1988 not only failed to remedy the weaknesses of the latter but ultimately undermined the success of the former (Adeney, 1989).

Public expenditure on such a scale under a government committed to privatization was the context in which the final stage in the history of the 'national champion' began. A further collapse of BL's market share and the prospect of further losses led to the intervention of the Department of Trade and Industry. In 1986 the company's part-time chairman, and the two senior managers who had taken on Edwardes's executive role after his return to Chloride at the end of his contract in 1983, were replaced. Combining both roles, on the Edwardes model, the DTI appointed another professional manager, the Canadian Graham Day, formerly chief executive of the heavy-loss-making British Shipbuilders. It was under Day's management that British Shipbuilders had been rationalized in preparation for privatization, which had become a key feature of Conservative government policy (Adeney, 1989).

Day proceeded to carry out a similar strategy to fulfil government objectives for the British motor industry. Jaguar, the small semi-luxury car maker, had already been sold on the Stock Exchange in 1984, although initially the government had retained a 'golden share' (revoked shortly after) to protect the company from corporate, especially foreign, raiders. In 1987 Leyland Trucks was sold to DAF, the Dutch CV manufacturer, while the bus division was disposed of in a management buyout, as was Unipart. In 1985 informal, secret meetings involving executives of Ford, BL and cabinet ministers explored merger. However, a political crisis, precipitated by the sale of the loss-making Westland Helicopters, raised the issue of foreign ownership of strategic British companies, creating a climate which torpedoed secret discussions involving Ford and senior political figures close to government. A resurgence of national feeling destroyed the possibility of a merger of the British car-making division with Ford. This was a development sought by the senior management at Dagenham anxious to withstand increasing import penetration. In particular they feared the growing threat posed not only by Japanese imports but in the longer term by inward investment and car production in Britain by Japanese companies (Adeney, 1989).

In 1988 Rover Group was sold to British Aerospace, the defence and property conglomerate, which itself comprised several former state-owned mergers between problem companies. The price of £150m was widely regarded as a gross undervaluation of the company's assets (and fell well below the figures mooted in the discussion involving Ford in 1985). The £520m cash injection from government was considered to be an overgenerous dowry, while tax concessions on Rover's losses and other concealed payments strengthened suspicions that political considerations were paramount in deciding Rover's fate (Adeney, 1989; *Independent on Sunday*, 9 August 1992). Three years later, in a conglomerate whose other divisions were also recording losses, Rover's market share in Britain slumped to no more than 13 per cent, while production was barely 0.4m and the workforce numbered 35,000.

(vi) Globalization and the role of multinationals

The ultimate demise of car and truck production by independent British-owned manufacturing companies was as remarkable for the speed with which the process occurred as for the scale and impact of that decline. That rapidity owned much to a combination of freer international trade and the growth of international competition. The effect on BLMC of rising import penetration on market share is shown in Table 8. From the early 1970s penetration by Japanese imports accounted for a small but rising share of new registrations, which led to an increasing concern among manufacturers in Britain. The result was an informal agreement between the SMMT and the Japanese manufacturers' association, whose members then held 9 per cent of the British car market, that a policy of 'prudent marketing' should limit imports voluntarily to no more than 11 per cent, an arrangement which continued to be observed (at the upper level) throughout the 1980s (Adeney, 1989).

Japanese imports exacerbated, rather than created, problems for the industry in Britain. Indirectly, however, the phenomenon of Japanese industrial expansion did have a considerable impact at a time when the British industry was at its most vulnerable. Built up rapidly during the 1960s behind tariffs at prohibitive levels, by the end of the decade Japan had become the world's second largest producer of motor vehicles. It consisted mainly of commercial vehicles and small cars exported on an increasing scale to the US, the Far East and Australia (Rhys, 1972). The response of the three American multinationals to Japanese competition in the US market was to increase investment in overseas subsidiaries and to move towards greater international integration of their operations. One effect of this was to intensify competition in Britain and Europe.

Beginning with the formation of Ford of Europe in 1967, Ford's policy – later emulated by General Motors and Chrysler – began as an exercise intended to achieve greater cooperation between the company's operations in Britain and Germany. Ten years later the strategy had evolved into a policy of regional integration of production and marketing based on international division of labour on a global scale. In Europe, meanwhile, the 1970s saw an increased level of industrial concentration, notably with the merger of Peugeot with Citroën. In 1979 the two largest motor manufacturers were General Motors (8.8m) and Ford (5.5m), but Japanese producers were third, fifth and tenth, including Toyota (3.0m) as third largest, followed by Volkswagen–Audi. The two largest French manufacturers, Peugeot–Citroën and Renault, were among the top ten, followed by Fiat (1.4m); British Leyland (0.6m) was fourteenth (Bardou *et al.*, 1982).

What were the effects of globalization on the motor industry in Britain? Its manifestations included a greater standardization of model range and the allocation of vehicle and component production between subsidiaries, based on comparative transaction costs. For example, the Ford Escort, launched in 1969, was manufactured both in Britain and Germany, although it was the Capri, introduced in 1977, which was the first Ford car to be conceived at the outset as a European car, built in cooperation between Ford plants in Britain and Continental Europe. In the 1980s the Fiesta, planned jointly by an Anglo-German team seconded from Dagenham and Cologne, exemplified the increasing levels of regional integration in progress. It was assembled in Germany and Spain; engine blocks were produced at Dagenham and carburettors in Northern Ireland. The proportion of locally-manufactured components in the three countries varied (Wood, 1988).

When General Motors began to rationalize production in 1979 car production and marketing were concentrated at Opel in Germany, and the manufacture of commercial vehicles in Britain. When in 1984 General Motors launched the J car (in Britain the Cavalier II), it comprised an engine made in Australia, either an automatic gearbox made in the US or a manual one made in Japan, a carburettor made in France, and pressings from Germany. The British contribution came to little more than oil filters, glass and wheels. The British content amounted to about 60 per cent, counting labour costs as roughly one-half (Adeney, 1989). With the power train manufactured elsewhere, as far as General Motors' operations are concerned by the early 1980s Britain had become little more than an assembly centre.

The trend towards 'sourcing' seriously affects the interpretation of trade statistics. Car imports from the EEC as a proportion of new owner sales in Britain rose from 20 per cent in 1974 to 38 per cent ten years later, and exceeded 40 per cent by the late 1980s; but this was largely attributable to British-based American assemblers obtaining an increasing proportion of their car sales in Britain supplied from plants in Europe. The combined figure for these tied imports by Ford and General Motors increased during that period from 1 to 22 per cent. Thus, whereas in 1973 the MNEs were net exporters of 200,000 cars, by the mid 1980s they had become net importers of around 350,000 (Jones, 1985; Bhaskar, 1984a) (see Table 9). Their strength in the British market since the 1970s was based as much on their role as the largest importers of Ford and General Motors vehicles sold as 'British' cars as on their superiority as manufacturers.

Furthermore, because of the American companies' practice of sourcing, the trade statistics understate the growth in imports. Whereas in 1973 Chrysler UK models sold in Britain embodied

Table 9 *Home car sales, tied imports and exports by US multinationals, 1976–89 (thousand units)*

	Ford			Vauxhall		
	UK Sales imports	Tied	Exports	UK Sales imports	Tied	Exports
1976	325	29	108			
1977	340	87	132			
1978	392	138	102			
1979	486	237	130	141	46	
1980	465	217	85	133	51	
1981	459	203	82	127	59	
1982	474	230	61	182	103	
1983	518	240	32	262	139	
1984	487	208	17	283	165	
1985	486	214	14	303	169	
1986	515	303	6	285	125	
1987	580	177	8	271	86	5
1988	584	249	7	304	119	1
1989	609	238	3	350	147	2

Sources: Bhaskar (1984a), pp. 529, 591, and SMMT.

97 per cent local content by value, by 1983 (as Talbot) the figure was 30 per cent. Over the same period the local content of Vauxhall cars fell from 98 to 22 per cent, compared with Ford's reduction from 88 to 22 per cent. By taking local content into account Jones calculated a tied car and component import figure of 4 per cent in 1974 which rose to 31 per cent ten years later. He estimated a 'true import content' figure for the British market in 1984 to have risen to 66 per cent, compared with official car import figures which showed stability at 57 per cent between 1979 and 1984 (Jones, 1985). The fall in exports by multinational subsidiaries was the consequence of corporate policies designed to limit intra-European trade by permitting plants in one country to export only to specific foreign markets. At the same time, the MNEs increased the export of kits for assembly in receiving countries. By 1983 Ford's net trade deficit from Britain reached £700m, that of General Motors £600m (Jones, 1985). Therefore, at a time when the British industry was struggling to maintain a

falling market share at home, the Trojan horse effect of tied imports and heavily-sourced cars which only appeared to be British was thus partly responsible for Leyland's inability to generate sales at levels which would support scale economies in production. From a national standpoint the MNEs were worsening Britain's trading balance on cars, which from 1975 went into the red.

One further indirect effect of the increasing strength of multinationals was that their reliance for basic research and development remained outside Britain. In this respect, throughout the 1970s the limited expenditure on R & D undertaken by BLMC/BL, also helped to put Britain well behind France and especially Germany, which benefited from R & D expenditure by American multinationals (Jones, 1983). Comparisons with spending in the US and Japan show expenditure on research and development in Britain to have been a fraction of the sums committed in those countries. The same is true for the number of scientists, engineers and other workers employed in motor-related R & D. The figure for Germany was 75 per cent greater than that for the UK, compared with a 10 per cent British lag behind France (Jones, 1983). If the investment of capital and human resources is taken to reflect the strength of each country's capacity for design engineering and the development of product technology, this evidence offers support to Whipp and Clark's contention, although it is disputed by Willman and Winch, that weaknesses in these respects hindered competitiveness (Whipp and Clark, 1986; Willman and Winch, 1987).

Was the impact of multinationals entirely negative? In assessing the effects of MNEs on the British industry it is important to consider their record of investment and employment creation (or maintenance), as well as their marketing policies. For while as traders the MNEs' policies were damaging to the British industry and to the balance of trade, Ford's record of investment based on higher unit profitability compared well with that of BLMC/BL, dependent on public expenditure to offset losses to provide net investment (see Table 10). On a rising trend, between 1973 and 1982 capital expenditure in Ford UK roughly equalled that of the British vehicle manufacturer. It was triple the investment made by Ford in other European countries and twice that undertaken in other subsidiaries outside the US (Bhaskar, 1984a).

Table 10 *Net profits after tax, and capital expenditure of major vehicle producers (£m) 1970–1982*

	British Leyland		Ford		Vauxhall		Chrysler Peugeot/Talbot	
	Profit	Cap. exp.	Profit	Cap. exp.	Profit	Cap. exp.	Profit	Cap. exp.
1970	−6	67	16	68	−9.4	11	−11	15
1971	16	50	−17	49	2.6	15	1	5
1972	22	42	28	32	−4.1	10	2	5
1973	26	63	28	42	−4	18	4	7
1974	−24	108	32	52	−18	32	−18	2
1975	−124	92	52	52	−13	14	−36	2
1976	44	114	7	56	−2	14	−43	2
1977	52	149	59	81	−2	9	−22	18
1978	38	233	116	163	2	32	−20	7
1979	−145	259	144	334	−31	32	−41	14
1980	−536	284	347	324	−83	22	−102	10
1981	−497	201	204	280	−57	12	−91	8
1982	−293	230	165	398	−39	12	−55	4

Source: Bhaskar (1984a), Vol. I, Table 8.1; Vol. II, Tables 9.13, 10.12, 11.5.

State subsidies were extended to Ford and Vauxhall, mainly through regional development programmes and investment grants in the form of interest relief. These implied a tacit recognition by government that on balance the employment provided by Ford's investment outweighed the effects of tied imports and sourcing. Of the £182m spent on the plant constructed at Bridgend in South Wales in 1972, about 40 per cent is estimated to have come from public funds. Thereafter subsidies were smaller, amounting to £177m for Ford and Vauxhall between 1976 and 1983. In 1976–9, however, government injected £162m into Chrysler's heavily loss-making Talbot subsidiary in an attempt to avoid unemployment (Bhaskar, 1984b). Unsuccessful as a policy, this measure also ran counter to the government's strategy of reducing the number of producers and promoting rationalization (Bhaskar, 1983; Young and Hood, 1977).

BLMC/BL was not the only company adversely affected by tied

imports and sourcing. The components branch of the motor industry supplied parts and accessories which accounted for 65 per cent of the material cost of BLMC/BL cars, as well as some proportion which made up 70 per cent of the material cost of Fords, 85 per cent of Vauxhalls and 71 per cent of Chrysler cars. Several of the firms which dominated the market – Lucas, Chloride, Dunlop, GKN, Automotive Products, and Automotive Engineering – virtually monopolized the home market for particular components, but the trend towards restricted vehicle exports and tied imports by the American multinationals stimulated a drive for exports by the component manufacturers.

In the 1970s the deficit on the balance of trade in cars was more than offset by the surplus from components. However, the fall in BL's production coupled with a rise in imported components by the MNEs led to a marked contraction of the market. One reaction of British component producers was to undertake direct investment in production facilities on the Continent, the source of imports, in order to protect sales and retrieve profitability. Even so, by the mid 1980s the balance of trade in motor components was also in deficit (Carr, 1990). Assessing the overall effects of the activities of multinationals, one historian's conclusion was that 'the deleterious effects of a sharp rise in tied imports, a decline in exports, a drastic diminution in local content and a reduction in car manufacturing capacity combined to accelerate the drift towards the industry's decline' (Church, 1986).

The economics of the international division of labour on which the MNEs' policies of the 1970s and 1980s were predicated had the effect of strengthening the industry in those countries where a combination of productivity, labour costs, exchange rates and profitability favoured location or relocation of production, although subsidies offered by governments seeking to attract investment were added to the equation. A comparison between Ford UK's performance and that of other Ford companies in Europe suggests that overall these factors placed the industry in Britain at a disadvantage during the 1970s and early 1980s. By European standards the performance of Ford UK was no more than average (Bhaskar, 1983). The productivity gap between Ford factories in Britain compared with those in Europe was due, in the opinion of Ford managers, not to differences between actual line speeds or production standards, which were similar, but in large measure to interruptions on the line. Compared with European plants, British factories recorded higher rates of industrial disputes, greater relaxation allowances, and permitted more non-productive time, which was often exceeded. A particular contrast was that BL had higher manning levels and lower work standards than European plants (Marsden, Morris, Willman and Wood, 1985).

Quality differences were also identified. In the mid 1970s Ford Fiestas and Escorts made in Britain attracted roughly twice the number of complaints concerning the same models built in Germany, while repair rates on the Cortina/Taunus were half as much again for the British-made cars than for those manufactured in Belgium. In 1981 a consumer survey of warranties revealed similar disparities between the quality and reliability of cars made in Britain with those made in Germany and especially in Japan (Bhaskar, 1979, 1983). Warranty costs of the new Metro and Maestro models exceeded those of comparable Ford and Vauxhall cars, and were ten times those of Nissan cars (Williams *et al.*, 1987). In a period when the quality of motor vehicles, as of other consumer goods, was subjected to increasing scrutiny by magazines and journals aimed specifically at consumers, and when increasingly systematic international comparisons promoted informed consumer choice, the weaknesses in British production created further difficulties for the marketing of British cars (Bhaskar, 1983).

Weaknesses specific to the British industry were exacerbated by a slowing down in the rate of growth of world vehicle production (Bardou *et al.*, 1982). The rapid rise of Japan to become the world's largest vehicle manufacturer in the 1980s, and an associated intensification of international competition and globalization of production added to the problem. The contraction of output from British factories resulted in merger, nationalization, and finally privatization. In 1988 Rover became a small and peripheral division of a large British conglomerate which, because of the financial arrangements entered into by the British government, the European Commission decreed must not be sold off by British Aerospace before 1993.

These developments coincided with a change in the equation affecting Britain's comparative advantage as a location for vehicle manufacture by foreign firms. The movement of the exchange rate, the more peaceable climate of industrial relations, a consequence partly of legislation and partly of recession, and the continuance of higher price and profit margins inside the British market, combined to encourage inward investment, which successive British governments actively sought. For Japanese manufacturers these advantages added to the prospect of access to the single European market planned for 1993 and made Britain an attractive focus for investment. The eclipse of the dwindling British motor industry meant, therefore, that more than ever the ability to translate comparative into competitive advantage in Britain came to depend on the financial resources, design and production technology, managerial methods, working practices and approaches to industrial relations conducted by American, French, and especially Japanese multinationals.

(vii) Explaining decline

By themselves none of the explanations which have been offered for decline, whether they emphasize adverse government policies, obstructive and militant labour, or organizational and managerial weaknesses, adequately account for the decline of the British motor industry. Each is necessary to appreciate the complex chronology and interaction between these various factors. Lewchuck's institutional approach, which stressed the system of atomistic competition and the centrality of the effort bargain to production, has been criticized for being too deterministic by oversimplifying the relationship between institutions and human behaviour. The model offers valuable insights into the industry's immediate post-war history, underlining the erosion of managerial control which continued after the BMC merger in 1952. At the same time, however, the sheer scale of the merger offered managers an opportunity to retrieve a measure of the shop floor control conceded during the war and its immediate aftermath.

The IRC's success in achieving an effective restructuring of the electrical engineering industry, which began with the merger of GEC with AEI in 1967, contrasts with the failure of the Leyland merger (Cowling, 1980). This not only points to the IRC's lack of power to enforce managerial change beyond the structural reform which resulted in the Leyland merger, but also underlines missed opportunities within the organization. Whereas overmanning and inefficient working practices were tackled immediately at GEC they remained a problem for BLMC. Although managers recognized the need for similar, though more far-ranging, changes, shop floor control in the car factories hindered managers' moves in that direction. By reducing further the complications presented by intercompany competition with respect to wages and conditions, the greater industrial concentration in the 1960s, when the British industry became virtually a monopoly, removed one of the difficulties of reforming the effort bargain. Another major barrier to change, which perpetuated the adverse effects of piecework payments, was the prevailing disarticulated system of industrial relations. In effect, negotiations were complicated by employers being at one remove from the trade unions, and shop stewards at one remove from both. Nonetheless, the survival of these institutional arrangements until their reform under the confrontational Edwardes management beginning in the late 1970s must be attributed partly to human failures, of managers and labour leaders.

Those who have emphasized the role of the trade unions and shop floor militancy in contributing to underutilization of plant, slow-speed working and strikes, notably Bhaskar, and Jones and Prais, likewise overlook the difficulties presented to Continental manufacturers by workers who were also uncooperative, though in different ways. Again this suggests that the effects on motor manufacturers in Britain of disruptive workers and of restrictive practices were those of degree. However, a comparison of industrial relations in German motor companies with those in Britain suggests that the differences had effects beyond those of lost production and lack of cooperation on the shop floor. The British system of industrial relations generated levels of uncertainty missing from the German system, with consequences for corporate planning beyond labour management.

Volkswagen was exceptional, in that after the Allies relinquished control the company remained in public ownership until the early 1960s. Thereafter the Federal Republic retained 20 per cent ownership, Lower Saxony held 15 per cent and the Volkswagen Foundation 5 per cent. Beginning in 1952, the Works Constitution

Act and the Collective Agreements Act were two pillars of the system of 'co-determination', designed to ensure that workers were represented on the supervisory boards in the ratio of one to three management representatives, increased in the 1970s to almost one in two, and that the law should be central to industrial relations. Even during the early post-war years the public company adopted informal arrangements not dissimilar to full co-determination as the basis for relations between managers and workers. Democratically elected Works Councils were given a legal monopoly of workers' representation, who used their rights under co-determination to ensure the recruitment of trade unionists. As trade unions (and shop stewards whom the unions attempted to insert into the structure of industrial relations in the late 1950s) lacked the legal status of Works Councils, the Councils maintained their key position.

Among the consequences of this system which gave legally enforceable workers' representation at workplace, and later at company level, was single union and company bargaining, centralized decision-making between Works Councils and companies, and an absence of interunion rivalry. From labour's standpoint there was some complaint that within this structure trade unionists were unable to exploit their position on supervisory and management boards to extract the most from employers (Streeck, 1984). Yet the ordered structure of industrial relations in the German car industry contrasted with the unregulated, individualistic character of industrial relations in Britain. Here the complexity and volatility of industrial relations were the combined result of centralized power held by an employers' association representing other engineering industries, and competing trade unions whose power, and that of workers generally, depended heavily on the exercise of shop floor action and strikes.

A key difference compared with the German system, and an important debilitating factor affecting the British industry, was an orderliness in relations between groups and institutions embedded in law. Such arrangements enabled companies to anticipate and plan in the knowledge that the law ruled out unpredictable, precipitate industrial action. The contrasting legacy of adversarial industrial relations in Britain generated both uncertainty and mutual distrust, reducing the likelihood of cooperation to effect internally initiated changes in management strategies. These were postponed until virtual bankruptcy, government intervention, and a relaxation of political constraints (though within financial control and targets) on managers recruited from outside the organization signalled a further repudiation of the long-established corporate culture.

Especially during the 1960s government, too, contributed to the uncertainty which discouraged fundamental long-term managerial changes. However, the emphasis by Bhaskar, Dunnett, and Pollard on the role of government in the industry's decline offers only a partial explanation. Evidence from international comparisons suggests that macroeconomic policies exacerbated, rather than caused, instability. Between 1968 and 1977, however, when government assumed a central role, political considerations affected the industry's development directly. The original strategy for BLMC, initiated by government through the IRC in 1968, failed partly because the choice of company and chief executive to lead the merger lacked the experience and the managerial support needed to transform the industry. Weaknesses here stemmed in part from a lack of professional and analytical skills, but important too were the prevailing assumptions and beliefs about what was possible, as well as the limited means to achieve objectives. Neither directors nor managers at Leyland had sought or planned for a restructuring of the entire British motor vehicle industry. The failure of strategy, in which government willed merger and rationalization while leaving implementation entirely to the new company in a political climate hostile to redundancies, illustrates the weaknesses of what Wilks called 'institutional insularity' (Wilks, 1990).

Wilks argued that throughout the post-war period government policies were the outcome of government–industry relations which were vitiated by the absence of institutional linkages, reflecting a British tradition of limited public authority in industrial affairs and a respect for the autonomy of business organizations. Reich concluded that undercapitalization, a high strike rate and poor management all resulted from the form that government policy took after 1945. International comparisons, he argued, showed that the critical difference between Britain and Germany, Italy and to a lesser extent France, is that only in Britain did liberal ideology survive the Second World War. Fascism and war on the Continent fostered discriminating ideologies and institutions, allowing scope for government intervention to promote national, economic and political interests. On the other hand, in Britain intervention by the state, when it occurred, was both constrained and non-discriminatory.

By treating American companies in Britain on equal terms with British-owned companies, Reich argues, government encouraged unrestricted inflows of foreign capital which were detrimental to the competitive position of the British industry. Furthermore, he argues that British government policies based on egalitarian principles created an advantage for the American subsidiaries. The allocation of steel, during the post-war period and at the time of the Korean War, favoured Ford, and later, the government underwrote Chrysler's losses in an attempted rescue. The American firms also possessed the option of withdrawing from the industry in Britain, and during the immediate post-war period this enabled them to disregard government advice on price control and profits. Reich suggests that the compliance of British firms was influenced by a perceived threat of nationalization, while later their approach to restructuring was softened by managers' interpretations of the government's willingness to rescue the Chrysler subsidiary as a reassuring sign for the survival of the British industry (Reich, 1990).

Most of Reich's new evidence to support his model, which breaks down in the 1960s, refers to the 1940s and early 1950s. Then Ford undoubtedly benefited from the prevailing liberal ideology at that time, but it is difficult to conclude that in a period of rapid growth in demand this was to the serious disadvantage of the British industry. Ford's post-war recovery and performance were spectacular, but from the mid 1930s that company possessed the critical advantages of a large, modern production plant, which had yet to produce at full car-making capacity during peacetime. Ford also possessed depth and ability in local management, and benefited from the resources for development, skills and experience of the parent company to call upon. Moreover, one reason why Ford proved to be so competitive within Britain whereas Volkswagen outpaced Ford in Germany was the corporate strategy chosen by managers in Dearborn, who at the end of the war regarded Ford in Britain as the European flagship. Ford's share of total car production in Britain reached 30 per cent; nonetheless, the superiority of productivity in the industry as a whole compared with European producers until the early 1960s suggests that productivity in British factories was not substantially different from that of Ford up to that time.

A much stronger case has been made by Wilks, who argues that from the 1960s the liberal ideology, which implied 'national treatment' for foreign subsidiaries, led government to rescue Chrysler and to remain passive when other American subsidiaries resisted government pressure to act in accordance with government employment and income policies that were constraining British companies' activities (Wilks, 1990). He concluded that the willingness to bail out Chrysler 'placed the future of the industry at least implicitly in the hands of the multinationals' (Wilks, 1990, *186*). This is a valid inference viewed in the light of BLMC's corporate weakness and the wider institutional structure of government including the civil service. Even after the crisis of 1975 heavy public investment in the company stopped short of extending discriminatory support comparable to that received by the national champions of other major Continental car manufacturing countries. While the state came to control the British industry in 1975, and since 1968 had acknowledged the importance of maintaining a British industry, tangible manifestation of government support was limited to providing funds for investment. The institutional dealings between firms and the Departments of Trade and Industry, Environment, Transport, Regional Development and the Treasury were conducted as 'transactions between insular elites'. Wilks concluded that the lack of contact between a secretive, non-specialist civil service on the one hand, and on the other uninformed managers, ineffectually represented at the industry level by the SMMT, resulted in minimal information flows and maximum propensity for mutual misunderstanding (Wilks, 1990).

One effect of this lack of awareness of the respective concerns, priorities and objectives was to preclude what has been called 'the politics of reciprocal consent' (Samuels, 1990), crucial to which was the need generally to ensure the cooperation of those whom the government sought to regulate. Instead government–industry relations were based on mutual suspicion and the politics of reciprocal incomprehension. Wilks distinguished between two levels at which industry–government relationships operated between 1975 and 1985, neither of which involved more than financial support and monitoring. One was the bureaucratic level, at which he described the relationship as 'distanced', the other was the 'arbitrary' relationship which characterized contacts at the ministerial levels. The defects of communication and understanding at both levels contributed to the confusion between political and industrial objectives when BLMC came under state control in 1975. The government accepted a strategy which, contrary to much of the evidence available, seemed to promise industrial revival through investment, improved industrial relations, some rationalization and minimal unemployment. The government subordinated economic criteria in defining industrial success and how to achieve it, to wider considerations of political economy, in particular to the protection of employment, regional development and the trade balance. This policy was reversed from 1977, culminating in privatization, 'the apotheosis of insularity' (Wilks, 1990, *176*).

Wilks's emphasis on the insular nature of relationships and Reich's stress on the weakening effect of the non-discriminatory policies of successive British governments imbued with the ethos of a traditional liberal, market ideology need to be put into an international context. Whereas Dunnett was critical of government because intervention undermined the competitive process, which he implies would have produced a creative response from the British industry, the criticism made by Wilks and Reich focused on the form which the intervention took, comparing the role of government in other countries involving the selection and systematic support of core firms or of a national champion.

Historians are not agreed on the extent of the contrast between government–industry relations in Britain and on the Continent, the extreme case most often cited being that of Germany. Abromeit (1990) stressed the liberal market ideology of successive post-war German governments, pointing out that contacts and communications between government and industry were good and that they focused mainly on questions concerning competitive structure and environmental regulation policies. He rejects the view that government support for industry was the product of a coherent industrial policy, let alone a strategy of industrial targeting or sectoral modernization. Measures were *ad hoc*, including fiscal measures to affect the climate for investment, the setting up of advisory bodies and the financing of research and development, and regional finance for restructuring declining industries.

Where government provided direct support, for Daimler and Benz for example, Abromeit emphasized that initiatives almost invariably originated from individual companies rather than from government. This, he argued, was evidence not of the power of trade associations but of the economic strength of large business organizations, whose influence owed more to the direct involvement of banks than to government–industry relations and discriminating government policies. Abromeit's account of successive German governments' attempts to avoid involvement and of intervention signalling 'crisis management', bears a distinct resemblance to government relations with the British motor industry.

Because British companies had remained insular their inability to cushion the cumulative effects of free trade and internationalization was in marked contrast to the options available to the multinationals. Tied imports and sourcing offered them some escape from the labour and production difficulties which also affected the industry in Britain. Such a strategy enabled Ford and Vauxhall to succeed in expanding their share of the British market, where prices and profit margins were high relative to the rest of Europe (Ashworth, Kay and Sharpe, 1982). None the less, Ford UK's inferior record compared with its European counterparts is evidence that it too experienced some of the debilitating effects of being part of a defective national economy. It thereby experienced government policies which were not only destabilizing to investment and indirectly contributed to the militancy of car workers, but also produced slower national economic growth than that experienced by other European countries, where real incomes were higher (Jones, 1981). Together these circumstances presented an economic, social, and political environment less conducive to the achievement of the highest European standards of manufacturing efficiency. In this respect the history of the decline of the motor industry is of wider significance for an understanding of the record of British manufacturing industry.

There are, however, certain factors the importance of which varied over time yet which were specific in contributing to the ultimate termination of Britain's only major independent motor manufacturer. Throughout the post-war period, but especially during the crucial years between the mid 1950s and the mid 1960s, BMC was producing models which were in demand at home and overseas, productivity levels were comparable still with those of manufacturers on the Continent. Corporate weakness, however, inhibited a policy of exploiting strength in the market, introducing structural and organizational changes affecting production and marketing, accompanied by investment in model development.

The particular difficulties presented by government policies and industrial relations to all motor manufacturers in Britain are not in doubt. Yet the rapid decline of the British motor industry during the 1970s was in part the outcome of repeated failures by managers to distinguish between short- and long-term problems. During the post-war boom which lasted until 1965 growth had concealed the industry's weaknesses as reported by the NAC and PEP in 1945 and 1950. Short-term instability in demand had been met by temporary reductions in capacity, partly by laying workers off, partly by allowing stoppages to drag on during recessions.

Thereafter, the years of static home demand were also attributed within the industry to government policies: the dip in exports to an overvalued currency which devaluation in 1967 appeared to have corrected when exports surged until 1970. This apparent failure on the part of British managers to distinguish short-term difficulties and their local causes from longer term trends was exacerbated by a lack of strategic planning. Furthermore, the investment that did take place during the 1960s and early 1970s was undertaken without vital information on production costs. This critical gap, crucial for designing cars to make profits for reinvestment, also precluded comparisons between the profitability of different models. Lack of information seriously hampered the formulation of informed production and marketing strategies. Simultaneously, and in part as a consequence, the inability to invest in new models led to a deterioration in the company's engineering and design capacity (Whipp and Clark, 1986). Lack of information, weakness of corporate integration and inadequate managerial resources were a combination which proved to be ill-suited to enable BMC, BMH or BLMC either to restructure themselves effectively or to adapt successfully to the rapidly changing internationally competitive economic environment.

These features were the legacy of corporate cultures established well before the Second World War, creating the limits within which managers exercised what economists have called 'bounded rationality', a concept which allows for rational intentions leading to unintended and less than optimal outcomes. The autocratic managerial approach of the founders of those companies which survived the competition of the interwar years was followed by a personal style adopted by successor managers (who were not family inheritors) from within those organizations. Even after the Leyland merger in 1968 the managerial style perpetuated was that characteristic of a personal enterprise in an industry and in an era which required a transition to some form of professional, managerial organization and control. In a world dominated by international and multinational business, international comparisons were central to corporate decisions on which, how, and where cars should be produced. The British companies lacked the organizational capacity to assess systematically their competitive environment and to respond. By contributing to a climate of uncertainty both government and labour added to the industry's problems, one effect of which was to discourage long-term planning. Yet without the introduction of accurate costing managers were in no position to recognize the point when their organization reached the critical level of vulnerability beyond which, unless fundamental changes in organization were made, a downward spiral would inevitably ensue.

The failure of the British motor industry to transform itself into an internationally competitive enterprise is explicable therefore mainly by three interacting factors. First were government policies in which political considerations constrained business decision-making and assisted the multinationals' strength in the domestic market. Second there was a system of industrial relations which was rooted neither in law nor in trade union power. Third, and fundamentally, there were historically rooted weaknesses in corporate structures and management which for so many years obscured the need for systematic planning and organizational change. When government finally took command during the late 1970s, the task of rescuing BLMC/BL had become more problematical as a result of simultaneous developments in the dynamics of the industry, notably the trend towards globalization and changes in the character of demand and competition in the domestic as well as in international markets. Neither nationalization nor privatization prevented Britain from becoming the first major car-producing country to relinquish a domestically owned independent national champion.

Bibliography

The place of publication is London unless otherwise indicated.

Abromeit, H. (1990) 'Government-industry Relations in West Germany', in Chick, M. (ed.), *Governments, Industries and Markets* (Aldershot).

Adeney, Martin (1989) *The Motor Makers.*

Alford, B. W. E. (1972) *Depression and Recovery? British Economic Growth.*

Alford, B. W. E. (1981) 'New industries for old? British industry between the wars' in Floud, R. and McCloskey, D. (eds), *The Economic History of Britain since 1700*, Vol. 2, *1860 to the 1970s* (Cambridge).

Alford, B. W. E. (1986) 'Lost opportunities: British business and businessmen during the First World War', in McKendrick, N. and Outhwaite, R. B. (eds), *Business Life and Public Policy* (Cambridge).

Alford, B. W. E. (1988) *British Economic Performance, 1945–1975* (Basingstoke).

Allen, G. C. (1926) 'The British Motor Industry', *London and Cambridge Economics Service*, LSE Special Memo, No. 18.

Andrews, P. W. S. and Brunner, E. (1955) *The Life of Lord Nuffield* (Oxford).

Armstrong, A. G. (1967) 'The motor industry and the British economy', *District Bank Review.*

Ashworth, M. H., Kay, J. A., and Sharpe, T. A. E. (1982) *Differentials between car prices in the United Kingdom and Belgium*, IFS Report, Series no. 2 (Institute for Fiscal Studies).

Bardou, J.-P., Chanaron, J. J., Fridenson, P., and Laux, J. M. (1982) *The Automobile Revolution: the Impact of an Industry.* (Translated from French by J. M. Laux) (Chapel Hill, North Carolina, US).

Barker, T. C. (1982) 'The Spread of Motor Vehicles before 1914' in Kindleberger and di Tella (eds), *Economics in the Long View*, Vol. 2.

Barnett, C. (1986) *The Audit of War: the Illusion and Reality of Britain as a Great Nation.*

Benn, Tony (1988) *Office Without Power, Diaries 1968–1972.*

Benn, Tony (1989) *Against the Tide, Diaries, 1973–76.*

Bevan, D. L. (1977) 'The Nationalized Industries', *The Economic System in the UK*, ed. Morris, D. (Oxford).

Beynon, H. (1973) *Working for Ford* (Harmondsworth).

Bhaskar, K. (1975) *Alternatives Open to the UK Motor Vehicle Industry* (Bath).

Bhaskar, K. (1979) *The Future of the UK Motor Industry.*

Bhaskar, K. (1983) *The Future of the UK and European Motor Industry* (Bath).

Bhaskar, K. *et al.* (1984a) *Research Report on the Future of the UK and the European Motor Industry*, Vols I and II (Bath).

Bhaskar, K. *et al.* (1984b) *State Aid to the European Motor Industry: a Report* (Norwich).

Blaich, F. (1981) 'The development of the distribution sector in the German car industry' in Okochi, Akio, Shimokawa, and Koichi (eds), *Development of Mass Marketing* (Tokyo).

Blaich, F. (1987) 'Why did the pioneer fall behind? Motorization in Germany between the wars' in Barker, T. (ed.), *The Economic and Social Effects of the Spread of Motor Vehicles.*

Bloomfield, G. (1978) *The World Automotive Industry.*

Bowden, S. M. (1991) 'Demand and supply constraints in the interwar car industry. Did the manufacturers get it right?' *Business History*, 33, 2.

Cannell, R. *et al.* (1984) *Ford of Europe: A Strategic Profile.*

Capie, F. (1983) *Depression and Protectionism: Britain between the Wars.*

Carr, Christopher (1990) *Britain's Competitiveness. The Management of the Motor Vehicle Components Industry.*

Carr, F. W. (1978) 'Engineering workers and the rise of labour in Coventry, 1914–1939' (Warwick, PhD thesis).

Castle, Barbara (1980) *The Castle Diaries.*

Caunter, C. F. (1957) *The History of Development of Light Cars*, HMSO.

Caunter, C. F. (1970) *The Light Car, a Technical History.*

Central Policy Review Staff (1975) *The Future of the British Car Industry*, HMSO.

Chandler, A. D. (1990) *Scale and Scope: The Dynamics of Industrial Capitalism.*

Channon, D. (1973) *The Strategy and Structure of British Enterprise* (Boston).

Chapman, A. L. and Knight, R. (1953) *Wages and Salaries in the United Kingdom 1920–38* (Cambridge).

Church, R. A. and Miller, M. (1977) 'The Big Three' in Barry Supple (ed.), *Essays in British Business History* (Oxford).

Church, R. A. (1977) 'Myths, Men and Motorcars', *Journal of Transport History*, IV, No. 2.

Church, R. A. (1978) 'Innovation, monopoly and supply of vehicle components in Britain, 1880–1930: the growth of Joseph Lucas Ltd', *Business History Review*, LII.

Church, R. A. (1979) *Herbert Austin: The British Motor Car Industry to 1941.*

Church, R. A. (1981) 'The Marketing of Automobiles in Britain and the United States before 1939', Okochi, A. and Koichi, S. (eds), *The Development of Mass Marketing* (Tokyo).

Church, R. A. (1982) 'Markets and Marketing in the British Motor Industry before 1914', *Journal of Transport History*, Spring 1982.

Church, R. A. (1986a) 'The Effect of American Multinationals on the British Motor Industry' in Levy Leboyer, M. and Teichova, A. (eds), *Multinationals in Historical Perspective* (Cambridge).

Church, R. A. (1986b) 'Family firms and managerial capitalism: the case of the international motor industry', *Business History*, 28, 2, 165–80.

Church, R. A. and Mullen, C. (1989) 'Cars and corporate culture: the view from Longbridge' in B. Tilson (ed.), *Made in Birmingham: Design and Industry, 1889–1989* (Brewin, Studley, Worcs).

Church, R. A. (1993) 'The mass marketing of motor cars before 1950: the missing dimension' in Tedlow, R. and Jones, G. (eds), *The Rise and Fall of Mass Marketing.*

Clack, G. (1967) *Industrial Relations in a British Car Factory* (Cambridge).

Clayden, Tim (1987) 'Trade unions, employers and industrial relations in the British motor industry', *Business History*, 29, 3, 304–24.

Cole, G. D. H. (1923) *Workshop Organisation.*

Collins, M. (1991) *Banks and Industrial Finance in Britain, 1830–1939.*

Coppock, D. J. (1956) 'The climacteric of the 1890s: a critical note', *Manchester School*, XXIV.

Cottrell, P. L. (1980) *Industrial Finance, 1830–1914. The Finance and Organisation of English Manufacturing Industry.*

Cowling, M. (1980) 'The Motor Industry' in idem, *Mergers and Economic Performance.*

Cowling, M. (1986) 'The Internationalization of Production and Deindustrialization', in Amin, A. and Goddard, J. (eds), *Technological Change, Industrial Restructuring and Regional Development.*

Croucher, R. (1982) *Engineers at War.*

Davenport-Hines, R. P. T. (1984) *Dudley Docker, the Life and Times of a Trade Warrior* (Cambridge).

Davy, J. (1967) *The Standard Car 1903–1963* (Coventry).

Department of Industry (1976) cmnd 6377 *The British Motor Vehicle Industry.*

Donnelly, T. and Thoms, D. (1990) 'Trade Unions, Management and the Search for Production in the Coventry Motor Car Industry, 1939–75', *Business History*, 31.

Donoghue, B. (1987) *Prime Minister: The Conduct of Policy under Harold Wilson and James Callaghan.*

Dunnett, P. J. S. (1980) *The Decline of the British Motor Industry.*

Durcan, J. W., McCarthy, W. E. J., and Redman, G. P. (1983) *Strikes in Post-war Britain: a study of stoppages of work due to industrial disputes, 1946–1973.*

Edelstein, M. (1976) 'Realized rates of return in UK home and overseas portfolio investment in the age of high imperialism', *Explorations in Economic History,* 13, 283–329.

Edelstein, M. (1982) *Overseas Investment in the Age of High Imperialism in the United Kingdom, 1850–1914.*

Edwardes, Michael (1983) *Back from the Brink.*

Edwards, P. (1982) 'Britain's changing strike problem', *Industrial Relations Journal,* 13, no. 2.

Elbaum, B. and Lazonick, W. (1986) 'An institutional perspective on British decline', *The Decline of the British Economy,* ed. Elbaum, B. and Lazonick, W. (Oxford).

Engelbach, C. R. F. (1927–28) 'Some notes on re-organizing a works to increase production', *Proceedings of the Institute of Automobile Engineers,* XXII.

Engelbach, C. R. F. (1933–4) 'Problems in manufacture', *Proceedings of the Institute of Automobile Engineers,* XXVIII.

Flanders, A. (1952) 'Industrial relations' in Worswick, G. N. and Ady, P. H. (eds), *The British Economy, 1945–50* (Oxford).

Foreman-Peck, J. (1979) 'Tariff protection and economies of scale: the British motor industry before 1939', *Oxford Economic Papers,* 31, No. 2.

Foreman-Peck, J. (1981a) 'The effect of market failure on the British motor industry before 1939', *Explorations in Economic History,* 18.

Foreman-Peck, J. (1981b) 'Exit, voice and loyalty as responses to decline: the Rover Company in the interwar years', *Business History,* 23, No. 2.

Foreman-Peck, J. (1982) 'The American challenge of the Twenties and the European motor industry', *Journal of Economic History,* XLII, No. 4.

Foreman-Peck, J. (1983) 'Diversification and the growth of the firm: the Rover company to 1914', *Business History,* 25, No. 2.

Foreman-Peck, J. (1985) 'Intra-firm trade in the international motor vehicle industry', in Casson, M. (ed.), *Multinational Companies and World Trade.*

Fridenson, P. (1978) 'The Coming of the Assembly Line to Europe' in W. Krohn (ed.), *The Dynamics of Science and Technology,* Vol. II (Dordrecht).

Friedman, A. L. (1977) *Industry and Labour: Class Struggle at Work and Monopoly Capitalism.*

Friedman, A. L. (1984) 'Management strategies, market conditions and the labour process', in F. J. Stephens (ed.), *Firms Organization and Labour.*

Friedman, H. and Meredeen, S. (1980) *The Dynamics of Industrial Conflict: Lessons from Ford.*

Frostick, Michael (1970) *Advertising the Motor Car.*

Gennard, J. and Steuer, M. D. (1971) 'The Industrial Relations of Foreign-owned Subsidiaries in the United Kingdom', *British Journal of Industrial Relations*, IX, 1.

Griffith, F. (1955) 'Why Austin Developed Unit Construction Transfer Machines', *The Machinist*, January.

Hackett, Dennis (1978) *The Big Idea. The Story of Ford in Europe* (Ford Motor Co.).

Hague, D. C. and Williamson, G. (1983) *The I. R. C. An Experiment in Industrial Intervention.*

Hannah, L. (ed.) (1976) *Management Strategy and Business Development.*

Hannah, L. (1983) *The Rise of the Corporate Economy.*

Harrison, A. E. (1981) 'Joint Stock flotation in the cycle, motor cycle and related industries, 1882–1914', *Business History*, 23.

Harrison, A. E. (1982) 'F. Hopper and Co: The Problem of Capital Supply in the Cycle Manufacturing Industry, 1891–1914', *Business History*, 24, 3–23.

Hinton, James (1973) *The First Shop Stewards' Movement.*

Holden, L. T. (1984) 'A History of Vauxhall Motors to 1950: Industry, Development and Local Impact on the Luton Economy' (M. Phil., Open University).

Hope, A. (1979) 'The Genius Today', *Autocar*, 25 August.

Hornby, William (1958) *Factories and Plant.*

Hounshell, D. A. (1984) *From the American System to Mass Production 1800–1932* (Baltimore).

House of Commons (1975) *British Leyland: the next decade* (The Ryder Report). HC 342, 1974/5.

House of Commons (1975) *The Motor Vehicle Industry*, 14th Report of the Trade and Industry Sub-Committee of the Expenditure Committee, HC 617.

House of Commons (1976) *Chrysler UK*, 8th Report of the Trade and Industry Sub-Committee of the Expenditure Committee, HC 146, 1975–6.

House of Commons (1977) *British Leyland*, Minutes of Evidence taken before the Expenditure Committee, HC 396, 1976–7.

House of Commons (1987) *The UK Components Industry*, Third Report of the Trade and Industry Select Committee, HC 407, 1986–7.

Hyman, Richard (1971) *The Workers' Union* (Oxford).

Imperial Economic Committee, Thirteenth Report (1936) *A Survey of the Trade in Motor Vehicles.*

Irving, R. J. (1975) 'New industries for old: some investment decisions of Armstrong Whitworth, 1900–1914', *Business History*, 17.

Jeffreys, J. B. (1945) *The Story of the Engineers.*

Jeremy, David (ed.) (1984–6) *A Biographical Dictionary of Business Leaders Active in Britain in the Period 1860–1980.*

Jones, D. T. (1981) *Maturity and Crisis in the European Car Industry.* Sussex European Papers No. 8, Brighton.

Jones, D. T. (1983) 'Technology and the UK Automobile Industry', *Lloyds Bank Review*, No. 148, April, 14–27.

Jones, D. T. (1984) 'Technology and the UK Automobile Industry', *Lloyds Bank Review*, April.

Jones, D. T. (1985) *The Import Threat to the UK Car Industry*, Science Policy Research Unit, Brighton.

Jones, D. T. and Prais, S. J. (1978) 'Plant Size and Productivity in the Motor Industry: Some International Comparisons', *Oxford Bulletin of Economics and Statistics*, 40, No. 2, May.

Kennedy, W. P. (1976) 'Institutional Response to Economic Growth: Capital Markets in Britain to 1914' in L. Hannah (ed.), *Management Strategy and Business Development: an Historical and Comparative Study*, pp. 151–83.

Khan, A. E. (1946) *Great Britain and the World Economy.*

Lambert, Z. E. and Wyatt, R. J. (1968) *Lord Austin, the Man.*

Laux, James (1976) *In First Gear* (Liverpool).

Law, C. M. (1985) 'The Geography of Industrial Rationalisation: The British Motor Car Industry, 1972–1982', *Geography*, 40, January.

Lewchuck, W. A. (1983) 'Fordism and the British Motor Car Employers, 1896–1932' in H. Gospel and G. Littler (eds), *Managerial Strategies and Industrial Relations.*

Lewchuck, W. A. (1984) 'The role of the British government in the spread of scientific management and Fordism in the interwar years', *Journal of Economic History*, 44, 355–61.

Lewchuck, W. A. (1985a) 'The Return to Capital in the British Motor Vehicle Industry', *Business History*, 27.

Lewchuck, W. A. (1985b) 'The origins of Fordism and alternative strategies: Britain and the United States, 1880–1930' in Tolliday, S. and Zeitlin, J. (eds), *Between Fordism and Flexibility, the International Motor Industry and its Workers* (Oxford).

Lewchuck, W. A. (1986) 'The Motor Vehicle Industry' in Elbaum, B. and Lazonick, W. (eds), *The Decline of the British Economy* (Oxford).

Lewchuck, W. A. (1987) *American Technology and the British Motor Vehicle Industry* (Cambridge).

Lloyd, I. (1978) *Rolls Royce, the Growth of a Firm.*

Lloyd, I. (1978) *Rolls Royce, Years of Endeavour.*

Locke, R. R. (1984) *The End of Practical Man: Entrepreneurship and Higher*

Education in Germany, France and Great Britain, 1880–1940, Vol. VIII ed. McKay, J. P. (Greenwich, Conn.).

Lyddon, D. (1983) 'Workplace organization in the British car industry', *History Workshop*, 15.

Mackay, D. J., Sladen, Janet P., and Halligan, Margaret J. (1984) *The UK Vehicle Manufacturing Industry: its Economic Significance* (PEIDA).

Marsden, David, Morris, Timothy, Willman, Paul, and Wood, Stephen (1985) *The Car Industry: Labour Relations and Industrial Adjustment.*

Mathias, P. (1983) second edn, *The First Industrial Nation.*

Maxcy, G. and Silberston, A. (1959) *The British Motor Industry.*

Maxcy, G. (1981) *The Multinational Motor Industry.*

Maxcy, G. (1958) 'The Motor Industry' in Cook, P. L. and Cohen, R. (eds), *Effects of Mergers.*

Melman, S. (1958) *Decision Making and Productivity* (Oxford).

Michie, R. C. (1981) 'Options, Concessions, Syndicates and the Provision of Venture Capital, 1880–1913', *Business History*, 23, 147–64.

Miller, M. and Church, R. A. (1979) 'Growth and Instability in the British Motor Industry between the Wars' in Aldcroft, D. H. and Buxton, C. *Instability and Industrial Development, 1919–1939.*

Ministry of Supply (1947) *National Advisory Council for the Motor Manufacturing Industry: Report of Proceedings* (HMSO).

Mitchell, B. R. (1962) *Abstract of European Historical Statistics.*

Morris, W. R. (1924) 'Policies that have built the Morris Motor Business', *System*, February.

Musson, A. E. (1978) *The Growth of British Industry.*

National Advisory Council, Ministry of Supply (1947) *Report and Proceedings Council, Motor Manufacturing Industry*, HMSO.

National Economic Development Council (1970) *Industrial Report by the Motor Manufacturing Development Council on the Economic Assessment to 1972.*

Nelson, W. H. (1967) *Small Wonder, the Amazing Story of the Volkswagen.*

Nicholson, T. R. (1983) *The Birth of the British Car Industry*, Vols I, II, III.

Nockolds, H. (1976) *Lucas, the First Hundred Years*, Vol. I.

Nubel, Otto (1987) 'The Beginnings of the Automobile in Germany' in Barker, T. (ed.), *The Economic and Social Effects of the Spread of Motor Vehicles.*

OECD (1987) *The Cost of Restricting Imports: the Automobile Industry.* Oliver, George (1971) *The Rover.*

Overy, R. J. (1973) 'Transportation and Rearmament in the Third Reich', *Historical Journal*, 16, 390–411.

Overy, R. J. (1975) 'Cars, roads and economic recovery', *Economic History Review*, XXVIII, 3, 466–83.

Overy, R. J. (1976) *William Morris, Viscount Nuffield.*

Pagnamenta, P. and Overy, R. J. (1984) *All Our Working Lives* (BBC, London.

Payne, P. L. (1988) *British Entrepreneurship in the Nineteenth Century* (second edn).

Pettigrew, A. (1979) 'On studying organisational cultures', *Administrative Science Quarterly*, 24, 4.

Plowden, W. E. (1971) *The Motor Car and Politics.*

Political and Economic Planning (PEP) (1950) Motor Vehicles, Engineering Report II.

Pollard, Sidney (1982) *The Wasting of the British Economy.*

Porter, M. (1989) *Competitiveness in the International Economy* (New York).

Pratten, C. and Silberston, A. (1967) 'International comparisons of labour productivity in the automobile industry, 1955–65', *Bulletin of the Oxford Institute of Statistics*, August 1967.

Pratten, C. (1971) *Economies of Scale in British Manufacturing Industry*, Cambridge.

Pryke, R. (1981) *The Nationalised Industries, Policies and Performance since 1968* (Oxford).

Rae, J. B. (1959) *American Automobile Manufacturers. The First Forty Years* (Philadelphia).

Reich, S. (1990) *Fruits of Fascism: Post-war Prosperity in Historical Perspective* (Cornell).

Report of the Liberal Industrial Inquiry (1928): Britain's Industrial Future.

Rhys, D. G. (1972) *The Motor Industry: An Economic Survey.*

Rhys, D. G. (1974) 'Employment Efficiency and Labour Relations in the British Motor Industry', *Industrial Relations Journal*, 5, No. 2.

Rhys, D. G. (1976) 'Concentration in the Inter-war Motor Industry', *Journal of Transport History*, New Series III, 4, 241–64.

Rhys, D. G. (1977) 'European mass-producing car makers and minimum efficient scale', *Journal of Industrial Economics*, XXV.

Rhys, D. G. (1988) 'Motor Vehicles' in Johnson, P. (ed.), *The Structure of British Industry.*

Richardson, H. W. (1961) 'The new industries between the wars', *Oxford Economic Papers*, XIII.

Richardson, H. W. (1965) 'Over-commitment in Britain before 1930', *Oxford Economic Papers*, XVII.

Richardson, Kenneth (1972) *Twentieth Century Coventry* (Coventry).

Rostas, L. (1948) *Corporative Productivity in British and American Industry* (Cambridge).

Rostow, W. W. (1963) *The Economics of Take-off into Sustained Growth.*

Royal Commission on Trade Unions and Employer Associations (1968) (Donavon Report), Cmd. 1623.

Salmon, E. A. (1975) 'Inside BL', *Management Today*, November.

Samuels, R. J. (1990) 'Business and the Japanese state', in Chick and Martin (eds), *Governments, Industries and Markets*, p. 37.

Sargant Florence, P. (1953) *Logic of British and American Industry*.

Sargant Florence, P. (1961) *Ownership, Control and Success of Large Companies*.

Saul, S. B. (1962) 'The Motor Industry in Britain to 1914', *Business History*, 5.

Saul, S. B. (1968) 'The Engineering Industry' in Aldcroft, D. H., *The Development of British Industry*.

Sedgwick, M. (1970) *Cars of the 1930s*.

Sedgwick, M. (1975) *Passenger Cars, 1924–1942*.

Silberston, A. (1958) 'The Motor Industry' in Burn, D. L. (ed.), *The Structure of British Industry* (Cambridge).

Silberston, A. (1965) 'The Motor Industry 1955–1964', *Oxford Bulletin of Economics and Statistics*, Vol. 27.

Skilleter, Paul (1988) 'The Thomas Papers', *Thoroughbred and Classic Cars*, June.

Sloan, Alfred, P., Jr (1967) *My Life with General Motors*.

SMMT, Society of Motor Manufacturers and Traders.

Starkey, Ken and McKinlay, Alan (1988) *Organizational Innovation, Competitive Strategy and the Management of Change in Four Major Companies* (Avebury).

Streeck, W. (1984) *Industrial Relations in West Germany*.

Sugden, Roger, 'The Warm Welcome for Foreign-owned Transnationals from recent British Governments', in Chick, M. (ed.), *Governments, Industries and Markets* (Aldershot).

Thomas, Sir Miles (1964) *Out on a Wing*.

Thomas, R. P. (1973) 'Style change and the automobile industry during the roaring twenties' in Cain, L. P. and Uselding, P., *Business Enterprise and Economic Change* (Chicago).

Thoms, David and Donnelly, Tom (1985) *The Motor Car Industry in Coventry since the 1890s*.

Thornhill, A. R. (1986) 'Industrial Relations in the British Motor Industry to 1939' (PhD, University of East Anglia).

Tiratsoo, N. (1992) 'The Motor Car Industry', in Mercer, H., Rollings, N., and Tomlinson, J. D., *Labour Governments and Private Industry* (Edinburgh).

Tolliday, S. (1983) 'Trade unions and shop floor bargaining in the British motor industry, 1910–1939', *Bulletin of the Society for the Study of Labour History*, 46, Spring.

Tolliday, S. (1985) 'Government, Employers and Shop Floor Organization in the British Motor Car Industry 1939–1969' in Tolliday, S. and Zeitlin, J. (eds), *Shop Floor Bargaining and the State* (Cambridge).

Tolliday, S. (1986) 'High tide and after: Coventry engineering workers and shop floor bargaining 1945–80' in Lancaster, A. and Mason, T. (eds), *Life and Labour in a Twentieth Century City: the Experience of Coventry* (Coventry).

Tolliday, S. (1987a) 'The failure of mass production unionism in the motor industry, 1914–1939' in Wrigley, C. (ed.), *A History of British Industrial Relations*, Vol. 2, *1914–1939*.

Tolliday, S. (1987b) 'Management and Labour, 1896–1939' in Tolliday, S. and Zeitlin, J. (eds), *The Automobile Industry and its Workers: between Fordism and Flexibility* (Cambridge).

Tolliday, S. (1991) 'Ford and "Fordism" in postwar Britain: enterprise management and the control of labour, 1937–1987' in Tolliday, S. and Zeitlin, J. (eds), *The Power to Manage*.

Turner, Graham (1971) *The Leyland Papers* (Birkenhead).

Turner, H. A., Clack, G. and Roberts, G. (1967) *Labour Relations in the Motor Industry*.

Tweedale, G. (1987) 'Business and investment strategies in the interwar British steel industry: case study of Hadfields Ltd. and Bean Cars', *Business History*, 29.

US Bureau of the Census (1976) *The Statistical History of the United States from Colonial Times to the Present* (New York).

US Bureau of Domestic and Foreign Commerce (1928) *Automotive Industry and Trade of Great Britain* (New York).

Von Tunzelman, G. N. (1978) 'Structural change and leading sectors in British manufacturing industry, 1907–68' in Kindleberger, C. P. and di Tella (eds), *Economics in the Long View*.

Waymark, P. (1983) *The Car Industry*.

Wells, L. T. (1974) 'Automobiles' in Vernon, R. (ed.), *Big Business and the State: Changing Relations in Western Europe*.

Whipp, R. (1987) 'Technology, Management, Strategic Change and Competitiveness', in Dorgham, M. A. (ed.), *Proceedings of the Fourth International Vehicle Design Congress* (Geneva).

Whipp, R. and Clark, P. (1986) *Innovation and the Automobile Industry, Product Process and Work Organization* (New York).

Whipp, R., Rosenfeld, R., and Pettigrew, A. (1987) 'Understanding Strategic Change Processes: Some Preliminary Findings' in Pettigrew, A. (ed.), *The Management of Strategic Change* (Oxford).

Whiting, R. C. (1983) *The View from Cowley: the Impact of Industrialization upon Oxford, 1918–38* (Oxford).

Wigham, E. (1973) *The Power to Manage*.

Wild, R. (1974) 'The origins and development of flow-line production', *Industrial Archaeology*, II.

Wilkins, Mira and Hill, Frank Ernest (1964) *American Business Abroad: Ford on Six Continents* (Detroit).

Wilks, S. (1984) *Industrial Policy and the Motor Industry* (Manchester).

Wilks, S. (1990) 'Institutional Insularity: Government and the British Motor Industry since 1945', in Chick, M. (ed.), *Governments, Industries and Markets* (Aldershot).

Williams, K. J., Williams, J. and Thomas, Dennis (1983) *Why are the British Bad at Manufacturing?*

Williams, K., Williams, J. and Haslam, C. (1987) *The Breakdown of Austin Rover* (Leamington Spa).

Willman, P. (1984) 'The Reform of Collective Bargaining and Strikes at BL Cars', *Industrial Relations Journal*, 15, No. 2.

Willman, P. (1987) 'Labour relations strategies at BL cars' in *The International Automobile Industry and its Workers: between Fordism and Flexibility*, ed. Tolliday, S. and Zeitlin, J. Z. (Oxford).

Willman, P. (1986) *Technological Change, Collective Bargaining and Industrial Efficiency* (Oxford).

Willman, P. and Winch, G. (1987) *Innovation and Management Control, Labour Relations at BL Cars* (Cambridge).

Wilson, Harold (1971) *The Labour Government, 1964–1970: a Personal Record.*

Wilson, Harold (1979) *The Final Term: the Labour Government, 1974–6.*

Wood, Jonathan (1988) *Wheels of Misfortune.*

Woollard, F. W. (1954) *The Principles of Flow Production.*

Wyatt, R. J. (1968) *The Motor for the Millions: the Austin Seven 1922–1939.*

Wyatt, R. J. (1981) *The Austin, 1905–52.*

Young, S. and Hood, N. (1977) *Chrysler UK: a Corporation in Transition* (New York).

Zeitlin, J. (1979) 'Craft control and the division of labour: engineers and compositors in Britain, 1890–1930', *Cambridge Journal of Economics*, 3, 263–74.

Zeitlin, J. (1980) 'The Emergence of Shop Steward Organisation and Job Control in the British Car Industry', *History Workshop*, 10.

Zeitlin, J. (1983) 'Workplace Militancy: a Rejoinder', *History Workshop*, 16.

Zeitlin, J. (1983) 'The Labour Strategies of British Engineering Employers, 1890–1922' in *Managerial Strategies and Industrial Relations*, ed. Gospel, H. and Littler, C.

Index

New Studies in Economic and Social History

Titles in the series available from Cambridge University Press:

1. M. Anderson
   Approaches to the history of the Western family, 1500–1914
2. W. Macpherson
   The economic development of Japan, 1868–1941
3. R. Porter
   Disease, medicine, and society in England: second edition
4. B.W.E. Alford
   British economic performance since 1945
5. A. Crowther
   Social policy in Britain, 1914–1939
6. E. Roberts
   Women's work 1840–1940
7. C. O'Grada
   The great Irish famine
8. R. Rodger
   Housing in urban Britain 1780–1914
9. P. Slack
   The English Poor Law 1531–1782
10. J.L. Anderson
    Explaining long-term economic change
11. D. Baines
    Emigration from Europe 1815–1930

12. M. Collins
Banks and industrial finance 1800–1939

13. A. Dyer
Decline and growth in English towns 1400–1640

14. R.B. Outhwaite
Dearth, public policy and social disturbance in England, 1550–1800

15. M. Sanderson
Education, economic change and society in England

16. R.D. Anderson
Universities and elites in Britain since 1800

17. C. Heywood
The development of the French economy, 1700–1914

18. R.A. Houston
The population history of Britain and Ireland 1500–1750

19. A.J. Reid
Social classes and social relations in Britain 1850–1914

20. R. Woods
The population of Britain in the nineteenth century

21. T.C. Barker
The rise and rise of road transport, 1700–1990

22. J. Harrison
The Spanish economy

23. C. Schmitz
The growth of big business in the United States and Western Europe, 1850–1939

24. R.A. Church
The rise and decline of the British motor industry

25. P. Horn
Children's work and welfare, 1780–1880

26. R. Perren
Agriculture in depression, 1870–1940

27. R.J. Overy
The Nazi economic recovery 1932–1938: second edition

Previously published as

Studies in Economic History

Titles in the series available from the Macmillan Press Limited

1. B.W.E. Alford
   Depression and recovery? British economic growth, 1918–1939
2. M. Anderson
   Population change in north-western Europe, 1750–1850
3. S.D. Chapman
   The cotton industry in the industrial revolution: second edition
4. N. Charlesworth
   British rule and the Indian economy, 1800–1914
5. L.A. Clarkson
   Proto-industrialisation: the first phase of industrialisation
6. D.C. Coleman
   Industry in Tudor and Stuart England
7. I.M. Drummond
   The gold standard and the international monetary system, 1900–1939
8. M.E. Falkus
   The industrialisation of Russia, 1700–1914
9. J.R. Harris
   The British iron industry, 1700–1850
10. J. Hatcher
    Plague, population and the English economy, 1348–1530
11. J.R. Hay
    The origins of the Liberal welfare reforms, 1906–1914

12. H. McLeod
Religion and the working classes in nineteenth-century Britain

13. J.D. Marshall
The Old Poor Law 1795–1834: second edition

14. R.J. Morris
Class and class consciousness in the industrial revolution, 1750–1850

15. P.K. O'Brien
The economic effects of the American civil war

16. P.L. Payne
British entrepreneurship in the nineteenth century

17. G.C. Peden
Keynes, the treasury and British economic policy

18. M.E. Rose
The relief of poverty, 1834–1914

19. J. Thirsk
England's agricultural regions and agrarian history, 1500–1750

20. J.R. Ward
Poverty and progress in the Caribbean, 1800–1960

Economic History Society

The Economic History Society, which numbers around 3,000 members, publishes the *Economic History Review* four times a year (free to members) and holds an annual conference.

Enquiries about membership should be addressed to

The Assistant Secretary
Economic History Society
PO Box 70
Kingswood
Bristol
BS15 5TB

Full-time students may join at special rates.

Immigration Federalism." University of Colorado Law Legal Studies Research Paper No. 07-06, accessed at http://ssm.com/abstract=96516

International Association of Chiefs of Police. 2007. *Police Chiefs Guide to Immigration*. Accessed Jan. 3, 2008 from http://www.theiacp.org/documents/pdfs/Publications/ChiefsGuidetoimmigration.pdf.

P... and Ryken Grattet. 2005. ...Law in Between: The Effects ...Organizational Imperviousness on ...e Policing of Hate Crime," *Social Problems* 52, pp. 337–359.

Katz, Charles and Vince Webb. *Policing Gangs in America*. New York: Cambridge University Press.

Kelling, George. 1999. *"Broken Windows" and Police Discretion*. Washington, D.C.: National Institute of Justice.

Lewis, Paul G., and S. Karthick Ramakrishnan. 2007. "Police Practices in Immigrant-Destination Cities: Political Control or Bureaucratic Professionalism?" *Urban Affairs Review* 42:6, pp. 874–900.

Major Cities Chiefs. 2006. *M C.C. Immigration Committee Recommendations for Enforcement of Immigration Laws by Local Police Agencies*. Retrieved 3 Jan 2008 from http://www.houstontx.gov/police/pdfs/mcc position.pdf.

Manning, Peter K. 2003. *Policing Contingencies*. Chicago: University of Chicago Press.

Massey, D. (ed.) 2008. *New Faces in New Places: The Changing Geography of American Immigration*. New York: Russell Sage Foundation.

McDonald, William F. 1997a. "Crime and Illegal Immigration: Emerging Local, State and Federal Partnerships," *NIJ Journal* (June). Washington D.C.: National Institute of Justice.

———. 1997b. "Illegal Immigration: Crime, Ramifications and Control (The American Experience)." In William F. McDonald ed., *Crime and Enforcement in the Global Village*. Cincinnati, OH: Anderson Publishers.

Passel, J.S. 2006. "The Size and Characteristics of the Unauthorized Migrant Population in the U.S.: Estimates Based on the March 2005 Current Population Survey." Retrieved 15 July 2007 from http://pewhispanic org/files/reports/6l.pdf.

Ramakrishnan, S. Karthick and Tom (Tak) Wong. 2007. "Immigration Policies Go Local: The Varying Responses of Local Governments to Undocumented Immigrants." Unpublished paper, University of California. Retrieved from http://www.law.berkeley.edu/centers/ewi/Ramakrishnan&Wongpaperfinal.pdf.

Romero, Mary and Marwah Serag. 2005. "Violation of Latino Civil Rights Resulting from INS and Local Police's Use of Race, Culture, and Class Profiling: The Case of the Chandler Roundup in Arizona," *Cleveland State Law Review* 52, pp. 75–96.

Singer, Audrey, Susan W. Hadwick, and Caroline B. Brettell (eds.) 2008. *Twenty-First Century Gateways*. Washington, DC: Brookings Institution.

Skogan, Wesley. 2006. *Police and Community in Chicago: A Tale of Three Cities*. New York: Oxford University Press.

Skolnick, Jerome. 1994. *Justice without Trial: Law Enforcement in Democratic Society*, rev. ed. New York: McMillan.

Spiro, Peter. 1997. "Learning to Live with Immigration Federalism," Connecticut *Law Review* 9, pp. 1627–36

Sudnow, David. 1965. "Normal Crimes: Sociological Features of the Penal Code in a Public Defender Office," *Social Problems*, Vol. 12, No. 3, pp. 255-276.

Sullivan, Bartholomew. 2008. Blackburn knocks Homeland immigration enforcement effort. *Memphis Commercial Appeal*, August 1.

Varsanyi, Monica W. 2008. Immigration policing through the backdoor: City ordinances, the 'right to the city' and exclusion of undocumented day laborers. *Urban Geography,* Vol. 29, No. 1, pp. 29–52.

Wilson, James Q. 1968. *Varieties of Police Behavior: The Management of Order in*

Eight Communities. Boston: Harvard University Press.

Zuniga, Victor, and Ruben Hernandez-Leon, eds. 2005. *New Destinations: Mexican Immigration in the United States.* New York: Russell Sage Foundation.

200

but in any case they cannot be shrugged off because elected officials and the public will increasingly expect that their police are prepared.

The case for the essential involvement of local police in counter-terrorism has been made in the United States by Kelling and Bratton (2006): The have argued that local police play a critical role in defeating terrorism, wh they go on to argue. They claim is not much different from other crime. They go on to argue. 'Counter-terrorism has to be woven into the everyday working of department. It should be included on the agenda of every meeting, new role must be imparted to officers on the street so that terrorism p becomes part of their everyday thinking' (Kelling and Bratton, 2006: tall order. We know that terrorist attacks are extremely rare events— even than murders, for example. And many police jurisdiction in the United States, would be unlikely to attract the terrorists' people in their community. They have been, and will be held a disaster occur. It makes sense, therefore, for them to pla Kelling and Bratton are correct to this extent: local police cann and even better sense to fold these plans into everyday p

But what should they actually do? In brief, we th intelligence about possible terrorist activity; (b) en are protected; and (c) be ready to respond in the of these is uncontroversial and will not be di discuss the first two tasks, both of which, in on prevention. We welcome this focus. there is another general point to be crimes where bringing perpetrators to guard against devoting the bulk of expense of effort on protecting terrorists might be congruent efforts exclusively, or even p be unproductive for reason targets, on the other ha require them to develo will always remain protect their most police. We will b

Regular as pre

any case, decades of criminological research have failed to establish a relationship between severe punishment and reduced crime. The best known example is the lack of statistical evidence that capital punishment deters murder. Offenders think they will not be caught and therefore do not take seriously the risk of severe punishment, or they do not care if they are caught because they are so drunk or enraged. Finally, the supply of offenders is never-ending. Five to ten percent of every new youth cohort will turn out to be regular offenders. So, however many offenders we arrest and imprison, others will soon take their place.

Some of the same reasons explain why it is dangerous to rely upon 'taking out' the terrorists—i.e. identifying them and then capturing or killing them—as the main defense against terrorism. Those who are willing to die for their beliefs are unlikely to be deterred by the risk of death or punishment. Catching them is difficult because terrorists are more careful than other criminals to conceal their activities. Even when their identities are known, they cannot always be caught, especially when they operate from overseas in countries sympathetic to their cause—witness the fruitless search for Osama bin Laden. They often cannot be tried in open court because of security concerns and they make very difficult prisoners, often turning their captivity into public relations disasters for their captors. Perhaps the greatest cost of imprisoning them is that their supporters feel justified in planning fresh outrages in order to force their release.

Killing terrorists carries even greater costs. It creates more bitterness among already hostile populations, making the underlying conflicts even harder to resolve. It justifies the terrorists' use of violence and supports the claim that they are fighting ruthless enemies. It turns them into martyrs and thus into potent recruiting symbols among the impressionable young men that terrorists seek to attract—young men who are currently streaming out of the madrassas in Pakistan, Saudi Arabia and parts of Indonesia.

None of this means that they should not be hunted down or punished once caught. They deserve to be punished for their crimes. It can also be effective to kill terrorist leaders, particularly when they are charismatic individuals, who hold considerable sway over their followers and who cannot easily be replaced. Killing these leaders might effectively decapitate the organization and leave its body to wither, saving the lives of many innocent people. However, much of this is beyond the capabilities or even interest of local police, whose primary concern surely is the prevention of terrorist attacks from occurring in their own communities.

In sum, the take-them-out mindset is an impediment to incorporating terrorism prevention into everyday police practice and thinking. But what of intelligence-led policing (Gill, 2000, Maguire, 2000)? Does this not offer a way to overcome the drawbacks of the normal take-them-out thinking?

INTELLIGENCE-LED POLICING

The term 'intelligence-led policing' was coined by the Kent Constabulary, which developed the concept in response to sharp increases in burglary and car theft at a time when police budgets were being cut. Senior managers believed that a small number of individuals were responsible for many of these crimes and that crime could best be cut by creating intelligence units to target the offenders for investigation and prosecution. They freed up resources for these units de-emphasizing the response to calls for service and, within 3 years, crime had dropped by one quarter. Intelligence-led policing is now the basis of the National Intelligence Model that has established new data collection and processing standards to be followed by the forty-three police forces in the United Kingdom.

In the United States, intelligence-led policing has captured attention as a way of combining discrete pieces of information about terrorist activities, that only make sense when considered together (Peterson, 2005). Popularized by the 9/11 Commission, intelligence-led policing can provide a way to 'join up the dots' (Gladwell, 2003). The New York Police Department is the leading exponent of intelligence-led policing to combat terrorism. It has more than 1,000 officers dedicated to counter-terrorism, it has hired intelligence and counter-terrorism experts, it has officers fluent in many foreign languages, it monitors news services and intelligence reports, and it has even stationed agents overseas in terrorism hot spots (Finnegan, 2005). No other police department in the United States can match this investment, though many large agencies, with hundreds or perhaps thousands of sworn officers, support an intelligence capacity. They might have a computerized database, intelligence officers, analysts, and an intelligence manager, though these are generally used to support investigations rather than to direct operations.

One fatal flaw of intelligence-led policing, especially the US version, is that it begins with the assumption that if the police simply collect as much information as they can, they will at some point identify suspicious activity (too many purchases of hydrogen peroxide for example), which will then lead to their destroying a terrorist cell or conspiracy. Much of this approach in the United States has also been accompanied by exhortations and reminders to people to report any suspicious activity or persons to a police hot line. Because this information is classified as 'secret' it is not known whether any information reported to a hot line has ever led to the discovery of a terrorist conspiracy. Furthermore, behaviors or events that are labeled as 'suspicious', are very vague, leaving open opportunities for individuals to exercise whatever prejudices or preconceptions they may have about what is suspicious or what a terrorist looks like. Under these circumstances, useless information is vastly more common than useful information. While the media often broadcast stories of intelligence successes resulting from tips received or surveillance undertaken, nobody hears about all the other people who were under surveillance, but to no result, and how many other apparently promising tips led nowhere.

Another flaw of intelligence-led policing is that it depends on individuals and agencies sharing information, which must then be collated and interpreted to produce intelligence. Indeed, the National Intelligence Model was designed to deal with just this problem, but there are many impediments to the timely sharing of terrorism information that the model cannot solve. One of these is that many local departments lack an intelligence capacity. They lack intelligence staff trained to a common curriculum and they lack appropriate technology (General Accounting Office, 2003). Many local agencies (again, particularly in the United States) even lack properly trained crime analysts, let alone intelligence analysts. In the general competition for resources, crime analysis must be considered more important than intelligence for most forces, simply because crime analysis can yield more obvious and consistent benefits for their everyday police work. As for technology, local forces may lack the computing equipment and software to facilitate a national intelligence data system and, even within the same force, there may be little interconnectivity among existing computer systems. Without such uniformity and interconnectivity, the dream of an electronic network across which the information collected can be quickly transmitted throughout the country remains just that—a dream.

An even greater impediment to information sharing than lack of technology or trained personnel might be human nature. Particularly in the early stages of an inquiry, investigators are likely to guard their information jealously. This is not just to prevent leaks that could jeopardize the investigation—secrecy is, after all, the hallmark of intelligence operations—but also for two other reasons. Investigators might doubt that 'outsiders' could help them and they would want to keep for themselves the considerable kudos resulting from the successful apprehension of terrorists. This might help to explain why the Organized Vehicle Crime Programme of the National Criminal Intelligence Service succeeded, at the cost of £1 million, in garnering only 184 items of information from local forces in a 2-year period—many of which were the results of specific requests made to police forces (Brown and Clarke, 2004; Brown et al., 2004).

COMMUNITY POLICING

'Local police officers have an everyday presence in the communities that they are sworn to protect. They 'walk the beat,' communicate regularly with the local residents and business owners, and are more likely to notice even subtle changes in the neighborhoods they patrol. They are in a better position to know responsible leaders in the Islamic and Arabic communities and can reach out to them for information or help in developing informants.' (Kelling and Bratton, 2006: 1)

As this statement makes clear, the prescription for obtaining vital information and earning the trust of communities is talking regularly and informally with key members of the community, and it is just one of many endorsements of the role of community policing in counter-terrorism. Community policing requires beat police officers to be assigned to particular neighborhoods so that they can spend considerable time there, getting to know residents or business owners and talking with them about local problems and troublesome individuals. It means they must be made responsible for reducing crime in their beats; that they must spend most of their working hours in these beats; and that they should pay close attention to what is bothering residents and business owners and do what they can to alleviate the problems. It requires management to select officers who are temperamentally suited to community policing, leaving them in place long enough to gain the trust of the community and to become familiar faces in the neighborhood; matching officers with neighborhoods—for example selecting officers who live close by or even in the neighborhoods they serve, and ensuring that they have the language skills to communicate with minority residents; allowing officers flexible work hours and, whenever possible, not pulling them from their neighborhoods for emergency duties elsewhere.

Finally, if they are to serve an intelligence function, officers must be trained in what signs to look for, and in sifting the few kernels of wheat from the overpowering chaff of useless information. Given the potential loss of life resulting from a terrorist attack, local communities might be less reticent in passing on information about suspicious activities than for conventional crime. In fact, gathering information through community policing has many advantages over traditional intelligence work. Specifically, it avoids: (a) undermining community trust though compiling unsubstantiated lists of suspects, (b) charges of profiling, phone-tapping and the legal and political encumbrances thereof, (c) costly and unproductive surveillance of suspects and places; (d) secret (and therefore suspect) operations and entrapment.

To ensure that community officers are meeting their goals, senior management will need to check the quality and frequency of intelligence reports that their officers supply. Management should also periodically check that officers are setting and meeting concrete crime and disorder reduction goals for their neighborhoods. This could mean that the force's crime analysis capabilities need to be strengthened by employing properly trained staff, providing them with up-to-date technology and preventing them from becoming mired in the production of routine reports (Clarke and Eck, 2003). Finally, managers will need to instill preventive values force-wide so that officers understand that problem solving is valued as much as detection and arrest and that it will be equally rewarded by recognition and promotion.

IMMIGRANT COMMUNITIES

Immigrant communities provide the basic conditions for new arrivals to find their way in a strange country, particularly when they cannot speak the language. By the same token, they make it easier for foreign terrorists to get bank accounts, credit cards, get money from abroad and find places to live. The first attack on the World Trade Center in 1993 was undertaken by individuals residing in a Jersey City immigrant community close to Manhattan and the 9/11 attackers all lived temporarily in or near immigrant areas that matched their ethnic and national backgrounds. So, there is little doubt that Al Qaeda's attacks were facilitated by the presence of immigrant communities in the United States, even if these communities were made use of inadvertently. In the UK immigrant communities, were the breeding grounds for the terrorists who attacked the London Underground in June 2005. Some of these communities might also have been a source of financial support for Al Qaeda. Al Qaeda's extensive revenue raising operations through charities and mosques in immigrant communities is well documented (Napoleoni, 2005). In some cases, it also seems that money raised within immigrant communities to assist charities in their home countries has been diverted into the hands of terrorists without the communities' knowledge.

It is clear, therefore, that in seeking information about possible terrorist attacks the police must pay special attention to immigrant communities, but heavy-handed or insensitive actions could easily make matters worse. Though the vast majority of immigrants are hostile to terrorism, they might feel threatened, become resentful and fail to cooperate with the authorities. These dangers are easier to avoid when community policing ideals inform the police approach rather than a take-them-out mindset, or even the application of intelligence-led policing. Community policing would also help protect immigrant communities from victimization resulting from the fear of terrorism. Every time there is news of a foiled terror plot, or whenever the terror alert is ramped up, immigrants become fearful—not just frightened of being victims of terrorism, but of being targeted by the authorities with further checks and restrictions and by the local population with hostility and even hate.

Protecting these communities and providing them with 'reassurance' (Innes, 2004, Morris, 2006), while at the same time ensuring they do not harbor or support terrorism, presents police with a difficult balancing act for several reasons, including that new immigrants often bring with them a fear and distrust of the police; many immigrants have little understanding of civil rights and law enforcement; language barriers prohibit effective communication and trust between immigrants and police, and immigrants fear that contact with police will threaten their immigration status.

Nevertheless, there is much the police can do to overcome these barriers and implement community policing successfully in immigrant communities. These actions include: establishing police sub-stations in larger communities; forging partnerships with schools, social services, and religious institutions to help younger immigrants, children of immigrants and elderly immigrants, and help keep them safe; using immigrant newspapers, religious institutions, and employers to communicate with those in immigrant communities who cannot attend community meetings; employing more interpreters and making police material available in the immigrants' languages; involving immigrant leaders in the design and implementation of cultural training for officers; working to overcome barriers preventing the recruitment of officers from these communities; clearly defining and publicizing policies of immigration law enforcement; and training community advocates on the role and policies of the police and training the media so that they can more accurately report the dialogues taking place between police and immigrants (Chapman and Scheider Undated).

PROTECTING VULNERABLE TARGETS

The police may be familiar with the difficulties in identifying possible terrorists, but they know much less about the equally difficult task of identifying and protecting vulnerable targets. They are not alone in this since governments, pundits and academics have all eschewed this subject (Clarke and Newman, 2006). They are quickly put off by some very difficult questions that immediately present themselves. How can society organize the enormous task, and afford the enormous cost, of retrofitting the vast number of potential terrorist targets with adequate security? If it is impossible to protect everything, how can the choice be narrowed, so that at least the most vulnerable targets are protected? When these are protected will not the terrorists simply attack the ones that have not yet been protected?

In *Outsmarting the Terrorists* (Clarke and Newman, 2006) we drew on the situational crime prevention theory for providing answers to these questions (Clarke, 2005) and in *Policing Terrorism: A Police Chief's Guide* (Clarke and Newman, (in press)) we reframed these answers for American police practice. We summarize here the main points for a broader police audience under the two headings of 'understanding the threat' and 'formulating a plan'.

UNDERSTANDING THE THREAT

Police must understand the nature of the threat if they are to formulate a plan for protecting targets from terrorism. The conceptual framework provided by situational crime prevention, discussed below, assists this understanding.

TREAT TERRORISM AS CRIME

It is sometimes argued that crime and terrorism are so different that the lessons in preventing crime can have little relevance in preventing terrorism. Is it not true that terrorists are better organized, more determined and more ruthless than ordinary criminals? Are they not also motivated by a 'higher cause' than most criminals who are usually seeking to benefit only themselves? Finally, is it not the case that acts of terrorism are better planned and on a larger scale than most acts of crime? Even if these points were true, the differences are merely ones of degree. Many of the acts of 'organized crime' are also well planned, large-scale and ruthless, and many terrorist operatives are as much motivated by common-place ambitions (e.g. gaining respect, earning a living and enjoying a life of excitement) as by the political ideals of their leaders. In any case, crime has very varied motives. Much of it is driven by greed, but other motives drive rape, homicide, vandalism and assaults, to name but a few examples. In fact, the most basic motivator of crime—to achieve a benefit—is also shared by terrorism. For all these reasons, we reject a hard and fast division between crime and terrorism and prefer to regard the latter as 'crime with a political motive' (Clarke and Newman, 2006).

CLEARLY DIFFERENTIATE BETWEEN DIFFERENT FORMS OF TERRORISM

Each different kind of terrorist attack must be analyzed separately. This is because, for example, suicide bombings in restaurants will have different requirements and constraints compared with suicide bombings in buses or trains. And both will differ greatly from hijackings of airliners or hostage takings at schools. These differences in terrorist methodology can be uncovered if the movements of a terrorist are traced, step by step, from the beginning to the end of his mission. As a result, the opportunities can be identified that terrorists must exploit in order to complete their attacks, and the decisions they make based on these, for example, their choice of target or weapon. It may be that there is insufficient information about how different terrorists implement their missions. In this case, police must 'think terrorist' by putting themselves in the shoes of the terrorist and imagining the steps needed to conduct a particular terrorist attack.

ANALYZE THE ATTRACTIVENESS OF TARGETS

Research in situational prevention has shown that thieves are attracted to particular products and not others. These attractive features of products have led Clarke (1999) to identify several characteristics that make products 'hot' to steal. Similarly, the terrorist must make a choice of a target and some are more attractive than others. In theory, he could attack anything, but in practice, his activities are constrained by money, location, accessibility to the target, disagreements with other operatives and many more. We have summarized the attractive features of a target by the acronym EVIL DONE (Clarke and Newman, 2006):

Exposed (the Twin Towers of the World Trade Center were sitting ducks)
Vital (electricity grids, transportation systems, communications)
Iconic (of symbolic value to the enemy, e.g. Buckingham Palace, Statue of Liberty)
Legitimate (terrorists' sympathizers cheered when Twin Towers collapsed)
Destructible (the Twin Towers were thought to be indestructible, but not by the 9/11 hijackers)
Occupied (Kill as many people as possible)
Near (Within reach of terrorist group, close to home)
Easy (the Murrah building in Oklahoma City was an easy target for McVeigh's car bomb placed within eight feet of its perimeter)

Armed with this elementary knowledge about the attractiveness of targets the police can then move to rule out many possible targets in their jurisdictions. Combined with an assessment of the expected loss should a target be attacked, the police, working with local businesses and other organizations, can collect information that tells them where the weak points are, and where potential terrorists would be most likely to direct their efforts. The collection of intelligence, therefore, in this enterprise, is never random, and as little useless information as possible is collected. It requires, of course, a lot of work getting to know the local community—it is simply community policing with a focus on target protection.

DO NOT SUCCUMB TO THE DISPLACEMENT ARGUMENT

It is often thought that the sole result of protecting the most vulnerable targets will be to displace attacks to unprotected ones. However, we know from studies in situational crime prevention that displacement is comparatively rare: it certainly does occur, but in a majority of cases it does not (Hesseling, 1994). For example, the passenger and baggage screening measures initially introduced in 1973 to prevent hijackings of aircraft between Cuba and the United States did not displace hijackings to other parts of the world (Clarke and Newman, 2006). Nor was there any apparent displacement to sabotage of airliners by smuggling bombs on board. Having said that, however, it must be recognized that the populations of terrorists (and criminals) do adjust their behavior over time to take account of security interventions that have been introduced. One example of adaptation is the plot uncovered in London in September 2006 to use liquid explosives on US bound airplanes where the terrorists had figured out that, despite the heightened security since 9/11, there was no ban on carrying liquids on board. In response to this new threat, the authorities were forced to introduce new restrictions on liquids. As soon as a security loophole is discovered it must be closed. In fact, we believe that leaving opportunities open for attack invites attack.

FORMULATING A PLAN

It will be clear from the above that any plan to protect targets must be long-term. This and other components of a protection plan are discussed below.

Develop Plans for Each Police Division (or Basic Command Unit)

Divisional commanders should be made responsible for drawing up plans for protecting targets in their jurisdictions. These plans should be revised each year in the light of progress made in the preceding year and in response to any newly emerging threats. The task should encompass two separate but related activities:

1. Identifying a small number of the most vulnerable targets and reducing this vulnerability, working with other stakeholders where necessary. For each target, police must think clearly about the kind of attack that is most likely and, by trying to think like a terrorist, consider how the attack would be undertaken and which specific vulnerabilities would be exploited.
2. Providing basic security advice for other possible targets.

The task of formulating the plan should be adequately resourced and each division should ensure that the responsible officers are properly trained in crime prevention and security procedures. The divisional plans should be reviewed by central command to ensure that boundary issues of omission or overlap are addressed.

Plan for the Long Term

It is possible to reduce specific forms of terrorism and to eliminate particular terrorist groups. In time, however, other terrorist groups will rise and new forms of attack will be developed. New forms of attack will also result from technological or social change, which produce new opportunities for terrorism. Police must, therefore, formulate a long-term plan for continuously analyzing target vulnerabilities in their jurisdictions, and for enhancing security where needed. In any case, the task of reducing opportunities for terrorism, which might seem impossible in the short term, becomes less daunting and more manageable when viewed as a long-term, probably permanent commitment.

Work Closely with the Private Sector

Because the private sector often owns or manages the majority of targets, the police must partner with businesses, industries and other nongovernmental agencies in reducing opportunities for terrorism. In persuading private sector partners to improve security in their spheres of influence, the police should look for solutions that also benefit normal business operations (so-called dual benefit solutions). A 'natural' private partner is the local security industry. In fact, security professionals are responsible for securing most of a jurisdiction's infrastructure, and they provide the visible crime control in the places where people spend much of their daily lives—at work, on public transport, in educational facilities and in shopping malls. They can also help police to identify needed resources, such as specialist consultants, when designing protection for some critical infrastructure, such as ports, reservoirs and water supply, and for facilities that need special handling, such as chemical factories or petroleum plants.

SUMMARY AND CONCLUSIONS

In the wake of the 9/11 attacks, terrorism has replaced crime as the greatest perceived threat to social order and, in the first 2 or 3 years after the attacks, it seemed as though intelligence agencies had usurped the police's role as the guardians of society. In the United States, this change in status was reflected in a diversion of funds from police to homeland security programs. More recently, things have begun to change again. Police leaders such as Kelling and Bratton (2006) have argued that police play a critical role in counter-terrorism because they are in the best position to learn about the emergence of local terrorist threats, to know which targets are most at risk, and to coordinate the first response to attacks. In this paper, we have focused on the first two of these functions, both concerned with prevention, which, because of the potential loss of life, is of great importance for terrorism. We have argued that an extension of community policing principles can best serve the first function (gathering intelligence), while situational crime prevention provides a useful framework for serving the second (the protection of vulnerable targets). To accommodate these functions, some police forces, especially in large cities with many attractive targets, might have to make considerable changes in their operating practices. They should embrace these changes because they are consistent with best practices in policing. They put a premium on prevention, on service to the community, on making full use of data and analysis, and on forming partnerships with other agencies and organizations, public and private. These practices will not only help meet the threat of terrorism, but will also help the police better serve their goals of fighting crime, protecting victims and providing reassurance to the public.

DISCUSSION QUESTIONS

1. Since 9/11, what has been done to increase terrorism prevention and response efforts among local police agencies?
2. Define terrorism and the alternative solutions of holding alleged terrorists before they are sentenced.
3. Analyze the pros and cons to information sharing among local and national intelligence agencies.
4. Discuss the controversy surrounding our counter-terrorism efforts primarily associated with the Patriot Act.

REFERENCES

Brown, R., and Clarke, R.V. 2004. "Police intelligence and theft of vehicles for export: Recent U.K. Experience." In Maxfield, M.G., and Clarke, R.V. (eds), *Understanding and Preventing Car Theft, Crime Prevention Studies*, vol.17. Monsey: Criminal Justice Press, pp. 173–192.

Brown, R., Clarke, R.V., and Sheptycki, J. 2004. *Tackling Organised Vehicle Crime: the role of NCIS, Findings 238*. London: Home Office.

Cauley, J., and Im, E.I. 1988. "Intervention Policy Analysis of Skyjackings and Other Terrorist Incidents." *American Economic Review* **78**(2): 27–31.

Chapman, R., and Scheider, M. Undated. *Community Policing for Mayors: A Municipal Service Model for Policing and Beyond*, Office of Community Oriented Policing Services. Washington, DC: U.S. Department of Justice, (Accessible at: www.cops.usdoj.gov).

Chauncey, R. 1975. "Deterrence: Certainty, Severity, and Skyjacking." *Criminology* **12**(4): 447–473.

Clarke, R.V. 1999. *Hot Products: Understanding, Anticipating and Reducing Demand for Stolen Goods, Police Research Series*, Paper 112. London: Home Office, (Accessible at: www.homeoffice.gov.uk/prgpubs.htm).

Clarke, R.V. 2005. "Seven Misconceptions of Situational Crime Prevention." In Tilley, N. (ed.), *Handbook of Crime Prevention and Community Safety*, Cullompton: Willan, 39–70.

Clarke, R.V., and Eck, J.E. 2003. *Become a Problem-solving Crime Analyst—In 55 Steps*, London: Jill Dando Institute of Crime Science, UCL.

Clarke, R.V., and Newman, G.R. 2006. *Outsmarting the Terrorists*, Westport CT: Praeger Security International.

Clarke, R.V., and Newman, G.R. Policing Terrorism: A Police Chief's Guide, Office of Community Policing Oriented Services. Washington, DC: U.S. Dept. of Justice, (In press).

Dugan, L., LaFree, G., and Piquero, A. 2005. "Testing a Rational Choice Model of Airline Hijackings." *Criminology* **43**(4): 1031–1066.

Enders, W., and Sandler, T. 1993. "The Effectiveness of Antiterrorism Policies: A Vector-Autoregression-Intervention Analysis." *American Political Science Review* **87**(4): 829–844.

Enders, W., and Sandler, T. 2000. "Is Transnational Terrorism Becoming More Threatening?" *Journal of Conflict Resolution* **44**(3): 307–332.

Enders, W., and Sandler, T. 2006. *The Political Economy of Terrorism*, Cambridge: Cambridge University Press.

Enders, W., Sandler, T., and Cauley, J. 1990. "UN Conventions, Technology and Retaliation in the Fight Against Terrorism: An Econometric Evaluation." *Terrorism and Political Violence* 2(1): 83–105.

Finnegan, W. 2005. "The Terrorism Beat: How is the NYPD Defending the City?" *New Yorker* **81**(21): 58–71.

General Accounting Office. 2003. *Efforts to Improve Information Sharing Need to be Strengthened, Report to the Secretary of Homeland Security*, GAO-03-760. Washington, DC: U.S. General Accounting Office.

Gill, P. 2000. *Rounding up the Usual Suspects? Developments in Contemporary Law Enforcement Intelligence*, Aldershot: Ashgate.

Gladwell, M. 2003. "Connecting the dots: the paradoxes of intelligence reform." *New Yorker* **March**(10): 83–88.

Heaton, R. 2000. "The Prospects for Intelligence-Led Policing: Some Historical and Quantitative Considerations." *Policing and Society* **9**: 337–355.

Hesseling, R.B.P. 1994. "Displacement: A Review of the Empirical Literature." In Clarke, RV (ed.), *Crime Prevention Studies*, Vol. 3. Monsey: Criminal Justice Press, 197–230, (Accessible at: www.popcenter.org).

Innes, M. 2004. "Reinventing Tradition? Reassurance, Neighbourhood Security and Policing." *Criminal Justice* **4**(2): 151–171.

Kelling, G.L., and Bratton, W.J. 2006. *Policing Terrorism, Civic Bulletin 43*. New York: Manhattan Institute.

Lum, C., Kennedy, L.W., and Sherley, A.J. 2006. The Effectiveness of Counter-terrorism Strategies: A Campbell Systematic Review, (Accessible at www.campbellcollaboration.org).

Maguire M. 2000. "Policing by Risks and Targets: Some Implications of Intelligence-Led Crime Control." *Policing and Society* **9**: 315–336.

Morris, J. 2006. *The National Reassurance Policing Programme: A Ten-site Evaluation, Findings 273*. London: Home Office.

Napoleoni, L. 2005. *Terror Incorporated: Tracing the Dollars Behind the Terror Networks*, New York: Seven Stories Press.

Peterson, M. 2005. *Intelligence-Led Policing: The New Intelligence Architecture*, Washington, DC: U.S. Dept. of Justice, Bureau of Justice Assistance.

12

Enforcing the Law: The Stress of Being a Police Officer

Judith A. Waters
William Ussery

The purpose of this chapter is to highlight the stressors involved in an occupation at potential risk – the profession of law enforcement. It reviews the history of police stress studies and describes prevention and treatment programs that have unfortunately not been sufficiently utilized because of the police culture. The documented symptoms of stress include digestive orders, cardiovascular disease, alcoholism, domestic violence, post-traumatic stress disorder, depression and suicide. While some police officers start their careers in excellent physical health, some retire early or even die from job-related stress disorders if the cumulative impact of stress exacts its toll. This chapter also offers a description of COP.2.COP a confidential hotline for officers and their families staffed by retired officers and licensed professionals.

THE NATURE OF THE "JOB"

On Monday, August 7, 2006, Detective Kieran J. Shields and his partner, Detective Dave Thompson were dispatched to Taylor Street in Orange, New Jersey, to investigate a shooting (Kelley and Holl, 2006). At the scene, Detective

Source: Judith A. Waters and William Ussery, "Enforcing the Law: The Stress of Being a Police Officer," Policing: An International Journal of Police Strategies and Management, vol 31:2. Copyright © 2007 Emerald Group Publishing Limited. Reprinted with permission.

Shields, 32, was shot to death, allegedly by a 19-year-old suspect. Despite the fact that Shields was wearing a bulletproof jacket, he was not protected. The shotgun blast penetrated both his neck and collarbone. Detective Shields, who came from a police family that included his own father, a retired officer from the Orange, New Jersey Police Department, had been recently promoted to detective after only four years on the force. He had already received several commendations and regularly volunteered his time to work with juvenile offenders. Detective Shields leaves a wife, two daughters (aged ten and seven) and an infant son. He grew up in Orange, developed his desire to be a police officer in Orange, joined the force and was promoted in Orange, and died in Orange.

Detective Shields was murdered at a time when the number of murders in the State of New Jersey had recently risen by 7 percent to 418 victims. According to the latest edition of the New Jersey Uniform Crime Report, 12 percent of these homicides were related to gang activity (cited in Schewber and Holl, 2006). Being killed or injured during the commission of a crime is one of the major challenges facing police officers and their families. In the August 9, 2006 edition of *The New York Times*, the Metro Briefing Section reported two deaths in a shooting in Queens, New York; the case of a man who died after a struggle with police officers in Pelham Manor, New York; the case of 12 people who were arrested on gang related charges; the case of a man who was killed and another who was wounded in Brooklyn; and the case of a man who was arrested for racing his car at 130 mph with another man on the Long Island Expressway. These reports were the only ones found to be interesting to the newspaper. They did not include all the dangerous domestic violence cases or the myriad other calls that occur on a daily basis when the community reaches out for police protection. On the very same day that Detective Shields' murder was reported (August 9, 2006), *The New York Times* also carried the story of two New Jersey Transit police officers who were suspended without pay for having sexual relations with a woman in their patrol car near Liberty Park in Jersey City on July 29, 2006. Although the two officers will not be charged with a sex crime since no coercion appears to have been involved, they will certainly face internal administration charges of "conduct unbecoming an officer". The outcome could easily include the loss of their jobs. Every day police officers are faced with the challenges of the job, plus the opportunities far less than professional behavior.

On August 10, 2006, a headline in the *New York Times* read "After Long Stress, Newsman in New Orleans Unravels" (Saulny, 2006). The story is about John McCusker, a photographer for *Times-Picayune*, who decided not to evacuate to Baton Rouge with the rest of the newspaper's staff. Using a kayak and even swimming through the muddy waters and debris, he took pictures of the dramatic aftermath of Hurricane Katrina. He also personally experienced the misery and trauma that he photographed, having lost all his belongings, his family's home, and the entire neighborhood where he had lived. The incident reported in the *New York Times* began as a traffic stop for erratic driving. However, when stopped, Mr. McCusker backed up and apparently used his car as a weapon to pin an officer between two cars before he sped away, subsequently driving into other cars. He was finally stopped again. Both times he begged the officers to shoot him. He said he just wanted to die. According to James Arey, Commander of the Negotiation Team of the New Orleans Police Department's Special Operations Division, McCusker made every effort to hurt the officers with his car. Arey pointed out that, "Our officers are well trained to recognize crises and attempts at suicide by cop" and that's what this was (p. A21).

The mass media image of police officers, outside of dramatic accounts of dangerous rescues and heroic responses to disasters, tends to focus on stories that will engage readers and sell newspapers. Consequently, stories of the bad cop, the brutal cop, the corrupt cop, and the tainted authority figures may make more interesting reading than the good cop just doing his job (Waters et al., 1982). On the other hand, creating a superman image can make life even more difficult for the officer than it normally would be.

In sum, police officers must be good psychologists at the same time they must secure the safety of the public and investigate the scene of a crime; address the needs of the victims, witnesses, and perpetrators; and face troubled individuals who may try to kill them or try to commit suicide. They must also be aware of the possibility that there are phantom assailants who are not immediately visible and they must still be able to keep their own reactions under control.

The events associated with Hurricane Katrina brought out both the best and the worst in the officers of the New Orleans Police Departments (CNN.com, September 13, 2005). In the days following the hurricane, officers performed acts of heroism in saving the victims of flooding, two officers committed suicide, and dozens (perhaps as many as 200) turned in their badges. The two officers who committed suicide were characterized as outstanding cops who used their own guns to take their lives. It should be noted that some of the officers who did not report for duty may have been trapped in their homes and were therefore unable to report to the command centers. In reality, large numbers of officers worked long hours, slept in their cars, went without normal sanitation facilities, and wore borrowed clothing because they had lost everything.

HISTORY OF POLICE STRESS STUDIES

The study of stress, the identification of contributing factors and symptoms, and the development of prevention and treatment programs began in earnest in the mid to late twentieth century (Lindemann, 1944; Mantell, 1994; Maslach and Jackson, 1979; Maslach, 1982; Mitchell, 1983; Mitchell and Everly, 1993; Reese, 1987; Russell and Beigel, 1990; Waters et al., 1982). While, in those early years, some police agencies did establish employee assistance programs, fund conferences, conduct research, and establish prevention programs, the incidence of police stress continued to escalate and affect many officers and their families. Most officers, however, have not utilized the services that were available due to the strong cultural influences of the law enforcement profession. In order to address cultural impediments, two factors have to be taken into account; confidentiality and the competence of the counselors. In 2000, in New Jersey, COP-2-COP, the first confidential hotline for police officers and their families was established. It utilizes retired police officers trained in assessment and in crisis intervention techniques to answer the phones (Ussery and Waters, 2006). These volunteer counselors conduct interviews that can lead to referrals to licensed mental health professionals who have police experience. So far, the hotline staff has answered over 18,000 calls. COP-2-COP was expanded following the events of September 11, 2001, to respond to the needs of the survivors of the World Trade Center disaster. Retired Police Lieutenant William Ussery, Clinical Supervisor of COP-2-COP, also went to New Orleans to assist in the Critical Incident Stress Debriefing process after Hurricane Katrina.

There is already sufficient evidence in the medical and mental health literature to demonstrate the relationships among various categories of life events, predisposing factors, and a broad spectrum of physical and psychological symptoms not only in populations-at-risk (e.g. law enforcement officers), but also in the general public. The symptoms that have been studied in police officers include poor job performance, increased accidents, sleep disturbances, marital discord, domestic violence, post-traumatic stress disorder, depression, suicide, alcohol and other drug abuse, ulcers and other digestive disorders, respiratory ailments, and cardiovascular disease. In the study of the consequences of the Oklahoma City Federal Building bombing (North et al., 1999), the researchers found elevated rates of post-traumatic stress disorder (PTSD) (American Psychiatric Association, 2000). The higher incidence of PTSD was associated more with some categories of survivors than others. These rates were often correlated with previous life experiences and the occupational tasks of at-risk groups. There is no doubt that police officers, as an occupational category, are exposed to more acute and chronic life stressors than most other occupations and are vulnerable to the development of most, if not all, of these symptoms.

The fact that police officers begin their careers in excellent physical health and retire early or die from job related stress disorders demonstrates the cost of continuous pressure and the need for ongoing emotional readjustment. While not everyone in a hazardous profession exhibits discernible symptoms of stress immediately following a traumatic incident, in the long run, the cumulative impact of stress exacts its toll. Of course, the cost associated with any stressful life event is a function of how each individual perceives that event. What may appear to be an exciting challenge to one person may seem like a threat to another. Also, since some people are capable of ventilating their feelings and discharging their emotions, they don't suffer as much as others from stressful life events. Suppressed emotions are often a precursor to the development of stress related disorders (Weisinger, 1985). Obviously, the inherent nature of police work precludes the immediate discharge of emotions. It is certainly not appropriate behavior for a police officer who has been given the responsibility of maintaining stability in others to ventilate in public. Another way of deflecting the influence of stressful life events is to develop effective coping mechanisms. A few individuals who don't appear to suffer from any symptoms include people who seem almost immune to stress. They may, in fact, be less sensitive to the human condition than people who do experience stress.

Hurricane Katrina has already been identified as the worst natural disaster in the history of the USA. More than one million Americans were forced to leave their homes. Many of them will never return (American Psychological

Association, 2006). According to The American Psychological Association (APA), the victims of natural disasters develop both psychological and physical health problems that are often mediated by the survivor's culture as well as by social and historic factors. Culture can determine just which events will be defined as traumatic and which will be down graded. Thus, the survivor can feel shame as well as anxiety for becoming upset by an experience that his/her culture does not identify as a traumatic event.

The responses to traumas fall into three stages (American Psychological Association, 2006). The first stage involves the immediate response, one that occurs in the direct aftermath of the disaster and coincides with emergency medical and humanitarian interventions. The next stage follows after the immediate emergency has passed. The third stage is comprised of the long-term responses that can emerge weeks, months, or even years after the actual event. It follows that psychological interventions must be matched to the stage as well as to the cultural background of the survivors.

In the early 1970s, Karl Goodin, Chief of the Cincinnati Police Department, gave some of the first seminars to address the issues of police work and stress. He stated that police work was one of the most stressful occupations. He went on to note that many officers suffer from health problems including heart attacks, depression, and suicide in numbers that are much higher than individuals in the business world or government service and that career police officers die at younger ages than members of other occupational categories. "Police culture leads officers to believe that they are a special population that has superhuman abilities and no weaknesses" when actually they are particularly vulnerable due to their need for constant vigilance. Not only does the individual officer deny his or her risk factors, but departments also ignore the problem. Within departments and academies, attention has always been paid to training for job related skills and to the need for up-to-date equipment. Less concern has been directed toward physical health and toward mental health and resiliency, proven tools for survival. While officer candidates have long been subjected to rigorous physical examinations, psychiatric screening has only been used recently. Moreover, current testing procedures are still underutilized and when they are used, the results are often misinterpreted.

The study of police stress coincides with the development of applied psychology following World War II. With the growth of community psychology, it was recognized that environmental and cultural factors have a strong influence on mental health, particularly responses to crises. Lindemann's (1944) early study of the survivors of the Coconut Grove nightclub fire led the way for research on the impact of traumatic events on the development of a broad spectrum of symptoms. Law enforcement officers were identified as an occupation-at-risk due to their actual exposure to threatening situations and to their need for constant vigilance with respect to the "phantom assailant" behind the next door. Unfortunately, police culture interfered and still interferes with obtaining accurate information about suicides. Police officers tend not only to avoid discussions about suicide, but also to be highly resistant to any form of educational prevention programs or treatment for imminent acts of self destruction.

The recognition of law enforcement as an occupation-at-risk for environmental, cultural, and personal factors did generate some prevention and treatment efforts such as Goodin's lectures. Mental health professionals began to teach in training academies and do "road shows" going to conferences or to individual departments for each shift. They also worked with officers referred through employee assistance programs designed to address the issues of officers involved in shootings. In 1982, Waters, Irons, and Finkle published a scale that identified the major stressors in police work and in their private lives that were most troubling to officers (Waters et al., 1982). However, it was not until the end of the year 2000 that the first hotline was opened to respond to officers in need of assistance (Ussery and Waters, 2006). Following a series of police suicides in New Jersey from 1996 to 1998, a group of community leaders was able to lobby the State Legislature successfully to create a bill that would establish and fund a dedicated hotline for law enforcement officers and their families. Thus, COP-2-COP was operational before the terrorist attacks of September 11, 2001.

The original mission of COP-2-COP was to provide a 24-hour hotline for officers and their families throughout New Jersey. Both confidentiality and integrity in practice was and are basic components of the program. COP-2-COP provides clinical assessment and peer support by the staff, all of whom are retired police officers who have volunteered their time and have been trained in crisis intervention. The staff is also prepared to deliver Critical Incident Stress Management sessions to first responders in times of tragedy. When a client needs further guidance, he or she is referred to a licensed mental health professional, an individual previously screened for prior experience working with law enforcement personnel. The reputation of COP-2-COP has made it a model for other emergency service crisis intervention programs. The success of COP-2-COP has been attributed to the rapid rapport and the therapeutic alliance formed between the clients served and the counselors. COP-2-COP has received recognition from the New Jersey Governor's Office, The New York City Police Department, The Port Authority Police Department of New York and New Jersey, The Federal Bureau of Investigation, The United States Secret Service, and *The New York Times*, as well as other publications.

THE POLICE STRESS MODEL

In order to design functional prevention programs and/or treat officers-at-risk, it is important to understand the predisposing factors, the nature of the stressful life events experienced by officers and both the transient and long term responses to these events (see Figure 1).

The predisposing factors begin with the biological status of the individual. While people outside of law enforcement are not usually required to pass comprehensive health examinations, police officers are given pre-employment "physicals". Thus, they begin their careers as healthy people, only to develop a broad range of stress related disorders during their careers. The second biological factor, current state of health, refers to the influence that being a working officer has on one's health. The longer an officer has been on the force, the more his resistance has been worn away. Psychological traits, states, and self

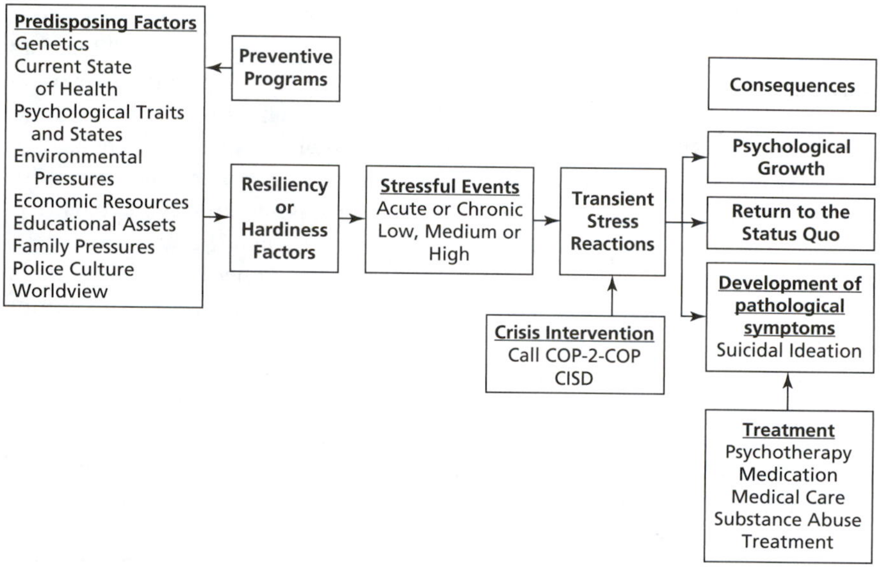

FIGURE 1 Police stress flowchart

expectations all influence the officer's ability to solve problems and address job related challenges and family issues. If the officer subscribes to the cultural stereotype of law enforcement, he or she will want to be a strong authority figure, and a perceptive problem solver. For many victims of crime, the officer is also the first psychologist on the scene (Waters, 2002). During emergencies such as September 11, 2001, and Hurricane Katrina, the police, firefighters and EMTs were truly the "first responders" (Ussery and Waters, 2006).

Many of the pressures experienced by officers are a product of environmental factors alone or a combination of psychological and environmental variables related to occupational issues. For example, one of the more obvious problems with a career in law enforcement is that it must inevitably involve shift work. Constant change of shifts (on a weekly or bi-weekly basis) leads to serious health problems. Changing sleep patterns, digestive system circadian rhythms, and other bodily functions affects both physical and psychological well-being. The process of readjustment to shift change schedules exacts a toll on each officer. In addition, normal family life is disrupted when the officer must sleep during the day or be absent from special events (e.g. holidays and birthdays) that conflict with his or her tour of duty.

For most officers, the roles and tasks associated with being a law enforcement officer can be debilitating. For each call, there is the potential for a violent confrontation with the ever-present possibility of being killed by an unknown assailant behind the next door. In responding to domestic violence calls (often 85 percent of an officer's normal duties), the couple who have been fighting with each other may both turn on the officer. Domestic violence cases are particularly dangerous since one or both combatants may also have been drinking and/or using drugs.

Police officers are always on duty. An officer once told me that going out to dinner with another officer or officers is like being taken to "The Last Supper" with all the officers sitting on one side of the table with their backs to the wall constantly surveying the room. The perpetual need for vigilance, even when off duty, also takes its toll on the officer's level of resilience.

Stressful life events include explosive, implosive and corrosive incidents. Police officers are faced with three types of stress: The explosive events (e.g. crimes in progress, terrorist situations such as September 11, 2001, and natural disasters) lead to acute and severe overt reactions, sometimes against other people. These reactions are often repressed in order for the officer to continue to fulfill his/her role of protecting the public. Long-term consequences follow when there is no intervention to reduce the impact of severe stress reactions. Some events have an implosive effect on the officer because of internal conflicts and the values that guided his/her choice of occupation.

The inability to "make a difference", the conflicts among family, and personal responsibilities, and job related considerations lead to the development of stress symptoms over a period of time. The daily tensions associated with police work have a corrosive effect, eroding confidence and wearing away at the individual's level of hardiness and resiliency. The essential problem, especially with corrosive events, is that officers do not engage in the type of self protective behaviors that could reduce the price of living a high risk lifestyle. Not only does the individual ignore these long term pressures but the department may also trivialize the negative consequences of police work. The implication is that only the weak suffer stress related symptoms. Hiding one's feelings becomes a badge of courage. Thus, the police culture combined with the reality of police work, even in the lowest crime rate areas, and the psychological factors that lead an individual to choose police work, all combine to create a situation that aggravates the inherent pressures of law enforcement.

Stress responses can be transient or chronic. On any particular day, officers face the normal challenges of the job ranging from the boredom of watching traffic to the potential danger of a domestic violence call to the guaranteed risk of a "break and entry" in progress. The event may literally be the "last straw" in a long career of tension filled days or it may be a situation of such magnitude that no one could have predicted the scope of its impact (e.g. September 11, 2001). Some of the events are acute and only have a short term impact while others can become chronic or are chronic by nature. The resolution of a short-term, low-level event is often a return to the "status quo". Not everyone reacts the same way to the events associated with law enforcement or to those associated with other high risk occupations. However, we have sufficient data to assume that each officer and the officer's family and supervisors should expect some sort of stress related response at one time or another, and do everything possible to address these situations with prevention programs and early interventions. Without some form of intervention, transient stress responses can develop into symptoms of physical and/or psychological pathology (e.g. suicidal ideation) requiring treatment. The resolution of even traumatic events can be psychological growth. When an individual is capable of coping with stressful events, he or she may actually develop new and effective stress reduction strategies and become stronger.

There are many types of prevention and treatment programs. In order to address the problems of police stress, academies and various other agencies and departments offer courses while the candidates are still in training, schedule speakers to work with each shift, and plan conferences for family members. Police psychologists are available to work with officers in need of counseling and with their spouses and children. Some programs are funded by federal and state sources, and some by private foundations. There are also Alcoholics Anonymous meetings specifically scheduled for officers.

Not all coping mechanisms are functional. For example, heavy alcohol consumption and substance abuse lead to more problems than they solve. Alan Leschner, former director of the National Institute on Drug Abuse, has stated on numerous occasions that there are two basic reasons for consuming alcohol or taking drugs, "to feel good and to feel better." Consequently, in an effort to self medicate, the officer may use alcohol, a dysfunctional coping mechanism that is closely associated with poor job performance, domestic violence, and eventually suicide. Despite the negative consequences, as a coping mechanism alcohol is condoned by the law enforcement culture. Joseph Wambaugh, a former police officer, now a novelist, has described "choir practice", the habit of gathering after a shift to drink and relax. Officers who retire sometimes even purchase police bars so that they can continue to see their peers. The problem is that alcohol consumption aggravates feelings of depression and decreases inhibitions. Alcoholism is related to marital discord, driving accidents, and medical disorders.

The question remains about what can be done to prevent police suicide and to reduce occupational stress and dysfunctional behavior in officers. The single most important factor for anyone who is recovering from a crisis is reliance on a dependable support group. Hopefully, the network must have the knowledge and skills to give good advice. In any case, concerned listening is the prime requisite for a counselor or for a friend. We turn a deaf ear most of the time. As a society, we have become accustomed to asking people how they feel without paying the slightest attention to the answer. Working in a drug therapeutic community (milieu therapy for addicts) requires that you actually stop and listen when inquiring about someone else's health. Failure to do so results in a "pull up", a form of chastisement for failure to comply with the rules of the house. We need to extend the practice of listening to all our relationships.

There are several reasons why police officers avoid contacting mental health professionals (Hackett and Violanti, 2003). First of all, there is a certain level of mistrust between officers and clinicians. Not only does the police culture militate against asking for help, but officers also question the competency of helpers outside of the field to understand the pressures of law enforcement. Trusting others, even family members, is also seen as a sign of weakness. In addition, there is also a tendency to ignore such symptoms of depression as a decrease in energy, feelings of sadness or worry, and the sense of desperation that permeates one's thought. Seeking help conflicts with the police image that is composed of individuals who are independent, competent, and trained to take care of dangerous situations, and to protect the public. Officers may also resist seeking help because they justifiably fear losing their jobs or suffering from other job actions. Specifically, police officers are seriously concerned about speaking to mental health professionals. They have legitimate cause for concern if they are later involved in court cases that address legal issues regarding their credibility. If an officer has seen a counselor and is later charged with using excessive force, the records can be subpoenaed. If an officer has filed a Workman's Compensation claim and the records have been released, these documents may no longer be considered privileged. Officers may also be concerned that their fitness for duty may be called to question if it becomes known that they have seen a counselor. They may not receive a promotion or be considered for a special assignment if there are mental health issues in the way and there are state guidelines that specify that an officer must be free of mental or emotional problems or free from psychopathology to qualify for certain jobs. Thus, officers with stress related problems have a realistic basis for their fears of job action. For an officer who has lost his or her job for cause, there are few viable alternatives in the outside world that utilize the skills acquired in police training or on the job. Officers are also afraid of being prescribed medications by psychiatrists to treat their symptoms. Part of their concern is due to the potential side effects of some antidepressants, and part is based on their own attitudes towards addicts. Officers worry that they will feel out of control or become slow in responding to emergencies. In some cases, they must also report that they are taking medications.

Police Culture and the Family

Police officers are often "too proud and too fearful" to seek assistance when it would do the most good for the officer or for his family (Kirschman, 2000, p. 221). The best way to label such behaviors is to invoke Freud's ubiquitous concept of denial. For example, many police officers deny the possibility that they could be so severely injured that they might need to retire early. Consequently, they rarely have any contingency plan for their future or their family's security. They are often so deeply affected by the negative aspects of their work lives that the negativity permeates their off duty experiences. Their unexpressed hostility overflows into their home lives and is rarely reduced by positive activities. The officer's children often bear the brunt of his or her criticism. Moreover, these attacks may be unrelated to the children's actual behavior. Some police officers see their children's independence as a challenge to their positions as authority figures and as marks of disrespect. Most police families live in constant fear. The spouses and children of police families worry about the danger that the officer faces every time he or she leaves the house. That growing fear is based on the fact that they don't know what will happen when the officer goes to work; neither does the officer. Detective Shields did not know. On the morning of September 11, 2001, no one could have anticipated the consequences to the first responders or the other victims of international terrorism. Since those days, we have all become more anxious than we once were. It is a normal way of life now. One would have to be very naïve to believe that terrorism can ever be completely prevented. Kirschman (2000) has summed up the challenge of police work for the family by saying that there is more to life than the badge. One of the greatest risks of police work is that cops become so inflated, narcissistic, and self involved that they chance alienating their real families by over investing their time and energy in the work family, which all too frequently turns out to be fickle and unsupportive. She suggests that, "One of the greatest risks to families is that they surrender their own identity in favor of the officer. The women in this book, especially, have had a hard time focusing on themselves and later regretted losing that focus" (Kirschman, 2000, p. 247).

Domestic Violence

Kirschman (2000) writes in her book, *I Love a Cop*, that domestic violence is the leading cause of injuries to women in the 15-44 age group. It is estimated that double the number of women are raped by husbands or ex-husbands than by strangers. Over 90 percent of the assaults on women are actually a function of their efforts to escape domestic violence. What is equally distressing is that the children are watching. Data suggest that between three and ten million American children witness domestic violence in their own homes. Clearly, home is no safe haven. Research indicates that between 40 to 70 percent of the men who attack women also attack the children. Many people will comply with a police officer's demands and show respect. The police follow a paramilitary model where orders are given and followed, sometimes without explanation. Many officers were in the armed forces. Finally, law enforcement, while undergoing some changes, is still predominantly a man's world and emphasizes traditional gender roles, applauding action over efforts at communication. Disrespecting their authority undermines their sense of self esteem.

Hanks (cited in Kirschman, 2000) postulates three categories of domestic abuse: Stress-related abuse, control related abuse, and special circumstances. In the case of stress-related abuse, the violence appears to follow a single crisis such as job loss or death of a family member. The violence is usually considered to be a serious problem by both partners. Both partners are also concerned that the children have been affected. The prognosis for behavioral change in this situation is optimistic. Control-related abuse, on the other hand, is an ongoing problem and can assume many faces. The perpetrator rarely takes responsibility for the situation and proceeds to blame the victim. Furthermore, the abuser seems to have no empathy for the victim and is only calmed by abject obedience. The spouse develops symptoms of post-traumatic stress disorder and feels trapped in the situation. Unfortunately, unless the abuser does take responsibility for his/her behavior, therapy may actually do more harm than good. In all three of the categories, there are two necessities: The abusers must be able to control their actions and the targets must learn how to keep themselves and their children free from harm. Parents must also learn to recognize the signs of psychological problems in the children such as depression, anxiety, suicidal ideation, sleep disorders, psychosomatic symptoms, conduct disorders and poor school performances that can result from domestic violence.

Treatment of a police officer involved in a case of domestic violence requires an investigation of charges of stalking, harassment, and physical abuse. Any officer identified either as a victim or perpetrator must be mandated to receive counseling (e.g. individual, couple, and family therapy as well as anger management sessions). The victims must be given protection.

What is particularly interesting to note is the fact that more police officers have been killed while intervening in cases of domestic violence than in the "war on drugs". Some of the very same officers trained in the procedures used to address domestic violence cases, actually go home and forget everything that they have learned.

It is important to report cases of domestic violence since one of the warning signs for future violence is a past history of violent acts, stalking behavior, and threats (McMurry, 1995). In cases of domestic violence, the threats and abuse may spread from the home and neighborhood to the spouse's job site because the perpetrator feels a need to control all aspects of the victim's life. In fact, the spouse's job itself is a source of stress to the perpetrator. The salary contributes to his or her financial independence and ability to leave the batterer at some time in the future. Consequently, the batterer is in danger of losing control over the situation.

SUICIDE

Even now, when we have already identified the sources of police stress and the dysfunctional responses that are associated with high risk occupations such as law enforcement, Reese (1987, p. xvi) points out that there remain "pockets of departmental and administrative resistance". Supervisors are not always trained to recognize the symptoms of stress, or if they are, they do not take appropriate action. Consequently, many of the ills associated with law enforcement such as alcohol abuse and marital conflict, fester until the results include physical illness, depression, domestic violence, and suicide. Although most departments provide officers with communications equipment, weapons, vehicles, and bullet resistant vests, Reese (1987, p. xix) notes that "we have not yet devised training programs that are capable of bullet-proofing the mind". In general, police departments tend to deny the very existence of psychological factors. Actually, as we have noted, police officers are at greater risk for suicide than other professions. Due to misreporting, however, the present statistics underestimate the scope of the problem. What we do know is that the suicide rate for Federal Bureau of Investigation agents is 116 percent above the national rate (Field and Jones, 1999, cited in Hackett and Violanti, 2003). In recent years, we have witnessed the aftermath of several critical incidents of such magnitude that post-traumatic stress disorder and the potential for suicide among first responders comes as no surprise. The world has been exposed to natural and manmade disasters for which we were surprisingly unprepared (e.g. The Oklahoma City Federal Building bombing, the events of September 11, 2001, the Tsunami, Hurricane Katrina, and terrorist activities around the world). Any survivor, officer or civilian, who has suffered as a result of one of these events needs proper critical incident debriefing procedures and referrals to experienced mental health professionals. Training in suicide prevention is also necessary for all departments.

In law enforcement, the prevention of suicide and other sequelae to traumatic events requires a strong support system. To the police officers, no one is better equipped to comprehend the pressures of law enforcement than another officer. Peer support programs are effective in terms of addressing many types of mental health problem. The concept of peer counseling is not a new idea. Law enforcement officers frequently gravitate toward more experienced colleagues who can serve as mentors in times of crisis. However, while law enforcement experience is critical and helps to establish rapport, training in the principles of crisis intervention and critical incident stress debriefing is also important.

The training of peer counselors should be conducted by mental health professionals with a knowledge of counseling skills, crisis intervention theory and practices, early warning signs of acute or chronic stress, suicide lethality assessment, the facts of alcohol and other drug abuse, and the issues of confidentiality. The peer counselor's mandate is to provide a safe, confidential climate for the client. It is also his or her responsibility to decide whether or not a referral to a licensed mental health professional should be the next step in the treatment process.

Peer counselors should be selected based on several criteria, including trustworthiness, sensitivity to the issues of racial diversity and other cultural factors, and the ability to command respect and establish rapport with clients quickly. Motivation is not sufficient. No intervention activity is better than the personnel who implement its policies.

The ripple effect of a suicide within a department spreads out to cover other officers, supervisors, members of the family, and friends. According to Mitchell (1983), the suicide of a peer is considered one of the most distressing incidents to face emergency service professionals. The question is always whether or not something could have been done to prevent the suicide. Could, for example, someone have recognized the causes or precipitating events? Were there substance abuse problems or threats of job loss due to inappropriate behavior? Did the individual actually threaten to kill him or herself? Was there a recent noticeable change in behavior such as a sudden decrease in job performance? Have there been problems with co-workers such as angry outbursts or atypical withdrawals? Among the predictors of suicide (Hackett and Violanti, 2003) are prior attempts, a family history of suicide, a major relationship breakdown such as separation or divorce, an internal investigation or actual criminal charges, and the availability of weapons.

The New York Post (July 12 2002) published the story of Daniel E. Steward, a 27-year-old New York City Fire Department medical technician, who hanged himself in the basement of his home on Long Island. He was deeply affected by the job of sifting through the rubble of "Ground Zero" searching for body parts. He left behind a distressing suicide note that described his heartache after removing body after body from the debris of the World Trade Center. Steward had been assigned to his duty for the two weeks immediately after September 11, 2001. However, he continued to search through the concrete and dust even on his days off until January of 2002. Although in the end, he only went to the site one day a week, the emotional trauma was already exacting a price. Despite the fact that "first responders" were being offered counseling in the months following 9/11, Steward only sought treatment on one occasion. Perhaps mandatory counseling for a longer period of time should have been utilized. There are, however, differing opinions on the value of coercion in requiring counseling (Waters, 2002). Steward, who was single, did not discuss his feelings or plans with any of his friends or co-workers.

In order to depict the type of officers who call the COP-2-COP hotline and yet maintain confidentiality, we have compiled two fictional case studies. The first case study involves an officer whose normal assignment was patrol. He was among the first officers to the World Trade Center just after the first tower collapsed. In describing the event, he said to us:

> We were up near a building to avoid the falling bodies. It was terrible. I saw a man or maybe it was a woman, I don't know which, split in half by a flagpole. I know now that they don't die or pass out before they hit the ground. I could see them trying to break their falls with their arms and legs outstretched just before they hit the ground.

The officer manifested persistent symptoms of post-traumatic stress disorder. He avoided the debriefing sessions by taking vacation time right after 9/11. Later, in his discussions with a COP-2-COP counselor, he reported that he still had flashbacks, nightmares, and re-experiences the events surrounding 9/11. He said that he would never forget the smell of death coming from the debris that was filled with human remains. The phone counselor advised the officer to accept an individual referral to a licensed therapist. At first he refused, however, after several more calls over a period of three weeks, the officer recognized that he was actually feeling some relief from the phone calls alone and acquiesced to individual treatment. He spent six months in treatment which resulted in marked improvement. Although the officer made significant changes in his lifestyle and reduced the severity of his symptoms, he was made aware that symptoms do reappear and that he would be free to return to treatment or to call the hotline again. The hotline counselor still calls him periodically to provide support and to check on the officer's stability. If alcohol consumption or drug abuse had been part of the officer's symptom syndrome, the therapist would have recommended either inpatient or outpatient substance abuse treatment. Treatment plans always reflect the needs of each caller and, when appropriate, may involve the families.

The second typical case involves the wife of a law enforcement officer who called COP-2-COP in order to get help for herself, for her husband, and for their children. She reported to the hotline counselor that she was afraid of her husband because of his angry threats and actual incidents of domestic violence. She was also concerned about the officer's personal safety since he had alluded to suicide as his best solution on several occasions. For her own safety, the wife had already had a restraining order taken out against the officer. However, the officer attempted repeatedly to coerce her into dismissing the restraining order. He said that it would cost him his job and the loss of the family's only source of income. The threat was very daunting since the wife was pregnant and worried about food and a place to live for herself and their two other children. The COP-2-COP staff informed the wife that if her husband did not violate the restraining order, he would not lose his job. The officer has, however, had his duty weapon removed and he has also been suspended from duty, due to the domestic violence complaint. He will be required, again by policy, to have a psychiatric evaluation and a "fit-for-duty" report. In all likelihood, the department will require that the officer have individual counseling sessions and attend a group anger management program. During the psychiatric evaluation, a history of alcohol and narcotics abuse was also uncovered. The substance abuse problem alone could jeopardize his job status. The next step should be some form of treatment. The exact nature would depend on the severity of the abuse. The COP-2-COP staff recognized the complexity of this police family's problems, but they remained focused on the needs of the client. In this case, the client is the wife, and first issue is the safety of the woman and her children. Domestic violence cases must be taken seriously since they can escalate rapidly from verbal threats to homicide. Even after a divorce, husbands (more than wives) have sought retribution for imagined affronts. What is particularly interesting is that the perpetrators are so convinced about the justice of their claims and their subsequent acts of violence that they don't even attempt to hide their identities or flee the scene (Waters et al., 2002). A personal sense of entitlement to punish their spouses or ex-spouses tends to override restraining orders and often results in murder and suicide.

The staff of COP-2-COP utilizes appropriate facilities and programs to provide support, safe refuges, and legal and practical advice to battered spouses. It should be remembered that all police officers know the location of shelters which are often in close proximity to the police department.

Domestic violence, murder, and suicide can be a product of burnout. Burnout, depression, and feelings of helplessness lead some officers to contemplate self-destructive acts while other officers develop hostility particularly towards the criminal element in their communities, especially when racism is involved.

Attitudes towards police officers range from praise and hero worship to almost joyous attempts to find flaws and dishonest behavior on the part of all officers. The families suffer the fall-out. Not only do the officers' schedules interfere with having a normal family life but the disruption of their circadian rhythms leads to temper tantrums and lack of patience. In an effort to improve the predictability of a family life and to enable officers to have some weekend time with their families, a number of departments have gone to 12-hour shifts and three- or four-day work weeks. In some cases, however, the plan backfired. The officers with predictable free time have taken second jobs!

DIVORCE

Police divorce is so prevalent that in some departments the rate ranges from 50 to 80 percent. With the rates in the general public on the rise, the gap is closing. Marriages that take place after the officer is already on the job last longer than those begun before the individual joins the force due to lack of false expectations.

HURRICANE KATRINA AND FAMILY CONFLICTS

The COP-2-COP staff assisted the Southern Law Enforcement Foundation in providing mental health support to police officers affected by both Hurricanes Katrina and Rita. The devastation of New Orleans was more than most people could have imagined or was depicted by the media. The disruption of regular police functions was a metaphor for the breakdown of society. The actual critical incident occurred when the hurricane had passed. The police were relieved from their regular shifts to stand by in the city. Most of them found rooms in vacant hotels or with friends or went to their own homes, if that was still possible. They had been told to return at 4:00 p.m. Unfortunately, some officers found themselves flooded out or marooned before returning to work. The stories of rapidly rising waters and the need to protect themselves from distraught citizens were overpowering. One officer swam with her month-old baby to "Headquarters" which was then at the Crystal Palace, the highest ground in the district. There were no communications since police radios, cell phones, and landlines were out. The same forces of nature, which prevented public transportation and communication, destroyed the chain of leadership in the department. There were reports of numerous police desertions which attracted widespread media coverage and public disdain. Many of these officers in the flood zones went home to protect their loved ones. They were torn between two oaths, "to protect and serve" and "to love, honor, and obey."

By now the public is aware that there were at least two suicides of officers in New Orleans. In one case, a respected officer with 32 years in the force, reportedly, was so distraught over the desertions and disorder that he took his own life. This is only one example of the extent of the disequilibrium during the attempt to restore calm that was further complicated by the lack of available mental health resources in the affected areas.

COPING STRATEGIES

Coping strategies can be categorized according to the source of the responsibility: The individual officer, or the department (Waters et al., 1982, p. 25). Individual coping strategies include:

- the development of a dependable support system;
- improved communication skills;
- a means of ventilating feelings appropriately;
- a regular exercise program with a minimal time expenditure of 30 minutes a session;
- a diet that contains elements necessary for optimal functioning and excludes elements that have negative values (e.g. a high fat diet);
- the development of other activities that provide for recreation, change of focus, and positive feedback;
- regular vacations;
- muscle relaxation exercises;
- meditation;
- the use of biofeedback; and
- participation in self-help groups.

Departmental strategies include:

- realistic job-related training in police functions;
- open communication channels between officers and supervisors;
- opportunities for meaningful input into departmental decisions whenever possible;
- reassessment of shift hours;
- constructive feedback on job performance;
- workshops on dealing with marital conflicts, good parenting procedures, and preparation for retirement, etc.;
- training for supervisors in good management techniques;
- opportunities for "debriefing" sessions at the end of the shift; and
- stress management training.

Notes: Since not all strategies will fit the lifestyles of all officers, each individual must select those techniques that are appropriate to his/her needs. More than one strategy is necessary to deal with the stresses of contemporary life.

THE COP-2-COP PROGRAM

The COP-2-COP program utilizes several components of successful crisis intervention strategies applied to other populations. For example, the stages in Robert's Seven Step Crisis Intervention Model are very similar to the COP-2-COP guidelines (Roberts, 1996). It should be noted, however, that many of the steps occur either simultaneously or are repeated during the process. For example, the first and second steps are difficult to separate:

(1) plan and conduct a crisis assessment (including measures of lethality);
(2) establish rapport and a therapeutic relationship;
(3) identify the caller's major problems including the precipitating events;
(4) deal with feelings. Be an active listener and validate the caller's emotions;
(5) generate and explore alternative coping strategies and skills;
(6) develop and formulate an appropriate action plan; and
(7) establish a follow-up plan and agreement.

Kanel suggests, "Although the ABC model of crisis intervention has a three stage approach, in an actual interview the components of one stage could be used at any time" (Kanel, 2007, p. 70). Sometimes during the interview process, the caseworker needs to be flexible and recognize the needs of the client and apply appropriate, timely interventions.

Since the COP-2-COP hotline staff is comprised of retired law enforcement officers helping other officers, establishing rapport and developing a therapeutic relationship is a comparatively simple task. Both the phone staff and the callers have similar backgrounds and occupational experiences, speak the same language, and are concerned with many of the same problems. The assessment guidelines used by the volunteers require answers to the following questions:

(1) the nature of the presenting problem;
(2) the severity of the situation and the length of time that the problem has existed;
(3) the actual impact on the officer's ability to function on the job and at home;
(4) the precipitants of the situation or the immediate cause of the problem;
(5) any past history or current substance abuse;
(6) other relevant aspects of past history;
(7) previous inpatient and/or outpatient psychiatric history; and
(8) current medical problems and medical history.

In another section of the initial interview, callers are asked about suicidal or homicidal ideations, whether or not they have access to their duty weapons, or any other firearms or lethal methods. The volunteers, as well as the clinicians who serve as referrals, have been trained and certified as trainers by John Violanti using a suicide prevention tool, "QPR." Written by Dr Paul G. Quinett in an instructional booklet entitled *Suicide, the Forever Decision*. The guidelines require that the staff:

- question anyone reporting suicidal tendencies or depression symptoms;
- persuade the person to seek further assistance; and
- refer the person to a mental health professional.

Throughout the assessment process, the staff expresses concern for the caller's feelings. They not only listen to what is being said and to the important issues that are being avoided, they also explore past coping strategies trying to separate the functional from the dysfunctional. During the assessment process, the staff members are careful not to interject their own suggestions. As any experienced therapist knows, clients frequently seek solutions to their problems from the counselor. Why should they do all the work necessary to solve a problem when a short cut is available? It is essential, however, that the callers develop their own solutions with guidance.

The caller's symptoms of depression often permeate the interview. When callers are asked what they do for entertainment, they may respond with descriptions of what they used to do. They may also report on their alcohol use at this point or discuss family problems including marital discord and admit to acts of even domestic violence.

The assessment process helps the staff to assist callers in developing a viable action plan. It is critical that each caller participates in the development of the plan so that a sense of personal control is reestablished and cognitive functioning is improved. The staff members try to set up parameters so that the callers are not overwhelmed by the enormity of their problems. The staff members also follow up on problem resolution by contacting the caller every ten days until they are convinced that the callers are stable. If necessary, they will call more frequently. The callback component is valued by both the clients and the staff. The clients appreciate the continuing concern and the staff members are rewarded by the clients' positive comments.

In order to build a list of competent and experienced licensed mental health professionals for referrals, 200 police departments in New Jersey were surveyed for the names of therapists who had been utilized in the past with success. The survey yielded 150 providers with expertise working with the law enforcement community. Even these professionals were given training on such topics as the police personality, post-traumatic stress disorder, and critical incident stress debriefing.

Following the events of September 11, 2001, other hotlines were put in place for survivors and for all the emergency service personnel affected by the disasters. The firefighters, police officers, and EMS teams were viewed as victims of a crime. Family members were also welcome to call.

SUMMARY

The image of police officers is that they are action oriented, problem solvers who are in control of their own emotions. They are supposed to be strong, resilient, and, of course, stoic. To be stoic means that they must remain unaffected by the violent and vicious behaviors that they encounter every day of the week. Feelings are addressed by repressing them. The price of readjustment ranges from simple irritability to heart attacks and suicide. The only way to address the problems is through screening, training, on going prevention programs, and early interventions and treatment based on programs such as the COP-2-COP model.

DISCUSSION QUESTIONS

1. List a couple of instances where disasters in the United States have caused law enforcement officers to experience stress. Discuss what programs have been created in the twenty-first century that are designed to help their situation.
2. Discuss what strong cultural influences would deter a cop from using a confidential mental health program.
3. Explain briefly how a person's culture can determine his or her behavior in a natural disaster.
4. Describe what the COP-2-COP program provides and discuss its success rates.

REFERENCES

American Psychological Association (2006), "APA's response to international and national crises: addressing diverse needs, 2005 Annual Report of the APA Policy and Planning Board", *American Psychologist*, Vol. 61 No. 5, pp. 513-21.

American Psychiatric Association (2000), *Diagnostic and Statistical Manual of Mental Disorders: DSM-IV TR*, Author, Washington, DC.

Hackett, D.P. and Violanti, J.M. (2003), *Police Suicide: Tactics for Prevention*, Charles C. Thomas, Springfield, IL.

Kanel, K. (2007), *A Guide to Crisis Intervention*, 3rd ed., Thomson, Belmont, CA.

Kelley, T. and Holl, J. (2006), "Suspect held in officer's shootings in Orange", *The New York Times*, pp. B1–B6.

Kirschman, E. (2000), *I Love a Cop: What Police Families Need to Know*, The Guilford Press, New York, NY.

Lindemann, E. (1944), "Symptomatology and management of acute grief", *Journal of Neurons and Mental Disease*, Vol. 181 No. 11, pp. 709–10.

Mantell, M.R. (1994), "Ticking bombs", *Psychology Today*, January/February, pp. 20–1.

Maslach, C. and Jackson, S. (1979), "Burned out cops and their families", *Psychology Today*, Vol. 12 No. 12, pp. 58–62.

Maslach, C. (1982), *Burnout: The Cost of Caring*, Prentice Hall, New York, NY.

McMurry, K. (1995), "Workplace violence: can it be prevented?", *Trial*, Vol. 31 No. 12, pp. 10-12. Mitchell, J.T. (1983), "When disaster strikes: the critical incident stress debriefing process", *Journal of Emergency Medical Services*, Vol. 8 No. 1, pp. 36-9.

Mitchell, J. and Everly, G. (1993), *Critical Incident Stress Debriefing: An Operations Manual for the Prevention of Traumatic Stress Among Emergency Services and Disaster Workers*, Chevron Publishing, Ellicott City, MD.

North, C.S., Nixon, S.J., Shariat, S., Mallonee, S., McMillen, J.C., Spitznagel, E.L. and Smith, E.M. (1999), "Psychiatric disorders among survivors of the Oklahoma City bombing", *Journal of the American Medical Association*, Vol. 282, pp. 755-62.

Reese, J. (1987), *A History of Police Psychological Services*, US Government Printing Office, Washington, DC.

Roberts, A.R. (1996), "Introduction: myths and realities regarding battered women", in Roberts, A.R. (Ed.), *Helping Battered Women: New Perspectives and Remedies*, Oxford University Press, New York, NY, pp. 3-12.

Russell, H.E. and Beigel, A. (1990), *Understanding Human Behavior for Effective Police Work*, Basic Books, New York, NY.

Saulny, S. (2006), "After long stress, newsman in New Orleans unravels", *The New York Times*, p. A21.

Schewber, N. and Holl, J. (2006), "Officials say slain detective and murder suspect crossed paths before", *The New York Times*, pp. B1-B6.

Waters, J. (2002), "Moving forward from September 11th. A stress/crisis/trauma model", *Brief Therapy and Crisis Intervention*, Vol. 2 No. 1.

Waters, J., Irons, N. and Finkle, E. (1982), "The police stress inventory: a comparison of events affecting officers and supervisors in rural and urban areas", *Police Stress*, Vol. 5 No. 1, pp. 18-25.

Waters, J.A., Lynn, R.I. and Morgan, K.I. (2002), "Workplace violence: prevention and intervention, theory and practice", in Rapp-Paglicci, L.A., Roberts, A.R. and Wodarski, J.S. (Eds), *Handbook of Violence*, John Wiley & Sons, Inc., New York, NY, pp. 378-413.

Ussery, W.J. and Waters, J.A. (2006), COP-2-COP hotlines: programs to address the needs of first responders and their families. Brief Treatment and Crisis Intervention.

Weisinger, H. (1985), *The Anger Workout Book*, Quill, New York, NY.

FURTHER READING

American Psychological Association (2001), "Response from APA [To Herbert et al., "Primum non nocere."]", *APA Monitor on Psychology*, Vol. 32 No. 10, pp. 4-8.

Black, J. (2000), "Personality testing and police selection. Utility of the "Big Fire", *New Zealand Journal of Psychology*, Vol. 29 No. 2, p. 24, available at: www.questia.com (accessed August 24, 2004).

Dohrenwend, B.S. (1978), "Social stress and community psychology", *American Journal of Community Psychology*, Vol. 6 No. 1, p. 2.

Everly, G.S., Lating, J.M. and Mitchell, J.T. (2000), "Innovations in group crisis intervention: critical incident stress debriefing (CISD) and critical incident stress management (CISM)", in Roberts, A.R. (Ed.), *Crisis Intervention*

Handbook: Assessment Treatment and Research, Oxford University Press, New York, NY, pp. 77-97.

Goode, E. (2001), "Some therapists fear services could backfire", *New York Times*, p. L21.

Herbert, J.D., Lilienfeld, S., Kline, J., Montomery, R., Lohr, J., Brandsma, L., Meadows, E., Jacobs, W.S., Goldstein, N., Gist, R., McNally, R.J., Acierno, R., Harris, M., Devilly, G.J., Bryant, R., Eisman, H.D., Kleinknecht, R., Rosen, G.M. and Foa, E. (2001), ""Primum non nocere" [Letter to the editors]", *APA Monitor on Psychology*, Vol. 32 No. 10, p. 4.

von der Kolk, B.A., Weisaeth, L. and von der Hart, O. (1996), "History of trauma in psychiatry", in von der Kolk, B.A., McFarlane, A.C. and Weisaeth, L. (Eds), Traumatic Stress: The Effects of Overwhelming Experience on Mind, Body, and Society, The Guilford Press, New York, NY.

Violanti, J.M. (1991), "Post trauma vulnerability: a proposed model", in Reese, J., Horn, J. and Dunning, C. (Eds), *Critical Incidents in Policing*, Government Printing Office, Washington, DC, pp. 365-72.

Violanti, J.M. (1996), *Police suicide: Epidemic in Blue*, Charles C. Thomas, Springfield, IL.

Waters, J. and Finn, E. (1995), "Handling client crises effectively on the telephone", in Roberts, A.R. (Ed.), *Crisis intervention and Time-Limited Cognitive Treatment*, Sage, Thousand Oaks, CA, pp. 251-89.

13

Less Than Lethal Use of Force

Gary M. Vilke and
Theodore C. Chan

Purpose – *Less lethal weapons have become a critical tool for law enforcement when confronting dangerous, combative individuals in the field. The purpose of this paper is to review the medical aspects and implications of three different types of less lethal weapons.*

Findings – *In general, these three different types of less lethal weapons have been effective for their intended use. Each type of less lethal weapon has a number of physiologic effects and specific medical issues that must be considered when the weapon is used. There is no clear evidence that these devices are inherently lethal, nor is there good evidence to suggest a causal link between sudden in-custody death and the use of irritant sprays or conducted energy devices.*

INTRODUCTION

Less lethal weapons have been a critical tool for law enforcement use when confronting dangerous, combative individuals in the field. Over the years, there have been many different less lethal devices used by law enforcement

Source: Gary M. Vilke and Theodore C. Chan, "Less Than Lethal Use of Force," Policing: An International Journal of Police Strategies and Management, vol 30:3.

officers. These weapons include impact projectile weapons, irritant sprays and conductive energy devices (CEDs), which occupy an intermediate level in the use of force continuum. Use of these technologies is thought to increase the safety of both the intended target individual by avoiding the use of lethal force, as well as the officer by facilitating the control of dangerous individuals. However, injuries and deaths have occurred following the use of such weapons which were previously known as "less-than-lethal." At times the injuries or deaths are directly linked to use of the devices, while in many cases, a causal link remains controversial.

Impact or blunt projectiles include bean bags and rubber bullets. These weapons are less lethal than firearms and allow a safe distance between the officer and subject. Irritant sprays and riot control agents, such as tear gas, mace (CN) and oleoresin capsicum (OC), have been used by law enforcement to facilitate compliance and temporarily incapacitate violent individuals or crowds. CEDs such as the Taser have become increasingly popular in law enforcement as a less lethal technology to temporarily subdue individuals. In this chapter, we review the different types of less lethal weapons, including their history, mechanisms of action, intended and other physiologic effects, and medical safety risks and precautions.

In addition, we review the research regarding the potential association of these devices with sudden in-custody deaths. This report includes a review of case reports, animal research and human research investigating this issue. In general, case reports of sudden deaths associated with these weapons cannot determine specific causality. Findings from animal research are limited in their applicability to humans. Even human studies investigating the physiologic effects of these devices may be limited depending on the specific conditions of the study subjects and how closely field conditions are replicated.

IMPACT PROJECTILES

Impact projectiles are used as an alternative to standard firearm rounds when trying to disperse a crowd from a distance or subdue a combative, dangerous individual without the use of lethal force. Modern day impact projectile weapons were first used during the Hong Kong Riots of the 1950s and 1960s, utilizing projectiles made of wood. Similar weapons were used during conflicts in Northern Ireland, Israel and Palestine in the 1970s and 1980s. Early devices included hard rubber missile-shaped projectiles that were difficult to direct, resulting in injuries to the head, face and chest. These projectiles have evolved into PVC-type bullets, modern-day blunt rubber bullets, and bean bag type rounds, which are currently in use by law enforcement agencies.

The action of the blunt impact projectile is to induce pain, irritation and minimal injury to the subject without causing any life-threatening injuries. In general, all involve a blunt type impact that can impart energies on the order of 100-200 Joules depending on the type of round and the distance from firing. The physiologic effects of blunt impact projectiles are directly related to anatomic location where the blunt impact projectile strikes the subject and induces blunt force trauma to the individual.

Case Reports, Reviews and Research Studies

The majority of the medical literature on this topic is based on case reports and case series. Both injuries and deaths have been reported with blunt impact projectiles which have caused injury by direct penetration into the body. Wawro and Hardy (2002) and Hardy report of a 56-year-old man who survived after his chest wall was penetrated by bean bag rounds fired from a 12 gauge shell at an unknown distance. Similar cases of intrathoracic bean bag penetration have also been reported by others, including penetration with intact bean bags as well as bean bag pellets when the bag fails (Charles *et al.*, 2002; Grange *et al.*, 2002). Suyama described 25 patients evaluated for injuries related to less lethal weapons implemented during a period of civil unrest in Cincinnati, Ohio. There were no deaths, but three patients required admission, including one with a pulmonary contusion, one with a liver laceration and one with an Achilles tendon rupture (Suyama *et al.*, 2003). de Brito *et al.* (2001) retrospectively reviewed five years of bean bag injuries in Los Angeles County Hospital and reported on 40 patients with one death from a massive hemothorax caused by chest penetration of the projectile.

In addition to penetrating trauma, blunt impact projectiles can also cause significant injury from blunt trauma. Chute and Smialak reported a case of a 61-year-old woman shot in the chest with a plastic bullet (AR-1 baton round) who subsequently collapsed, suffered cardiac arrest and died. Autopsy showed she had sustained multiple rib fractures to the left chest, an underlying lung laceration, and heart lacerations that led to significant bleeding into the chest cavity. The cause of death was reported as blunt force injuries of chest due to plastic bullet wound (Chute and Smialek, 1998).

Several studies have looked at the injury patterns from the use of plastic and rubber bullets. Their conclusions all tend to show that while generally regarded as less lethal weapons, significant injuries including death can occur when the weapons strike the chest, abdomen, or head. Millar *et al.* reviewed 90 patients who had sustained injuries to various parts of their bodies, concluding that the eyes, face, skull, bones, and brain are at greatest risk of injury from rubber bullets. The distance at which the rubber bullets resulted in serious injury ranged from 17 to 25 meters (Millar *et al.*, 2005). Hughes reviewed 29 cases of injuries from a new plastic baton round in Northern Ireland. There were no fatalities, but seven patients required admission (Hughes *et al.*, 2005). Steele retrospectively reviewed patients presenting to six hospitals during a one-week period of civil unrest in Northern Ireland who were injured by plastic bullets. He reported a total of 155 patients with 172 injuries, no fatalities, but 42 admissions, with three to intensive care. Of those in intensive care, one had globe rupture and multiple facial fractures, one had a laparotomy for three perforations of the small bowel and the third required splenectomy for a splenic laceration (Steele *et al.*, 1999). Ritchie and Gibbons reported on 80 subjects injured by rubber bullets, with four who died, three from ventricular dysrhythmias secondary to cardiac contusion and one from a hemopneumothorax. An additional 19 patients required hospitalization for significant chest wounds (Ritchie and Gibbons, 1990).

Commotion cordis is a rare occurrence when a direct blow to the chest causes a sudden fatal disturbance of cardiac rhythm in the absence of demonstrable signs of significant mechanical injury to the heart. Although no in-custody death cases associated with impact projectiles have been specifically attributed to commotion cordis, blunt impact weapons generate energies that are on the order of those that have induced commotion cordis in other situations (such as an individual struck to the chest with a baseball). Therefore, one could speculate that these devices would have the same risk of causing ventricular fibrillation (VF) and sudden death.

Overall, impact projectiles have been used widely and effectively as less lethal weapons. From the medical perspective, injuries and rare deaths have been directly related to the blunt traumatic force delivered by the projectile onto the individual. While efforts continue to focus on reducing this risk, it is unlikely that such injuries can be completely eliminated given that these devices are designed to deliver pain and irritation through blunt force.

IRRITANT SPRAYS

Irritant sprays include agents like CN, CS, and OS (pepper spray), which can be used to disperse large gatherings or to temporarily incapacitate individuals. These agents are commonly dispersed as gases, smoke or aerosols, and therefore, may affect users as well as subjects.

CN was first synthesized in 1871. It was used in World War I as well as served as the primary tear gas used by law enforcement and the military up through the 1950s. It is a colorless crystalline substance that can be disseminated in a smoke form from an explosive device, such as a grenade, or propelled as a liquid or powder. It acts as an irritant smoke when in contact with skin or mucous membrane tissues such as the eyes, nasal passages, oral cavity, and airway. Symptoms of exposure include sneezing, rhinorrhea, coughing and increased airway secretions, as well as burning sensations of the nasal passages and airways. Oral cavity and gastrointestinal exposure can result in the sensation of burning in the mouth, increased salivation, gagging, nausea, and vomiting. Ocular exposure to CN causes a burning sensation in the eye, injection of the conjunctiva, eye irritation, photophobia, and tearing. Similarly, skin contact can result in burning, irrigation, and erythema.

CS is an irritant agent first synthesized in 1928, and replaced CN as the standard riot control irritant agent in the US Army in 1959. Because of its perceived improved effectiveness, it had replaced CN in most law enforcement agencies in the USA by the late 1950s as well. CS is typically disseminated by dispersion of the powder or solution by explosion, spray or smoke. Because of its insoluble nature, decontamination of buildings or other items after exposure can be challenging. CS also has a high-flammability rating and has been noted to have caused some structure fires (Danto, 1987).

The clinical effects that may be seen with the use of CS are similar to those of CN, resulting in irritation and inflammation of the skin, airways, and mucous membrane tissues on exposure. The effects typically start within minutes of exposure and continue as long as the person is exposed to the material. After minutes of exposure, a sensation of skin burning will typically occur, particularly over moistened or freshly shaven areas. The degree of symptoms tends to worsen based on concentration and duration of exposure. Increased exposure can have symptoms progress to gagging and vomiting, more skin and mucous membrane burning and subjective tightness in the chest. These symptoms improve after removal of the exposure and gradually resolve over 30-60 minutes, but skin erythema may last up to several hours. However, if the exposure is with a high concentration of CS, under high temperature or humid conditions, severe erythema along with edema and skin vesication can occur, typically occurring within the first hour. Tolerance to CS has been demonstrated from prolonged or repeated exposures (Punte *et al.*, 1963; Bestwick *et al.*, 1972).

During the riots in Washington DC in 1968, firefighters were often exposed to CS when they entered buildings in which the agent had been previously used. Movement around the building and use of water hoses re-aerosolized the material, causing erythema and edema on the skin of a number of firefighters (Rengstorff and Mershon, 1969a). In workers with repeated exposure and sensitization to CS, acquired contact dermatitis has occurred, confirmed by skin testing. Symptoms ranged from simple erythema to large vesicles and bullae. No pulmonary symptoms were reported (Shmunes and Taylor, 1973).

OC or pepper sprays are derived from the natural oily extract of pepper plants in the genus capsicum. The use of OC spray by law enforcement agencies increased in the 1980s as the use of CS was on the decline, and by the 1990s, the majority of states had legalized OC spray use by the public (Smith and Greaves, 2002). Concentrations of OC may range from 1 to 15 percent, with the commercially available OC typically being about 1 percent in concentration. Delivery modes include liquid stream spray, aerosol spray, and powder delivered as a projectile.

OC spray can cause direct irritation to the eyes, skin and mucous membranes. The onset of symptoms is almost instantaneous, causing burning and tearing of the eyes, as well as eye spasm, ranging from involuntary blinking to sustained closure of the eyelids. Cutaneous symptoms may include flushing, tingling and intense burning sensation of the skin, particularly over recently shaved areas. Mucous membrane exposure, especially of the nasal passages, will cause irritation, rhinorrhea and congestion, with some subjects reporting nausea. Exposure of the airway and respiratory tract to aerosolized OC causes tingling, coughing, gagging and shortness of breath, as well as a transient laryngeal paralysis and a temporary inability to speak (Steffee *et al.*, 1995).

Case Reports and Reviews

CN and CS: A few cases of severe allergic reactions have been reported with CN, particularly following a previous exposure. One case was reported in a military recruit who had been previously exposed to CN 17 years earlier which manifested as minimal itching at that time. Following a repeated exposure, he developed generalized itching, which progressed over the next several hours to generalized erythema all parts of his body except the face portion which had been covered by a mask. He developed a fever of 103 and by 48 hours had diffuse vesication and edema, followed ultimately by sloughing of much of his skin, but recovered (Queen and Standler, 1941). Other cutaneous reactions have been reported as well (Madden, 1951).

Thorburn reported on the medical complications associated with prolonged exposure to CN in a prison where there were recurrent and prolonged exposures in closed spaces with limited ventilation. Cutaneous complications included first and second degree burns. Treatment with steroids and bronchodilators for laryngotracheo-bronchitis, inflammation of the airway, was needed in several patients, but none reported any permanent damage. All eye complaints were transient and required no specialized treatment, resulting in no corneal injuries or permanent damage (Thorburn, 1982).

Chapman and White reported on a prisoner who was found dead under his bunk 46 hours after a reported prolonged CN gassing of inmates in cells with no ventilation. The deceased inmate was found in rigor mortis and on autopsy was noted to have evidence of inflammation and damage to his airway and lungs (Chapman and White, 1978). Another reported death occurred after closed room exposure with an estimated ten times the lethal concentration. On autopsy, there were similar findings as with the previous case (Punte *et al.*, 1963).

Park and Giammona report a case in which CS tear gas canisters were fired into a house resulting in a four-month-old infant being exposed for two-to-three hours. The infant required hospital admission for frequent suctioning of upper airway secretions and was treated with steroids and antibiotics as well as positive pressure ventilation for respiratory distress and wheezing. He was ultimately discharged home fully recovered after 28 days (Park and Giammona, 1972). Thomas *et al.* reported on nine marines involved with strenuous exercise and exposure to CS in field training who developed a transient pulmonary syndrome. They presented with cough, shortness of breath, hemoptysis and hypoxia, with some requiring close monitoring and treatment for hypoxia, but all nine recovered and demonstrated normal lung function within a week after the exposure (Thomas *et al.*, 2002). Hu reported a case of exposure in an asthmatic who developed semi-chronic symptoms of cough and shortness of breath for up to two years after the exposure. Her FEV1 (Forced Expiratory Volume in 1 second) at four weeks post exposure was 62 percent of predicted and her forced vital capacity was 78 percent. At one and a half years after exposure, her FEV1 was 128 percent of predicted, with a 16 percent drop with brisk exercise in cool air (Hu and Christiani, 1992). Based on the report, it is difficult to determine if her subjective symptoms of dyspnea were related to her underlying chronic asthma rather than the CS exposure.

The use of CS has resulted in reports of eye injuries, particularly when a tear gas cartridge is discharged at close range. In some cases, particles of agglomerated CS were driven into the eye tissue by the force of the dispersion device, typically a blast. In these cases, chemical reaction damage of the cornea was noted over the course of months a year, which are characteristically different than blast injuries from particles other than CS (Levine and Stahl, 1968).

OC: Since OC spray is commonly used by many law enforcement agencies, there are many case reports and case series of deaths and injuries following OC use (Steffee *et al.*, 1995; Granfield *et al.*, 1994; Pollanen *et al.*, 1998; O'Halloran and Frank, 2000). Amnesty International claims that over 90 persons have died after exposure to pepper spray in the USA since the early 1990s (Amnesty International, 2005). Granfield *et al.* (1994) reported 30 cases of in-custody death following OC exposure, in which drugs and underlying natural diseases were a significant factor in a majority of these cases. O'Halloran and Frank (2000) reported of 21 cases of restraint in-custody death, of which ten of the restraint episodes were preceded by use of OC spray, and Pollanen *et al.* (1998) reported 21 in-custody restraint deaths of which four had been sprayed with OC.

However, a causal connection between OC exposure and death remains controversial. There is no definitive evidence that OC is inherently lethal. In almost all of these cases of reported deaths associated with OC, the OC spray was determined not to have been the cause of death, with the exception of only one case. In that patient, Steffee *et al.* reported that a person who had a history of asthma and was sprayed with OC spray 10–15 times suffered a sudden cardio-respiratory arrest. Autopsy revealed severe epithelial lung damage with the cause of death attributed to severe bronchospasm probably precipitated by the use of pepper spray (Steffee *et al.*, 1995).

Billmire described a four-week-old healthy infant who was sprayed in the face with a 5 percent OC spray when a key chain self-defense canister accidentally discharged. The child had sudden onset of gasping respirations, epistaxis, apnea, and cyanosis. The child required mechanical ventilation and extraocorporeal membrane oxygen support. The child was discharged home after a 13-day hospitalization (Billmire *et al.*, 1996). An 11-year-old boy required intubation and ventilation four hours after exposure for severe croup (upper airway inflammation) that resulted from intentional inhalation of OC spray. He was extubated two days later and recovered uneventfully (Winograd, 1997).

Since OC is typically directed towards the face, symptoms often involve the eyes. Corneal abrasions have been reported in up to 7 percent by Watson *et al.* (1996) and 8.6 percent of cases by Brown *et al.* (2000). These findings have been noted as transient and do not require any additional treatment beyond decontamination with water irrigation. These temporary ocular injuries were also reported by Vesaluoma *et al.* (2000).

Research Studies

CN and CS: There is limited human research on the risks of CN in terms of inducing disability or death. Although permanent eye damage has been reported associate with the use of CN at close range, it is challenging to separate out whether the damage is from the CN or the actual weapon. However, at harassing or standard field concentrations, there is no evidence that CN causes permanent eye injury. Holland performed human studies in which 0.5 milligram of CN placed on subjects' skin for 60 minutes caused irritation and erythema, as compared with CS which had no effects when used in amounts of less than 20 milligram. Skin vesication was seen with the same dose of CN when the skin was moist, whereas no vesication occurred with CS at levels of 30 milligram or less (Holland and White, 1972).

There is little evidence that CS results in any permanent lung damage even after several exposures to field concentrations (Blain, 2003). In 36 subjects exposed to CS, Bestwick *et al.* (1972) found no change in tidal volume, peak flow or vital capacity when comparing pre-exposure values to those measured immediately afterward and at 24 hours post-exposure. In another study on human subjects, Punte *et al.* (1963) reported that individuals subjected to daily exposures to CS showed no changes in airway resistance immediately following, as four or ten days after CS exposure.

In terms of other types of injuries, human studies have been performed to assess the effects of CS on skin using different concentrations and assessing the effects of various ambient temperatures and humidity levels. Subjects developed first and second degree burns at different levels and the authors concluded that many variables affect the likelihood of blistering, making risk assessment difficult to predict (Hellreich *et al.*, 1967, 1969). Human ocular exposures of 0.1 or 0.25 percent CS carried in different solutions caused the inability to open the eyes for 10–135 seconds. Evaluation after the exposure via slit lamp examination noted a transient conjunctivitis, but no corneal damage (Rengstorff and Mershon, 1969a, b).

OC: Because of its ability to block pain sensation and itching, capsaicin has been studied in many different clinical conditions, including treatment of psoriasis, osteoarthritis, post-herpetic neuralgia, and diabetic neuropathy. These capsaicin-related pharmacotherapies have typically been associated with topical application of the agent. Given its ability to induce cough, capsaicin has also been utilized to study the cough reflex and the pulmonary system, as well as to assess the efficacy of various cough suppressants (Foster *et al.*, 1991).

Some animal and *in-vitro* human tissue studies have suggested that capsaicin increases airway resistance and bronchoconstriction (Lundberg *et al.*, 1983; Hansson *et al.*, 1992). However, clinical studies in humans with nebulized capsaicin are less definitive. Fuller reported that inhaled nebulized capsaicin resulted in a temporary increase in airway resistance that was dose-dependent, maximal at 20 seconds, and lasting less than 60 seconds (Fuller *et al.*, 1985). Blanc *et al.* (1991) and Collier and Fuller (1984) both reported no significant decrease in FEV1 in subjects who inhaled nebulized capsaicin at concentrations sufficient to induce cough. However, direct bronchoconstriction caused by capsaicin may be masked by cough and deep inhalation as both have bronchodilatory effects. In fact, doses of inhaled capsaicin low enough to not induce coughing have been shown to cause changes in airway resistance and pulmonary function (Fuller, 1991; Maxwell *et al.*, 1987; Hathaway *et al.*, 1993).

Unlike capsaicin, data on the human effects of OC spray are limited, particularly any interventional data (Ross and Siddle, 1996). A number of observational reports have been published assessing safety of OC spray use, including a two-year joint study by the FBI and US Army that reported that OC spray was not associated with any long-term health risks (Onnen, 1993).

Chan *et al.* conducted a randomized, cross-over controlled trial in 35 volunteer human subjects who were exposed to either OC spray or placebo propellant without OC, followed by a ten minute period of being placed in either the sitting or prone maximal restraint position. Pulmonary function testing was performed and arterial blood gases sampled during this time. OC exposure did not result in abnormal pulmonary dysfunction, hypoxemia or hypoventilation when compared to placebo in either the sitting or restraint positions. However, there was an increase in mean heart rate and blood pressure in subjects exposed to OC that did not occur in the placebo group. The investigators concluded that OC spray did not result in any evidence of respiratory compromise with and without restraint that would make place subjects at risk for asphyxiation from OC exposure. The changes in cardiovascular parameters, however, indicated the need for additional study (Chan *et al.*, 2002). Beyond clinical research in the laboratory setting, OC spray use has been widespread and a number of epidemiologic studies have reported on its use and safety.

The California State Attorney General reported that no fatal consequences occurred in over 23,000 exposures to OC spray. Watson *et al.* reviewed 908 exposures to OC spray that had occurred locally and found that fewer than 10 percent of subjects required any medical attention, and more specifically less than 1 percent had respiratory complaints requiring medical treatment. None of these patients were determined to have any significant injuries. Additionally, no fatalities were reported in either of these studies (Watson *et al.*, 1996; Lundgren, 1996).

Overall, OC spray has been used hundreds of thousands of times with no long-term health effects reported. Although there are case reports of death following use, in the large majority of cases other causes such as drug intoxication, excited delirium or underlying medical condition, have been implicated as the primary cause of death in the large majority of these cases. Moreover, clinical and epidemiologic studies on OC have yet to report any compelling evidence that OC is inherently dangerous or lethal.

CONDUCTIVE ENERGY DEVICES

CEDs were introduced into the law enforcement force continuum in the late 1970s. CED is a generic term referring to any device to subdue and control an individual by delivering electrical energy to the subject. The most well-known CED is the Taser® (Thomas A. Swift Electric Rifle) energy device, but others on the market include the Stinger stun gun and the remote activated custody control (RACC) belt®. There are other electronic belts, shields, and a host of hand-held contact stun guns available to law enforcement. Many of these products are also available to the general public.

In the past decade, the Taser has become the most popular incapacitating neuromuscular device on the market with an estimated 10 percent of all police officers in this country currently carrying the device (Hamilton, 2005). According to Taser International®, Tasers have been purchased by over 9,000 police departments in the USA and abroad. The manufacturer asserts that the device helps officers avoid the use of deadly force while lowering the risk of injury to users. It has been reported that the device has been used on over 150,000 volunteers during training sessions and on over 100,000 subjects by law enforcement officers in actual field confrontations, though the true total number of uses is unknown (Taser International, 2006).

The Taser X26 is a handheld device resembling a handgun intended to be used on subjects up to 21 feet away. The energy output of the device is 26 watts total, 1.76 joules per pulse, at 1.62 milliamps, and 50,000 volts. It utilizes an automatic timing mechanism to apply the electric charge for 5 seconds. The device initially propels two probes at a velocity of 180 feet per second. The electrical energy is discharged through a sequence of dampened sine-wave current pulses each lasting about 11 microseconds. This energy is neither pure AC nor pure DC, but probably akin to rapid fire, low amplitude DC shocks.

CEDs work by incapacitating volitional control of the body. These weapons create intense involuntary contractions of skeletal muscle, causing subjects to lose the ability to directly control the actions of their voluntary muscles. CEDs directly stimulate motor nerve and muscle tissue, overriding central nervous system control and causing incapacitation regardless of the subject's mental focus, training, size, or drug intoxication state. Subjects report painful shock-like sensations and the feeling that all of their muscles are contracting at once. During the CED discharge, subjects are unable to voluntarily perform motor tasks, however they remain conscious with full memory recall.

This effect terminates as soon as the electrical discharge is halted. Immediately after the taser shock, subjects are usually able to perform at their physical baseline. There is no known permanent lasting effect on the muscular system aside from any injuries that may result from an associated fall. There is a large experience of police trainees who have been tasered as part of their training. Most reported that the experience was unpleasant and declined to be re-tasered. A few subjects described a tingling sensation in the area under the probe sites lasting a few minutes after being tasered (Koscove, 1985). There is some residual muscle soreness reported by some who have been tasered.

CED effects vary depending on the particular device used, body location of and distance between the probes, and the condition of subject. For example, probes spread apart over a larger distance on the subject's body will have a greater effect because it allows for the electrical discharge to affect a larger portion of the body (Fish and Geddes, 2001). The effects of these devices have been reported to increase with the duration of application such that prolonged exposures may result in some sensation of fatigue and weakness even after the discharge is halted (Robinson et al., 1990). On the other hand, CEDs may fail to have their intended effect if the probes do not make adequate contact with the body, the probe spread is not wide enough thereby only affecting local muscle groups, or if the device fails to discharge.

Case Reports and Reviews

There has been a great deal of publicity in the lay press recently regarding in-custody deaths in subjects following use of the Taser (Hamilton, 2005). Amnesty International claims that more than 70 persons have died after Taser deployment by law enforcement. Some have postulated that the electrical discharge of CEDs on the body can induce life-threatening heart conduction abnormalities or cardiac dysrhythmias, disrupt normal respiration or cause metabolic derangements that could lead to death. However, there is limited research on the direct physiologic effects of CEDs and a direct causal connection between CEDs and the reported fatalities remains controversial.

Kornblum and Reddy examined 16 deaths that were associated with Taser use over a five-year period. All of these cases involved young men with a history of drug abuse who were behaving in a bizarre or unusual fashion drawing police attention. The ultimate cause of death was determined to be drug overdose in the majority of cases. The authors suggest that most of the subjects died after being in a manic, agitated, combative state, known as agitated delirium. Drug intoxication itself caused or predisposed the subjects to have increased risk for sudden death, and that the taser was not likely the causative factor. There was one case, however, in which Taser was felt to be contributory. In this case, the subject had a history of cardiac disease, for which he had been told to get a pacemaker, but had not done so. On autopsy he had a diseased heart and lethal levels of PCP in his system, but the cause of death was listed as cardiac arrhythmia due to sick sinus syndrome, mitral valve prolapse, and electrical (Taser) stimulation while under the influence of PCP (Kornblum and Reddy, 1991). Overall, the authors of the report concluded that the Taser in and of itself did not cause death, but may have contributed in this one case.

In a prospective case review conducted by Ordog in Los Angeles in the mid-1980s, 218 patients who presented to the emergency department after being shot with a taser were evaluated. These patients were then compared with 22 similar patients who were shot by police with 0.38 caliber handguns during the same time period. In 76 percent of the cases in which the Taser was utilized, subjects display bizarre and uncontrollable behavior.

Ninety-five percent were men and 86 percent had a history of recent phencyclidine (PCP) use. The mortality rate in the taser group in this study was 1.4 percent (3 of 218 patients) and the morbidity rate was 0 percent. All three patients who died arrived to the emergency department in asystole, had high levels of PCP in their system and went into cardiac arrest shortly after being tasered, ranging anywhere from 5 to 25 minutes after taser deployment. The medical examiner's reports on all three cases listed PCP toxicity as the cause of death, with no signs of myocardial damage, airway obstruction, or other fatal pathologic findings. Of the 22 patients shot with the 0.38 special, 50 percent of them died and 50 percent had varying degrees of serious morbidity (Ordog *et al.*, 1987).

Strote *et al.* evaluated deaths associated with Taser use found via a search of Lexis-Nexis and Google. They identified 71 deaths associated with Taser use, with 28 (39 percent) having autopsy reports available. The average age was 34.8 years, all were male, and 39 percent were White, 46 percent were Black, and 14 percent were Hispanic. No deaths were found to occur directly because of Taser use, but 21 percent reported a possible contributory component. Causes of death was felt to be directly drug related in 57 percent of cases, with 68 percent of the cases having cocaine or methamphetamine use. Excited delirium was either directly or indirectly responsible in 57 percent of cases and 46 percent of cases had significant pre-existing cardiac disease reported (Strote *et al.*, 2005).

Mehl reported a case of a miscarriage in a 32-year-old pregnant woman at approximately 8-10 weeks gestation one week after she had received a Taser activation. One probe lodged above the uterus in the abdomen, and the other in the left thigh. Reports of the duration of shock varied from 3 to 10 seconds. She fell to the ground and was reportedly unable to move for 5 minutes afterwards. One day later she began having vaginal spotting that continued for 7 days and was subsequently diagnosed with an incomplete miscarriage. Pathology analysis of the tissue from a uterine curettage revealed products of conception with extensive hemorrhage, necrosis, and inflammation. Though a temporal relationship is suggested between the Taser activation and miscarriage, no clear cause and effect relationship can be established (Mehl, 1992).

Research

Human research on the effects and safety of CEDs is limited, with most physiologic investigations having been conducted in animal models. One of the reasons for the limited human studies is the requirement that such studies be approved by local human research protection committees, which are often wary of these devices because of preconceived notions based on media and press reports. In fact, the approval of the original devices was not based on actual human or animal studies, but rather theoretical calculations of the physical effects of dampened sinusoidal pulses, for which the US Consumer Product Safety Commission concluded that the taser should not be lethal to a normal healthy person (Obrien, 1991).

One of the more common concerns regarding CEDs is whether these devices can cause cardiac dysrhythmias or cardiac standstill. The development of dysrhythmias or standstill would then cause the heart to not pump blood to the rest of the body, resulting in sudden death. The two main cardiac rhythm disturbances that are of greatest concern are VF, which is the lack of organized electrical activity and contraction of heart muscle cells, and asystole, which is the absence of any electrical activity.

For externally applied current, the fibrillatory current (the current that produces VF in human beings) is believed to be a function of the duration, frequency, and magnitude of the current, as well as the patient's body weight and the timing in the cardiac cycle during which the current is applied (Koscove, 1985; Ferris *et al.*, 1936; Kouwenhoven *et al.*, 1959). The threshold for VF in men for externally applied, 60 Hertz current has been proposed to be 500 milliamps for shocks of less than 200 microseconds duration, and 50 milliamps for shocks of more than two seconds (Koscove, 1985). The longer a current flows, the greater the chance a shock will occur during the vulnerable part of the cardiac cycle (early ventricular repolarization which is approximately 10-20 percent of the cardiac cycle) (Forrest *et al.*, 1992). The Taser X26 carries a current of 2.1 milliamps for a duration of 0.0004 seconds (Taser International, 2006).

Additionally, resistance is also going to play a role into how much current actually flows for a given voltage (voltage = current × resistance). The lower the resistance, the larger the current that will flow. The total resistance of the body is the sum of internal resistance plus twice the skin resistance as current enters and exits the body (Forrest *et al.*, 1992). A skin effect is known to exist when high-frequency electricity is used as these currents tend to stay near the surface of a conductor. Since the Taser devices use very high-frequency electricity, the output of the Taser is believed to stay near the skin and muscle surface of the body and not penetrate deeply to the internal organs, such as the heart (Bleetman *et al.*, 2004).

A porcine study published by Roy in 1989 used an older model stun gun that produced high voltages (> 100,000 volts) and short duration pulses (< 20 microseconds). The investigators compared five different models of stun gun with varying energies. The average value of the current applied during each shock was calculated to be 3.8 milliamps. When towels were placed between the skin and the electrodes to simulate clothing, the maximum current spike was 190 milliamps with a pulse length of 20 microseconds. Using two anesthetized normal healthy pigs, the investigators were able to induce VF when the leads of the stun gun were applied directly to the heart or to the chest of one of the animals in which a cardiac pacemaker had been implanted. Important to note was that these adverse effects were immediate, not delayed. The authors surmised that the mechanism of action inciting VF was not pacemaker inhibition, but rather fibrillatory current directly accessing the heart via the pacemaker leads. This device's shock also produced cardiac standstill when applied through layers of simulated clothing over a prolonged period. However, these findings only occurred with the two stun gun models delivering the highest energy. There were no cardiac effects seen with the lower energy units. This study demonstrated that VF was indeed possible, but only at very high-energy outputs and when the electrical discharge occurred directly over or with direct access to the heart (Roy and Podgorski, 1989).

More recently, McDaniel and Stratbucker studied the Air Taser and Advanced Taser M26 in five anesthetized dogs with an average weight of 54 pounds. Over 200 electrical discharges of the devices placed directly over the chest failed to induce VF in any of the animals. The authors did note that when both probes were placed directly over the heart they were able to pace the heart similar to a pacemaker, but still did not induce VF (McDaniel *et al.*, 2000).

Stracbucker *et al.* studied 13 adult domestic pigs by applying Taser-like electrical discharge to the thorax similar to human use of the device, and then gradually increased the energy output above that level until VF was achieved. The investigators did not induce VF in the pigs until levels of energy 20 times that of the standard Taser level. When using energy levels below that threshold, 43/43 discharges did not induce VF (Stracbucker et al., 2003).

In another animal study, McDaniel *et al.* evaluated the cardiac effects on nine pigs shocked using a device that delivered an electrical discharge identical in waveform and charge to the Taser X26 device. The electrodes were placed across the thorax of the animals using the barbs that matched the probes used by the standard device. The animals were shocked for 5 seconds, simulating field use of the device. The study used gradually increasing amounts of charge delivered to identify two levels. The first being the lowest amount of charge required to induce VF at least once, called the VF threshold. The second defined as the highest discharge that could be applied five times without inducing VF called the maximum safe level. The authors then compared this value to the standard device discharge and the ratio of the two values to determine the safety index. The study found that the electrical discharge required to induce VF was 15 to 42 times the energy output of a standard Taser discharge. This safety factor increased with the size and weight of the subject. The conclusion of the authors was that discharge levels output by fielded Taser devices have an extremely low probability of inducing VF (McDaniel *et al.*, 2005).

In one of very few studies in human subjects, Levine *et al.* conducted a study monitoring 67 subjects electrocardiographically immediately before and after Taser shock during police training sessions. The investigators reported no changes in cardiac rhythm, ECG morphology, or presence aberrantly conducted beats following the taser discharge. Mean heart rate increased by just over 19.4 beats/minute following the taser shock, but no abnormal cardiac dysrhythmias were identified (Levine *et al.*, 2005).

Recently, Ho *et al.* evaluated 66 volunteer subjects who received a standard five second Taser activation at a training course. The authors obtained venous blood samples before, immediately after, and 16 hours and 24 hours after activation. The blood samples were analyzed for troponin, myoglobin, lactate, potassium, glucose, blood urea nitrogen, creatinine, and creatine kinase levels. There were no significant changes from baseline values of the electrolyte or blood urea/creatinine ratio.

There was an increase in the serum bicarbonate and creatinine kinase levels at 16 and 24 hours. Serum myoglobin levels were elevated at all three time intervals post-Taser activation, but the troponin levels all remained < 0.3 nanograms per millilitre except for a single 24 hour post exposure level. That subject was evaluated at a hospital by a cardiologist, with no evidence of myocardial infarction or cardiac disability found. The troponin level returned to normal eight hours later (Ho *et al.*, 2006).

The potential for life-threatening cardiac dysrhythmias or cardiac muscle damage to occur as a result of the electrical discharge from current Taser devices appears to be low based on the available studies. However, there may be theoretical risks to patients with pacemakers or underlying cardiac disease, and the effect of recurrent or prolonged taser discharges remains unclear.

To date, little research has been conducted on the non-cardiac effects of the Taser. An air force study published by Jauchem et al. investigated the metabolic effects of repeated taser activations on sedated swine that received five-second Taser activations alternating with five seconds of rest for three continuous minutes. The animals demonstrated transient, clinically insignificant increases in potassium and sodium, a significant decrease in blood pH (increase in acid level) that returned toward normal after 1 hour, a significant rise in blood lactate that returned to baseline after 2 hours, and a significant rise in whole blood pCO2 that returned to baseline after 1 hour. The correlation of these results to use in humans, where far fewer applications are utilized, is unknown (Jauchem *et al.*, 2005).

More recently, the respiratory effects of the Taser were studied in 32 human subjects who underwent a 5 second Taser discharge. In this study, pulmonary function, ventilation, oxygenation and carbon dioxide elimination were monitored in human volunteers up to 1 hour after the Taser shock. Overall, ventilation and respiratory rate actually increased during the first 10 minutes, then returned to baseline levels. The subjects did continue to breathe during the 5 second shock. There was no evidence of abnormally low oxygen or elevated carbon dioxide levels in the blood following the shock, suggesting the Taser had no detrimental impact on respiratory function (Chan, SAEM 2007). The effect of Taser discharges on neurologic function remain to be studied.

CONCLUSION

Impact projectiles, irritant spray agents, and CEDs are important in the use of force armamentarium for law enforcement when dealing with violent, combative individuals who place themselves and the general public at risk. While associated with rare cases of sudden in-custody deaths, it is unclear what causal connection may exist between these less lethal technologies and reported fatalities. In many instances, individuals were in conditions which placed them at high risk for sudden death regardless of what force was utilized. In addition, a combination of force methods may have been utilized in these cases. Further research is needed to study the impact of these weapons on human physiology, as well as the underlying condition of those individuals who come in contact with law enforcement and are at greatest risk.

DISCUSSION QUESTIONS

1. Compare the physiologic effects and specific medical issues of the use of lethal and less-than-lethal weapons.
2. List a couple of reasons why animal research vs. human research regarding the lethal weapon physiologic effects are limited.
3. What three parts of the body if penetrated with a less-than-lethal weapon could cause death?
4. Discuss the differences of CS, CN, and OC and if they have prolonged effects.
5. Define what a CED is and discuss why it is so popular among police officers.

REFERENCES

Amnesty International (2005), available at: web.amnesty.org (accessed March 28, 2005).

Bestwick, F.W., Holland, P. and Kemp, K.H. (1972), "Acute effects of exposure to ortho-chlorobenzylidene malononitrile (CS) and the development of tolerance", *British Journal of Industrial Medicine*, Vol. 29, pp. 298–306.

Billmire, D.F., Vinocur, C., Ginda, M., Robinson, N.B., Panitch, H., Friss, H., Rubenstein, D. and Wiley, J.F. (1996), "Pepper-spray-induced respiratory failure treated with extracorporeal membrane oxygenation", *Pediatrics*, Vol. 98 No. 5, pp. 961–3.

Blain, P.G. (2003), "Tear gases and irritant incapacitants. 1-chloroacetophenone, 2-chlorobenzylidene malononitrile and dibenz[b,f]-1,4-oxazepine", *Toxicological Reviews*, Vol. 22 No. 2, pp. 103–10.

Blanc, P., Liu, D., Juarez, C. and Boushey, H.A. (1991), "Cough in hot pepper workers", *Chest*, Vol. 99, p. 27.

Bleetman, A., Steyn, R. and Lee, C. (2004), "Introduction of the Taser into British policing. Implications for UK emergency departments: an overview of electronic weaponry", *Emergency Medicine Journal*, Vol. 21, pp. 136–40.

Brown, L., Takeuchi, D. and Challoner, K. (2000), "Corneal abrasions associated with pepper spray exposure", *American Journal of Emergency Medicine*, Vol. 18 No. 3, pp. 271–2.

Chan, T.C., Vilke, G.M., Clausen, J., Clark, R.F., Schmidt, P., Snowden, T. and Neuman, T. (2002), "The effect of oleoresin capsicum 'pepper spray' inhalation on respiratory function", *Journal of Forensic Science*, Vol. 47 No. 2, pp. 299–304.

Chapman, A.J. and White, C. (1978), "Death resulting from lacrimatory agents", *Journal of Forensic Science*, Vol. 23, pp. 527–30.

Charles, A., Asensio, J., Forno, W., Petrone, P., Roldan, G. and Scott, R.P. (2002), "Penetrating bean bag injury: intrathoracic complication of a nonlethal weapon", *Journal of Trauma*, Vol. 53 No. 5, pp. 997–1000.

Chute, D.J. and Smialek, J.E. (1998), "Injury patterns in a plastic (AR-1) Baton fatality", *American Journal of Forensic Medicine and Pathology*, Vol. 19 No. 3, pp. 226–9.

Collier, J.G. and Fuller, R.W. (1984), "Capsaicin inhalation in man and the effects of sodium cromoglycate", *British Journal of Pharmacology*, Vol. 81, p. 113.

Danto, B.L. (1987), "Medical problems and criteria regarding the use of tear gas by police", *American Journal of Forensic Medicine and Pathology*, Vol. 8, pp. 317–22.

de Brito, D., Challoner, K.R., Sehgal, A. and Mallon, W. (2001), "The injury pattern of a new law enforcement weapon: the police bean bag", *Annals of Emergency Medicine*, Vol. 38 No. 4, pp. 383–90.

Ferris, L.P., King, B.G. and Spence, P.W. (1936), "Effects of electrical shock on the heart", *Transactions of the American Institute of Electrical Engineering.*, Vol. 55, pp. 498–515.

Fish, R.M. and Geddes, L.A. (2001), "Effects of stun guns and tasers", *Lancet*, Vol. 358, p. 687.

Forrest, F.C., Saunders, P.R., McSwinney, M. and Tooley, M.A. (1992), "Cardiac injury and electrocution", *Journal of the Royal Society of Medicine*, Vol. 85, p. 642.

Foster, G., Yeo, W.W. and Ramsay, L.E. (1991), "Effect of sulindac on the cough reflex of healthy subjects", *British Journal of Clinical Pharmacology*, Vol. 31, pp. 207–8.

Fuller, R.W. (1991), "Pharmacology of inhaled capsaicin in humans", *Resp. Med.*, Vol. 85, p. 31, supplementary A.

Fuller, R.W., Dixon, C.M.S. and Barnes, P.J. (1985), "Bronchoconstrictor response to inhaled capsaicin in humans", *Journal of Applied Physiology*, Vol. 58 No. 4, p. 1080.

Granfield, J., Onnen, J. and Petty, C.S. (1994), *Pepper Spray and in Custody Deaths*, Executive Brief: Science and Technology, International Association of Chiefs of Police and National Institute of Justice, Alexandria, VA.

Grange, J.T., Kozak, R. and Gonzalez, J. (2002), "Penetrating injury from a less-lethal bean bag gun", *Journal of Trauma*, Vol. 52 No. 3, pp. 576–8.

Hamilton, A. (2005), "From zap to zzzz. Time", available at: www.time.com/time/magazine (accessed March 28, 2005).

Hansson, L., Wollmer, P., Dahlback, M. and Karlsson, J.A. (1992), "Regional sensitivity of human airways to capsaicin-induced cough", *American Review of Respiratory Disease*, Vol. 145, p. 1191.

Hathaway, T.J., Higenbottam, T.W., Morrison, J.F.J., Clelland, C.A. and Wallwork, J. (1993), "Effects of inhaled capsaicin in heart-lung transplant patients and asthmatic subjects", *American Review of Respiratory Disease*, Vol. 148, p. 1233.

Hellreich, A., Goldman, R.H., Bottiglieri, N.G. and Weimer, J.T. (1967), "The effects of thermally-generated CS aerosols on human skin", Technical Report 4075, Medical Research Laboratories, Edgewood Arsenal, MD.

Hellreich, A., Mershon, M.M., Weimer, J.T., Kysor, K.P. and Bottiglieri, N.G. (1969), "An evaluation of the irritant potential of CS aerosols on human skin under tropical climactic conditions", Technical Report 4252, Medical Research Laboratories, Edgewood Arsenal, MD.

Holland, P. and White, R.G. (1972), "The cutaneous reactions produced by o-chlorobenzylidene malononitrile and 1-chloroacetophenone when applied directly to the skin of human subjects", *British Journal of Dermatology*, Vol. 86, pp. 150–4.

Ho, J.D., Miner, J.R., Lakireddy, D.R., Bultman, L.L. and Heegaard, W.G. (2006), "Cardiovascular and physiologic effects of conducted electrical weapon discharge in resting adults", *Academic Emergency Medicine*, Vol. 13 No. 6, pp. 589–95.

Hu, H. and Christiani, D. (1992), "Reactive airways dysfunction after exposure to teargas", *Lancet*, Vol. 339, p. 1535.

Hughes, D., Maguire, K., Dunn, F., Fitzpatrick, S. and Rocke, L.G. (2005), "Plastic baton round injuries", *Emergency Medicine Journal*, Vol. 22 No. 2, pp. 111–2.

Jauchem, J.R., Sherry, C.J., Fines, D.A. and Cook, M.C. (2005), "Acidosis, lactate, electrolytes, muscle enzymes, and other factors in the blood of sus scrofa following repeated TASER exposures", *Forensic Science International*, Vol. 161 No. 1, pp. 20–30.

Kornblum, R. and Reddy, S. (1991), "Effects of the Taser in fatalities involving police confrontation", *Journal of Forensic Science*, Vol. 36 No. 2, pp. 434–48.

Koscove, E. (1985), "The Taser Weapon: a new emergency medicine problem", *Annals of Emergency Medicine*, Vol. 14 No. 12, pp. 1205–98.

Kouwenhoven, W.B., Knickerbocker, G.G. and Chestnut, R.W. (1959), "AC shocks of varying parameters affecting the heart", *Transactions of the American Institute of Electrical Engineering (Communications and Electronics)*, Vol. 78, pp. 163–9.

Levine, R.A. and Stahl, C.J. (1968), "Eye injury caused by tear gas weapons", *American Journal of Ophthalmology*, Vol. 65, pp. 497–508.

Levine, S., Sloane, C., Chan, T., Vilke, G. and Dunford, J. (2005), "Cardiac monitoring of subjects exposed to the taser", *Academic Emergency Medicine*, Vol. 13 No. 5, p. S47.

Lundberg, J.M., Martling, C.R. and Saria, A. (1983), "Substance P and capsaicin-induced contraction of human bronchi", *Acta Physiologica Scandanavia*, Vol. 119, p. 49.

Lundgren, D.E. (1996), "Oleoresin capsicum (OC) usage reports: summary information", Report of the California State Attorney General.

McDaniel, W., Stratbucker, R. and Smith, R. (2000), "Surface application of taser stun guns does not cause ventricular fibrillation in canines", *Proceedings of the Annu. Int. Conf. IEEE. Eng. Med. Biol. Soc., Chicago, IL.*

McDaniel, W., Stratbucker, R., Nerheim, M. and Brewer, J. (2005), "Cardiac safety of neuromuscular incapacitating devices", *PACE*, pp. s284–7, Supplement 1.

Madden, J.F. (1951), "Cutaneous hypersensitivity to tear gas (chloroacetophenone)", *AMA Archives of Dermatology and Syphilology*, Vol. 63, p. 133.

Maxwell, D.L., Fuller, R.W. and Dixon, C.M.S. (1987), "Ventilatory effects of inhaled capsaicin in man", *European Journal of Pharmacology*, Vol. 31, p. 715.

Mehl, L. (1992), "Electrical injury from tasering and miscarriage", *Acta Obstetricia et Gynecologica Scandanavica*, Vol. 1, pp. 118–23.

Millar, R., Rutherford, W.H., Jonston, S. and Malhotra, V.J. (2005), "Injuries caused by rubber bullets: a report on 90 patients", *British Journal of Surgery*, Vol. 62, pp. 480–6.

Obrien, D. (1991), "Electronic weaponry-a question of safety", *Annals of Emergency Medicine*, Vol. 20 No. 5, pp. 583–7.

O'Halloran, R.L. and Frank, J.G. (2000), "Asphyxial death during prone restraint revisited: a report of 21 cases", *American Journal of Forensic Medicine and Pathology*, Vol. 21 No. 1, pp. 39–52, Erratum in: *American Journal of Forensic Medicine and Pathology*, Vol. 21 No. 2, p. 200.

Onnen, J. (1993), "Oleoresin capsicum", International Association of Chiefs of Police Executive Brief, p. 1.

Ordog, G., Wasserberger, J., Schlater, T. and Balasubramanium, S. (1987), "Electronic gun (taser) injuries", *Annals of Emergency Medicine*, Vol. 16 No. 1, pp. 73–8.

Park, S. and Giammona, S.T. (1972), "Toxic effects of tear gas on an infant following prolonged exposure", *American Journal of Diseases of Children*, Vol. 123, pp. 245–6.

Pollanen, M.S., Chaisson, D.A., Cairns, J.T. and Young, J.G. (1998), "Unexpected death related to restraint for excited delirium: a retrospective study of deaths in police custody and in the community", *Canadian Medical Association Journal*, Vol. 158, pp. 1603–7.

Punte, C.L., Owens, E.J. and Gutentag, P.J. (1963), "Exposures to ortho-chlorobenzylidene malononitrile", *Archives of Environmental Health, Vol. 6*, pp. 72–80.

Queen, F.B. and Standler, T. (1941), "Allergic dermatitis following exposure to tear gas (chloroacetophenone)", *Journal of the American Medical Association*, Vol. 117, p. 1879.

Rengstorff, R.H. and Mershon, M.M. (1969a), "CS in trioctyl phosphate: effects on human eyes", Technical Report 4376, Medical Research Laboratories, Edgewood Arsenal, MD.

Rengstorff, R.H. and Mershon, M.M. (1969b), "CS in water: effects on human eyes", Technical Report 4377, Medical Research Laboratories, Edgewood Arsenal, MD.

Ritchie, A.J. and Gibbons, J.R.P. (1990), "Life threatening injuries to the chest caused by plastic bullets", *British Medical Journal*, Vol. 301, p. 1027.

Robinson, M.N., Brooks, C.G. and Renshaw, G.D. (1990), "Electric shock devices and their effects on the human body", *Medicine, Science and the Law*, Vol. 30 No. 4, pp. 285–300.

Ross, D. and Siddle, B. (1996), "Use of force policies and training recommendations: based on the medical implications of oleoresin capsicum", PPCT Research Review, Belleville, IL.

Roy, O. and Podgorski, A. (1989), "Tests on a shocking device—the stun gun", *Medical and Biological Engineering and Computing*, Vol. 27, pp. 445–8.

Shmunes, E. and Taylor, J.S. (1973), "Industrial contact dermatitis: effects of the riot control agent ortho-chlorobenzylidene malononitrile", *Archives of Dermatology*, Vol. 107, pp. 150–5.

Smith, J. and Greaves, I. (2002), "The use of chemical incapacitant sprays: a review", *Journal of Trauma*, Vol. 52 No. 3, pp. 595–600.

Steele, J.A., McBride, S.J., Kelly, J., Dearden, C.H. and Rocke, L.G. (1999), "Plastic bullet injuries in Northern Ireland: experiences during a week of civil disturbance", *Journal of Trauma*, Vol. 46 No. 4, pp. 711–4.

Steffee, C.H., Lantz, P.E., Flannagan, L.M., Thompson, R.L. and Jason, D.R. (1995), "Oleoresin capsicum (pepper) spray and 'in-custody deaths'", *American Journal of Forensic Medicine and Pathology*, Vol. 16 No. 3, pp. 185–92.

Stracbucker, R., Roeder, R. and Nerheim, M. (2003), "Cardiac safety of high voltage Taser X26 waveform", *Proceedings of the 25th Annual International Conference of the IEEE EMBS, Cancun, Mexico*, pp. 3261–2.

Strote, J., Campbell, R., Pease, J., Hamman, M.S. and Hutson, R. (2005), "The role of tasers in police restraint-related deaths", *Annals of Emergency Medicine*, Vol. 46 No. 3, p. s85.

Suyama, J., Panagos, P.D., Sztajnkrycer, M.D., FitzGerald, D.J. and Barnes, D. (2003), "Injury patterns related to use of less-lethal weapons during a period of civil unrest", *Journal of Emergency Medicine*, Vol. 25 No. 2, pp. 219–27.

Taser International (2006), available at: www.taser.com (accessed May 3, 2006).

Thomas, R.J., Smith, P.A., Rascona, D.A., Louthan, J.D. and Gumpert, B. (2002), "Acute pulmonary effects from o-chlorobenzylidenemalontrile 'tear gas': a unique exposure outcome unmasked by strenuous exercise after a military training event", *Military Medicine*, Vol. 167, pp. 136–9.

Thorburn, K.M. (1982), "Injuries after use of the lacrimatory agent chloroacetophenone in a confined space", *Archives of Environmental Health*, Vol. 37, pp. 182–6.

Vesaluoma, M., Muller, L., Gallar, J., Lambiase, A., Moilanen, J., Hack, T., Belmonte, C. and Tervo, T. (2000), "Effects of oleoresin capsicum pepper spray on human corneal morphology and sensitivity", *Investigative Ophthalmology and Visual Science*, Vol. 41, pp. 2138–47.

Watson, W.A., Stremel, K.R. and Westdorp, E.J. (1996), "Oleoresin capsicum (cap-stun) toxicity from aerosol exposure", *Annals of Pharmacotherapy*, Vol. 30, pp. 733–5.

Wawro, P.A. and Hardy, W.R. (2002), "Penetration of the chest by less-than-lethal 'beanbag' shotgun rounds", *Journal of Trauma*, Vol. 52 No. 4, pp. 767–8.

Winograd, H.L. (1997), "Acute croup in an older child: an unusual toxin origin", *Clinical Pediatrics*, Vol. 16, pp. 884–7.

PART III

Courts

In 2011, two cases made headlines due to their convoluted stories and celebrity connections: the Casey Anthony case and the Dr. Conrad Murray case. Casey Anthony was accused of murdering her two-year-old daughter, while Dr. Conrad Murray was accused of involuntary manslaughter of the world famous singer Michael Jackson. After the trial, Casey Anthony was found not guilty, and Dr. Conrad Murray was found guilty and sentenced to four years in prison. Although the public looks on these cases as examples of how the court system functions, they do not actually provide an accurate depiction of the courts.

The reality is that the typical American courtroom is not what the public saw in either of these trials. Most lower criminal courts in city courtrooms have little of the quiet dignity one expects to see when decisions concerning individual freedom and justice are made. The scene is usually one of noise and confusion as attorneys, police, and prosecutors mill around conversing with one another and making bargains to keep the assembly line of the criminal justice process in operation. One might see a judge accepting guilty pleas and imposing sentences at a rapid pace, going through the litany of procedure in rote fashion.

THE COURTROOM WORKGROUP

The picture the public sees of the courts is what they saw during the trials of Casey Anthony and Dr. Conrad Murray. Trials such as these make people believe that the courts operate as a true adversarial system, where the prosecutor and the defense attorney are sworn enemies, only remaining civil to stay in the good graces of the neutral judge. In reality the prosecutor, defense attorney, and judge make up the courtroom workgroup. This group is characterized by cooperation, efficiency, and the well-being of the group over all. The prosecutor and the defense attorney work together to determine the charge and sentence of a defendant, then the judge signs off on their agreement. All the while, no member of the group is trying to trick or deceive any other member.

Although it may seem that trials are quite common, and that the prosecutor wants to bring defendants to trial, so he or she can bring them to justice, they are actually quite uncommon. The preferred method of efficiency for the courtroom workgroup is plea-bargaining. Marc Galanter's chapter, "The Vanishing Trial," explains that trials have been seriously declining since the mid-1980s. His data show that there has been a decline in the total number of trials and in the number of cases ended by trials. This means that more and more cases are ended by plea-bargains. Court data show that more than 90 percent of all cases are plea-bargained. The courtroom workgroup plea-bargaining provides not only optimal efficiency, but each member of the group benefits from it. Prosecutors gain a relatively easy conviction, even in cases in which there may not have been enough evidence to convince a jury to convict the defendant. They also save time and resources by disposing of cases and recommending a punishment without the need for time-consuming trial preparations. Defense attorneys benefit from plea-bargaining by saving the time involved in pretrial preparation, earning their fees quickly, and moving on to the next income-producing case. Also, it helps public defenders cope with large and often growing caseloads. Judges, too, avoid time-consuming trials and are spared the prospect of determining what sentence to impose on the defendant. By plea-bargaining, they can adopt the sentence recommended by the prosecutor in consultation with the defense attorney, provided the sentence fits within the range of sentences that the judge believes is appropriate for a given crime and offender. Defendants also have great incentives to plea-bargain because their cases are completed quickly, and they can participate in establishing a definite punishment rather than facing the uncertainty of a judge's discretionary sentencing decision after trial.

Although all the members of the courtroom workgroup work together, they each have distinct powers and responsibilities. These powers define the positions of each of the court actors and illustrate how the members of the group need to work together to maximize the efficiency of the courts. By examining each member's position, you can see how the reality of their jobs differs from the illusion the public has.

THE PROSECUTOR

Prosecutors are powerful because from the time of arrest to the final disposition of a case, prosecutors can make a variety of decisions that will largely determine a defendant's fate. The prosecutor chooses the cases to be prosecuted, selects the charges that are to be brought into the courtroom, recommends the bail amount required for pretrial release, approves any negotiated agreements made with the defendant, and urges judges to impose particular sentences. The prosecutor possesses significant discretion to make such decisions without direct interference from either the law or other actors in the justice system. David Bjerk's chapter, "Prosecutorial Discretion: Making the Crime Fit the Penalty," demonstrates this by presenting empirical evidence that illustrates how prosecutors often use their discretion to avoid mandatory minimum sentences. Specifically, he discusses how prosecutors in states that have "three-strike laws" will often prosecute offenders for lesser crimes that are not covered by the law. Because most local prosecutors are elected officials, their decisions may be responsive to changes in public opinion. For some office holders, it is a matter of reelection, while others feel they are obliged to follow the will of the people in holding an office of public trust. This can be seen through the Casey Anthony case and Dr. Conrad Murray case. Even though the prosecutor may not have had the best evidence to convict Casey Anthony of the murder of her daughter, he still thought it would be best to take the case to trial because by not prosecuting Casey Anthony he risked upsetting the public due to the highly publicized nature of the investigation. The same could be said for the case against Dr. Conrad Murray. Accusations against physicians are generally handled in civil court, but because the victim was Michael Jackson, the prosecutor could have been pressured into finding someone at fault for his death. A prosecutor's decisions might also be affected by their caseload. Adam Gershowitz and Laura Killinger's chapter, "The State Never Rests," asserts that when prosecutors have excessive caseloads, they make decisions that harm the defendants, victims, and public at large. They argue that when prosecutors have a large caseload, they have a hard time properly identifying defendants that are less culpable and deserving of a more lenient plea-bargain.

Throughout the justice process, prosecutors have links with the other actors in the system, and these relationships shape the prosecutors, decisions. Prosecutors may, for example, recommend bail amounts and sentences that demonstrate their understanding of and support for particular judges' preferences. In front of "tough" judges, prosecutors may make "tough" recommendations; however, they are likely to modify their arguments for a judge who favors leniency or rehabilitation. Likewise, the other actors in the system may adjust their decisions and actions to solidify their relationships with the prosecutor. Police officers' investigation and arrest practices are likely to reflect their understanding of the prosecutor's priorities. Thus, prosecutors influence the decision of others in the criminal justice process while also shaping their own actions to preserve and reinforce their relationships with police, defense attorneys, and judges. The actors of the court work together, despite what the Casey Anthony and Dr. Conrad Murray trials show. If you were to go strictly off of what these headline-making cases show, you would believe that trials are common and that the defense attorney is the defender of injustice, while the prosecutor is the state's representation in the fight against crime; however, George Cole's chapter, "Decision to Prosecute," explains that this image could not be further from the truth. In reality the courts function as a team. Cole discusses that a prosecutor's decision to prosecute depends on the cooperation of many court actors.

Prosecutors gain additional power from the fact that their decisions and actions are confidential and hidden from public view. For example, a prosecutor and defense attorney may strike a bargain outside the courtroom whereby the prosecutor reduces a charge in exchange for a guilty plea or drops a charge altogether if the defendant agrees to seek psychiatric help. In such instances, the justice system reaches a decision about a case in a way that is nearly invisible to the public.

DEFENSE ATTORNEYS

Defense attorneys elicit strong public impressions, both positive and negative. On the one hand, they are viewed as defenders of liberty, with a duty to keep the burden of proof on the state. As such, they are involved in a constant searching and creative questioning of official decisions at all stages of the justice process. On the other hand, they are seen as somehow "soiled" by their clients, engaged in shady practices to free clients from the rightful demands of the law. The public retains the more tarnished image. For example, Casey Anthony's defense attorney, Jose Baez, is respected, but often reviled, for defending a woman who many believe to be a murderer.

Defense attorneys face unique difficulties in their work. Their duty typically involves preparing clients and their relatives for the likelihood of conviction and punishment. Defense lawyers also struggle with the fact that criminal practice does not pay well. Public defenders have relatively low salaries, and attorneys appointed to represent poor defendants are paid small sums. If privately retained attorneys do not demand payment from their clients at the start of the case, they may later find themselves trying to persuade the defendants' relatives to pay—because many convicted offenders have no incentive to pay for unsuccessful legal services while sitting in prison. Abraham Blumberg's chapter, "The Practice of Law as Confidence Game: Organization and Co-Optation of a Profession," discusses how defense attorneys secure their fees. He also demonstrates that defense attorneys are not defenders of injustice that work hard to prove their clients' innocence, but rather a court actor that tries to convince his or her client and their families that the best option is to plead guilty to please the judge and prosecutor. To perform their jobs enthusiastically and derive satisfaction from their careers, defense attorneys must focus on goals other than money. That these attorneys are usually on the losing side of cases can make it especially difficult for them to feel like successful professionals. The vast majority of these attorneys are not featured on the six o'clock news.

Defense attorneys face additional pressures. If they mount a vigorous defense and gain acquittal for their client, the community may blame them for using "technicalities" to keep a criminal on the streets. After the jury returned a not guilty verdict in the Casey Anthony trial, lead attorney Jose Baez, as well as other attorneys on the case, received numerous threats. The wife of one of the attorneys involved in Casey Anthony's defense, Cheney Mason, felt so threatened that she called 911 to report the threatening phone calls and unplugged their telephone. In addition, if defense attorneys embarrass the prosecution in court, they may harm their prospects for reaching cooperative plea agreements on behalf of future clients. As previously discussed, cooperation among the court actors is crucial. If a defense attorney is not able to cooperate with the prosecutor, he or she may have a hard time obtaining clients. Thus, criminal practice can impose significant financial, social, and psychological burdens. As a result, many attorneys get "burned out" after a few years and few criminal law specialists stay in the field past the age of 50.

TO BE A JUDGE

When the public watched the courtroom proceedings of the Casey Anthony trial and the Dr. Conrad Murray trial, they expected that the judge was a neutral arbiter between the state and the accused; and if either of them was convicted, the judge would provide a fair, unbiased sentence. Americans believe that the judge, more than any other person in the system, symbolizes and is expected to embody justice, thereby ensuring that the right to due process is respected and that the defendant is treated fairly. The judge's black robe and gavel symbolize the impartiality the public expects from our courts. Judges are supposed to act both inside and outside the courthouse according to a well-defined role designed to prevent involvement in anything that could tarnish the judiciary's reputation. The public expects judges to make careful, consistent decisions that uphold the ideals of equal justice for all citizens; however, this image of judges devoting themselves to careful deliberations and thoughtful decisions does not reflect the daily reality for most American judges. Lower court judges can face significant caseloads that require them to quickly exercise discretion in the disposition and punishment of minor offenses with little supervision from any higher court. Because of the unending flow of cases, they operate with assembly-line precision.

All judges are addressed as "Your Honor," and we must rise to our feet in deference whenever they enter or leave the courtroom. This respect and deference is not based on any certainty that each judge is highly qualified and fair. In some jurisdictions, judges are sometimes chosen for reasons that have little to do with either their legal qualifications or their judicial manner. Instead, they may be chosen because of their political connections, friendships with influential officials, or financial contributions to political parties. There is a strong reform movement to place men and women of quality on the bench. Reformers urge that selection of judges on a nonpolitical basis will produce higher quality, more efficient, more independent, and consequently more impartial and fair members of the judiciary. In opposition are those who argue that in a democracy the voters should elect the people charged with carrying out public policies, including judges. They contend that people chosen by their fellow citizens can better handle the steady stream of human problems confronting the judges of the nation.

The judge, just like the prosecutor and defense attorney, is a member of the courtroom workgroup. By belonging to the workgroup, the judge puts the well-being of the group first, which suggests that in reality the judge is not a neutral arbiter but is on the side of the group. Consequently, judges' sentences tend to be very routine, so routine, in fact, that any constant member of the court such as the court clerk, bailiff, or court reporter, would be able to tell you what a particular judge's sentence would be given the crime and the defendant's criminal history. This is all made possible by the fact that the general public does not usually pay attention to what the courts are doing; however, occasionally there are headline-making cases that can affect a judge's sentencing patterns. If we look at Dr. Conrad Murray's trial, we can see an example of this. Dr. Conrad Murray was on trial for involuntary manslaughter, the maximum sentence for which was four years in prison. It might be expected that a defendant who committed this crime, and had no criminal history, would probably receive a sentence of one or two years in prison and one or two years of probation or community service; however, it is possible that due to the highly publicized nature of this case, Dr. Conrad Murray was sentenced to the maximum of four years. This case may not be considered routine because the public was watching and every decision that the judge made was scrutinized. With this in mind the judge may have given a sentence that was harsher than he would have given to any other defendant. This could take away from the illusion of the impartial judge that doles out justice fairly.

THE PROBLEM WITH HEADLINE-MAKING CASES

Judging by the number of news stories dedicated to cases such as Casey Anthony's and Dr. Conrad Murray's, it appears that the public becomes enthralled with cases that make headlines. The trouble with this, however, is that these cases give the public false impressions of how the courts really function. They see the prosecutor and defense attorney arguing over what actually happened, and if and how the defendant should be punished. They also see the jury diligently listening; and if the defendant is found guilty, they see the judge hand down a sentence. The problem lies in what the public does not see. They do not see that more than 90 percent of cases are plea-bargained. They do not see that few cases actually make it to trial, meaning that juries rarely have to deliberate. And they certainly do not see that the court actors cooperate to maximize efficiency. It is because of cases such as these that if the public were to see the courts on an average day, they would be thoroughly surprised.

WRITING ASSIGNMENTS

1. How does the reality of the court's behavior differ from the illusion the public has?
2. What are the implications of the local legal culture, and how do they explain both the behavior of actors in the system and how the system functions?
3. Discuss the importance and role of discretion on the judicial process. Should we try to limit discretion?
4. What are the collective beliefs about how judicial decisions occur?

14

The Decision to Prosecute

George F. Cole

The prosecuting attorney works within the context of an exchange system of clientele relationships that influence decision making. In this case study I explore the nature of these relationships and link politics to the allocation of justice.

This paper is based on an exploratory study of the Office of Prosecuting Attorney, King County (Seattle), Washington. The lack of social–scientific knowledge about the prosecutor dictated the choice of this approach. An open-ended interview was administered to one-third of the former deputy prosecutors who had worked in the office during the ten-year period 1955–1965. In addition, interviews were conducted with court employees, members of the bench, law-enforcement officials, and others having reputations for participation in legal decision making. Over fifty respondents were contacted during this phase. A final portion of the research placed the author in the role of observer in the prosecutor's office. This experience allowed for direct observation of all phases of the decision to prosecute so that the informal processes of the office could be noted. Discussions with the prosecutor's staff, judges, defendants' attorneys, and the police were held so that the interview data could be placed within an organizational context.

Source: "The Decision to Prosecute," by George F. Cole in Law and Society Review Vol 4:3, p. 313–343.

The primary goal of this investigation was to examine the role of the prosecuting attorney as an officer of the legal process within the context of the local political system. The analysis is therefore based on two assumptions. First, that the legal process is best understood as a subsystem of the larger political system. Because of this choice, emphasis is placed upon the interaction and goals of the individuals involved in decision making. Second, and closely related to the first point, it is assumed that broadly conceived political considerations explained to a large extent "who gets or does not get—in what amount—and how, the good (justice) that is hopefully produced by the legal system."[1] By focusing upon the political and social linkages between these systems, it is expected that decision making in the prosecutor's office will be viewed as a principal ingredient in the authoritative allocation of values.

THE PROSECUTOR'S OFFICE IN AN EXCHANGE SYSTEM

While observing the interrelated activities of the organizations in the legal process, one might ask, "Why do these agencies cooperate?" If the police refuse to transfer information to the prosecutor concerning the commission of a crime, what are the rewards or sanctions that might be brought against them? Is it possible that organizations maintain a form of "bureaucratic accounting" that, in a sense, keeps track of the resources allocated to an agency and the support returned? How are cues transmitted from one agency to another to influence decision making? These are some of the questions that must be asked when decisions are viewed as an output of an exchange system.

The major findings of this study are placed within the context of an exchange system.[2] This serves the heuristic purpose of focusing attention upon the linkages found between actors in the decision-making process. In place of the traditional assumptions that the agency is supported solely by statutory authority, this view recognizes that an organization has many clients with which it interacts and upon whom it is dependent for certain resources. As interdependent subunits of a system, then, the organization and its clients are engaged in a set of exchanges across their boundaries. These will involve a transfer of resources between the organizations that will affect the mutual achievement of goals.

The legal system may be viewed as a set of interorganizational exchange relationships analogous to what Long has called a community game.[3] The participants in the legal system (game) share a common territorial field and collaborate for different and particular ends. They interact on a continuing basis as their responsibilities demand contact with other participants in the process. Thus, the need for cooperation of other participants can have a bearing on the decision to prosecute. A decision not to prosecute a narcotics offender may be a move to pressure the U.S. Attorney's Office to cooperate on another case. It is obvious that bargaining occurs not only between the major actors in a case—the prosecutor and the defense attorney—but also between the clientele groups that are influential in structuring the actions of the prosecuting attorney.

Exchanges do not simply "sail" from one system to another but take place in an institutionalized setting that may be compared to a market. In the market, decisions are made between individuals who occupy boundary-spanning roles and who set the conditions under which the exchange will occur. In the legal system, this may merely mean that a representative of the parole board agrees to forward a recommendation to the prosecutor, or it could mean that there is extended bargaining between a deputy prosecutor and a defense attorney. In the study of the King County prosecutor's office, it was found that most decisions resulted from some type of exchange relationship. The deputies interacted almost constantly with the police and criminal lawyers; the prosecutor was more closely linked to exchange relations with the courts, community leaders, and the county commissioners.

THE PROSECUTOR'S CLIENTELE

In an exchange system, power is largely dependent upon the ability of an organization to create clientele relationships that will support and enhance the needs of the agency. For, although interdependence is characteristic of the legal system, competition with other public agencies for support also exists. Because organizations operate in an economy of scarcity, the organization must exist in a favorable power position in relation to its clientele. Reciprocal and unique claims are made by the organization and its clients. Thus, rather than being oriented toward only one public, an organization is beholden to several publics, some visible and others seen clearly only from the pinnacle of leadership. As Gore notes when these claims are "firmly anchored inside the organization and the lines drawn taut, the tensions between conflicting claims form a net serving as the institutional base for the organization."[4]

An indication of the stresses within the judicial system may be obtained by analyzing its outputs. It has been suggested that the administration of justice is a selective process in which only those cases that do not create strains in the organization will ultimately reach the courtroom.[5] As noted in Figure 1, the system operates so that only a small number of cases arrive for trial, the rest being disposed of through reduced charges, *nolle prosequi*, and guilty pleas.[6] Not indicated are those cases removed by the police and prosecutor prior to the filing of charges. As the focal organization in an exchange system, the office of the prosecuting attorney makes decisions that reflect the influence of its clientele. Because of the scarcity of resources, market-like relationships, and the organizational needs of the system, prosecutorial decision making emphasizes the accommodations made to the needs of participants in the process.

Justice Court (Cases filed)	3,700
Felonies	2,471
Gross misdemeanors	629
Misdemeanors	574
Traffic violations	20
Game violations	6

Superior Court (Bound over)	774
Plead guilty	510
Plead innocent	240
Dismissed	24
Found guilty	216
Found innocent	24

Justice Court (Reduced to misdemeanor)	1,697
Plead guilty	1,595
Plead innocent	4
Dismissed	98
Found guilty	3
Found innocent	1

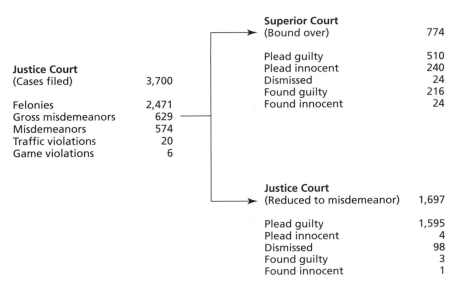

FIGURE 1 Disposition of Felony Cases, King County, 1964

Police

Although the prosecuting attorney has discretionary power to determine the disposition of cases, this power is limited by the fact that usually he is dependent upon the police for inputs to the system of cases and evidence. The prosecutor does not have the investigative resources necessary to exercise the kind of affirmative control over the types of cases that are brought to him. In this relationship, the prosecutor is not without countervailing power. His main check on the police is his ability to return cases to them for further investigation and to refuse to approve arrest warrants. By maintaining cordial relations with the press, a prosecutor is often able to focus attention on the police when the public becomes aroused by incidents of crime. As the King County prosecutor emphasized, "That [investigation] is the job for the sheriff and police. It's their job to bring me the charges." As noted by many respondents, the police, in turn, are dependent upon the prosecutor to accept the output of their system; rejection of too many cases can have serious repercussions affecting the morale, discipline, and work load of the force.

A request for prosecution may be rejected for a number of reasons relating to questions of evidence. Not only must the prosecutor believe that the evidence will secure a conviction, but he must also be aware of community norms relating to the type of acts that should be prosecuted. King County deputy prosecutors noted that charges were never filed when a case involved attempted suicide or fornication. In other actions, the heinous nature of the crime, together with the expected public reaction, may force both the police and prosecutor to press for conviction when evidence is less than satisfactory. As one deputy noted, "In that case [murder and molestation of a six-year-old girl] there was nothing that we could do. As you know the press was on our back and every parent was concerned. Politically, the prosecutor had to seek information."

Factors other than those relating to evidence may require that the prosecutor refuse to accept a case from the police. First, the prosecuting attorney serves as a regulator of caseloads not only for his own office, but for the rest of the legal system. Constitutional and statutory time limits prevent him and the courts from building a backlog of untried cases. In King County, when the system reached the "overload point," there was a tendency to be more selective in choosing the cases to be accepted. A second reason for rejecting prosecution requests may stem from the fact that the prosecutor is thinking of his public exposure in the courtroom. He does not want to take forward cases that will place him in an embarrassing position. Finally, the prosecutor may return cases to check the quality of police work. As a former chief criminal deputy said, "You have to keep them on their toes, otherwise they get lazy. If they aren't doing their job, send the case back and then leak the situation to the newspapers." Rather than spend the resources necessary to find additional evidence, the police may dispose of a case by sending it back to the prosecutor on a lesser charge, implement the "copping out" machinery leading to a guilty plea, drop the case, or in some instances send it to the city prosecutor for action in municipal court.

In most instances, a deputy prosecutor and the police officer assigned to the case occupy the boundary-spanning roles in this exchange relationship. Prosecutors reported that after repeated contacts they got to know the policemen whom they could trust. As one female deputy commented, "There are some you can trust, others you have to watch because they are trying to get rid of cases on you." Deputies may be influenced by the police officer's attitude on a case. One officer noted to a prosecutor that he knew he had a weak case, but mumbled, "I didn't want to bring it up here, but that's what they [his superiors] wanted." As might be expected, the deputy turned down prosecution.

Sometimes the police perform the ritual of "shopping around," seeking to find a deputy prosecutor who, on the basis of past experience, is liable to be sympathetic to their view on a case. At one time, deputies were given complete authority to make the crucial decisions without coordinating their activities with other staff members. In this way the arresting officer would search the prosecutor's office to find a deputy he thought would be sympathetic to the police attitude. As a former deputy noted, "This meant that there were no departmental policies concerning the treatment to be accorded various types of cases. It pretty much depended upon the police and their luck in finding the deputy they wanted." Prosecutors are now instructed to ascertain from the police officer if he has seen another deputy on the case. Even under this more centralized system, it is still possible for the police to request a specific deputy or delay presentation of the case until the "correct" prosecutor is available. Often a prosecutor will gain a reputation for specializing in one type of case. This may mean that the police will assume he will get the case anyway, so they skirt the formal procedure and bring it to him directly.

An exchange relationship between a deputy prosecutor and a police officer may be influenced by the type of crime committed by the defendant. The prototype of a criminal is one who violates person and property. However, a large number of cases involve "crimes without victims." This term refers to those crimes generally involving violations of moral codes, where the general public is theoretically the complainant. In violations of laws against bookmaking, prostitution, and narcotics, neither actor in the transaction is interested in having an arrest made. Hence, vice control men must drum up their own business. Without a civilian complainant, victimless crimes give the police and prosecutor greater leeway in determining the charges to be filed.

One area of exchange involving a victimless crime is that of narcotics control. As Skolnick notes, "The major organizational requirement of narcotics policing is the presence of an informational system."[7] Without a network of informers, it is impossible to capture addicts and peddlers with evidence that can bring about convictions. One source of informers is among those arrested for narcotics violations. Through promises to reduce charges or even to *nolle pros.*, arrangements can be made so that the accused will return to the narcotics community and gather information for the police. Bargaining observed between the head of the narcotics squad of the Seattle police and the deputy prosecutor who specialized in drug cases involved the question of charges, promises, and the release of an arrested narcotics pusher.

In the course of postarrest questioning by the police, a well-known drug peddler intimated that he could provide evidence against a pharmacist suspected by the police of illegally selling narcotics. Not only did the police representative want to transfer the case to the friendlier hands of this deputy, but he also wanted to arrange for a reduction of charges and bail. The police officer believed that it was important that the accused be let out in such a way that the narcotics community would not realize that he had become an informer. He also wanted to be sure that the reduced charges would be processed so that the informer could be kept on the string, thus allowing the narcotics squad to maintain control over him. The deputy prosecutor, on the other hand, said that he wanted to make sure that procedures were followed so that the action would not bring discredit on his office. He also suggested that the narcotics squad "work a little harder" on a pending case as a means of returning the favor.

Courts

The ways used by the court to dispose of cases is a vital influence in the system. The court's actions affect pressures upon the prison, the conviction rate of the prosecutor, and the work of probation agencies. The judge's decisions act as clues to other parts of the system, indicating the type of action likely to be taken in future cases. As noted by a King County judge, "When the number of prisoners gets to the 'riot point,' the warden puts pressure on us to slow down the flow. This often means that men are let out on parole and the number of people given probation and suspended sentences increases." Under such conditions, it would be expected that the prosecutor would respond to the judge's actions by reducing the inputs to the court either by not preferring charges or by increasing the pressure for guilty pleas through bargaining. The adjustments of other parts of the system could be expected to follow. For instance, the police might sense the lack of interest of the prosecutor in accepting charges; hence they will send only airtight cases to him for indictment.

The influence of the court on the decision to prosecute is very real. The sentencing history of each judge gives the prosecutor, as well as other law enforcement officials, an indication of the treatment a case may receive in a courtroom. The prosecutor's expectation as to whether the court will convict may limit his discretion over the decisions on whether to prosecute. "There is great concern as to whose court a case will be assigned. After Judge ——— threw out three cases in a row in which entrapment was involved, the police did not want us to take any cases to him." Since the prosecutor depends upon the plea-bargaining machinery to maintain the flow of cases from his office, the sentencing actions of judges must be predictable. If the defendant and his lawyer are to be influenced to accept a lesser charge or the promise of a lighter sentence in exchange for a plea of guilty, there must be some basis for belief that the judge will fulfill his part of the arrangement. Because judges are unable formally to announce their agreement with the details of the bargain, their past performance acts as a guide.

Within the limits imposed by law and the demands of the system, the prosecutor is able to regulate the flow of cases to the court. He may control the length of time between accusation and trial; hence he may hold cases until he has the evidence that will convict. Alternatively, he may seek repeated adjournment and continuances until the public's interest dies; problems such as witnesses becoming unavailable and similar difficulties make his request for dismissal of prosecution more justifiable. Further, he may determine the type of court to receive the case and the judge who will hear it. Many misdemeanors covered by state law are also violations of a city ordinance. It is a common practice for the prosecutor to send a misdemeanor case to the city prosecutor for processing in the municipal court when it is believed that a conviction may not be secured in justice court. As a deputy said, "If there is no case—send it over to the city court. Things are speedier, less formal, over there."

In the state of Washington, a person arrested on a felony charge must be given a preliminary hearing in a justice court within ten days. For the prosecutor, the preliminary hearing is an opportunity to evaluate the testimony of witnesses, assess the strength of the evidence, and try to predict the outcome of the case if it is sent to trial. On the basis of this evaluation, the prosecutor has several options: he may bind over the case for trial in superior court; he may reduce the charges to those of a misdemeanor for trial in justice court; or he may conclude that he has no case and drop the charges. The presiding judge of the Justice Courts of King County estimated that about 70 percent of the felonies are reduced to misdemeanors after the preliminary hearing.

Besides having some leeway in determining the type of court in which to file a case, the prosecutor also has some flexibility in selecting the judge to receive the case. Until recently the prosecutor could file a case with a specific judge. "The trouble was that Judge ——— was erratic and independent, [so] no one would file with him. The other judges objected that they were handling the entire work load, so a central filing system was devised." Under this procedure cases are assigned to the judges in rotation. However, as the chief criminal deputy noted, "The prosecutor can hold a case until the 'correct' judge comes up."

Defense Attorneys

With the increased specialization and institutionalization of the bar, it would seem that those individuals engaged in the practice of criminal law have been relegated, both by their profession and by the community, to a low status. The urban bar appears to be divided into three parts. First there is an inner circle, which handles the work of banks, utilities, and commercial concerns; second, another circle includes plaintiffs' lawyers representing interests opposed to those of the inner circle; and finally, an outer group scrapes out an existence by "haunting the courts in hope of picking up crumbs from the judicial table."[8] With the exception of a few highly proficient lawyers who have made a reputation by winning acquittal for their clients in difficult, highly publicized cases, most of the lawyers dealing with the King County prosecutor's office belong to this outer ring.

In this study, respondents were asked to identify those attorneys considered to be specialists in criminal law. Of the nearly 1,600 lawyers practicing in King County, only 8 can be placed in this category. Of this group, 6 were reported to enjoy the respect of the legal community, while the others were accused by many respondents of being involved in shady deals. A larger group of King County attorneys will accept criminal cases, but these lawyers do not consider themselves specialists. Several respondents noted that many lawyers, because of inexperience or age, were required to hang around the courthouse searching for clients. One Seattle attorney described the quality of legal talent available for criminal cases as "a few good criminal lawyers and a lot of young kids and old men. The good lawyers I can count on my fingers."

In a legal system where bargaining is a primary method of decision making, it is not surprising that criminal lawyers find it essential to maintain close personal ties with the prosecutor and his staff. Respondents were quite open in revealing their dependence upon this close relationship to pursue their careers successfully. The nature of criminal lawyer's work is such that his saleable product or service appears to be influence rather than technical proficiency in the law. Respondents hold the belief that clients are attracted partially on the basis of the attorney's reputation as a fixer, or as a shrewd bargainer.

There is a tendency for ex-deputy prosecutors in King County to enter the practice of criminal law. Because of his inside knowledge of the prosecutor's office and friendships made with court officials, the former deputy feels that he has an advantage over other criminal law practitioners. All of the former deputies interviewed said that they took criminal cases. Of the eight criminal law specialists, seven previously served as deputy prosecutors in King County and the other was once a prosecuting attorney in a rural county.

Because of the financial problems of the criminal lawyer's practice, it is necessary that he handle cases on an assembly-line basis, hoping to make a living from a large number of small fees. Referring to a fellow lawyer, one attorney said, "You should see ———. He goes up there to Carroll's office with a whole fistful of cases. He trades on some, bargains on others, and never goes to court. It's amazing but it's the way he makes his living." There are incentives, therefore, to bargaining with the prosecutor and other decision makers. The primary aim of the attorney in such circumstances is to reach an accommodation so that the time-consuming formal proceedings need not be implemented. As a Seattle attorney noted, "I can't make money if I spend my time in a courtroom. I make mine on the telephone or in the prosecutor's office." One of the disturbing results of this arrangement is that instances were reported in which a bargain was reached between the attorney and deputy prosecutor on a "package deal." In this situation, an attorney's clients are treated as a group; the outcome of the bargaining is often an agreement whereby reduced charges will be achieved for some, in exchange for the unspoken assent by the lawyer that the prosecutor may proceed as he desires with the other cases. One member of the King County bar had developed this practice to such a fine art that a deputy prosecutor said, "When you saw him coming into the office, you knew that he would be pleading guilty." At one time this situation was so widespread that the "prisoners up in the jail had a rating list which graded the attorneys as either 'good guys' or 'sellouts.' "

The exchange relationship between the defense attorney and the prosecutor is based on their need for cooperation in the discharge of their responsibilities. Most criminal lawyers are interested primarily in the speedy solution of cases because of their precarious financial situation. Because they must protect their professional reputations with their colleagues, judicial personnel, and potential clientele, however, they are not completely free to bargain solely with this objective. As one attorney noted, "You can't afford to let it get out that you are selling out your cases."

The prosecutor is also interested in the speedy processing of cases. This can only be achieved if the formal processes are not implemented. Not only does the pressure of his caseload influence bargaining, but also the legal process, with its potential for delay and appeal, creates a degree of uncertainty that is not present in an exchange relationship with an attorney with whom you have dealt for a number of years. As the presiding judge of the Seattle District Court said, "Lawyers are helpful to the system. They are able to pull things together, work out a deal, keep the system moving."

Community Influentials

As part of the political system, the judicial process responds to the community environment. The King County study indicated that there are different levels of influence within the community and that some people had a greater interest in the politics of prosecution than others. First, the general public is able to have its values translated into policies followed by law-enforcement officers. The public's influence is particularly acute in those gray areas of the law where full enforcement is not expected. Statutes may be enacted by legislatures defining the outer limits of criminal conduct, but they do not necessarily mean that laws are to be fully enforced to these limits. There are some laws defining behavior that the community no longer considers criminal. It can be expected that a prosecutor's charging policies will reflect this attitude. He may not prosecute violations of laws regulating some forms of gambling, certain sexual practices, or violations of Sunday Blue Laws.

Because the general public is a potential threat to the prosecutor, staff members take measures to protect him from criticism. Respondents agreed that decision making occurs with the public in mind—"Will a course of action arouse antipathy toward the prosecutor rather than the accused?" Several deputies mentioned what they called the "aggravation level" of a crime. This is a recognition that the commission of certain crimes, within a specific context, will bring about a vocal public reaction. "If a little girl, walking home from the grocery store, is pulled into the bushes and indecent liberties taken, this is more disturbing to the public's conscience than a case where the father of the girl takes indecent liberties with her at home." The office of the King County prosecuting attorney has a policy requiring that deputies file all cases involving sexual molestation in which the police believe the girl's story is credible. The office also prefers charges in all negligent homicide cases where there is the least possibility of guilt. In such types of cases the public may respond to the emotional context of the case and demand prosecution. To cover the prosecutor from criticism, it is believed that the safest measure is to prosecute.

The bail system is also used to protect the prosecutor from criticism. Thus it is the policy to set bail at a high level with the expectation that the court will reduce the amount. "This looks good for Prosecutor Carroll. Takes the heat off of him, especially in morals cases. If the accused doesn't appear in court the prosecutor can't be blamed. The public gets upset when they know these types are out free." This is an example of exchange where one actor is shifting the responsibility and potential onus onto another. In turn, the court is under pressure from county jail officials to keep the prison population down.

A second community group having contact with the prosecutor is composed of those leaders who have a continuing or potential interest in the politics of prosecution. This group, analogous to the players in one of Long's community games, is linked to the prosecutor because his actions affect their success in playing another game. Hence community boosters want either a crackdown or a hands-off policy toward gambling, political leaders want the prosecutor to remember the interests of the party, and business leaders want policies that will not interfere with their own game.

Community leaders may receive special treatment by the prosecutor if they run afoul of the law. A policy of the King County office requires that cases involving prominent members of the community be referred immediately to the chief criminal deputy and the prosecutor for their disposition. As one deputy noted, "These cases can be pretty touchy. It's important that the boss knows immediately about this type of case so that he is not caught 'flat-footed' when asked about it by the press."

Pressure by an interest group was evidenced during a strike by drugstore employees in 1964. The striking unions urged Prosecutor Carroll to invoke a state law that requires the presence of a licensed pharmacist if the drugstore is open. Not only did union representatives meet with Carroll, but picket lines were set up outside the courthouse protesting his refusal to act. The prosecutor resisted the union's pressure tactics.

In recent years, the prosecutor's tolerance policy toward minor forms of gambling led to a number of conflicts with Seattle's mayor, the sheriff, and church organizations. After a decision was made to prohibit all forms of public gaming, the prosecutor was criticized by groups representing the tourist industry and such affected groups as the bartenders' union, which thought the decision would have an adverse economic effect. As Prosecutor Carroll said, "I am always getting pressures from different interests—business, the Chamber of Commerce, and labor. I have to try and maintain a balance between them." In exchange for these considerations, the prosecutor may gain prestige, political support, and admission into the leadership groups of the community.

SUMMARY

By viewing the King County Office of Prosecuting Attorney as the focal organization in an exchange system, data from this exploratory study suggests the marketlike relationships that exist between actors in the system. Because prosecution operates in an environment of scarce resources and because the decisions have potential political ramifications, a variety of officials influence the allocation of justice. The decision to prosecute is not made at one point, but rather the prosecuting attorney has a number of options he may employ during various stages of the proceedings. But the prosecutor is able to exercise his discretionary powers only within the network of exchange relationships. The police, court congestion, organizational strains, and community pressures are among the factors that influence prosecutorial behavior.

DISCUSSION QUESTIONS

1. What is the prosecutor's role in the exchange system?
2. Describe the relationship between the prosecutor and the police. What factors influence a prosecutor's decision to refuse a case from the police?
3. How does the judge influence the prosecutor's decision to prosecute?
4. What advantages does the defense attorney have for cooperating with the prosecutor?
5. Describe the ways the community can influence a prosecutor's decision to prosecute.

NOTES

1. James R. Klonoski and Robert I. Medelsohn, "The Allocation of Justice: A Political Analysis," *Journal of Public Law* 14 (May 1965): 323–342.

2. William M. Evan, "Toward a Theory of Inter-Organizational Relations," *Management Science* 11 (August 1965): 218–230.

3. Norton Long, *The Polity* (Chicago: Rand McNally, 1962), p. 142.

4. William J. Gore, *Administrative Decision-Making* (New York: John Wiley, 1964), p. 23.

5. William J. Chambliss, *Crime and the Legal Process* (New York: McGraw-Hill, 1969), p. 84.

6. The lack of reliable criminal statistics is well known. These data were gathered from a number of sources, including King County, "Annual Report of the Prosecuting Attorney," State of Washington, 1964.

7. Jerome L. Skolnick, *Justice Without Trial* (New York: John Wiley, 1966), p. 120.

8. Jack Ladinsky, "The Impact of Social Backgrounds of Lawyers on Law Practice and the Law," *Journal of Legal Education* 16 (1963): 128.

15

Prosecutorial Discretion: Making the Crime Fit the Penalty

David Bjerk

This chapter empirically documents one way in which prosecutorial discretion may be used to dampen the effects of mandatory minimum sentencing laws. Specifically, prosecutors can use their discretion over prosecution charges to circumvent a mandatory minimum sentencing law for some defendants by prosecuting defendants who were initially arrested for the crime targeted by the sentencing law for lesser crimes not covered by the law. I document the use of such discretion with respect to several state "three-strikes"-type repeat-offender laws imposed throughout the 1990s, and I find that prosecutors become significantly more likely to lower a defendant's prosecution charge to a misdemeanor when conviction for the initial felony arrest charge would lead to sentencing under a three-strikes law. Moreover, accounting for such behavior is important, as I show that failure to do so can lead to overstating the effects of these laws on average sentencing by almost 30 percent.

Source: David Bjerk, "Prosecutorial Discretion: Making the Crime Fit the Penalty," Journal of Law and Economics 48: 591–625.

I INTRODUCTION

The use of mandatory minimum sentencing laws has become quite widespread throughout the United States. By 1994, at least one version of a mandatory minimum sentencing law was on the books in all 50 states, in the District of Columbia, and with the federal government. The motivation for these laws has primarily been to provide a simple and politically viable means of increasing the expected sentence for individuals who commit certain crimes through limiting the sentencing discretion available to actors within the judicial system.

While mandatory minimum sentencing laws appear to significantly curtail the discretionary influence judges have over the minimum sentences they impose on convicted criminals, the point has been raised that these laws may simply shift the discretion to other actors in the judicial process, namely, prosecutors. As stated by the Bureau of Justice Assistance, "The concern is that (sentencing) guidelines have merely shifted discretion from parole boards, prison officials, and judges to prosecutors." However, this report goes on to say that "[l]ittle evidence exists to document how much this (shifting of discretion) has occurred."

Understanding the role of prosecutorial discretion with respect to mandatory minimum sentencing laws is important for two primary reasons. First, any future legislative policy regarding sentencing guidelines must take into account the degree to which the effects of these guidelines will be affected by the mitigating actions available to agents within the court, specifically, prosecutors. Second, understanding the role of prosecutorial discretion is important with regard to the theoretical crime literature. Most theoretical crime models assume that lawmakers can determine both the probability of conviction and the sentence given conviction and that finding and convicting another criminal is relatively more expensive than increasing the sentence imposed on a convicted criminal. As discussed by Gary Becker and others, efficient deterrence in such a world is to impose the maximal possible sentence on all individuals convicted for each crime but to find and convict only a minimal number of offenders. But if lawmakers do not have absolute authority in determining how arrested offenders are sentenced and the preferences of other actors in the judicial system do not always align with those of lawmakers, then the above result will not hold. As shown by James Andreoni and Luigi Frazoni, when agents in the judicial system have some discretion over sentencing beyond that of legislators, it may be more socially efficient to make sentences reflect the social cost of the crime.

This paper adds to the literature on mandatory minimum sentencing laws in two primary ways. First, it provides formal empirical evidence documenting that one way in which prosecutors react to mandatory minimum sentencing laws is by systematically becoming more likely to prosecute those arrested for crimes targeted by these laws for lesser crimes not covered by these laws. Specifically, with respect to one type of mandatory minimum sentencing law, namely, "three-strikes-type" repeat-serious-offender laws, I show that following the imposition of these laws, prosecutors become almost twice as likely to prosecute three-strikes arrestees for lesser misdemeanor crimes not covered by the laws. Moreover, further results suggest that such behavior is the result of prosecutors using their discretion to partially circumvent three-strikes laws owing to their own constraints and preferences, not simply in response to changes in behavior by other actors within the judicial system.

The second contribution of this paper is to show the importance of accounting for this type of prosecutorial discretion over prosecution charges when estimating the effects of mandatory minimum sentencing laws on average sentencing. With respect to the three-strikes laws examined here, I show that failing to account for the type of prosecutorial discretion discussed above will lead to substantially overstating the effect of these laws on average sentencing. In particular, a naive estimate of the effect of these laws, where the ability of prosecutors to selectively lessen prosecution charges is not accounted for, will lead to overstating the effect of these laws on average sentencing by almost 30 percent.

II PREVIOUS LITERATURE REGARDING THE EFFECTS OF MANDATORY MINIMUM SENTENCING LAWS

As discussed in the introduction, a variety of mandatory minimum sentencing laws have been implemented throughout the United States over the last couple of decades. This section briefly reviews the findings and conclusions of some of the more recent literature related to prosecutor behavior with respect to these laws.

At the federal level, the United States Sentencing Commission (USSC) found that of a sample of defendants whose arrest offenses appeared to be covered by one of the federal mandatory minimum sentencing laws imposed in the late 1980s, over 25 percent were tried or sentenced under alternate charges that either had lower or no mandatory minimum sentence. The USSC also found that for 45 percent of drug defendants for whom weapons enhancements were found appropriate, no weapons charges were filed. Moreover, for 63 percent of defendants for whom increased punishments were possible because of prior felony convictions, increased minimums were not sought or obtained.

At the state level, Michael Tonry summarizes the findings concerning several state-level mandatory sentencing laws. In interpreting these findings he concludes that "[t]he people who operate the criminal justice system generally find mandatory minimum sentencing laws too inflexible for their taste and take steps to avoid what they consider unduly harsh, and therefore, unjust, sentences" and that "[p]rosecutors often avoid application of mandatory sentencing laws simply by filing charges for different, but roughly comparable, offenses that are not subject to mandatory sentences."

The idea that mandatory minimum sentencing laws cause actors in the judicial system, particularly prosecutors, to change their behavior in order to mitigate the effects of these laws is not a new one. In fact, one of the main reasons Congress repealed almost all of the existing mandatory federal sentences for drug offenses in 1970 was because there was a feeling that "the severity of existing penalties, involving in many instances minimum mandatory sentences, [has] led in many instances to reluctance on the part of the prosecutors to prosecute some violations, where the penalties seem to be out of line with the seriousness of the offenses."

While the studies examined by Tonry provide a good deal of anecdotal and descriptive evidence regarding prosecutor behavior and defendant outcomes following the imposition of mandatory minimum sentencing laws, most do not provide rigorous statistical evidence documenting how prosecutor behavior adjusts to mandatory minimum sentencing laws. More specifically, the previous studies of the effects of mandatory minimum sentencing laws generally do not explicitly test the statistical significance of any changes in prosecutor behavior following the imposition of the minimum sentencing laws or test whether these behavioral changes were directed primarily toward only those defendants targeted by the sentencing laws.

Daniel Kessler and Anne Piehl use more rigorous statistical methods in their evaluation of the effects of California's Proposition 8, a repeat-offender mandatory minimum sentencing law passed in 1982. They find that for defendants prosecuted for robbery, a crime eligible for sentencing under Proposition 8, the mean sentence for repeat offenders increased by over 50 percent relative to those of nonrepeat offenders subsequent to the passage of Proposition 8. Moreover, they also found that the mean sentence for repeat offenders prosecuted for grand larceny, a similar but lesser crime than robbery, which was not covered by Proposition 8, also showed a small but significant increase relative to those of nonrepeat offenders following passage of the sentencing law. By contrast, the mean sentence for repeat offenders prosecuted for drug possession, a crime not eligible for sentencing under Proposition 8, actually decreased slightly relative to those of nonrepeat offenders following the imposition of Proposition 8.

Like Tonry, Kessler and Piehl interpret their results as showing that prosecutor discretion can play an important role following the imposition of a mandatory minimum sentencing law. However, Kessler and Piehl's conclusions differ from those of Tonry concerning the specific way in which prosecutorial discretion matters. While Tonry emphasizes prosecutors using their discretion over prosecution charges to mitigate the overall effect of mandatory minimum sentencing laws on actual sentencing, Kessler and Piehl interpret their evidence as showing that prosecutors use their discretion over sentence lengths (presumably through plea bargain offers) to increase the sentences of defendants who committed lesser but similar crimes not covered by the new laws. In concluding, Kessler and Piehl say that their findings suggest that "increases in statutory sentences result in more punishment, not less punishment, than the simple statement of the laws would suggest" and that their findings reject "the null hypothesis that actors in the criminal justice system seek to undo changes in laws."

III THE REACTION OF PROSECUTORS TO MANDATORY MINIMUM SENTENCING LAWS

While Kessler and Piehl's interpretation of their evidence is somewhat at odds with Tonry's conclusions, their actual findings do not necessarily provide evidence against the mitigating behavior on the part of prosecutors as suggested by Tonry. For example, say prosecutors react to a mandatory minimum sentencing law targeting some crime A in the manner suggested by Tonry. To take an extreme case, say that the law has no effect on sentencing, but it causes prosecutors to use their discretion over prosecution charges to circumvent this law for defendants with less serious criminal records arrested for crime A (specifically, those who would have received a sentence less than the mandatory minimum if they had been arrested and convicted for crime A before the imposition of the law) by prosecuting these defendants for some lesser but related crime B not covered by the law. Therefore, even if the law does not increase the sentence for any criminals arrested for crime A, the average sentence for those convicted for crime A will rise following the imposition of the law because the lower bound on sentences will be truncated from below at a higher level. Moreover, if these defendants who were arrested for crime A but prosecuted and convicted for crime B all receive longer sentences than the average individual arrested and convicted for crime B, the mean sentence for those convicted for crime B will also rise following the imposition of the mandatory minimum sentencing law. Note that these implications exactly correspond with the findings of Kessler and Piehl but arise not because prosecutors use their discretion over sentence lengths to increase sentencing for those arrested and convicted for crime A and the related but lesser crime B, but rather because prosecutors use their discretion over prosecution charges to mitigate the effects of the sentencing law targeting crime A.

In general, within the context of mandatory minimum sentencing laws, the role and importance of prosecutorial discretion remains unresolved. In this section, I directly examine whether prosecutors use their discretion over prosecution charges to lessen the initial arrest charges for some defendants in reaction to one type of mandatory minimum sentencing law—namely, the state three-strikes-type repeat-serious-offender laws passed in several states throughout the 1990s.

A. Data and Definitions

The data used for this analysis come from *State Court Processing Statistics 1990–2000*. This Bureau of Justice Statistics data set tracks a sample of defendants arrested for state felony offenses, weighted to be representative of the nation's 75 most populous counties. The data set contains detailed information for each individual's case, including the date of arrest, the initial arrest charge, whether the individual was prosecuted for a felony or a misdemeanor, the demographic and criminal history characteristics of the defendant, the final disposition of the case, any conviction charges, and any sentence imposed. The general sample used in this paper consists of all cases that were not pending and contained valid data regarding the initial arrest charge, whether the eventual prosecution charge was a felony or a misdemeanor, the adjudication outcome, and any eventual conviction charges.

As stated above, the laws I will examine in this analysis are several state three-strikes sentencing laws that were passed throughout the 1990s. Although there are substantial differences in the particular laws passed in each of the states, the general purpose of these laws was similar: they were meant to impose prison sentences on serious repeat offenders for longer periods of time than the existing laws dictated. As shown in Table 1, between 1990 and 1996, some version of a three-strikes law passed in 12 of the 24 states contained in the data set used here. As can be seen in Table 2, these three-strikes laws cover many different crimes and have very different eligibility criteria. Therefore, unlike laws targeting gun possession or drug sales, determining which individuals in the data set were arrested for and/or convicted for the crimes targeted by the three-strikes laws is not straightforward. To make this determination, for each state in the data set that passed a three-strikes-type sentencing law between 1990 and 1996, the crimes covered by the law and the criminal history required by the law were used to define the criteria that an individual must meet to be eligible for the law in that state. If an individual's initial arrest charge and criminal history appear to satisfy the criteria for his or her home state's three-strikes law, then this individual is said to be in the group arrested for a three-strikes crime. Similarly, if an individual's conviction charge and criminal history appear to satisfy the criteria for his or her home state's three-strikes law, this individual is said to be in the group convicted for a three-strikes crime.

One constraint of this data set is that the information regarding arrest (conviction) charges and prior criminal history is not as specific as the criteria specified by the three-strikes laws. In particular, while the *State Court Processing Statistics* data set categorizes arrest and conviction charges according to only 14 different crime categories, there are many more arrest and conviction charge possibilities in the actual judicial system. Moreover, while the judicial system has extensive details concerning each arrested individual's criminal history, the criminal history data captured by the data set include only the number of previous felony convictions, the number of previous violent-felony convictions, the number of previous misdemeanor convictions, and the number of previous jail or prison stays. Table 2 shows how I dealt with these constraints when defining who was arrested (convicted) for a three-strikes crime. For example, the Florida three-strikes law states that a defendant is eligible for three-strikes sentencing if he or she is convicted three times for any of the following crimes: any forcible felony, aggravated stalking, aggravated child abuse, lewd or indecent conduct, and escape. For this analysis, a defendant from Florida is coded to have been arrested (convicted) for a three-strikes crime if his or her arrest (conviction) charge is for murder, rape, robbery, assault, or another violent crime and he or she had two or more prior violent-felony convictions.

Note that these definitions imply that a defendant with an arrest (conviction) charge and a criminal history that fit his or her state's three-strikes law is said to be arrested (convicted) for a three-strikes crime regardless of whether he or she was arrested before or after the three-strikes law was passed. In this way, these laws are treated like mandatory minimum sentencing laws targeting other crimes, such as drug sales or firearms possession, where the targeted crime was defined both before and after the law. Also, note that since these laws differ across states, the definitions imply that defendants arrested (convicted) for the same crime and with the same criminal history need not both be said to be arrested (convicted) for a three-strikes crime if they come from different home states and their home states' three-strikes laws differ. Furthermore, since a defendant needs to both be arrested (convicted) for a crime covered by his or her state's three-strikes law and have the criminal history that fits his or her state's three-strikes law, defendants who are from the same state and both arrested (convicted) for a crime covered by their state's three-strikes law may not both be said to be arrested (convicted) for a three-strikes crime if they have different criminal histories.

It is important to note that there is likely to be considerable measurement error concerning those who are defined to be arrested (convicted) for a three-strikes crime versus those who are defined to be arrested (convicted) for other crimes. As mentioned previously, the actual criteria required to be eligible for three-strikes sentencing are generally more specific than what is contained in the *State Court Processing Statistics* data used here. This means that some individuals are likely classified as being arrested for a three-strikes crime when they should not be and some individuals are classified as being arrested for an "other" crime when they should be in the three-strikes group. For example, in the case of Florida, an individual arrested for a violent felony who was previously convicted for a different violent felony and an escape will be eligible for three-strikes sentencing under Florida law but will not be classified as such in this analysis (since escape is likely in the "other" category in the *State Court Processing Statistics* data). Such measurement error will mean that any differences in outcomes between those classified as being arrested for three-strikes crimes and those arrested for "other" crimes will likely cause any estimated differences in treatment between the two groups to understate the true differences, as some individuals classified as arrested for "other" crimes are actually being treated like three-strikes arrestees.

Table 1 Three-Strikes Laws Passed 1990–96

State	Features of Three-Strikes Legislation	Year of Implementation	Law	Features of Preexisting Sentencing Laws
California	Mandatory doubling of sentence for any felony if one prior serious or violent-felony conviction; mandatory life without parole for 25 years for any third felony conviction if two prior serious or violent-felony convictions	1994	Cal. Penal Code § 667	Life with no parole eligibility before 20 years for third violent-felony conviction where separate prison terms were served for the first two; life with no parole for fourth violent-felony conviction
Florida	Added new category of "violent career criminal" to existing habitual offender statute; for third conviction for specified violent offense, life if first-degree felony, 30–40 years if second-degree felony, 10–15 years if third-degree felony	1995	Fla. Stat. Ann. § 775.084	Categories of habitual felony offender and habitual violent offender; range of enhanced sentences
Georgia	Mandatory life without parole for second specified violent-felony conviction	1995	Ga. Code Ann. § 17-10-7	On fourth felony conviction, offender must serve maximum time imposed and not be eligible for parole until maximum sentence served
Indiana	Mandatory life without parole for second specified violent-felony conviction	1994	Ind. Code § 35-50-2-8.5	Habitual offender law requiring enhanced sentencing on third felony conviction
Maryland	Life without parole for fourth violent-felony conviction for which separate prison terms were served for the first three	1994	Md. Code Ann., art. 27, § 643B	Same law, except that carjacking and armed carjacking were not on the list of offenses receiving this sentence
New Jersey	Mandatory life without parole for third conviction for certain violent felonies	1995	N.J. Stat. Ann. § 2C:43-7.1	Rarely invoked "persistent offender" provision allowing sentence one degree higher than the conviction offense on third conviction for first-, second-, or third-degree felonies

Pennsylvania	Mandatory minimum enhanced sentence of 10 years for second conviction for crime of violence and 25 years for third such conviction	1995	Penn. Consol. Stat. Ann. § 42-9714	Mandatory minimum enhanced sentence of 5 years for second or subsequent conviction for certain specified crimes of violence
Tennessee	Mandatory life without parole for second conviction for designated violent felonies; same for third conviction for other violent felonies	1994	Tenn. Code Ann. § 43-35-120	mandatory life without parole for third violent-felony conviction
Utah	Second- and third-degree felony offenders sentenced as first-degree felons and first-degree felons not eligible for probation if they have two prior convictions for any felony and a present conviction for a violent felony	1995	Utah Code Ann. § 76-3-203.5	Second- and third-degree felonies receive enhanced sentence of 5 years to life if offender has two prior convictions at least as severe as second-degree felonies
Virginia	Mandatory life without parole on third conviction for specified violent felonies or drug distribution charges	1994	Va. Code Ann. § 19.2-297.1	No parole eligibility if convicted of three separate violent felonies
Washington	Mandatory life without parole on third conviction for specified violent felonies	1993	Wash. Rev. Code Ann. § 9.94A.392	Number of prior convictions factored into offender score on state's sentencing guidelines
Wisconsin	Mandatory life without parole on third conviction for specified serious offenses	1994	Wisc. Stat. Ann. § 939.62	For repeat felony offenders, up to 10 years can be added to sentences of 10 years or more; 6 years can be added to sentences of 1–10 years

SOURCES. —John Clark, James Austin, & D. Alan Henry, Three Strikes and You're Out: A Review of State Legislation, exhibit 10 (1997); and Thomas B. Marvell & Carlisle Moody, The Lethal Effects of Three-Strikes Laws, 30 J. Legal. Stud. 89 n.27 (2001).

Table 2 Descriptions of State Three-Strikes Laws and the Laws as Captured by Data

	Actual Three-Strikes-Eligible Crimes	Strikes Needed to Be "Out"	Three-Strikes Crimes as Defined in Analysis
Alabama	No three-strikes law passed in 1990s	. . .	. . .
Arizona	No three-strikes law passed in 1990s	. . .	. . .
California	Any felony if one prior conviction was for murder, rape, lewd act on child, continual sex abuse of child, penetration by foreign object, sexual penetration by force, sodomy by force, oral copulation by force, robbery, attempted murder, assault with deadly weapon on peace officer, assault with deadly weapon by an inmate, assault with intent to rape or rob, felony resulting in bodily harm, arson causing bodily injury, carjacking, exploding device with intent to injure or murder, kidnapping, mayhem, arson, burglary of occupied dwelling, grand theft with firearm, drug sales to minors, any felony with deadly weapon	2	Arrest (conviction) for any felony if one or more previous violent-felony convictions
Washington, D.C.	No three-strikes law passed in 1990s	. . .	. . .
Florida	Any forcible felony, aggravated stalking, aggravated child abuse, lewd or indecent conduct, escape	3	Arrest (conviction) for murder, rape, robbery, assault, or other violent crime if two or more prior violent-felony convictions
Hawaii	No three-strikes law passed in 1990s	. . .	. . .

Georgia	Murder, armed robbery, kidnapping, rape, aggravated child molestation, aggravated sodomy, aggravated sexual battery	2	Arrest (conviction) for murder, rape, robbery, or other violent (not including assault) if one or more prior violent convictions
	Any felony	4	Any felony arrest (conviction) if three or more previous felony convictions
Indiana	Murder, rape, sexual battery with weapon, child molestation, arson, robbery, burglary with weapon or resulting in serious injury, drug dealing	3	Arrest (conviction) for murder, rape, robbery, other violent crime (not including assault), burglary with possession of weapon, or drug trafficking, if two or more prior violent-felony convictions or two or more prior drug convictions or one or more violent-felony and one or more prior drug convictions
Illinois	No three-strikes law passed in 1990s	. . .	. . .
Kentucky	No three-strikes law passed in 1990s	. . .	. . .
Maryland	Murder, rape, robbery, first- or second-degree sexual offense, arson, burglary, kidnapping, carjacking, manslaughter, use of firearm in felony, assault with intent to murder, rape, rob, or commit sexual offense	4, with prison terms served for first three strikes	Arrest (conviction) for murder, rape, robbery, other violent crime (not including assault), burglary, or use of weapon in commission of a felony, if three or more prior violent-felony convictions and three or more prior prison terms

SOURCES.—Definitions of three-strikes crimes in each state are from John Clark, James Austin, & D. Alan Henry, Three Strikes and You're Out: A Review of State Legislation (1997).

Table 3 Defendant Characteristics

Characteristic	Arrested for Three-Strikes Crime		Arrested for "Other" Felony	
	N	Coefficient	*N*	Coefficient
Arrested for violent crime	1,726	.48 (.012)	21,729	.24 (.003)
Arrested for property crime	1,726	.28 (.010)	21,729	.34 (.003)
Arrested for drug crime	1,726	.21 (.010)	21,729	.34 (.003)
Arrested for other felony	1,726	.09 (.007)	21,729	.08 (.002)
Age (years)	1,726	31.4 (.190)	21,672	29.1 (.065)
Percentage black	1,726	.54 (.014)	15,644	.41 (.003)
Percentage Hispanic	1,280	.30 (.013)	15,644	.28 (.004)
Percentage female	1,721	.07 (.006)	21,694	.16 (.003)
Number of prior convictions	1,709	7.22 (.150)	21,591	2.80 (.033)
Number of prior felony convictions	1,753	3.54 (.730)	21,670	.97 (.015)
Mean sentence (months)	1,658	30.3 (2.11)	20,336	12.0 (.32)
Percentage convicted	1,726	.73 (.011)	21,729	.73 (.003)
Percentage prosecuted for misdemeanor	1,726	.06 (.006)	21,729	.13 (.002)

Finally, note that because of how I defined the group of defendants arrested for three-strikes crimes, the group of defendants arrested for felonies other than three-strikes crimes are not always arrested for lesser crimes. However, as can be seen in Table 3, defendants arrested for three-strikes crimes are more likely to have been arrested for violent crimes, have more lengthy criminal histories, are given longer jail sentences, and are less likely to be prosecuted for misdemeanors than are defendants arrested for other felonies.

B. Empirical Evaluation of Prosecutor Response to Three-Strikes Laws

As discussed above, if prosecutors have discretion over prosecution charges, they may respond to a law increasing the mandatory minimum sentence for certain crimes by prosecuting a greater fraction of those arrested for the targeted crimes for lesser crimes not covered by the law. In order to examine whether such behavior occurs with respect to these three-strikes laws, we need to estimate how the proportion of individuals arrested for three-strikes crimes that are prosecuted for lesser non-three-strikes crimes changes following the imposition of the three-strikes laws. The difficulty in performing this analysis is that the data set used here does not provide specific information on the prosecution charge. Rather, it only provides information concerning whether the defendant was in the end prosecuted for a felony or a misdemeanor. However, since all defendants in the data set were initially arrested for felonies, and none of the three-strikes laws apply to misdemeanors, any defendant in this data set who was prosecuted for a misdemeanor can be said to have been prosecuted for a lesser crime than his or her initial arrest charge and prosecuted for a crime that was not eligible for three-strikes sentencing. Therefore, in analyzing whether three-strikes laws appear to cause prosecutors to become less likely to prosecute individuals for three-strikes crimes, I examine whether there is an increase in the proportion of three-strikes arrestees who were prosecuted for misdemeanors following the imposition of the three-strikes laws.

This definition of "lesser" crimes as being misdemeanors will also tend to cause measurement error in the true group of interest because in many states, prosecutors can choose to prosecute individuals arrested for three-strikes crimes for other lesser felonies not covered by their states' three-strikes laws. Since such individuals will be erroneously evaluated as being both arrested and prosecuted for a three-strikes crime in this analysis, such measurement error will generally cause the results in this paper to understate the true degree to which prosecutors alter their use of discretion over prosecution charges in response to three-strikes laws. In other words, the results discussed below likely miss some instances of prosecutors downgrading the arrest charge and thereby avoiding three-strikes sentencing. Hence, these results provide a lower-bound estimate on the degree to which prosecutors respond to three-strikes laws by prosecuting eligible individuals for lesser crimes not covered by the laws.

Table 4 shows the proportions of felony defendants prosecuted for misdemeanors before and after the imposition of three-strikes laws. The table reports that the proportion of defendants arrested for three-strikes crimes who were prosecuted for misdemeanors rose from 5.5 percent before the passage of three-strikes laws to 9.3 percent after their passage. This change represents an increase of over 70 percent, statistically significant at the 1 percent level. By comparison, of the defendants who resided in states that passed three-strikes laws but who were arrested for felonies other than three-strikes crimes, the proportion prosecuted for misdemeanors stayed roughly constant, moving from 12.9 percent before the passage of the three-strikes laws to 12.2 percent after their passage. This means that, relative to other felony defendants,

Table 4 Probability of being Prosecuted for a Misdemeanor

Defendants	Prelaw		Postlaw		
	N	Coefficient	*N*	Coefficient	Difference
Arrested for three-strikes crime	1,289	.055 (.007)	437	.093 (.014)	.038** (.015)
Arrested for "other" felony	15,281	.129 (.003)	6,448	.122 (.004)	−.007 (.005)
Difference in difference					.045** (.016)

** Significant at the 1% level.

defendants arrested for three-strikes crimes became 4.5 percentage points more likely to be prosecuted for a lesser misdemeanor charge following the imposition of three-strikes laws. This increase is statistically significant at the 1 percent level.

Of all the three-strikes laws passed throughout the time period examined here, California's was not only one of the most broadly targeted but also one of the most severe in terms of the penalties it prescribed. Because of this, any behavioral changes by California prosecutors or other actors in the California judicial system in response to this law may have been significantly larger than analogous changes in other states. California also contributes the most three-strikes defendants to the data set. It is important to assess whether the estimates in Table 4 are simply picking up radical changes in California. However, this does not appear to be the case. The changes in prosecution charges following the implementation of a three-strikes law in California are similar to those in the other three-strikes states. Hence, the results shown in Table 4 do not appear to be driven solely by changes in the California judicial process following the imposition of the three-strikes laws.

IV WHY DO PROSECUTORS LESSEN PROSECUTION CHARGES FOR THREE-STRIKES ARRESTEES?

The findings presented above show that three-strikes arrestees become more likely to be prosecuted for lesser charges when conviction for their arrest charge would lead to sentencing under a three-strikes mandatory minimum sentencing law. This finding is certainly consistent with many of the studies discussed previously that emphasize prosecutors' (or prosecutor offices') attempting to circumvent mandatory minimum sentencing laws for some defendants because of their own preferences and constraints. However, it may also be true that these apparent changes in prosecutor behavior are simply an outcome or response to changes in criminal, police, judge, jury, and/or defense attorney behavior. This section attempts to examine this issue in more detail.

A. Direct Evidence Concerning Prosecutorial Discretion

The California three-strikes law not only covers a broader range of defendants and proscribes harsher sentences than most other states, but it also provides prosecutors with another method for circumventing the three-strikes law not generally available (at least officially) in other states. Specifically, California prosecutors can circumvent the California three-strikes law unofficially, by lessening the prosecution charge in the manner described above, or officially, by dropping a previous felony conviction, or "strike."

Jennifer Edwards Walsh examines the criteria California prosecutors use when deciding for whom to apply this added discretion over previous strikes. In a direct survey of district attorney offices in 25 of the 58 California counties (accounting for over 75 percent of the state's total share of three-strikes convictions), Walsh finds that 92 percent of the district attorney offices had used their discretion to drop a strike in a three-strikes case. The most common reason given by the district attorney offices for why they would choose to strike a previous three-strikes conviction in a three-strikes case was that the arrest offense "was trivial in nature" (74 percent), followed by the prior strike's being "remote in time" (65 percent), "defendant has no recent criminal history" (65 percent), and "prior strikes all from singular incident" (65 percent) "Case likely to end in acquittal" placed eighth out of the 10 choices, with 43.5 percent. Hence, California prosecutors choose to circumvent the three-strikes law by striking previous strike convictions for defendants who are arrested for lesser crimes and have more remote and less serious criminal histories.

If it is believed that prosecutors use criteria similar to these when choosing to lessen prosecution charges, then Walsh's findings support the notion that the changes in prosecution charge outcomes shown in the previous section are the result of prosecutors attempting to circumvent three-strikes laws because of their own constraints and preferences. Given the relative strength of the California law, and if prosecutors use their charging discretion to circumvent three-strikes laws, then why do California prosecutors not appear to change their prosecution behavior more drastically than prosecutors in other three-strikes states?

The answer to this question may be that this ability to drop a previous strike means that even if California prosecutors attempt to circumvent their three-strikes law more often than prosecutors in other states, they are not necessarily more likely to lessen prosecution charges in order to do so, as they have this other official method at their disposal. However, it is certainly possible that prosecutors in states other than California find less official ways to drop prior strikes in order to mitigate the impact of three-strikes laws.

Therefore, the foregoing discussion simply reveals that lessening prosecution charges may be one of several ways in which prosecutors can use their discretion in an effort to circumvent three-strikes laws. Therefore, the similarity between changes in prosecution practices in California and other three-strikes states is not necessarily surprising.

B. Changes in Criminal and Police Behavior

One stated motivation for three-strikes laws has often been to increase the expected sentence for repeat offenders committing serious crimes in order to deter them from committing another serious crime. Given this deterrence goal, the question can be asked whether the increase in the proportion of three-strikes defendants prosecuted for misdemeanors following the imposition of the three-strikes laws reflects changes in the behavior of some repeat criminals and/or changes in police arresting behavior, not prosecutors attempting to circumvent the laws. For example, if the laws deter repeat offenders from committing the more serious three-strikes crimes, then the group arrested for three-strikes crimes should comprise a "less severe" group of offenders after the law. Then, even if prosecutors do not change their behavior concerning how "serious" a repeat-offender defendant must be in order to be prosecuted for a felony, a greater proportion of defendants arrested for three-strikes crimes would be prosecuted for misdemeanors following the imposition of three-strikes laws. Hence, rather than a changing severity standard necessary to be prosecuted for a three-strikes crime, deterrence effects that result in compositional changes in the group arrested for three-strikes crimes could possibly explain the findings shown in Table 4.

However, the deterrence effects of three-strikes laws are more likely to work in the opposite direction than just posited. Three-strikes laws should arguably have a greater deterrence effect on repeat offenders thinking of committing less serious three-strikes crimes since the lesser crimes are presumably only marginally worthwhile without the law. Therefore, if anything, the group of three-strikes defendants is likely to be composed of offenders committing more serious crimes after the law. Without changes to prosecutor behavior, such a compositional change would lead to fewer three-strikes arrestees being prosecuted for misdemeanors after the law—a result inconsistent with the results shown in Table 4.

More generally, we can see if the relative proportion of all those arrested for three-strikes crimes falls after the imposition of the three-strikes laws by regressing the proportion of defendants in the data set who were arrested for three-strikes crimes in each year in each state on a dummy for whether a three-strikes law had yet been passed in that state, a dummy for whether a three-strikes law was ever passed in that state, and year dummies. The coefficient on the dummy variable for whether a three-strikes law had yet been passed is insignificantly different from zero, which indicates that the proportion of defendants arrested for three-strikes crimes in a state did not change significantly after the passage of a three-strikes law.

There are very few significant changes in the characteristics of defendants arrested for three-strikes crimes following the imposition of the three-strikes laws. In fact, relative to contemporaneous changes in the composition of the group of defendants arrested for other felonies in three-strikes states, the passage of three-strikes laws did not significantly alter the composition of the group arrested for three-strikes crimes on any relevant dimension except that a slightly greater proportion was arrested for drug crimes. However, this increase is not large enough to account for the change in prosecutor behavior. This means the increase in the proportion of three-strikes arrestees arrested for drug crimes following the imposition of three-strikes laws does not drive the earlier findings concerning changes in misdemeanor prosecutions.

While this evidence is clearly not conclusive of three-strikes laws' having no deterrence effects, a lack of deterrence is plausible for several reasons. First, the particulars of each of the laws may make it difficult for repeat serious offenders to be able to properly calculate the change in the expected cost to further criminal behavior. Moreover, it may take several years for criminals to adjust their behavior to changes in sentencing policy, and these deterrence effects may not have had time to manifest themselves postlaw in the time frame available with these data. Finally, repeat offenders may discount their future so heavily and/or be such poor decision makers that even substantial changes in sentencing do not affect their behavior.

C. Changes in Judge and Jury Behavior

Another argument concerning the results shown in Table 4 is that these results may not be due to prosecutors' using their discretion to circumvent the laws for some defendants but rather to prosecutors' adjusting their behavior in response to changes in judge and/or jury behavior. Specifically, juries may react to a three-strikes law by becoming less likely to convict all defendants prosecuted for three-strikes crimes after the passage of the law. Similarly, judges may react to the law by using their control over the judicial proceedings to make it more difficult to convict any defendant prosecuted for three-strikes crimes after the passage of the law.

If it is true that changes in judge or jury behavior cause the conviction rates for three-strikes prosecutions to fall following the imposition of three-strikes laws, then prosecutors may decide to prosecute a greater proportion of three-strikes arrestees for misdemeanors not to avoid the law but rather to avoid the now uniformly higher acquittal probability associated with three-strikes prosecution charges. To attempt to evaluate if this explanation is true, I first examine whether individuals prosecuted for a three-strikes crime are more likely to be acquitted at trial following the imposition of three-strikes laws.

Defendants arrested for three-strikes crimes are no more likely to be acquitted at trial after the imposition of the three-strikes laws. Moreover, the other specifications show that this result is true even after controlling for a variety of other defendant characteristics that may affect conviction rates and may be changing over time owing to changes in which defendants prosecutors decide to bring to trial.

While these results are consistent with the hypothesis that judges and juries do not change their behavior with respect to convicting three-strikes defendants after the passage of three-strikes laws, they are not necessarily conclusive. Specifically, if prosecutors alter their decision of who to bring before a jury in response to juries becoming less likely to convict defendants being prosecuted for three-strikes crimes, then it is still possible that conviction rates for three-strikes defendants would not change drastically following the implementation of the laws.

D. Changes in Defense Attorney Behavior

Another possibility is that three-strikes arrestees become more likely to be prosecuted for misdemeanors after the imposition of three-strikes laws is not because of any changes in prosecutor behavior but because of changes in defense attorney behavior. More specifically, prosecutors may have offered misdemeanor plea bargain opportunities at similar rates before and after the imposition of the three-strikes laws but because of the longer sentences associated with conviction for three-strikes crimes following the imposition of three-strikes laws, defense lawyers (and their clients) may simply become more likely to accept these misdemeanor plea bargain offers after the imposition of three-strikes laws. It is then this higher acceptance rate that accounts for the increased likelihood that three-strikes arrestees are prosecuted for misdemeanors following the imposition of the three-strikes laws.

Those defendants arrested for three-strikes crimes did not become any more likely to resolve their cases through plea bargaining after the passage of a three-strikes law.

It is possible that defense lawyers became more willing to accept plea bargains following the passage of the three-strikes laws but that prosecutors became less likely to offer them. Such behavior could potentially explain the lack of change in the fraction of cases resolved through plea bargains discussed above. However, such a process would not account for the increase in the fraction of three-strikes arrestees being prosecuted for misdemeanors following the imposition of three-strikes laws. Therefore, it seems unlikely that the changes in prosecution charge outcomes observed in Table 4 are primarily due to changes in defense attorney behavior.

V SUMMARY AND CONCLUSION

This paper emphasizes the importance of accounting for prosecutorial discretion when analyzing the effects of mandatory minimum sentencing laws. In particular, prosecutors generally have the discretion to prosecute a defendant for a lesser charge than the initial arrest charge, and the use of such discretion can have dramatic effects on sentencing with respect to mandatory minimum sentencing laws, as conviction for a crime targeted by the sentencing law can result in a substantially different sentence than a conviction for a lesser but related crime not covered by the law.

In analyzing the use of this type of prosecutorial discretion with respect to several three-strikes-type sentencing laws implemented throughout the 1990s, I find that prosecutors become almost twice as likely to lower a felony arrest charge to a misdemeanor for the purposes of prosecution when conviction on the initial arrest charge would have lead to sentencing under a three-strikes law. Moreover, the available evidence suggests that prosecutors generally initiate such behavior because of their own preferences and resource constraints, not as a reaction to changes in behavior by criminals, judges, juries, or defense lawyers. However, such behavioral changes by these other actors in the judicial system cannot be ruled out, and a more explicit examination of these actors provides an important avenue for further research.

Taking into account this use of prosecutorial discretion was also shown to have very important implications for estimating the average effect these three-strikes laws have on sentencing. In particular, while I find that the three-strikes laws examined here appear to significantly increase the average sentence for being arrested for a three-strikes crime, failing to take into account prosecutorial discretion over prosecution charges will lead to overstating this increase by almost 30 percent. Therefore, this paper reveals not only that prosecutors do alter their discretionary behavior in response to three-strikes laws but also that this increased use of discretion has substantive and meaningful implications for analyzing the overall effects of these laws on sentencing.

In generalizing these findings to other mandatory minimum sentencing laws, it is worth noting that three-strikes laws target individuals arrested for serious crimes with extensive criminal histories. Since prosecutors may be less inclined to let these serious offenders back out on the street, the use of prosecutor discretion to circumvent three-strikes laws may be much more rare than the use of prosecutor discretion to circumvent mandatory minimum sentences targeting less serious crimes, such as drug or firearm possession. Hence, the effects of prosecutorial discretion with respect to three-strikes sentencing laws may provide a lower bound on the degree to which prosecutor discretion is used to mitigate the effects of mandatory minimum sentencing laws.

The findings of this paper suggest that, besides some of the ethical concerns that have been raised concerning certain mandatory minimum sentencing laws, these laws may also be associated with pushing judicial discretion to less visible parts of the judicial system. Moreover, where advocates of mandatory minimum sentencing laws argue that such laws can decrease sentencing variation across criminals who commit similar crimes (and have similar criminal histories) and eradicate overly lenient sentencing, such arguments do not appear to be completely true, as prosecutorial discretion over the prosecution charge can possibly lead to even more variation in sentencing and certainly will lead to even shorter sentences for some individuals than would have occurred without such laws. Therefore, if society desires to systematically increase the sentences for criminals who commit certain crimes, policies that allow for judges to retain some flexibility, such as the Federal Sentencing Commission Guidelines, which give sentencing ranges and allow deviations from the guidelines if the reasons are specified, may be a more effective and transparent means of reaching this objective.

DISCUSSION QUESTIONS

1. In what ways do prosecutors circumvent the intended legislation of three-strikes or repeat offender minimum mandatory sentencing guidelines?
2. How does prosecutorial discretion affect the overstating of laws on average sentencing?
3. Why did Congress repeal the mandatory federal sentences for drug offenses in 1970?
4. How do "other" crimes cause any estimated difference in classification of three-strikes arrests?
5. What ethical concerns are raised because of prosecutorial discretion?

BIBLIOGRAPHY

Anderson, James M.; Kling, Jeffrey R.; and Stith, Kate. "Measuring Interjudge Sentencing Disparity: Before and after the Federal Sentencing Guidelines." *Journal of Law and Economics* 42 (1999): 271–307.

Andreoni, James. "Reasonable Doubt and the Optimal Magnitude of Fines: Should the Penalty Fit the Crime?" *RAND Journal of Economics* 22 (1991): 385–95.

Becker, Gary S. "Crime and Punishment: An Economic Approach." *Journal of Political Economy* 76 (1968): 169–217.

Blumstein, Alfred; Cohen, Jacqueline; Martin, Susan E.; and Tonry, Michael, eds. *Research on Sentencing: The Search for Reform.* Washington, D.C.: National Academy Press, 1983.

Bureau of Justice Assistance. National Assessment of Structured Sentencing. Washington, D.C.: U.S. Department of Justice, 1996.

Clark, John; Austin, James; and Henry, D. Alan. *Three Strikes and You're Out: A Review of State Legislation.* Washington D.C.: National Institute of Justice, September 1997.

Eisenstein, James; Flemming, Roy B.; and Nardulli, Peter F. *The Contours of Justice: Communities and Their Courts.* Boston: Little, Brown, 1988.

Franzoni, Luigi Alberto. "Negotiated Enforcement and Credible Deterrence." *Economic Journal* 109 (1999): 509–35.

Kessler Daniel P., and Piehl, Anne Morrison. "The Role of Discretion in the Criminal Justice System." *Journal of Law, Economics, and Organization* 14 (1998): 256–76.

Knapp, Kay A. "Arizona: Unprincipled Sentencing, Mandatory Minimums, and Prison Crowding." *Overcrowded Times* 2 (1991): 10–12.

LaCasse, Chantale, and Payne, A. Abigail. "Federal Sentencing Guidelines and Mandatory Minimum Sentences: Do Defendants Bargain in the Shadow of the Judge?" *Journal of Law and Economics* 42 (1999): 245–70.

Loftin, Colin; Heumann, Milton; and McDowall, David. "Mandatory Sentencing and Firearms Violence: Evaluating an Alternative to Gun Control." *Law and Society Review* 17 (1983): 287–318.

Marvell, Thomas B., and Moody, Carlisle. "The Lethal Effects of Three-Strikes Laws." *Journal of Legal Studies* 30 (2001): 89–106.

Nelson, Blake. "The Minnesota Sentencing Guidelines: The Effects of Determinate Sentencing on Disparities in Sentencing Decisions." *Law and Inequality* 10 (1992): 217–51.

Shepherd, Joanna M. "Fear of the First Strike: The Full Deterrent Effect of California's Two- and Three-Strikes Legislation." *Journal of Legal Studies* 31 (2002): 159–201.

Tonry, Michael. *Sentencing Matters.* New York: Oxford University Press, 1996.

U.S. Department of Justice. Bureau of Justice Statistics. *State Court Processing Statistics, 1990–2000: Felony Defendants in Large Urban Counties* (computer file). Conducted by the Pretrial Services Resource Center. 2nd ICPSR ed. Ann Arbor, Mich.: Inter-university Consortium for Political and Social Research, 2000.

United States Sentencing Commission. *Special Report to the Congress: Mandatory Minimum Penalties in the Federal Criminal Justice System*. Washington D.C.: The Commission, 1991.

Walsh, Jennifer Edwards. "'In the Furtherance of Justice': The Effect of Discretion on the Implementation of California's Three Strikes Law." Paper presented at the American Political Science Association annual meeting, Atlanta, September 2–5, 1999.

16

The Practice of Law as Confidence Game

Organization Co-Optation of a Profession

Abraham S. Blumberg

Central to the adversary system is the defense attorney, who will engage the prosecution in a "fight" to ensure that the defendant's rights are protected and that the case is presented to the judge and jury in the best possible light. What happens when the professional environment of the criminal lawyer moderates the adversarial stance? Bargain justice occurs when it is believed to be in the best interests of both the prosecutor and the defense to avoid the courtroom confrontation. Abraham Blumberg argues that the defense attorney acts as a double agent, to get the defendant to plead guilty.

Source: "The Practice of Law as Confidence Game: Organization Co-Optation of a Profession" by Abraham S. Blumberg. Law and Society Review 1: 15–39.

A recurring theme in the growing dialogue between sociology and law has been the great need for a joint effort of the two disciplines to illuminate urgent social and legal issues. Having uttered fervent public pronouncements in this vein, however, the respective practitioners often go their separate ways. Academic spokesmen for the legal profession are somewhat critical of sociologists of law because of what they perceive as the sociologist's preoccupation with the application of theory and methodology to the examination of legal phenomena, without regard to the solution of legal problems. Further, it is felt that "contemporary writing in the sociology of law . . . betrays the existence of painfully unsophisticated notions about the day-to-day operations of courts, legislatures, and law offices." Regardless of the merit of such criticism, scant attention—apart from explorations of the legal profession itself—has been given to the sociological examination of legal institutions, or their supporting ideological assumptions. Thus, for example, very little sociological effort is expended to ascertain the validity and viability of important court decisions, which may rest on wholly erroneous assumptions about the contextual realities of social structure. A particular decision may rest upon a legally impeccable rationale; at the same time it may be rendered nugatory or self-defeating by contingencies imposed by aspects of social reality of which the lawmakers are themselves unaware.

Within this context, I wish to question the impact of three recent landmark decisions of the United States Supreme Court, each hailed as destined to effect profound changes in the future of criminal law administration and enforcement in America. The first of these, *Gideon* v. *Wainwright*, 372 U.S. 335 (1963), required states and localities henceforth to furnish counsel in the case of indigent persons charged with a felony. The Gideon ruling left several major issues unsettled, among them the vital question: What is the precise point in time at which a suspect is entitled to counsel? The answer came relatively quickly in *Escobedo* v. *Illinois*, 378 U.S. 478 (1964), which has aroused a storm of controversy. Danny Escobedo confessed to the murder of his brother-in-law after the police had refused to permit retained counsel to see him, although his lawyer was present in the station house and asked to confer with his client. In a 5 to 4 decision, the court asserted that counsel must be permitted when the process of police investigative efforts shifts from merely investigatory to that of accusatory: "when its focus is on the accused and its purpose is to elicit a confession—our adversary system begins to operate, and, under the circumstances here, the accused must be permitted to consult with his lawyer."

As a consequence, Escobedo's confession was rendered inadmissible. The decision triggered a national debate among police, district attorneys, judges, lawyers, and other law-enforcement officials, which continues unabated, as to the value and propriety of confessions in criminal cases. On June 13, 1966, the Supreme Court in a 5 to 4 decision underscored the principle enunciated in *Escobedo* in the case of *Miranda* v. *Arizona*. Police interrogation of any suspect in custody, without his consent, unless a defense attorney is present, is prohibited by the self-incrimination provision of the Fifth Amendment.

Regardless of the relative merit of the various shades of opinion about the role of counsel in criminal cases, the issues generated thereby will be in part resolved as additional cases move toward decision in the Supreme Court in the near future. They are of peripheral interest and not of immediate concern in this paper. However, the *Gideon, Escobedo*, and *Miranda* cases pose interesting general questions. In all three decisions, the Supreme Court reiterates the traditional legal conception of a defense lawyer based on the ideological perception of a criminal case as an *adversary, combative* proceeding, in which counsel for the defense assiduously musters all the admittedly limited resources at his command to *defend* the accused. The fundamental question remains to be answered: Does the Supreme Court's conception of the role of counsel in a criminal case square with social reality?

The task of this paper is to furnish some preliminary evidence toward the illumination of that question. Little empirical understanding of the function of defense counsel exists; only some ideologically oriented generalizations and commitments. This paper is based upon observations made by the writer during many years of legal practice in the criminal courts of a large metropolitan area. No claim is made as to its methodological rigor, although it does reflect a conscious and sustained effort for participant observation.

★ ★ ★

COURT STRUCTURE DEFINES ROLE OF DEFENSE LAWYER

The overwhelming majority of convictions in criminal cases (usually over 90 percent) are not the product of a combative, trial-by-jury process at all, but instead merely involve the sentencing of the individual after a negotiated, bargained-for plea of guilty has been entered. Although more recently the overzealous role of police and prosecutors in producing pretrial confessions and admissions has achieved a good deal of notoriety, scant attention has been paid to the organizational structure and personnel of the criminal court itself. Indeed, the extremely high conviction rate produced without the features of an adversary trial in our courts would tend to suggest that the "trial" becomes a perfunctory reiteration and validation of the pretrial interrogation and investigation.

The institutional setting of the court defines a role for the defense counsel in a criminal case radically different from the one traditionally depicted. Sociologists and others have focused their attention on the deprivations and social disabilities of such variables as race, ethnicity, and social class as being the source of an accused person's defeat in a criminal court. Largely overlooked is the variable of the court organization itself, which possesses a thrust, purpose, and direction of its own. It is grounded in pragmatic values, bureaucratic priorities, and administrative instruments. These exalt maximum production and the particularistic career designs of organizational incumbents, whose occupational and career commitments tend to generate a set of priorities. These priorities exert a higher claim than the stated ideological goals of "due process of law," and are often inconsistent with them.

Organizational goals and discipline impose a set of demands and conditions of practice on the respective professions in the criminal court to which they respond by abandoning their ideological and professional commitments to the accused client, in the service of these higher claims of the court organization. All court personnel, including the accused's own lawyer, tend to be co-opted to become agent-mediators who help the accused redefine his situation and restructure his perceptions concomitant with a plea of guilty.

Of all the occupational roles in the court, the only private individual who is officially recognized as having a special status and concomitant obligations is the lawyer. His legal status is that of "an officer of the court" and he is held to a standard of ethical performance and duty to his client as well as to the court. This obligation is thought to be far higher than expected of ordinary individuals occupying the various occupational statuses in the court community. However, lawyers, whether privately retained or of the legal-aid, public defender variety, have close and continuing relations with the prosecuting office and the court itself through discreet relations with the judges via their law secretaries or "confidential" assistants. Indeed, lines of communication, influence, and contact with those offices, as well as with the Office of the Clerk of the Court, the Probation Division, and the press, are essential to present and prospective requirements of criminal law practice. Similarly, the subtle involvement of the press and other mass media in the court's organizational network is not readily discernible to the casual observer. Accused persons come and go in the court system schema, but the structure and its occupational incumbents remain to carry on their respective career, occupational, and organizational enterprises. The individual stridencies, tensions, and conflicts a given accused person's case may present to all the participants are overcome, because the formal and informal relations of all the groups in the court setting require it. The probability of continued future relations and interaction must be preserved at all costs.

This is particularly true of the "lawyer regulars"—that is, those defense lawyers, who by virtue of their continuous appearances in behalf of defendants, tend to represent the bulk of a criminal court's nonindigent case work load, and those lawyers who are not "regulars," who appear almost casually in behalf of an occasional client. Some of the lawyer "regulars" are highly visible as one moves about the major urban centers of the nation; their offices line the back streets of the courthouses, at times sharing space with bondsmen. Their political "visibility" in terms of local clubhouse ties, reaching into the judge's chambers and the prosecutor's office, is also deemed essential to successful practitioners. Previous research has indicated that the "lawyer regulars" make no effort to conceal their dependence upon police, bondsmen, and jail personnel. Nor do they conceal the necessity for maintaining intimate relations with all levels of personnel in the court setting as a means of obtaining, maintaining, and building their practice. These informal relations are the *sine qua non* not only of retaining a practice but also in the negotiation of pleas and sentences.

The client, then, is a secondary figure in the court system as in certain other bureaucratic settings. He becomes a means to other ends of the organization's incumbents. He may present doubts, contingencies, and pressures which challenge existing informal arrangements or disrupt them; but these tend to be resolved in favor of the continuance of the organization and its relations as before. There is a greater community of interest among all the principal organizational structures and their incumbents than exists elsewhere in other settings. The accused's lawyer has far greater professional, economic, intellectual, and other ties to the various elements of the court system than he does to his own client. In short, the court is a closed community.

This is more than just the case of the usual "secrets" of bureaucracy which are fanatically defended from an outside view. Even all elements of the press are zealously determined to report on that which will not offend the board of judges, the prosecutor, and probation, legal-aid, or other officials, in return for privileges and courtesies granted in the past and to be granted in the future. Rather than any view of the matter in terms of some variation of a "conspiracy" hypothesis, the simple explanation is one of an ongoing system handling delicate tensions, managing the trauma produced by law enforcement and administration, and requiring almost pathological distrust of "outsiders" bordering on group paranoia.

The hostile attitude toward "outsiders" is in large measure engendered by a defensiveness itself produced by the inherent deficiencies of assembly-line justice, so characteristic of our major criminal courts. Intolerably large caseloads of defendants, which must be disposed of in an organizational context of limited resources and personnel, potentially subject the participants in the court community to harsh scrutiny from appellate courts and other public and private sources of condemnation. As a consequence, an almost irreconcilable conflict is posed in terms of intense pressures to process large numbers of cases, on the one hand, and the stringent ideological and legal requirements of "due process of law," on the other hand. A rather tenuous resolution of the dilemma has emerged in the shape of a large variety of bureaucratically ordained and controlled "work crimes," shortcuts, deviations, and outright rule violations adopted as court practice in order to meet production norms. Fearfully anticipating criticism on ethical as well as legal grounds, all the significant participants in the court's social structure are bound into an organized system of complicity. This consists of a work arrangement in which the patterned, covert, informal breaches and evasions of "due process" are institutionalized but are, nevertheless, denied to exist.

These institutionalized evasions will be found to occur to some degree in all criminal courts. Their nature, scope, and complexity are largely determined by the size of the court and the character of the community in which it is located—for example, whether it is a large, urban institution or a relatively small rural county court. In addition, idiosyncratic, local conditions may contribute to a unique flavor in the character and quality of the criminal law's administration in a particular community. However, in most instances a variety of stratagems are employed—some subtle, some crude, ineffectively disposing of what are often too-large caseloads. A wide variety of coercive devices are employed against an accused client, couched in a depersonalized, instrumental, bureaucratic version of due process of law, and which are in reality a perfunctory obeisance to the ideology of due process. These include some very explicit pressures which are exerted in some measure by all court personnel, including judges, to plead guilty and avoid trial. In many instances the sanction of a potentially harsh sentence is utilized as the visible alternative to pleading guilty, in the case of recalcitrants. Probation and psychiatric reports are "tailored" to organizational needs, or are at least responsive to the court organization's requirements for the refurbishment of a defendant's social biography, consonant with his new status. A resourceful judge can, through his subtle domination of the proceedings, impose his will on the final outcome of a trial. Stenographers and clerks, in their function as record keepers, are on occasion pressed into service in support of a judicial need to "rewrite" the record of a courtroom event. Bail practices are usually employed for purposes other than simply assuring a defendant's presence on the date of a hearing in connection with his case. Too often, the discretionary power as to bail is part of the arsenal of weapons available to collapse the resistance of an accused person. The foregoing is a most cursory examination of some of the more prominent "shortcuts" available to any court organization. There are numerous other procedural strategies constituting due process deviations, which tend to become the work-style artifacts of a court's personnel. Thus, only court "regulars" who are "bound in" are really accepted; others are treated routinely and in almost a coldly correct manner.

The defense attorneys, therefore, whether of the legal-aid, public defender variety or privately retained, although operating in terms of pressures specific to their respective role and organizational obligations, ultimately are concerned with strategies which tend to lead to a plea. It is the rational, impersonal elements involving economies of time, labor, expense, and a superior commitment of the defense counsel to these rationalistic values of maximum production of court organization that prevail in his relationship with a client. The lawyer "regulars" are frequently former staff members of the prosecutor's office and utilize the prestige, know-how, and contacts of their former affiliation as part of their stock-in-trade. Close and continuing relations between the lawyer "regular" and his former colleagues in the prosecutor's office generally overshadow the relationship between the regular and his client. The continuing colleagueship of supposedly adversary counsel rests on real professional and organizational needs of a *quid pro quo*, which goes beyond the limits of an accommodation or *modus vivendi* one might ordinarily expect under the circumstances of an otherwise seemingly adversary relationship. Indeed, the adversary features which are manifest are for the most part muted and exist even in their attenuated form largely for external consumption. The principals, lawyer and assistant district attorney, rely upon one another's cooperation for their continued professional existence, and so the bargaining between them tends usually to be "reasonable" rather than fierce.

FEE COLLECTION AND FIXING

The real key to understanding the role of defense counsel in a criminal case is to be found in the area of the fixing of the fee to be charged and its collection. The problem of fixing and collecting the fee tends to influence to a significant degree the criminal court process itself, and not just the relationship of the lawyer and his client. In essence, a lawyer–client "confidence game" is played. A true confidence game is unlike the case of the emperor's new clothes wherein that monarch's nakedness was a result of inordinate gullibility and credulity. In a genuine confidence game, the perpetrator manipulates the basic dishonesty of his partner, the victim or mark, toward his own (the confidence operator's) ends. Thus, "the victim of a con scheme must have some larceny in his heart."

Legal service lends itself particularly well to confidence games. Usually, a plumber will be able to demonstrate empirically that he has performed a service by clearing up the stuffed drain, repairing the leaky faucet or pipe—and therefore merits his fee. He has rendered, when summoned, a visible, tangible boon for his client in return for the requested fee. A physician, who has not performed some visible surgery or otherwise engaged in some readily discernible procedure in connection with a patient, may be deemed by the patient to have "done nothing" for him. As a consequence, medical practitioners may simply prescribe or administer by injection a placebo to overcome a patient's potential reluctance or dissatisfaction in paying a requested fee, "for nothing."

In the practice of law there is a special problem in this regard, no matter what the level of the practitioner or his place in the hierarchy of prestige. Much legal work is intangible either because it is simply a few words of advice, some preventive action, a telephone call, negotiation of some kind, a form filled out and filed, a hurried conference with another attorney or an official of a government agency, a letter or opinion written, or a countless variety of seemingly innocuous and even prosaic procedures and actions. These are the basic activities, apart from any possible court appearance, of almost all lawyers, at all levels of practice. Much of the activity is not in the nature of the exercise of the traditional, precise professional skills of the attorney such as library research and oral argument in connection with appellate briefs, court motions, trial work, drafting of opinions, memoranda, contracts, and other complex documents and agreements. Instead, much legal activity, whether it is at the lowest or highest "white shoe" law firm levels, is of the brokerage, agent, sales representative, lobbyist type of activity, in which the lawyer acts for someone else in pursuing the latter's interests and designs. The service is intangible.

The large-scale law firm may not speak as openly of their "contacts," their "fixing" abilities, as does the lower-level lawyer. They trade instead upon a facade of thick carpeting, walnut paneling, genteel low pressure, and superficialities of traditional legal professionalism. There are occasions when even the large firm is on the defensive in connection with the fees they charge because the services rendered or results obtained do not appear to merit the fee asked. Therefore, there is a recurrent problem in the legal profession in fixing the amount of fee and in justifying the basis for the requested fee.

Although the fee at times amounts to what the traffic and the conscience of the lawyer will bear, one further observation must be made with regard to the size of the fee and its collection. The defendant in a criminal case and the material gain he may have acquired during the course of his illicit activities are soon parted. Not infrequently the ill-gotten fruits of the various modes of larceny are sequestered by a defense lawyer in payment of his fee. Inexorably, the amount of the fee is a function of the dollar value of the crime committed and is frequently set with meticulous precision at a sum which bears an uncanny relationship to that of the net proceeds of the particular offense involved. On occasion, defendants have been known to commit additional offenses while at liberty on bail, in order to secure the requisite funds with which to meet their obligations for payment of legal fees. Defense lawyers condition even the most obtuse clients to recognize that there is a firm interconnection between fee payment and the zealous exercise of professional expertise, secret knowledge, and organizational "connections" in their behalf. Lawyers, therefore, seek to keep their clients in a proper state of tension, and to arouse in time the precise edge of anxiety which is calculated to encourage prompt fee payment. Consequently, the client attitude in the relationship between defense counsel and an accused is in many instances a precarious admixture of hostility, mistrust, dependence, and sycophancy. By keeping his client's anxieties aroused to the proper pitch, and establishing a seemingly causal relationship between a requested fee and the accused's ultimate extrication from his onerous difficulties, the lawyer will have established the necessary preliminary groundwork to assure a minimum of haggling over the fee and its eventual payment.

In varying degrees, as a consequence, all law practice involves a manipulation of the client and a stage management of the lawyer–client relationship so that at least an *appearance* of help and service will be forthcoming. This is accomplished in a variety of ways, often exercised in combination with each other. At the outset, the lawyer-professional employs with suitable variation a measure of sales puff which may range from an air of unbounding self-confidence, adequacy, and dominion over events, to that of complete arrogance. This will be supplemented by the affectation of a studied, faultless mode of personal attire. In the larger firms, the furnishings and office trappings will serve as the backdrop to help in impression management and client intimidation. In all firms, solo or large-scale, an access to secret knowledge and to the seats of power and influences is inferred, or presumed to a varying degree as the basic vendable commodity of the practitioners.

The lack of visible end product offers a special complication in the course of the professional life of the criminal court lawyer with respect to his fee and in his relations with his client. The plain fact is that an accused in a criminal case always "loses" even when he has been exonerated by an acquittal, discharge, or dismissal of his case. The hostility of an accused which follows as a consequence of his arrest, incarceration, possible loss of job, expense, and other traumas connected with his case is directed, by means of displacement, toward his lawyer. It is in this sense that it may be said that a criminal lawyer never really "wins" a case. The really satisfied client is rare, since in the very nature of the situation even an accused's vindication leaves him with some degree of dissatisfaction and hostility. It is this state of affairs that makes for a lawyer–client relationship in the criminal court which tends to be a somewhat exaggerated version of the usual lawyer–client confidence game.

At the outset, because there are great risks of nonpayment of the fee, due to the impecuniousness of his clients, and the fact that a man who is sentenced to jail may be a singularly unappreciative client, the criminal lawyer collects his fee *in advance*. Often, because the lawyer and the accused both have questionable designs of their own upon each other, the confidence game can be played. The criminal lawyer must serve three major functions, or stated another way, he must solve three problems. First, he must arrange for his fee; second, he must prepare and then, if necessary, "cool out" his client in case of defeat (a highly likely contingency); third, he must satisfy the court organization that he has performed adequately in the process of negotiating the plea, so as to preclude the possibility of any sort of embarrassing incident which may serve to invite "outside" scrutiny.

In assuring the attainment of one of his primary objectives, his fee, the criminal lawyer will very often enter into negotiations with the accused's kin, including collateral relatives. In many instances, the accused himself is unable to pay any sort of fee or anything more than a token fee. It then becomes important to involve as many of the accused's kin as possible in the situation. This is especially so if the attorney hopes to collect a significant part of a proposed substantial fee. It is not uncommon for several relatives to contribute toward the fee. The larger the group, the greater the possibility that the lawyer will collect a sizeable fee by getting contributions from each.

A fee for a felony case which ultimately results in a plea, rather than a trial, may ordinarily range anywhere from $550 to $1,500. Should the case go to trial, the fee will be proportionately larger, depending upon the length of the trial. But the larger the fee the lawyer wishes to exact, the more impressive his performance must be, in terms of his stage-managed image as personage of great influence and power in the court organization. Court personnel are keenly aware of the extent to which a lawyer's stock-in-trade involves the precarious stage management of an image which goes beyond the usual professional flamboyance, and for this reason alone the lawyer is "bound in" to the authority system of the court's organizational discipline. Therefore, to some extent, court personnel will aid the lawyer in the creation and maintenance of that impression. There is a tacit commitment to the lawyer by the court organization, apart from formal etiquette, to aid him in this. Such augmentation of the lawyer's stage-managed image as this affords is the partial basis for the *quid pro quo* which exists between the lawyer and the court organization. It tends to serve as the continuing basis for the higher loyalty of the lawyer to the organization; his relationship with his client, in contrast, is transient, ephemeral, and often superficial.

DEFENSE LAWYER AS DOUBLE AGENT

The lawyer has often been accused of stirring up unnecessary litigation, especially in the field of negligence. He is said to acquire a vested interest in a cause of action or claim which was initially his client's. The strong incentive of possible fee motivates the lawyer to promote litigation which would otherwise never have developed. However, the criminal lawyer develops a vested interest of an entirely different nature in his client's case: to limit its scope and duration rather than do battle. Only in this way can a case be "profitable." Thus, he enlists the aid of relatives not only to assure payment of his fee, but he will also rely on these persons to help him in his agent-mediator role of convincing the accused to plead guilty, and ultimately to help in "cooling out" the accused if necessary.

It is at this point that an accused-defendant may experience his first sense of "betrayal." While he had perhaps perceived the police and prosecutor to be adversaries, or possibly even the judge, the accused is wholly unprepared for his counsel's role performance as an agent-mediator. In the same vein, it is even less likely to occur to an accused that members of his own family or other kin may become agents, albeit at the behest and urging of other agents or mediators, acting on the principle that they are in reality helping an accused negotiate the best possible plea arrangement under the circumstances. Usually, it will be the lawyer who will activate next of kin in this role, his ostensible motive being to arrange for his fee. But soon latent and unstated motives will assert themselves with entreaties by counsel to the accused's next of kin to appeal to the accused to "help himself" by pleading. *Gemeinschaft* sentiments are to this extent exploited by a defense lawyer (or even at times by a district attorney) to achieve specific secular ends, that is, of concluding a particular matter with all possible dispatch.

The fee is often collected in stages, each installment usually payable prior to a necessary court appearance required during the course of an accused's career journey. At each stage, in his interviews and communications with the accused, or in addition, with members of his family, if they are helping with the fee payment, the lawyer employs an air of professional confidence and "insidedopesterism" in order to assuage anxieties on all sides. He makes the necessary bland assurances, and in effect manipulates his client, who is usually willing to do and say the things, true or not, which will help his attorney extricate him. Since the dimensions of what he is essentially selling, organizational influence and expertise, are not technically and precisely measurable, the lawyer can make extravagant claims of influence and secret knowledge with impunity. Thus, lawyers frequently claim to have inside knowledge in connection with information in the hands of the district attorney, police, or probation officials or to have access to these functionaries. Factually, they often do, and need only to exaggerate the nature of their relationships with them to obtain the desired effective impression upon the client. But, as in the genuine confidence game, the victim who has participated is loath to do anything which will upset the lesser plea which his lawyer has "conned" him into accepting.

In effect, in his role as double agent, the criminal lawyer performs an extremely vital and delicate mission for the court organization and the accused. Both principals are anxious to terminate the litigation with a minimum of expense and damage to each other. There is no other personage or role incumbent in the total court structure more strategically located, who by training and in terms of his own requirements, is more ideally suited to do so than the lawyer. In recognition of this, judges will cooperate with attorneys in many important ways. For example, they will adjourn the case of an accused in jail awaiting plea or sentence if the attorney requests such action. While explicitly this may be done for some innocuous and seemingly valid reason, the tacit purpose is that pressure is being applied by the attorney for the collection of his fee, which he knows will probably not be forthcoming if the case is concluded. Judges are aware of this tactic on the part of lawyers, who, by requesting an adjournment, keep an accused incarcerated a while longer as a not too subtle method of dunning a client for payment. However, the judges will go along with this, on the ground that important ends are being served. Often, the only end served is to protect a lawyer's fee.

The judge will help an accused's lawyer in still another way. He will lend the official aura of his office and courtroom so that a lawyer can stage-manage an impression of an "all-out" performance for the accused in justification of his fee. The judge and other court personnel will serve as a backdrop for a scene charged with dramatic fire, in which the accused's lawyer makes a stirring appeal in his behalf; with a show of restrained passion, the lawyer will intone the virtues of the accused and recite the social deprivations which have reduced him to his present stage. The speech varies somewhat, depending on whether the accused has been convicted after trial or has pleaded guilty. In the main, however, the incongruity, superficiality, and ritualistic character of the total performance is underscored by a visibly impassive, almost bored reaction on the part of the judge and other members of the court retinue.

Afterward, there is a hearty exchange of pleasantries between the lawyer and district attorney, wholly out of context in terms of the supposed adversary nature of the preceding events. The fiery passion in defense of his client is gone, and the lawyers for both sides resume their offstage relations, chatting amiably and perhaps including the judge in their restrained banter. No other aspect of their visible conduct so effectively serves to put even a casual observer on notice that these individuals have claims upon each other. These seemingly innocuous actions are indicative of continuing organizational and informal relations, which, in their intricacy and depth, range far beyond any priorities or claims a particular defendant may have.

Criminal law practice is a unique form of private law practice since it really only appears to be private practice. Actually it is bureaucratic practice, because of the legal practitioner's enmeshment in the authority, discipline, and perspectives of the court organization. Private practice, supposedly, in a professional sense, involves the maintenance of an organized, disciplined body of knowledge and learning; the individual practitioners are imbued with a spirit of autonomy and service, the earning of a livelihood being incidental. In the sense that the lawyer in the criminal court serves as a double agent, serving higher organizational rather than professional ends, he may be deemed to be engaged in bureaucratic rather than private practice. To some extent the lawyer-client "confidence game," in addition to its other functions, serves to conceal this fact.

THE CLIENT'S PERCEPTION

The "cop-out" ceremony, in which the court process culminates, is not only invaluable for redefining the accused's perspectives of himself, but also in reiterating publicly in a formally structured ritual the accused person's guilt for the benefit of significant "others" who are observing. The accused not only is made to assert publicly his guilt of a specific crime, but also a complete recital of its details. He is further made to indicate that he is entering his plea of guilt freely, willingly, and voluntarily, and that he is not doing so because of any promises or in consideration of any commitments that may have been made to him by anyone. This last is intended as a blanket statement to shield the participants from any possible charges of "coercion" or undue influence that may have been exerted in violation of due process requirements. Its function is to preclude any later review by an appellate court on these grounds, and also to obviate any second thoughts an accused may develop in connection with his plea.

However, for the accused, the conception of self as a guilty person is in large measure a temporary role adaptation. His career socialization as an accused, if it is successful, eventuates in his acceptance and redefinition of himself as a guilty person. However, the transformation is ephemeral, in that he will, in private, quickly reassert his innocence. Of importance is that he accept his defeat, publicly proclaim it, and find some measure of pacification in it. Almost immediately after his plea, a defendant will generally be interviewed by a representative of the probation division in connection with a presentence report which is to be prepared. The very first question to be asked of him by the probation officer is: "Are you guilty of the crime to which you pleaded?" This is by way of double affirmation of the defendant's guilt. Should the

Table 1 Defendant Responses as to Guilt or Innocence After Pleading Guilty (Years: 1962, 1963, 1964; $N = 724$)

Nature of Response		Number of Defendants
Innocent (manipulated)	"The lawyer, judge, police, or D.A. 'conned me' "	86
Innocent (pragmatic)	"Wanted to get it over with" "You can't beat the system" "They have you over a barrel when you have a record"	147
Innocent (advice of counsel)	"Followed my lawyer's advice"	92
Innocent (defiant)	"Framed"—Betrayed by "complainant," "police," "squealers," "lawyer," "friends," "wife," "girlfriend"	33
Innocent (adverse social data)	Blames probation officer or psychiatrist for "bad report," in cases where there was prepleading investigation	15
Guilty	"But I should have gotten a better deal" Blames lawyer, D.A., police, judge	74
Guilty	Won't say anything further	21
Fatalistic (doesn't press his "innocence," won't admit "guilt")	"I did it for convenience" "My lawyer told me it was only thing I could do" "I did it because it was the best way out"	248
No response		8
Total		724

defendant now begin to make bold assertions of his innocence, despite his plea of guilty, he will be asked to withdraw his plea and stand trial on the original charges. Such a threatened possibility is, in most instances, sufficient to cause an accused to let the plea stand and to request the probation officer to overlook his exclamations of innocence. Table 1 is a breakdown of the categorized responses of a random sample of male defendants in Metropolitan Court during 1962, 1963, and 1964 in connection with their statements during presentence probation interviews following their plea of guilty.

It would be well to observe at the outset that of the 724 defendants who pleaded guilty before trial, only 43 (5.94 percent) of the total group had confessed prior to their indictment. Thus, the ultimate judicial process was predicated upon evidence independent of any confession of the accused.

As the data indicate, only a relatively small number (95) out of the total number of defendants actually will even admit their guilt following the copout ceremony. However, even though they have affirmed their guilt, many of these defendants felt that they should have been able to negotiate a more favorable plea. The largest aggregate of defendants (373) were those who reasserted their "innocence" following their public profession of guilt during the cop-out ceremony. These defendants employed differential degrees of fervor, solemnity, and credibility, ranging from really mild, wavering assertions of innocence which were embroidered with a variety of stock explanations and rationalizations, to those of an adamant, "framed" nature. Thus, the "innocent" group, for the most part, were largely concerned with underscoring for their probation interviewer their essential "goodness" and "worthiness," despite their formal plea of guilty. Assertion of innocence at the postplea stage resurrects a more respectable and acceptable self-concept for the accused defendant who has pleaded guilty. A recital of the structural exigencies which precipitated his plea of guilt serves to embellish a newly professed claim of innocence, which many defendants mistakenly feel will stand them in good stead at the time of sentence, or ultimately with probation or parole authorities.

Relatively few (33) maintained their innocence in terms of having been "framed" by some person or agent-mediator, although a larger number (86) indicated that they had been manipulated or conned by an agent-mediator to plead guilty, but as indicated, their assertions of innocence were relatively mild.

A rather substantial group (147) preferred to stress the pragmatic aspects of their plea of guilty. They would only perfunctorily assert their innocence and would in general refer to some adverse aspect of their situation which they believed tended to negatively affect their bargaining leverage, including in some instances a prior criminal record.

One group of defendants (92), while maintaining their innocence, simply employed some variation of a theme of following "the advice of counsel" as a covering response to explain their guilty plea in the light of their new affirmation of innocence.

The largest single group of defendants (248) were basically fatalistic. They often verbalized weak suggestions of their innocence in rather halting terms, wholly without conviction. By the same token, they would not admit guilt readily and were generally evasive as to guilt or innocence, preferring to stress aspects of their stoic submission in their decision to plead. This sizeable group of defendants appeared to perceive the total court process as being caught up in a monstrous organizational apparatus, in which the defendant's role expectancies were not clearly defined. Reluctant to offend anyone in authority, fearful that clear-cut statements on their part as to their guilt or innocence would be negatively construed, they adopted a stance of passivity, resignation, and acceptance. Interestingly, they would in most instances invoke their lawyer as being the one who crystallized the available alternatives for them and who was therefore the critical element in their decision-making process.

In order to determine which agent-mediator was most influential in altering the accused's perspectives as to his decision to plead or go to trial (regardless of the proposed basis of the plea), the same sample of defendants were asked to indicate the person who first suggested to them that they plead guilty. They were also asked to indicate which of the persons or officials who made such a suggestion was most influential in affecting their final decision to plead. Table 2 indicates the breakdown of the responses to the two questions.

It is popularly assumed that the police, through forced confessions, and the district attorney, employing still other pressures, are most instrumental in the inducement of an accused to plead guilty. As Table 2 indicates, it is actually the defendant's own counsel who is most effective in this role. Further, this phenomenon tends to reinforce the extremely rational nature of criminal law administration, for an organization could not rely upon the sort of idiosyncratic measures employed by the police to induce confessions and maintain its efficiency, high production, and overall rational-legal character. The defense counsel becomes the ideal agent-mediator since, as "officer of the court" and confidant of the accused and his kin, he lives astride both worlds and can serve the ends of the two as well as his own.

While an accused's wife, for example, may be influential in making him more amenable to a plea, her agent-mediator role has, nevertheless, usually been sparked and initiated by defense counsel. Further, although a number of first suggestions of a plea came from an accused's fellow jail inmates, he tended to rely largely on his counsel as an ultimate source of influence in his final decision. The defense counsel being a crucial figure in the total organizational scheme for constituting a new set of perspectives for the accused, the same sample of defendants was asked to indicate at which stage of their contact with counsel the suggestion of a plea was made. There are three basic kinds of defense counsel available in Metropolitan Court: legal-aid, privately retained counsel, and counsel assigned by the court (but may eventually be privately retained by the accused).

The overwhelming majority of accused persons, regardless of type of counsel, related a specific incident which indicated an urging or suggestion, either during the course of the first or second contact, that they plead guilty

Table 2 Role of Agent-Mediators in Defendant's Guilty Plea

Person or Official	First Suggested Plea of Guilty	Influenced the Accused Most in His Final Decision to Plead
Judge	4	26
District attorney	67	116
Defense counsel	407	411
Probation officer	14	3
Psychiatrist	8	1
Wife	34	120
Friends and kin	21	14
Police	14	4
Fellow inmates	119	14
Others	28	5
No response	8	10
Total	724	724

Table 3 Stage (Contact) at Which Each Type of Counsel Suggests that Defendant Plead Guilty (*N* = 724)

	Privately Retained		Legal-Aid		Assigned		Total	
Contact	*N*	%	*N*	%	*N*	%	*N*	%
First	66	35	237	49	28	60	331	46
Second	83	44	142	29	8	17	233	32
Third	29	15	63	13	4	9	96	13
Fourth or more	12	6	31	7	5	11	48	7
No response	0	0	14	3	2	4	16	2
Total	190	100	487	100[a]	47	101[a]	724	100

[a]Rounded percentage.

to a lesser charge if this could be arranged. Of all the agent-mediators, it is the lawyer who is most effective in manipulating an accused's perspectives, notwithstanding pressures that may have been previously applied by police, district attorney, judge, or any of the agent-mediators that may have been activated by them. Legal-aid and assigned counsel would apparently be more likely to suggest a possible plea at the point of initial interview as response to pressures of time. In the case of the assigned counsel, the strong possibility that there is no fee involved may be an added impetus to such a suggestion at the first contact.

In addition, there is some further evidence in Table 3 of the perfunctory, ministerial character of the system in Metropolitan Court and similar criminal courts. There is little real effort to individualize, and the lawyer's role as agent mediator may be seen as unique in that he is in effect a double agent. Although, as "officer of the court" he mediates between the court organization and the defendant, his roles with respect to each are rent by conflicts of interest. Too often these must be resolved in favor of the organization which provides him with the means for his professional existence. Consequently, in order to reduce the strains and conflicts imposed in what is ultimately an overdemanding role obligation for him, the lawyer engages in the lawyer–client "confidence game" so as to structure more favorably an otherwise onerous role system.

CONCLUSION

Recent decisions of the Supreme Court, in the area of criminal law administration and defendants' rights, fail to take into account three crucial aspects of social structure which may tend to render the more libertarian rules as nugatory. The decisions overlook (1) the nature of courts as formal organization, (2) the relationship that the lawyer "regular" *actually* has with the court organization, and (3) the character of the lawyer–client relationship in the criminal court (the routine relationships, not those unusual ones that are described in "heroic" terms in novels, movies, and television).

Courts, like many other modern large-scale organizations, possess a monstrous appetite for the co-optation of entire professional groups as well as individuals. Almost all those who come within the ambit of organization authority find that their definitions, perceptions, and values have been refurbished, largely in terms favorable to the particular organization and its goals. As a result, recent Supreme Court decisions may have a long-range effect which is radically different from that intended or anticipated. The more libertarian rules will tend to produce the rather ironic end result of augmenting the *existing* organizational arrangements, enriching court organizations with more personnel and elaborate structure, which in turn will maximize organizational goals of "efficiency" and production. Thus, many defendants will find that courts will possess an even more sophisticated apparatus for processing them toward a guilty plea!

DISCUSSION QUESTIONS

1. How does the structure of the court determine the role of the defense lawyer?
2. In what ways are the fee fixing and collecting of defense lawyers different from other professions? How does the process of fixing and collecting fees show the occurrence of a lawyer-client "confidence game"?
3. How does the defense lawyer act as a double agent?
4. Blumberg provides data on which agent-mediator first suggested pleading guilty, and who was the most influential in the decision to plead guilty. What does the data show, and how does this lend evidence to the argument that the defense lawyer acts as a double agent?
5. The three Supreme Court cases mentioned show that the Supreme Court has a certain conception of the role of counsel. Does the Supreme Court's conception of the role of counsel match with the reality of the role of counsel?

17

The State (Never) Rests

Gershowitz and Killinger

Although dozens of scholars have documented the appalling underfunding of indigent defense in the United States, virtually no attention has been paid to the overburdening of prosecutors. In many large jurisdictions, prosecutors handle caseloads that are as large as those handled by public defenders. Counter-intuitively, when prosecutors shoulder excessive caseloads, it is criminal defendants who are harmed. Because overburdened prosecutors do not have sufficient time and resources for their cases, they fail to identify less culpable defendants who are deserving of more lenient plea bargains. Prosecutors also lack the time to determine which defendants should be transferred to specialty drug courts where they have a better chance at rehabilitation. Overwhelmed prosecutors commit inadvertent (though still unconstitutional) misconduct by failing to identify and disclose favorable evidence that defendants are legally entitled to receive. And excessive prosecutorial caseloads lead to the conviction of innocent defendants because enormous trial delays encourage defendants to plead guilty in exchange for sentences of time-served and an immediate release from jail. This chapter documents the excessive caseloads of prosecutors' offices around the country, and it demonstrates how the overburdening of prosecutors harms criminal defendants, victims, and the public at large.

INTRODUCTION

In recent decades, legal scholars have devoted enormous attention to two problems in the American criminal justice system: the appalling underfunding

Source: "The State (Never) Rests: How Excessive Prosecutorial Caseloads Harm Criminal Defendants" by Adam M. Gershowitz and Laura R. Killinger, from Northwestern University Law Review, Vol. 105, No. 1. Reprinted by special permission of Northwestern University School of Law, Northwestern University Law Review.

of indigent defense and intentional prosecutorial misconduct. Both problems are deeply troubling, and the academic literature helpfully serves to spotlight the problems and encourage reform. Remarkably, however, there is virtually no scholarship focusing on the opposite side of the coin. Scholars have failed to notice that prosecutors in large counties are often as overburdened as public defenders and appointed counsel. In some jurisdictions, individual prosecutors handle more than one thousand felony cases per year. Prosecutors often have hundreds of open felony cases at a time and multiple murder, robbery, and sexual assault cases set for trial on any given day. Prosecutors in many large cities have caseloads far in excess of the recommended guidelines that scholars often cite to criticize the caseloads of public defenders. Quite simply, many prosecutors are asked to commit malpractice on a daily basis by handling far more cases than any lawyer can competently manage.

Not only have scholars neglected to analyze excessive prosecutorial caseloads, they have also failed to consider how those caseloads result in inadvertent prosecutorial error. While there is an enormous (and important) literature analyzing intentional prosecutorial misconduct, the reality is that most prosecutorial misconduct is accidental. While some of these cases involve unscrupulous prosecutors, far more often the errors are inadvertent because prosecutors are too busy to properly focus on their cases or because they have not received proper guidance from senior lawyers who are terribly overburdened themselves.

The ramifications of excessive prosecutorial caseloads extend throughout the criminal justice system and, perhaps surprisingly, are most harmful to criminal defendants. Excessive caseloads lead to long backlogs in court settings, including trials, and bottom-line plea bargain offers. Defendants who have been unable to post bail thus remain incarcerated for months because overburdened prosecutors do not have time to focus on their cases. Jails accordingly remain overcrowded, resulting in not only great expense to taxpayers but also terrible conditions of confinement for defendants who are awaiting trial. Worse yet, excessive prosecutorial caseloads delay trials for months or even years, leading some defendants who would have exercised their trial rights to simply plead guilty and accept a sentence of time served. Some innocent defendants plead guilty to crimes they have not committed simply to get out of jail.

Because they are overburdened, prosecutors—who are sworn to achieve justice, not to win at all costs—lack the time and resources to carefully assess which defendants are most deserving of punishment. In rare cases, this means prosecutors will be unable to separate the innocent from the guilty. In far more cases, overburdened prosecutors will be unable to distinguish the most culpable defendants from those who committed the crimes but are not deserving of harsh punishment. For example, when a defendant is charged with robbery, prosecutors with time to look into the case might discover that, although the defendant was present at the crime scene, he was a small-time player tagging along with more serious criminals. Or prosecutors might learn that a defendant charged with theft had a very low IQ or that he stole to support his family rather than for more illicit purposes. In those cases, prosecutors who have time to dig into cases may be willing to plea bargain to lower charges or sentences. This is particularly important when, as too often is the case, the indigent defendant is represented by an overburdened defense lawyer who did not conduct any investigation or who lacked the time to bring the relevant information to the prosecutor's attention. When prosecutors are overburdened, there is less chance that they will separate out the least culpable defendants.

Excessive prosecutorial caseloads also harm victims. Here the problem is easy to visualize. Overburdened prosecutors have little time to meet with victims and thus may not receive factual information from them that would help to convict or sentence the guilty party. If they do have the opportunity to contact victims, overburdened prosecutors may be rushed for time and seem aloof or uncaring. Victims thus may be denied the therapeutic justice they seek from the criminal justice process.

Finally, excessive caseloads harm the public as well. As every first year law student knows, defendants are presumed innocent and prosecutors face a tough burden of proving defendants guilty beyond a reasonable doubt. While this burden is important to protect the innocent and curb governmental power, the open secret in criminal justice circles is that most criminal defendants are in fact guilty. Overburdened prosecutors who lack the time to thoroughly investigate cases, subpoena witnesses, meet with experts, and complete a host of other tasks will find themselves disadvantaged at trial. Guilty defendants who should be convicted go free because prosecutors lack the time and resources necessary to win at trial.

Although excessive prosecutorial caseloads should be an obvious concern for defendants, victims, and the public, solving the problem is a difficult task. While legislatures may sometimes grudgingly allocate greater funding for prosecutors, appropriating more money to prosecutors can unfairly disadvantage already underfunded indigent defense lawyers, who are unlikely to receive comparable funding increases. Additionally, because prosecutors' offices are so drastically understaffed, modest budget increases would have little impact on the enormous overburdening of prosecutors. Accordingly, we suggest a bolder approach whereby overburdened prosecutors and indigent defense lawyers make a coordinated request for drastically increased funding for the criminal justice system at large, rather than for their individual offices.

Part I of this Essay reviews the caseloads of prosecutors in some of the largest district attorneys' offices in the nation. While not every large prosecutor's office is overburdened, Part I also demonstrates that many offices are woefully understaffed. Part II then explains how excessive prosecutorial caseloads harm defendants, victims, and the public at large. Part III offers an approach for reducing prosecutorial caseloads to more manageable levels.

I. PROSECUTORS IN LARGE JURISDICTIONS OFTEN HAVE EXCESSIVE CASELOADS

Although there are more than 2300 prosecutors' offices throughout the United States, a comparatively small number of district attorneys' offices in major cities handle a huge number of America's criminal prosecutions. Though these large district attorneys' offices are all organized somewhat differently, they have one thing in common: far too few prosecutors are tasked with handling far too many cases. As we explain in this Part, prosecutors in many large cities are asked to handle excessive caseloads that run afoul of advisory guidelines for criminal defense attorneys. Prosecutors are also asked to make do with grossly inadequate support staff. Unfortunately, tough economic times over the past few years have only made the situation worse.

A. Standards Suggest Prosecutors Should Not Handle More than 150 Felonies or 400 Misdemeanors per Year

In 1968, a national commission created by the Department of Justice studied the problem of excessive public defender caseloads and adopted a recommendation that defenders handle no more than 150 felonies *or* 400 misdemeanors in any year. In subsequent years, these guidelines have been widely endorsed by criminal justice organizations, the American Bar Association, and academic commentators. While the recommended caseloads are far from perfect, there is widespread agreement that, roughly speaking, limiting defense counsel to no more than 150 felonies *or* 400 misdemeanors ensures that they have sufficient time to devote to each of their cases.

In the over forty years since these guidelines for criminal defense caseloads were established, no organization has stepped forward with comparable caseload limits for prosecutors. It is beyond the scope of our project to offer an ideal case load limit for prosecutors, but it is quite plausible to suggest that the guidelines should be similar to those recommended for defense attorneys. Arguably, prosecutors are in a position to handle slightly more cases than defense attorneys because they do not have to chase down leads in an effort to establish an effective defense. On the other hand, prosecutors have many obligations, such as handling arraignments or meeting with victims, which defense attorneys do not have to shoulder. While we are not sure of the exact caseloads prosecutors should handle, we are confident that it should be similar to the number recommended for defense attorneys.

Of course, as most criminal justice observers know, many public defenders and appointed counsel violate the recommended caseload limits. Scholars have rightly characterized enormous public defender caseloads of 500 or 600 annual cases per lawyer as a "national crisis" and "outrageous." Unfortunately, many large prosecutors' offices also have caseloads that rise to this crisis level and beyond.

B. Prosecutors in Large Counties Are Regularly Tasked with Hundreds or Even Thousands of Felony Cases per Year

In 2006, prosecutors in Harris County, Texas, surveyed the largest district attorneys' offices in the nation to determine the sizes of their staffs and the numbers of cases they handle. Although the data showed that a few offices have reasonable workloads, many large counties had caseloads far in excess of recommended guidelines for public defenders.

As Table 1 demonstrates, prosecutors in many large counties handle far more cases than guidelines recommend. For example, although defense lawyer

Table 1 Cases per Prosecutor in Large District Attorneys' Offices in 2006

County	Prosecutors	Felonies	Misdemeanors	Felonies per Prosecutor	Misdemeanors per Prosecutor	Total Filings per Prosecutor
Los Angeles, CA	1020	68,654	125,580	67	123	190
Cook, IL (Chicago)	800	60,000	265,000	75	331	406
New York, NY (Manhattan)	532	11,190	111,055	21	209	230
Kings, NY (Brooklyn)	413	12,514	98,725	30	239	269
Maricopa, AZ	343	40,000	5000	117	15	132
San Diego, CA	310	18,888	27,654	61	89	150
Miami-Dade, FL	283	36,286	54,974	128	194	322
Philadelphia, PA	283	15,515	54,485	55	193	247
Queens, NY	276	5274	57,938	19	210	229
Orange, CA	249	19,011	50,233	76	202	278
Harris, TX (Houston)	238	39,154	69,494	165	292	457
San Bernardino, CA	219	20,187	38,459	92	176	268
Riverside, CA	217	15,518	21,197	72	98	169
Dallas, TX	217	24,251	53,637	112	247	359
Broward, FL (Ft. Lauderdale)	194	15,720	68,301	81	352	433
Wayne, MI (Detroit)	188	13,000	4000	69	21	90
Sacramento, CA	185	11,491	20,759	62	112	174
Santa Clara, CA	185	8729	25,164	47	136	183
Suffolk, NY (Long Island)	177	2930	33,889	17	191	208
King, WA (Seattle)	163	9815	16,000	60	98	158
Tarrant, TX (Fort Worth)	155	15,328	27,752	99	179	278
Alameda, CA (Oakland)	151	9731	26,165	64	173	238
Bexar, TX (San Antonio)	146	10,188	32,314	70	221	291
Clark, NV (Las Vegas)	135	22,420	32,678	166	242	408
Middlesex, MA (Cambridge)	113	720	38,000	6	336	343

guidelines provide that attorneys should handle no more than 150 felonies *or* 400 misdemeanors, the average caseload in Clark County, Nevada, was 166 felonies *and* 242 misdemeanors for every prosecutor in the office. The workload for Harris County, Texas prosecutors was even higher, with an average of 165 felonies *and* 292 misdemeanors for each prosecutor in the office.

Unfortunately, the data in Table 1 vastly understate the scope of the problem by assuming that every prosecutor in the office handles an equal number of cases. This assumption is not correct. Each large district attorney's office has numerous prosecutors and attorneys whose specialized roles leave them handling very small caseloads or no cases at all. In turn, the overwhelming bulk of cases are handled by a smaller core group of "in-the-trenches" prosecutors, whose case numbers are drastically higher than the averages listed in Table 1. To put the actual workload of these prosecutors in perspective, consider all of the attorneys in large district attorneys' offices who are not handling day-to-day cases: First, there are management prosecutors who are responsible for supervisory functions and do not personally handle many cases. Such management prosecutors include the elected district attorney, the first-assistant district attorney who fills the role of chief operating officer and handles day-to-day management matters, and bureau chiefs who oversee departments and are personally responsible for only a handful of very high-profile cases. Second, in many large district attorneys' offices, there are line prosecutors, or assistant district attorneys, whose sole responsibilities include revoking bonds for defendants who have failed to show up for court or performing "intake" by drafting warrants and answering police officers' questions. These prosecutors handle isolated pieces of cases, but they do not have to prepare cases for trial. Finally, there are prosecutors who exclusively handle complicated matters, such as white-collar fraud or death-penalty cases and therefore have unusually low caseloads.

In sum, while large district attorneys' offices have hundreds of prosecutors on staff, many of the prosecutors do not handle run-of-the-mill cases. The bulk of felony and misdemeanor cases are therefore left to a smaller group of prosecutors. For example, the Philadelphia District Attorney's Office informed us that fewer than half of their prosecutors (roughly 150 of 309 attorneys) handle pending cases that are set for trial. It is this group of in-the-trenches prosecutors who are particularly overburdened. In some jurisdictions, the workload of these prosecutors is truly staggering. One extreme example is Harris County, Texas, where some prosecutors are handling upwards of 1500 felonies per year and over 500 felonies at any one time. A brief description of the office's structure highlights the problem.

The Harris County District Attorney's Office assigns three felony prosecutors to each of its felony courts. On average, each felony court receives about 2000 new filings per year. The senior prosecutor in each court serves primarily in a supervisory role and personally handles only about a dozen of the court's most serious cases. Almost all of that court's 2000 felony cases are split between the other two prosecutors. The second-most senior prosecutor (the "number two prosecutor") is responsible for the more serious crimes: noncapital murders, sexual assaults, child abuse, robberies, and other serious felonies. These cases are the most complicated and therefore the most time-consuming. In a given year, the number two prosecutor handles about 500 serious felonies. The remaining 1500 felony cases—drug offenses, burglaries, assaults, and various other crimes—are assigned to the most junior prosecutor. At any one time, this junior prosecutor, who typically has about two years of prosecutorial experience under his belt, has about 500 open cases to handle. While these cases are less complicated, over the span of a year, a junior prosecutor in a felony courtroom handles ten times the number of felony cases than is recommended for public defenders.

The situation is similarly dire in other large district attorneys' offices. In Cook County, Illinois, the average felony prosecutor has 300 or more open cases at any one time. In a given year, many felony prosecutors there handle between 800 and 1000 total cases. In Tarrant County, Texas, home of Fort Worth, prosecutors handle upwards of 150 felony cases at any one time, and misdemeanor prosecutors juggle between 1200 and 1500 matters apiece. In Philadelphia County, Pennsylvania, prosecutors working in the Major Trials Unit or the Family Violence Sexual Assault Unit have open caseloads of 250 cases.

Although it may not be the *most* overburdened prosecutor's office in the country, the Clark County District Attorney's Office in Las Vegas, Nevada, truly puts the problem in perspective. The entire Clark County criminal justice system is terribly overburdened. In 2009, a report by an outside indigent defense consultant demonstrated that Clark County public defenders cleared 215 cases per year, in addition to dealing with other open cases. Almost any reasonable observer would conclude that Clark County public defenders are overburdened. The Nevada Supreme Court even contemplated imposing caps on public defenders' caseloads. Yet very little attention has been paid to the fact that prosecutors in Clark County have more cases than public defenders. In 2009, the District Attorney's Office filed more than 70,000 felonies and misdemeanors. After budget cuts and excluding attorneys whose sole job was to screen cases, the Clark County District Attorney's Office had only 90 prosecutors to handle those 70,000 filings, a ratio of nearly 800 cases per prosecutor.

Although prosecutors have long been overburdened in some jurisdictions, events over the last few years have greatly exacerbated the problem. As scholars have observed, criminal filings have tended to increase rather than contract. This may be due to new laws being placed on the books, more aggressive law enforcement with respect to particular crimes, or economic downturns leading to increased crime rates. Whatever the cause, filings in many prosecutors' offices are on the rise. For example, in Dallas County, Texas, felony filings increased by more than 10% between 2005 and 2009. Matters were far worse in Harris County, Texas, where filings rose by more than 20% over a three-year period. In San Bernardino County, California, total case filings rose by more than 20% in just the two-year period between 2006 and 2008. Indeed, in the entire State of California, criminal case filings increased by more than 100,000 between 2005 and 2006. In New York State, criminal case filings rose by nearly 200,000 between 2004 and 2008. As filings have skyrocketed, however, most large district attorneys' offices have not been in a position to hire additional prosecutors to keep pace. The Bureau of Justice Statistics found that, while the number of attorneys in prosecutors' offices nationwide rose consistently during the 1990s, the numbers plateaued in 2001 and actually declined slightly thereafter. Accordingly, as total case filings have increased over the past decade, the workloads of individual prosecutors have grown in turn.

Even worse, the economic downturn has led a number of district attorneys' offices to reduce the number of prosecutors through hiring freezes or even layoffs. In Detroit, the Wayne County District Attorney's Office was forced to reduce its total number of prosecutors—through a hiring freeze and layoffs—by a stunning forty-eight people between 2008 and 2010, a 25% reduction. In Las Vegas, the Clark County District Attorney's Office suffered a similarly drastic cut from 135 prosecutors in 2006 to 102 prosecutors by 2010. Budget cuts forced the Cook County State's Attorney's Office to cut forty prosecutors and fifty staff in 2008. In Seattle, the King County District Attorney's Office was forced to cut eighteen prosecutor positions in 2008. In San Bernardino, California, the District Attorney's Office eliminated sixteen prosecutor positions between 2006 and 2010. In Phoenix, the Maricopa County District Attorney's Office has not replaced sixteen prosecutors who have left the office in the last two years. Other counties, including Harris County, Broward County, and Miami–Dade County, have also been forced to cut prosecutors in recent years.

C. Inadequate Support Staff

Although excessive caseloads are indefensible, the burden on individual prosecutors would be lessened if large district attorneys' offices had adequate support staff to help prosecutors handle the cases. For instance, paralegals are helpful in keeping track of files, drafting and responding to simple motions, and conducting legal research. Investigators are crucial in finding missing witnesses, serving subpoenas, and doing other background investigation. Victim–witness coordinators also serve a useful purpose in keeping victims apprised of court hearings and listening to family concerns. This is to say nothing of the secretaries and other basic support staff needed to answer phones, make copies, and keep the office running. It is well-known that public defender offices around the country must make do with inadequate support staff, but resources are also inadequate in district attorneys' offices.

For example, the four largest counties in Texas handle a combined total of more than 270,000 criminal cases per year. Yet, they have fewer than thirty-five paralegals combined to work on all of those cases. The Cook County District Attorney's Office is the second largest prosecutor's office in the nation and handles hundreds of thousands of cases per year with fewer than ten paralegals on staff.

Although large prosecutors' offices tend to have more investigators than paralegals, the numbers are still woefully inadequate. In 2006, the ten largest prosecutors' offices in the country represented a population of nearly forty million people and handled well over a million cases, but they had a combined total of only 1,043 investigators on staff. On average, then, in those ten district attorneys' offices, there were more than 1000 cases per investigator. In Clark County, Nevada—which had 29,308 felonies and 41,298 misdemeanors in 2009—there are only twenty investigators for the whole office, and most of their time is spent serving subpoenas because the office does not have enough process servers to contact all of the witnesses. In Seattle, the King County District Attorney's Office handled nearly 15,000 criminal cases without a single investigator on staff. And in Miami–Dade County, there were more than 4500 cases per investigator. Worse yet, the total number of investigators in Miami–Dade County has since dropped from twenty to fourteen, resulting in a ratio of more than 6100 cases for every investigator on staff in 2009.

Table 2 Cases per Investigator in the Ten Largest Prosecutors' Offices In 2006

County	Population	Total Cases	Investigators	Case per Investigation
Los Angeles, CA	9,935,475	194,234	280	694
Cook, IL	5,303,683	325,000	177	1836
Harris, TX	3,693,050	108,648	59	1841
Maricopa, AZ	3,635,528	45,000	49	918
Orange, CA	2,988,072	69,234	119	582
San Diego, CA	2,933,462	46,542	131	355
Kings, NY	2,486,235	111,239	99	1,124
Miami-Dade, FL	2,376,014	91,260	20	4563
Dallas, TX	2,305,454	77,888	59	1320
Queens, NY	2,241,600	63,212	50	1264
Totals:	37,898,573	1,132,257	1043	1086

D. Why Has So Little Attention Been Paid to the Overburdening of Prosecutors?

Given that there are dozens of scholarly articles and scores of newspaper features dissecting the indigent defense crisis, skeptical observers might wonder why, if prosecutors' caseloads are in fact so excessive, they have received so little attention from academics and the news media.

Let us begin first with the news media. One overly simplistic explanation for lack of media interest is that reporters are politically liberal and therefore more interested in stories of unfairness to criminal defendants than to overworked prosecutors. Perhaps there is a tiny kernel of truth to this explanation, but by and large it is unsatisfying. A more plausible explanation for the lack of media attention to prosecutorial caseloads is that defense lawyers are in a far better position to generate press coverage for themselves.

Over the last few decades, lawyers for indigent defendants have raised legal challenges to excessive workloads in a variety of forms ranging from ineffective assistance of counsel claims to declaratory judgment actions seeking structural reform. Although these legal challenges have mostly been unsuccessful, the attendant publicity has been enormous. For instance, when a class action lawsuit against New York's public defender system was argued before the state's highest court in early 2010, the *New York Times* ran a lengthy article highlighting the terrible representation received by one defendant. Moreover, much of the indigent defense litigation has been spearheaded by corporate law firms seeking pro bono litigation experience for their junior associates. These law firms—including powerhouses like Covington & Burling LLP, Arnold & Porter LLP, Kirkland & Ellis LLP, and Davis Polk & Wardell LLP—have public relations experience and media contacts that can be used to create publicity. By contrast, these litigation and publicity options are not available to prosecutors. Even if prosecutors had an interest in filing a suit to contend that their workloads were excessive, they would lack the requisite elements of a case and controversy. While indigent defendants can point to violations of the Sixth and Fourteenth Amendments, which give them access to the courthouse, prosecutors have no such constitutional hook.

More importantly, overburdened prosecutors would be unlikely to file such cases even if they were justiciable. Because elected district attorneys are often politicians who work behind the scenes with state and county bodies to procure funding, they are unlikely to want to provoke a public fight over their budgets and workloads. Rather, elected district attorneys would likely prefer to maintain a good working relationship with the other elected officials that fund them, and line prosecutors who want to keep their jobs must follow this unspoken lead. On the other hand, public defender offices typically have more contentious relationships with county and state officials and have less reason to be publicly polite. To an even greater degree, appointed lawyers have the autonomy to file litigation and start a media firestorm. The appointed lawyers with the interest and savvy to file systemic indigent defense litigation are often excellent lawyers who have paying clients they could serve instead of doing appointed work. As such, these appointed counsel effectively operate as independent contractors and can stir up controversy with little fear of retribution from state and county officials.

The lack of academic interest in excessive prosecutorial caseloads is harder to explain than the lack of litigation. Again, the argument that most academics are liberal and have more interest in criminal defendants than in government agents is superficial and largely unhelpful. A more telling explanation derives from the shared background of many law professors. The traditional route to academia does not run through state prosecutors' offices.

While there are undoubtedly numerous criminal law professors who worked as federal prosecutors before entering academia, federal prosecutors have vastly greater resources than their state counterparts. Academics who were formerly federal prosecutors therefore likely did not personally experience the crushing caseloads faced by assistant district attorneys in overburdened county prosecutors' offices. By contrast, there are a number of prominent criminal justice scholars who served as public defenders in state courts prior to entering the academy. The past experiences of these former public defenders may be the driving force for their passion and some of their indigent defense scholarship.

★ ★ ★

In sum, there is considerable evidence that prosecutors' offices in many large counties are woefully understaffed. Prosecutors in many counties are regularly called upon to handle two or three times the caseloads that have been recommended for defense lawyers. In a smaller number of jurisdictions, prosecutors are handling ten times as many cases as criminal justice organizations, the American Bar Association, and academics find acceptable for defense lawyers. Additionally, prosecutors must handle these massive caseloads without adequate investigative or paralegal support. Because little scholarly and press attention has been paid to the overburdening of prosecutors, policymakers have not been forced to confront how excessive caseloads harm defendants, victims, and the public at large.

II. HARM CAUSED BY EXCESSIVE PROSECUTORIAL CASELOADS

Excessive prosecutorial caseloads result in serious problems throughout the criminal justice system. Most obviously, as we discuss below in sections B and C, excessive caseloads harm crime victims, who feel ignored by busy prosecutors, and the public at large, which is disserved when overwhelmed prosecutors lack the time and resources to handle cases against clearly guilty defendants. Less apparent, but even more pernicious, is the harm that excessive prosecutorial caseloads work on criminal defendants. As we explain below in section A, overburdening prosecutors results in longer sentences for less culpable offenders, longer delays in the dismissal of charges against the innocent, fewer disclosures of exculpatory evidence by prosecutors, and more guilty pleas by innocent defendants in exchange for sentences of time served and release from jail. Somewhat counterintuitively, overburdening prosecutors is more harmful than helpful to criminal defendants.

A. Harm to Criminal Defendants

Conventional wisdom holds that defendants benefit when prosecutors have huge caseloads. The logic is simple: if prosecutors are overburdened, they will not have time to competently prosecute all of their cases and will not bring many cases to trial. By this logic, prosecutors accordingly must plea bargain cases on terms more favorable to defendants to shrink their dockets. To a certain extent, this conventional wisdom is correct. The entire class of criminal defendants—thousands of defendants in large jurisdictions—likely receives better plea deals from overburdened prosecutors. However, many other effects of excessive prosecutorial caseloads tend to harm criminal defendants, particularly those who are less culpable or even wholly innocent.

1. *Overburdened Prosecutors Cannot Always Identify the Least Culpable Offenders and Afford Them Sentencing Reductions.*—First, consider how excessive caseloads prevent prosecutors from giving sentencing breaks to the defendants who truly deserve them, while simultaneously giving discounts to the undeserving. In a jurisdiction where prosecutors are not overburdened, assume that the going rate for a run-of-the-mill armed robbery is ten years' imprisonment. Of course, not all robberies are the same. Prosecutors adjust the ten-year average sentence up or down depending on the facts they discover during their pretrial investigations. In the case of Robber *A*, prosecutors with adequate time and resources may learn that although police found him inside the bank while the crime was being committed, he was actually a minor player in the robbery who had fallen in with a bad crowd after having previously been a good student. The prosecutor might therefore be willing to offer Robber *A* a plea deal carrying five years' incarceration, well under the going rate of ten years. On the other hand, looking at Robber *B*'s paper record, prosecutors might initially think he is entitled to a sentencing break as well; he is charged with stealing a relatively small amount of money and has only one prior criminal conviction for a simple assault that occurred over five years ago. If prosecutors had the time to conduct a proper investigation, however, they might discover that Robber *B* pointed his shotgun directly at the victims' heads and that he was the ringleader of the robbery. Moreover, the victim of Robber *B*'s previous crime might inform prosecutors that Robber *B* had broken his nose and cheekbones and that the case was pleaded down to simple assault (rather than aggravated assault) only because Robber *B* had agreed to provide testimony against another perpetrator. With this information in hand, prosecutors might decide that Robber *B* should serve the going rate of ten years or perhaps more. In sum, with time and resources to investigate their cases, prosecutors are able to carefully differentiate between defendants and to tailor plea bargain offers accordingly.

Now consider what might have happened if the cases of Robbers *A* and *B* had been handled by overburdened prosecutors. Although the going rate for "average" robberies should be ten years, in jurisdictions with overburdened prosecutors the typical punishment may be closer to eight years because defense attorneys can bargain more aggressively knowing that trial is very unlikely. Even though they are overburdened, prosecutors nevertheless try to differentiate between offenders the best they can. But they must make do with less information. They will not have time to personally interview the bank tellers, meet with Robber *B*'s previous victim, or learn that Robber *A* is regarded in the community as a good kid who was only a passive participant in the robbery. While Robber *A*'s attorney may convey this information, prosecutors may discount the defense attorney's description as self-serving without neutral witnesses to attest to it. Accordingly, based primarily on the paper record in front of them, overburdened prosecutors might determine that both Robbers *A* and *B* are entitled to slight discounts on the going rate—say, seven years instead of ten. In the case of Robber *A*, the overburdened prosecutor will therefore offer a plea-bargained sentence in excess of what the defendant deserves. And in the case of Robber *B*, the prosecutor will offer a plea-bargained sentence that is far lower than what the defendant deserves. In both cases, overburdened prosecutors fail to achieve the most just result.

A similar problem occurs when prosecutors have little time or information before exercising their broad authority to transfer defendants to specialty drug courts. These courts are designed to treat and rehabilitate nonviolent offenders rather than incarcerate them and have become popular in recent years. For example, consider how prosecutors are likely to handle a defendant who has been charged with prostitution for the third time. On the surface, the defendant may not seem like a good candidate for transfer to a specialty drug court because she is a recidivist and is not even charged with a drug crime. A busy prosecutor is therefore likely to spend only a few minutes on the case, offer a plea bargain carrying a short jail sentence, and then move on to the next case.

Yet if the prosecutor had time to conduct a closer investigation, he might discover that the defendant's real problem is not prostitution but an underlying drug addiction. Our defendant engages in prostitution only to support her drug habit and has been arrested for crack possession in the past. But for her drug habit, she would have a good chance of living a productive life. She has ties to the community, a high school degree, and appears to be intelligent and capable of handling a regular job. If the prosecutor were to transfer her to the drug court, she would be subject to drug testing, would participate in meetings with probation officers, and would stand a better chance of escaping the cycle of trading sex for drugs. Yet because her case appears typical and the overburdened prosecutor has dozens of other cases to manage that day, our defendant may not have the chance to attend drug court. She will almost certainly plead guilty, spend time in jail, and start the cycle all over again following her release. The negative effects of this cycle impact not only the defendant but also the community, which presumably would prefer to transform a drug user into a productive member of society rather than tolerate recidivism.

2. Excessive Caseloads Hinder Prosecutors from Turning Over Brady *Material to Criminal Defendants.*—As detailed above, excessive caseloads prevent prosecutors from exercising their discretion to achieve the most just and beneficial outcomes. In those instances, prosecutors do not necessarily err but are nonetheless unable to achieve the good results that they likely could accomplish with reasonable caseloads. Perhaps more troubling than these failures of discretion is that excessive caseloads lead prosecutors to run afoul of their constitutional obligations and commit inadvertent prosecutorial misconduct. Overburdened prosecutors likely fail to comply with several constitutional and statutory obligations; as explained below, the most pervasive are so-called *Brady* violations.

Under the doctrine established in *Brady v. Maryland*, prosecutors are required to disclose favorable evidence that tends to either exculpate the defendant or impeach witnesses against him. This makes *Brady* at once one of the most important obligations imposed on prosecutors and one of the most common claims by criminal defendants in appealing their convictions. Academic commentators are critical of *Brady* violations, and when the violations are intentional, such criticism is justified. What most commentators fail to recognize, however, is that the overwhelming majority of *Brady* violations are unintentional and occur because prosecutors are overburdened or have received inadequate guidance from supervising prosecutors, who themselves are overburdened. Of course, inadvertent failure to turn over *Brady* material is still a constitutional violation and can be just as damaging to criminal defendants as intentional violations. But unlike intentional violations, which can only be stopped by snuffing out the covert actions of manipulative prosecutors, inadvertent *Brady* violations can be reduced by limiting prosecutorial caseloads and providing resources for better training.

A few hypothetical, but all too common, situations illustrate the problem of inadvertent *Brady* violations. Imagine a felony prosecutor in a large district attorney's office with 200 open felony cases, four of which are set for trial each week. Though the prosecutor strives to give the defense attorney in each case notice of *Brady* material (and other more mundane matters) a few weeks in advance of trial, it is difficult to keep up with the workload, and our prosecutor must make choices about which cases to prioritize. Believing that three of the four cases set for trial on, for example, June 1, will plea bargain, she focuses most of her attention on the case that she thinks is most likely to go to trial. Unfortunately, our prosecutor is not clairvoyant, and by the time May 28 arrives, one of the cases she thought would plea bargain fails to settle. The prosecutor is, of course, not totally unprepared. She has served subpoenas for likely witnesses and reviewed the other evidence in the file. But being prepared for trial requires much more than that. Our prosecutor must have in-depth meetings with the key witnesses and closely study the entire case file. With only a few days before trial, she must scramble to be ready in time. And in scrambling to get ready, the overburdened prosecutor can easily overlook *Brady* material that she should turn over to the defendant. Our overburdened prosecutor might fail to realize in her last-minute meeting that the witness's story now conflicts with something he said when speaking to the police many months ago. Or she may be fully aware of evidence that impeaches government witnesses and decide to delay producing it out of fear that disclosing witness identities too far in advance of trial will lead to witness tampering. In the hectic period before trial, prosecutors may simply forget to turn over evidence of which they are personally aware. The list of possible scenarios is endless, but the key point is the same in each permutation: prosecutors who have hundreds of open cases and are not sure which will actually go to trial will inadvertently overlook *Brady* material as they scramble to be ready for trial at the last minute.

More disturbing than simple oversights are instances in which junior prosecutors do not even realize they have a legal obligation to turn over evidence.

In extremely busy district attorneys' offices, prosecutors are quickly saddled with enormous responsibilities very early on. While these young prosecutors surely learned about the *Brady* doctrine in law school, they may fail to recognize actual *Brady* obligations when they arise in the real world. For instance, a junior prosecutor who has tried only a few serious felonies may neglect to disclose that a domestic violence victim initially told a police officer that her bruises were from falling down rather than from being hit by her abuser. The junior prosecutor may simply not realize that such evidence is *Brady* material. In a properly staffed district attorney's office, a supervising prosecutor likely would catch the error and ensure that the State complies with the *Brady* doctrine's requirements. In overburdened prosecutors' offices, however, supervisors may fail to correct errors because they too are overwhelmed and lack the time to provide the hands-on guidance that is necessary to avoid inadvertent misconduct.

3. Excessive Caseloads Prevent Prosecutors from Promptly Dismissing Cases with Weak Evidence or Cases Where the Defendant Is Innocent.—More crime is committed, and more suspects are arrested, than could possibly be processed through the criminal justice system. Most prosecutors' offices (even those that are overburdened) work hard to screen out weak cases early on before charges are filed. Still, prosecutors file charges against thousands of defendants each year only to later discover that the defendants are innocent or that the cases are too weak to bring to trial. While these defendants are certainly happy to have the charges against them dropped, for many defendants the dismissals do not happen until weeks or months after charges were initially filed. If the defendants are too poor to post bond, as more than 30% of criminal defendants are, they will be incarcerated for those weeks or months. With jails across the country overcrowded, these defendants are often forced to live in squalid conditions with poor medical care, awful food, and the risk of violence and death. While this problem is unavoidable to a certain extent, it is magnified in jurisdictions where prosecutors carry excessive caseloads.

The overarching story is fairly simple: when prosecutors carry excessive caseloads, they handle them in a triage fashion. Prosecutors do not look ahead to cases that will come to a boil in weeks or months; they live in the here and now. If evidence is lurking in a case file that will ultimately lead to a defendant's case being dismissed, it will linger there until the prosecutor has time to focus on the matter. The fewer cases the prosecutor has, the sooner the charges against innocent defendants will be dismissed.

The situation is more nuanced when prosecutors are pushed to dismiss cases by proactive defense attorneys. Often defense lawyers raise legitimate legal or factual questions about a case shortly after charges are filed. While a defense attorney's inquiries and concerns are not enough to justify outright dismissal of a case, they are sufficient to spur the prosecutor to investigate the facts and witnesses more closely. If the prosecutor has a manageable caseload, she will likely conduct this investigation very quickly. Ethical prosecutors have no interest in continuing to lock up innocent defendants. And efficient prosecutors have no desire to keep cases on the docket that could easily and justifiably be dismissed. If the prosecutor has an unreasonable caseload, however, she may not dig into the case until absolutely necessary, which may be just before the case is set for another status hearing or, worse yet, trial. Innocent defendants may thus languish in jail for longer than necessary.

Of course, there is a flip side to this story. One might argue that if prosecutors had more manageable caseloads they might not abandon some of the weak cases that they presently dismiss after charges are filed. After all, from an ethical standpoint, prosecutors only need to believe there is probable cause in order to bring a case forward to a jury. If prosecutors had more time to work on marginal cases, increased resources might actually lower dismissal rates. While this argument seems compelling, it likely accounts for a comparatively small number of cases. First, prosecutors typically make their reputations by trying cases and winning those trials. Thus they have little incentive to push weak cases to trial when they run significant risk of losing. Second, at least when it comes to felonies, it seems unlikely that prosecutors are presently dismissing cases outright that they would try if they had greater resources. While prosecutors may be willing to plea bargain serious felony cases when their evidence is weak, political pressure and a strong sense of justice likely prevents prosecutors from outright dismissing charges against violent felony defendants they believe to be guilty. Thus, it is difficult to see how increased resources will lead prosecutors to drastically decrease the number of cases they dismiss.

In sum, while prosecutors by and large succeed at removing weak cases from the criminal justice system, innocent defendants (and those who are guilty but for which proof is lacking) are charged with crimes every day. Unfortunately, excessive caseloads prevent prosecutors from moving swiftly. Many defendants therefore languish in jail for weeks or months. Excessive prosecutorial caseloads thus harm innocent defendants and exacerbate jail overcrowding and unsafe conditions of confinement.

4. *Excessive Caseloads Lead to the Conviction of the Innocent.*—Innocent defendants are regularly convicted of crimes, both at trial and as a result of their own guilty pleas. Though it is rare that innocence is later established, it seems easy to blame the prosecutors who win wrongful convictions against the innocent. But in the context of excessive caseloads it is just as easy to see how innocent defendants slip through the cracks.

a. Prosecutors lack the time and resources to discover who is innocent.—Start with two basic truths about the criminal justice system: (1) most criminal defendants are guilty and (2) most criminal defendants lie to prosecutors and claim to be innocent. Understandably, prosecutors are skeptical of most claims of innocence. And because prosecutors are overburdened, they have little time to devote to each case. The little time prosecutors do have is strategically spent trying to convict defendants they firmly believe to be guilty rather than exploring undocumented theories that could exculpate other defendants. Moreover, even when prosecutors do take the time to inquire into defendants' claims of innocence, they may only have time to conduct cursory investigations that are unlikely to be successful. Prosecutors may try to track down alibi or self-defense witnesses that the defendant claims support his version of events, but when such witnesses have not come forward on their own, they are often hard to locate. Furthermore, because a considerable amount of violent crime is committed in minority neighborhoods where even law-abiding citizens fear the police, witnesses with helpful exculpatory information may be unwilling to come forward. This problem is even worse when the witnesses themselves are involved in criminal activity. And the problem is particularly vexing in border states where perfectly honest and otherwise law-abiding witnesses may be illegal immigrants afraid to speak with prosecutors out of fear of deportation. If prosecutors' offices had greater resources to hire investigators who could interact with the community and be seen as partners, then prosecutors might have a more realistic chance of finding witnesses to support the claims of innocent defendants.

Without sufficient time and resources, however, prosecutors often ask defense attorneys to shoulder the burden of investigating claims of innocence. Overburdened prosecutors who are skeptical of innocence claims (most of which are untruthful) ask defense attorneys to find the key witnesses that support their clients' claims and to have those witnesses sign affidavits swearing to the information. If the defense attorney is competent and not overburdened herself, there is nothing inherently wrong with this approach. The problem, of course, is that many public defenders or appointed counsel representing indigent defendants are overburdened as well. Worse yet, in some jurisdictions, compensation for appointed counsel representing indigent defendants is capped for each case, thereby encouraging defense attorneys to take more cases and creating a financial incentive to avoid spending much time working to prove their client's innocence. Overburdened, incompetent, or lazy defense attorneys are therefore unlikely to fare much better than overburdened prosecutors in uncovering compelling evidence that defendants are truly innocent.

In many instances, defense attorneys will come forward with some evidence that, if properly developed, might be sufficient to raise reasonable doubt. In other words, defense attorneys are unlikely to hand prosecutors "smoking gun" evidence so compelling that it leads prosecutors to dismiss charges on the spot. Rather, defense attorneys might come forward with phone numbers for supposed alibi witnesses so that the prosecutors can contact them. Or defense attorneys might ask prosecutors to hear from witnesses who challenge police officers' accountings of how a traffic stop occurred. In other cases, defense attorneys might ask prosecutors to dismiss charges because they believe a key witness has mental health problems or because they claim that the victim in a domestic violence case will now recant her original testimony. Such evidence is not immediately exculpatory, and it may not turn out to be exculpatory at all after it is investigated so it is likely shelved when prosecutors are managing hundreds of other cases. When prosecutors finally find the time to focus on the case, witnesses or key evidence may be gone. Thus the needle-in-the-haystack defendant who deserves to be acquitted, either because he is factually innocent or because there are legitimate questions about the evidence against him, may ultimately be convicted.

b. Innocent defendants plead guilty in exchange for sentences of time served and an immediate exit from jail.—Most innocent defendants who are wrongfully convicted are not the victims of prosecutorial misconduct or inept defense lawyering. Rather, most innocent defendants are convicted because they knowingly and voluntarily pleaded guilty to offenses they did not commit. But why would an innocent defendant plead guilty? The simple answer is that excessive caseloads lead to long trial backlogs and short-sentence plea bargain offers. Innocent defendants thus can plead guilty to sentences of time served and simply leave jail.

When prosecutors have excessive caseloads, it is logistically impossible for every defendant who asserts his innocence to be afforded a timely, quick jury trial. Excessive prosecutorial caseloads therefore lead to many poor defendants who cannot afford bail, including innocent defendants, languishing in jail for months or even years awaiting trial. When innocent defendants are charged with the most serious crimes and face decades in prison, it makes sense for them to wait their turn for trial. If a defendant is found not guilty at trial, the time he spent in pretrial detention will be nowhere close to the sentence he would have received had he pleaded guilty and been convicted.

But when innocent defendants are charged with misdemeanors or low-level felonies, the time in jail while waiting for trial may actually exceed the sentence they would receive if they pleaded guilty. For example, imagine that a defendant is charged with burglary for breaking into a garage and stealing tools. The defendant has no resources with which to post bond. Although prosecutors do not know it, the eyewitness placing the defendant at the scene is mistaken. Moreover, the case against the defendant is so weak that if it proceeded to trial, a decent defense attorney would rip it apart: there was only one eyewitness, it was nighttime, police presented the mug shots in a suggestive fashion, and the defendant was found blocks away from the scene and was not in possession of any of the stolen property. If the defendant wants to continue waiting for a trial, he will almost certainly be acquitted. However, the defendant has already been in jail for a month, and the prosecutor is willing to offer a plea bargain for the one month the defendant has already served. While the innocent defendant does not want to admit to a crime he did not perpetrate, he ultimately pleads guilty simply to get out of jail.

Moreover, the collateral consequences of pleading guilty, such as stigma or harm to employment prospects, are unlikely to deter innocent defendants from pleading guilty. If an individual has already spent weeks in jail awaiting trial, any stigma or embarrassment has probably already attached. While pleading guilty may require the defendant to meet with a parole officer or undergo random urinalysis, the added stigma of conviction is likely of little consequence when his family and friends already knew that he was locked up in jail. Perhaps more importantly, defendants who are too poor to post bond are not likely to have their career prospects hindered by pleading guilty to a crime. They are unlikely to apply to medical school or law school, and in most instances they are not concerned that elite Fortune 500 companies are unlikely to hire individuals with burglary convictions. Instead, because these individuals are likely competing for manual labor jobs or low-paying employment in the service industry, pleading guilty to a crime they did not commit, particularly a misdemeanor, will not have much effect on their employment prospects. Innocent defendants thus have good reasons (and few obstacles) to plead guilty to crimes they did not commit.

* * *

Although it is counterintuitive, excessive prosecutorial caseloads are very damaging to criminal defendants. Overburdened prosecutors have trouble exercising their discretion as effectively as they might like. Less culpable defendants therefore do not receive sentencing discounts that they would receive from less-burdened prosecutors. Candidates for drug treatment courts may not be transferred to those courts because overburdened prosecutors fail to recognize worthy defendants. Well-meaning but overburdened prosecutors fail to disclose *Brady* material to defendants and likely run afoul of other constitutional and statutory obligations. Excessive caseloads hinder prosecutors from promptly dismissing weak cases, leaving innocent defendants imprisoned for far longer than necessary. And overburdened prosecutors may unknowingly offer too-good-to-refuse plea bargain offers to innocent defendants, encouraging the innocent to plead guilty to crimes they did not commit. While the entire class of criminal defendants might receive some plea bargaining benefit from overwhelmed prosecutors, excessive prosecutorial caseloads may well cause more harm than good to a host of criminal defendants.

B. Harm to Victims

Excessive prosecutorial caseloads are also damaging to the victims of crime. When prosecutors are overburdened, they are unable to spend much time with victims or even to meet with them at all. Prosecutors thus fail to acquire useful information that could be used to convict the guilty and ensure that they are adequately punished. Perhaps more troubling, overburdened prosecutors who do not have time to communicate with victims will leave them feeling victimized again, denying victims the therapeutic justice they seek from the criminal justice system.

There are many ways in which victims are ignored by the process. They are not informed that offenders have been arrested or charged. Even if they are aware of an arrest, victims may not be notified when the defendant makes bail. Often, victims are not informed of court settings or plea bargain offers, nor notified, in some jurisdictions, that the defendant has been convicted and sentenced. It is not surprising that victims believe they should be kept informed about what is happening in their cases. Nor is it shocking that victims become upset when key steps in the process occur without their knowledge. Just as crime victims want to receive respect and apologies from the offenders who harmed them, so too do victims want a certain amount of attention and respect from the criminal justice process. When victims are informed about the process and hear a sympathetic voice acknowledge that they have been wronged, they can begin to heal faster.

Many large district attorneys' offices have tried to keep victims better informed by hiring victim–witness coordinators or by instituting policies requiring prosecutors to make contact with victims and seek their input before plea bargaining cases. Yet, these policies face enormous obstacles, largely because of excessive caseloads. When an office has tens of thousands of cases each year but only a handful of victim–witness coordinators, many victims are likely to slip through the cracks. The same is true when prosecutors lack the time to meet with victims or even to talk with them by phone. Even if prosecutors can meet with some victims, the sheer number of cases likely makes it difficult to differentiate among victims and to remember to contact them again. Of course, most prosecutors probably do not intentionally ignore victims. They would likely prefer to have time to meet with them, update them on their cases, and offer encouragement. Whether or not the prosecutor on a given case has the best of intentions, a crime victim who receives minimal attention from an overburdened prosecutor almost certainly leaves the process feeling victimized by the criminal justice system.

C. Harm to the Public at Large

Although it is fairly obvious, no discussion of excessive prosecutorial caseloads would be complete without mention of the harm such caseloads do to the public at large. Although the current system ensures that most guilty defendants either plead guilty or are convicted at trial, it is undoubtedly true that excessive caseloads result in a substantial number of guilty defendants being wrongfully acquitted or receiving plea bargain offers that are far too generous. Such windfalls to defendants encourage politicians to enact criminal justice "reforms" that actually cause more harm than good.

1. Overburdened Prosecutors Fail to Attain Convictions for Guilty Defendants at Trial.—Because the American criminal justice system believes (wisely, in our opinion) that it is better for ten guilty people to go free rather than for one innocent person to be convicted, there will always be some guilty defendants who escape justice. Yet, there is a significant difference between freeing the guilty because they were not proven "guilty beyond a reasonable doubt" and letting the guilty escape justice because prosecutors lack the time and resources to properly prepare their cases. Unfortunately, in jurisdictions with overburdened prosecutors, even clearly guilty defendants are acquitted at trial.

Criminal cases can fall apart for dozens of reasons when time and resources are limited. Prosecutors may be unable to locate key witnesses in advance of trial. Witnesses may need hours of trial preparation that prosecutors lack the time to provide. Prosecutors may not have time to search out the best expert witnesses or the money to hire the ones they do find. Faced with huge numbers of cases, prosecutors may lack the time to prepare effective presentations of complicated scientific testimony from ballistics to breathalyzer results. Or prosecutors might simply miss an obvious and important detail about a case because they lacked the time to visit the crime scene before trial.

Of course, public defenders and appointed counsel in many jurisdictions face the exact same obstacles in defending indigent criminal defendants. We do not mean to suggest that the overburdening of defense lawyers is not a problem or that prosecutors should be given greater resources than defense lawyers. We only mean to assert that just as the lack of defense resources results in the occasional conviction of the innocent, it is also true that the lack of prosecutorial resources sometimes allows the guilty to escape conviction.

The problem posed by lack of prosecutorial resources is more apparent in the instances where defendants are wealthy enough to retain private attorneys. While some of these defendants receive the same level of representation that would be provided by public defenders, in many instances defendants who spend a lot of money on private lawyers get what they pay for. In some cases, prosecutors are simply no match for well-funded defense lawyers with adequate time to devote to their cases.

Drunk driving prosecutions provide a good example. Wealthy defendants who spend $20,000 or $30,000 to hire lawyers specializing in drunk driving defense are buying time and attention for their cases. The defense lawyer will have time to visit the scene where the sobriety tests were conducted to check for irregularities. He will be able to blow up photographs or maps to highlight the questionable conditions under which the tests were conducted. The defense will have the chance to thoroughly investigate the background of the officer who conducted the tests, the crime lab where blood samples were processed, and the chemist who ran the analysis. And the defense will also be able to retain the services of skilled expert witnesses who can cast doubt on the validity of breathalyzer tests in general and how they were applied in that particular case.

By contrast, an overburdened prosecutor will not have time to personally visit the crime scene, nor will she have an investigator who she can task to do so. The prosecutor will also lack the time and money to magnify photographs or create helpful visual displays. Worse yet, the prosecution's expert witness is likely to be a chemist from the local crime lab who himself is juggling dozens of other cases and likely will not have time for a detailed meeting to discuss his testimony in advance of trial. In these circumstances, it is not difficult to see how a factually guilty defendant might evade conviction.

2. Overburdened Prosecutors Plea Bargain the Cases of Some Guilty Defendants for Sentences That Are Far Too Low.—While excessive prosecutorial caseloads lead to some number of guilty defendants being acquitted at trial, the far more significant problem is guilty defendants receiving plea bargains that are too lenient. As we explained in Part II.A above, some defendants receive lighter plea deals than they deserve because prosecutors lack the time to thoroughly investigate an offender's case and criminal history to discover that he is deserving of considerably greater punishment. We do not repeat that analysis here but instead extend it to cases in which prosecutors know that a defendant deserves a longer sentence but lack the time and resources to staunchly advocate for that penalty. Put simply, in an unknown (though likely substantial) number of cases, prosecutors knowingly agree to plea deals carrying sentences well below what they believe the defendants deserve because of the caseload pressures that they face.

Consider again the typical prosecutor who has multiple cases set for trial on a given day and is carrying hundreds of other open felony matters. Imagine that the prosecutor has made a plea bargain offer of ten years' imprisonment to a robbery defendant with a lengthy criminal history. The prosecutor firmly believes that the defendant will receive at least a fifteen year sentence if he is convicted at trial. The prosecutor thus should hold firm on her plea bargain offer and proceed to trial if the defendant refuses to accept ten years' incarceration. If the prosecutor proceeds to trial on this robbery case, however, it will likely take three entire days to try the case. That will be three days the prosecutor will lose in terms of preparing subpoenas, interviewing witnesses, researching the law, responding to motions, and getting up to speed on the other cases sitting on her desk. The defense lawyer, if he is remotely worth his salt, is aware of this problem. The defense lawyer will therefore respond to the prosecutor's bottom line plea bargain with a lower counteroffer. If that counteroffer is ridiculously low—say three years, in response to the prosecutor's offer of ten years—even an overburdened prosecutor will likely reject it. But if the offer is only slightly lower—say seven years instead of the prosecutor's bottom line offer of ten years—it is easier for the prosecutor to acquiesce and to accept a deal below her bottom line than for her to sacrifice three days of her time.

The prosecutor can justify accepting the much lower plea bargain by telling herself that if she had insisted on going to trial, it would have hindered her from managing the hundreds of other cases on her docket and would have made it nearly impossible to prepare her other trial cases. This rationalization is even more persuasive to a prosecutor if her other defendants committed more serious offenses such as murders and rapes. Put simply, for even the most hardworking and committed prosecutors, excessive caseloads make it impossible to hold firm on every plea bargain offer and credibly threaten to go to trial. Prosecutors therefore plea bargain cases for less than what they believe many defendants deserve.

3. Windfalls to Clearly Guilty Defendants Encourage Politicians to Enact Criminal Justice "Reforms" That Are Actually Harmful.—When guilty defendants are acquitted at trial or receive lighter-than-justified plea bargains, the harm extends beyond those offenders themselves. Windfalls to obviously guilty defendants fuel the ratcheting up of criminal law by encouraging legislatures to add new crimes to the books and increase punishments. In turn, this trend causes the United States to lock up more people and spend more money on jails and prisons, all while ignoring the underlying problem of the underfunding of prosecutors and indigent defense lawyers.

In the vast majority of cases where prosecutors agree to lighter plea bargains than defendants actually deserve, the cases disappear into the system never to be heard from again. But in a few rare cases, particularly those in which a defendant received probation or a short prison sentence and later committed a new high-profile offense, the news media can seize on the issue. For example, a news story may announce that today's vehicular manslaughter defendant never received jail time for her previous drunk driving charges. In short order, politicians may come forward with legislation to increase punishment ranges or impose mandatory minimums.

As scholars have detailed, such legislation is often harmful. Mandatory minimum sentences prevent judges from individualizing justice to less culpable defendants who deserve mercy. Longer punishments separate offenders from their families, thus increasing the number of children in urban areas who go through their entire childhoods without male parents. The public must spend more tax money on jails and prisons.

To be sure, harmful criminal justice legislation is not solely attributable to the backlash following lenient plea bargain deals. And, of course, in some instances there are good public policy arguments for increasing sentencing ranges or imposing mandatory minimums. Our point here is not to wade too deeply into that debate but simply to note that excessive prosecutorial caseloads can result in unanticipated backlashes for sentencing policy.

III. SOLUTIONS TO THE EXCESSIVE CASELOAD PROBLEM

Although it appears clear that defendants, victims, and the public at large are harmed by excessive prosecutorial caseloads, remedying the problem is difficult. It would be a mistake for legislatures to simply appropriate more money for prosecutors' offices and leave public defenders' offices underfunded. Moreover, it is not beneficial for prosecutors and public defenders to each complain to legislative bodies that the other is undeserving of funding increases. When prosecutors and public defenders bicker with each other over funding, it is too easy for legislatures to deny both offices the funds they need. Accordingly, a more productive approach would be for overburdened prosecutors and public defenders to make joint proposals for a major influx of money to properly fund the criminal justice system.

A. Simply Appropriating More Money for More Prosecutors Is the Wrong Approach

An initial reaction to data showing excessive prosecutorial caseloads is to suggest that district attorneys' offices simply hire more prosecutors. Such a proposal is a difficult sell (because money is finite and legislatures have many competing concerns), but it is at least plausible. Politicians' interests are often aligned with prosecutors' needs because the former want to be viewed as "tough on crime" and therefore want to take credit for incarcerating criminals.

Thus, while legislatures would rather enact symbolic measures that look good and cost no money, if district attorneys' offices place enough pressure on legislatures to fund greater staff and resources, there is a chance that district attorneys will get some of what they request.

The biggest problem with simply hiring more prosecutors is that doing so would have adverse effects on the rest of the criminal justice system. Increasing the number of prosecutors without a corresponding increase in public defenders would exacerbate the indigent defense problem. Defense lawyers would still be overburdened and would be in a worse position because they would then be facing prosecutors who were better resourced and thus better prepared for trial and less interested in plea bargaining.

A second objection to simply appropriating money for new prosecutors is that there would be no guarantee that the allotted money would be used to reduce existing caseloads. Prosecutors' offices may use the added manpower to simply file more charges. At present, overburdened prosecutors' offices likely decline charges for minor criminal infractions that they simply lack the manpower to prosecute. Increasing the number of prosecutors may thus result in increased prosecution of low-level drug or prostitution cases without any real reduction in the caseloads of existing prosecutors.

A third objection is that elected district attorneys in large offices (who are primarily administrators and typically do not handle actual cases) may view new staff as an opportunity to enhance their political reputations rather than reduce existing caseloads. At present, most local district attorneys have no choice but to use almost all of their budgets to handle violent crime. A sudden influx of new staff might lead elected prosecutors to create new departments or to allocate new lawyers to pet projects that will make political hay. For example, very few county district attorneys' offices have the resources to handle long-term, paper-intensive, white-collar crime cases. Yet, in today's political climate, many elected district attorneys would surely like to have robust white-collar divisions that focus on high-profile issues such as mortgage fraud or investment malfeasance. Similarly, as it has become politically popular to "go green," elected prosecutors might like to expand the size of their environmental divisions. Or district attorneys may simply be animal lovers who want to expand departments that focus on animal cruelty. All of these are worthwhile projects, but directing resources to new areas will do little to reduce the enormous caseloads facing existing prosecutors.

B. Providing Additional Resources for both Prosecutors and Indigent Defense Lawyers Is the Better Approach

A far better approach to dealing with the overburdening of prosecutors is for legislatures to provide additional funding for both prosecutors and defense attorneys. This approach has the virtue of guaranteeing that resources will be used to help overburdened prosecutors without disadvantaging indigent defendants. This, of course, is easier said than done.

The first key obstacle, as noted above, is that legislatures are often unreceptive to spending any money, even on prosecutors. Yet this problem can be overcome when prosecutors can convince politicians that additional funding is in the public interest or that additional funding will bolster the politicians' law-and-order credentials. The second obstacle, procuring complementary funding for indigent defense and maintaining it into the future, is much more difficult. Despite decades of indigent defense scholarship arguing that a large influx of money is needed and even court rulings demanding greater funding, legislatures have been hostile to funding increases. And even when legislatures do provide greater funding, the increases are sometimes rescinded shortly thereafter because public defenders' offices are an attractive target for cuts in cash-strapped times. There are ways to circumvent this problem, though.

One option is to directly tie additional indigent defense funding to the added resources for prosecutors. By coupling prosecutor funding with indigent defense funding, legislatures likely would find it easier to spend money on indigent defense. In fact, this idea has proved successful in some jurisdictions. As Professor Ron Wright has documented, prosecutors and public defenders in Tennessee were able to convince the legislature to appropriate additional funding for both departments by simultaneously submitting weighted caseload information documenting their workloads.

Admittedly, this approach initially seems counterintuitive. Like other budget priorities, there is a finite amount of money that legislatures have to spend on criminal justice. Money devoted to indigent defense is money not spent on prosecutors, prisons, or judges. Indeed, in collecting the data for this Essay, we spoke with a number of prosecutors who thanked us for taking up their fight against the public defenders who are trying to take "their" resources. As opposed to further bickering between the prosecutors' and defenders' offices, which only makes it easy for legislators to deny both departments the funding they have requested, we suggest that a better approach would be for prosecutors and public defenders to make a combined pitch, arguing that the criminal justice system is underfunded as a whole. As Professor Wright has pointed out, in areas such as corrections, legislatures are already accustomed to "hearing the funding requests of complementary players in a single system and sometimes require a coordinated budget request from them." Scholars have suggested that dribs and drabs of additional funding are insufficient to fix the indigent defense problem and that only an enormous budgetary increase can effect significant change. The same logic applies to overburdened prosecutors. Arguing with county funding boards over trifling funding increases (or fighting to stave off reductions) will not change the status quo for either prosecutors or public defenders. Rather, both public defenders' and overburdened prosecutors' offices need a game-changing funding increase. By making a joint proposal for a large funding increase, public defenders and prosecutors might be in a better position to shake loose the large and much-needed sums of money that legislatures would otherwise refuse to dole out.

CONCLUSION

Although scholars have long decried the excessive caseloads of public defenders and appointed counsel, little attention has been paid to the huge caseloads handled by prosecutors in many large counties. Across the country, many prosecutors are tasked with handling five or even ten times as many cases as guidelines recommend for public defenders. Obviously, excessive prosecutorial caseloads are harmful to victims, who receive little attention to their cases, and the public at large, which must tolerate guilty defendants being acquitted. But the problem is much bigger than that.

Excessive prosecutorial caseloads are also very damaging to criminal defendants. Because overburdened prosecutors lack adequate time and resources, they fail to recognize less culpable defendants who are deserving of more lenient plea bargains or would be better served by being transferred to specialty drug courts where they would have a better chance at rehabilitation. From a purely legal standpoint, overwhelmed prosecutors commit inadvertent (though still unconstitutional) misconduct by failing to identify and disclose favorable evidence that defendants are legally entitled to receive. Finally, excessive prosecutorial caseloads harm innocent defendants. Busy prosecutors take far longer to recognize weak cases and dismiss charges against innocent defendants. And excessive caseloads delay trials, leading innocent defendants to plead guilty in exchange for sentences of time served and an immediate release from jail.

The solution to the problem of overburdened prosecutors is, of course, increased funding. Yet, legislatures must be cautious not to bolster prosecutors' offices at the expense of public defenders. Considerably greater funding is therefore necessary for prosecutors as well as public defenders.

DISCUSSION QUESTIONS

1. How does the number of cases the average prosecutor handles per year compare to the recommended number of cases a public defender should have per year? Why were these recommendations made?
2. What is the importance of adequate support staff for the prosecutor's office?
3. Why has so little attention been paid to the overburdening of prosecutors when so much attention has been paid to the overburdening of indigent defenders?
4. Discuss the harms that are caused to criminal defendants, victims, and the public at large by excessive prosecutorial caseloads.
5. What solutions does Gershowitz propose for the problem of prosecutorial overburdening?

18

The Vanishing Trial

Marc Galanter

This chapter traces the decline in the portion of cases that are terminated by trial and the decline in the absolute number of trials in various American judicial fora. The portion of federal civil cases resolved by trial fell from 11.5 percent in 1962 to 1.8 percent in 2002, continuing a long historic decline. More startling was the 60 percent decline in the absolute number of trials since the mid 1980s. The makeup of trials shifted from a predominance of torts to a predominance of civil rights, but trials are declining in every case category. A similar decline in both the percentage and the absolute number of trials is found in federal criminal cases and in bankruptcy cases. The phenomenon is not confined to the federal courts; there are comparable declines of trials, both civil and criminal, in the state courts, where the great majority of trials occur. Plausible causes for this decline include a shift in ideology and practice among litigants, lawyers, and judges. Another manifestation of this shift is the diversion of cases to alternative dispute resolution forums. Within the courts, judges conduct trials at only a fraction of the rate that their predecessors did, but they are more heavily involved in the early stages of cases. Although virtually every other indicator of legal activity is rising, trials are declining not only in relation to cases in the courts but to the size of the population and the size of the economy. The consequences of this decline for the functioning of the legal system and for the larger society remain to be explored.

Source: Adapted from Marc Galanter, "The Vanishing Trial: An Examination of Trials and Related Matters in Federal and State Courts," Journal of Empirical Legal Studies, vol 1:3.

I. THE NUMBER OF CIVIL TRIALS

This project reflects the growing awareness of a phenomenon that runs counter to the prevailing image of litigation in the United States. Over the past generation or more, the legal world has been growing vigorously. On almost any measure—the number of lawyers, the amount spent on law, the amount of authoritative legal material, the size of the legal literature, the prominence of law in public consciousness—law has flourished and grown. It seems curious, then, to find a contrary pattern in one central legal phenomenon, indeed one that lies at the very heart of our image of our system—trials. The number of trials has not increased in proportion to these other measures. In some, perhaps most, forums, the absolute number of trials has undergone a sharp decline. A sense of the change can be gathered from Table 1, which charts the number of civil trials in the federal courts by nature of suit at 10 year intervals from 1962 to 2002.

As illustrated by Table 1, dispositions have increased by a factor of five—from 50,000 to 258,000 cases. But the number of civil trials in 2002 was more than 20 percent lower than the number in 1962—some 4,569 now to 5,802 then. So the portion of dispositions that were by trial was less than one-sixth of what it was in 1962—1.8 percent now as opposed to 11.5 percent in 1962.

The drop in civil trials has not been constant over the 40-year period; it has been recent and steep. In the early part of our period, there was an increase in trials, peaking in 1985, when there were 12,529. From then to now, the number of trials in federal court has dropped by more than 60 percent and the portion of cases disposed of by trial has fallen from 4.7 percent to 1.8 percent.

A substantial portion of the cases that reach the trial stage terminate before the trial is completed. In 1988, some 24 percent of all cases reaching trial were disposed of "during" trial—28 percent of jury trials and 19 percent of bench trials. By 2002, when the number of cases reaching the trial stage had fallen by 60 percent, the percentage disposed of "during" trial dropped to 18 percent, with little difference between jury and bench trials. As fewer cases managed to survive until the trial stage, those that began a jury trial were more resistant to being deflected from pursuing the trial through to its conclusion.

The decline in the rate of civil trials in the post-World War II federal courts continues and accentuates a long historic trend away from trial as the mode of disposing of civil cases. In 1938, the year that the Federal Rules of Civil Procedure took effect, 18.9 percent of terminations were by trial.

In his study of litigation in the St. Louis Circuit Court from 1820 to 1970, Wayne McIntosh observes:

> During the first 100 years of the study period, the percentage of cases culminating in a contested hearing or trial remained fairly steady (around 25 to 30 percent). After 1925, though, the average skirted downward into

Table 1 Civil Trials in U.S. District Courts at 10-Year Intervals, 1962–2002

	Dispositions	Jury Trials	Bench Trials	All Trials	Trials as % of Dispositions	Jury Trials as % of Dispositions	Bench Trials as % of Dispositions	Case Type as % of All Trials	Case Type as % All Jury Trials	Case Type as % of All Bench Trials	Jury Trials as % of All Trials
1962											
Civil	50,320	2,765	3,037	5,802	11.5%	5.5%	6.0%	100.0%	100.0%	100.0%	47.7%
Torts	19,254	2,238	946	3,184	16.5%	11.6%	4.9%	54.9%	80.9%	31.1%	70.3%
Torts, diversity	12,353	1,834	342	2,176	17.6%	14.8%	2.8%	37.5%	66.3%	11.3%	84.3%
Contracts	14,981	303	818	1,121	7.5%	2.0%	5.5%	19.3%	11.0%	26.9%	27.0%
Contracts, diversity	4,529	279	474	753	16.6%	6.2%	10.5%	13.0%	10.1%	15.6%	37.1%
Prisoner	3,118	0	96	96	3.1%	0.0%	3.1%	1.7%	0.0%	3.2%	0.0%
Civil rights	317	11	42	53	16.7%	3.5%	13.2%	0.9%	0.4%	1.4%	20.8%
Labor	2,479	31	199	230	9.3%	1.3%	8.0%	4.0%	1.1%	6.6%	13.5%
I.P.	1,595	6	163	169	10.6%	0.4%	10.2%	2.9%	0.2%	5.4%	3.6%
1972											
Civil	90,177	3,361	4,807	8,168	9.1%	3.7%	5.3%	100.0%	100.0%	100.0%	41.1%
Torts	25,952	2,451	1,114	3,565	13.7%	9.4%	4.3%	43.6%	72.9%	23.2%	68.8%
Torts, diversity	15,232	1,997	409	2,406	15.8%	13.1%	2.7%	29.5%	59.4%	8.5%	83.0%
Contracts	18,200	507	1,203	1,710	9.4%	2.8%	6.6%	20.9%	15.1%	25.0%	29.6%
Contracts, diversity	9,361	480	821	1,301	13.9%	5.1%	8.8%	15.9%	14.3%	17.1%	36.9%
Prisoner	15,802	27	431	458	2.9%	0.2%	2.7%	5.6%	0.8%	9.0%	5.9%
Civil rights	5,023	116	651	767	15.3%	2.3%	13.0%	9.4%	3.5%	13.5%	15.1%
Labor	4,936	25	353	378	7.7%	0.5%	7.2%	4.6%	0.7%	7.3%	6.6%
I.P.	2,223	10	183	193	8.7%	0.4%	8.2%	2.4%	0.3%	3.8%	5.2%
1982											
Civil	184,835	4,771	6,509	11,280	6.1%	2.6%	3.5%	100.0%	100.0%	100.0%	42.3%
Torts	30,630	2,439	1,050	3,489	11.4%	8.0%	3.4%	30.9%	51.1%	16.1%	69.9%
Torts, diversity	19,085	1,913	391	2,304	12.1%	10.0%	2.0%	20.4%	40.1%	6.0%	83.0%
Contracts	59,977	890	1,492	2,382	4.0%	1.5%	2.5%	21.1%	18.7%	22.9%	37.4%

(*continued*)

Table 1 (*continued*)

	Dispositions	Jury Trials	Bench Trials	All Trials	Trials as % of Dispositions	Jury Trials as % of Dispositions	Bench Trials as % of Dispositions	Case Type as % of All Trials	Case Type as % All Jury Trials	Case Type as % of All Bench Trials	Jury Trials as % of All Trials
Contracts, diversity	22,457	856	1,112	1,968	8.8%	3.8%	5.0%	17.4%	17.9%	17.1%	43.5%
Prisoner	25,864	180	716	896	3.5%	0.7%	2.8%	7.9%	3.8%	11.0%	20.1%
Civil rights	14,821	707	1,456	2,163	14.6%	4.8%	9.8%	19.2%	14.8%	22.4%	32.7%
Labor	9,836	126	481	607	6.2%	1.3%	4.9%	5.4%	2.6%	7.4%	20.8%
I.P.	4,305	58	214	272	6.3%	1.3%	5.0%	2.4%	1.2%	3.3%	21.3%
1992											
Civil	230,171	4,279	3,750	8,029	3.5%	1.9%	1.6%	100.0%	100.0%	100.0%	53.3%
Torts	44,754	1,799	657	2,456	5.5%	4.0%	1.5%	30.6%	42.0%	17.5%	73.2%
Torts, diversity	32,279	1,422	257	1,679	5.2%	4.4%	0.8%	20.9%	44.7%	10.4%	84.7%
Contracts	52,006	745	768	1,513	2.9%	1.4%	1.5%	18.8%	17.4%	20.5%	49.2%
Contracts, diversity	22,746	679	564	1,243	5.5%	3.0%	2.5%	15.5%	15.9%	15.0%	54.6%
Prisoner	44,247	359	696	1,055	2.4%	0.8%	1.6%	13.1%	8.4%	18.6%	34.0%
Civil rights	21,136	889	772	1,661	7.9%	4.2%	3.7%	20.7%	20.8%	20.6%	53.5%
Labor	15,557	82	252	334	2.1%	0.5%	1.6%	4.2%	1.9%	6.7%	24.6%
I.P.	5,491	84	96	180	3.3%	1.5%	1.7%	2.2%	2.0%	2.6%	46.7%
2002											
Civil	258,876	3,006	1,563	4,569	1.8%	1.2%	0.6%	100.0%	100.0%	100.0%	65.8%
Torts	49,588	782	289	1,071	2.2%	1.6%	0.6%	23.4%	26.0%	18.5%	73.0%
Torts, diversity	27,563	639	85	724	2.6%	2.3%	0.3%	15.8%	21.3%	5.4%	88.3%
Contracts	38,085	371	338	709	1.9%	1.0%	0.9%	15.5%	12.3%	21.6%	52.3%
Contracts, diversity	22,285	342	251	593	2.7%	1.5%	1.1%	13.0%	11.4%	16.1%	57.7%
Prisoner	56,693	292	199	491	0.9%	0.5%	0.4%	10.7%	9.7%	12.7%	59.5%
Civil rights	40,881	1,234	290	1,524	3.7%	3.0%	0.7%	33.4%	41.1%	18.6%	81.0%
Labor	15,864	69	121	190	1.2%	0.4%	0.8%	4.2%	2.3%	7.7%	36.3%
I.P.	7,872	120	65	185	2.4%	1.5%	0.8%	4.0%	4.0%	4.2%	64.9%

SOURCE: Annual Reports of the Administrative Office of the U.S. Courts, Table C-4.

> the 15 percent range. [Figures] . . . reveal that the shift from adjudication to bargaining is. . . wholesale and not restricted to any one issue.

In a study of trial courts in two California counties at 20-year intervals from 1890 to 1970, Lawrence Friedman and Robert Percival found that trials in Alameda County dropped from 36 percent of the sampled civil cases in 1890 to 16.1 percent in 1970; and in rural San Benito County from 25.8 percent in 1890 to 10.7 percent in 1970. In their study of civil litigation in Los Angeles Superior Court, Molly Selvin and Patricia Ebener compared samples of cases from the era before World War II (1915–1940) and the postwar era (1950–1979).

> We. . .observed changes in the method by which cases are terminated. More cases were disposed of by the court in the earlier sample than later, and 16 percent of these cases were tried. In the cases filed since 1950 more settled or were dismissed by the plaintiff. Fewer had court dispositions and very few were tried.

A. Bench Trials and Jury Trials

In the course of the rise and then fall in the number of federal civil trials, the makeup of these trials changed. More of them are before juries and fewer are bench trials. In 1962, there was a slight preponderance of bench trials, which grew until the early 1980s. Starting in 1990, the number of bench trials fell sharply, so that by 2002, jury trials made up almost two-thirds (65.8 percent) of all civil trials. Indeed, measuring against 1962, the number of bench trials has fallen by 49 percent from 3,037 to 1,563, while the number of jury trials has increased by 8.7 percent from 2,765 to 3,006. Jury trials fell precipitously in 2002 (by 17 percent from the 3,632 in 2001), nearing their 1962 level. In 2003, jury trials numbered 2,603, 5.9 percent below the 1962 total.

B. Civil Rights Trials

As contract and tort trials fell from comprising 74 percent of all trials in 1962 to 38 percent in 2002, what replaced them? Largely, it was civil rights: in 1962, there were only 317 civil rights dispositions; in 2002, there were 40,881. In 1962, civil rights accounted for less than 1 percent of all civil trials; in 2002, they were just over a third of all trials (1,543 of 4,569) and 41 percent of jury trials (1,234 of 3,006). This is particularly remarkable in light of the required diversion of many civil rights cases through the Equal Employment Opportunities Commission and the readiness of courts to grant summary judgment in such cases. For 30 years, even as the portion of cases tried has fallen, civil rights has remained the type of case most likely to reach trial: trials were 19.7 percent of all civil rights dispositions in 1970 and 3.8 percent in 2002.

C. Prisoner Petitions

The other large new batch of trials is prisoner petitions. The prison population multiplied six times from 1962 (218,830) to 2001 (1,324,465). Together with the jail population of 631,240, there were almost 2 million total inmates in 2001.

These numerous prisoners share with other Americans an increase in rights consciousness. America's love affair with imprisonment has multiplied this class of claimants, who have vexing grievances, unlimited time, few competing recreations, and very low opportunity costs (but very few resources for litigation).

The rate of prisoner petitions rose rapidly during the 1960s from 12 per 1,000 prisoners in 1962 to over 80 per 1,000 in the early 1970s. But these petitions, unpopular with judges and politicians, have not kept pace with the growth of the prison population. The rate has been falling for 30 years to about 44 per 1,000 in 2001. In that time, there was a sharp decline in habeas corpus petitions from over 66 percent of the total in 1970 to 43 percent in 2002. Civil rights claims replaced habeas corpus as the largest category of prisoner cases in 1978 until such claims were curtailed by the Prison Litigation Reform Act of 1995 (PLRA).

The PLRA was enacted to decrease the amount of prisoner litigation in the federal courts. Although it did not change much of the substantive law underlying prisoner claims, the PLRA changed both the procedures and remedies available to prisoners in federal courts. The PLRA accomplishes this through three chief measures: (1) by requiring that inmates exhaust all available administrative grievance procedures before filing a claim in district court; (2) by imposing filing fees and court costs on inmates, regardless of indigency; and (3) by requiring that district courts review prisoner complaints before docketing, or as soon as practicable thereafter, and dismiss them if they "fail to state a claim upon which relief may be granted; or. . .seek monetary relief from a defendant who is immune from such relief." The increased exhaustion and screening requirements are the strongest explanations for the decrease in prisoner trials because both mechanisms serve to eliminate complaints before they reach the trial stage. The PLRA also imposes limits on damages and attorney fees, and allows for nonresponse by defendants without fear of admitting to the allegations. Moreover, at the same time Congress passed the PLRA, it imposed new restrictions on offices receiving federal legal funding, prohibiting them from representing inmates.

The result is that the PLRA suppressed trials even more than it suppressed filings. Margo Schlanger estimates that from the mid-1990s until 2001, "[f]ilings are down about forty percent—but trials are down fifty percent." The great surge of prisoner filings had driven the number of trials from 96 in 1962 to over 1,000 in 1984, peaking at 1,235 in 1996, and falling to 491 in 2002. The trials in 1962 were all bench trials. Prior to 1970, only a handful of prisoner trials were before juries, but the portion of jury trials grew, surpassing the number of bench trials in every year since 1999. In 2002, 59 percent of prisoner trials were before juries.

The rate of trials is low: at its peak in 1970, 4.5 percent of prisoner petition terminations were by trial; just 1 percent were by trial in 2002. From a mere 1.7 percent of trials in 1962, prisoner petitions made up one-sixth (16.3 percent) of all trials and almost a quarter (24.7 percent) of all bench trials at their high point in 1996. Even after their suppression by the PLRA, they form 12.7 percent of trials: one out of every eight bench trials and almost one out of ten jury trials. The continued prominence of prisoner cases as a portion of trials reflects not only the growth in prison populations but also the greater decline in the rate of trials of other types of cases.

D. Trials Before Magistrates

Could the apparent decline in trials reflect a shift in who is conducting the trials? The federal courts are also staffed by magistrate judges, who since 1979 are empowered to try cases if the parties consent to trial before the magistrate. The current system of magistrate judges was created by the Federal Magistrates Act of 1968. It replaced the office of U.S. commissioner and conferred on magistrates three basic categories of judicial responsibility: (1) all the powers and duties formerly exercised by the U.S. commissioners; (2) the trial and disposition of "minor" (i.e., misdemeanor) criminal offenses; and (3) "additional duties," including pretrial and discovery proceedings in civil and criminal cases, preliminary review of habeas corpus petitions, and services as a special master. In 1976, Congress increased the scope of magistrate authority, further conferring on magistrates the ability to hear and determine any pretrial matters in civil or criminal cases (with eight listed exceptions). In 1979, Congress authorized magistrates to try and enter final judgment in any civil case with the consent of the parties, and expanded trial jurisdiction to extend to all federal misdemeanors. Amendments in 1996 clarified that review of final orders of a magistrate judge were limited to the courts of appeal, and further amendments in 2000 enlarged the class of criminal cases that magistrates could enter judgment on and granted magistrates civil and criminal contempt authority.

The number of civil cases terminated by magistrate judges multiplied by five from some 2,452 in 1982 to 12,710 in 2002. The number of trials before magistrates rose from 570 in 1979 (the first year for which data is available) to 1,919 in 1996, but then fell steadily to 959 in 2002. (The fall continued in 2003, during which there were 867 magistrate trials.)

The percentage of magistrate dispositions by trial has fallen. In 1982, the first year for which a computation is possible, one-third (33.6 percent) of all magistrate civil dispositions were by trial. But as the number of dispositions by magistrates increased, the portion tried has fallen, so that in 2002 only 7.5 percent were by trial.

Unfortunately, the magistrate disposition and trial data do not tell us about the types of cases (nature of suit) in which these dispositions and trials occur. Thus, we cannot specify the composition of magistrate trials and we do not know if this composition has changed over time and whether it parallels or complements the composition of trials before judges.

II. THE CHANGING CHARACTER OF TRIALS: TIME AND COMPLEXITY

As we busy ourselves counting trials, we should not overlook the possibility that what constitutes a trial may have changed over the years. Lawrence Friedman reminds us that in earlier eras trials were often brief and perfunctory. The elaboration of procedure, the enlargement of evidentiary possibilities, and the increased participation of lawyers have made the trial more complex and refined than its remote ancestors. It is widely believed that within the period covered here, the cases that are tried have become more complex and consume larger investments of resources. Unfortunately, we do not have longitudinal data from the federal courts on such features as the amount of discovery, number of motions, number of lawyers, number of objections, number of witnesses, and so forth. Studies of other courts suggest that complexity, investment, and length of trial are connected. In their study of Los Angeles Superior Court, Selvin and Ebener note that from their earlier (1915–1949) to their later (1950–1979) period, the number of events in filed cases increased as did the portion of cases with discovery and that the length of trials "dramatically increased." "In the earlier sample of civil filings, 60 percent of the trials lasted no longer than one day. Since 1950, only 20 percent of all trials took one day or less."

A Canadian study also suggests a connection between case complexity and the decline of trials. In Toronto from 1973 to 1994, the number of trials fell (both absolutely and as a portion of dispositions) while the number of plaintiffs per case, the number of motions per case, the number of defenses, and the length of time consumed by cases all increased. As an overall indicator of complexity, the researchers measured the average physical bulk of the court files produced in cases commenced in every fifth year of their study. There were some 106 files per storage box of cases commenced in 1973–1974, but only 24 cases per (equally tightly-packed) box of cases commenced in 1988–1989.

Few measures of complexity are available for cases in federal courts. Civil trials that lasted four days or more were 15 percent of trials in 1965 and 29 percent of trials in 2002; trials of three days or more rose from 27 percent to 42 percent over the same amount of time. This shift to longer trials is produced by an increase in the number of the longest trials combined with a shrinking of the number of short trials.

Several studies suggest that the number and length of trials are connected with the size of verdicts, that is, with the amount at stake. If the decline in the number of trials involves the squeezing out of smaller cases, then we might expect shorter trials to become less frequent and a corresponding increase in the portion of longer trials and in the size of verdicts. Examining jury verdicts in Cook County, Illinois, and at several California sites in the 1980s, Mark Peterson observed:

> The trends over all cases suggest that the median jury award is related to the number of jury trials. Usually the median award moved in the

opposite direction from changes in the number of trials: When the number of trials fell, the median increased; when the number of trials increased, the median decreased. This relationship suggests that the total number of jury trials changed primarily because the number of smaller cases (*i.e.*, those that involved modest damages) increased or decreased at different times.

Peterson's study was updated through 1994 by Eric Moller, who found that the number of jury trials fell in 11 of 15 sites—in many cases substantially. From 1985 to 1994, the number of verdicts in Los Angeles fell from 459 to 292; in San Francisco, 115 to 57; and in Cook County, Illinois, 699 to 468. As fewer cases were tried, the size of verdicts increased. The causality here may run in both directions: not only would the settlement or abandonment of smaller cases tend to produce larger awards, but higher awards could provide greater inducements for defendants to avoid trial.

In recent data on the state courts of general jurisdiction in the nation's 75 most populous counties, the association of lower trial numbers with higher awards is more ambiguous. From 1992 to 2001, the number of trials in these courts declined dramatically by 47 percent, but the amount awarded to winning plaintiffs underwent a striking decline overall: the median jury award fell 43 percent from $65,000 in 1992 to $37,000 in 2001. But specific categories of cases displayed different patterns. For example, the number of product liability trials decreased by 76 percent, while the median jury award increased by 288 percent (from $140,000 to $543,000). However, premises liability trials decreased by 52 percent, while the median jury award fell by 17 percent (from $74,000 to $61,000). Rather than obeying a single hydraulic principle, specific kinds of cases seem to have distinctive careers.

Another factor that may be associated with cost and complexity is the length of time it takes a case to reach trial. In 1963, the median time from filing to disposition by trial was 16 months; in 2002 the median time was over 20 months. The time from filing to termination either with "no court action" or "before pretrial" has remained relatively constant over the years (six to seven months in the former; seven to eight months in the latter); however, the median time from filing to disposition "before or during pretrial" has fallen from 18 months in 1963 to only 13 months in 2002. Although the disposal of cases during pretrial has become more expeditious, cases proceeding to trial have been taking longer to move through the courts.

One measure of higher investment in tried cases that amplifies the stakes and complexity of trials is the burgeoning of "scientific jury selection" and a panoply of associated techniques involving mock trials, focus groups, and other devices for selecting juries and tailoring advocacy to them. From its beginnings in the early 1970s, the jury consulting industry has grown substantially. It was estimated that in 1982 there were about 25 jury consultants in the United States; in 1994 there were 10 times as many. Another account concluded that in 1999 there were "over 700 people who call themselves jury consultants and over 400 firms offering these types of service." Revenues in 2000 were estimated at about $400 million. The industry's growth during a period in which there are fewer and fewer jury trials may reflect the thinning of lawyers' trial experience. One consultant observes: "It's only going to get bigger, because more and more lawyers will get to be sixty years old, having tried only five or ten cases."

III. FROM FILING TO TRIAL

Interestingly, although the number and rate of trials has fallen, judicial involvement in case activity—at least on some level—has increased. Although the portion of cases that terminate "during or after pretrial" has fallen only slightly from 15 percent in 1963 to 11 percent in 2002, the number of cases that terminated "before pretrial" (but with some type of court action) rose from 20 percent in 1963 to 68 percent in 2002. Clearly, courts are more involved in the early resolution of cases than they used to be.

In 1963, more than half (55 percent) terminated before the occurrence of any "court action." By 2002, only 19 percent terminated at this stage. The big change came in the late 1980s, when the number of cases moving into the "before pretrial" stage began a dramatic increase, so that today nearly 70 percent of cases terminate at this stage as opposed to some 20 percent in 1962.

This tells us that cases are departing the court at an earlier stage, but not how. Both popular speech and a great deal of scholarly discourse proceed as if the universe of disposition is made up of trial and settlement, so that a decline in trials must mean an increase in settlements. Analyzing dispositions in federal courts from 1970 to 2000, Gillian Hadfield concludes that "a smaller percentage of cases were disposed of through settlement in 2000 than was the case in 1970." What increased as trials disappeared was not settlement, but nontrial adjudication. This is consistent with a documented increase in the prevalence of summary judgment. Comprehensive and continuous data are not available, but a Federal Judicial Center (FJC) study provides a glimpse of the change. Comparing a sample of cases in six metropolitan districts over the period 1975–2000, the researchers found that the portion of cases terminated by summary judgment increased from 3.7 percent in 1975 to 7.7 percent in 2000. Assuming that these districts were not grossly unrepresentative, we can juxtapose these figures with our data on trials. In 1975, the portion of disposition by trial (8.4 percent) was more than double the portion of summary judgments (3.7 percent), but in 2000 the summary judgment portion (7.7 percent) was more than three times as large as the portion of trials (2.2 percent).

Analyzing the earlier studies of summary judgment activity and his own study of the Eastern District of Pennsylvania from 2000–2003, Stephen Burbank estimates that:

> the rate of case terminations by summary judgment in federal civil cases nationwide increased substantially in the period from 1960 and 2000,

from approximately 1.8 percent to approximately 7.7 percent. There is evidence, however, that the termination rate—indeed, the rate of activity more generally—under this supposedly uniform rule ranes substantially in different ports of the country and in different types of cases.

In the Eastern District of Pennsylvania, Burbank found that summary judgments increased from 4.1 percent to 4.7 percent of terminations from 2000 to 2003 while trials dropped from 2.5 percent to 1.0 percent. Thus Burbank's figures, like those of the FJC, suggest that we have moved from a world in which dispositions by summary judgment were equal to a small fraction of dispositions by trial into a new era in which dispositions by summary judgment are a magnitude several times greater than the number of trials.

IV. CIVIL FILINGS

A. General

We have been talking about dispositions. Do these changing patterns of dispositions merely reflect changes in filings? Clearly, the decline in trials is not simply a reflection of the cases coming to the federal courts, for the number of trials has declined while the number of filings has increased fivefold. Nor is the decline in trials simply a function of the changing makeup of a docket with fewer of the types of cases that are most likely to get tried and more of the types that rarely go to trial. There are many more civil rights cases (the most trial-prone category) and no appreciable decline in the absolute number of torts cases (the next most trial prone). In 2002, these two categories together made up 37 percent of all district court filings and 35 percent of dispositions, down from 45.5 percent of filings and 38.8 percent of dispositions in 1962. Instead, we see the drop in trial rates occurring in every category, suggesting that the difference lies in what happens in court rather than in a change in the makeup of the caseload.

Filings are the most direct link between courts and the wider society, so they are the place where we can observe changes in this linkage. From 1962 to 1986, filings per million persons increased steadily from about 260 per million persons to four times that; then they fell for six years and then began to fluctuate in the same range—at more than three times the 1960s level.

Filings rose more quickly than the population, but they declined in relation to the size of the economy. Filings per billion dollars of gross domestic product peaked in the mid 1980s at more than twice their 1962 level, but by 2002 they had fallen part of the way back to their 1962 level.

B. Class Actions

One particular sort of filing that deserves special mention is class actions. It is striking that the pattern of class-action filings, falling through the 1980s but rising steeply in the 1990s, is the mirror image of the pattern of the number of trials depicted earlier. Class-action filings fall during the late 1970s and early 1980s when trial numbers reach unprecedented peaks; class-action filings rise from the mid 1990s when trial numbers are falling to unprecedented lows. When we disaggregate class actions by case type we see that this "U" represents two movements: the downward swing tracks the withering of civil rights class actions and the upward swing is driven by two major changes—a newfound willingness to permit tort class actions and a surge of securities class actions following Congress's 1995 attempt to curtail such cases.

Trials in class-action cases are quite rare. The adjudication in class actions tends to occur at pretrial stages—rulings on certification of the class, discovery, motions to dismiss—or after settlement in fairness hearings. It has long been observed that the low trial rate in class actions reflects the high stakes that such cases represent for defendants. Recent developments suggest that corporate defendants, with the help of sections of the plaintiffs' bar, have learned to use the class-action device as an instrument to manage the risk of multiple claims. This provides a useful reminder that the rate of trials may reflect changing strategies by *defendants* as well as by plaintiffs.

There may be an indirect but important connection between class-action numbers and trial numbers: lawyers who file claims as class actions remove a large number of claims from the possibility of being tried individually and replace them with a much smaller number of cases in a category that very rarely eventuates in a trial. So when lawyers undertake to bundle claims in "high trial" areas like torts and civil rights into class actions, we might expect fewer trials. Conversely, the withering of civil rights class actions may be reflected in the great surge of filings and trials in individual civil rights cases.

C. Multi-District Litigation

Another device for bundling large numbers of cases in the federal courts is transfer by the Judicial Panel on Multi-District Litigation (JPML). The JPML has its origins in the Coordinating Committee for Multiple Litigation for the United States District Courts, established in 1962 by Chief Justice Earl Warren to find a way to efficiently deal with more than 2,000 treble-damage antitrust actions, containing more than 25,000 claims for relief, filed in 36 district courts against heavy electrical equipment manufacturers. To deal with these actions, the Committee introduced two major innovations: (1) discovery was coordinated on a national basis, including the creation of a central document depository for use by all the parties; and (2) certain actions were transferred and consolidated for trial. The overall impact of the Committee on this litigation was remarkable: only nine cases went to trial, and only five of those to judgment. Based on that success, the JPML was established in 1968 as a way to coordinate national discovery in other multi-district litigations.

Essentially, the JPML is authorized to transfer actions pending in two or more district courts "involving one or more common questions of fact" to a single district court for consolidated or coordinated pretrial proceedings.

Transfer may be initiated either by motion of a party or by the panel on its own initiative. In theory, once pretrial activity takes place, the cases are returned to their originating districts.

But in fact, most cases are resolved at the MDL stage. "Experience shows that few cases are remanded for trial: most MDL is settled in the transferee court." The percentage of cases remanded is typically in the low single digits.

The number of litigations (i.e., sets of cases) filed with the JPML has risen gradually over time, but there is no evident increase in the number of cases comprising them or the number that involve class-action allegations. Nor is there any evident trend in the dominant subject matters, apart from the decline of anti-trust litigations and the increase in litigations that do not fall within the specified classifications.

V. FEDERAL FORUMS APART FROM CIVIL LITIGATION

A. Criminal Cases and Trials

Some observers have suspected that the decline in civil trials is a response to increasing business on the criminal side of the federal courts. The criminal caseload (measured by the number of defendants) has risen, though more modestly than civil caseloads, from 33,110 in 1962 to 76,827 in 2002. This is about half the rate of increase on the civil side. The pressure to dispose of these cases expeditiously has increased due to the strictures of the 1974 Speedy Trial Act. We occasionally do hear of courts refusing to try civil cases because of the press of criminal business, but one thing that has not happened is the occurrence of more criminal trials. Not only are a smaller percentage of criminal dispositions by trial—under 5 percent in 2002 compared with 15 percent in 1962—but the absolute number of criminal trials has diminished: from 5,097 in 1962 to 3,574 in 2002, a drop of 30 percent.

Are the factors impelling fewer civil trials also at work on the criminal side? Or are there other reasons for the decline of criminal trials? One distinctive feature that may account for the decline in criminal trials is the implementation of determinate sentencing in the federal courts. The federal sentencing guidelines were created by the Sentencing Reform Act of 1984 and went into effect on November 1, 1987. Essentially, they produce a determinate sentencing range by creating two values—a criminal history score based on past criminal conduct and an offense level based on the severity of the instant offense—and then use these values as axes to locate the appropriate sentencing range (expressed in months) on a grid known as the sentencing table. Unless the court determines that a departure from the given sentencing range is warranted due to factors not adequately addressed by the guidelines, the court is bound by the limits of the guideline range. The sentence created is non-parolable, and the availability of good-time credit while in prison is limited, thus enhancing the determinacy and the severity of the guidelines. The guidelines offer an incentive to avoid trial in the form of a criminal-offense-level reduction (one axis of the sentencing grid) for what is termed "acceptance of responsibility." Although proceeding to the guidelines which state that it is only in "rare situations" that the incentive can be preserved after exercising this option.

Gauging the impact of the sentencing guidelines on the number of criminal trials in the federal courts is difficult because many other changes in the criminal justice system have taken place concurrently. Congress has enacted more statutes with mandatory minimum sentences and increased funding for law enforcement, while Department of Justice policies regarding plea and prosecution strategies have changed as well. Although it is difficult to specify conclusions about the direct impact of the sentencing guidelines on trial rates, it is unmistakable that the number of criminal trials has decreased since the implementation of the guidelines. From 1962 to 1991, the percentage of trials in criminal cases remained steady between approximately 13 percent to 15 percent. However, since 1991, the percentage of trials in criminal cases has steadily decreased (with the exception of one slight increase of 0.06 percent in 2001): from 12.6 percent in 1991 to less than 4.7 percent in 2002. That the guidelines contributed to this decline is consistent with the assumption that systemwide implementation of the guidelines did not take place until at least the beginning of the 1990s, due both to constitutional challenges and an overall period of adjustment.

Early studies suggested that the presence of the guidelines increased the rate of trials. One study found that although the systemwide rate of trials remained virtually unchanged by 1990, there was an increase in trial activity for drug and firearms cases (where the penalties were most severe), but a decrease in the amount of trial activity for fraud and related cases. Another early study noted a general increase in the amount of trial activity after the implementation of the guidelines, and an ABA survey of district court judges published in 1992 found that 73 percent of those who responded believed that the guidelines increased the number of trials. However, a study published in 1991 by the U.S. Sentencing Commission found that there was no appreciable difference in the rate of trials due to the sentencing guidelines.

Indeed, there was an increase in trial activity for drug cases from 1987 to 1990; the percentage of drug cases that went to trial increased from 16.1 percent to 18.6 percent. Meanwhile, trial rates for violent crimes (homicide, robbery, and assault) and fraud-related crimes (fraud, embezzlement, and forgery) either remained relatively consistent or decreased slightly: 18.7 percent to 19.1 percent in the former, 10.9 percent to 8.5 percent in the latter. However, beginning in 1991, the total number of cases—drug cases included—that went to trial began to steadily decrease, as noted above. Drug trials as a percentage of total drug defendants fell to 10 percent in 1995 and only 4.1 percent in 2002; trials for violent crime defendants fell to 13.7 percent in 1995 and 6.6 percent in 2002; while trials for defendants accused of fraud-related offenses fell to 6 percent in 1995 and 4.2 percent in 2002.

There has been no noticeable increase in the length of federal criminal trials. The number of trials longer than one day was lower in 2002 than at any point in the previous 30 years. Trials longer than three days make up a larger portion of all trials than they once did, but there are actually fewer of them than there have been since the early 1970s.

B. Bankruptcy

Our figures on the federal district courts do not include bankruptcy. The volume of bankruptcy filings is considerably larger than the volume of filings in the district courts and has been growing more rapidly. However, while bankruptcy filings have multiplied, Elizabeth Warren's research indicates a shrinkage of trial activity that parallels those in the civil and criminal jurisdictions of the district courts. Professor Warren describes a modest increase in the number of adversarial proceedings from 1985 to 2002, but the portion of adversary proceedings terminated "during or after trial" fell from 16.4 percent in 1985 to 4.8 percent in 2002. In 1985, there were 9,287 trials in bankruptcy court; by 2002, there were 3,179—barely more than a third of the total in 1985. Like their Article III brethren, bankruptcy judges preside over fewer trials: in 1985, the average was 37 trials; in 2002 it was about 10.

C. Administrative Adjudication

A significant portion of all adjudication takes place not in the courts, but in various administrative tribunals and forums. The federal government had 1,370 administrative law judges in 2001—more than double the 665 authorized Article III district court judgeships. An uncounted number of similar positions exist in the states. Further research should be undertaken to ascertain the amount and features of this administrative adjudication and whether there are trends that are related to those observed in courts. One provocative foray is the work of Steven L. Schooner, who documents a dramatic drop in protests and contract appeals connected to government procurement over the course of the 1990s. Protests at the General Accounting Office decreased by half over the course of the decade; cases docketed at the five largest agency boards of contract appeals fell to a third or less of their earlier peaks. Again we see parallels to the drop in adjudication in the courts, but can only wonder if these agency forums are typical and how the declines in these various settings are related.

VI. COURT RESOURCES

The presence of larger caseloads, (presumptively) more complex cases, more elaborate pretrial proceedings, and longer trials invites us to imagine that the decline in trials is attributable to resource constraints that disable courts from conducting as many trials as they used to. The appeal of the resource explanation is highlighted by recent cuts in both federal and state courts. Before embracing this view we should recall that in the 1980s a smaller number of district judges with fewer auxiliaries and more meager resources managed to conduct more than twice as many trials as their present-day counterparts. The trends are mixed, but it is difficult to conclude that there are fewer resources relative to demand, at least for the trial courts in the federal system. The number of Article III judges in the district courts has grown from 279 (of 307 authorized) in 1962 to 615 (of 665 authorized) in 2002. They were assisted by 92 senior judges and more than 500 magistrates. However, this increase has fallen short of the increase in caseload. Filing per sitting judge has more than doubled, from 196 in 1962 to 443 in 2002.

Concurrently, the number of non-Article III personnel and total expenditures grew more rapidly. In 1962, there were 5,602 nonjudicial personnel employed by the federal judiciary; in 1992 (the last year that figures were available), that number had grown to 25,947. Judicial expenditures increased from $246 million (1996 dollars) in 1962 to $4.254 billion (1996 dollars) in 2002.

So the decline in trials is accompanied by a larger judicial establishment of which judges form a smaller portion. In 1962 there were 18.9 nonjudicial employees for each Article III district court judge. This fell slightly by 1972 (17.8) but jumped to 28.3 in 1982 and 45.9 in 1992. No figures are available after 1992, but the pattern of total spending by the judiciary suggests that the ratio is larger than ever.

Although the 1962 starting date was picked to maximize the comparability of data, it turns out to have an additional advantage—it lies at the very beginning of a set of momentous changes in the technology of legal work. Such technology had been fairly stable and unchanging since the turn of the last century, when legal work was reshaped by the telephone, the typewriter, comprehensive legal publication, and new research devices like digests and citators. Not much had changed by 1960; perhaps the only noticeable innovation in the first half of the century was the introduction of loose-leaf services. But starting in 1960, there was an accelerating succession of new technologies—photo-reproduction, computerization, fax machines, online data services, overnight delivery, electronic mail, teleconferencing, and so forth—that multiplied the amount of information that could be assembled and manipulated by legal actors. The lawyers who represent parties that appear in federal court work in larger entities, law firms or legal staffs, and come to the courts with enlarged capacities for record keeping, retrieval, and communication. The courts themselves enjoy a similar enhancement of capacity to record, find, examine, and disseminate information.

VII. TRIALS ON APPEAL

Theodore Eisenberg's pioneering exploration of the relationship between trials and appeals finds that tried cases in the federal courts are appealed at roughly four times the rate of cases terminated without trials. Nevertheless, because there are so few tried cases, tried cases form only a small fraction of those appealed—about one in eight in the years 1987–1996. And as the proportion of tried cases falls, the portion of concluded appeals that are from trials falls and so does the absolute number of appellate decisions in tried cases.

Plaintiffs appeal at a higher rate than defendants in nontried cases; defendants appeal more against trial outcomes and they succeed at a higher rate than plaintiffs. Tried cases are thus more likely to be subject to appeal than cases decided without trial and appealed tried cases are more likely to be reversed than appealed nontried cases. What sorts of grounds are the basis for these reversals? Are cases that enter the law reports more likely to be those involving a trial? Or a reversal? Are these changing as the number of trials diminishes?

The body of reported cases continues to expand. In spite of restrictions on publication, the annual increment of published federal cases increased from 5,782 pages in 1962 to 13,490 pages in 2002, an increase of 133 percent. Curiously, as the body of case law becomes ever larger, the presence of authoritative pronouncements of law at the peak of the hierarchy is thinned out. The Supreme Court of the United States decides fewer cases—less than half as many as 20 years ago—and its decisions are marked by less consensus. So doctrine multiplies as decisive adjudication wanes.

VIII. OTHER FORUMS

A. The Number of Trials in State Courts

The great preponderance of trials, both civil and criminal, take place in the state courts. But data about the number, subject, and characteristics of state trials has been scarce and not readily comparable from one state to another. In their symposium paper, Brian Ostrom, Shauna Strickland, and Paula Hannaford of the National Center for State Courts have assembled an unprecedented bank of state trial data into comparable form.

Trials in the courts of general jurisdiction of 21 states (and the District of Columbia) that contain 58 percent of the U.S. population for the years 1976 to 2002 provide a picture of trends in the state courts that overall bear an unmistakable resemblance to the trends in federal courts we have been examining. The portion of cases reaching jury trial declined from 1.8 percent to 0.6 percent of dispositions and bench trials fell from 34.3 percent to 15.2 percent. The absolute number of jury trials is down by one-third and the absolute number of bench trials is down 6.6 percent.

In trials in the nine states (and Puerto Rico) that counted general civil trials (that is, tort, contract, and real property) separately from 1992 to 2002, we see an even more pronounced 44 percent drop in the absolute number of jury trials, while bench trials drop 21 percent. Here the fall in trials is accounted for in part by a fall in the number of dispositions, which decline by 21 percent.

So the portion of cases disposed of by bench trials ends where it begins, at 4.3 percent, while jury trials fall from 1.8 percent to 1.3 percent of dispositions.

The pattern of decline is confirmed by another sampling of state court activity that provides a more precise picture of the parties, claims, and outcomes of trials. Under the sponsorship of the Bureau of Justice Statistics of the U.S. Department of Justice, the National Center for State Courts tracked the trial activity in state courts of general jurisdiction in the 75 most populous counties in the years 1992, 1996, and 2001. The researchers counted all the tort, contract, and real property trials (presumably, those that were resolved by trial, since we are given judgment amounts). In 1992, there were 22,451 trials in these counties. In 2001, there were only 11,908, a 47 percent reduction. Tort trials were down 31.8 percent and contracts trials were down 61 percent. During these same years, tort trials in federal courts decreased by 37.6 percent and federal contract trials were down 47.7 percent.

The attrition of trials in the decade covered was substantial in both state and federal courts, and across different case types. During this decade, state trials were decreasing at a greater rate than trials in federal courts, suggesting that the decline in trials is not driven by some factor peculiar to the federal courts, such as the increase in filings or appellate court endorsement of summary judgment.

On the criminal side, the trial rate has moved in the same direction in the state courts as in the federal courts. From 1976 to 2002, the overall rate of criminal trials in courts of general jurisdiction in the 22 states for which data is available dropped from 8.5 percent of dispositions to 3.3 percent. The decrease was similar in jury trials (from 3.4 percent to 1.3 percent) and bench trials (from 5.0 percent to 2.0 percent). Although dispositions grew by 127 percent in these courts, the absolute number of jury trials fell by 15 percent and of bench trials by 10 percent. The patterns of attrition resemble those in the federal courts, where criminal trials fell from 15.2 percent to 4.7 percent of dispositions in those years.

It might be supposed that the decline in the percentage of criminal trials reflects an increase in the proportion of lesser crimes and a decline in the presence of felonies, but in the 13 states that provide separate figures for felonies, trials as a portion of felony dispositions fell from 8.9 percent in 1976 to 3.2 percent in 2002. The absolute number of felony jury trials remained fairly constant, but in 2002 they made up only 2.2 percent of the larger number of felony dispositions, compared to 5.2 percent in 1976. The number of bench trials dropped substantially: in 2002, bench trials were only 1 percent of felony dispositions, down from 3.7 percent in 1976.

Although the state data is less comprehensive, it is sufficiently abundant to indicate that the trends in state court trials generally match those in the federal courts. In both there is a decline in the percentage of dispositions that are by jury trial and bench trial. In both there is a decline in the absolute number of jury trials and bench trials. In the federal courts, nonjury trials have declined even more dramatically than jury trials; in the state courts, it is jury trials that are shrinking faster.

B. The Number of ADR Proceedings

One of the most prominent explanations of the decline of trials is the migration of cases to other forums. Thomas Stipanowich has pulled together the elusive data about the prevalence and growth of ADR, including both court-annexed programs and free-standing forums (e.g., the American Arbitration Association, Center for Public Resources, JAMS). To these we might add forums within organizations—so-called internal dispute resolution (IDR)—a category that overlaps the "free-standing" one to the extent that organizations retain these providers to administer or staff their programs.

How much does ADR/IDR affect the trial dockets of the courts? Once cases are filed in court, they may be deflected into mediation or arbitration with the encouragement of the court. Much of the most visible ADR occurs not as an alternative to filing, but after a case is filed in court. Stipanowich reports that in 2001, some 24,000 cases were referred to some form of ADR in the federal courts. That would be about one-seventh of the number of dispositions that year. How this affected the number or rate of trials remains to be learned. In 1992, arbitration accounted for only 1.7 percent of contract dispositions and 3.5 percent of tort dispositions in the state courts in the nation's 75 largest counties.

Alternatively, claimants may pursue matters in noncourt forums without filing a case in court. They may do this either on their own volition or under the constraint of a mandatory arbitration clause. We know that a significant number of claims are kept out of the courts by such clauses, but we do not know how many. Data on the caseload of these free-standing forums is elusive. One of the oldest and best established of these is the American Arbitration Association (AAA). During the period that contract filings in federal court grew spectacularly, the AAA's Commercial Arbitration Docket underwent a corresponding growth from less than 1,000 cases in 1960 to 11,000 in 1988. In the 1990s, when contracts filings tumbled in both federal and state courts, the AAA docket remained steady and even began to increase late in the decade; by 2002 there were something over 17,000 of them.

Overall, the caseload of ADR institutions remains small in comparison to that of the courts. A RAND Institute of Civil Justice study of Los Angeles estimated that the entire "private" caseload in 1993 was about one-twentieth of the caseload of the public courts (including small claims). But recourse to ADR forums was growing rapidly while court caseloads were stable. Privately handled cases were larger: some 60 percent involved claims of $25,000 or more, while only 14 percent of public claims were that large. This implies that private dockets contained almost one-fifth of the large cases. Not all of these would necessarily have gone to court earlier, but we see here diversion of cases away from the courts that is of a magnitude that might contribute significantly to the decline of trials in public courts. Los Angeles boasted an atypically rich variety of private dispute handlers, so these findings are provocative rather than representative. They also alert us to refine our formulation of the vanishing trial phenomenon. As Stipanowich observes, several prominent sectors of arbitration have increasingly acquired features associated with public litigation—for example, securities arbitration has acquired an organized specialist bar, discovery, published decisions, and punitive damages. In such instances, perhaps we should think of the relocation of trials outside public courts rather than the disappearance of trials.

IX. CAUSES AND CONSEQUENCES

A. Causes of the Trial Implosion

For a long time, the great majority of cases of almost every kind in both federal and state courts have terminated by settlement. This reflects the exigencies of litigation, which lead parties to trade off the possibility of preferred outcomes for avoidance of the costs and risks of proceeding through trial. It also reflects the architecture of the system, which has capacity to give full treatment to only a minority of the matters entitled to invoke it. Instead, it relies on a combination of cost barriers (not only out-of-pocket expenditures, but queues and risk) to induce parties to abandon claims or negotiate a settlement on the basis of the signals and markers that it generates. We would expect that as the population of claims increases more rapidly than the capacity of the system to provide full treatment, the portion receiving that treatment would decrease. What we are seeing since the late 1980s is not only a continuation in the shrinkage of *percentage* of cases that go to trial, but a shrinkage of the *absolute number* of cases that go to trial. The diminishment of the trial element in the work of the courts reflects and is entwined with many other changes. At the risk of underestimating the complexity of this process, let me attempt a rough foray into causes of the decline on the one hand and consequences of that decline on the other.

The first cluster of explanations are what might be called diminished-supply arguments, that is, that cases did not eventuate in trials because they did not get to court in the first place or, having come to court, they have departed for another forum. Not getting to court may be part of the explanation. Filings have been going down, especially in the state courts. This may reflect fewer unresolved grievances, or a change in estimations of cost and likely success by claimants or by lawyers who might have represented them. But the declines in filings are more modest than the declines in trials. For example, in the 10 states there is data for, the total number of cases (tort, contract, and real property) disposed of in 2002 (a rough indicator of the number of filings a year or two earlier) was down 21 percent from 1992, presumably leaving more resources for conducting trials in the remaining cases, but the number of trials in these states fell by 27 percent.

In any event, the diminished-supply explanation appears quite inapplicable to the federal courts. Filings dropped from their record high of 273,056 in 1985 (also the record year for trials) to a recent low of 207,094 in 1991 and since then have fluctuated mostly in the upper part of that range—approximately five times as great as filings in 1962. In comparison with the state data discussed above, federal filings rose by 19 percent from 1992 to a new record high in 2002. During that decade, civil trials declined by 43 percent. Some observers have proposed that the drop in trials in federal courts is attributable to a shift of filings away from types of cases with high trial rates. But civil rights and torts, the two most trial-prone categories, together comprised 39 percent of all filings in 1962 and 37 percent of a much larger total in 2002.

A more persuasive line of argument is the diversion argument—that the claims and contests are there but they are in different forums. In the discussion of ADR above, we saw that there seems to be some substance to this, but it should be kept in mind that the decline in trials is very general, across the board, and is not confined to sectors or localities where ADR has flourished.

A third explanation might be called the economic argument, that is, that going to trial has become more costly as litigation has become more technical, complex, and expensive. Rising costs of increasingly specialized lawyers, the need to deploy expensive experts, jury consultants, and all the associated expenses have priced some parties out of the market. For those who can afford to play, the increased transaction costs enlarge the overlap in settlement ranges. More and more of the players in the legal arena are corporate actors who view participation in the legal arena in terms of long-term strategy. Increasingly, they regard much legal involvement as just another business input, one that must be subjected to cost controls. One part of such control is alternative sourcing—diverting what might have been in the courts into alternative forums.

Litigant strategizing about trials is affected by perceptions of their costs and outcomes and, in particular, by the perception that awards (and therefore risks) are increasing in size. As we noted earlier, the evidence about award size is mixed. As trial becomes more rare and more expensive, it makes sense that smaller cases would leave the field and awards in the fewer claims that go to trial and prevail would be higher. The departure of smaller cases is compatible with the increasing length of trials, the increasing frequency of appeals, the relatively greater decline of bench trials, and with reports from Jury Verdict Research of constantly rising awards, reports whose representativeness is suspect on other grounds. Yet the 75 county studies provide substantial contrary evidence that awards may be falling rather than rising.

However, litigants respond not to what is happening in the courts but to what they *believe* is happening. The perception of higher awards complements the widespread view in defense circles that trials are not only expensive, but are risky because juries are arbitrary, sentimental, and "out of control," and reinforces strategies of settlement to avoid trial. We know from several studies that the media are far more likely to report verdicts for plaintiffs and large awards than defendant verdicts, small awards, or the reduction or reversal of awards. Notwithstanding occasional efforts to debunk some of the "litigation explosion" legends, the regular consumer of media reports would be badly misinformed about the number of product liability and medical malpractice cases, the size of jury awards, the incidence of punitive damages, and the regularity with which corporate defendants succeed in defeating individual claimants. Whatever the source of the skewed coverage, the audience receives the reassuring message that David generally manages to best Goliath, as well as the disturbing corollary that undeserving or spurious Davids are thick on the ground. This pattern of media bias also suggests that the public greatly overestimates the number of trials and does not perceive the recent and drastic decline. This may well hold true for a very large section of legal professionals, as well.

The diminished supply, diversion, and cost arguments focus on the assessments, incentives, and strategies of the parties. Another set of explanations focuses on institutional factors, on the courts themselves. One such explanation is the notion that courts lack the resources to hold more trials. The increase in expenditure and in nonjudicial personnel throws some doubt on this. And the history suggests that with fewer judges and personnel and far less money, the federal courts 20 years ago were conducting more than twice as many civil trials. Even given an increase in mandatory noncivil matters and postulating increased complexity of cases, it seems doubtful that lack of court resources is a major constraint on the number of trials.

Courts are not only worked on by external forces, but are the site and source of changing institutional practice and of ideology that inspires and justifies that practice. Modern procedure has conferred on trial court judges broader unreviewed (and perhaps unreviewable) discretion. This discretion has been used to shape a new style of judging, frequently referred to as managerial judging. "[T]he discretion of trial judges has expanded partly because of increased complexity but even more so from the multiplication of discretionary procedural, evidentiary and management decisions." The expansion of managerial judging enlarges the discretion of trial judges and diminishes the control of appellate judges:

> Managerial decisions involve a different, and more expansive, sort of discretion than purely legal decisions. For one thing, a judge's managerial decisions typically are insulated from appellate review, because they are interlocutory in nature, often are made off the record, and, in any event, typically are subject to a lenient "abuse of discretion" standard of review. But the difference between legal decisions and managerial ones runs much deeper. When "judges make legal decisions, the parties have an opportunity to marshal arguments based on an established body of principles. . . ." [M]anagerial discretion is different in nature. Judges deciding how to manage cases on their dockets have a wide array of tactics available and, indeed, choose to exercise their supervisory discretion in widely disparate ways, even when handling the same exact case.

These institutional changes flow from and reinforce changes in judicial ideology. Trial judges are equipped with enhanced discretionary power in order to resolve cases and clear dockets. In the 1970s, as institutional pressures focused measures of judges' performance on their control over caseload, influential judges and administrators of the federal courts embraced the notion that judges were problem solvers and case managers as well as adjudicators. Training programs emphasized the role of the judge as mediator, producing settlements by actively promoting them. This turn to judges as promoters of settlement and case managers was endorsed by the amendment of Rule 16 of the Federal Rules of Civil Procedure in 1983 and by the enactment of the Civil Justice Reform Act in 1990.

B. Trial Lawyers and Judges

As the number of judges and lawyers grows and the number of trials falls, the fund of trial experience of both judges and lawyers is diminished. The stock of judicial experience with trials is diminished. In 1962, there were 39 trials for each sitting federal district judge (18.2 criminal and 20.8 civil). Twenty-five years later in 1987, near the height of the boom in trials, there were 35.3 trials (13.0 criminal and 22.3 civil) for each sitting district judge. In 2002, there were just 13.2 trials (5.8 criminal and 7.4 civil) for each sitting district judge—roughly one-third as many as in 1962. It is not only district judges that are conducting fewer trials: Elizabeth Warren reports that trials per bankruptcy judge declined from about 37 per year in 1985 to 10 per year in 2002.

These figures overstate the number of trials actually conducted by sitting district judges. If every magistrate trial event occurred in a separate case and that case did not also include a trial conducted by a district judge, the total number of trials held by district judges in 2002 would be something like 3,610. But since there were some cases in which both a magistrate and a district judge presided over trials, the number of such cases should be added to the 3,610 to determine the number of trials conducted by district judges. Not all of these judges were sitting judges. Some trials were conducted by senior judges, a category whose numbers have grown more rapidly than the roster of sitting judges. In 1973, there were 80 senior district judges, one for every 4.8 sitting district judges; in 2002, there were 285 senior judges, one for every 2.2 sitting judges.

It is harder to track the shrinkage of trial experience among lawyers. During the 1962–2002 period, the number of lawyers roughly tripled. The number of lawyers per 100,000 persons grew from 160.4 in 1970 to 366.0 in 2002.

It seems undeniable that the average lawyer has less trial experience. But within that larger lawyer population, the stock of experienced trial lawyers is diminished. The membership of the Association of Trial Lawyers of America, which includes a very substantial portion of lawyers who regularly represent individual plaintiffs at trial, is at roughly the same level as in the early 1980s. The rise of programs for training trial lawyers through simulations (e.g., NITA) suggests a corresponding shrinkage of opportunities for "on-the-job" training.

Kevin McMunigal argues that diminished trial experience results in an atrophy of advocacy skills that may both lessen future trials, as inexperienced lawyers are unwilling to undertake the risk of trial, and also distort settlements as lawyers without trial experience are less able to evaluate cases accurately. The decline in the centrality of trial advocacy to lawyers' work (and its replacement by pretrial maneuver) is registered in the language used by practitioners: by the 1970s, lawyers described themselves as "litigators" in contradistinction to "trial lawyers."

C. Consequences of the Trial Implosion

Every other part of the legal world grows: there are more statutes, more regulations, more case law, more scholarship, more lawyers, more expenditure, more presence in public consciousness. In all these respects the growth of the legal world outstrips that of the society or the economy. But trials are shrinking, not only in relation to the rest of the legal world, but relative to the society and the economy. From 1962 to 2002, federal trials per million persons fell by 49 percent; from 1976 to 2002, trials in 22 state courts of general jurisdiction fell by 33 percent.

Since the economy was growing more rapidly than the population, the number of trials per billion dollars of gross domestic product (GDP) has fallen more steadily and precipitously. By 2002 federal civil trials per billion of GDP were less than one-quarter as many as in 1962, even though spending on law as a portion of GDP had increased during that period.

What difference does it make? Aren't we just as well off with fewer trials?

Do fewer trials mean less law or worse law? Trials are not exactly an endangered species—at least for now. But their presence has diminished. In 2002, there were 20 percent fewer federal civil trials than in 1962 and about 30 percent fewer criminal trials. Trials as a portion of federal dispositions are a fraction of their earlier levels—roughly one-third for criminal cases and one-eighth for civil cases. Trends in the state courts over the past quarter-century point to a comparable decline of trials there.

As trials shrink as a presence within the legal world, they are displaced from the central role assigned them in the common law. Although, as Lawrence Friedman observes, there was never a time when trial was the modal way of resolving civil cases, common law procedure has been defined by the presence of this discreet plenary event, to which all else was prelude or epilog. But now we see a great elaboration of pretrial adjudication, of alternatives to trial, and of posttrial procedures. The number of disputes increases and the amount of legal doctrine proliferates, but they are connected by means other than trial.

The decline in trials may have some direct distributive effects. Eisenberg and Farber computed the win rates at trial and overall for various pairings of parties in nonpersonal injury diversity cases from 1986 to 1994. They found that corporate parties were far more successful both as plaintiffs and defendants than were individual parties. Generally, in each pairing of party types, plaintiffs prevailed in settlement more frequently than they did at trial—with a single exception. That exception was when an individual plaintiff faced a corporate defendant; in that pairing, which went to trial at the highest rate, plaintiffs did better at trial. We do not know how much of this advantage remains after 10 more years of declining trials.

More generally, how is the character of the law changed by the absence of trials? Legal contests become more like those in the civil law, not a single plenary event, but a series of encounters with more judicial control, more documentary submissions, and less direct oral confrontation. Settlements entail "bargaining in the shadow of the law," so the influence of legal doctrine is present, but is thoroughly mixed with considerations of expense, delay, publicity and confidentiality, the state of the evidence, the availability and attractiveness of witnesses, and a host of other contingencies that lie beyond the substantive rules of law. It is "the law" in its broad sense of process that casts the shadow, not merely its doctrinal core.

The signals and markers that provide guidance for settlements derive increasingly from pronouncements that are not connected with an authoritative determination of facts. What does this do to the clarity of signals? Are clear signals better than fuzzy ones?

Several studies suggest that in the absence of trials, the decision-making process of adjudication may get swallowed up by the surrounding bargaining process. This dissolution of legal standards is evident in Janet Cooper Alexander's description of securities class-action litigation as "a world where all cases settle." In such a world, "it may not even be possible to base settlement on the merits because lawyers may not be able to make reliable estimates of expected trial outcomes.... There is nothing to cast a shadow in which the parties can bargain." Judges preside over routine settlements that reflect not legal standards but the strategic position of the repeat players.

Marygold Melli, Howard Erlanger, and Elizabeth Chambliss observed that in the child support arena they explored, there was a

> question of who is in fact casting the shadow of the law. The expectation of what a particular judge would set for child support had to be determined from the cases in his or her court—most of which involved settlement. The shadow of the law, therefore, was cast by the agreements of the parties. It seems that, rather than a system of bargaining in the shadow of the law, divorce may well be one of adjudication in the shadow of bargaining.

Judith Resnik found in the prevalence of consent decrees—in which judges (in effect) delegate official power to the negotiators before the bench—another example of the supposedly central and independent formal process of adjudication becoming subordinated to the supposedly penumbral process of bargaining that surrounds it. In all these instances the absence of an authoritative determination of facts transforms adjudication into a spiral of attribution in which supposedly autonomous decisionmakers take cues from other actors who purport to be mirroring the decisions of the former.

Indeed, the portion of the shadow cast by formal adjudication may be shrinking. Although the number of appeals has increased, the number subject to intensive full-dress review has declined. More appeals are decided on the basis of briefs alone, without oral argument. Appellate courts decide many more of their cases without published opinions or without any opinion at all. And increasingly they ratify what the courts below have done.

The decline of trials is occurring in a setting in which the amount of law is increasing rapidly. There are more federal regulatory statutes, more agencies, more staff, more enforcement expenditures, and more rules. A rough measure of the sheer quantity of rules may be derived from the number of pages added to the *Federal Register* each year: in 1960 there were 14,477 pages added; in 2002, 80,322 pages. There were comparable increases in the amount of regulation by state and local government.

The corpus of authoritative legal material has grown immensely over our period. The amount of published commentary that glosses this authoritative material has grown apace. The number of law reviews has multiplied and the average output of each has grown. The number of entries in the *Index to Legal Periodicals and Books* grew from 22,031 in 1982 to 382,428 in 2002. Parallel to the growth of these scholarly sources was a proliferation of less formal channels of legal information. The profusion of legal materials has outrun these printed sources. Since their inception in 1973, online databases have multiplied access to legal materials.

What is the relation between this profusion of legal information and the shrinking number of trials? Apparently, of the increasingly more numerous reported cases, a smaller portion reflect adjudication in which there was a trial. And the secondary literature, which in almost every subject continues to grow at an even faster rate than the number of reported cases, presumably analyzes materials that are generated in nontrial formats. So we have a growth in the amount of legal doctrine that is increasingly independent of trials.

In a realm of ever-proliferating legal doctrine, the opportunities for arguments and decisions about the law are multiplied, while arguments and decisions become more detached from the texture of facts—at least from facts that have weathered the testing of trial. The general effects of judicial activity are derived less from a fabric of examples of contested facts and more from an admixture of doctrinal exegesis, discretionary rulings of trial judges, and the strategic calculations of the parties. Contests of interpretation replace contests of proof. Paradoxically, as legal doctrine becomes more voluminous and more elaborate, it becomes less determinative of the outcomes produced by legal institutions.

Again, it is necessary to emphasize that the vanishing trial phenomenon includes not only a decline in trials within the core legal institutions but also a diffusion and displacement of trial-like things into other settings—administrative boards, tribunals, ADR forums, and so forth. Although trials in court become less attractive and/or available to litigants, legal counters are invoked in more settings. In these other forums, public law is both extended and blurred; there is more legal flesh and less bones to give it shape. At the same time that courts are a declining site of trials, they are, at least potentially, an increasing site of supervisory oversight of the trial process elsewhere. As adjudication is diffused and privatized, what courts do is changing as they become the site of a great deal of administrative processing of cases, along with the residue of trials in high-stakes and intractable cases. The consequences of these developments and the shape of the legal system to which they are leading remain hidden from us.

DISCUSSION QUESTIONS

1. Why have federal trials dropped by more than 60 percent since 1985?
2. What types of trials have risen and how has Congress impacted such types of trials?
3. Explain how the Judiciary has contributed to the decline of trials.
4. Explain the differences between civil and criminal jury trial numbers in state and federal courts.
5. What consequences have become apparent from the decline of trials?

PART IV

Corrections

Prison comes to mind most often when people think of corrections. This is understandable given the history of corrections and the folklore about prison life, and the fact that incarceration is the most visible part of the process. Many of us have seen the looming walls, barbed wire fences, and searchlights of a prison. The prison is also brought to our attention by the media whenever there is inmate unrest or an escape. And it is the prison that legislators and politicians speak about when they debate changes in the penal code or appropriations for corrections. Yet for students of criminal justice, it should be no surprise that less than one-third of offenders under supervision are in prison and jails. Most offenders are punished in the community through probation, intermediate sanctions, facilities, and organizations responsible for the management of people accused or convicted of criminal offenses.

COMMUNITY CORRECTIONS

Since the early nineteenth century, supervision in the community has been recognized as an appropriate punishment for some offenders. Its popularity dropped as Americans became weary of crime in the 1980s. Legislatures began passing tough sentencing laws and stipulated that incarceration should be the priority punishment; however, more recently criminal justice scholars recognized that many imprisoned offenders, if properly supervised, could be punished in a more cost effective manner in the community.

Beside prisons and jails, corrections include probation, halfway house, education and work release, boot camps, parole supervision, counseling, and community services. One of the biggest debates on community corrections is whether or not they are effective. In his chapter "What Works? Questions and Answers about Prison Reform," Martinson examines the effectiveness of different types of community corrections by discussing empirical studies done on each type of program. He discusses studies on a multitude of different programs, including individual and group counseling, probation and parole, educational training, and many other forms of community corrections. Community corrections can also include programs that help inmates successfully reenter society. Travis and Petersilia further discuss prisoner reentry in their chapter, "Reentry Reconsidered: A New Look at an Old Question." They stress the current necessity for reentry programs, and examine the potential benefits to certain reentry programs. Effectiveness is not the only debate that comes with community corrections though. Safety of the everyday citizen is also discussed in association with the use of community corrections.

With the state of our economy, cutting costs is essential. Billions of dollars are currently being spent to incarcerate more individuals for longer periods of time. In fact, due to the increase in sentence lengths, inmates are getting older, which presents new challenges to the criminal justice system. In their chapter, "The Aging Inmate," Rikard and Rosenberg consider the challenges that older inmates present and how the criminal justice system should deal with the increase in the age of inmates. By increasing the use of intermediate sanctions, the criminal justice system could not only save money, but it could also lessen the overwhelming burden on the prisons. Morris and Tonry argue the need for intermediate sanctions in their chapter, "Between Prison and Probation: Toward a Comprehensive Punishment System." They discuss that intermediate sanctions can be used to punish offenders that do not need the restrictions of prison and offenders who need more restrictions than those offered by probation.

Many of the alternatives to incarceration rely on advances in technology such as electronic anklets, video surveillance, or global positioning systems. These alternatives rely on cheap and inexpensive invasive measures, such as regular urine and blood testing. New technologies in community corrections offer possibilities of reduced costs and better efficiency; however, these electronic supervision tools also have the possibility of causing problems. They could break, fail to report violations, or cause officers more stress. With electronic-supervision technology, there is also the question of privacy. Many argue that those under community supervision have lost their right to privacy, while others argue that this type of technology simply infringes on the privacy of individuals too much. Although new technology offers endless possibilities for the future of community corrections, the possibility of technological malfunction and privacy issues leave many concerned.

PRISON PRIVATIZATION MOVEMENT

To save money the federal and state governments have been exploring the privatization of certain aspects of their systems. The number of state and federal prisons has been increasing and one area that has been pursued, with some success, is the privatization of prisons. In addition to cost saving, there is evidence that private prisons are safer, may offer better and more diverse programs, and outperform public-run facilities on a number of other indicators. Lukemeyer and McCorkle offer evidence to support this as they detail the increase in prison privatization in their chapter, "The Privatization of Incarceration."

In the United States, private prisons are growing. We now have more than 260 correctional facilities housing about 99,000 inmates. With the growth of private prisons come questions as to their costs and benefits. Many would argue that the greatest appeal of private prisons is their promise of cost effectiveness. Studies conducted by the prison industry show that private prisons may be more cost effective; however, studies conducted by unbiased sources have shown that this may not actually be the case. These studies revealed that private prisons give the impression of being less expensive because they take only healthy inmates that will not be expensive to house.

In the wake of a three-prisoner escape from a minimum/medium security for-profit prison in Arizona that led to the murder of a couple, questions have been circulating about the security of private prisons. The public fears that an incident like the one in Arizona could occur at any other private prison. Studies on the safety of private prisons show mixed reviews. While some find that private prisons have fewer incidences of escapes and inmate disturbances, others find that they have higher incidences of inmate escapes. Due to the concerns over cost and safety, many would argue that the jury is still out on private prisons.

MENTAL ILLNESS

Many researchers and policy makers believe that an increase in incarceration is the result of deinstitutionalizing mental illness. As mental health facilities have closed more prisons have opened, and individuals that may have been fit for the former find themselves in the latter. Public perceptions of the mentally ill have changed and with a bevy of high-profile incidents, concerns over the link between mental illness and violent behavior has grown. In his chapter, "Mental illness, crime, and violence: Risk, context, and social control," Markowitz examines the role of deinstitutionalization of mental illness and the potential impact it has had on public perceptions.

Currently, rates of mental illness are higher in prison than in the community at large. Studies have shown that the majority of local jail inmates and state and federal inmates have symptoms of serious mental health illnesses. This is occurring at a rapid rate due to the slashing of mental health budgets in order to continue to build more prisons. Now the people that would traditionally be placed in a mental health facility are being sentenced to prison. The problem is that prisons were never built to handle the treatment of serious mental illness. Prisons tend to be ill-equipped to appropriately treat these mentally ill inmates. As a result, these inmates receive little or no meaningful treatment.

WOMEN IN PRISON

Overall, crime in the United States is declining, but female crime is increasing. This increase in female offending has resulted in an increase in female incarceration and brought with it a number of issues that are not accompanied with male incarceration. Females cope with incarceration differently than men and need different programs, facilities, health-care, and supervision. Many women are new or expecting mothers when they enter prison and develop prison families. Additionally, incarcerated women are disproportionately victimized by inmates and prison staff. Each of these issues along with some explanations on why female crime is increasing is discussed further by Baker and colleagues in their chapter "The Unique Experience of Female Offenders."

In the past three decades, the number of women in prison has increased over 800 percent, with two-thirds of these women being incarcerated for non-violent crimes. The war on drugs can account for some of this dramatic increase, as a substantial number of incarcerated women are there for drug offenses. Prisons were not prepared to handle a larger female inmate population. This means that women in prison are not getting the proper programs and conditions that are necessary for them. For example, the number of women giving birth in prisons has increased substantially. The newborn babies are allowed to stay in the facility with the new mother for about 12 to 18 months; however, only nine states have prison nursery programs. With an increase in the amount of women that are pregnant in prison comes a need for greater cleanliness and hygienic standards. Many studies have recommended implementing programs so that facilities can take proper care of the infants being born, as well as for the prisons to reevaluate how their facilities are cleaned and maintained. Unfortunately, with the collapse of the economy, budgets are being slashed, especially prison budgets. Many states are closing down multiple prisons to save money, which means that improving the standards of women prisons is low on the priority list.

The corrections system has seen significant changes in the last few decades. Not only has there been an increase in the number of community corrections programs, especially with the rise of technology, but there have also been many unexpected changes to the characteristics of the prison inmates and the type of prison they are housed in. All these changes have brought many debates along with them, mostly concerning the safety of society, and how to handle the newer inmates. A ough changes should be made in prisons and community corrections, bec of modifications of the corrections system, the unfortunate state of the ec ny is not helping the situation. Instead of making changes to the existing s to better them, states are closing facilities.

WRITING ASSIGNMENTS

1. pro or con position to the itermediate punishments, probation. Do they arise necessity, out of planning evaluation, or stem from our dards of justice?

hat is community corrections nd what role might it play in the future of corrections in the United States?

3. Discuss some of the new challenges facing corrections today. What might be done to assuage some of the problems each of these challenges brings?
4. Prisons are not equipped to handle the growing female inmate and mentally ill inmate populations. What changes should be made to the prison system to be better suited for these inmates?

19

Between Prison and Probation: Toward a Comprehensive Punishment System

Norval Morris
Michael Tonry

With record-high incarceration rates and overwhelming probation caseloads, Morris and Tonry argue for the need for intermediate punishments. These sanctions can be used in the community to punish offenders who do not require the restrictions of prison as well as offenders who require more restrictions than those imposed by probation.

There [are now] more than 1,000,000 Americans aged 18 and over in prison and jail, and more than 2,500,000 on parole or probation. If one adds those on bail or released awaiting trial or appeal and those serving other punishments such as community service orders, the grand total under the control of the criminal justice system exceeds four million, nearly 2 percent of the nation's adult population.

The pressure of these numbers on insufficient and mostly old penal institutions and on sparsely staffed probation offices has sharpened interest in all punishments lying between the prison and the jail at one end and insufficiently supervised probation at the other—there is general agreement about the need to develop and expand "intermediate punishments" but the path to that end is far from clear.

There are two main lines of argument. First, it is submitted that there has been a failure in this country to develop and institutionalize a range of punishments lying between incarceration and probation. That argument can stand *alone* and would support an expansion of intermediate punishments without considering any questions of sentencing processes. The selection between those properly committed to prison and those sentenced to intermediate punishments cannot be based alone on the gravity of their crimes or the lengths of their criminal records, nor can the choice between probation and an intermediate punishment.

The second line of argument takes the matter further: for certain categories of offenders now in prison, some though not all could better be sentenced to intermediate punishments, and for certain categories of offenders now on probation, some though not all could be better subjected to more intensive controls in the community than probation now provides.

The first argument is obvious enough and does not deny the conventional wisdom; indeed, such is the extent of current experimentation with intermediate punishments that the ground is fertile and the time precisely right for their growth. The second argument will meet with more opposition since it seems to contradict the intuitive sense that like cases should be treated alike, that crimes of equal severity committed by criminals with equal criminal records should be punished identically. We regard this position as an erroneous application of principles of "just dessert." A comprehensive and just sentencing system requires principled "interchangeability" of punishment of "like" cases, some going to prison, some receiving an intermediate punishment. Similarly, there must be principled interchangeability of punishment of like cases, with some being put on probation while others receive the more intensive control or qualitatively different experience of an intermediate punishment.

• • •

[The following is a bare statement of our recommendations:]

- Intermediate punishments should be applied to many criminals now in prison and jail and to many criminals now sentenced to probation or a suspended sentence.
- Intermediate punishments must be rigorously enforced; they should not, as is too often the present case, be ordered absent adequate enforcement resources.
- Breaches of conditions of intermediate punishments must be taken seriously by the supervising authority and, in appropriate cases, by

the sentencing judge, if these punishments are to become credible sanctions.

- The fine should be greatly expanded, in amount and in frequency, both as a punishment standing alone and as part of a punishment package. Fines must be adjusted to the offender's financial capacity (to be achieved by a system of "day fines") and must be collected; this requires innovative assessment and enforcement arrangements, since at present fines are set too low, do not sufficiently match the means of the offender, and are too often not collected.
- The use of community service orders, standing alone or as part of a punishment package, should be greatly increased. Such punishments are applicable to the indigent and to the wealthy; they have much to contribute provided, as for other intermediate punishments, they are vigorously supervised and enforced.
- Intensive probation is a mechanism by which reality can be brought to all intermediate punishments. Allied to house arrest, treatment orders, residential conditions up to house arrest, buttressed by electronic monitoring where appropriate, and paid for by fees for service by the offender where that is realistic, intensive supervision has the capacity both to control offenders in the community and to facilitate their growth to crime-free lives.
- Current sentencing reforms, both proposals and developments, devote inadequate attention to intermediate punishments. Sentencing guidelines, legislative or voluntary, shaped by a sentencing commission or by a court system, must provide better guidance to the judiciary in the use of intermediate punishments if a comprehensive sentencing system is to be developed. In particular:
  1. there is a range of offense–offender relationships in which incarcerative and intermediate punishments are equally applicable;
  2. there is a range of offense–offender relationships in which intermediate punishments and lesser community-based controls are equally applicable;
  3. the sentencing judge requires adequate information about the offender and his financial and personal circumstances to decide on the applicability to each convicted offender of a fine, of a community service order, of a treatment or residential order, of intensive supervision, or of a split sentence involving incarceration and an intermediate punishment—or a mixture of several of these punishments;
  4. the judge should retain ultimate responsibility for the decision on the "back-up" sentence, that is, on what should be done if the conditions of an intermediate punishment are not adhered to.
- As intermediate punishments become part of a comprehensive sentencing system, their efficacy must be critically evaluated so that, in time, an effective treatment classification may emerge.

THE OVERUSE OF IMPRISONMENT AND PROBATION

The figures again: 1,000,000 in prison and jail, over 2,500,000 on probation. How many of these would be better subjected to intermediate punishments cannot be precisely calculated but that the number is large can be confidently affirmed.

Who among the sentenced offenders now in prison or jail need not be there? One way to get at this question is to define the criteria that justify incarceration and then to ask how many in prison and jail do not meet those criteria.

Some years ago, one of us argued in *The Future of Imprisonment* that prison is an appropriate punishment only when one or more of the following three conditions is fulfilled:

- Any lesser punishment would depreciate the seriousness of the crime or crimes committed.
- Imprisonment is necessary for deterrence, general or special.
- Other less restrictive sanctions have been frequently or recently applied to this offender.

We hope it is not stubborn persistence in error that leads us to reaffirm allegiance to those propositions. They track ideas offered by the American Law Institute's *Model Penal Code* and by the American Bar Association's *Standards for Criminal Justice*. Both of these organizations and many other commentators on sentencing have expressed a preference for parsimony in incarceration with a presumption against that punishment unless it be necessary for one or more of these three purposes: to affirm the gravity of the crime, to deter the criminal and others who are like-minded, or because other sanctions have proved insufficient.

Judged by these criteria there are many in prison and jail who need not be there, who are at a shallow end of severity of crime and have criminal records that do not trigger any one of these selecting criteria. How many is a matter of guesswork. Prison wardens differ in their estimates, but it is common to hear talk of 10 to 15 percent. And there are other straws in the wind of this assessment.

In practice, there is another reason, and an increasingly popular reason, why convicted criminals are imprisoned. The sentencing judge may be skeptical that imprisoning a given criminal is necessary to reaffirm any behavioral standards, may doubt that it will have either a general or special deterrent effect, and may doubt that imprisonment will prove any more effective, whatever its purposes, than any other punishment. But this, at least, the judge knows: an offender who is in prison will not be committing any crimes against other than the prison community. Incapacitation plays an increasing role in the sentencing decision and may in considerable part account for the present overcrowding of penal institutions.

Incapacitation is a function of risk-assessment. This becomes clear when "caps" are put on prison populations or on jail populations by court orders pursuant to Eighth Amendment suits. Those running the prisons or jails have frequently had to arrange, and have arranged, early release programs, freeing many who otherwise would be in prison or jail. Wisely they select for such release the lower-risk offenders, those who seem most likely to avoid crime, at least during the remainder of the period to which they had been sentenced. This, of course, is exactly what parole boards do, particularly when they are guided by parole prediction tables such as the "salient factor score" developed for the federal parole system. There are many now in prison who have a low likelihood of future criminality, particularly if that prediction is confined to crimes of personal violence.

In the broad sense, then, there are certainly prisoners who in terms of risk to society or other punitive purpose need not serve the prison terms now imposed. Within that group a number need never have been so sentenced had there existed a sufficient range of intermediate punishments to provide community protection from them.

Even more certainly, of the more than 2 million convicted offenders now sentenced to probation there are many who should be under closer supervision than ordinary probation provides and also many who by fines or by community service should make larger amends for their crimes than ordinary probation now provides. It would be misleading to suggest with any attempt at precision what that number might be, since it is in large part a function of what community-based treatment and control resources are available. But when one finds caseloads of 200 and more per probation officer in some of our cities, it is clear both that probation is often a merely token sanction providing scant community protection and that the number of probationers meriting middle-range intermediate punishment is large.

We have, in short, created a punishment system that is polarized and ill-adapted to the gradations of severity of crime and magnitude of future threat that are the grist of the mill of our criminal courts. Between overcrowded prisons and even more overcrowded probation, there is a near-vacuum of appropriate and enforced middle-range punishments. . . . Unless and until such intermediate punishments are developed and institutionalized, there can be no comprehensive punishment system suited to the realities of crime and criminals in this country.

THE UNDERUSE OF INTERMEDIATE PUNISHMENTS

At last, there is an experiment with a day-fine system in this country, decades after it became entrenched in many European punishment systems. At last, federal fines have been raised to realistic levels, decades after the threats of white-collar crime and organized crime were understood. Some countries now treat the fine as their main punishment for quite serious crime; such a thought is brushed aside in the United States, a country otherwise dedicated to the power of the economic incentive. Why not, then, let the fine serve as a powerful penal disincentive rather than a mere adjunct to other punishments?

The reasons for the neglect of the fine as a weapon against other than minor crime are not clear. That the fine is an insufficiently used punishment is, however, clear beyond argument. It is seen as ineffective against the wealthy and inapplicable to the poor. Far too often, when a fine is imposed it is not collected, and this holds true in federal as well as state and local courts.

All that is now affirmed is that a system of fines graduated to the severity of the crime and the capacity of the criminal to pay, if imposed and collected, is an essential part of a comprehensive punishment system. The knowledge base exists to develop and implement such a system. Widespread experimentation has taken place in this country with various methods of assessing, imposing, and collecting fines and other countries have moved toward implementing such systems.

Unlike the other intermediate punishments we shall consider, the development of an effective system of fines could be achieved cheaply, without the development of any large-scale enforcement mechanisms. This is one area of the criminal justice system to which the private sector can make a significant contribution—and to its own profit. Private financial institutions are good at collecting debts; the courts are not.

All who have studied criminal punishments in this country, be they from the bleeding-hearted left or the lantern-jawed right, lament the state of the fine. There is less unanimity concerning the underuse of the other punishments in the middle range between prison and probation, but in our view the cases are equally strong.

The community service order is analogous to the fine, clearly applicable to the indigent, for whom a fine may be inappropriate, but also suited, either alone or as an adjunct to other punishments, to many who can and should pay fines. Later we tell the story of experimentation with this punishment in this country and abroad; for the time being all that is being suggested is that one important way in which the criminal can make amends to the community he has wronged—make a contribution to it given that he has inflicted injury on it—is by providing some form of community service that is needed and that otherwise would not be provided. In the destroyed inner-city areas there is much need for rehabilitation of otherwise unusable housing; there is unlimited work to be done to preserve our heritage of natural resources; our hospitals and all our community services stand in need of assistance—it seems obvious that there is ample opportunity here for some offenders, as part of their punishment or as their punishment, to give of their labor and skills to our benefit and possibly also to theirs.

Intermediate punishments encompass a wide diversity of community-based treatments and controls of the convicted offender, ranging from house arrest, to halfway houses, to intensive probation with conditions of treatment or control vigorously enforced and, if appropriate, backed up by the emerging technology of electronic and telephonic monitoring. . . . The probation order has become the punishment of choice for a wide swath of crimes. Like prison, inadequately supplied with the resources to fulfill its mission, probation has been overwhelmed by numbers. But, this reality apart, it has come to be realized that many offenders require closer supervision than the usual probation order provides. Hence the development of these more intensive controls, combining elements of police supervision and casework assistance. . . . For some criminals, as a punishment standing alone, for others, as part of a larger punishment package, community-based punishments stand in urgent need of further development as a necessary and integral part of a comprehensive punishment system.

THE ENFORCEMENT OF INTERMEDIATE PUNISHMENTS

As we surveyed experimentation with intermediate punishments, one pattern emerged which may go far to explain their small role in punishment policy and practice: an enthusiastic reformer, a judge as in the origins of the community service order, or an agency as in much experimentation with intensive supervision probation, seeks and finds funds to launch an experimental program of intermediate punishments. It "works well": the early enthusiasm of a new initiative leads the sentencing court and the community in which it is established to be satisfied with its observed results. It does not have a high failure rate; it is hard to know, however, whether the failure rate would have been higher or lower if some other punishment had been imposed on the same offenders. There is always the possibility that the new initiative skimmed the least threatening offenders from the pool of convicted offenders possibly suited to this new punishment; at any event, those who launch it and those who are subject to it feel [good] about it. It is written up in some popular literature and often featured on local or national television, usually with excessive claims of success. Then the task of building it into the larger punishment system in the city or state where it was established begins—and usually ends. The enthusiasm of the early reformers dissipates; they move on to other pastures. The other punishment agencies, prison and probation, are not excited by this new competition for their clientele, even though they recognize their overload. Bureaucratic inertia dominates. The "reform" is allowed quietly to die.

We draw two morals from this oft repeated experience. First, the designers and administrators of new initiatives must face and overcome daunting organizational, political, financial, and bureaucratic problems if new programs are to be institutionalized and their promised benefits achieved. Second, and more important for our purposes here, the development of a comprehensive punishment system requires the dedication of appreciable resources of men and women, money and materials, to the implementation and enforcement of a range of intermediate punishments if we are to move beyond experimentation.

• • •

It may be true that, in the long run, a punishment system making appropriate use of a range of punishments from probation through the middle range of punishments and on to imprisonment may be less expensive than one that relies excessively on prison; but that will be true, if at all, in the very long run. Community-based controls are labor intensive if they are to be effective. If the convicted offender is to be supervised effectively, with or without the assistance of electronic or similar monitoring, with or without, for example, regular drug testing, supervising officers cannot carry a large caseload. The "alternatives to imprisonment" movement sailed under false colors when it claimed immediate savings; prison budgets decline only when substantial numbers are taken out of the prison so that a prison or a wing of a prison may be closed—and that does not seem an immediate likelihood in most American jurisdictions.

And there is another aspect of reality that is not usually stressed by those who advocate this type of development of our punishment system: the intermediate punishment must be rigorously enforced, it must be "backed up" by enforcement mechanisms that take seriously indeed any breach of the conditions of the community-based sanction. This does not mean, for example, that the addict who once relapses in a treatment program must by that fact and without more be incarcerated; but it does mean that this relapse must be taken seriously and that there is a real possibility of the imposition of a prison term because of the relapse.

If a fine is imposed, adjusted to the criminal's financial circumstances and potential, and time given to pay if necessary, it is of the first importance that an effective and determined enforcement machinery be in place. It seems unnecessary to make such a point, but the record of failure to collect fines in the federal system, and similar experience in state and local fining practice, compel such a stressing of the obvious.

Here too the law must keep its promises. The promise of intermediate punishments demands for its fulfillment resources adequate to their support and sufficient for their determined enforcement.

SENTENCING TO INTERMEDIATE PUNISHMENTS

Concerns for justice and fairness in sentencing will lead, in time, probably within 25 years, to the creation in most American states of comprehensive systems of structured sentencing discretion that encompass a continuum of punishments from probation to imprisonment, with many intermediate punishments ranged between. These systems may take the form of the sentencing guidelines now in place in Minnesota, Washington, and elsewhere, or they may take some other form, but they will all provide for interchangeability of punishments for like-situated offenders. They will establish ranges of interchangeable punishments, bounded by considerations of desert, that are presumed to be applicable to the cases governed by each range, subject to the right of the judge to impose some other sentence if he provides written reasons for so doing; the adequacy and appropriateness of those reasons will be subject to review by appellate courts that will consult a body of case law, a common law of sentencing, for guidance.

These predictions may seem millenarian, but they are the foreseeable extension of developments and practices that are already in place. Anyone who in 1970 predicted the radical changes in American sentencing practices that have taken place since that date would have seemed even more romantic than we do now. The developments that underlay the past two decades of evolution in American sentencing practices will continue to shape reform for decades to come in the directions that we have identified. . . .

In 1970 the indeterminate sentencing systems in the United States, federal and state, had continued virtually unchanged from at least 1930 and looked much the same everywhere. Premised at least in theory on commitment to the values of individualized sentencing and rehabilitative correctional programs, indeterminate sentencing systems gave officials wide-ranging discretion and freedom from external controls over their decisions. Criminal statutes and common law doctrines defined the elements of crimes. Statutes established maximum terms of probation and imprisonment, and maximum amounts of fines, that could be imposed. Occasionally, but rarely, the statutes established mandatory minimum prison terms for persons convicted of particular crimes. Prosecutors had complete control over charging and plea bargaining. Judges had little-fettered discretion to "individualize punishment" in deciding who received probation and who was sentenced to jail or prison, and, for those to be confined, to set minimum or maximum terms, and sometimes both. Parole boards, subject only to statutory provisions on parole eligibility, generally when a third of the maximum term had been served, decided who was released from prison prior to the expiration of their terms, when, and under what conditions.

None of these decisions—charging and plea bargaining, sentencing, paroling—was governed by legal or administrative decision rules and only rarely did these decisions raise issues cognizable in the appellate courts. Well-established doctrines based on notions of separation of powers and deference to administrative expertise led appellate courts to refuse to review prosecutorial and parole decisions on the substantive merits. Equivalent notions of comity between judges and deference to the better information of the trial judge caused appellate courts to accord extreme deference to the discretionary sentencing decisions of the trial judge.

When courts did consider appeals from parole and prosecutorial decisions, which was uncommon before 1970, the cases generally involved procedural issues. When appellate courts considered sentence appeals in the few states where such appeals were allowed, few sentences were overturned and they tended to be such gross departures from standard practice that the appeals courts felt comfortable concluding that they constituted an "abuse of discretion" or that they "offended the conscience."

In effect, prosecutors, judges, and parole boards were accountable for their decisions in individual cases only to their political constituencies and their consciences. Few would have guessed in 1970 that nearly every facet of indeterminate sentencing in theory and in practice would be decisively repudiated within a decade.

• • •

The theoretical attacks were most influentially advanced by Francis Allen in his 1964 book, *The Borderland of Criminal Justice*, and in 1974 by Norval Morris in *The Future of Imprisonment*. Their arguments had two major elements. First, from an ethical perspective, it is simply wrong to take or extend the state's criminal law powers over individuals for, ostensibly, their own good, especially in light of pessimistic findings on the correctional systems' abilities to rehabilitate offenders. Second, from a psychological perspective, it defies common experience to imagine that coerced participation in treatment programs will often facilitate personal growth and change. Generally, self-improvement is voluntary; coupling participation in treatment programs with a likelihood of earlier release motivated prisoners to participate, but often it did not motivate them to change.

Taken together, these critiques greatly undermined indeterminate sentencing and the practices and institutions that went with it. It is not easy to defend a major set of social institutions that are portrayed as based on unsound empirical, ethical, and psychological premises, as characterized by racial and class bias, by arbitrariness, by lawlessness, and by unfairness, and as conspicuously ineffective at achieving the larger social purposes of reducing crime and rehabilitating offenders—and few tried.

Hence American sentencing institutions and practices underwent more extensive and more radical changes between 1975 and 1985 than in any other decade in our history. Most of the changes attempted to structure or eliminate the discretionary decisions exercised by public officials. Although new initiatives affecting decision making by judges and prosecutors were not uncommon, it was the parole boards, the institutions that in theory based their decisions on rehabilitative predictions and assessments, that experienced the most drastic changes.

• • •

Many of the sentencing innovations since the midseventies have not achieved their proponents' aims. Mandatory sentencing laws, for example, had at best a modest short-term deterrent effect on the crimes they affect and usually produced very little change in sentencing practices. For serious crimes, the one- or two-year minimum sentence usually prescribed was generally less than would normally be imposed even without a mandatory sentencing law.

For less serious offenses and offenders, lawyers and judges could usually devise a method for circumventing the mandatory sentence when its imposition seemed to them unduly harsh.

Voluntary guidelines for sentencing fared little better. Voluntary guidelines were voluntary in two senses; their development by judges was self-initiated and not in furtherance of a statutory directive, and whether and to what extent judges followed them was entirely in the hands of each individual judge. In most jurisdictions, voluntary guidelines seem to have had little effect on sentencing. Although courts in more than 40 states established voluntary guidelines between 1975 and 1980, in most places they were soon abandoned or soon became dead letters.

Statutory determinate sentencing laws did somewhat better and in some states, notably North Carolina and California, they seem to have reduced sentencing disparities and made sentencing somewhat more predictable. In other states, however, like Illinois and Indiana, the new laws offered no meaningful constraints on judicial discretion and proved to be no improvement on the indeterminate sentencing systems they replaced.

Parole guidelines in some jurisdictions, such as Minnesota and the federal system, accomplished much of what their creators had in mind. Consistently applied, they made release dates more predictable and served to even out disparities in the lengths of prison sentences meted out by judges. Their major shortcoming from a reform perspective was that they affect only those offenders who are sent to prison and accordingly have no effect whatever on the question of who is sentenced to prison or on what happens to those who are not imprisoned.

The sentencing reform initiative of the future is the combination of the sentencing commission and presumptive sentencing guidelines that Judge Frankel first proposed in 1972 as a solution to the lawlessness that he decried, that Minnesota first implemented in 1980, and that other jurisdictions have elaborated as the years have passed. Presumptive sentencing guidelines establish presumptions that govern judges' decisions whether to imprison an offender and, if so, for how long. The judge may conclude that special circumstances justify some other sentence or, in other words, that the presumption should be rejected. If so, the judge must explain his reasoning and its adequacy is subject to review by appeal of sentence to a higher court. Careful evaluations of the experience in Minnesota and later Washington showed that presumptive sentencing guidelines could reduce sentencing disparities, reduce differences in sentencing patterns associated with race, increase consistency in sentencing statewide, and make sentencing much more predictable, so that state sentencing policies could be related in a meaningful way to the availability of prison beds and other correctional resources.

Presumptive sentencing guidelines appear to be a way to address most of the major critiques of indeterminate sentencing. They reduce disparities and the potential for decisions based on invidious considerations of race and class. They provide decision rules to guide the sentencing choices judges make. Judges are made accountable because they must comply with the guidelines' presumptions or give reasons for doing something else. Sentence appeals become meaningful because appellate judges have some basis for assessing the correctness of the trial judge's decisions and the reasons that are invoked to justify them.

The wisdom of Judge Frankel's proposal, and the core of the sentencing commission idea, was its combination of the sentencing commission, sentencing guidelines, and appellate sentence review. All three elements were crucial. The creation of an administrative agency responsible for formulation of sentencing policy provided an institution much better situated than any legislature to accumulate specialized expertise to develop comprehensive sentencing policies and sufficiently removed from the glare of day-to-day legislative politics to approach these often controversial matters in a principled and thoughtful way. The resulting sentencing guidelines for the first time provided an instrument for the expression of finely tuned standards for exercise of the punitive powers of the state, and their presumptive character required that judges give reasons for their decisions to depart from the guidelines' presumptions. Those reasons, in turn, for the first time in this country provided the material for development of principled appellate review of sentences. . . .

A comprehensive sentencing system must provide guidance to judges in choosing among all available sentencing options, including probation, prison, and all the intermediate punishments that fall between them in severity and intrusiveness. . . . There is, however, one threshold that must be crossed before such a system becomes a viable possibility—the prison or probation, something or nothing, simplicities of too much present thought must be rejected.

• • •

Here we simply set out the components of a comprehensive sentencing system.

1. The principle of interchangeability of punishments must be recognized.
2. The "in/out" line must be erased to eliminate the false dichotomous prison-or-nothing simplicities.
3. In place of a two-part in-or-out sentencing grid, there should be at least four graded categories of punishment presumptions: "out," "out unless . . . ," "in unless . . . ," and "in."
4. Within the governing purposes *of* sentencing established by policymakers, the guidelines should permit the judge to look to the applicable purposes of punishment to be served *at* sentencing in choosing among the available interchangeable punishments.
5. The principle of interchangeability should be recognized for all crimes for which the presumptive prison sentence (for those cases where the applicable purposes at sentencing will best be served by incarceration) is two years or less.

6. The system should provide guidance for all sentencing decisions for all felonies and misdemeanors.
7. The choice among interchangeable punishments is for the judge to make, not the offender.

The preceding list does not address all of the issues our proposals raise. For example, it does not explain how the exchange rates between different punishments are to be determined or calculated, or how judges are to know what the governing purposes are *at* sentencing. We discuss such problems later. We believe, however, that they are simpler than at first appears and that their apparent difficulty results mainly from their novelty.

Our mission is to explain how in principle and in practice a comprehensive sentencing system, which incorporates a rich variety of intermediate punishments linked to one another and to probation and prison by a principle of interchangeability, can be established and implemented. Before we turn to that fuller explication and justification, a critical issue of justice as fairness must be mentioned and its implications noted.

Fitting intermediate punishments into a principled sentencing system has proved to be the Achilles heel of both sentencing reform proposals and practice. The central reason for this is (somewhat unexpectedly given the general human capacity to tolerate the sufferings of others with a degree of equanimity) a sense of unfairness when it is suggested that two equally undeserving criminals should be treated differently—since differently here means that one will be treated more leniently than the other.

The conceptual keystone of the argument is that a developed punishment theory requires recognition that precise equivalency of punishment between equally undeserving criminals in the distribution of punishments is in practice unattainable and is in theory undesirable. We argue that all that can be achieved is a rough equivalence of punishment that will allow room for the principled distribution of punishments on utilitarian grounds, unfettered by the miserable aim of making suffering equally painful. . . .

The first consequence is that it now becomes possible to move appreciable numbers who otherwise would be sentenced to prison into community-based intermediate punishments, having a roughly equivalent punitive bite but serving both the community and the criminal better than the prison term. It also becomes possible to move appreciable numbers who otherwise would be sentenced to token probationary supervision into intermediate punishments that exercise larger controls over them and provide us with larger social protection from their criminality. The advantages are obvious; it is a liberating idea—but it has its problems, theoretical and practical.

First, the theoretical problem. If appropriate guidance is to be given the sentencing judge under such a system of punishment, some "exchange rates" between punishments to achieve this rough equivalence must be stated in advance. There exist a few fledgling efforts to state these exchange rates; we believe that a principled system of punishment can be defined in which rough equivalence of punitive bite and identity of process in relation to stated purposes of punishment provide the necessary guidance to the judge and also give both the appearance and the reality of fairness to the community and to the convicted offender.

Among the practical problems that accompany such a purposive introduction of intermediate punishments into the body of a punishment system, none is more troublesome than its impact on existing class and race biases.

At present black adult males per hundred thousand are more than seven times as likely to be in prison as white adult males. The reasons for this are deeply rooted in history, social structure, and social attitudes; but it also seems clear that the criminal justice systems of this country—federal, state, and local—make some contribution to this sad result. Are we really proposing the introduction of a punishment system that by its expansion of intermediate punishments will make this racial skewing worse? At first blush it would appear so.

Take two addict-criminals convicted of selling relatively small amounts of cocaine on a number of separate occasions. Each has once before been convicted of illegal possession of marijuana. Each is aged 20. Criminal A is in college, the son of a loving and supportive middle-class family, living in a district where space is available in drug treatment programs. Criminal B has never met his putative father, lives in a high-rise apartment in a slum area with his mother and his two much younger siblings, welfare being their major financial support. The waiting list at the available drug treatment center is long, the waiting time three months.

You know the pigmentation of the two hypothetical but far from unreal criminals.

Are we really suggesting that Criminal B serve a jail or prison term with the hope that thereafter he can be fitted into a drug treatment program, while Criminal A should pay a substantial fine, be under intensive probationary supervision with a condition of regular attendance at a drug treatment program where he is tested regularly to ensure that he is drug-free, and be subjected possibly to house arrest in the evenings and weekends—electronically monitored if that be necessary? This will, of course, be the likely result. Is it unprincipled? We think not.

The criminal justice system lacks both resources and capacity to take on the task of rectification of social inequalities of race or class. It will do well if it does not exacerbate them. To insist that Criminal A go to jail or prison because resources are lacking to deal sensibly with Criminal B is to pay excessive tribute to an illusory ideal of equality. That is not the way equality of opportunity and equality of punitive pain is to be achieved; it is to be achieved by efforts to provide within the criminal justice system for Criminal B what exists for Criminal A, and to intercede by means other than the criminal justice system to eradicate the inequalities that generate the present discrimination.

The comprehensive punishment system we propose will, we believe, in the longer run reduce the impact of race and class on sentencing practice. The more clearly the exchange rates between punishments and the purposes each is to serve can be articulated in advance, the more possible it will be to reduce race and class biases in the selection of sanctions. Strong racial and class prejudices, conscious and less perceived, already drive sentencing practice; the substitution of purposive principles framed independently of race and class but necessarily having race and class correlates will make matters better, not worse.

DISCUSSION QUESTIONS

1. Summarize Morris and Tonry's recommendations for intermediate punishments.
2. Describe Morris and Tonry's criteria for incarceration as an appropriate punishment. According to their criteria, how many offenders in prison or in jail do not need to be there?
3. Why do intermediate punishments have such a small role in punishment policy and practice?
4. Discuss Morris and Tonry's components of a comprehensive sentencing system.
5. What are the theoretical and practical problems with the comprehensive punishment system Morris and Tonry propose?

20

What Works? Question and Answers about Prison Reform

Robert Martinson

Publication of this article in 1974 framed the debate about rehabilitation as a correctional goal. This recidivism-based research was much cited by practitioners and policy makers alike, as the reason for shifting to determinate sentences and for limiting discretionary release on parole. While Martinson fought to correct what he felt was a misinterpretation of this influential work, it is credited with reducing the role of treatment programs.

• • •

One of the problems in the constant debate over "prison reform" is that we have been able to draw very little on any systematic empirical knowledge about the success or failure that we have met when we *have* tried to rehabilitate offenders, with various treatments and in various institutional and non-institutional settings. The field of penology has produced a voluminous research literature on this subject, but until recently there has

Source: Robert Martinson, "What Works? Questions and Answers About Prison Reform," The Public Interest, No. 35, p. 22–54.

been no comprehensive review of this literature and no attempt to bring its findings to bear, in a useful way, on the general question of "What works?" My purpose in this essay is to sketch an answer to that question.

THE TRAVAILS OF A STUDY

• • •

What we set out to do in this study was fairly simple, though it turned into a massive task. First we undertook a six-month search of the literature for any available reports published in the English language on attempts at rehabilitation that had been made in our corrections systems and those of other countries from 1945 through 1967. We then picked from that literature all those studies whose findings were interpretable—that is, whose design and execution met the conventional standards of social science research. Our criteria were rigorous but hardly esoteric: A study had to be an evaluation of a treatment method, it had to employ an independent measure of the improvement secured by that method, and it had to use some control group, some untreated individuals with whom the treated ones could be compared. We excluded studies only for methodological reasons: They presented insufficient data, they were only preliminary, they presented only a summary of findings, their results were confounded by extraneous factors, they used unreliable measures, one could not understand their descriptions of the treatment in question, they drew spurious conclusions from their data, their samples were undescribed or too small or provided no true comparability between treated and untreated groups, or they had used inappropriate statistical tests and did not provide enough information for the reader to recompute the data. Using these standards, we drew from the total number of studies 231 acceptable ones, which we not only analyzed ourselves but summarized in detail so that a reader of our analysis would be able to compare it with his independent conclusions.

These treatment studies use various measures of offender improvement: recidivism rates (that is, the rates at which offenders return to crime), adjustment to prison life, vocational success, educational achievement, personality and attitude change, and general adjustment to the outside community. We included all of these in our study, but in these pages I will deal only with the effects of rehabilitative treatment on recidivism, the phenomenon which reflects most directly how well our present treatment programs are performing the task of rehabilitation. The use of even this one measure brings with it enough methodological complications to make a clear reporting of the findings most difficult. The groups that are studied, for instance, are exceedingly disparate, so that it is hard to tell whether what "works" for one kind of offender also works for others. In addition, there has been little attempt to replicate studies; therefore one cannot be certain how stable and reliable the various findings are. Just as important, when the various studies use the term "recidivism rate," they may in fact be talking about somewhat different measures of offender behavior—i.e., "failure" measures such as arrest rates or parole violation rates, or "success" measures such as favorable discharge from parole or probation. And not all of these measures correlate very highly with one another. These difficulties will become apparent again and again in the course of this discussion.

With these caveats, it is possible to give a rather bald summary of our findings: *With few and isolated exceptions, the rehabilitative efforts that have been reported so far have had no appreciable effect on recidivism.* Studies that have been done since our survey was completed do not present any major grounds for altering that original conclusion. What follows is an attempt to answer the questions and challenges that might be posed to such an unqualified statement.

EDUCATION AND VOCATIONAL TRAINING

1. *Isn't it true that a correctional facility running a truly rehabilitative program—one that prepares inmates for life on the outside through education and vocational training—will turn out more successful individuals than will a prison which merely leaves its inmates to rot?*

If this is true, the fact remains that there is very little empirical evidence to support it. Skill development and educational programs are in fact quite common in correctional facilities, and one might begin by examining their effects on young males, those who might be thought most amenable to such efforts. A study by New York State (1964) found that for young males as a whole, the degree of success achieved in the regular prison academic education program, as measured by changes in grade achievement levels, made no significant difference in recidivism rates. The only exception was the relative improvement, compared with the sample as a whole, that greater progress made in the top seven per cent of the participating population—those who had high I.Q.'s, had made good records in previous schooling, and who also made good records of academic progress in the institution. And a study by Glaser (1964) found that while it was true that, when one controlled for sentence length, more attendance in regular prison academic programs slightly decreased the subsequent chances of parole violation, this improvement was not large enough to outweigh the associated disadvantage for the "long-attenders": Those who attended prison school the longest also turned out to be those who were in prison the longest. Presumably, those getting the most education were also the worst parole risks in the first place.

• • •

In sum, many of these studies of young males are extremely hard to interpret because of flaws in research design. But it can safely be said that they provide us with no clear evidence that education or skill development programs have been successful.

TRAINING ADULT INMATES

When one turns to adult male inmates, as opposed to young ones, the results are even more discouraging. There have been six studies of this type; three of them report that their programs, which ranged from academic to prison work experience, produced no significant differences in recidivism rates, and one—by Glaser (1964)—is almost impossible to interpret because of the risk differentials of the prisoners participating in the various programs.

Two studies—by Schur (1948) and by Saden (1962)—do report a positive difference from skill development programs. In one of them, the Saden study, it is questionable whether the experimental and control groups were truly comparable. But what is more interesting is that both these "positive" studies dealt with inmates incarcerated prior to or during World War II. Perhaps the rise in our educational standards as a whole since then has lessened the differences that prison education or training can make. The only other interesting possibility emerges from a study by Gearhart (1967). His study was one of those that reported vocational education to be non-significant in affecting recidivism rates. He did note, however, that when a trainee succeeded in finding a job related to his area of training, he had a slightly higher chance of becoming a successful parolee. It is possible, then, that skill development programs fail because what they teach bears so little relationship to an offender's subsequent life outside the prison.

One other study of adults, this one with fairly clear implications, has been performed with women rather than men. An experimental group of institutionalized women in Milwaukee was given an extremely comprehensive special education program, accompanied by group counseling. Their training was both academic and practical; it included reading, writing, spelling, business filing, child care, and grooming. Kettering (1965) found that the program made no difference in the women's rates of recidivism.

Two things should be noted about these studies. One is the difficulty of interpreting them as a whole. The disparity in the programs that were tried, in the populations that were affected, and in the institutional settings that surrounded these projects makes it hard to be sure that one is observing the same category of treatment in each case. But the second point is that despite this difficulty, one can be reasonably sure that, so far, educational and vocational programs have not worked. We don't know why they have failed. We don't know whether the programs themselves are flawed, or whether they are incapable of overcoming the effects of prison life in general. The difficulty may be that they lack applicability to the world the inmate will face outside of prison. Or perhaps the type of educational and skill improvement they produce simply doesn't have very much to do with an individual's propensity to commit crime. What we do know is that, to date, education and skill development have not reduced recidivism by rehabilitating criminals.

THE EFFECTS OF INDIVIDUAL COUNSELING

2. *But when we speak of a rehabilitative prison, aren't we referring to more than education and skill development alone? Isn't what's needed some way of counseling inmates, or helping them with the deeper problems that have caused their maladjustment?*

This, too, is a reasonable hypothesis; but when one examines the programs of this type that have been tried, it's hard to find any more grounds for enthusiasm than we found with skill development and education. One method that's been tried—though so far, there have been acceptable reports only of its application to young offenders—has been individual psychotherapy. For young males, we found seven such reported studies. One study, by Guttman (1963) at the Nelles School, found such treatment to be ineffective in reducing recidivism rates; another, by Rudoff (1960), found it unrelated to *institutional* violation rates, which were themselves related to parole success. It must be pointed out that Rudoff used only this indirect measure of association, and the study therefore cannot rule out the possibility of a treatment effect. A third, also by Guttman (1963) but at another institution, found that such treatment was actually related to a slightly *higher* parole violation rate; and a study by Adams (1959b and 1961b) also found a lack of improvement in parole revocation and first suspension rates.

• • •

There have been two studies of the effects of individual psychotherapy on young incarcerated *female* offenders, and both of them (Adams, 1959; Adams, 1961) report no significant effects from the therapy. But one of the Adams studies (1959) does contain a suggestive, although not clearly interpretable, finding: If this individual therapy was administered by a psychiatrist or a psychologist, the resulting parole suspension rate was almost two-and-a-half times *higher* than if it was administered by a social worker without this specialized training.

There has also been a much smaller number of studies of two other types of individual therapy: counseling, which is directed towards a prisoner's gaining new insight into his own problems, and casework, which aims at helping a prisoner cope with his more pragmatic immediate needs. These types of therapy both rely heavily on the empathetic relationship that is to be developed between the professional and the client. It was noted above that the Adams study (1961b) of therapy administered to girls, referred to in the discussion of individual psychotherapy, found that social workers seemed better at the job than psychologists or psychiatrists. This difference seems to suggest a favorable outlook for these alternative forms of individual therapy. But other studies of such therapy have produced ambiguous results. Bernsten (1961) reported a Danish experiment that showed that socio-psychological counseling combined with comprehensive welfare measures—job and residence placement, clothing, union and health insurance membership, and financial aid—produced an improvement among some short-term male offenders, though not those in either the highest-risk or the lowest-risk categories. On the other hand, Hood, in Britain (1966), reported generally non-significant results with a program of counseling for young males. (Interestingly enough, this experiment *did* point to a mechanism capable of changing recidivism rates. When boys were released from institutional care and entered the army directly, "poor risk" boys among both experimentals *and* controls did better than expected. "Good risks" did worse.)

So these foreign data are sparse and not in agreement; the American data are just as sparse. The only American study which provides a direct measure of the effects of individual counseling—a study of California's Intensive Treatment Program (California, 1958), which was "psychodynamically" oriented—found no improvement in recidivism rates.

• • •

GROUP COUNSELING

Group counseling has indeed been tried in correctional institutions, both with and without specifically psychotherapeutic orientation. There has been one study of "pragmatic," problem-oriented counseling on *young* institutionalized males, by Seckel (1965). This type of counseling had no significant effect. For adult males, there have been three such studies of the "pragmatic" and "insight" methods. Two (Kassebaum, 1971; Harrison, 1964) report no long-lasting significant effects. (One of these two did report a real but short-term effect that wore off as the program became institutionalized and as offenders were at liberty longer.) The third study of adults, by Shelley (1961), dealt with a "pragmatic" casework program, directed towards the educational and vocational needs of institutionalized young adult males in a Michigan prison camp. The treatment lasted for six months and at the end of that time Shelley found an improvement in attitudes; the possession of "good" attitudes was independently found by Shelley to correlate with parole success. Unfortunately, though, Shelley was not able to measure the *direct* impact of the counseling on recidivism rates. His two separate correlations are suggestive, but they fall short of being able to tell us that it really is the counseling that has a direct effect on recidivism.

With regard to more professional group *psychotherapy*, the reports are also conflicting. We have two studies of group psychotherapy on young males. One, by Parsons (1966), says that this treatment did in fact reduce recidivism. The improved recidivism rate stems from the improved performance only of those who were clinically judged to have been "successfully" treated; still, the overall result of the treatment was to improve recidivism rates for the experimental group as a whole. On the other hand, a study by Craft (1964) of young males designated "psychopaths," comparing "self-government" group psychotherapy with "authoritarian" individual counseling, found that the "group therapy" boys afterwards committed *twice* as many new offenses as the individually treated ones. Perhaps some forms of group psychotherapy work for some types of offenders but not others; a reader must draw his own conclusions, on the basis of sparse evidence.

With regard to young females, the results are just as equivocal. Adams, in his study of females (1959a), found that there was no improvement to be gained from treating girls by group rather than individual methods. A study by Taylor of borstal (reformatory) girls in New Zealand (1967) found a similar lack of any great improvement for group therapy as opposed to individual therapy or even to no therapy at all. But the Taylor study does offer one real, positive finding: When the "group therapy" girls *did* commit new offenses, these offenses were less serious than the ones for which they had originally been incarcerated.

• • •

As with the question of skill development, it is hard to summarize these results. The programs administered were various; the groups to which they were administered varied not only by sex but by age as well; there were also variations in the length of time for which the programs were carried on, the frequency of contact during that time, and the period for which the subjects were followed up. Still, one must say that the burden of the evidence is not encouraging. These programs seem to work best when they are new, when their subjects are amenable to treatment in the first place, and when the counselors are not only trained people but "good" people as well. Such findings, which would not be much of a surprise to a student of organization or personality, are hardly encouraging for a policy planner, who must adopt measures that are generally applicable, that are capable of being successfully institutionalized, and that must rely for personnel on something other than the exceptional individual.

TRANSFORMING THE INSTITUTIONAL ENVIRONMENT

3. *But maybe the reason these counseling programs don't seem to work is not that they are ineffective* per se, *but that the institutional environment* outside *the program is unwholesome enough to undo any good work that the counseling does. Isn't a truly successful rehabilitative institution the one where the inmate's whole environment is directed towards true correction rather than towards custody or punishment?*

This argument has not only been made, it has been embodied in several institutional programs that go by the name of "milieu therapy." They are designed to make every element of the inmate's environment a part of his treatment, to reduce the distinctions between the custodial staff and the treatment staff, to create a supportive, non-authoritarian, and non-regimented atmosphere, and to enlist peer influence in the formation of constructive values. These programs are especially hard to summarize because of their variety; they differ, for example, in how "supportive" or "permissive" they are designed to be, in the extent to which they are combined with other treatment methods such as individual therapy, group counseling, or skill development, and in how completely the program is able to control all the relevant aspects of the institutional environment.

One might well begin with two studies that have been done of institutionalized adults, in regular prisons, who have been subjected to such treatment; this is the category whose results are the most clearly discouraging. One study of such a program, by Robison (1967), found that the therapy did seem to reduce recidivism after one year. After two years, however, this effect disappeared, and the treated convicts did no better than the untreated. Another study, by Kassebaum, Ward, and Wilner (1971), dealt with a program which had been able to effect an exceptionally extensive and experimentally rigorous transformation of the institutional environment. This sophisticated study had a follow-up period of 36 months, and it found that the program had no significant effect on parole failure or success rates.

The results of the studies of youth are more equivocal. As for young females, one study by Adams (1966) of such a program found that it had no significant effect on recidivism; another study, by Goldberg and Adams (1964), found that such a program *did* have a positive effect. This effect declined when the program began to deal with girls who were judged beforehand to be worse risks.

As for young males, the studies may conveniently be divided into those dealing with juveniles (under 16) and those dealing with youths. There have been five studies of milieu therapy administered to juveniles. Two of them—by Laulicht (1962) and by Jesness (1965)—report clearly that the program in question either had no significant effect or had a short-term effect that wore off with passing time. Jesness does report that when his experimental juveniles did commit new offenses, the offenses were less serious than those committed by controls. A third study of juveniles, by McCord (1953) at the Wiltwych School, reports mixed results. Using two measures of performance, a "success" rate and a "failure" rate, McCord found that his experimental group achieved both less failure *and* less success than the controls did. There have been two positive reports on milieu therapy programs for male juveniles; both of them have come out of the Highfields program, the milieu therapy experiment which has become the most famous and widely quoted example of "success" via this method. A group of boys was confined for a relatively short time to the unrestrictive, supportive environment of Highfields; and at a follow-up of six months, Freeman (1956) found that the group did indeed show a lower recidivism rate (as measured by parole revocation) than a similar group spending a longer time in the regular reformatory. McCorkle (1958) also reported positive findings from Highfields. But in fact, the McCorkle data show, this improvement was not so clear: The Highfields boys had lower recidivism rates at 12 and 36 months in the follow-up period, but not at 24 and 60 months. The length of follow-up, these data remind us, may have large implications for a study's conclusions. But more important were other flaws in the Highfields experiment: The populations were not fully comparable (they differed according to risk level and time of admission); different organizations—the probation agency for the Highfields boys, the parole agency for the others—were making the revocation decisions for each group; more of the Highfields boys were discharged early from supervision, and thus removed from any risk of revocation. In short, not even from the celebrated Highfields case may we take clear assurance that milieu therapy works.

In the case of male youths, as opposed to male juveniles, the findings are just as equivocal, and hardly more encouraging. One such study by Empey (1966) in a residential context did not produce significant results. A study by Seckel (1967) described California's Fremont Program, in which institutionalized youths participated in a combination of therapy, work projects, field trips, and community meetings. Seckel found that the youths subjected to this treatment committed *more* violations of law than did their non-treated counterparts.

• • •

So the youth in these milieu therapy programs at least do no worse than their counterparts in regular institutions and the special programs may cost less. One may therefore be encouraged—not on grounds of rehabilitation but on grounds of cost-effectiveness.

WHAT ABOUT MEDICAL TREATMENT?

4. *Isn't there anything you can do in an institutional setting that will reduce recidivism, for instance, through strictly medical treatment?*

A number of studies deal with the results of efforts to change the behavior of offenders through drugs and surgery. As for surgery, the one experimental study of a plastic surgery program—by Mandell (1967)—had negative results. For non-addicts who received plastic surgery, Mandall purported to find improvement in performance on parole; but when one reanalyzes his data, it appears that surgery alone did not in fact make a significant difference.

One type of surgery does seem to be highly successful in reducing recidivism. A twenty-year Danish study of sex offenders, by Stuerup (1960), found that while those who had been treated with hormones and therapy continued to commit both sex crimes (29.6 per cent of them did so) and non-sex crimes (21.0 per cent), those who had been castrated had rates of only 3.5 per cent (not, interestingly enough, a rate of zero; where there's a will, apparently there's a way) and 9.2 per cent. One hopes that the policy implications of this study will be found to be distinctly limited.

As for drugs, the major report on such a program—involving tranquilization—was made by Adams (1961b). The tranquilizers were administered to male and female institutionalized youths. With boys, there was only a slight improvement in their subsequent behavior; this improvement disappeared within a year. With girls, the tranquilization produced worse results than when the girls were given no treatment at all.

THE EFFECTS OF SENTENCING

5. *Well, at least it may be possible to manipulate certain gross features of the existing, conventional prison system—such as length of sentence and degree of security—in order to affect these recidivism rates. Isn't this the case?*

At this point, it's still impossible to say that this is the case. As for the degree of security in an institution, Glaser's (1964) work reported that, for both youth and adults, a less restrictive "custody grading" in American federal prisons was related to success on parole; but this is hardly surprising, since those assigned to more restrictive custody are likely to be worse risks in the first place. More to the point, an American study by Fox (1950) discovered that for "older youths" who were deemed to be good risks for the future, a minimum security institution produced better results than a maximum security one. On the other hand, the data we have on youths under 16—from a study by McClintock (1961), done in Great Britain—indicate that so-called Borstals, in which boys are totally confined, are more effective than a less restrictive regime of partial physical custody. In short, we know very little about the recidivism effects of various degrees of security in existing institutions; and our problems in finding out will be compounded by the probability that these effects will vary widely according to the particular *type* of offender that we're dealing with.

The same problems of mixed results and lack of comparable populations have plagued attempts to study the effects of sentence length. A number of studies—by Narloch (1959), by Bernsten (1965), and by the State of California (1956)—suggest that those who are released earlier from institutions than their scheduled parole date, or those who serve short sentences of under three months rather than longer sentences of eight months or more, either do better on parole or at least do no worse. The implication here is quite clear and important: Even if early releases and short sentences produce no improvement in recidivism rates, one could at least maintain the same rates while lowering the cost of maintaining the offender and lessening his own burden of imprisonment. Of course, this implication carries with it its concomitant danger: the danger that though shorter sentences cause no worsening of the recidivism rate, they may increase the total amount of crime in the community by increasing the absolute number of potential recidivists at large.

• • •

More important, the effect of sentence length seems to vary widely according to type of offender. In a British study (1963), for instance, Hammond found that for a group of "hard-core recidivists," shortening the sentence caused no improvement in the recidivism rate. In Denmark, Bernsten (1965) discovered a similar phenomenon: That the beneficial effect of three-month sentences as against eight-month ones disappeared in the case of these "hard-core recidivists." Garrity found another such distinction in his 1956 study. He divided his offenders into three categories: "pro-social," "anti-social," and "manipulative." "Pro-social" offenders he found to have low recidivism rates regardless of the length of their sentence; "anti-social" offenders did better with short sentences; the "manipulative" did better with long ones. Two studies from Britain made yet another division of the offender population, and found yet other variations. One (Great Britain, 1964) found that previous offenders—but not first offenders—did better with *longer* sentences, while the other (Cambridge, 1951) found the *reverse* to be true with juveniles.

To add to the problem of interpretation, these studies deal not only with different types and categorizations of offenders but with different types of institutions as well. No more than in the case of institution type can we say that length of sentence has a clear relationship to recidivism.

DECARCERATING THE CONVICT

6. *All of this seems to suggest that there's not much we know how to do to rehabilitate an offender when he's in an institution. Doesn't this lead to the clear possibility that the way to rehabilitate offenders is to deal with them* outside *an institutional setting?*

This is indeed an important possibility, and it is suggested by other pieces of information as well. For instance, Miner (1967) reported on a milieu therapy program in Massachusetts called Outward Bound. It took youths 15½ and over; it was oriented toward the development of skills in the out-of-doors and conducted in a wilderness atmosphere very different from that of most existing institutions. The culmination of the 26-day program was a final 24 hours in which each youth had to survive alone in the wilderness. And Miner found that the program did indeed work in reducing recidivism rates.

But by and large, when one takes the programs that have been administered in institutions and applies them in a non-institutional setting, the results do not grow to encouraging proportions. With casework and individual counseling in the community, for instance, there have been three studies; they dealt with counseling methods from psycho-social and vocational counseling to "operant conditioning," in which an offender was rewarded first simply for coming to counseling sessions and then, gradually, for performing other types of approved acts. Two of them report that the community-counseled offenders did no better than their institutional controls, while the third notes that although community counseling produced fewer arrests per person, it did not ultimately reduce the offender's chance of returning to a reformatory.

• • •

PSYCHOTHERAPY IN COMMUNITY SETTINGS

There is some indication that individual psychotherapy may "work" in a community setting. Massimo (1963) reported on one such program, using what might be termed a "pragmatic" psychotherapeutic approach, including "insight" therapy and a focus on vocational problems. The program was marked by its small size and by its use of therapists who were personally enthusiastic about the project; Massimo found that there was indeed a decline in the recidivism rate. Adamson (1956), on the other hand, found no significant difference produced by another program of individual therapy (though he did note that arrest rates among the experimental boys declined with what he called "intensity of treatment"). And Schwitzgebel (1963, 1964), studying other, different kinds of therapy programs, found that the programs *did* produce improvements in the attitudes of his boys—but, unfortunately, not in their rates of recidivism.

And with *group* therapy administered in the community, we find yet another set of equivocal results. The results from studies of pragmatic group counseling are only mildly optimistic. Adams (1965) did report that a form of group therapy, "guided group interaction," when administered to juvenile gangs, did somewhat reduce the percentage that were to be found in custody six years later. On the other hand, in a study of juveniles, Adams (1964) found that while such a program did reduce the number of contacts that an experimental youth had with police, it made no ultimate difference in the detention rate. And the attitudes of the counseled youth showed no improvement. Finally, when O'Brien (1961) examined a community-based program of group psychotherapy, he found not only that the program produced no improvement in the recidivism rate, but that the experimental boys actually did worse than their controls on a series of psychological tests.

PROBATION OR PAROLE VERSUS PRISON

But by far the most extensive and important work that has been done on the effect of community-based treatments had been done in the areas of probation and parole. This work sets out to answer the question of whether it makes any difference how you supervise and treat an offender once he has been released from prison or has come under state surveillance in lieu of prison. This is the work that has provided the main basis to date for the claim that we do indeed have the means at our disposal for rehabilitating the offender or at least decarcerating him safely.

One group of these studies has compared the use of probation with other dispositions for offenders; these provide some slight evidence that, at least under some circumstances, probation may make an offender's future chances better than if he had been sent to prison. Or, at least, probation may not worsen those chances. A British study, by Wilkins (1958), reported that when probation was granted more frequently, recidivism rates among probationers did not increase significantly. And another such study by the state of Michigan in 1963 reported that an expansion in the use of probation actually improved recidivism rates—though there are serious problems of comparability in the groups and systems that were studied.

• • •

Quite a large group of studies deals not with probation as compared to other dispositions, but instead with the type of treatment that an offender receives once he is *on* probation or parole. These are the studies that have provided the most encouraging reports on rehabilitative treatment and that have also raised the most serious questions about the nature of the research that has been going on in the corrections field.

Five of these studies have dealt with youthful probationers from 13 to 18 who were assigned to probation officers with small caseloads or provided with other ways of receiving more intensive supervision (Adams, 1966—two reports; Fiestman, 1966; Kawaguchi, 1967; Pilnick, 1967). These studies report that, by and large, intensive supervision does work—that the specially treated youngsters do better according to some measure of recidivism. Yet these studies left some important questions unanswered. For instance, was this improved performance a function merely of the number of contacts a youngster had with his probation officer? Did it also depend on the length of time in treatment? Or was it the quality of supervision that was making the difference, rather than the quantity?

INTENSIVE SUPERVISION: THE WARREN STUDIES

The widely reported Warren studies (1966a, 1966b, 1967) in California constitute an extremely ambitious attempt to answer these questions. In this project, a control group of youths, drawn from a pool of candidates ready for first admission to a California Youth Authority institution, was assigned to regular detention, usually for eight to nine months, and then released to regular supervision. The experimental group received considerably more elaborate treatment. They were released directly to probation status and assigned to 12-man caseloads. To decide what special treatment was appropriate within these caseloads, the youths were divided according to their "interpersonal maturity level classification," by use of a scale developed by Grant and Grant. And each level dictated its own special type of therapy.

• • •

"Success" in this experiment was defined as favorable discharge by the Youth Authority; "failure" was unfavorable discharge, revocation, or recommitment by a court. Warren reported an encouraging finding: Among all but one of the "subtypes," the experimentals had a significantly lower failure rate than the controls. The experiment did have certain problems: The experimentals might have been performing better because of the enthusiasm of the staff and the attention lavished on them; none of the controls had been *directly* released to their regular supervision programs instead of being detained first; and it was impossible to separate the effects of the experimentals' small caseloads from their specially designed treatments, since no experimental youths had been assigned to a small caseload with "inappropriate" treatment, or with no treatment at all. Still, none of these problems were serious enough to vitiate the encouraging prospect that this finding presented for successful treatment of probationers.

This encouraging finding was, however, accompanied by a rather more disturbing clue. As has been mentioned before, the experimental subjects, when measured, had a lower *failure* rate than the controls. But the experimentals also had a lower *success* rate. That is, fewer of the experimentals as compared with the controls had been judged to have successfully completed their program of supervision and to be suitable for favorable release. When my colleagues and I undertook a rather laborious reanalysis of the Warren data, it became clear why this discrepancy had appeared. It turned out that fewer experimentals were "successful" because the experimentals were actually committing more offenses than their controls. The reason that the experimentals' relatively large number of offenses was not being reflected in their failure rates was simply that the experimentals' probation officers were using a more lenient revocation policy. In other words, the controls had a higher failure rate because the controls were being revoked for less serious offenses.

So it seems that what Warren was reporting in her "failure" rates was not merely the treatment effect of her small caseloads and special programs. Instead, what Warren was finding was not so much a change in the behavior of the experimental youths as a change in the behavior of the experimental *probation officers*, who knew the "special" status of their charges and who had evidently decided to revoke probation status at a lower than normal rate. The experimentals continued to commit offenses; what was different was that when they committed these offenses, they were permitted to remain on probation.

The experimenters claimed that this low revocation policy, and the greater number of offenses committed by the special treatment youth, were *not* an indication that these youth were behaving specially badly and that policy makers were simply letting them get away with it. Instead, it was claimed, the higher reported offense rate was primarily an artifact of the more intense surveillance that the experimental youth received. But the data show that this is not a sufficient explanation of the low failure rate among experimental youth; the difference in "tolerance" of offenses between experimental officials and control officials was much greater than the difference in the rates at which these two systems detected youths committing new offenses. Needless to say, this reinterpretation of the data presents a much bleaker picture of the possibilities of intensive supervision with special treatment.

"TREATMENT EFFECTS" VERSUS "POLICY EFFECTS"

This same problem of experimenter bias may also be present in the predecessors of the Warren study, the ones which had also found positive results from intensive supervision on probation; indeed, this disturbing question can be raised about many of the previously discussed reports of positive "treatment effects."

This possibility of a "policy effect" rather than a "treatment effect" applies, for instance, to the previously discussed studies of the effects of intensive supervision on juvenile and youthful probationers. These were the studies, it will be recalled, which found lower recidivism rates for the intensively supervised.

• • •

One must conclude that the "benefits" of intensive supervision for youthful offenders may stem not so much from a "treatment" effect as from a "policy" effect—that such supervision, so far as we now know, results not in rehabilitation but in a decision to look the other way when an offense is committed. But there is one major modification to be added to this conclusion. Johnson performed a further measurement (1962b) in his parole experiment: He rated all the supervising agents according to the "adequacy" of the supervision they gave. And he found that an "adequate" agent, whether he was working in a small *or* a large caseload, produced a relative improvement in his charges. The converse was not true: An *in*adequate agent was more likely to produce youthful "failures" when he was given a *small* caseload to supervise. One can't much help a "good" agent, it seems, by reducing his caseload size; such reduction can only do further harm to those youths who fall into the hands of "bad" agents.

So with youthful offenders, Johnson found, intensive supervision does not seem to provide the rehabilitative benefits claimed for it; the only such benefits may flow not from intensive supervision itself but from contact with one of the "good people" who are frequently in such short supply.

INTENSIVE SUPERVISION OF ADULTS

The results are similarly ambiguous when one applies this intensive supervision to adult offenders. There have been several studies of the effects of intensive supervision on adult parolees. Some of these are hard to interpret because of problems of comparability between experimental and control groups (general risk ratings, for instance, or distribution of narcotics offenders, or policy changes that took place between various phases of the experiments), but two of them (California, 1966; Stanton, 1964) do not seem to give evidence of the benefits of intensive supervision. By far the most extensive work, though, on the effects of intensive supervision of adult parolees has been a series of studies of California's Special Intensive Parole Unit (SIPU), a 10-year-long experiment designed to test the treatment possibilities of various special parole programs. Three of the four "phases" of this experiment produced "negative results." The first phase tested the effect of a reduced caseload size; no lasting effect was found. The second phase slightly increased the size of the small caseloads and provided for a longer time in treatment; again there was no evidence of a treatment effect. In the fourth phase, caseload sizes and time in treatment were again varied, and treatments were simultaneously varied in a sophisticated way according to personality characteristics of the parolees; once again, significant results did not appear.

The only phase of this experiment for which positive results were reported was Phase Three. Here, it was indeed found that a smaller caseload improved one's chances of parole success. There is, however, an important caveat that attaches to this finding: When my colleagues and I divided the whole population of subjects into two groups—those receiving supervision in the North of the state and those in the South—we found that the "improvement" of the experimentals' success rates was taking place primarily in the North. The North differed from the South in one important aspect: Its agents practiced a policy of returning both "experimental" and "control" violators to prison at relatively high rates. And it was the North that produced the higher success rate among its experimentals. So this improvement in experimentals' performance was taking place only when accompanied by a "realistic threat" of severe sanctions.

• • •

THE EFFECTS OF COMMUNITY TREATMENT

In sum, even in the case of treatment programs administered outside penal institutions, we simply cannot say that this treatment in itself has an appreciable effect on offender behavior. On the other hand, there is one encouraging set of findings that emerges from these studies. For from many of them there flows the strong suggestion that even if we can't "treat" offenders so as to make them do better, a great many of the programs designed to rehabilitate them at least did not make them do *worse*. And if these programs did not show the advantages of actually rehabilitating, some of them did have the advantage of being less onerous to the offender himself without seeming to pose increased danger to the community. And some of these programs—especially those involving less restrictive custody, minimal supervision, and early release—simply cost fewer dollars to administer. The information on the dollar costs of these programs is just beginning to be developed but the implication is clear: *that if we can't do more for (and to) offenders, at least we can safely do less.*

There is, however, one important caveat even to this note of optimism: In order to calculate the true costs of these programs, one must in each case include not only their administrative cost but also the cost of maintaining in the community an offender population increased in size. This population might well not be committing new offenses at any greater rate; but the offender population might, under some of these plans, be larger in absolute *numbers*. So the total number of offenses committed might rise, and our chances of victimization might therefore rise too. We need to be able to make a judgment about the size and probable duration of this effect; as of now, we simply do not know.

DOES NOTHING WORK?

7. *Do all of these studies lead us irrevocably to the conclusion that nothing works, that we haven't the faintest clue about how to rehabilitate offenders and reduce recidivism? And if so, what shall we do?*

We tried to exclude from our survey those studies which were so poorly done that they simply could not be interpreted. But despite our efforts, a pattern has run through much of this discussion—of studies which "found" effects without making any truly rigorous attempt to exclude competing hypotheses, of extraneous factors permitted to intrude upon the measurements, of recidivism measures which are not all measuring the same thing, of "follow-up" periods which vary enormously and rarely extend beyond the period of legal supervision, of experiments never replicated, of "system effects" not taken into account, of categories drawn up without any theory to guide the enterprise. It is just possible that some of our treatment programs *are* working to some extent, but that our research is so bad that it is incapable of telling.

Having entered this very serious caveat, I am bound to say that these data, involving over two hundred studies and hundreds of thousands of individuals as they do, are the best available and give us very little reason to hope that we have in fact found a sure way of reducing recidivism through rehabilitation. This is not to say that we found no instances of success or partial success; it is only to say that these instances have been isolated, producing no clear pattern to indicate the efficacy of any particular method of treatment. And neither is this to say that factors *outside* the realm of rehabilitation may not be working to reduce recidivism—factors such as the tendency for recidivism to be lower in offenders over the age of 30; it is only to say that such factors seem to have little connection with any of the treatment methods now at our disposal.

From this probability, one may draw any of several conclusions. It may be simply that our programs aren't yet good enough—that the education we provide to inmates is still poor education, that the therapy we administer is not administered skillfully enough, that our intensive supervision and counseling do not yet provide enough personal support for the offenders who are subjected to them. If one wishes to believe this, then what our correctional system needs is simply a more full-hearted commitment to the strategy of treatment.

It may be, on the other hand, that there is a more radical flaw in our present strategies—that education at its best, or that psychotherapy at its best, cannot overcome, or even appreciably reduce, the powerful tendency for offenders to continue in criminal behavior. Our present treatment programs are based on a theory of crime as a "disease"—that is to say, as something foreign and abnormal in the individual which can presumably be cured. This theory may well be flawed, in that it overlooks—indeed, denies—both the normality of crime in society and the personal normality of a very large proportion of offenders, criminals who are merely responding to the facts and conditions of our society.

This opposing theory of "crime as a social phenomenon" directs our attention away from a "rehabilitative" strategy, away from the notion that we may best insure public safety through a series of "treatments" to be imposed forcibly on convicted offenders. These treatments have on occasion become, and have the potential for becoming, so draconian as to offend the moral order of a democratic society; and the theory of crime as a social phenomenon suggests that such treatments may not be only offensive but ineffective as well. This theory points, instead, to decarceration for low-risk offenders—and, presumably, to keeping high-risk offenders in prisons which are nothing more (and aim to be nothing more) than custodial institutions.

But this approach has its own problems. To begin with, there is the moral dimension of crime and punishment. Many low-risk offenders have committed serious crimes (murder, sometimes) and even if one is reasonably sure they will never commit another crime, it violates our sense of justice that they should experience no significant retribution for their actions. A middle-class banker who kills his adulterous wife in a moment of passion is a "low-risk" criminal; a juvenile delinquent in the ghetto who commits armed robbery has, statistically, a much higher probability of committing another crime. Are we going to put the first on probation and sentence the latter to a long term in prison?

Besides, one cannot ignore the fact that the punishment of offenders is the major means we have for *deterring* incipient offenders. We know almost nothing about the "deterrent effect," largely because "treatment" theories have so dominated our research, and "deterrence" theories have been relegated to the status of a historical curiosity. Since we have almost no idea of the deterrent functions that our present system performs or that future strategies might be made to perform, it is possible that there is indeed something that works—that to some extent is working right now in front of our noses, and that might be made to work better—something that deters rather than cures, something that does not so much reform convicted offenders as prevent criminal behavior in the first place. But whether that is the case and, if it is, what strategies will be found to make our deterrence system work better than it does now, are questions we will not be able to answer with data until a new family of studies has been brought into existence. As we begin to learn the facts, we will be in a better position than we are now to judge to what degree the prison has become an anachronism and can be replaced by more effective means of social control.

DISCUSSION QUESTIONS

1. What did the studies conducted on educational and vocational training show? Did the results differ for young inmates and adult inmates?
2. Did any of the studies on individual or group counseling show a reduction in recidivism?
3. What is milieu therapy and did it have any effect on recidivism?
4. What were the results of the studies conducted on sentence length and degree of security?
5. Describe all of the different types of community treatment that were discussed. Did any of those treatments have an effect on recidivism?
6. What can we conclude about the types of programs that our criminal justice system has?

21

The Aging Inmate

R.V. Rikard and
Ed Rosenberg

During the past 30 years, American prisons have experienced rapidly expanding numbers of inmates, including more who are elderly. Elderly inmates present unique management challenges to the extent they experience age-specific adjustments and adaptations to prison life. Accommodating this "special needs" population, which places a disproportionate strain on available correctional resources, raises both prison environment and policy-level questions. Although some advocate early and/or medical release for older inmates who are seen as no longer posing a threat to society, state and federal correctional data indicate that early release is not a dominant trend. This article reviews the causes of the growth in the older male inmate population and then applies tools from gerontology to provide a perspective for evaluating current or prospective correctional system responses and programs, and to raise issues and suggest policies that might benefit older inmates as well as correctional systems.

A three-decade convergence of trends in the American correctional system has led to significant growth in the population of aging inmates. As the number of aging inmates grows, so do financial and facilities costs to state departments of correction (DOCs) and the Federal Bureau of Prisons (FBOP). Even if forethought was given to the growth of this "special

Source: R.V. Rikard and Ed Rosenberg, "Aging Inmates: A Convergence of Trends in the American Criminal Justice System," Journal of Correctional Health Care vol. 13 no. 3 150–162.

needs" inmate population, current federal and state budget difficulties hinder the ability to address the environmental, health-related, and social needs of these inmates.

This article has five goals. First, the increase in the number of older persons in America and in U.S. prison systems will be documented, an operational definition of the aging inmate will be provided, and the characteristics of this special needs population will be described. Second, a historical review presents the convergence of three trends that have led to an increase in the aging inmate population. Third, the increasing costs of caring for and managing this population will be described, showing the increasing financial burden aging inmates place on state DOCs and the FBOP. Fourth, policies and programs that state DOCs and the FBOP use to manage and provide care for aging inmates will be described. Finally, a gerontological perspective, focusing on age, period, and cohort effects, will be presented and employed to suggest a disaggregation of aging inmate care and management issues that will optimize policy and program responses. A multidisciplinary approach should both enhance our understanding of aging inmate issues and challenges and help us evaluate potential policy responses.

THE GRAYING OF AMERICA: DEMOGRAPHICS AND DEFINITIONS

In 1900, only 4% of Americans were age 65 or older (Hooyman & Kiyak, 1999). By 2000 the older population had more than tripled, to about 13% of the U.S. population. Over the same period, life expectancy increased from 47 to 78 years, due largely to advances in medical science and technology. As 80 million baby boomers (those born between 1946 and 1964) become the new generation of senior citizens, the population age 65+ will roughly double (Hooyman & Kiyak, 1999). By the time all the baby boomers have turned 65, about 1 in 5 Americans will be in that age group.

Increases in life expectancy have not bypassed prison populations. Although several factors contribute to the size of the elderly inmate population, the number of older inmates and the percentage of the incarcerated population they comprise will grow rapidly. Formby and Abel (1997) note that in 1990, approximately 19,610 persons age 55 and older were incarcerated in state and federal correctional institutions; in 2 years this number grew to 23,025 older inmates, and to 25,004 in 1993. Texas saw an estimated 86% increase in the older inmate population from 1994 to 1998, compared to a 35.4% increase in the general prison population for the same given time period (Schreiber, 1999). Zimbardo (1994) found that in 1994 elderly inmates represented 4% of the total prison population in California. However, by 2020, California will see a projected increase in its elderly inmate population of more than 200%. Other authors have estimated that by 2020, older inmates will represent 21% to 33% of the U.S.

prison population (Chaneles, 1987; Durham, 1994; Neeley, Addison, & Craig-Moreland, 1997).

The increase in the number and percentage of aging inmates is due in part to medical advances. Yet such inmates often have long histories of alcohol and drug abuse, insufficient diet, and lack of medical care (Williams, 2001). The combination of physical and mental declines makes aging inmates, on the average, 10 to 11.5 years older physiologically than their nonincarcerated age peers (Doughty, 1999; Southern Legislative Conference, 1998). This is why most recent studies consider either age 50 or 55 as the onset of old age for inmates (Aday, 1994a, 2003; Auerhahn, 2002; Barnes, 1999; Bouplon, 1999; Durham, 1994; Goetting, 1983, 1984a, 1984b, 1985; Holeman, 1998; Merianos, Marquart, Damphouse, & Hebert, 1997; Morton, 1992; Rosefield, 1993; Wheeler, Connelly, & Wheeler, 1995; Zimbardo, 1994). For our purposes, then, an elderly male inmate is defined as age 50+.

Compared to younger inmates, older inmates have poorer health, especially regarding chronic conditions, substance abuse, and psychological disorders (Aday, 1994a; Bouplon, 1999; Rosefield, 1993). Formby and Abel (1997) found that older inmates suffered an average of three chronic illnesses during their incarceration. Because of health and other aging-related needs, older prisoners are up to 3 times more costly to maintain than younger inmates; older inmates use more prescription drugs than younger inmates and spend twice as much time in medical facilities (Morton, 1992; Sheppard, 2001). Older inmates also are more likely to have committed violent crimes; 75% are still serving time for their first offense (Sheppard, 2001). This is at least in part because of the greater odds of parole or release of nonviolent offenders in the same age cohort.

THE CRIME CONTROL MODEL IN CRIMINAL JUSTICE

Before the Vietnam War years, correctional policy and sentencing guidelines were based on the rehabilitative model, which emphasized treatment programs to reform the "sick" offender. Griset (1991) notes that a medical model was frequently invoked to treat the offender for an indeterminate time until the inmate was considered "well." However, after the socially turbulent 1960s there were changes in sentencing policies prompted by antirehabilitationists' claims that inmates were not "sick" and that the criminal justice system could not "prescribe a cure" through treatment in the correctional system (Griset, 1991).

The passage of the 1984 Federal Sentencing Reform Act provides further evidence of the shift from rehabilitation toward incapacitation (King & Mauer, 2001; Rausch, 1996). The Act implemented mandatory minimum sentences and specified periods of incarceration for specified federal offenses. By the mid-1990s, 13 states had passed their own form of sentencing reform acts (Flynn, Flanagan, Greenwood, & Krisberg, 1995; Mackenzie, 2001). In 1994, the Federal Violent Crime Control and Law Enforcement Act was passed, allocating $9.7 billion for prison construction and $6 billion for prevention programs. The largest impact of this bill was its mandate that 50% of the funding for all programs go to states that adopted truth-in-sentencing laws, including the condition that such laws require offenders to serve at least 85% of their sentence before being eligible for release (Violent Crime Control, 1994). Judicial discretion in sentencing was virtually eliminated—no longer could judges or prosecutors consider such factors as age, health, or perceived risk to the community. This shift in the dominant rationale for imprisonment keeps more convicts incarcerated for longer periods of time, leading to growth in the proportion of older inmates (Auerhahn, 2002).

Thus, beginning after the Vietnam War years and continuing to the present, there has been a movement in the criminal justice system away from an overarching philosophy of rehabilitation toward one of incapacitation. Indicators of this shift include mandatory sentencing, "three-strikes" programs, and various "get-tough" crime policies. These factors—more sentences, longer sentences, mandatory sentences—when coupled with medical advances that keep aging inmates alive longer, have led to the current growth of the older inmate population (Chaneles, 1987; Flynn et al., 1995; Holeman, 1998; Merianos et al., 1997; Zimbardo, 1994).

The challenge of the aging inmate thus results from multiple trends: the historical evolution of America's criminal justice philosophy, the resultant explosion of the prison population, and the significant current and future growth of the older inmate population. Additionally, this challenge must be addressed in an era of large federal deficits and shrinking state budgets. Given the convergence of these trends and the disproportionate costs of incarcerating older inmates, an examination of the policies and programs of state DOCs, the FBOP, and independent organizations should shed light on current approaches to managing, housing, and caring for older inmates.

THE CHALLENGE: NUMBERS AND COSTS

If federal and state policies remain unchanged there will be a significant growth in the number of older inmates, a population with disproportionate medical needs and costs. Adequate equipment and services needed to provide medical care for aging inmates include 24-hour nursing coverage, infirmary beds, physician availability, pharmacy, laboratory, x-ray, and rehabilitative physical care resources (Rosefield, 1993). For the elderly offender, kidney dialysis costs at least $122 per treatment; a pacemaker implant costs $15,000 to $50,000 (Krane, 1999a, 1999b).

Thus, the responsibility of federal and state correctional departments to provide adequate medical care and housing for older inmates will be more complex—and more expensive—than ever. In fact, at both the federal and state levels, the cost of inmate health care has increased dramatically. The FBOP spends more than $400 million annually to imprison and care for elderly inmates (Holeman, 1998). However, states also bear the burden of providing care for the aging inmate population. For example, Pennsylvania's spending on prison health services grew from $1.23 million in 1973 to $16.7 million in 1986, largely because of older inmate expenses such as eyeglasses, dentures, open-heart surgery, and care for the terminally ill (Chaneles, 1987). More than a decade ago, Zimbardo (1994) found the annual cost to incarcerate an inmate age 60+ in California to be about $69,000, compared to $21,000 for an inmate age 30. A 50-year-old person convicted in 1994 who serves a 25-year sentence at an average cost of $60,000 per year would cost the state of California about $1.5 million. More recently, a Georgia study (Georgia Department of Corrections, 2000) found that inmates age 50+, who represent only 6% of the incarcerated population, consume more than 12% of the inmate health care budget. Consequently, the mean annual cost was $69,000 per older inmate.

STATE AND FEDERAL POLICIES AND PROGRAMS

In discussing the management and care of elderly inmates, there are two areas of general interest for both scholars and practitioners: release and reintegration, and prison facility design and management (Drummond, 1999; Duckett, Fox, Harsha, & Vish, 2001; Goetting, 1983; Holeman, 1998; Ornduff, 1996; Yates & Gillespie, 2000). However, current policies and programs at state and federal levels exhibit little consensus regarding either release or management of the aging inmate (Adams, 1995; Aday, 2003; Coalition, 1998; Drummond, 1999; Duckett et al., 2001; Goetting, 1983; Ornduff, 1996; Yates & Gillespie, 2000). What follows is a review of current policies and programs employed to care for the aging inmate population.

"Compassionate"/Medical/Nonmedical Early Parole

Perhaps the most controversial aging inmate issue is release from prison before serving the complete term of incarceration (Goetting, 1983; Ornduff, 1996). Early release usually occurs for one of two reasons: terminal illness or record of incarcerated behavior. Medical parole, also known as "compassionate" release, refers to the release of an inmate who suffers from a terminal disease and whose remaining life expectancy is within a specified threshold (Ornduff, 1996). As Russell (1994) noted in her survey of all 50 states, the District of Columbia, and the FBOP, only Kansas, Maine, and the District of Columbia allowed medical release of inmates. In some other states, medical release for the elderly inmate is valid only during the term of illness or until death. If the medical condition improves, medical parole is revoked and the inmate is returned to the correctional atmosphere, a practice found in Georgia, New York, Ohio, Oklahoma, Oregon, and Texas (Russell, 1994).

When examining this perhaps morally justifiable approach from a financial standpoint, one can question whether state DOCs are merely cost-shifting, transferring the economic burden of the ailing inmate from correctional facilities to the inmate's family or, more commonly, community health and social services. Ornduff (1996) notes that states disagree on where the prisoner may go after being released on medical parole. Delaware's relatively stringent policy mandates the inmate be released on medical parole only when arrangements have been made for the treatment of the person in some other institution. Montana's moderate policy requires that the prisoner agree to a designated facility recommended by the state parole board. Connecticut's lenient medical release policy permits inmate release into an environment "suitable to his medical health," which can include the residence of the inmate's family. Thus there is no clear medical parole policy that all—or even most—state DOCs follow.

There are currently few early release policies for chronically but nonterminally ill aging inmates. As noted above, such inmates are a financial burden on correctional systems, yet are likely to remain incarcerated barring a change in criminal justice system policy. Therefore an area of future research could focus on policy adaptations that address not only medical parole but also an overall cost-effective integration of services (vs. cost-shifting) for these aging parolees. Innovative policies or programs that result from such initial efforts can serve as a guide for national policy development.

One such innovative program for nonterminally ill aging inmates that challenges the public opinion trend is the Project for Older Prisoners (POPS; Aday, 2003; Coalition, 1998; Drummond, 1999; Duckett et al., 2001; Goetting, 1983; Yates & Gillespie, 2000). Founded in 1989, POPS operates primarily through law schools in the District of Columbia and five states: Louisiana, Maryland, Michigan, North Carolina, and Virginia. The stated goals are to reduce prison overcrowding and costs to taxpayers. As of 2002, POPS had counseled more than 500 older inmates and won release for nearly 100, with no reported recidivism (Duckett et al., 2001; Florida House, 1999; Goetting, 1983; Yates & Gillespie, 2000).

To be eligible for the POPS program, an inmate must be at least 55, have served the average time of his or her sentence, and be deemed no longer a present danger. The victim or victim's family must agree to the inmate's early release (Coalition, 1998; Drummond, 1999; Duckett et al., 2001; Goetting, 1983; Yates & Gillespie, 2000). On the inmate's release a POPS volunteer—typically a law school student—is assigned to work with the former inmate to establish a network of reintegrative support services, such as Social Security or the Veterans Administration.

The POPS program is creative and apparently effective, yet limited in geographic reach, and the basic requirements for inmate selection are quite specific (Ornduff, 1996). Expansion of POPS to all other states could yield a cost-effective and arguably humane reduction in the number of elderly inmates. The success of current POPS programs plus data showing that released elderly inmates have the lowest rates of recidivism of any age category support further exploration of this idea (Florida House of Representatives, 1999; Turley, 1989; Yates & Gillespie, 2000; Zimbardo, 1994).

Prison Facility Design and Management

If the aging inmate is not to be released, a key question is whether aging inmates should be segregated from or consolidated into the general inmate population. There is no uniform policy from any of the state DOCs regarding consolidation versus segregation. According to a 1997 National Institute of Corrections study on the health needs of aging inmates, 23 states have specific services for older inmates. Of these 23 states, 15 provide segregated medical facilities for elderly inmates (U.S. Department of Justice, 1997). Moreover, scholars do not agree on whether aging inmates should be consolidated into or segregated from the general inmate population (Adams, 1995; Aday, 1994a, 1994b, 2003; Duckett et al., 2001; Goetting, 1984a, 1985; Johnson, 1988; Merianos et al., 1997; Neeley et al., 1997; Ornduff, 1996; Rosefield, 1993; Wiegand & Burger, 1979; Yates & Gillespie, 2000).

A prison management perspective asks whether the presence of aging inmates improves the atmosphere of a facility or makes them potential victims for younger inmates. Support for consolidation comes from prison administrators who believe that older inmates have a calming effect on younger inmates (Adams, 1995; Aday, 1994b, 2003; Ornduff, 1996; Yates & Gillespie, 2000). However, Ornduff (1996) and Johnson (1988) found that prison administrators consider "older" inmates to be 35 to 50 years old. Additionally, administrators prefer consolidation because it allows the older inmates to participate in work details and educational/vocational programs, and because it provides easier access to the aging inmate for family and friends (Adams, 1995; Aday, 1994b; Goetting, 1983; Ornduff, 1996; Yates & Gillespie, 2000). Thus, the safety issue is not directly addressed.

There are also arguments favoring segregation of older inmates. Segregation minimizes the odds that older inmates will fall prey to younger, more aggressive inmates (Adams, 1995; Aday, 1994b, 2003; Ornduff, 1996; Yates & Gillespie, 2000). Segregation also provides elderly inmates the opportunity to build friendships and support networks with their age peers, reducing feelings of loneliness and despair and building self-respect (Adams, 1995; Goetting, 1984b; Morton, 1992; Ornduff, 1996; Yates & Gillespie, 2000). Age-based segregation allows the designation of one central unit that can be adapted as an "elder-friendly" physical environment, with such features as fewer stairwells, more ramps and handrails, lower bunks or bunk assignments, quiet and well-lit communal areas, and nonwaxed floors to reduce falls. These and other physical environment modifications in a segregated geriatric unit address older inmates' safety needs and physical limitations (Bouplon, 1999; Duckett et al., 2001; Neeley et al., 1997; Rosefield, 1993; Wiegand & Burger, 1979).

States' Response to Parole, Facility Design, and Management

Our review of state policies for older inmate segregation/consolidation found that some state DOCs have developed programs to meet the housing and management needs of aging inmates. Eighteen states provide age-segregated facilities. Eight states and the FBOP consolidate older inmates into the general inmate population. The remaining 24 states have no documented segregation/consolidation policy. The housing programs of five states, covering the range of residential arrangements from "most" to "least" accommodating, are described below.

Ohio. Ohio has six correctional facilities that house older inmates, the majority being located at Hocking Correctional Facility (HCF), a 450-bed age-segregated facility for inmates 50 years of age or older (Ohio Department of Rehabilitation and Correction, 1997). Programming for older inmates at HCF includes (a) prerelease programming, in which inmates receive a "Golden Buckeye Card" as well as information on how to file for Social Security benefits, listings of area human service providers, and job-seeking skills; (b) vocational building and property maintenance training courses; (c) Maturing With Understanding While Behind Bars, a program that educates inmates on the physical, psychological, and social issue of aging; (d) adult basic education and literacy courses; and (5) Self Care, a program that provides material on medical issues and problems of aging, as well as recognizing and dealing with issues of aging (Ohio, 1997).

In conjunction with these programs, HCF has developed correctional staff training programs that emphasize age sensitivity, legal issues, grieving, death and dying, prerelease and aftercare, supervision of older prisoners, programming, and medical and nutritional concerns (Ohio, 1997). When necessary, the Ohio DOC provides nursing home placement. Although there are strict guidelines for placement, aging inmates are placed in nursing homes if they need assistance with two or more Activities of Daily Living (ADL; described below). Currently there are no halfway houses for older inmates.

Pennsylvania. At the time of this writing, Pennsylvania had one correctional facility—State Correctional Institute at Laurel Highlands—that segregates older inmates from the general prison population. Inmates are eligible to reside at State Correctional Institute at Laurel Highlands when they turn 55. These elderly inmates have access to age-targeted medical services (including substance abuse), psychological counseling (e.g., death and dying issues), and a reintegration program called Life Skill, which develops skills necessary for older inmates to successfully reintegrate into their communities (Aday, 2003).

Virginia. Virginia has one specialized facility for inmates age 55 and older. Deerfield Correctional Center provides assisted living care, skilled nursing care, and special training for guards who interact with older inmates. Because of the increasing costs of caring and providing housing for elderly inmates, Virginia state officials place the inmates in extramural assisted living care; the state pays $30 per day per aging inmate, versus $100 per day to maintain the same inmate inside the prison facility (Baker, 1999; Florida Corrections Commission, 2001).

Florida. The Florida DOC evaluates inmates based on their overall medical classification. It does not have an age-specific set of policies and procedures, except those relating to its specialized (e.g., segregated) facility at River Junction, which was legislatively designated a geriatric facility in 2000. The legislation, however, stipulates that inmates qualify for transfer to River Junction only if they are "generally healthy." This biases assignment to River Junction in favor of "relatively younger" older inmates. The River Junction Correctional Institution staff complete a required training program titled Aging Inmate Supervision. In addition, an Elder Abuse, Neglect, and Exploitation program has been approved by the Florida Department of Elder Affairs for correctional officer training (Correctional Medical Authority, 2000; Florida Corrections Commission, 2001).

Montana. Montana lacks a policy on housing aging inmates and does not provide a separate facility for them. However, the Montana State University–Bozeman nursing program has a cooperative program with the Montana DOC wherein nurses intern at the Montana State Prison. This allows nursing students to learn about geriatric medicine and reduces DOC costs, because elderly inmates do not need to be transported out of the prison for medical care (Boswell, 2001).

APPLYING A GERONTOLOGICAL PERSPECTIVE

As the American population ages, gerontology becomes a more relevant field of study. As the American prison population ages, it becomes more likely that a gerontological perspective can inform criminal justice policies and political action. This section addresses four topics: how age is defined (how people are "age-graded"), how differences between younger and older persons are explained, how the functional status of the older inmate is assessed, and a theoretical model of the relationship between the inmate and his environment.

Defining Age

Using chronological age to identify older inmates or to make them eligible for certain programs or resources, as many scholars and policy makers have done, may need to be reconsidered. Most people are familiar with defining age chronologically. One advantage to such a definition is that it provides easily measured thresholds for social activities, opportunities, or privileges. It also allows us to precisely allocate people to life stages, such as teenager (ages 13-19 inclusive) and elderly (age 65 and over). On the other hand, defining age chronologically is an imperfect measure of life stage or ability. Of particular relevance to the issue of aging inmates is the fact that, although health does in general decline with age, chronological age may not be the best predictor of inmate health and thus of inmate needs. Consequently, resources targeted to prisoners "of a certain age" are likely to benefit some prisoners who do not need them and omit others who do.

A second way of age-grading is biological/physiological. People are assigned to age categories (e.g., young, middle-aged, old) based on biological traits and physiological indicators (e.g., cardiovascular fitness, neuromuscular response, bone density, or chronic health problems such as high blood pressure, diabetes, and prostate or breast cancer). A third age-grading method addresses functional age. This focuses on one's ability to perform necessary tasks (e.g., personal hygiene, job) and is related to but not identical to physiological aging.

Chronological age is a highly reliable indicator but not necessarily a valid one regarding physiological status and functionality. If the best use of resources is to assist all who need assistance and no one who doesn't, allocating resources based on chronological age is a mistake.

Explaining Differences Between Older and Younger People: Age, Period, and Cohort Effects

When trying to understand how people change as they age or why older and younger people differ, gerontologists often use age, period, and cohort effects as analytical tools. An age, or maturation, effect is a change that occurs essentially because of the aging process. Physiological changes, such as graying hair or immune system deterioration, are examples. Some challenges posed by the increase in numbers of older inmates are largely age effects: changes in health status, needs, and costs together with a growing need for environmental adaptations such as ramps, handrails, or widened doorways.

A period or historical effect is a change across a population because of a historical event. For example, the passage of Social Security changed the nature of retirement and image of retirees in America, and it can be argued that the entire population underwent and was affected by these changes. For our purposes, period effects would include the 1970s shift from a rehabilitation model to an incapacitation model in the criminal justice system, which led to a prison construction boom. The Sentencing Reform Act (1984) and the Law Enforcement Act (1994) toughened and extended sentences and reduced judges' discretion. At the confluence of these events we find a prescription for an increase in older inmates: more prisoners, more prison beds, more lifers, and less parole.

A cohort effect typically refers to differences between generations that can be attributed essentially to the unique experiences of each generation during its formative years. In prison, for example, different cohorts may view the Con

(Convict's) Code—an unwritten set of values and norms that guide de facto prison life and is passed down orally from senior inmates to new arrivals—differently. Senior inmates are no longer viewed by more junior inmates, relatively unquestioningly, as wiser and more steeped in prison culture, and thus older inmates are no longer guaranteed the respect and protection historically mandated by the Con Code. Thus, generational differences in the value accorded the Con Code are making consolidated (age-integrated) prison life more problematic for older inmates (Clemmer, 1958; Sykes, 1971).

It is important for criminologists and decision makers to determine which effect best explains aging inmate issues and challenges. For instance, an age effect, such as increased need for dialysis as the older inmate population rises, will continue as long as prisons hold significant numbers of older inmates. Such ongoing needs must be addressed and planned for, essentially, in perpetuity. A cohort effect, however, means that a trait or need that characterizes today's older prisoners essentially "belongs" to that generation, and as it dies out the trait or need may disappear as well. Thus a cohort explanation implies a short-term need that should be addressed now but which may not be an ongoing drain on resources. Finally, a period effect tells us that there are historical events (e.g., the shift from a rehabilitation model to an incapacitation model) that created current conditions, and thus new historical events (e.g., changes in policy or law) can change the conditions.

Assessing Inmate Age

For more than 30 years gerontologists have assessed functionality via two indexes: Activities of Daily Living (ADL) and Instrumental Activities of Daily Living (IADL). The ADL instrument measures the level of functional independence regarding bathing, dressing, toileting, transferring (e.g., into and out of bed or a chair), continence, and feeding (Katz, Ford, Moskowitz, Jackson, & Jaffe, 1963). The IADL instrument assesses functional ability in using the telephone, shopping, food preparation, housekeeping, laundry, mode of transportation, responsibility for medications, and ability to handle finances (Lawton & Brody, 1969). Both indexes are used to assess older persons' needs and thus the residential placement and types of services they require and that will be reimbursed.

Although one or more IADL categories may not be applicable to the prison environment, or may need to be adapted, these instruments have proven over the years to be reliable and valid means of assessing functionality and thus the need for assistance.

The Older Inmate and His Environment

The Person-Environment Model (Lawton & Nahemow, 1973) illustrates how differing levels of personal competence and environmental press influence behavior and affect. For people to function successfully and have positive affect, there must be an approximate balance between competence and press. The relevance for those charged with responding to the challenges posed by increasing numbers of older inmates is that unacceptable imbalances between personal competence and environmental press can be addressed either by increasing competence or by decreasing press. Thus the problems caused by growing numbers of elderly prisoners can be addressed by teaching new behaviors or problem-solving skills or by modifying the residential prison environment to reduce its press on aging inmates.

CONCLUSIONS

We contend that applying gerontological tools—particularly the analysis of age, period, and cohort effects—can help untangle the multiple causes that have contributed to the growth and, especially, the challenges of an aging inmate population. Such analysis also can help evaluate the odds of and reasons for the success of extant or proposed programs and policies, and ideally will inform future studies of aging inmates. We conclude by highlighting three focal concerns for aging inmates and then offer policy recommendations.

Three Concerns

Inmate capacity. *The quantity issue.* For three decades, due largely to the shift from a rehabilitation to an incapacitation model of crime control, America has been building prisons, tightening laws and sentencing restrictions, and imposing longer sentences. Current state budget shortfalls are forcing states to adjust. Options now under consideration include closing prisons, laying off correctional officers, delaying new prison construction, and cutting inmate education programs (Butterfield, 2002). Thus, because of legislation, we now find rapidly rising numbers and percentages of older inmates, whose aging leads to higher and increasingly burdensome costs.

Prison environment. *The quality issue.* Age effects include physical and mental health needs, adult protective services, and adapted housing. These are real needs and entail additional costs. There are also period effects—the shift to a crime control model led to a prison building boom, but it appears the needs of aging inmates were not taken into account in new prison construction.

Probation and parole. *The reintegration issue.* Tight budgets are leading states to reconsider sentencing and parole (Butterfield, 2002). Several studies show recidivism is inversely related to age at time of release. But most states have no programs like POPS, specifically designed to help older offenders adjust back into civilian life. Cost-cutting measures, such as eliminating GED and vocational education courses for inmates, hinder reintegration. Older parolees often qualify for one or more state assistance programs but may not know they are available or how to access them. Finally, family support is less likely for older offenders; either family has died or cannot accommodate the older person's needs, or family members were the victims and are understandably reluctant to support the perpetrator.

Policy Recommendations

Based on our use of a gerontological perspective to examine the growth of the aging inmate population, we make five policy recommendations. First, to the extent the crime control model is not changed and sentencing/parole policies are not age-targeted, existing and new prisons must prepare to adapt to increasing numbers of older inmates by providing age-targeted physical plant adaptations, staffing and staff training, and programming for inmates. Second, future research should focus on new policies that not only address medical parole for aging inmates but also focus on the placement of aging parolees that proves to be the most cost-effective for all social service agencies. Third, new policies or programs that are outcomes of the previously mentioned research should serve as a guide for a national policy. Fourth, age-specific reintegration programs should be encouraged and supported: parole officers should be trained to help meet the needs of older parolees, and halfway houses should be able to accommodate their environmental needs. The POPS program could serve as a national model for such programs. Finally, states should consider exempting older inmates, who are least likely to reoffend, from parole once released.

In the best of all possible worlds, core values and philosophies guide policy development, and policy is accurately and effectively operationalized in programming at national, state, and local levels. In reality, it seems that the conditions that have led to a rapid rise in older inmates and their housing in facilities designed for younger persons are gradually and sporadically being ameliorated, and we welcome this, even if it is happening for financial or political reasons or reasons not directly related to criminal justice philosophy or society's moral position on incarceration. We hope that our recommendations, based on an integration of criminal justice and gerontological analysis, might serve as a more overarching and integrated guide to inform the policy and practice of incarceration in America.

DISCUSSION QUESTIONS

1. What is your view on the release of elderly inmates that cause little to no threat to society?
2. Should the state and federal government solely carry the financial burden of the elderly inmate? Or should this financial burden be shifted to the inmate's family?
3. Discuss how the advances in science and health-care have impacted the increased number and percentage of aging inmates.

4. Briefly discuss POPS and why it has been so effective in other states and the reasons why some states have not adopted it.
5. Describe the major problems and issues that prisons face today.

REFERENCES

Adams, J. E. (1995). The incarceration of the older inmate. *Nova Law Review, 19*(2), 455–475.

Aday, R. H. (1994a). Aging in prison: A case study of new elderly offenders. *International Journal of Offender Therapy and Comparative Criminology, 38*, 79-91.

Aday, R. H. (1994b). Golden years behind bars. *Federal Probation, 58*(2), 1-19.

Aday, R. H. (2003). *Aging prisoners: Crisis in American corrections*. Westport, CT: Praeger.

Auerhahn, K. (2002). Selective incapacitation, three strikes, and the problem of aging prison populations: Using simulation modeling to see the future. *Criminology, 1*, 353-388.

Baker, D. P. (1999, July 3). Virginia opens special prison for aging inmates: Harsher sentences, parole rules expected to boost number of ailing people behind bars. *Dallas Morning News*, p. B4.

Barnes, M. (1999, June 21). Aging inmates present problems: Prison population grays with nation. *Fayetteville Observer*, p. 6.

Boswell, E. (2001). *Montana's elderly inmates set off national survey—Prisoner care leads to collaboration*. Bozeman: Montana State University Press.

Bouplon, R. A. (1999). *1999 annual report*. Tallahassee, FL: Florida Corrections Commission.

Butterfield, F. (2002, January 21). Tight budgets force states to reconsider crime and penalties. *New York Times*, p. A1.

Chaneles, S. (1987). Growing old behind bars. In K. C. Haas & G. P. Alpert (Eds.), *The dilemmas of corrections: Contemporary readings* (pp. 548-554). Prospect Heights, IL: Waveland Press.

Clemmer, D. (1958). The prison community. In E. J. Latessa, A. Holsinger, J. W. Marquart, & J. R. Sorensen (Eds.), *Correctional contexts: Contemporary and classical readings* (Vol. 2, pp. 83-87). Los Angeles: Roxbury Press.

Coalition for Federal Sentencing Reform. (1998). *Executive summary*. Alexandria, VA: National Center on Institutions and Alternatives.

Correctional Medical Authority. (2000). *Annual report of the CMA—Incarcerating elderly and aging inmates: Medical and mental health implications*. Tallahassee, FL: Author.

Doughty, P. (1999). *A concern in corrections: Special health needs*. Oklahoma City, OK: Oklahoma Department of Corrections.

Drummond, T. (1999). US: Cellblock senior. *Times Magazine (US)*, p. 60.

Duckett, N., Fox, T. A., Harsha, T. C., & Vish, J. (2001). *Issues in Maryland sentencing—The aging Maryland prison population*. College Park, MD: Maryland State Commission on Criminal Sentencing Policy.

Durham, A. M. (1994). *Crisis and reform: Current issues in American punishment*. New York: Little, Brown.

Florida Corrections Commission. (2001). Status report on elderly offenders. In Florida Corrections Commission, *2001 annual report*. Tallahassee, FL: Author.

Florida House of Representatives, Criminal Justice and Corrections Council,

Committee on Corrections. (1999). *An examination of elder inmates services: An aging crisis.* Tallahassee, FL: Author.

Flynn, E. E., Flanagan, T., Greenwood, P., & Krisberg, P. (1995). Three-strikes legislation: Prevalence and definition. *Critical Criminal Justice Issues* (National Institute of Justice Report 158837, pp. 122-133). Washington DC: National Institute for Justice.

Formby, W. A., & Abel, C. F. (1997). Elderly men in prison. In J. I. Kosberg & L. W. Kaye (Eds.), *Elderly men: Special problems and professional challenges* (p. 317). New York: Springer.

Georgia Department of Corrections. (2000). *Georgia's aging inmate population.* Atlanta, GA: Author.

Goetting, A. (1983). The elderly in prison issues and perspectives. *Journal of Research in Crime and Delinquency, 20,* 291-309.

Goetting, A. (1984a). The elderly in prison: A profile. *Criminal Justice Review, 9*(2), 14-24.

Goetting, A. (1984b). Prison program and facilities for elderly inmates. In E. S. Newman, D. J. Newman, & M. L. Gewirtz (Eds.), *Elderly criminals* (pp. 169-176). Cambridge, MA: Oelgeschlager, Gunn, & Hain.

Goetting, A. (1985). Racism, sexism, and ageism in the prison community. *Federal Probation, 44*(3), 10-22.

Griset, P. (1991). *Determinate sentencing: The promise and the reality of retributive justice.* Albany, NY: State University of New York Press.

Holeman, B. (1998). Nursing homes behind bars: The elderly in prison. *Coalition for Federal Sentencing Reform, 2,* 1-4.

Hooyman, N., & Kiyak, H. A. (1999). *Social gerontology: A multidisciplinary approach* (5th ed., Vol. 520). Needham Heights, MA: Allyn & Bacon.

Johnson, E. H. (1988). Care for elderly inmates: Conflicting concerns and purposes in prisons. In B. McCarthy & R. Langworthy (Eds.), *Older offenders: Perspectives in criminology and criminal justice* (pp. 157-163). New York: Praeger.

Katz, S., Ford, A. B., Moskowitz, R. W., Jackson, B. A., & Jaffe, M. W. (1963). Studies of illness in the aged. The index of ADL: A standardized measure of biological and psychosocial function. *Journal of the American Medical Association, 185,* 914-919.

King, R. S., & Mauer, M. (2001). *Aging behind bars: "Three strikes" seven years later.* Washington, DC: The Sentencing Project.

Krane, J. (1999a, April 12). Demographic revolution rocks U.S. prisons. *APBnews,* p. 4.

Krane, J. (1999b, April 12). Should elderly convicts be kept in prison? *APBnews,* p. 5.

Lawton, M. P., & Brody, E. M. (1969). Assessment of older people: Self-maintaining and instrumental activities of daily living. *Gerontologist, 9,* 179-186.

Lawton, M. P., & Nahemow, L. (1973). Ecology and the aging process. In C. Eisdorfer and M. P. Lawton (Eds.), *Psychology of adult development and aging.* Washington, DC: American Psychological Association.

Mackenzie, D. L. (2001). *Sentencing and corrections in the 21st century: Setting the stage for the future* (NCJ report 189089). Washington, DC: U.S. Department of Justice, Office of Justice Programs, National Institute of Justice.

Merianos, D. E., Marquart, J. W., Damphouse, K., & Hebert, J. L. (1997). From the outside in: Using public health data to make inferences about older inmates. *Crime and Delinquency, 43,* 298-313.

Morton, J. (1992). *An administrative overview of the older inmate.* Washington, DC: U.S. Department of Justice, National Institute of Corrections.

Neeley, C. L., Addison, L., & Craig-Moreland, D. (1997). Addressing the needs of elderly offenders. *Corrections Today, 59*(5), 120-123.

Ohio Department of Rehabilitation and Correction. (1997). *Older offenders: The Ohio initiative*. Columbus, OH: Author.

Ornduff, J. S. (1996). Releasing the elderly inmate: A solution to prison overcrowding. *Elder Law Journal, 4*, 20.

Rausch, S. P. (1996). Foreword: Current issues in prison management. *Criminal Justice Review, 21*, 1-19.

Rosefield, H. A. (1993). The older inmate—Where do we go from here? *Journal of Prison and Jail Health, 12*, 51-58.

Russell, M. P. (1994). Too little, too late, too slow: Compassionate release of terminally ill prisoners. Is the cure worse than the disease? *Widener Journal of Public Law, 3*, 799-828.

Schreiber, C. (1999, July 19). Behind bars: Aging prison population challenges correctional health system. *NurseWeek*, p. 3.

Sheppard, R. (2001, April 9). Growing old inside. *Maclean's*, pp. 30-33.

Southern Legislative Conference of the Council of State Governments. (1998). *SLC special series report: The aging inmate population*. Atlanta, GA: Author.

Sykes, G. M. (1971). The society of captives. In E. J. Latessa, A. Holsinger, J. W. Marquart, & J. R. Sorensen (Eds.), *Correctional contexts: Contemporary and classical readings* (Vol. 2, pp. 88-109). Los Angeles: Roxbury Press.

Turley, J. (1989, October 9). Prisons aren't nursing homes. *New York Times*, p. A17.

U.S. Department of Justice, National Institute of Corrections. (1997). *Prison medical care: Special needs populations and cost control*. Longmont, CO: Author.

Violent Crime Control and Law Enforcement Act of 1994. (1994). HR 3355. Washington, DC: United States Department of Justice.

Wheeler, M., Connelly, M., & Wheeler, B. (1995). *The aging of prison populations: Directions for Oklahoma*. Oklahoma City, OK: Oklahoma Department of Corrections.

Wiegand, D., & Burger, J. C. (1979). The elderly offender and parole. *Prison Journal, 59*, 48-57.

Williams, D. (2001, May 12). Aging inmates raise prison costs. *The Augusta Chronicle*, p. 3.

Yates, J., & Gillespie, W. (2000). The elderly and prison policy. *Journal of Aging & Social Policy, 11*(2-3), 167-175.

Zimbardo, P. (1994). *Transforming California's prisons into expensive old age homes for felons: Enormous hidden costs and consequences for California's taxpayers*. San Francisco: Center on Juvenile and Criminal Justice.

22

The Privatization of Incarceration

Anna Lukemeyer
Richard C. McCorkle

The number of state and federal prisoners has increased dramatically over the past 30 years, but public willingness to finance prisons has not kept pace. One response has been a renewed interest in privately managed prisons. Proponents of privatization contend that private contractors, unencumbered by government procurement and personnel procedures, can provide better quality prison services at lower costs. This article uses the 1995 Census of State and Federal Adult Correctional Facilities *to examine claims of improved quality. The authors find that privately managed prisons perform better on some, but not all, measures of quality of confinement. Specifically, bivariate comparisons suggest that private facilities outperform both state and federal facilities in terms of the proportion of institutions that are able to avoid inmate assaults on staff members or other inmates. Even when the authors controlled for other causal variables, private prisons remained significantly less likely than federal prisons to experience violence.*

Source: Anna Lukemeyer, Richard C. McCorkle, "Privatization of Prisons Impact on Prison Conditions," The American Review of Public Administration vol. 36 no. 2 189–206.

Thirty years ago, state and federal prisons housed slightly fewer than 220,000 prisoners. By 2003, the number of prisoners had grown to approximately 1,470,045—an increase of nearly 700%. Public willingness to finance prisons and prison services, however, has not kept pace with this population growth. One response to these developments has been a renewed interest in privately managed prisons. By 2000, more than 100 privately managed, secure adult facilities were in operation or under construction. Proponents of privatization contend that private contractors, unencumbered by government procurement and personnel procedures, can provide better quality of prison services at lower costs. Others contend that factors such as limited competition and little scope for innovative cost savings make it unlikely that privately managed prisons can deliver on this promise. This article reviews the literature concerning privatizers' claims of improved quality. Then, using the *Census of State and Federal Adult Correctional Facilities*, the article provides an overview of differences among public and private prisons on various dimensions associated with quality of confinement. Finally, we assess whether, controlling for other potential causal factors, private prisons do better than public on one important element of quality: avoiding violence among inmates.

PRIVATIZATION OF PRISONS: POLICY ARGUMENTS

Joel (1993) identifies four types of privatization of prisons. The first and most common form is government contracting for individual prison services such as medical care, food services, or staff training. Most states contract for at least one private service (Cox & Osterhoff, 1993). The second form of privatization involves private employment of prison inmates. Private construction and financing of prisons represents the third type of privatization. In the fourth type, which may be combined with the third type, a government enters into a contract with a private corporation to provide complete private management of a prison facility. This fourth, and arguably most controversial, type of privatization is the focus of this article.

Joel (1993) describes the process that a government typically follows when it contracts for private management of a prison facility. The government begins the process by issuing a request for proposals specifying performance criteria. After receiving responses from private contractors, government officials evaluate the responses, select a private firm, and negotiate a contract for managing the facility. The private contractor is typically paid a per diem fee for each prisoner (Joel, 1993).

By the mid-1980s, private (frequently nonprofit) operation of juvenile detention centers and adult prerelease and work release centers was common. In addition, in the 1980s states began contracting for operation of adult prisons and jails. Although most were minimum security, some housed medium and maximum security prisoners. By 1997, McDonald and colleagues reported the existence of 142 secure adult facilities (McDonald, Fournier, Russell-Einhorn, & Crawford, 1998).

Interest in private management of prisons has grown as a part of a larger interest in privatization of government services in general. Proponents of privatizing government services contend that the competition of the marketplace fosters efficiency and flexibility among private sector actors. Governments, in contrast, have little incentive to innovate or cut costs. Consequently, proponents of privatization argue, service delivery alternatives that allow increased use of private sector resources and competition are often superior (Benson, 1998; Morgan & England, 1988).

Proponents of prison privatization contend that private contractors, unencumbered by rigid procurement and personnel procedures, can construct, supply, and staff a prison more quickly and efficiently. Thus, proponents argue, private contractors can provide prison services at lower cost than the public sector (Benson, 1998; Joel, 1993; Logan, 1990; see also McDonald et al., 1998). Furthermore, in addition to cost savings, some policy analysts contend that private sector innovation and flexibility will allow contractors to increase the quality of prison facilities and services (see, e.g., Logan, 1990).

Not all analysts agree that these benefits will be realized in practice. Some argue that rather than leading contractors to improve quality, the profit motive will result in cost cutting detrimental to security and prisoners' well-being (Donahue, 1989; see also Logan, 1990; McDonald et al., 1998). Donahue (1989) points out that high entry costs may discourage private contractors from entering the market. If sufficient competition does not develop among private contractors, then government contracting need not result in either cost reductions or quality improvements (Donahue, 1989). Even in the presence of competitive pressure, Donahue contends, the nature of prison management simply may not provide sufficient scope for innovations and cost savings if quality is to be maintained. O'Hare, Leone, and Zegans (1990) argue that it is difficult for the same producer to simultaneously generate both cost reduction and product improvement. Unless government pursues a strategy of deliberately inviting innovation, the contracting process can generate pressure to cut costs at the expense of improvements in quality (O'Hare et al., 1990). Finally, scholars note that despite the existence of contractual provisions securing the welfare of prisoners, private prison management has historically been characterized by brutality and abuse (DiIulio, 1990; Durham, 1993; see also McDonald et al., 1998).

PRIVATIZATION: EMPIRICAL RESEARCH

Costs

Relatively few systematic studies of the effect of privatization on costs have been done, and these have been characterized as contradictory and inconclusive (McDonald, 1990; McDonald et al., 1998). A 1985 study of public and private juvenile detention centers concluded that cost differences between them were "minuscule." McDonald (1990) compared the costs of federally operated and privately operated Immigration and Naturalization Service (INS) detention centers. He found the average estimated cost per inmate in the private centers to be 7% to 19% lower than the average cost per bed in the federally operated centers. In 1989, due to a sharp increase in residents at the federal centers, the average cost of the private centers exceeded that of the government by about 14%. McDonald reported that an earlier study found that private contractors' per capita, per diem costs exceeded the costs of the INS-run detention centers by 17%. Later studies have been similarly contradictory (Austin & Coventry, 2001; McDonald et al., 1998).

Logan and McGriff (1989) report what is still perhaps the most rigorous comparison of public and private costs. Logan and McGriff compared the cost to the county of the operation of the recently privatized Hamilton County (Tennessee) Penal Farm with the estimated cost of operating the penal farm had it remained under direct county management. The estimate of the costs of direct county operation included those costs, such as employee benefits and capital depreciation, that are frequently omitted in government accounts of costs. Logan and McGriff concluded that private operation of the prison resulted in savings to the county of at least 4% to 8%.

McDonald and his colleagues (1998) argue that the results of the existing studies of cost differences must be viewed with caution, however. They explain the difficulties as follows:

> Comparing public and private prisons' costs is complicated for a variety of reasons. Comparable public facilities may not exist in the same jurisdiction. Private facilities may differ substantially from other government facilities in their functions. . . . Or they may differ in their age, design, or the security needs of the inmates housed, all of which affect the costs of staffing them. Cost comparisons are also difficult because public and private accounting systems were designed for different purposes; that is, public systems were not designed principally for cost accounting. Spending to support imprisonment is often borne and reported by agencies other than the correctional department and calculation of these costs is often difficult for lack of data. The annual costs of "using up" the physical assets are not counted in the public sector, as capital expenditures are generally valued only in the year that they are made, rather than being spread across the life of the assets. Nor is the cost to the taxpayer of contracting readily apparent from tallies of payments to contractors. Governments incur expenses for contract procurement, administration, and monitoring; for medical costs above amounts capped by contracts; and for sentence computation, transportation, and other activities performed by governments. Cost comparisons often fail to account for such expenditures. (p. iv)

After a detailed review of the literature, they conclude that "available data do not provide strong evidence of any general pattern" and "drawing conclusions about the inherent superiority of one or the other mode of provision . . . is premature" (p. v).

Quality

Prisons differ significantly in terms of the quality of living conditions and services that they provide to inmates (DiIulio, 1987). Prison management appears to be a significant determinant of the quality of prison life (DiIulio, 1987; McCorkle, Miethe, & Drass, 1995). Although many object to private ownership or management of the nation's prisons on ethical grounds, the argument that privatization will result in innovative and improved management of the nation's prisons is, at bottom, an empirical claim. Objective evaluation of that claim can aid, but need not determine, the debate.

In addition to anecdotal reports of improvements in quality of prison conditions resulting from privatization, three early, more formal studies suggested proponents' claims of improved quality might, in fact, be realized in practice. Brakel (1988) distributed a questionnaire to inmates of the Hamilton County Penal Farm following its privatization. Thomas and Logan (1993) summarize Brakel's results as follows:

> Brakel found that the private prison was more highly rated by inmates on its physical improvements, upkeep, and cleanliness; staff competence and character; work assignments; chaplain and counsellor services; requests and grievances; correspondence and telephone; and outside contracts. Other areas had a balance of positive and negative evaluations (e.g. safety, security, classification, medical care, food, education, discipline, and legal access). Two areas received mostly negative ratings: recreation and release procedures (but the latter remained under county, not private, control). Six prisoners who had been in the prison under the previous administration by county employees were able to make, collectively, twenty-eight explicit before and after comparisons. Of these, twenty-four favored the private prison and four favored the previous county administration. (pp. 226-227)

Hatry, Brounstein, and Levinson (1993) compared a privately operated adult minimum security prison to a similar state-operated prison. They also examined two pairs of matched juvenile secure treatment facilities. The researchers visually inspected each facility, surveyed inmates and staff, interviewed administrators, and gathered data from agency records. They rated the facilities in terms of their physical condition, security, educational and other programs, inmates' health, and indicators of rehabilitation. They found that the privately operated facilities rated slightly higher on a majority of these indicators. Hatry and colleagues proposed two possible explanations for the apparent advantage of the private institutions. First, they noted that the private staff were younger and less experienced. Although one might expect performance to improve with experience, the researchers speculated that "youthful enthusiasm" prevailed over "job burnout" (p. 199). In support of this conclusion, they observed that the staff in the private facilities appeared more enthusiastic and interested in working with inmates. Second, Hatry and colleagues noted that the privately operated institutions appeared to have more flexible management. They suggested that these two factors made the private institutions less harsh for both staff and inmates.

Finally, Logan (1991) studied a privately operated women's prison in New Mexico. He compared it to a state institution that had housed virtually the same women in the preceding year and to a federal women's prison. Logan conceptualized the quality of confinement as being composed of eight dimensions: (a) security against escapes and importation of contraband, (b) inmate and staff safety, (c) ability to preserve order within the prison, (d) medical, psychological, and dental care, (e) opportunities for work, training, and education, (f) justice in the enforcement of prison rules, (g) conditions of confinement such as population density, food, recreation, noise, and so forth, and (h) prison management. Logan compiled data from records, surveys of staff members and inmates, and site visits to the prisons.

Logan (1991) found that all three prisons were well run, and the indicators showed no large differences in their quality of confinement. The private and state prisons were comparable on more dimensions than either was superior. Nevertheless, where differences did occur they tended to favor the private prison. Logan developed a summary measure of the indicators for each of the eight dimensions of quality. He found that the private prison outscored the state on all dimensions but medical and related care and that the private facility outscored the federal prison on all but justice.

With respect to management, Logan (1991) found that the warden and other managers at the private prison reported more flexibility in personnel matters and in buying equipment. Staff members at the private facility were characterized as being more aware that their advancement depended on performance. Authority in the private facility was less hierarchical and more decentralized in comparison to the state institution. Staff reported that they had more responsibility and that decisions were made more quickly and flexibly. Logan reported that the private staff had higher morale. In short, Logan found differences in management that conformed to expectations of privatization advocates.

In 1998, Gaes, Camp, and Saylor reviewed eight studies (including Logan's) in which the researchers evaluated the quality of confinement at one or a few private institutions. The studies used a variety of methods including surveys of inmates and staff, audits and site visits, and analysis of official data concerning recidivism, inmate assaults, escapes, and other performance indicators. In general, these studies tended to report results favoring the private facilities. Nevertheless, Gaes et al. (1998) suggest that serious methodological flaws limit the value of these studies.

> Most of the studies do not use a variety of different measurement approaches, fail to study equivalent inmate populations or have insufficient information on the comparability of the offenders; use inappropriate or no statistics; and use a single point in time rather than a longitudinal assessment. Most also fail to explain the nature of private innovation, the impact of privatization on the entire system, or how innovation affects performance in terms of cost and quality of operations. (p. 31)

Therefore, Gaes and colleagues conclude that we do not yet have sufficient data to make generally applicable statements about whether privatization does in fact result in improved prison performance.

Recently, Austin and Coventry (2001) drew on a 1997 national survey of private state prisons to compare private and public institutions on a variety of measures of performance. They report that the privately operated prisons were similar to public facilities in terms of both provision of—and inmate participation in—work programs. Private institutions tended to provide somewhat more counseling and educational programs, and inmate participation in educational programs was higher in the private institutions. Private and public prisons followed similar staffing patterns. The private facilities tended to greater proportions of minority employees but lower levels of staffing overall. Private prisons reported a substantially higher rate of inmate-on-inmate assaults (35.1 per 1,000 inmates versus 25.4 for public prisons). Rates of other types of disturbances—assaults on staff, riots, fires, other disturbances, and inmate deaths—were remarkably similar.

Because there are few maximum security private prisons, Austin and Coventry (2001) also presented data for comparisons limited to medium or minimum security public and private facilities. The findings remained much the same on all the dimensions except assaults. In this comparison, private facilities reported higher rates of inmate-on-staff assaults than public prisons (12.2 per 1,000 inmates and 8.2 per 1,000, respectively), and the gap between private and public rates of inmate-on-inmate assaults increased somewhat (33.5 and 20.2, respectively).

In short, like the evidence concerning the impact of privatization on costs, the evidence concerning the impact of private management on the quality of prison conditions remains inconclusive. A number of case study researchers have concluded that private management leads to improvements, albeit sometimes modest ones, on many indicators of quality. Nevertheless, other researchers have criticized these studies as methodologically weak and lacking in generalizability. Finally, a recent national survey suggests that private facilities do less well in one important dimension—controlling inmate assaults.

"Creaming"

Although Logan (1991) and Hatry and colleagues (1993) report management differences, such as greater flexibility and higher staff morale, that might lead to better conditions in private prisons, others suggest that private advantages with respect to quality of confinement, to the extent that they exist at all, are more likely the result of creaming. That is, they contend, private prisons are more likely to house inmates who are more tractable and less likely to pose disciplinary problems. There is some evidence that this is the case. Ohio and Texas, for example, place only medium or minimum security inmates in privately operated prisons (Cummins, 2000; Hallett & Hanauer, 2001). Colorado law prevents placing inmates in private prisons if they present "a high potential for escape or violence" (Raher, 2002).

Nevertheless, although private institutions appear less likely to house the highest risk inmates, they routinely incarcerate those that do, in fact, pose a significant risk of violence or escape. In an Abt Associates survey, state correctional administrators reported that they sent violent inmates to more than two thirds of the private facilities under contract (McDonald et al., 1998). Moreover, the distinction between maximum and medium classifications is not consistent across jurisdictions. Inmates classified as medium security risk in one jurisdiction (and therefore appropriate for placement in a private facility) may be judged maximum in another, and even medium security facilities may house substantial numbers of high-risk offenders (McDonald et al., 1998). Thus, whether and to what extent differences in prison conditions can be attributed to private institutions' housing more tractable inmates rather than to better management remains uncertain.

RESEARCH QUESTION

As the previous section shows, the impact, if any, of privatization on quality of prison conditions and performance remains open to debate. Most of the studies have been limited to a small number of institutions. Austin and Coventry (2001) present a broadly based comparison of public and private institutions, but their evaluation controls only for security level. Many other factors affect prison conditions and quality of confinement. Broadly stated, our long-term research question is whether, controlling for other causal factors, privatization has resulted in improvements in prison conditions and performance. In this article, we first present an overview of differences among private and public prisons. Then we assess, in a multivariate context, how well private prisons do on one important element of quality: controlling violence among inmates.

RESEARCH METHOD

Data and Variables

The data for this study were taken from the 1995 *Census of State and Federal Adult Correctional Facilities* collected by the U.S. Department of Justice, Bureau of Justice Statistics (1998). The census includes data from 112 federally operated prisons, 1,278 state or locally operated prisons and community-based facilities, and 110 privately operated institutions. The census includes men's, women's, and coed prisons. In addition to prisons whose primary purpose was general adult confinement, the census includes a number of institutions with specialized functions. These include boot camps, reception and classification facilities, hospitals and medical treatment facilities, work release and prerelease centers, and others. Here, we limit our analysis to the 873 predominantly male public and private institutions that report general adult confinement as their primary purpose: 93 federal prisons, 762 state facilities, and 18 privately operated institutions.

This study assesses differences between publicly and privately managed prisons on certain indicators of quality of confinement. We distinguish private from public management and within public management, federal from state. The dependent variable is quality of prison conditions and services. DiIulio (1990) suggests measuring this variable in terms of three dimensions: order, amenities, and service. He defines order as "the absence of individual or group misconduct behind bars that threatens the safety of others." Amenities means "anything intended to increase the inmates' comfort—clean living quarters, good food, color television sets." Service includes "anything intended to enhance the inmates' lifetime prospects—programs in remedial reading, vocational training, work opportunities, and so on" (p. 170).

The data contained variables allowing measurement of two of these dimensions: order and services. We operationalized order in terms of reported violent incidents among inmates, specifically, inmate assaults on inmates and inmate assaults on guards. We present variables measuring two aspects of inmate violence. First, because a proportion of facilities report no inmate violence, we used a dummy variable to identify whether the institution experienced any violence. This allowed us to look at the proportion within each sector (federal, state, or private) that experienced some violence. We also looked at the rate, per 1,000, of inmate assaults on inmates plus inmate assaults on guards: A higher value on this measure represents a decrease in order and therefore a decrease in the quality of confinement.

The service dimension is measured by two variables: (a) the percentage of inmates on June 30, 1995, enrolled in educational programs, including adult basic education, secondary education (General Equivalency Diploma [GED]), special education, vocational training, college courses, and study release programs (i.e., release into the community to attend school) and (b) the number of program staff members (educational staff, counselors, chaplains, etc.) per 100 prisoners. A higher value on these measures represents an increase in the quality of confinement.

Analysis

Using a simple difference of means (or proportions) *t* test, we first compared private to federal management and private to state management on each of the measures of order and services described above. Then we used a probit analysis to examine, in a multivariate context, differences among federal, state, and private facilities with respect to the occurrence of any violence. As controls, we included a number of variables identified in previous research as affecting levels of inmate violence: age of institution, size of inmate population, degree of crowding, presence or absence of a court order based on prison conditions, guard-to-inmate ratio, percentage of prisoners who are racial or ethnic minorities, racial composition of staff compared to racial composition of inmates, percentage of prisoners in maximum security custody, percentage of prisoners who are women, geographic region, extent of educational programs, and the institution's physical security level (McCorkle et al., 1995).

FINDINGS

Table 1 presents basic demographic characteristics of the prisons by type of management (private, federal, or state). In general, privately operated prisons are, on average, smaller and less crowded than federal or state prisons. In terms of racial composition of inmates, however, private facilities look much like state prisons. About half of inmates in both private and state prisons are African American (53% and 50%, respectively), and about 10% are Hispanic. In contrast, African Americans make up a smaller proportion of federal prisoners (33%), and Hispanic inmates are a larger proportion of the federal population (20%).

In terms of the ratio of guards to prisoners, private facilities fall about midway between state and federal facilities: Federal facilities have 14.8 correctional staff members per 100 prisoners, private have 21.1, and state have 25.6. Private prisons also seem to occupy a middle ground between federal and state prisons with respect to the security level of the physical facility. Of the state institutions, fully 70% are rated medium security or higher (27.4% are maximum and 42.6% are medium security). In contrast, higher security facilities make up a smaller percentage of private institutions (44%) and an even smaller percentage of federal institutions (35%). Although federal and private institutions are comparable in their proportion of medium security facilities, a higher proportion of private (16.7%) than federal (8.6%) institutions are rated maximum security. Nevertheless, there are only 18 private institutions in the data set. Therefore, percentage comparisons are of somewhat questionable utility. In terms of absolute numbers, there are 3 maximum security private prisons and 8 federal. There are 5 medium security private prisons and 25 federal. In terms of security level of inmates actually housed, inmates requiring maximum security custody make up approximately the same smaller proportion of private and federal prisoners (6.9% and 8.8%, respectively). In contrast, at 16.7%, the proportion of maximum security inmates in state prisons is substantially higher.

Table 1 Adult General Confinement Men's Prisons (1995)[a] Characteristics by Type of Management (*n* = 873)

	Private (n = 18)		Public: Federal (n = 93)		Public: State (n = 762)	
	M	*SD*	*M*	*SD*	*M*	*SD*
Size (average daily population of inmates)	440	434	762	497***	927	922***
Crowding (average daily population/rated capacity)	0.89	0.10	1.27	0.41***	1.02	0.25***
High security (% of institutions rated medium or maximum security)	44		35		70**	
Correctional staff (per 100 inmates)	21.1	11.7	14.8	20.8	25.6	14.7
Female (% of inmates)	2.9	7.0	0.1	0.8	0.4	2.3
African American (% of inmates)	52.9	29.0	33.4	14.6**	49.7	21.7
Hispanic (% of inmates)	10.0	24.8	20.4	15.2	10.1	12.9
Maximum security custody (% of inmates)	6.9	23.5	8.8	23.4	16.7	28.7*
Age of institution (in years)	20.2	28.0	21.7	23.7	32.5	33.0*

SOURCE: Authors' calculations from *Census of State and Federal Adult Correctional Facilities, 1995* (U.S. Department of Justice, 1998).

a. All adult general confinement prisons in which 75% or more of the inmate population was male on June 30, 1995.

*$p < .10$ (difference of means *t* test, two-tailed; federal compared to private or state compared to private).

**$p < .05$ (difference of means *t* test, two-tailed; federal compared to private or state compared to private).

***$p < .01$ (difference of means *t* test, two-tailed; federal compared to private or state compared to private).

Table 2 presents differences among private, federal, and state prisons in terms of the variables measuring quality of confinement. Turning first to the services dimension, our two measures present slightly different findings. With respect to percentage of inmates in educational programs, our findings are similar to those of Austin and Coventry (2001). In comparison to state prisons, a greater proportion of inmates in private prisons are participating in educational or vocational education programs (22% and 32%, respectively). There is virtually no difference between private and federal facilities on this measure. With respect to program staff, however, private prisons are lower than both state and federal institutions. Private prisons provide 4.3 program staff members per 100 prisoners, whereas state prisons provide 5.1. At 6.8 program staff members per 100 inmates, federal prisons have the highest ratio.

Table 2 Adult General Confinement Men's Prisons (1995) Indicators of Quality of Confinement by Type of Management (n = 848)

	Private		Public: Federal		Public: State	
	M	*SD*	*M*	*SD*	*M*	*SD*
Services						
Program (educational and treatment) staff (per 100 inmates)	4.26	2.71	6.83	4.65***	5.10	3.43
	n = 17		n = 69		n = 713	
In class (% of inmates enrolled in educational or vocational education programs)	31.66	22.52	29.96	19.25	21.72	15.71*
	n = 18		n = 90		n = 746	
Order						
Violence:[a]						
Rate—all facilities (per 1,000 inmates)	30.71	53.32	20.63	28.37	38.27	59.89
	n = 18		n = 93		n = 737	
Percentage of institutions reporting any violence[b]	61.11		81.72		80.87	
	n = 18		n = 93		n = 737	
Rate—only facilities with any violence (per 1,000 inmates)	50.26	61.26	25.24	29.48	47.33	63.30
	n = 11		n = 76		n = 596	

Inmate assaults on inmates:						
Percentage of institutions reporting any[b]	55.56		79.57*		78.59*	
	$n = 18$		$n = 93$		$n = 738$	
Rate—only facilities with such assaults (per 1,000 inmates)	48.98	56.36	12.83	12.20*	32.78	41.70
	$n = 10$		$n = 74$		$n = 580$	
Inmate assaults on staff:						
Percentage of institutions reporting any[b]	38.89		64.52*		65.23**	
	$n = 18$		$n = 93$		$n = 745$	
Rate—only facilities with such assaults (per 1,000 inmates)	9.01	7.54	16.15	19.84*	19.23	35.74**
	$n = 7$		$n = 60$		$n = 486$	

SOURCE: Authors' calculations from *Census of State and Federal Adult Correctional Facilities,* 1995 (U.S. Department of Justice, 1998).

a. Total of inmate assaults on inmates and inmate assaults on guards.

b. Reported n = total number of institutions (both those reporting and those not reporting violence or such assaults) for each category (private, federal, or state).

*$p < .10$ (difference of means t test, two-tailed; federal compared to private or state compared to private).

**$p < .05$ (difference of means t test, two-tailed; federal compared to private or state compared to private).

***$p < .01$ (difference of means t test, two-tailed; federal compared to private or state compared to private).

The second section of Table 2 compares private to state and federal prisons in terms of their ability to maintain order, specifically, their success in controlling inmate violence. Looking just at the rate of violent incidents per 1,000 inmates, at 30.7 incidents per 1,000, private prisons fall between federal (20.6 per 1,000) and state (38.3 per 1,000). If one looks at the percentage of institutions that experience any instances of violence, however, the private prisons appear significantly better than either federal or state. More than one third of the private institutions (38.9%) experienced no incidents of violence in 1995, compared to only about 20% of the federal or state institutions. Among the institutions that experienced some violence, private institutions and state institutions had similar rates (about 50.3 and 47.3 per 1,000, respectively), and both rates were substantially higher than the rate at federal institutions (25.2 per 1,000).

Table 2 thus presents interesting findings concerning violence. Most federal and state institutions experience some violence. They differ primarily in the level of that violence, with federal facilities experiencing, on average, a rate of violence about half that of the state facilities. Private prisons present a more complex picture. A substantial minority—more than one third—report no violent incidents. Among those with violence, however, the average rate is the highest of the three sectors—slightly higher than state institutions and almost twice the rate of federal. This suggests, on its face, that a subset of private institutions are doing well at avoiding violence, whereas another subset are doing no better than state prisons and considerably worse than federal. This finding is important because it demonstrates that the advantages, if any, of private management with respect to avoiding inmate violence are not automatic or universal. Determining what factors and circumstances differentiate more and less successful privatizations represents an important avenue for further research.

As Table 2 shows, the patterns are much the same if we separate violence into its two components: inmate-on-inmate assaults and inmate-on-staff assaults. A greater proportion of private than state and federal institutions were able to avoid both types of assaults. Almost half of the private institutions reported no inmate-on-inmate assaults (compared to less than a quarter of the federal and state institutions), and more than 60% of the private facilities reported no inmate-on-staff assaults (compared to about 35% of state and federal). Limiting the analysis only to institutions reporting some assaults reveals the same bifurcation among private prisons with respect to inmate-on-inmate assaults that we found with respect to violence overall: Although a greater proportion of private prisons are able to avoid inmate-on-inmate violence altogether, among institutions experiencing violence, private institutions have the highest rate of inmate-on-inmate assaults. The pattern is not repeated with respect to inmate-on-staff assaults, however. Even limiting the analysis to institutions with assaults, private prisons report the lowest rate of inmate-on-staff assaults.

These findings present a somewhat different picture than Austin and Coventry (2001), who found that private institutions experienced considerably more inmate-on-inmate assaults. Our findings suggest that although a subset of private prisons may have higher rates of inmate-on-inmate assaults, in some dimensions private institutions may have an advantage. It appears that a higher proportion of private institutions are successful at avoiding any occurrences of violence (either inmate on inmate or inmate on staff) than either federal or state prisons. Furthermore, even among institutions with violence, private institutions are better able to control inmate-on-staff assaults.

Of course, the comparisons in Table 2 do not control for other variables that may affect incidence and rates of violence. For instance, private prisons have advantages over both federal and state prisons in terms of size, crowding, and percentage of female inmates, and these likely affect incidence and rates of violence. Furthermore, a number of writers have suggested that private prisons are housing the more manageable cream of the prisoner population. The remainder of this article addresses whether in fact these apparent private successes with respect to restraining violence remain when other factors are controlled.

Among the control variables, age of facility, size, racial composition of inmates, presence or absence of a court order, region, and educational staff-to-inmate ratio are all significantly related to probability of violence. As expected, facilities that are older, larger, or under court order are more likely to experience violence, as are facilities with a higher proportion of minority inmates. Prisons with a higher proportion of male inmates are also more likely to experience violence. Perhaps contrary to popular perception, prisons in the traditional southern states show a lower probability of violence when other variables are held constant.

The results contain two unexpected findings. First, crowding is negatively related to occurrence of violence. Previous results with respect to crowding have been inconclusive, however (McCorkle et al., 1995). Second, a higher educational staff-to-inmate ratio is associated with a higher probability of violence. This result is somewhat contradictory to earlier findings that inmate participation in educational programs decreases the rate of violence (McCorkle et al., 1995).

With respect to type of management, privately managed prisons maintain an advantage over federal prisons in avoiding inmate violence, even when other potentially causal factors are controlled. State prisons are also more likely to experience violence, but that finding is not statistically significant.

Looking first at inmate-on-inmate assaults, we see again that even controlling for other potentially causal factors, privately managed prisons are more able to avoid such assaults entirely. Federal prisons show a .12 increase in the probability of such assaults, and state prisons show a .13 increase.

Federal prisons are again significantly more likely than private prisons to experience this type of assault, with a .20 difference in probability. No significant differences exist between private and state facilities, however. Among the control variables, their impact is similar in terms of direction and significance to their impact in the model of inmate-on-inmate violence.

CONCLUSION

This article presents a review of the literature and findings concerning the impact of private operation on prison conditions and performance. Like the studies before it, it provides some evidence that privately managed prisons perform better on some, but not all, measures of quality of confinement. Specifically, bivariate comparisons suggest that private facilities outperform state facilities in terms of the proportion of inmates in educational programs and that private facilities outperform both state and federal facilities in terms of the proportion of institutions that are able to avoid inmate assaults (either on staff or on other inmates) entirely. It is surprising that even when we controlled for other potentially causal variables, private prisons remained significantly less likely than federal prisons to experience any violence. Furthermore, decomposing violence into inmate-on-inmate and inmate-on-staff assaults revealed that private prisons do significantly better than federal prisons on both of these measures.

With respect to state prisons, however, the results were less clear. Although private prisons remained less likely than state institutions to experience violence in general, only the findings with respect to inmate-on-inmate violence even approached statistical significance. This suggests that differences on the control variables or other chance factors may explain a good part of the private prisons' apparent advantages over state prisons.

Even with respect to federal prisons, our findings must be viewed with caution. We present data for only 1 year. This, with the relatively small number of private prisons, raises the possibility that our findings reflect a temporary chance event rather than an enduring phenomenon. Furthermore, the possibility that the private prison advantage is due to creaming remains. Although we were able to control for some inmate characteristics associated with violence (race, gender, and the security classification), other potentially important variables (e.g., age, type of offense, time to release) were not available in this data set.

Despite their methodological shortcomings, however, a number of studies (including ours) have found evidence that privately managed prisons provide a better quality of confinement, at least along certain dimensions. Furthermore, in two case studies (Hatry et al., 1993; Logan, 1991), the authors found that management in private facilities was less hierarchical and more flexible. Employees had more responsibility and were more aware that their advancement depended on performance (Logan, 1991). Thus, there is some evidence to support advocates' claims that privatization leads to more responsive management and more responsible staff, and previous research suggests that management factors can be important determinants of the quality of confinement (McCorkle et al., 1995).

Perhaps the most interesting finding, however, arises from the bivariate comparisons in which we decomposed violence into the probability of experiencing any violence and, conditioned on experiencing violence, the rate of such violence. High proportions of both federal and state prisons experienced some violence. These two sectors differed primarily in the rate of violence. Among private prisons, on the other hand, a smaller proportion experienced any violence, and the multivariate analysis suggests that—particularly with respect to inmate-on-inmate assaults—this difference cannot entirely be attributed to differences on control variables.

Furthermore, even though as a group private prisons were less likely to experience any violence, private prisons with violence exhibited the highest rates of violence. This suggests that among private prisons there may be two subgroups: one group that is very effective in controlling violence and one that is much poorer. Thus, an important question for further research is what distinguishes those private prisons that are more successful. A number of writers have suggested that the terms of the contract and the type and strength of oversight are important. Whether this or some other factor is at work here remains to be investigated.

DISCUSSION QUESTIONS

1. Does privatization of prisons mean that the government is giving up its responsibility?
2. Will privatization solve the costs and overcrowding problems in state and federal prisons?
3. In Logan's survey explain why private prisons were favored in all dimensions except medical and related care.
4. Is "creaming" a problem? Does this mean that our government gets the more difficult inmates?
5. The quality of confinement is said to be better in the private sector, but is there reason to believe that this quality will continue?

REFERENCES

Austin, J., & Coventry, G. (2001). *Emerging issues on privatized prisons* (NCJ 181249). Washington, DC: Bureau of Justice Assistance.

Benson, B. (1998). *To serve and protect: Privatization and community in criminal justice.* New York: New York University Press.

Brakel, S. J. (1988). Prison management, private enterprise style: The inmates' evaluation. *New England Journal on Civil and Criminal Confinement, 14,* 175-244.

Cox, N., & Osterhoff, W. (1993). The public private partnership: A challenge and an opportunity for corrections. In G. Bowman, S. Hakim, & P. Seidenstat (Eds.), *Privatizing correctional institutions* (pp. 113-130). New Brunswick, NJ: Transaction.

Cummins, E. C. (2000). Private prisons in Texas, 1987-2000: The legal, economic, and political influences on policy implementation. *Dissertation Abstracts International, 61*, 4543. (University Microfilms No. AAT 9993972)

Dauber, E., & Schichor, D. (1979). A comparative exploration of prison discipline. *Journal of Criminal Justice, 7*, 21-36.

DiIulio, J., Jr. (1987). *Governing prisons*. New York: Free Press.

DiIulio, J., Jr. (1990). A duty to govern: A critical perspective on the private management of prisons and jails. In D. McDonald (Ed.), *Private prisons and the public interest* (pp. 155-178). New Brunswick, NJ: Rutgers University Press.

Donahue, J. (1989). *The privatization decision*. New York: Basic Books.

Durham, A., III. (1993). The future of correctional privatization: Lessons from the past. In G. Bowman, S. Hakim, & P. Seidenstat (Eds.), *Privatizing correctional institutions* (pp. 33-50). New Brunswick, NJ: Transaction.

Gaes, G., Camp, S., & Saylor, W. (1998). Appendix 2: Comparing the quality of publicly and privately operated prisons, a review. In D. McDonald, E. Fournier, M. Russell-Einhorn, & S. Crawford (Eds.), *Private prisons in the United States: An assessment of current practice*. Boston: Abt Associates.

Hallett, M., & Hanauer, A. (2001). Selective celling: Inmate population in Ohio's private prisons. *Policy Matters Ohio*. Retrieved June 2, 2004, from http://www.policymattersohio.org/pris.html/.

Hatry, H., Brounstein, P., & Levinson, R. (1993). A comparison of privately and publicly operated corrections facilities in Kentucky and Massachusetts. In G. Bowman, S. Hakim, & P. Seidenstat (Eds.), *Privatizing correctional institutions* (pp. 193-212). New Brunswick, NJ: Transaction.

Hewitt, J. D., Poole, E. D., & Regoli, R. M. (1984). Self-reported and observed rule-breaking in a prison: A look at disciplinary response. *Justice Quarterly, 1*, 437-447.

Joel, D. (1993). The privatization of secure adult prisons: Issues and evidence. In G. Bowman, S. Hakim, & P. Seidenstat (Eds.), *Privatizing correctional institutions* (pp. 51-74). New Brunswick, NJ: Transaction.

Logan, C. (1990). *Private prisons: Cons and pros*. New York: Oxford University Press.

Logan, C. (1991). *Well kept: Comparing quality of confinement in a public and private prison*. Washington, DC: National Institute of Justice.

Logan, C., & McGriff, B. (1989). *NIJ Report No. 216*. Washington, DC: National Institute of Justice.

Mandell, B. R. (2002). The privatization of everything. *New Politics, 9*, 83-112.

McCorkle, R., Miethe, T., & Drass, K. (1995). The roots of prison violence: A test of deprivation, management, and the "not-so-total" institution models. *Crime and Delinquency, 41*, 317-331.

McDonald, D. (1990). The costs of operating public and private correctional facilities. In D. McDonald (Ed.), *Private prisons and the public interest* (pp. 86-106). New Brunswick, NJ: Rutgers University Press.

McDonald, D., Fournier, E., Russell-Einhorn, M., & Crawford, S. (1998). *Private prisons in the United States: An assessment of current practice*. Cambridge, MA: Abt Associates.

Morgan, D., & England, R. (1988). The two faces of privatization. *Public Administration Review, 48*, 979-987.

O'Hare, M., Leone, R., & Zegans, M. (1990). The privatization of imprisonment: A managerial perspective. In D. McDonald (Ed.), *Private prisons and the public interest* (pp. 130-154). New Brunswick, NJ: Rutgers University Press.

Raher, S. (2002). *Private prisons and public money: Hidden costs borne by Colorado's taxpayers* [mimeograph]. Denver: Colorado Criminal Justice Reform Coalition.

Thomas, C., & Logan, C. (1993). The development, present status, and future potential of correctional privatization in America. In G. Bowman, S. Hakim, & P. Seidenstat (Eds.), *Privatizing correctional institutions* (pp. 213-240). New Brunswick, NJ: Transaction.

Toone, R. (2002). *Protecting your health and safety: A litigation guide for inmates.* Montgomery, AL: Southern Poverty Law Center.

U.S. Department of Justice, Bureau of Justice Statistics. (1998). *Census of state and federal adult correctional facilities, 1995* (conducted by U.S. Department of Commerce, Bureau of the Census) [computer file]. Ann Arbor, MI: Interuniversity Consortium for Political and Social Research [producer and distributor].

23

Mental Illness, Crime, and Violence: Risk, Context, and Social Control

Fred E. Markowitz

In this chapter, I review theory and research on the relationship between mental illness, crime, and violence. I begin by discussing the larger backdrop of deinstitutionalization of mental illness and its consequences for the criminal justice system in both individual and macro-level terms. I then compare public perceptions of dangerousness associated with mental illness with individual-level studies that assess the risk of violence and criminal behavior among those with mental illness. I review key findings as to the role of certain psychotic symptoms, social demographic characteristics, and the context in which violence unfolds. Finally, I discuss recent efforts at managing persons with mental illness who violate the law, focusing on the limitations of diversionary programs.

Source: Fred E. Markowitz, "Mental illness, crime, and violence: Risk, context, and social control," Aggression and Violent Behavior Volume 16, Issue 1, Pages 36–44.

1. INTRODUCTION

High-profile shootings at schools, universities, and government buildings bring public attention to the problem of mental illness and violence. Visible homeless persons with mental illness and substance abuse problems are commonplace in urban areas. In this article, I provide an overview of the perceptions, realities, and processes surrounding these issues by organizing and reviewing research related to the study of mental illness violence, and crime. Specifically, I address the following questions: How has the nature of mental health care changed in such a way that has led to more people with mental illness in jails and prisons than in hospitals? What are the pathways by which persons with mental illness end up there? What is the public perception of violence among the mentally ill compared to objective assessments of the risk? Finally, how effective are recent efforts at addressing the problem of mental illness in the criminal justice system?

In an effort to integrate our understanding of these issues, I begin by discussing major developments in legal and treatment systems that manage persons with severe mental illness. I then examine recent research on public perceptions of dangerousness among persons with mental illness. Next, I review research on the relationship between mental illness, crime, and violence, focusing on individual, macro, and situational processes. Finally, I discuss recent legal and social policy initiatives related to mental illness and violence.

2. DEINSTITUTIONALIZATION, MENTAL ILLNESS, AND THE CRIMINAL JUSTICE SYSTEM

2.1. Deinstitutionalization

Until the 1960s, substantial numbers of persons with mental illness were treated in large, publicly funded hospitals. Based on the National Institute of Mental Health (NIMH) estimates, in 1960, about 563,000 beds were available in U.S. state and county psychiatric hospitals (314 beds per 100,000 persons), with about 535,400 resident patients. By 1990, the number of beds declined to about 98,800 (40 per 100,000) and the number of residents to 92,059 (National Institute of Mental Health, 1990). By 2005, there were only 17 public psychiatric beds available per 100,000 persons, despite increases in the population and estimates that about 50 beds per 100,000 are needed for minimal treatment capacity (Torrey, Kennard, Eslinger, Lamb, & Pavle, 2010). Several factors contributed to the drop in inpatient capacity. First, medications were developed, which controlled the symptoms of the most debilitating mental disorders (e.g., schizophrenia). Second, an ideological shift, advocating a more liberal position on confinement, led to states adopting stricter legal standards for involuntary commitment (dangerousness to self or others) that are not frequently used. Third, and perhaps most important, fiscal policy changed, including the shifting of costs for mental health care from states to the federal government (Medicare, Medicaid, Social Security Disability Income), followed by budget cuts and substantial underfunding of community mental health services (Gronfein, 1985; Issac & Armat, 1990; Kiesler & Sibulkin, 1987; Mechanic & Rochefort, 1990; Redick, Witkin, Atay, & Manderscheid, 1992; Weinstein, 1990). These trends and associated policies are generally referred to as the deinstitutionalization of the mentally ill.

The sharp decline in public psychiatric hospital capacity has been offset to some extent by inpatient units in private psychiatric and general hospitals, as well as by moving patients to nursing homes. An important component to the changing nature of psychiatric hospitalization is the increased role of general hospitals. Emergency rooms and psychiatric units in general hospitals provide acute treatment for those with mental illness and can bill Medicaid for doing so (Mechanic, McAlpine, & Olfson, 1998). Although these hospitals contribute to treatment capacity, they still do not provide the longer term care that public psychiatric hospitals did. Moreover, recent studies show changes in how psychiatric hospitalization is accessed, with many disadvantaged patients not admitted to private hospitals because of an inability to pay for their care (Lincoln, 2006). Paradoxically, federal rules prohibit patients aged 21–64 with Medicaid from receiving care in specialized psychiatric hospitals. Therefore, capacity for maintaining and treating America's mentally ill, especially the most severely impaired and economically disadvantaged patients, has been substantially diminished (Ehrenkranz, 2001; Lamb & Bachrach, 2001; Torrey, 1995, 1997).

As hospitals closed and the number of beds reduced, many patients were discharged from state hospitals into the community. Others, as a result of stricter standards for involuntary commitment, were not even admitted—an "opening of the back doors" and "closing of the front doors." Moreover, in the early 1960s the average length of stay was about 6 months, but by the early 1990s it had declined to about 15 days (National Institute of Mental Health, 1990). By 2007, it was less than 10 days. Meanwhile, the rate of admissions from the early to mid 2000s has increased slightly (Manderscheid, Atay, & Crider, 2009). This indicates that patients are often stabilized (i.e., given medication) and released, without adequate follow-up treatment and support (Weinstein, 1990). Not surprisingly, substantial numbers of these patients end up being readmitted. This has been referred to as the "revolving door" phenomenon (Kiesler & Sibulkin, 1987).

Historically, psychiatric hospitals have functioned as a source of control of persons who are unable to care for themselves and whose behavior may be threatening to the social order (Grob, 1994; Horwitz, 1982). In the early 1990s, the public mental health care system crossed a threshold where the majority of expenditures previously directed toward state hospital inpatient care were now directed toward community-based services (Lutterman & Hogan, 2000). An important consequence of reduced hospital capacity is that a large portion of persons with severe mental illness now live in urban areas with less supervision and support. Although some do well, many lack "insight" into their disorders, go untreated, or have difficulty complying with medication regimens, and are unable to support themselves (Mechanic, 2008). This presents considerable difficulties for families and others who are often unable or unwilling to deal with persons whose behavior may at times be unmanageable or threatening (Avison, 1999; Karp, 2001).

2.2. Mental Illness and the Criminal Justice System

Very early research demonstrated the interdependence of the mental health and criminal justice systems (Penrose, 1939). More recently, in the aftermath of deinstitutionalization, prisons and jails have supplanted public psychiatric hospitals as institutions of social control of the mentally ill (Liska, Markowitz, Bridges-Whaley, & Bellair, 1999). Studies have examined frequency of arrest, jail, and imprisonment among people admitted into psychiatric hospitals before and during deinstitutionalization (Adler, 1986; Arvanites, 1988; Belcher, 1988; Cocozza, Melick, & Steadman, 1978; Steadman, Monohan, Duffee, Hartstone, & Robbins, 1984; Steadman, Fabiasak, Dvoskin, & Holohean, 1987; Steadman, McCarty, & Morrisey, 1989). Studies from the 1970s and 1980s found that the percentage of patients with prior arrests increased (Arvanites, 1988; Melick, Steadman, & J.J. Cocozza, 1979a; Melick, Steadman, & J.C. Cocozza, 1979b). Studies of imprisonment reported an overall increase in the percentage of prison inmates with prior mental hospitalization (Steadman et al., 1984, 1978). Many researchers thus concluded that the mentally ill are being overarrested and warehoused in city and county jails (Adler, 1986; Lamb & Grant, 1982; Palermo, Smith, & Liska, 1991; Pogrebin & Regoli, 1985; Teplin, 1984, 1990).

More recent nationally representative surveys of state and federal prisoners, jail inmates, and probationers are consistent with earlier research, indicating that persons who report "currently" or "ever having a mental or emotional condition" are overrepresented in all those groups (Ditton, 1999). One study estimates that up to 16% of persons in prisons and jails may have a mental illness, many of whom have committed serious offenses (Ditton, 1999). That is over 300,000 persons, a rate (for men) which is about 4 times higher than the general population. Thus, it is estimated that there are now more than three times as many persons with mental illness in jails and prisons than in psychiatric hospitals (Torrey et al., 2010). The most recent study puts the estimate of the percentage of inmates with a history of mental health problems in jails at 64% and at 56% for state prison inmates, with 50–60% reporting current symptoms (James & Glaze, 2006). In terms of types of offenses, Silver, Felson, & VanEseltine (2008) found that, among prison inmates, those with serious mental illness were somewhat overrepresented among those incarcerated for assaultive violence and sexual crimes, but not property, and other types of crime.

Because of a lack of appropriately trained staff and screening procedures, many persons are retained in jails and prisons without adequate treatment.

These inmates are less likely than others to be released on bail, more likely to experience abuse from guards and other inmates, and are at an increased risk of suicide (Torrey, 1995). Thus, corrections facilities serve, in part, as rather dysfunctional alternatives to psychiatric hospitals. Although many jails and prisons provide mental health services, and several communities have programs to divert mentally ill offenders from jail to treatment (discussed below), the availability of these services and programs is limited relative to the need for them (Fisher, 2003; Goldstrom, Henderson, Male, & Manderscheid, 1998; Morris, Steadman, & Veysey, 1997; Steadman, Morris, & Dennis, 1995).

2.3. The Role of Homelessness

Homelessness is an important pathway to incarceration among the mentally ill. Studies estimate that approximately one-third of homeless persons meet diagnostic criteria for a major mental illness (Jencks, 1994; Lamb, 1992; Shlay & Rossi, 1992). Including substance-related disorders, the figure is closer to 75%. Consequently, surveys of jail and prison inmates find that mentally ill offenders are more likely than other inmates to have been homeless at the time of arrest and in the year before arrest (DeLisi, 2000; James & Glaze, 2006; McCarthy & Hagan, 1991). Because of a lack of community treatment programs and limited staffing (critical for monitoring medication compliance), personal resources, and social supports, many mentally ill homeless persons are at increased risk of police encounters and arrest for not only "public order" types of offenses, such as vagrancy, intoxication, or disorderly conduct, but also for more serious types of crimes, such as assault (Dennis & Steadman, 1991; Estroff, Zimmer, Lachotte, & Benoit, 1994; Fisher, Silver, & Wolff, 2006; Fisher et al., 2006; Hiday, 1995; Hiday, Swanson, Swartz, Borum, & Wagner, 2001; Lamb & Weinberger, 2001; McGuire & Rosenbeck, 2004; Mechanic & Rochefort, 1990; Silver et al., 2008; Teplin, 1994).

The presence of homeless persons and associated public order offenses may be a source of neighborhood disorder, generating fear and reducing social cohesion among neighborhood residents, thus facilitating more serious crime, such as robbery (see Markowitz, Bellair, Liska, & Liu, 2001; Sampson, Raudenbush, & Earls, 1997; Skogan, 1990). High levels of urban disorder, including the visibility of homeless mentally ill persons, has led many cities to take aggressive policing approaches that, at times, may contribute to the overrepresentation of mentally ill persons in jails and prisons.

The vulnerability of homeless mentally ill persons also increases their risk of being the victims of crime, well beyond the rates generally found by the National Crime Victimization Surveys (Choe, Jeanne, Teplin, & Abram, 2008; Dennis & Steadman, 1991; Teplin, McClelland, Abram, & Weiner, 2005). They are easier targets for offenders. Insights from routine activities theory suggest that homeless persons have reduced levels of "capable guardianship" necessary to protect themselves from crime (Felson, 2002; Hagan & McCarthy, 1998). Moreover, the likelihood of victimization among homeless mentally ill persons is increased because of the risks of victimization associated with alcohol use more generally (Felson & Burchfield, 2004). Altogether, mental illness and homelessness creates "criminogenic" situations.

A macro-level study by Markowitz (2006) showed that, across U.S. cities, higher public inpatient psychiatric capacity was associated with fewer homeless persons and lower crime and arrest rates. Moreover, pooled analyses of states from the 1980s to the late 1990s showed that increases in the proportion of private, for-profit psychiatric hospital beds was associated with an increase in the size of jail populations as well as suicide rates (Yoon, 2011; Yoon and Bruckner, 2009). The exact effect of reduced public hospital capacity on homelessness, crime, and arrest rates may be difficult to predict however, since this effect likely depends on the availability and quality of a variety of fragmented community-based treatment and housing services, of which data are not systematically compiled in the same way that hospital data is. In these studies, per capita spending on community mental health services shows no effect on crime and arrest rates and is associated with an increase in the size of jail populations, but it offsets the effect of loss of public inpatient capacity on suicide rates. Unfortunately, macro-level data do not allow estimates of the proportion of jail and prison inmates with mental illness. One study, comparing two jails in different catchment areas, one with higher levels of community-based mental health services, found no difference in the prevalence of mental illness across the two jails (Fisher, Packer, Simon, & Smith, 2000). Together, although limited in scope, the findings from these studies suggest that provision of greater community-based mental health services alone may not be sufficient to reduce the number of persons with mental illness in jail.

3. PUBLIC PERCEPTIONS OF DANGEROUSNESS ASSOCIATED WITH MENTAL ILLNESS

3.1. The Changing Nature of Public Understanding of Mental Illness

There is both 'good news' and 'bad news' when it comes to public understanding of mental illness generally. Early research in the 1950s, based on a nationally representative survey, asked respondents the open-ended question: When you hear someone say that a person is 'mentally ill,' what does that mean to you? Results showed that Americans had a somewhat narrow view of mental illness, with the majority associating mental illness with psychosis. For example, respondents indicated that mental illness means that "persons are not in touch with reality" or "live in their own world." Respondents also used colloquial terms such as "nuts," "deranged," or "out of one's mind" to describe mental illness (Starr, 1955). In 1996, the same question was asked again in a nationally representative survey. This time, fewer persons gave answers reflecting psychosis (35%) and more persons gave responses reflecting other disorders such as anxiety/depression (34%), personality disorders, substance abuse, or cognitive impairment, suggesting that the public's conceptions of mental illness has broadened beyond stereotypical conceptions associated with psychotic disorders and is seen as something less alien and extreme (Phelan, Link, Stueve, & Pescosolido, 2000).

Other recent research used vignettes that described persons who fit the criteria for one of several mental illnesses (schizophrenia, major depression, and substance dependence) and asked respondents whether they thought "the person was likely to have mental illness?" About 88% said "yes" when presented with a description of a person with schizophrenia, and about 69% said "yes" when a person with major depression was described. When asked specifically whether they thought the person was "likely to have depression," 95% said "yes" (Link, Monahan, Stueve, & Cullen, 1999; Link, Phelan, Bresnahan, Stueve, & Pescosolido, 1999). Also, Americans are more likely to attribute the causes of disorders such as schizophrenia and depression to chemical imbalances, genetic factors, and stressful life circumstances, rather than to "bad character," "the way the person was raised," or "God's will" (Martin, Pescosolido, & Tuch, 2000). Together, these findings suggest that public understanding of the causes of mental illness has become somewhat more sophisticated and consistent with professionals' views.

3.2. Perceptions of Dangerousness

However, the 'bad news,' concurrent with these favorable developments, is that there has been an increase in the proportion of persons who associate mental illness with dangerousness, violence, and unpredictability. In 1950, when asked what 'mental illness' means to them, about 7% of respondents mentioned violent manifestations or symptoms, compared to 12% in 1996. Also, those who think of mental illness in terms of psychosis are more likely to associate mentally ill persons with dangerousness and are less willing to live near them, socialize with them, work with them, have a group home for the mentally ill nearby, or have someone with mental illness marry into their family, i.e., they want to have greater 'social distance.' Moreover, perceptions of dangerousness increase support for coercive measures to treat persons with mental illness, such as involuntary commitment (Pescosolido, Monahan, Link, Stueve, & Kikuzawa, 1999).

Paradoxically, public understanding of mental illness has apparently increased, yet perceptions of persons with psychotic disorders as dangerous have increased as well. A likely possible explanation is that media images and high publicity surrounding certain violent events have created misunderstanding of the actual risk of violence. While there has been a good deal of research on how mental illness is presented in the mass media, in terms of inaccurate depictions and overemphasis on violence (Corrigan, 2005; Wahl, 1995), the link between media portrayals and attitudes toward mental illness has not been fully examined. However, one study found that highly publicized college campus shootings may lead to increases in fear among college students of being a victim of violent crime on campus (Kaminski, Koons-Witt, Thompson, & Weiss, 2010).

3.3. Causal Attributions

Recent research has examined the effects of beliefs about the causes of mental illness and perceptions of dangerousness on attitudes toward persons with mental illness. Survey studies using experimental vignettes examined the impact of causal attributions and perceptions of dangerousness on responses toward persons with mental illness (Corrigan, Markowitz, Watson, Rowan, & Kubiak, 2003). This research has shown that when the onset of mental illness is viewed as being under one's control (e.g., as a result of drug use), persons are more likely to avoid, withhold help, and endorse coercive treatment. Also, when persons are seen as responsible for causing their condition, this leads to decreased feelings of pity and increased feelings of anger and fear. Anger, fear, and lack of pity, in turn, lead to rejecting responses, such as social avoidance and increased support for the use of coercive control. The findings also show that information about dangerousness increases the likelihood of discriminatory responses. However, findings from this study also suggested that those who are more familiar with mental illness are more likely to offer interpersonal help and less likely to avoid people with psychiatric disorders (Corrigan et al., 2003). Taken together, this research suggests that certain beliefs about mental illness may increase discrimination toward persons with mental illness, resulting in social exclusion, and further limiting employment and housing opportunities, all of which may then worsen psychiatric conditions and may thus exacerbate the likelihood of aggressive behavior.

In an innovative study among police officers in a major metropolitan area, Watson, Corrigan, and Ottati (2004) showed that when suspects are described as having schizophrenia, they are viewed not only as less responsible for their condition and more in need of help but also as potentially more dangerous. This highlights the paradoxes inherent in attitudes toward persons with mental illness—on one hand, increased understanding of mental illness and its causes, yet increased fear and stigma on the other. A limitation of the study was that it did not indicate the type of behavior the suspect was exhibiting. Also, given the lack of real-life context in these types of studies, it may be difficult to evaluate to what extent educating police officers and others on mental illness and diagnostic labels would help them manage situations in such a way that minimizes escalation of conflict, leading to violence.

4. INDIVIDUAL-LEVEL RESEARCH ON MENTAL ILLNESS AND THE LIKELIHOOD OF VIOLENCE AND CRIME

4.1. Treatment Sample Studies

Given public perceptions and conflicting interests among advocacy groups, the risk of violence among persons with mental illness has been a somewhat ideologically charged issue, with some emphasizing increased risk as a way of highlighting the need for better and more compulsory treatment, and others downplaying the risk of violence as a way of reducing stigma and discrimination that may worsen a person's psychiatric condition (Monahan, 1992; Torrey, Stanley, Monahan, & Steadman, 2008). Much research has examined the direct relationship between mental disorder and the likelihood of violent and criminal behavior. One major study—The MacArthur Violence Risk Assessment Study—compared the frequency of violence among patients discharged from inpatient treatment units with that of a "matched" sample of persons living in the same (often disadvantaged) neighborhoods (Monahan et al., 2001). The study found a higher risk of violence among persons with mental illness that had co-occurring substance abuse disorders. This suggested that mental illness affects violence indirectly by increasing the likelihood of substance abuse. The most recent and comprehensive study, including over 1400 adult patients with schizophrenia sampled from 57 clinical sites in 24 states showed that about 19% reported violent behavior in the last 6 months, a rate much greater than would be expected in the general population (Swanson et al., 2006).

One of the limitations of studying persons who are in treatment is that they may be 'selected' into treatment because they are inclined toward disruptive behavior, thus producing somewhat of an upward bias in the prevalence of violence among persons with, for example, conditions such as schizophrenia or bipolar disorder. However, persons with these types of disorders are the most likely among those with mental illness to receive specialty treatment at some point in the lifetimes (Wang, Demler, & Kessler, 2002). On the other hand, as in the MacArthur study, persons with schizophrenia with low insight and paranoid symptoms are significantly less likely to take part in studies, and may thus contribute to an underestimate of the risk of violence (Torrey et al., 2008). It is not clear exactly to what extent these types of countervailing biases affect estimates of the likelihood of violence among persons with mental illness.

4.2. Community Sample Studies

One influential study that used data from the New York metropolitan area included those in treatment and a community sample and asked about self-reported violent behavior and arrests. This study also included data on respondents' official arrest records (Link, Andrews, & Cullen, 1992). It showed that those who were either new, ongoing, or former patients, including many with schizophrenia, bipolar disorder, and major depression are at an increased risk of violence and arrest compared to those with no treatment history (Link et al., 1992). In this case, while estimates of arrests are more objective, there is still the problem of the validity of self-reported aggressive behavior. However, in general, studies have shown that self-reports are valid, but that there may be a tendency for racial minorities to underreport violent behavior (Hindelang, Hirschi, & Weis, 1981). In an effort to overcome this, Link et al. (1992) employed controls for social desirability bias to correct for underreporting, along with controls for demographic variables, including race. An important limitation to this study is that a significant portion of those with mental illness go untreated; therefore, treatment history itself is an imperfect indicator of mental health status (Kessler et al., 2005).

The best, larger scale studies use diagnostic criteria to establish the prevalence of mental illness, irrespective of treatment history and also include self-reported measures of violence. They yield similar findings to the studies above. Using data from the Epidemiological Catchment Area (ECA) study, Swanson, Holzer, Ganju, & Jono (1990) found that violent behavior, including hitting, throwing things, and use of weapons in the last year was found among 25% of those who met the DSM criteria for a mental disorder, compared to only 2% of those with no mental disorder. Studies using data from Israel and Finland with comparable measures, yielded similar results (Link, Monahan, et al., 1999; Link, Phelan, et al., 1999; Tiihonen, Isohanni, Rasanen, Koiranen, & Moring, 2007).

It is important to note, however, that persons with mental illness are not only more likely to engage in violent behavior, but, controlling for their own violent behavior, are also more likely to be the victims of violence (Choe et al., 2008; Silver, Arseneault, Langley, Caspi, & Moffitt, 2005; Teplin et al., 2005). This is understandable, given that violent encounters are most often a two-way street—one person initiates violence while the other engages in violence as a means of responding to threats or in retaliation for perceived harm (Tedeschi & Felson, 1994). Furthermore, people with severe mental illnesses such as schizophrenia, bipolar disorder, or major depression are at increased risk of death by not only suicide but also homicide (Hiroeh, Appleby, Mortensen, & Dunn, 2001).

4.3. Symptoms Associated with Violence

Both the treatment sample and general population studies show that, in many cases, those experiencing certain "positive" psychotic or "threat control/override" symptoms (e.g., delusional thinking and hallucinations) are at an increased risk of violence (Elbogen & Johnson, 2009; Swanson, 1994; Link, Monahan, et al., 1999; Link, Phelan, et al., 1999; Swanson et al., 1996; Swanson et al., 2006; Teasdale, 2009). Consistent with symbolic interactionist theory, persons experiencing these symptoms may accept irrational thoughts as real, misperceiving the actions of others (including family members or police officers) as threatening and respond aggressively (Link, Monahan, et al., 1999; Link, Phelan, et al., 1999). In contrast, patients with "negative" symptoms (e.g., social withdrawal) are at a lower risk of violence. Moreover, one study finds the effect of threat-control override symptoms is limited to men (Teasdale, Silver, & Monahan, 2006). These studies also show that the risk of violence is increased among those with multiple disorders, those with co-occurring substance use/dependence disorders, and noncompliance with medication regimens that reduce troublesome symptoms (Swartz et al., 1998).

Despite emphasis on symptoms, other problems associated with mental illness must be taken into account. Matejkowsi, Solomon, & Cullen (2008) found that, among 95 persons with severe mental illness who were convicted of murder in Indiana between 1990 and 2002, most were raised in households with significant family dysfunction, had extensive histories of substance abuse and criminality, and had received little treatment for their mental and substance use disorders. Furthermore, some nonviolent criminal behavior among homeless persons with mental illness may be considered "survival" crimes, such as shoplifting and trespassing. Also, some crime may result from "antisocial" personalities that are a part of some mental illnesses (Hiday, 1997).

4.4. Demographic Factors

Very importantly, in the community studies discussed above, the association between mental disorder and violence or arrest holds after controlling for demographic factors. In fact, the risk of violence among those with mental illness is at par with or exceeded by the risk associated with simply being male, younger, or a disadvantaged racial minority. In terms of public perceptions, demographic variables, while perhaps contributing to fear of crime (Quillian & Pager, 2001), are likely seen as unchangeable, while mental illness may be regarded, to a certain extent, as something the person "brought on themselves," thus outweighing demographic variables that compound perceived risk. Therefore, persons may be more likely to discriminate based on the knowledge that someone has mental illness, for fear of disturbing behavior, than based on demographic characteristics, that, when taken together, determine the risk of violence to a greater extent. The interaction among demographic variables and mental illness in their impact on risk and perceptions of dangerousness remains to be fully examined.

5. COMMUNITY CONTEXT: THE ROLE OF SOCIALLY DISORGANIZED NEIGHBORHOODS IN VIOLENCE AMONG PERSONS WITH MENTAL ILLNESS

5.1. Social Disorganization and Mental Illness

Theories that explain crime generally can be applied to understand crime and violence among persons with mental illness. Key to this approach is understanding how mental illness enhances the effects of crime-causing variables. One important explanation is that seriously mentally ill persons have long been more likely to reside in disadvantaged urban areas, as a result of the downward drift in socioeconomic status that mental illness often leads to (Faris & Dunham, 1939). Currently, as a result of deinstitutionalization, lack of long-term care facilities, and selection processes that limit job and residential opportunities, many mentally ill and homeless persons reside in group homes, shelters, or single-room occupancy hotels, or in subsidized housing, all of which are more likely to be located in "socially disorganized" neighborhoods. These are neighborhoods where there are more economically disadvantaged persons, there is greater racial diversity, and there are more fragmented families. Social disorganization theory predicts that neighborhood disorganization leads to weakened social cohesion, thereby lessening the ability of communities to exert both formal and informal control over the behavior of their residents, resulting in increased crime (Bursik & Grasmick, 1993; Markowitz et al., 2001; Sampson & Groves, 1989; Sampson et al., 1997). Moreover, in these types of neighborhoods, cultural norms regarding violent retaliation in disputes are prevalent (Anderson, 2000). Following from this line of thinking, studies show that, for persons with mental illness, living in such neighborhoods increases the risk of criminal offending beyond individual demographic characteristics, highlighting the role of criminogenic contexts in facilitating violence (Silver, 2000a,b; Silver, Mulvey, & Monahan, 1999).

5.2. Police Encounters

In the face of limited treatment options, disturbing behavior that might have been dealt with medically prior to deinstitutionalization is now more likely to be treated as criminal behavior. For example, even though police may recognize some disruptive behavior as resulting from mental illness, they often have little choice but to use "mercy bookings" as a way to get persons into mental health treatment. Police officers are among those most likely to deal with persons with mental illness in crisis situations and are now one of the main sources of referral of persons into mental health treatment (Engel & Silver, 2001; Lamb, Weinberger, & DeCuir, 2002). Also, police, who see troublesome situations through the lens of their role as "law enforcers" are motivated to maintain their authority in conflict situations, often invoking the power of arrest to do so (Watson & Angell, 2007).

In the wake of deinstitutionalization, these processes have led some to argue that mental illness has been "criminalized" (Lamb & Weinberger, 1998; Lamb et al., 2002; Steury, 1991; Teplin, 1990). The evidence in support of the criminalization hypothesis comes primarily from the systematic observation of police–citizen encounters that show mentally ill suspects are more likely to be arrested than their nonmentally ill counterparts (Teplin, 1984). However, a more recent study of police–citizen encounters in 24 police departments in three metropolitan areas elaborates on those findings (Engel & Silver, 2001). That study showed that other factors, not considered in previous research, such as whether suspects are under the influence of drugs, are noncompliant, fight with officers or others, as well as the seriousness of their offense predicts the likelihood of arrest among mentally ill suspects. Consistent with that research, Kaminski (2007), using pooled time series data of the 50 states for the period 1972 to 1996 found that the number of mentally ill persons released each year from state and county mental hospitals was related to rates of lethal violence against the police. An important implication of these studies is that if mentally ill persons are overrepresented in criminal justice settings, it is not solely attributable to discriminatory treatment on the part of police, but due, in part, to a greater likelihood of arrest-generating behavior. Many cities have attempted to mitigate the potential for conflict in police encounters with mentally ill citizens by implementing crisis-intervention training (CIT) programs. However, it is difficult to fully assess their effectiveness. Some studies indicate that while CIT improves police understanding of mental illness, it may not reduce, for example, the use of force and the likelihood of arrest (Compton, Bahora, Watson, & Oliva, 2008). Factors, such as the availability of nonjail treatment, may offset effects of CIT.

6. SITUATIONAL DYNAMICS: THE ROLE OF STRESS AND CONFLICTED RELATIONSHIPS IN VIOLENCE AMONG PERSONS WITH MENTAL ILLNESS

6.1. Stress and Conflicted Relationships

Research on the role of stress and mental illness has been brought to bear on understanding part of the reason that persons with mental illness are at an increased risk of violent behavior and victimization. This research is guided by the logic of the stress process model, the dominant approach to understanding the social patterns of psychological distress—more common, sub-clinical symptoms of anxiety and depression (Mirowsky & Ross, 2003). The theory holds that stress (or life strains) places persons at risk of psychiatric illness and that stress is socially distributed, principally according to socioeconomic status, gender, age, and marital status. Moreover, social support and other coping resources (e.g., self-efficacy) mitigate the effects of stress on well-being. Hiday (1995) was among the first to develop a model that applies these insights to violence and serious mental illness. In her model, economic disadvantage not only places persons at risk for developing symptoms of mental illness, but also because of the disadvantage that mental illness creates, persons with mental illness experience greater levels of stress and conflict. Aggressive behavior becomes both an externalized expression of symptoms and a way of coping with conflict, fear, and goal-blockage—especially in socially disorganized neighborhoods where violence is more common.

The findings of several studies are consistent with the stress model. Using ECA data, Silver and Teasdale (2005) find that, controlling for social demographic variables, stressful life events (e.g., disruptions or changes in employment, relationships, and living situations) in the past year and impaired social support explained a significant portion of the association between mental/

substance disorders and violence. Although untested, it is likely that disputes with intimates surrounding involuntary treatment, efforts to control disruptive behavior, and financial disagreements may facilitate violent behavior (Estroff et al., 1994). In fact, similar to violence committed by nonmentally ill persons, family members are highly likely to be the targets of violence involving persons with mental illness (Estroff et al., 1994).

Similarly, DeCoster and Heimer (2001) find that violent behavior is a response to stressful life events and an externalized expression of depressive symptoms among young adults. Since stressful life events are structured by social background factors, notably social class, these types of studies link criminological and mental health research by suggesting an important pathway by which disadvantaged persons become involved in serious violence. Moreover, depressive symptoms weaken family attachments, which, in turn, can lead to further depression and aggressive behavior (DeCoster & Heimer, 2001). This is consistent with research that shows that not only are social relationships important for reducing symptoms, but that, unfortunately, symptoms may erode the quality of social relationships (Markowitz, 2001). One way this operates is through aggressive behavior.

7. PUBLIC POLICY RESPONSES

7.1. Community Treatment Alternatives

In recognition of the risk of violence and criminalization of mental illness, there have been increased efforts to provide services within correctional settings and support for community treatment alternatives, such as intensive case management, jail diversion programs, including mental health courts, and legally mandated assisted outpatient treatment (Compton et al., 2008; Dvoskin, 1994; Morris et al., 1997; Morris et al., 1997; Steadman et al., 1995, 1999; Watson, Hanrahan, Luchins, & Lurigio, 2001). These types of programs take a variety of forms: some with mental health professionals involved at the scene of a disturbance and diversion taking place prior to arrest, others with diversion taking place after arrest (involving special mental health courts), or crisis intervention training for police to manage persons in crisis situations and help them get into treatment facilities, rather than into jail (Reuland & Cheney, 2005). Such programs require effective coordination between law enforcement, judges, prosecutors, and mental health professionals. However, the cultural orientations of these groups can be at odds—public order, authority maintenance, and punishment versus treatment. The evidence regarding the effectiveness of these often uncoordinated programs is somewhat limited in terms of symptom improvement, quality of life, and likelihood of re-offending, according to the findings of a large (n = 2000), national, randomized, multi-site study (Broner, Lattimore, Cowell, & Schlenger, 2004; Fisher, 2003; Mechanic, 2008). However, one recent study using random assignment of subjects to a post-booking jail diversion program found that those in the program experienced reduced contact with the criminal justice system over a 12-month evaluative period (Case, Steadman, Dupuis, & Morris, 2009). Reductions were greatest among those with a criminal history. However, no improvements were shown regarding symptoms, suggesting that these types of programs may have more a public safety, rather than public health benefit.

7.2. Outpatient Civil Commitment

The majority of states' laws allow for mandatory assisted outpatient treatment (outpatient civil commitment, or AOT) for those who lack the capacity to care for themselves, many of whom are at risk of homelessness and criminal behavior (Appelbaum, 2005). However, relatively few states implement the law or have a comprehensive system of treatment programs to accompany it. There have been some attempts to gauge the effectiveness of AOT. One study of 78 patients in New York City did not show any differences in outcomes between those who received court-ordered mental health services and those who received non-court-ordered services (Steadman, 2001). However, that study excluded persons with a history of violence. Another study of several thousand patients throughout New York State that had been considered for court-ordered treatment as a result of troublesome behavior reported significant improvements in service use and community living among those under an AOT order compared to those not under such an order (Van Dorn et al., 2010). However, patients were not randomly assigned to AOT. Moreover, one implication of these studies is that it may simply be the availability of services, rather than the court-order per se that led to improved outcomes.

Unless implemented on a significant scale, these types of programs may be insufficient to take the place of public institutions focusing specifically on the inpatient care of persons with serious mental illness and substance abuse disorders. Moreover, these types of programs are likely to be most effective when they address a wide set of issues that are required to facilitate recovery from mental illness more generally, including illness management, employment, housing, substance abuse, and trauma intervention (Osher & Steadman, 2007; Watson et al., 2001). This has led Fisher, Roy-Bujnowski, et al. (2006) and Fisher, Silver, and Wolff (2006) to argue there has been an overemphasis on "need for services" in reducing violence among mentally ill persons rather than on the more general factors that lead to criminal behavior, such as the failure to make normative life course transitions, economic disadvantage, and criminogenic lifestyles that can accompany mental illness.

8. CONCLUSION

In sum, public psychiatric hospital capacity is an important source of control of those whose behavior or public presence may at times threaten the social order. This capacity has been reduced dramatically over the last several decades. In the absence of this capacity, many persons with mental illness have fallen through the cracks of community based services, which can be effective, but are often fragmented and require active engagement on the part of persons who require them, yet may not recognize the need to do so. Unfortunately, this leads to an increased risk of homelessness and involvement in the criminal justice system, as well as victimization. The problem is especially pronounced among those who are economically disadvantaged, who are more likely to reside in 'disorganized' neighborhoods, where stress and cultural differences in dispute resolution enhance the risk of crime.

Concurrently, public perception of violence among persons with mental illness has increased over the last several decades. Despite an apparent improvement in understanding the nature and causes of mental illness, there is the tendency to associate mental disorders, especially psychosis, with an increased likelihood of violence. As such, the general public's perceptions are not entirely out of line with objective assessments of risk. Unfortunately, perceptions of violence are a significant component to the stigma associated with mental illness which likely adds to the devaluation and discrimination that many persons who are diagnosed—yet are not violent—experience. Stigma and social rejection, in turn, limits social opportunities, such as jobs, housing, and social networks for persons with mental illness, which, to some extent, serve as protective factors in reducing stress, and thereby reducing the risk of violence.

The proportion of persons with mental illness who are at risk of violence or other criminal behavior is modest. In the aggregate, the risk translates into appreciable increases in the rates of violent and other types of crime, resulting in substantially greater numbers of persons with mental illness who find their way into the criminal justice system—a system that was not intended for therapeutic purposes, but has been forced to adapt by becoming the nation's largest residential facility for the mentally ill. High quality, well-coordinated community mental health services that focus on both symptom reduction and social-economic well-being (e.g., housing and employment) may reduce the number of mentally ill persons who end up in jails and prisons. In response to this significant social problem, Congress has enacted the Mentally Ill Offender Treatment and Crime Reduction Reauthorization and Improvement Act of 2008, intended to provide more funding for local programs that will help divert persons from the criminal justice system into mental health treatment. Such efforts require tremendous initiative on the part of policy makers and local agencies, and are likely to be limited in their development and effectiveness relative to the scale of the problem. An important next step for research is to compile systematic data at the community level on such services in order to assess their aggregate impact. Also, national jail survey data needs to make offenders' city-level identifiers available to researchers so that aggregate estimates of the proportion of persons with mental illness in jails in a given city can be computed and linked with data on mental health services and examined across a number of cities.

DISCUSSION QUESTIONS

1. Discuss the pros and cons of deinstitutionalization. Is it the reason for the mental illness crises today?
2. Describe three ways in which you would solve the homelessness and mental illness problems in today's society.
3. Analyze the implications of releasing the mentally ill back into society and discuss the necessary medical treatments after release.
4. Do you think that by educating our elected officials and law enforcement it will have a positive impact on this issue?

REFERENCES

Adler, F. (1986). Jails as a repository for former mental patients. *International Journal of Offender Therapy and Comparative Criminology, 30*, 225–236.

Anderson, E. (2000). *Code of the streets: Decency, violence, and the moral life of the inner city*. New York: W.W. Norton & Co.

Appelbaum, P.S. (2005). Assessing Kendra's law: Five years of outpatient commitment in New York. *Psychiatric Services, 56*, 791–792.

Arvanites, T.M. (1988). The impact of state mental hospital deinstitutionalization on commitment for incompetency to stand trial. *Criminology*, 26, 307–320.

Avison, W.R. (1999). The impact of mental illness on the family. *Handbook of the Sociology of Mental Health* (pp. 495–515).

Belcher, J.R. (1988). Are jails replacing the mental health system for the homeless mentally Ill? *Community Mental Health Journal*, 24, 185–194.

Broner, N., Lattimore, P. K., Cowell, A. J., & Schlenger, W.E. (2004). Effects of diversion on adults with co-occurring mental illness and substance use: Outcomes from a national multi-site study. *Behavioral Sciences and the Law*, 22, 519–542.

Bursik, R.J., Jr., & Grasmick, H.G. (1993). *Neighborhoods and crime: The dimensions of effective community control*. Lexington.

Case, B., Steadman, H.J., Dupuis, S.A., & Morris, L.S. (2009). Who succeeds in jail diversion programs for persons with mental illness? A multi-site study. *Behavioral Sciences and the Law*, 27, 661–674.

Choe, B.A., Jeanne, Y., Teplin, L.A., & Abram, K.M. (2008). Perpetration of violence, violent victimization, and severe mental illness: Balancing public health concerns. *Psychiatric Services, 59*, 153–164.

Cocozza, J., Melick, M.E., & Steadman, H.J. (1978). Trends in violent crime among ex-mental patients. *Criminology*, 16, 317–334.

Compton, M.T., Bahora, M., Watson, A.C., & Oliva, J.R. (2008). A comprehensive review of extant research on crisis intervention team (CIT) programs. *The Journal of the American Academy of Psychiatry and the Law, 36* (1), 47–55.

Corrigan, P.W. (2005). *On the stigma of mental illness*. Washington, DC: American Psychological Association.

Corrigan, P.W., Markowitz, F.E., Watson, A., Rowan, D., & Kubiak, M.A. (2003). Attribution and dangerousness models of public discrimination against persons with mental illness. *Journal of Health and Social Behavior, 44*, 162–179.

DeCoster, S., & Heimer, K. (2001). The relationship between law violation and depression: An interactionist analysis. *Criminology, 39*, 799–836.

DeLisi, M. (2000). Who is more dangerous? Comparing the criminality of adult homeless and domiciled jail inmates: A research note. *International Journal of Offender Therapy and Comparative Criminology, 44*, 59–69.

Dennis, D.L., & Steadman, H. J. (1991). *The criminal justice system and severely mentally ill homeless persons: An overview. Report prepared for the Task Force on Homelessness and Severe Mental Illness*. Delmar, NY: Policy Research Associates.

Ditton, P.M. (1999). Mental health and treatment of inmates and probationers. *Bureau of Justice Statistics Special Report* NCJ 174463, July.

Dvoskin, J.A. (1994). Using intensive case management to reduce violence by mentally ill persons in the community. *Hospital and Community Psychiatry*, 45, 679–684.

Ehrenkranz, S.M. (2001). Emerging issues with mentally ill offenders: Causes and social consequences. *Administration and Policy in Mental Health*, 28, 165–180.

Elbogen, E.B., & Johnson, S.C. (2009). The intricate link between violence and mental disorder: Results from the National Epidemiologic Survey on Alcohol and Related Conditions. *Archives of General Psychiatry*, 66, 152–161.

Engel, R.S., & Silver, E. (2001). Policing mentally disordered suspects: A reexamination of the criminalization hypothesis. *Criminology, 39*, 225–252.

Estroff, S., Zimmer, C., Lachotte, W., & Benoit, J. (1994). The influence of social networks and social support on violence by persons with serious mental illness. *Hospital & Community Psychiatry, 45*, 669–679.

Faris, R.E.L., & Dunham, H. W. (1939). *Mental Disease in Urban Areas*. Chicago: University of Chicago Press.

Felson, M. (2002). *Crime and Everyday Life* (3rd ed.). Thousand Oaks, CA: Sage.

Felson, R.B., & Burchfield, K. B. (2004). Alcohol and the risk of physical and sexual assault victimization. *Criminology, 42*, 837–860.

Fisher, W. H. (2003). *Community based interventions for criminal offenders with severe mental illness*. New York: Elsevier.

Fisher, W.H., Packer, I.K., Simon, L.J., & Smith, D. (2000). Community mental health services and the prevalence of severe mental illness in local jails: Are they related? *Administration and Policy in Mental Health*, 27, 1573–3289.

Fisher, W.H., Roy-Bujnowski, K., Grudzinskas, A.J., Clayfield, J.C., Banks, S., & Wolff, N. (2006). Patterns and prevalence of arrest in a statewide cohort of mental health care consumers. *Psychiatric Services*, 57, 1623–1628.

Fisher, W.H., Silver, E., & Wolff, N. (2006). Beyond criminalization: Toward a criminologically informed framework for mental health policy and services research. *Administration and Policy in Mental Health & Mental Health Services Research, 33*, 544–557.

Goldstrom, I., Henderson, M.J., Male, A., & Manderscheid, R.W. (1998). Jail mental health services: A national survey. *Mental Health, United States* (pp. 176–187). Washington, DC: U. S. Department of Health and Human Services.

Grob, G. N. (1994). *The mad among us: A history of the care of America's mentally ill*. New York: Free Press.

Gronfein, W. (1985). Psychotropic drugs and the origins of deinstitutionalization. *Social Problems*, 32, 437–455.

Hagan, J., & McCarthy, B. (1998). *Mean streets: Youth crime and homelessness*. New York: Cambridge University Press.

Hiday, V.A. (1995). The social context of mental illness and violence. *Journal of Health and Social Behavior*, 36, 122–137.

Hiday, V.A. (1997). Understanding the connection to mental illness and violence. *International Journal of Law and Psychiatry*, 20, 399–417.

Hiday, V.A., Swanson, J.W., Swartz, M.S., Borum, R., & Wagner, H.R. (2001). Victimization: A link between mental illness and violence? *International Journal of Law and Psychiatry*, 24, 559–572.

Hindelang, M.J., Hirschi, T., & Weis, J.G. (1981). *Measuring delinquency*. Thousand Oaks, CA: Sage.

Hiroeh, U., Appleby, L., Mortensen, P.B., & Dunn, G. (2001). Death by homicide, suicide and other unnatural causes in people with mental illness. *Lancet, 358*, 2110–2112.

Horwitz, A. V. (1982). *The social control of mental illness*. New York: Academic Press.

Issac, R. J., & Armat, V.C. (1990). *Madness in the streets: How psychiatry and law abandoned the mentally ill.* New York: Free Press.

James, D.J., & Glaze, L.E. (2006). *Mental health problems of prison and jail inmates.* Washington, D.C.: U.S. Department of Justice, Bureau of Justice Statistics.

Jencks, C. (1994). *The Homeless*. Cambridge, MA: Harvard University Press.

Kaminski, R.J. (2007). *The Impact of Deinstitutionalization on Police Homicide Victimization*. Paper presented at the American Society of Criminology, Atlanta, November 14–17.

Kaminski, R.J., Koons-Witt, Barbara A., Thompson, Stewart N., & Weiss, D. (2010). The impacts of the Virginia Tech and Northern Illinois University shootings on fear of crime on campus. *Journal of Criminal Justice, 38*, 88–98.

Karp, D. A. (2001). *The burden of sympathy: How families cope with mental illness.* New York: Oxford University Press.

Kessler, R.C., Demler, O., Frank, R.G., Olfson, M., Pincus, H.A., & Walters, E.E. (2005). Prevalence and treatment of mental disorders, 1990 to 2003. *The New England Journal of Medicine*, 352, 2515–2523.

Kiesler, C.A., & Sibulkin, A.E. (1987). *Mental hospitalization: Myths and facts about a national crisis*. Newbury Park, CA: Sage.

Lamb, H.R. (1992). *Deinstitutionalization in the nineties in treating the homeless mentally ill.* Washington, DC: American Psychiatric Association.

Lamb, H.R., & Bachrach, L.L. (2001). Some perspectives on deinstitutionalization. *Psychiatric Services*, 52, 1039–1045.

Lamb, H.R., & Grant, R. (1982). The mentally ill in an urban jail. *Archives of General Psychiatry, 39*, 17–22.

Lamb, H.R., & Weinberger, L.E. (1998). Persons with severe mental illness in jails and prisons: A review. *Psychiatric Services*, 49, 483–492.

Lamb, H.R., & Weinberger, L.E. (2001). *Deinstitutionalization: Problems and Promise*. San Francisco: Jossey-Bass.

Lamb, H.R., Weinberger, L.E., & DeCuir, W.J. (2002). The police and mental health. *Psychiatric Services, 53*, 1266–1271.

Lincoln, A. (2006). Psychiatric emergency room decision-making, social control, and the 'undeserving sick'. *Sociology of Health & Illness, 28*, 54–75.

Link, B.G., Andrews, H., & Cullen, F.T. (1992). The violent and illegal behavior of mental patients reconsidered. *American Sociological Review, 57*, 275–292.

Link, B.G., Monahan, J., Stueve, A., & Cullen, F.T. (1999). Real in their consequences: A sociological approach to understanding the association between psychotic symptoms and violence. *American Sociological Review, 64*, 316–332.

Link, B., Phelan, J., Bresnahan, M., Stueve, A., & Pescosolido, B.A. (1999). Public conception of mental illness: Labels, causes, dangerousness, and social distance. *American Journal of Public Health, 89*, 1328–1333.

Liska, A.E., Markowitz, F.E., Bridges-Whaley, R., & Bellair, P.E. (1999). Modeling the relationships between the criminal justice and mental health systems. *The American Journal of Sociology, 104*, 1744–1775.

Lutterman, T., & Hogan, M. (2000). State mental health agency controlled expenditures and revenues for mental health services, FY 1981 to FY 1997. Mental Health, United States, 2000. Washington, DC: U.S. Department of Health and Human Services.

Manderscheid, R.W., Atay, J. E., & Crider, R.A. (2009). Changing trends in state psychiatric hospital use from 2002 to 2005. *Psychiatric Services, 60*, 29–34.

Markowitz, F.E. (2001). Modeling processes in recovery from mental illness: Relationships between symptoms, life satisfaction, and self-concept. *Journal of Health and Social Behavior, 42*, 64–79.

Markowitz, F.E. (2006). Psychiatric hospital capacity, homelessness, and crime and arrest rates. *Criminology, 44*, 45–72.

Markowitz, F.E., Bellair, P.E., Liska, A.E., & Liu, J. (2001). Extending social disorganization theory: Modeling the relationships between cohesion, disorder, and fear. *Criminology, 39*, 293–320.

Martin, J.K., Pescosolido, B.A., & Tuch, S.A. (2000). Of fear and loathing: the role of 'disturbing behavior,' labels, and causal attributions in shaping public attitudes toward persons with mental illness. *Journal of Health and Social Behavior, 41*, 208–223.

Matejkowsi, J.C., Solomon, P.L., & Cullen, S.W. (2008). Characteristics of persons with severe mental illness who have been incarcerated for murder. *The Journal of the American Academy of Psychiatry and the Law, 36*, 74–86.

McCarthy, B., & Hagan, J. (1991). Homelessness: A criminogenic situation. *British Journal of Criminology, 31*, 393–410.

McGuire, J.F., & Rosenbeck, R.A. (2004). Criminal history as a prognostic indicator in the treatment of homeless people with severe mental illness. *Psychiatric Services, 55*, 42–48.

Mechanic, D. (2008). Mental health and social policy: Beyond managed care. Boston, MA: Allyn and Bacon.

Mechanic, D., McAlpine, D., & Olfson, M. (1998). Changing patterns of psychiatric inpatient care in the United States, 1988–1994. Archives of General Psychiatry, 55, 785–791.

Mechanic, D., & Rochefort, D. A. (1990). Deinstitutionalization: An appraisal of reform. *Annual Review of Sociology, 16*, 301–327.

Melick, M.E., Steadman, H.J., & Cocozza, J.J. (1979a). Explaining the increased crime rate of mental patients: The changes in clientele of State hospitals. *The American Journal of Psychiatry, 135*, 816–820.

Melick, M.E., Steadman, H.J., & Cocozza, J.C. (1979b). The medicalization of criminal behavior among mental patients. *Journal of Health and Social Behavior, 20*, 228–237.

Mirowsky, J., & Ross, C.E. (2003). *Social Causes of Psychological Distress* (2nd ed.). 2003. New York: Aldine de Gruyter.

Monahan, J. (1992). Mental disorder and violent behavior: perceptions and evidence. *The American Psychologist, 47*, 511–521.

Monahan, J., Steadman, H.J., Silver, E., Applebaum, P., Robbins, P., Mulvey, et al. (2001). *Rethinking risk assessment:*

The MacArthur study of mental disorder and violence. New York: Oxford University Press.

Morris, S.M., Steadman, H.J., & Veysey, B.M. (1997). Mental health services in United States jails. *Criminal Justice and Behavior, 24*, 3–19.

National Institute of Mental Health. (1990). *Mental Health, United States*. Washington, DC: U.S. Government Printing Office.

Osher, F.C., & Steadman, H.J. (2007). Adapting evidence-based practices for persons with mental illness involved with the criminal justice system. *Psychiatric Services, 58*, 1472–1478.

Palermo, G.B., Smith, M.B., & Liska, F.J. (1991). Jails versus mental hospitals: A social dilemma. *International Journal of Offender Therapy and Comparative Criminology, 35*, 97.

Penrose, L. (1939). Mental disease and crime: Outline of a comparative study of European statistics. *The British Journal of Medical Psychology, 18*, 1–15.

Pescosolido, B. A., Monahan, J., Link, B.G., Stueve, A., & Kikuzawa, S. (1999). The public's view of the competence, dangerousness, and need for legal coercion of persons with mental health problems. *American Journal of Public Health, 89*, 1339–1345.

Phelan, J.C., Link, B.G., Stueve, A., & Pescosolido, B.A. (2000). Public conceptions of mental illness in 1950 and 1996: What is mental illness and is it to be feared? *Journal of Health and Social Behavior, 41*, 188–207.

Pogrebin, M.R., & Regoli, R.M. (1985). Mentally disordered persons in jail. *Journal of Community Psychology, 13*, 409–412.

Quillian, L., & Pager, D. (2001). Black neighbors, higher crime? The role of racial stereotypes in evaluations of neighborhood crime. *The American Journal of Sociology, 107*, 717–767.

Redick, R.W., Witkin, M.J., Atay, J., & Manderscheid, R.W. (1992). Specialty mental health system characteristics. *Mental Health, United States, 1992* (pp. 1–141). Washington, DC: USDHHS.

Reuland, M., & Cheney, J. (2005). *Enhancing success of police-based diversion programs for people with mental illness*. Delmar, New York: GAINS Center.

Sampson, R.J., & Groves, W.B. (1989). Community structure and crime: Testing social disorganization theory. *The American Journal of Sociology, 94*, 774–802.

Sampson, R.J., Raudenbush, S. W., & Earls, F. (1997). Neighborhoods and violent crime: A multilevel study of collective efficacy. *Science, 277*, 918–924.

Shlay, A. B., & Rossi, P. H. (1992). Social science research and contemporary studies of homelessness. *Annual Review of Sociology, 18*, 129–160.

Silver, E. (2000a). Extending social disorganization theory: A multilevel approach to the study of violence among persons with mental illnesses. *Criminology, 38*, 301–332.

Silver, E. (2000b). Race, neighborhood disadvantage, and violence among persons with mental disorders: The importance of contextual measurement. *Law and Human Behavior, 24*, 449–456.

Silver, E., Arseneault, L., Langley, J., Caspi, A., & Moffitt, T. (2005). Mental disorder and violent victimization in a total birth cohort. *American Journal of Public Health, 95*, 2015–2021.

Silver, E., Felson, R., & VanEseltine, M. (2008). The relationship between mental health problems and violence among criminal offenders. *Criminal Justice and Behavior, 35*, 405–426.

Silver, E., Mulvey, E.B., & Monahan, J. (1999). Assessing violence risk among discharged patients: Towards an ecological approach. *Law and Human Behavior, 23*, 235–253.

Silver, E., & Teasdale, B. (2005). Mental disorder and violence: An examination of stressful life events and impaired social support. *Social Problems, 52*, 62–78.

Skogan, W. G. (1990). *Disorder and decline: Crime and the spiral decay of American neighborhoods*. New York: Free Press.

Starr, S. (1955). *The public's ideas about mental illness*. Chicago: National Opinion Research Center.

Steadman, H.J. (2001). Assessing the New York City involuntary outpatient commitment pilot program. *Psychiatric Services, 52*, 330–336.

Steadman, H.J., Cocozza, J. J., & Veysey, B.M. (1999). Comparing outcomes for diverted and nondiverted jail detainees with mental illnesses. *Law and Human Behavior, 23*, 615–627.

Steadman, H.J., Fabiasak, S., Dvoskin, J., & Holohean, E.J. (1987). A survey of mental disability among state prison inmates. *Hospital & Community Psychiatry, 38*, 1086–1090.

Steadman, H.J., McCarty, D.W., & Morrisey, J.P. (1989). *The mentally ill in jail*. New York: Guilford.

Steadman, H.J., Monohan, J., Duffee, B., Hartstone, E., & Robbins, P.C. (1984). The impact of state mental hospital deinstitutionalization on U.S. prison populations, 1968-1978. *The Journal of Criminal Law and Criminology, 75*, 474–490.

Steadman, Henry J., Morris, S. M., & Dennis, D.L. (1995). The diversion of mentally ill persons from jails to community-based services: A profile of programs. *American Journal of Public Health, 85*, 1630–1635.

Steury, E.H. (1991). Specifying "criminalization" of the mentally disordered misdemeanant. *The Journal of Criminal Law and Criminology, 82*, 334–359.

Swanson, J.R., Borum, R., Swartz, M., & Monahan, J. (1996). Psychotic symptoms and disorders and the risk of violent behavior in the community. *Criminal Behavior and Mental Health, 6*, 317–332.

Swanson, J. W. (1994). Mental disorder, substance abuse, and community violence: An epidemiological approach. In J. Monahan & H. J. Steadman (Eds.), *Violence and mental disorder: Developments in risk assessment*. Chicago: University of Chicago Press.

Swanson, J.W., Holzer, C. E., III, Ganju, V.K., & Jono, R.T. (1990). Violence and psychiatric disorder in the community: Evidence from the epidemiological catchment area surveys. *Hospital and Community Psychiatry, 41*, 761–770.

Swanson, J.W., Swartz, M.S., Van Dorn, R.A., Elbogen, E.B., Wagner, H.R., Rosenheck, R.A., et al. (2006). National study of violent behavior in persons with schizophrenia. *Archives of General Psychiatry, 63*, 490–499.

Swartz, M.S., Swanson, J.W., Hiday, V.A., Borum, R., Wagner, H.R., & Burns, B.J. (1998). Violence and severe mental illness: The effects of substance abuse and nonadherence to medication. *The American Journal of Psychiatry, 155*, 226–231.

Teasdale, B. (2009). Mental disorder and violent victimization. *Criminal Justice and Behavior, 36*(5), 513–535.

Teasdale, B., Silver, E., & Monahan, J. (2006). Gender, threat/control-override delusions and violence. *Law and Human Behavior, 30*, 649–658.

Tedeschi, J.T., & Felson, R.B. (1994). *Violence, aggression, and coercive actions*. Washington, DC: American Psychological Association.

Teplin, L.A. (1984). Criminalizing mental disorder: The comparative arrest rate of the mentally ill. *The American Psychologist, 39*, 794–803.

Teplin, L.A. (1990). The prevalence of severe mental disorder among male urban jail detainees: Comparison with the Epidemiological Catchment Area Program. *American Journal of Public Health, 80*, 663–669.

Teplin, L.A. (1994). Psychiatric and substance abuse disorders among male urban jail detainees. *American Journal of Public Health, 84*, 290–293.

Teplin, L.A., McClelland, G.M., Abram, K.M., & Weiner, D.A. (2005). Crime victimization in adults with severe mental illness: Comparison with the national crime victimization survey. *Archives of General Psychiatry, 62*, 911–921.

Tiihonen, J., Isohanni, M., Rasanen, P., Koiranen, M., & Moring, J. (2007). Specific major mental disorders and criminality: A 26-year prospective study of the 1966 northern Finland birth cohort. *The American Journal of Psychiatry, 154*, 840–845.

Torrey, E.F. (1995). Jails and prisons: America's new mental hospitals. *American Journal of Public Health, 85*, 1611–1613.

Torrey, E.F. (1997). *Out of the shadows: Confronting America's mental illness crisis.* New York: John Wiley and Sons.

Torrey, E.F., Kennard, A.D., Eslinger, D., Lamb, R., & Pavle, J. (2010). *More mentally ill persons are in jails and prisons than hospitals: A survey of the states.* Arlington, VA: Treatment Advocacy Center.

Torrey, E.F., Stanley, J., Monahan, J., & Steadman, H.J. (2008). The MacArthur Violence Risk Assessment Study revisited: Two views ten years after its initial publication. *Psychiatric Services, 59*, 147–152.

Van Dorn, R.A., Swanson, J.W., Swartz, M.S., Wilder, C.M., Moser, L.L., Gilbert, A.R., et al. (2010). Continuing medication and hospitalization outcomes after assisted outpatient treatment in New York. *Psychiatric Services, 61*, 982–987.

Wahl, O.F. (1995). *Media Madness: Public Images of Mental Illness*. New Brunswick, NJ: Rutgers University Press.

Wang, P.S., Demler, O., & Kessler, R.C. (2002). Adequacy of treatment for serious mental illness in the United States. *American Journal of Public Health, 92*, 92–98.

Watson, A.C., & Angell, B. (2007). Applying procedural justice theory to law enforcement's response to persons with mental illness. *Psychiatric Services, 58*, 787–793.

Watson, A.C., Corrigan, P.W., & Ottati, V. (2004). Police officer attitudes and decisions regarding persons with mental illness. *Psychiatric Services, 55*, 46–53.

Watson, A., Hanrahan, P., Luchins, D., & Lurigio, A. (2001). Mental health courts and the complex issue of mentally ill offenders. *Psychiatric Services, 52*, 477–481.

Weinstein, R.M. (1990). Mental hospitals and the institutionalization of patients. *Research in Community and Mental Health, vol. 6.* (pp. 273–294) Greenwich, CT: JAI Press.

Yoon, J. (2011). Effect of increased private share of inpatient psychiatric resources on jail population growth: Evidence from the United States. *Social Science and Medicine, 72*, 447–455.

Yoon, J., & Bruckner, T.A. (2009). Does deinstitutionalization increase suicide? *Health Services Research, 44*, 1385–1405.

24

Reentry Reconsidered

A New Look at an Old Question

Jeremy Travis
Joan Petersilia

Prison policy influences the social fabric of the community, and has a strong interrelationship with social policy and other areas of public law. This discussion illustrates the legislative role in sentencing, and the failure to understand the ways in which the political system impacts the daily wheels of justice. Increased or mandated sentencing fails to consider the issue of how to integrate offenders back into mainstream society.

Last year, about 585,000 individuals—nearly 1,600 a day—left state and federal prisons to return home. On one level, this is not particularly noteworthy. Ever since prisons were built, prisoners have faced the challenge of moving from confinement in correctional institutions to liberty on the street. Yet, as we argue in this article, from a number of policy perspectives, the age-old issue of prisoner reintegration has taken on critical importance as we enter the new century. Furthermore, we believe that a renewed research and policy focus on the phenomenon of prisoner reentry can breathe life into old debates about the purposes of punishment, the relationship between offenders and society, and the consequences of the arrest, incarceration, and return of offenders.

We first view the reentry phenomenon through a jurisprudential lens. We argue that a reentry perspective sheds light on three natural experiments in justice policy: namely, the fourfold increase in per capita rates of incarceration, the disintegration of a unified sentencing philosophy, and the weakening of parole as a coherent approach to prisoner reintegration. We then discuss recent changes in the profile of returning prisoners. Third, we examine linkages between the reentry phenomenon and five related social policy domains. Finally, we explore some implications of this reentry perspective for the development of new policies.

SENTENCING POLICY THROUGH A REENTRY LENS

Over the past generation, sentencing policy in the United States has been characterized by three interrelated developments, one well known, two less so: the growth in imprisonment rates, the fragmentation of sentencing philosophy, and the weakening of parole. Taken together, they have had profound consequences on the reintegration of released prisoners.

The Growth of Imprisonment

The per capita rate of imprisonment in America hovered at about 110 per 100,000 from 1925 to 1973, with little variation (Blumstein & Beck, 1999). Starting in 1973, however, the rate of imprisonment has grown steadily, so that our rate is now 476 per 100,000, over four times the 1973 level (Beck, 2000a). State prisons now house 1.2 million people (Beck, 2000a). There are an additional 596,485 people in local jails, a threefold increase since 1980 (Bureau of Justice Statistics, 2000a).

There has been a nearly parallel growth in the size of the population under parole supervision. In 1980, there were 220,000 people on parole, serving the remainder of their prison sentences under community supervision. By 1999, that number had grown to 713,000, a more than a threefold increase. Similarly, the probation population increased between 1980 and 1999, from 1.2 million to 3.8 million (Bureau of Justice Statistics, 2000a).

As a natural, predictable consequence of the nation's experiment with increased levels of imprisonment, more people leave prison to return home, typically under some form of criminal justice supervision. As Figure 1 shows, the number of people released from state and federal prisons has increased from 154,000 in 1980 to about 585,000 in 2000. Because the average length

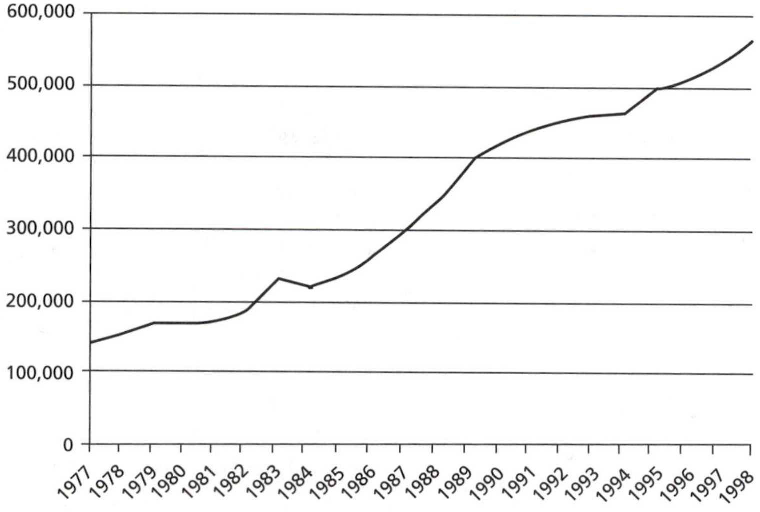

FIGURE 1 Sentenced prisoners released from State and Federal Jurisdictions, 1977–1998

Source: BJS, National Prisoner Statistics data series (NPS-1)

of prison stay has also increased over time, there has been a slight lag between intake levels and release levels in the prison systems. But by 1998 there were similar numbers admitted (615,000) as released (547,000) (Beck, 2000b; Bureau of Justice Statistics, 2000b). Furthermore, now that the nation's prison population is moving toward equilibrium, and even declining in some states, we can expect that the reentry cohorts may soon peak as well.

In summary, the burden on the formal and informal processes that should work together to support successful reintegration of prisoners has increased enormously. On one level, if the capacity to manage reintegration had kept pace with the flow of released prisoners—as the capacity to incarcerate has basically kept pace with the increase in detained prisoners—then, perhaps, the reentry phenomenon today would be no different than in times past. To borrow the language of the assembly line, the throughput would simply be at a higher level of production. But, as will be shown . . . the exponential increase in release cohorts has placed exponentially greater strains on the communities where prisoner removal and return are concentrated. And the philosophical and operational capacity to manage the higher production of released prisoners has not kept pace.

The Fragmentation of Sentencing Philosophy

A second, lesser-known development in our sentencing philosophy has been what Michael Tonry (1999, p. 1) called the "fragmentation of American sentencing policy." A generation ago, we had a unifying national sentencing philosophy, what Tonry called "a distinctly American approach to sentencing and corrections, usually referred to as indeterminate sentencing, and it had changed little in the preceding 50 years" (p. 1). Under this approach, all states provided judges with broad ranges of possible sentences, authorized the release of prisoners by parole boards, supervised prisoners after release, and explicitly embraced rehabilitation of offenders as the goal of corrections (Tonry, 1999).

That philosophy came under attack from the left and right ends of the political spectrum. Liberals critiqued indeterminate sentencing by judges and discretionary release decisions by parole boards as presenting opportunities for distortions of justice. Widely disparate sentences for similar offenses and similar offenders were critiqued as violating fundamental principles of fairness. The unreviewable nature of the decisions was seen as presenting opportunities for disparate racial outcomes. And the lingering uncertainty regarding the culmination of a prison term, dependent on the seemingly arbitrary decision of a parole board, was critiqued as adding unnecessary stress to the period of imprisonment (Frankel, 1973).

The criticism from the right was equally fierce. The imposition of indeterminate sentences, with low minimum and high maximum prison terms, was criticized as a fraud on the public. A resurgent belief in "just desserts," the idea that criminal behavior warrants a punishment proportionate to the offense, resonated with a new public belief that the criminal justice system was too lenient (Hirsch, 1976; Wilson, 1975). A review of the literature on the effectiveness of rehabilitation, captured in the famous phrase "nothing works," weakened the intellectual underpinning of the stated purpose of sentencing and correction (Martinson, 1974). Finally, the use of early release as a mechanism to manage burgeoning prison populations strained public confidence in the integrity of the governmental process for managing the severity of punishment (Wright, 1998).

Under attack from left and right, the philosophy of indeterminate sentencing, once embraced by all 50 states and enshrined in the Model Penal Code, lost its intellectual hold on U.S. sentencing policy. Beginning with the abolition of parole in Maine in 1975, "nearly every state has in some way repudiated indeterminate sentencing" and replaced it with a variety of state experiments (Tonry, 1996, p. 4; Tonry, 1999). As of 1998, 17 states had created sentencing commissions, quasi-independent administrative bodies that have designed sentencing grids that significantly constrain judicial sentencing discretion (Rottman et al., 2000). Legislation creating mandatory minimum sentences has been enacted in all 50 states (Austin et al., 1995). Three-strikes laws have lengthened prison terms for persistent offenders in 24 states (Austin et al., 1999). Forty states have enacted truth-in-sentencing laws requiring that violent offenders serve at least 50% of their sentences in prison; of these 40 states, 27 and the District of Columbia require violent offenders to serve at least 85% of their sentences in prison (Ditton & Wilson, 1999).

These developments in U.S. sentencing philosophy can be analyzed from a number of different perspectives. One could analyze their effects on the level of incarceration, the profile of the prison population, plea bargaining practices, or prosecutorial discretion, to name a few. A reentry perspective focuses attention on the impact of these developments on the process of release and reintegration—on the timing of the release decision, the procedures for making the release decision, the preparation of the prisoner for release, the preparation of the prisoner's family and community for his release, supervision after release, and the linkages between in-prison and post-release activities.

For example, as a result of these changes in sentencing philosophy, fewer prisoners are being released because of a parole board decision (see Table 1). In 1990, 39% were released to supervision by parole board action, and 29% by mandatory release; by 1998, those figures had been reversed, and 26% were released by parole board decision, and 40% by mandatory release (Beck, 2000b). With widespread adoption of truth-in-sentencing statutes, these trends can be expected to continue, so that release by parole board will become a vestige of a bygone era, retained in some states but in others, reserved for an aging prison cohort sentenced under the old regime.

The policy and research questions posed by this development have implications for corrections management. Does the absence of a discretionary release process remove an incentive for good behavior? If so, can the loss of that incentive be replaced with another, equally effective incentive? Does the automatic nature of release diminish the prisoner's incentive to find a stable residence or employment on the outside, the factors that traditionally influenced release decisions? Does a mandatory release policy increase or decrease a correctional agency's coordination between life in prison and planning for life outside of prison? Does mandatory release remove the ability of a parole board to revisit the risk posed by the offender, once his prison behavior has been observed? The psychological literature on coping and adaptation in prison concludes that long-term imprisonment may cause depression, anxiety, and mental breakdown (Liebling, 1999). If more inmates are "maxing out," the parole board has no ability to correct for risk-related variables that may have presented themselves during imprisonment. And, if parole boards have little authority to extend inmate sentences, what role does that leave for victims? Recent research shows that more than 70% of parole boards now invite victims to attend the parole hearing (Petersilia, 1999). As parole boards release

Table 1 Inmate Releases Decisions, 1990–1998

	RELEASED TO SUPERVISION				
Year	Parole Board	Mandatory Release	Other Conditional	Expiration of Sentence	Other
1990	39.4	28.8	15.5	12.7	3.6
1995	32.3	39.0	10.1	14.5	4.0
1996	30.4	38.0	10.2	16.7	4.7
1997	28.2	39.7	10.4	16.8	4.9
1998	26.0	40.4	11.2	18.7	3.7

SOURCE: Beck, 2000a.

fewer prisoners in the future, these victims' rights become less meaningful (Herman &Wasserman, 2001).

The absence of a dominant sentencing philosophy has also left the current sentencing regime—actually, a national crazy quilt made up of piecemeal sentencing reforms—without a public rationale that would explain the relationship between imprisonment and release. Under the old regime, it was straightforward: when a prison sentence was imposed (under a variety of justifications), the amount of time served would depend on a later determination of release readiness. Release decisions and postrelease supervision were part and parcel of the sentencing framework. Under a just-desserts model, for example, the purpose of a period of postrelease supervision is unclear. Under a mandatory minimum sentence, why should an offender serve any more time in the community? If prisons started to look more like jails, with fixed-date releases, what is the rationale for any supervision after release? Why not just show the prisoners the door when they have served their time?

THE WEAKENING OF PAROLE

The increase in incarceration and fragmentation of our sentencing philosophy have created strains on the raison d'etre and management of parole agencies. Reflecting the notion of a continuous flow from prison to community, with a focus on the endpoint of rehabilitation and reintegration, the word parole actually has two operational meanings: it refers both to the agency making a release decision (the parole board) and the agency supervising the offender in the community (typically the "division of parole").

A focus on returning prisoners does not begin with a discussion of parole populations, however, because some prisoners are released without supervision. Returning to Table 1, we see that in 1998, 18.7% of the released prisoners were released because their sentence had expired, and another 3.7% were released without supervision, meaning that 22.4% of the 1998 release cohort of 547,000—or about 123,000—left prison with no legal supervision. This form of release is increasing steadily as determinate sentencing reforms take hold—in 1990, only 16.3% of the released cohort were released without supervision, meaning that about 69,000 left prison unconditionally that year (Beck, 2000b).

There are two views of this development. On the one hand . . . parole supervision has not been proven effective at reducing new arrests, and has been shown to increase technical violations (Petersilia &Turner, 1993). Intensive supervision program clients are subject to much closer surveillance than others under supervision, and more of their violations may come to official attention, resulting in more returns to jail or prison. If noncompliance with technical conditions signaled that offenders were "going bad," then returning them to incarceration might prevent future crime. However, research on the issue has shown no support for the argument that violating offenders on technical conditions suppressed new criminal arrests (Petersilia & Turner, 1993). So, simply increasing parole supervision does not lead to fewer crimes. Therefore, why force more offenders into an ineffective system of supervision? Perhaps, as James Austin (2001) argued, certain offenders who pose low risks should simply be released.

On the other hand, if the transition from prison life to community life is difficult, and if some form of supervision can make that transition more effective, then the loss of a legal connection would appear counterproductive. This view becomes particularly compelling when one considers the stories of prisoners who serve the last years of their sentence in maximum security, then are released to the street without supervision because they reached the end of their sentence. And from purely a public safety standpoint, the status of parole allows law enforcement greater search and seizure powers, and a quick way to remove offenders from the street if they commit a new crime. In this view, both society and ex-offenders stand to benefit from legal supervision.

The increase in prison populations has had the predictable impact on parole caseloads without proportionate increases in resources. As discussed earlier, in 1999 there were 713,000 individuals on parole (or other form of conditional release), more than triple the number on parole in 1980 (Bureau of Justice Statistics, 2000a). Spending has not kept pace with this growth in supervision caseloads. In the 1970s, parole officers handled caseloads averaging 45 offenders; today, most officers are responsible for about 70 parolees (Rottman et al., 2000). At the same time, per capita spending per parolee has decreased from more than $11,000 per year in 1985 to about $9,500 in 1998 (J. P. Lynch & Sabol, 2001).

The nature of parole supervision has shifted over the past two decades as well. The parole field has uneasily accommodated two potentially conflicting objectives, one more akin to social work, one more akin to law enforcement. The introduction of new surveillance technologies, particularly urine testing and electronic monitoring, has provided enhanced capacity to detect parole violations and, thereby, to increase the rate of revocations of liberty (Kleiman, 1999). Signaling a shift in emphasis, recent surveys of parole officers show that more of them prioritize the law enforcement function of parole, rather than its service or rehabilitation functions (M. Lynch, 1998).

For these and other reasons, the rate of parole violations has increased significantly over recent years. In 1985, 70% of parolees successfully completed their parole term; by 1997, that number had dropped to 44%. Conversely, the percentage of those who fail on parole has increased from less than a third of all parolees in 1985 to 54% in 1997 (Petersilia, 1999). Almost 9% of all parolees nationally are counted as absconding-meaning their whereabouts are unknown to parole agents (Bonczar & Glaze, 1999).

This rise in rates of parole failures, coupled with an increasing base of parole populations, has had profound impacts on the nation's prison population. In 1980, parole violators constituted 18% of prison admissions; they now constitute 37% of prisoners coming in the front door. In 1998, this meant that 207,000 of the 565,000 people admitted to prison were parole violators, individuals who had either been returned to prison on a technical violation or for committing a new offense (Beck, 2000a).The combination of this increase with the leveling off of new prison commitments from new convictions means that parole revocations are now a significant factor in the rising prison populations.

Just as the collapse of a unifying sentencing philosophy has resulted in enormous state variation in punishment regimes, it has also resulted in wide differences in parole practices. For example, in California, 65% of the individuals admitted to that state's prisons in 1997 were parole violators; in Florida, parole violators accounted for 12% of new admissions; in Pennsylvania, 33% (Petersilia, 1999). Nationally, parole violators serve on average another 5 months in prison (Austin et al., 2000).

Taken together, these three developments paint a picture of a system that has lost its way. More people are going to prison under differing sentencing philosophies and returning home through a system of reintegration that has diminished capacity to perform that function and now serves more to return reentry failures to prison's front door. One need not engage in illusions about the capacity of this population to obey the law to conclude that the constructs of philosophy, law, policy, and practice are out of alignment. A return to the preexisting arrangement is unlikely; nor is it necessarily desirable in all respects. But, in our view, any sentencing regime should retain a focus on the reintegration goal. No matter what punishment philosophy sends prisoners to prison, no matter how their release is determined, with few exceptions they all come back. It is hard to find a coherent reentry philosophy in the current state of affairs.

THE PROFILE OF REENTERING PRISONERS

The profile of returning prisoners is changing in ways that pose new challenges to successful reentry. The basic demographics have not changed much over the past 20 years. The parole population is mostly male, although the number of incarcerated females has risen steadily over the past decade. Their median age is 34; the median education level is 11th grade. More than half (55%) of the returning offenders in 1998 were White, while 44% were African-American. Twenty-one percent of offenders on parole in 1998 were Hispanics, who may be of any race (Bonczar & Glaze, 1999).

One characteristic that has changed is the crime for which the offenders were convicted. Reflecting the arrest activities of the "war on drugs," the percentage of released offenders who had been convicted of drug offenses increased significantly during the past 20 years. More than one third (35%) of prisoners released to parole in 1997 had been incarcerated for a drug offense, up from 28% in 1990 and 12% in 1985. Over the same time period, the percent of parolees who had been convicted of violent offenses declined. In 1997, about a quarter of offenders coming into parole had convictions for violent offenses, down from a third (35%) in 1985 (Beck, 2000b).

The profile of returning prisoners is changing in other respects. Due to shifting sentencing policies, including mandatory minimums and truth-in-sentencing laws, the average length of stay in prison is increasing. Those released to parole in 1997 served an average of 27 months in prison—5 months longer than those released in 1990 (Beck, 2000b). This longer time in prison translates into a longer period of detachment from family and other social networks, posing new challenges to the process of reintegration.

More sobering is the decrease in the preparation of these prisoners for their release. As shown in Figure 2, in 1997 approximately a third of the inmates about to be released participated in vocational (27%) or educational (35%) programs—down from 31% and 43%, respectively, in 1991.The level of participation in prerelease planning did not decline, but only 12% of prisoners about to be released participate in prerelease planning at all. Of the entire prison population, an estimated 7% report participation in prison industries, whereas 24% are altogether idle (Austin et al., 2000).

The inescapable conclusion is that we have paid a price for prison expansion, namely a decline in preparation for the return to community. There is less treatment, fewer skills, less exposure to the world of work, and less focused attention on planning for a smooth transition to the outside world.

Another important perspective is that the growing numbers of returning offenders are increasingly concentrated in neighborhoods already facing enormous disadvantage. A majority of prisoners are released into counties that contain the central cities of metropolitan areas. In 1996, an estimated two thirds of the 489,000 state prison releases were released into these counties. Fewer

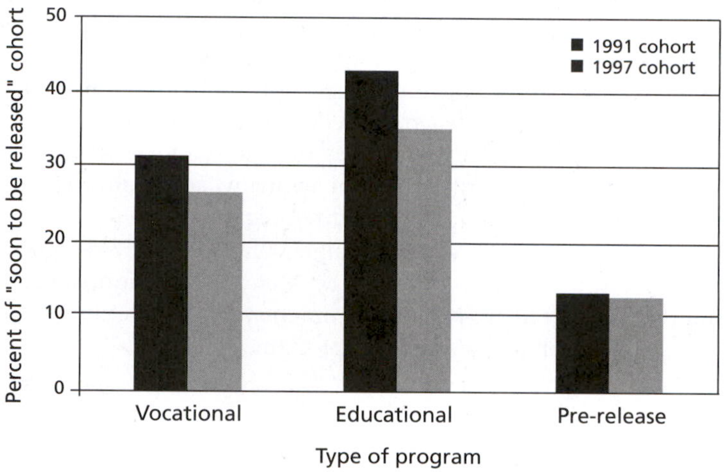

FIGURE 2 Offenders to Be Released in the Next 12 Months: Percent Participating in Prison Programs, 1991 and 1997 (based on preliminary analysis of data for forthcoming Urban Institute Crime Policy Report).

than 50% of 220,000 prisoners were released into these counties in 1984 (J. P. Lynch & Sabol, 2001). Presumably, the releases are more highly concentrated within the central cities of these core counties than they are in the nearby suburbs. And the central cities typically are less wealthy than neighboring areas, and they face other challenges such as loss of labor market share to suburban regions (J. P. Lynch & Sabol, 2001).

Research also suggests high concentrations of prisoners in a relatively small number of neighborhoods within the central cities of the core counties. For example, J. P. Lynch and Sabol (2001) have conducted analyses using data on Ohio state prisoners from Cuyahoga County, which includes the city of Cleveland. More than two thirds of the county's prisoners and most of the block groups with high rates of incarceration come from Cleveland. Concentrations are such that three tenths of 1% of the block groups in the county account for approximately 20% of the county's prisoners. In such "high-rate" block groups, somewhere between 8% and 15% of the young Black males are incarcerated on a given day.

High rates of removal and return of offenders may further destabilize disadvantaged neighborhoods. Recent research by Todd Clear and Dina Rose indicates that high incarceration and return rates may disrupt a community's social network, affecting family formation, reducing informal control of children and income to families, and lessening ties among residents. Clear, Rose, and Ryder (2001) also argue that when removal and return rates hit a certain tipping point, they may actually result in higher crime rates, as the neighborhood becomes increasingly unstable and less coercive means of social control are undermined.

However, the question of whether incarceration policies of the past 15 years have had a beneficial or detrimental effect on the social capital of communities is far from settled (J. P. Lynch & Sabol, 2000b). Alternative theories suggest that this tipping point may differ across communities and that, in some cases—particularly in very high-poverty, high-crime areas—incarceration may be an effective tool for controlling crime. Research shows that residents in these communities want a greater police presence and more attention to the chronic crime problems surrounding them. We do not yet know the relative benefits of removal and returns in various types of communities—there are clearly incapacitation benefits to crime control in many communities, but those may erode without a focus on reentry and reintegration.

In sum, the prisoners moving through the high-volume, poorly-designed assembly line that has, in many respects, lost a focus on reintegration, are less well prepared individually for their return to community, and are returning to communities that are not well prepared to accept them.

SOCIAL POLICY DIMENSIONS OF REENTRY

A focus on reentry highlights connections between criminal justice policy and other social policy domains that are provocative and suggest new directions for research and policy. In this section, we set aside issues of criminal justice policy—e.g., the purposes of punishment—and examine, instead, the overlapping considerations with other policy domains.

Health Policy

The population moving through correctional facilities in the United States presents serious health problems; the question is how to coordinate criminal justice and health policies in ways that improve health outcomes and, secondarily, justice outcomes. Interestingly, a period of incarceration often has positive consequences for the health status of a prisoner—in part because adequate health care is constitutionally required, but also because the food and living environment are more conducive to better health outcomes than many situations in the community. Yet the consequences for a prisoner's mental health may be adverse, and for substance abusers the effects of incarceration depend heavily on the management of the risk of relapse.

The overlap between the public health population and the criminal justice population is striking. For example, as Hammett (2001) shows, nearly one quarter of all people living with HIV or AIDS, one third living with Hepatitis C, and one third with tuberculosis in the United States in 1997 were released from a correctional facility (prison or jail) that year. These data suggest that correctional facilities could provide efficient access to large numbers of people posing serious public health risks, but embracing this challenge would require reconfiguration of the health and justice professions. For criminal justice policymakers, attention would need to be paid to diagnostic screening and treatment capabilities in all prisons and jails. From a reentry perspective, the two professions would need careful collaboration to ensure a smooth transition of care from prison or jail to community health care. Whether this capacity exists, and whether criminal justice supervision could increase the likelihood of healthy outcomes, are open questions.

Some 80% of the state prison population report a history of drug and/or alcohol use, including 74% of the "soon-to-be-released" prisoners (Beck, 2000b; Mumola, 1999). However, in-prison treatment is not readily available to those who need it. Despite a significant infusion of federal monies to fund treatment in state prisons, only 10% of state inmates reported participating in professional substance abuse treatment since admission, down from 25% in 1991 (Bureau of Justice Statistics, 1999). (When one includes participation in drug abuse programs, such as self-help groups and educational programs, the participation rates increase to 24% of the 1997 prison population, down from 30% in 1991 [Bureau of Justice Statistics, 1999].) Of the soon-to-be-released group who were using drugs in the month prior to incarceration, only 18% had participated in treatment since prison admission. And only 22% of the alcohol abusers had participated (Beck, 2000b).

The concern about the connections between criminal justice policy and drug treatment policy is brought into sharp focus by two distinct research findings. First, there is a significant body of evaluation literature demonstrating that in-prison drug treatment in the period leading up to release can, if combined with treatment in the postrelease period, significantly reduce both drug use and recidivism (Harrison, 2001). So, careful planning of treatment programs, along with supervision during reentry, will enhance health and safety. The second research finding comes from research on the brain. This research concludes "addiction is a brain disease" (Leshner, 1998, p. 2). Consequently, the return of a former addict to his old neighborhood places him at high risk of relapse, in part because the old haunts act as a trigger to his brain mechanisms and heighten the cravings. So, the criminal justice policy of requiring a parolee to return to his community may merely be placing a recovering addict at the crossroads of greatest risk.

Inmates with mental illness are also increasingly being imprisoned—and ultimately, being released. In 1998, the Bureau of Justice Statistics estimated that 16% of jail or prison inmates reported either a mental condition or an overnight stay in a mental hospital (Ditton, 1999). There are relatively few public mental health services available, and studies show that even when they are available, mentally ill individuals fail to access available treatment because they fear institutionalization, deny that they are mentally ill, or distrust the mental health system (Lurigio, 2001). Untreated mentally ill individuals may engage in criminal behaviors that eventually lead to arrest and conviction.

FAMILY AND CHILD WELFARE POLICY

One of the undeniable aspects of imprisonment is that relationships with family are strained. Not surprisingly, then, the increase in incarceration has significant consequences for family and child welfare policy. Most prisoners are parents—about one half of the men and two thirds of the women. According to the Bureau of Justice Statistics, in 1999 more than 1.5 million minor children in the United States had a parent who was incarcerated, an increase of more than a half million since 1991. About 7% of all African-American children currently have a parent in prison (Mumola, 2000).

Incarceration has consequences for child rearing. When fathers are imprisoned, about 90% of their children remain in the custody of their mothers. When mothers are incarcerated, however, fewer than a third of their children stay with their fathers, placing new demands on the extended family, peer networks, and child welfare systems (Hagan & Dinovitzer, 1999).

The high rates of incarceration in poor neighborhoods create a high level of ongoing disruption in family relationships. Sometimes, the removal of a family member is a good outcome—someone who has been violent in the home, draining resources to support a drug habit, or otherwise posing negative consequences for the family's well-being. But the removal of large numbers of mostly male young adults also drains the community of a key ingredient of social capital—community men. These complex relationships, combined with the great distance between many prisons and prisoners' communities, require creative management on the part of the families and the private and governmental support systems that could minimize the harm to children and families.

The reentry perspective focuses policy attention on the moment of release. How is the family prepared for this moment? How is the prisoner prepared? If there is a history of dysfunction, whose responsibility is it to minimize the harm? Particularly in the instance of domestic violence or child abuse, what is the role of the state and the police in managing the reentry safely?

WORKFORCE PARTICIPATION

The current strong economy presents unusual opportunities for linkages between ex-offenders and the world of work. Approximately two thirds of prisoners had a job just prior to their incarceration (J. P. Lynch & Sabol, 2000a). However, released offenders have very low employment rates, suggesting that incarceration may reduce the employability and future earnings of young men (Western, Kling, & Weiman, 2001). The stigma of incarceration makes ex-inmates unattractive for entry-level or union jobs; civil disabilities limit ex-felons access to skilled trades or the public sector; and incarceration undermines the social networks that are often necessary to obtain legitimate employment. Moreover, Nagin and Waldfogel (1998) found that the effect of imprisonment on employment and future earnings is particularly pronounced for inmates over age 30, suggesting that as the prison and parole population ages, employment prospects become bleaker.

Civic Participation

In many ways, prisoners leave prison with only part of their debt to society paid. Much more is owed, and it may never be paid off. For example, one of the traditional consequences of a felony conviction has been the loss of voting rights. The laws of 46 states and the District of Columbia contain such stipulations. Fourteen states permanently deny convicted felons the right to vote. Eighteen states suspend the right to vote until the offender has completed the sentence and paid all fines. As a result, some 4 million Americans, 1.4 million of whom are African American (equaling 13% of the Black male adult population), are disenfranchised in this way (Fellner & Mauer, 1998).

In a spate of laws beginning in the late 1980s, a number of states now require that sex offenders be registered with the police upon release from prison, and/or that the community be notified in some way that a sex offender is living in the neighborhood. Today, every state requires convicted sex offenders to register with law enforcement on release (so-called Megan's laws).

These kinds of disqualifications and burdens (for a review, see Petersilia, 1999) constitute a very real component of the punishment—taken together, they reflect a philosophy akin to internal exile under which ex-offenders are cut off from civic participation, banned from certain employment opportunities, and required to display their status as ex-offender when required.

Racial Disparities

No discussion of imprisonment would be complete without a focus on the impact of incarceration on different racial groups. Bonczar and Beck (1997) calculated that in 1991, an African-American male had a 29% chance of being incarcerated at least once in his lifetime, 6 times higher than that for White males. In fact, the Bureau of Justice Statistics estimated that 9% of Black males in their late 20s and 3% of Hispanic males in their late 20s were in prison at the end of 1999 (Beck, 2000a). Looked at differently, more than one third of Black male high school dropouts were in prison or jail in the late 1990s; a higher percentage of this group were imprisoned than employed (Western & Pettit, 2000).

The consequences of imprisonment on minority communities—and our democracy—are profound. Just the impact on voting rights and civic participation generally is very disturbing. Denying large segments of the minority population the right to vote will likely alienate them further and spawn beliefs about the state that are contentious (Clear, Rose, & Ryder, 2001). Greater alienation and disillusionment with the political process also erodes residents' feelings of commitment and makes them less willing to participate in local activities. This is important because our most effective crime fighting tools require community collaboration and active engagement (Sherman et al., 1997). An increase in alienation between the community and the agencies of justice will make it more difficult for those agencies to turn back to communities and ask for assistance in neighborhood-based approaches (Petersilia, 2000).

It strikes us that this abbreviated summary of some of the data presented at the Reentry Roundtable that we co-hosted in October 2000 (most of which are found in the articles in this volume) argue strongly for strategic engagement between these varied policy sectors and criminal justice policy using the moment of reentry as the focal planning point. For example, the high degree of public health concerns presented by the criminal justice population is a compelling case for coordination of health care in the prison and in the community. Similarly, the creation of seamless treatment systems for returning prisoners with histories of substance abuse would keep a significant number of offenders from returning to prison. The linkage between prison-based work and community-based work also seems manageable, particularly in a low-unemployment economy. Furthermore, we applaud the work underway in a number of states to reconsider the reach of the current voter disqualification laws. Finally, we hope that the new community focus on reentry, with geo-coded data, and analysis of the impact of imprisonment and reentry on poor, minority communities can provide a new dimension to the ongoing debate about the impact of criminal justice on our pursuit of racial justice.

IMPLICATIONS OF THE REENTRY PERSPECTIVE

We find the reentry perspective helpful in shining light into the dusty corners of some old debates about criminal justice policy. We have three particular corners in mind: the logic of parole, the mission of corrections, and the allocation of public and private responsibilities for the reintegration of offenders. Our overarching conclusion resembles the rallying cry of welfare reformers—we think we should abolish the system of parole as we know it, and replace it with a new system focused squarely on the goal of reintegration.

The Logic of Parole

Parole has both operational and jurisprudential meanings for criminal justice policy. At an operational level, it refers both to a method of making release decisions and a form of community supervision. As this article has demonstrated, we have concluded that both operational meanings of the word have lost political ground in recent years. We think a reentry analysis makes a compelling case for a reconsideration of the jurisprudential logic of parole as well. The central tenet of our parole system is the idea that a prisoner is expected to serve a portion of his sentence in the community, and he risks return to prison—often for the remainder of his sentence—if he fails to meet certain conditions.

We would substitute a new, two-part jurisprudential logic, namely that (a) completion of a prison sentence represents payment of a debt to society, and (b) every substantial period of incarceration should be followed by a period of managed reentry. In other words, we think it is important to decouple the rationale for the imposition of a sentence to imprison for a period of time from the rationale for community supervision for a period of time. The former should be justified in terms of deterrence, retribution, rehabilitation or incapacitation, the traditional underpinnings of a criminal sentence; the latter should be justified in terms of reintegration. In this view, if a criminal sentence requires imprisonment, the sentence would be served when the prison phase is completed. After completion of the prison sentence, the reentry phase would begin. For released prisoners who pose little risk and can accomplish reintegration easily, the reentry phase could be quite short, perhaps as short as a month. For those who pose greater risks and face greater difficulty reestablishing themselves, the reentry phase would be longer, but upper bounds would be established proportionate to both the risk and the original offense.

Supervision during this period would be the responsibility of a new, community-based entity . . . The expectations placed on the returning prisoner would be related to successful reintegration—for example, getting a job, staying sober, attending mental health counseling, or making restitution to the victim. Failure to meet expectations during this period of managed reentry would not result in return to prison, as in traditional parole jurisprudence, because the sentence has been served with the completion of the prison term. Rather, as with drug courts, failure could result in graduated sanctions, up to a short deprivation of liberty, if those sanctions are demonstrably effective at changing behavior. In this system, if the released prisoner commits a new crime, it would be treated as a new crime to be prosecuted in a traditional manner, not as a violation of a condition of release as often happens now.

There are important and interesting experiments in this new approach to the task of reintegration. The Wisconsin Sentencing Commission articulated this risk-based philosophy in its final report and Wisconsin has launched pilot projects to test these ideas (Smith & Dickey, 1999). Washington state has embraced a risk-based approach to postprison supervision (Lehman, in press). The new concept of a reentry court reflects these principles as well (Travis, 2000). As originally proposed, reentry courts would have the authority to impose sanctions for failure to meet conditions associated with a reintegration plan, but not on the theory that the original sentence remains in effect. These courts would also provide a public forum that would underscore the importance of the work of reintegration for the offender and the community alike.

We recognize that some sentencing reforms, such as the federal system's, have implemented a new status of "supervised release" to replace parole, but we prefer a new conceptualization of the connection between the reintegration mandate and our sentencing jurisprudence, not a reinstatement of parole under a different name.

For our proposal to take full shape, two revisions to a state's sentencing framework would be required. First, the duration of the criminal sentence would be defined as coinciding with completion of the prison term. The truth-in-sentencing philosophy reflects this idea somewhat, but with an emphasis on creating a fixed prison term. In our proposal, by contrast, we would still allow for early completion of a prison term (and thereby early completion of the criminal sentence) upon a showing of good conduct in prison in order to create incentives for conforming behavior in prison life. Second, a new legal status of reentry supervision would be created, with upper time limits, and incentives for early completion. During this period following prison release, the power of the state to revoke liberty would be statutorily limited to a system of graduated, parsimonious sanctions related to failures to meet reentry conditions. We believe these statutory clarifications would reflect a public recognition of the need to reintegrate returning prisoners into our society.

THE MISSION OF CORRECTIONS

We think that the departments of corrections should also embrace the new mission of reintegrating returning prisoners. To do this, corrections agencies would be expected (and funded) to create a seamless set of systems that span the boundaries of prison and community. For example, corrections agencies would create linkages between in-prison jobs training and community-based employment and job training and between in-prison health care and community-based health care. They would be expected to link mental health services on both sides of the wall, or to work with community-based domestic violence services when a prisoner with a history of spousal abuse is released. They would be expected to give a prisoner the tools to succeed—for example, identification, driver's license, access to social security or other benefits, or housing, upon release. Where necessary, the department of corrections would be authorized to purchase services to ensure a smooth transfer of responsibility, for example, the first few months' rent if no private housing is available, or transitional mental health counseling to help cushion the shock of return, if community-based care is not available.

Just as welfare reform forced welfare agencies to shift from a dependency model to a model of transition to independence, so too a reentry perspective should force corrections agencies to take practical steps to move prisoners toward independence. In the case of welfare reform, this shift meant that welfare agencies invested in child care, job training, and employee assistance programs—whatever it took to move the client from welfare to work. Similarly, we would expect corrections agencies to make strategic investments in transitional services to move prisoners toward independence. The necessary step here is that corrections agencies must embrace reintegration as a goal, and we note with interest that the Ohio Department of Rehabilitation and Corrections, under the leadership of Reginald Wilkinson, has officially adopted this new mandate (Wilkinson, in press).

ALLOCATION OF RESPONSIBILITIES FOR REINTEGRATION

Who is responsible for successful reintegration? Clearly, the released prisoner has an important role to play, a role that we think is enhanced if made visible and explicit, as in a reentry court. We have also argued that a corrections agency has a role to play, creating a seamless linkage between in-prison programs and community programs to increase the chances of successful reintegration. Yet, our reentry analysis suggests that many of the key activities are distinctly local. For example, this discussion implies that the health, child welfare, job placement, drug treatment, and other service entities need to be mobilized to support prisoner reintegration. Most of these are city- or county-level functions and therefore require the leadership of the mayor or other executive. In our traditional configuration of responsibilities, we have oddly placed responsibility for "reentry management" in a state agency, typically a parole division or a corrections agency. Yet, we have also created community supervision functions in probation or pretrial release agencies, which are often county or city based. These artificial distinctions are barriers to reentry management.

We think it's important to move these activities as close to the community as possible. This is where the problems and assets can be found—the risks to relapse can be identified here; the positive power of social networks can be found here. Ultimately, reentry management should be community-based, with a focus on marshalling community resources to assist in successful reintegration. The legal status of the individual—whether on parole, probation, or pretrial release, whether adult or juvenile—matters somewhat, but we could envision a community supervision system that embraced all types of individuals, in all types of legal relationships with the criminal justice system. We are impressed by the idea of a community justice development organization, now being developed by the Center for Alternative Sentencing and Employment Services (CASES) in New York City. This idea borrows from the successes of community development corporations over the past 20 years that have managed the creation of housing, employment opportunities, and economic growth as intermediaries between federal, state, and local governments responsible for those functions and community institutions that are sometimes better at carrying them out. The researchers and planners at CASES have analyzed the probation and parole caseloads of certain neighborhoods and have asked a simple question: Why can't supervision of those individuals be organized along neighborhood lines, with much of the supervisory responsibility devolved to a community-based entity?

The creation of a community-based intermediary working on criminal justice issues could conceivably win the trust of the community and coalesce community capacity such as churches, small businesses, service providers, schools, and civic institutions to support the work of reintegration of returning prisoners. This new entity could broker the relationship between those institutions and the formal agencies of the justice system. The state system could then devolve the supervision functions of reentry management to the community justice development corporation and retain responsibility for the imposition of sanctions to a reentry court or other backstop system. The function of the government employees now called parole officers would be redefined in this new paradigm. Some of those functions would be performed by community justice corporation employees; other functions more related to enforcement of conditions of reentry would be performed under the auspices of the reentry court or other governmental entity. As with drug courts, it would be important that "carrots and sticks" be used in concert to produce the desired behavioral outcomes.

In sum, we find this reentry perspective suggests new ways of thinking about the underpinnings of our concept of parole, a new mandate for corrections, and a new mission at the local level to coalesce public and private capabilities to increase positive outcomes of the reentry process. This realignment of philosophy and operational capacity is not just about crime policy; it is ultimately about community well-being. And maybe good crime policy results will follow.

DISCUSSION QUESTIONS

1. How have the growth of imprisonment, the fragmentation of sentencing philosophy, and the weakening of parole affected the reintegration of released prisoners?
2. Describe the profile of the typical reentering prisoner. How has this profile changed over the years?
3. Explain how the five social policy domains affect the reentry process.
4. What are the policy implications of the reintegration perspective?

REFERENCES

Austin, J. (2001). Prisoner reentry: Current trends, practices, and issues. *Crime & Delinquency*, 47, 314–334.

Austin, J., Bruce, M. A., Carroll, L., McCall, P. L., & Richards, S.C. (2000, November). *The use of incarceration in the United States.* Paper prepared for the annual meeting of the American Society of Criminology, San Francisco.

Austin, J., Clark, J., Hardyman, P., & Henry, D. A. (1999). Impact of "three strikes and you're out." *Punishment & Society,* 1, 131–162.

Austin, J., Jones, C., Kramer, J., & Renninger, P. (1995). *National Assessment of Structured Sentencing, Final Report.* (Bureau of Justice Statistics Publication No. NJS 167557). Washington, DC: U.S. Department of Justice, Bureau of Justice Assistance.

Beck, A. (2000a). *Prisoners in 1999.* Bureau of Justice Statistics Bulletin. (Bureau of Justice Statistics Publication No. NCJ 183476). Washington DC: U.S. Department of Justice, Bureau of Justice Statistics.

Beck, A. (2000b, April 13). *State and Federal Prisoners Returning to the Community: Findings from the Bureau of Justice Statistics.* Paper presented at the First Reentry Courts Initiative Cluster Meeting, Washington DC. For more information, see http://www.ojp.usdoj.gov/bjs/pub/pdf/sfprc.pdf

Blumstein, A., & Beck, A. (1999). Population growth in U.S. prisons, 1980–1996. In M. Tonry and J. Petersilia (Eds.), *Prisons.* Chicago: University of Chicago Press.

Bonczar, T.P., & Beck, A. (1997). *Lifetime Likelihood of Going to State or Federal Prison.* In Bureau of Justice Statistics, Special Report. (Bureau of Justice Statistics Publication No. NCJ 160092). Washington, DC: U.S. Department of Justice, Bureau of Justice Statistics.

Bonczar, T.P., & Glaze, L.E. (1999). *Probation and Parole in the United States, 1998.* In Bureau of Justice Statistics bulletin. (Bureau of Justice Statistics Publication No. NCJ 178234.) Washington, DC: U.S. Department of Justice, Bureau of Justice Statistics.

Bureau of Justice Statistics. (1999). *Correctional Populations in the United States, 1997.* Washington, DC: U.S. Department of Justice, Bureau of Justice Statistics.

Bureau of Justice Statistics. (2000a, June 23). *Correctional population trends.* Washington, DC: U.S. Department of Justice, Bureau of Justice Statistics. Retrieved February 22, 2001, from the World Wide Web: http://www.ojp.usdoj.gov/bjs/keytabs.htm

Bureau of Justice. (2000b, August 2). *Sentenced prisoners admitted to State or Federal jurisdiction.* Washington, DC: U.S. Department of Justice, Bureau of Justice Statistics. Retrieved February 22, 2001, from the World Wide Web: http://www.ojp.usdoj.gov/bjs/dtdata.htm#justice

Bureau of Justice. (2000c, June 9). *Total sentenced prisoners released from state or federal jurisdiction.* Available: http://www.ojp.usdof.gov/bjs/dtdata.htm#justice

Clear, T., Rose, D.R., & Ryder, J.A. (2001). Incarceration and the community: The problem of removing and returning offenders. *Crime & Delinquency*, 47, 335–367.

Ditton, P.M. (1999). *Mental Health and Treatment of Inmates and Probationers.* In Bureau of Justice Statistics, Special Report. (Bureau of Justice Statistics Publication No. NCJ 174463). Washington, DC: U.S. Department of Justice, Bureau of Justice Statistics.

Ditton, P.M., & Wilson, D.J. (1999). *Truth and Sentencing in State Prisons.* In

Bureau of Justice Statistics, Special Report. (Bureau of Justice Statistics Publication No. NCJ 170032). Washington, DC: U.S. Department of Justice, Bureau of Justice Statistics.

Fellner, J. & Mauer, M. (1998). *Losing the Vote: The Impact of Felony Disenfranchisement Laws in the United States* (Criminal Justice Briefing Sheet No. 1046). Washington, DC: The Sentencing Project. Available: http:// www .sentencingproject.org/pubs/ pubs.html#9080

Frankel, M. (1973). *Criminal Sentences: Law Without Order.* New York: Hill and Wang.

Hagan, J. & Dinovitzer, R. (1999). Collateral consequences of imprisonment for children, communities, and prisoners. In M. Tonry and J. Petersilia (Eds.), *Prisons.* Chicago: University of Chicago Press.

Hammett, T. M. Health-related issues in prisoner reentry. *Crime & Delinquency*, 47, 390–409.

Harrison, L. D. (2001). The revolving prison door for drug-involved offenders: Challenges and opportunities. *Crime & Delinquency*, 47, 462–484.

Herman, S., & Wasserman, C. (2001). A role for victims in offender reentry. *Crime & Delinquency*, 47, 428–445.

Hirsch, A. von. (1976). *Doing Justice: The Choice of Punishments.* (Rep. of the Committee for the Study of Incarceration). New York: Hill and Wang.

Kleiman, M. (1999). *Getting Deterrence Right: Applying Tipping Models and Behavioral Economics to the Problems of Crime Control. Perspectives on Crime and Justice: 1998–1999 Lecture Series,* 3. (Bureau of Justice Statistics Publication No. NCJ 178244). Washington, DC: National Institute of Justice.

Lehman, J. D. (in press). Re-inventing community corrections in Washington state. *Corrections Management Quarterly,* 5(3).

Leshner, A. I. (1998). "Addiction is a brain disease—and it matters." *National Institute of Justice Journal,* No. 237, 2–6.

Liebling, A. (1999). Prison suicide and prisoner coping. In M. Tonry and J. Petersilia (Eds.), *Prisons.* Chicago: University of Chicago Press.

Lurigio, A. Effective services for parolees with mental illnesses. *Crime & Delinquency*, 47, 446–461.

Lynch, J. P., & Sabol, W. J. (2000a. December 5). *Analysis of Bureau of Justice Statistics Data: Survey of Inmates of State Correctional Facilities, 1991 and 1997.* Urban Institute First Tuesdays presentation, Washington DC.

Lynch, J. P., & Sabol, W.J. (2000b). Prison use and social control. In *Policies, Processes and Decisions of the Criminal Justice System.* Washington, DC: U.S. Department of Justice.

Lynch, J. P,. & Sabol, W. J. (2001). Prisoner reentry in perspective (Urban Institute Crime Policy Report). In *Crime policy report.* Washington, DC: Urban Institute Press.

Lynch, M. (1998). Waste managers? New penology, crime fighting, and the parole agent identity. *Law and Society Review,* 32, 839–869.

Martinson, R. (1974). What works? Questions and answers about prison reform. *Public Interest,* 35, 22–45.

Mumola, C. J. (1999). *Substance abuse and treatment, state and federal prisoners, 1997.* In Bureau of Justice Statistics, special report (Bureau of Justice Statistics Publication No. NCJ 172871). Washington, DC: U.S. Department of Justice, Bureau of Justice Statistics.

Mumola, C. J. (2000). *Incarcerated Parents and Their Children.* In Bureau of Justice Statistics, special report (Bureau of Justice Statistics Publication No. NCJ 182335). Washington, DC: U.S.

Department of Justice, Bureau of Justice Statistics.

Nagin, D., & Waldfogel, J. (1998). The effects of conviction on income through the life cycle. *International Review of Law and Economics*, 18, 25–40.

Petersilia, J. (1999). Parole and prisoner reentry in the United States. In M. Tonry and J. Petersilia (Eds.), *Prisons.* Chicago: University of Chicago Press.

Petersilia, J. (2000). When prisoners return to the community: Political, economic, and social consequences. In *Sentencing & Corrections, Issues for the 21st Century,* 9. (Bureau of Justice Statistics Publication No. NCJ 184253). Washington, DC: National Institute of Justice.

Petersilia, J., & Turner, S. (1993). Intensive probation and parole. In M. Tonry and J. Petersilia (Eds.), *Crime and Justice: A review of research* (Vol. 17). Chicago: University of Chicago Press.

Rottman, D. B., Flango, C. R, Cantrell, M. T., Hansen, R., & LaFountain, N. (2000). *State Court Organization 1998.* (Bureau of Justice Statistics Publication No. NCJ 178932). Washington, DC: U.S. Department of Justice, Bureau of Justice Statistics.

Sherman, L., Gottfredson, D., MacKenzie, D., Eck, J., Reuter, P., & Bushway, S. (1997). *Preventing Crime: What Works, What Doesn't, What's Promising.* College Park: University of Maryland Press.

Smith, M. E., & Dickey, W. J. (1999). Reforming sentencing and corrections for just punishment and public safety. In *Sentencing & Corrections, Issues for the 21st Century*, 4. (Bureau of Justice Statistics Publication No. NCJ 175724). Washington, DC: National Institute of Justice.

Tonry, M. (1996). *Sentencing Matters.* New York: Oxford University Press.

Tonry, M. (1999). The fragmentation of sentencing and corrections in America. In *Sentencing & Corrections, Issues for the 21st Century*, 1. (Bureau of Justice Statistics Publication No. NCJ 175721). Washington, DC: National Institute of Justice.

Travis, J. (2000). But they all come back: Rethinking prisoner reentry. In *Sentencing & Corrections, Issues for the 21st Century*, 7. (Bureau of Justice Statistics Publication No. NCJ 181413). Washington, DC: National Institute of Justice.

Western, B., Kling, J. R., & Weiman, D. F. The labor market consequences of incarceration. *Crime & Delinquency,* 47, 410–427.

Western, B., & Pettit, R. (2000) Incarceration and racial inequality in men's employment. *Industrial and Labor Relations Review,* 54, 3–16.

Wilkinson, R.A. (2001). Offender reentry: A storm overdue. *Corrections Management Quarterly*, 5(3).

Wilson, J.Q. (1975). *Thinking About Crime.* New York: Vintage Books.

Wright, R.F. (1998). *Managing Prison Growth in North Carolina through Structured Sentencing.* National Institute of Justice, Program Focus. (Bureau of Justice Statistics Publication No. NCJ 168944). Washington, DC: National Institute of Justice.

25

The Unique Experience of Female Prisoners

Thomas Baker, Laura Bedard, and Marc G. Gertz

Despite an overall decline in crime in the United States female offending and incarceration has been increasing. Numerous theories have been put forth to explain this increase in offending. This chapter discusses some of these ideas. In addition, this chapter describes some of the demographic shifts and details of female offending and incarceration over recent decades. Female incarceration presents challenges not present in the male correctional setting. With commentary from the former warden of a female correctional institution, we detail the unique experiences of females from offending through incarceration.

INTRODUCTION

Explaining female offending once was considered unnecessary. Whereas male crime was seen as ubiquitous and, at least at the most minor levels, to be expected-boys being boys-female offending was thought of as an aberration – something abnormal and literally unladylike. A shift in this line of thought occurred in the 60's and 70's. Crime has often been considered a male, especially young male, phenomenon. But females now make up a considerable proportion of criminal offenders. Women are now responsible for more crimes

Source: "The Unique Experience of Female Offenders" By Thomas Baker, Laura Bedard, and Marc G. Gertz. Reprinted by permission of the authors.

than at any other time in history- they account for approximately 25 percent of offenses according to the 2009 Uniform Crime Report. Additionally, they are being incarcerated at record rates. In 2009 the Bureau of Justice Statistics reported that females constituted 18 percent of the correctional population (this includes probation, parole, house arrest etc). While this is still a relatively small portion of the overall inmate population, it is a dramatic increase. In 1990, females comprised only 14 percent of inmates. That means in a 20 year period this population exploded by 22.2 percent. This occurred even though the total rate of crime declined during the same time period. Understanding the dynamics of this aberrational increase is critical to devising ways to dampen the swell in female offending.

A push to understand the unique circumstances of female offending arose with the popularity of feminism in the late 60's and 70's. Theories that explored an individual's level of strain or the ability of the government and communities to control individuals were popular. Researchers began questioning whether the same male-oriented theories that were being used to explain offending and to develop crime control policies were as effective at explaining female offending and controlling female crime. The fact is that women face different strains and different government and community controls than men. For example, females mature biologically and psychologically faster than males. These differences create a path for females from offending into incarceration that is quite unique. These differences have implications for the rate of female incarceration, the nature of female offending, and their incarceration experience (especially for incarcerated mothers) which are the 4 main sections of this chapter:

- Increase in Female Offending and Incarceration
- The Nature of Female Offending
- The Incapacitation of Females
- Incarcerating Mom

Each of the above topics is explored in depth with the goal of examining the rather unique phenomenon of female offending while describing the experience of female inmates with a special insight from a former warden of a female prison.

EXAMINING THE INCREASE IN FEMALE OFFENDING AND INCARCERATION

Well-established theories and prominent theorists predicted a dramatic increase in offending and subsequent incarceration as a result of the sharp increases in offending experienced during the 1980's. To the surprise of many, the boom did not transpire and instead a remarkable drop in crime occurred during the 1990's and 2000's. This drop in crime was tempered by

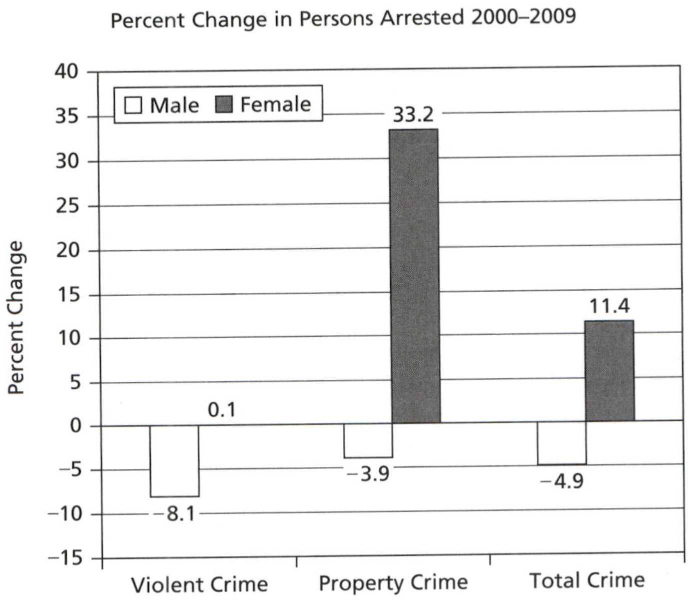

an unsettling fact: female offending grew at a rate faster than males. Over the past decade (2000-2009), the percent of males arrested for crime dropped: violent crime dropped just over 8 percent, property crime decreased nearly 4 percent and total crime decreased approximately 5 percent. During that same decade, the female trend went in the opposite direction: violent crime increased 0.1 percent, property crime increased over 33 percent and total crime increased over 11 percent.

In the two decade period from 1990-2009, in almost every year the percent of females incarcerated in correctional facilities (state and federal) grew at a pace faster than males. The percent increase in the male population only exceeded that of the female population in 4 years of that 2 decade period and only 6 times in the prior 3 decades. (There is some suggestion that this surge in female offending is slowing. In 2009, the most recent year for which there is data, there was approximately a 1 percent *decrease* in the number of females incarcerated in correctional facilities throughout the U.S.)

A number of explanations have been offered for these shifts in female offending and incarceration. The media, beginning in the 1970's, described these increases as a *negative* consequence of the strongly championed women's liberation movement. As more females left the home and rejected the traditional gender roles of home-maker and house-wife and instead began entering the workplace, they now had increased opportunity to be both the victims and perpetrators of crimes.

Others see this conclusion as a clear aberration from the theoretical and empirical literature. They point to findings that employment and wealth are two of the better predictors for decreases in offending. They note that females are far more vulnerable to economic inequality as a result of the patriarchal power structure of the U.S. This subjugation and inequality, they propose, is

Annual % Change in Federal and State Incarceration 1977–2009

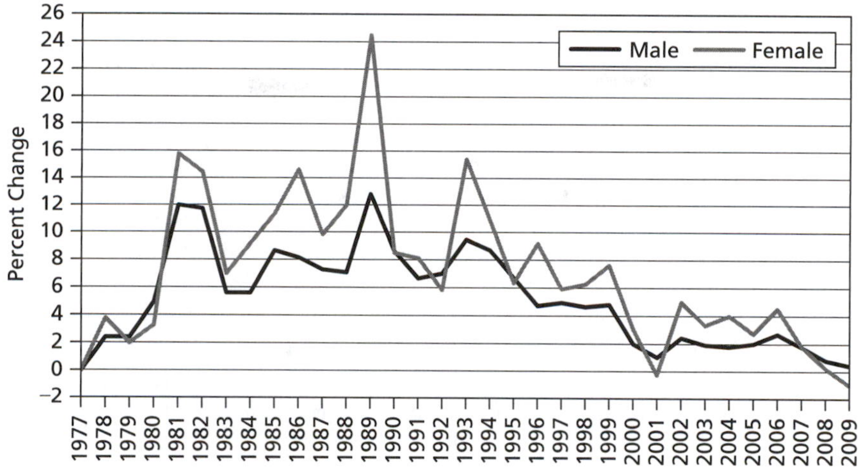

the real reason why, for example, many economically marginalized women are forced into minor property offenses for survival.

Researchers also theorize that increases in offending may be a result of increases in victimization. It is proposed that sexual and physical abuse in the home leads females from otherwise conventional and traditional lifestyles into criminal offending. These researchers posit, for example, that abuse-physical, sexual, or otherwise- may cause young females to run away to the streets where they turn to crimes such as prostitution and drug dealing as a means to survive. These concepts can be broken down into two theoretical frameworks: The Gender Equality Hypothesis and Gender Inequality Hypothesis. The figure shows the theoretical elaboration of the two hypotheses.

This separate attempt at explaining female offending rejects traditional theoretical explanations. Many researchers have questioned the efficacy of using traditional sociological theories researched and theorized by men were adequate for explaining female offending. Gendered explanations of criminal offending support different propositions for female offending than traditionally male dominated theories and tests. The locus of traditional theory and research on male offending may not, necessarily, have been done for misogynistic reasons. Rather when these theories initially were proposed, the rate of female offending was so low as not to be given much consideration. This ignorance of female offending, many feminists claim, has led to misconceptions

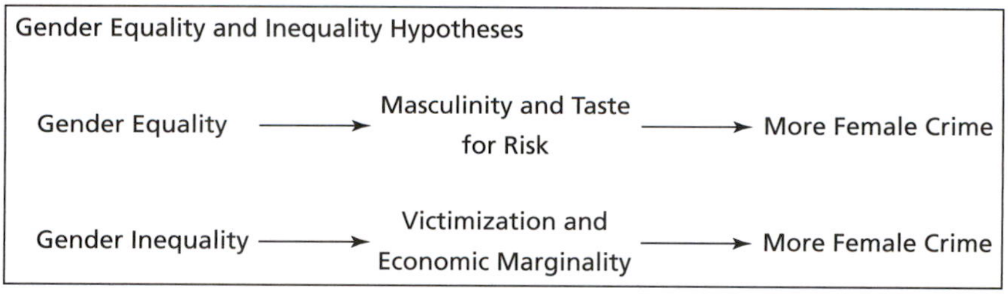

or at least to overgeneralizations. "While such elements as learning, peer influences, social control, family attachment and supervision, individual strain and opportunity are essential in the understanding of crime for both males and females … these factors have variant influences within and across gender." (Miller and Mullins, 2006). Traditional conceptualizations of causes of offending may be relevant to females, but the paths they take to become strained or the attachment they have to their families, or the supervision to which they should be subjected, may be qualitatively and quantitatively different from males. The ubiquity, or generalizability across genders of some of criminology's more respected and highly regarded theories is in doubt and further examination seems necessary.

This movement towards seeking a more nuanced, gender-based understanding of female crime and incarceration prompted Daly (1998), Miller and Mullins (2006), and others to posit typologies to try to describe the complex relationship between gender and offending. Three of these areas are described below.

GENDERED LIVES

This typology focuses on the relationship between gender and all social practices as a way to understand female offending. It looks at the differences in how men and women experience society. For example, it examines how gender impacts social practices such as making friends, relating sexually, parenting, surviving hardship, and finding purpose. This model explores how these gender-determined different social experiences affect aspects of life, such as committing crime. It explores how many typical gender social roles encourage offending-such as typical male roles-or discourage offending-as in the case of typical female roles.

Gendered pathways to lawbreaking

This conceptual framework places primary emphasis on the different lawbreaking path that men and women take. It identifies, for example, the female path to offending that occurs as a result of prior victimization. But, prior victimization is not the only unique path to crime for females. Researchers actually note that placing too much emphasis on this pathway risks ignoring other gender-influenced events along the way, including economic marginality, school experiences, structural dislocation and drug and alcohol use (Miller and Mullins, 2006).

Gendered Crime

To identify the effect of gender on offending, this approach takes into account structural characteristics that may affect females and their criminal offending. For example, high crime neighborhoods make it more likely females will be exposed to drugs and violence and less likely they will have positive social networks to provide outlets for their emotions and to help them pursue desired goals. Societal structures also may affect the types of offenses women commit.

According to this conceptualization, male domination of crime means that the ability of females to offend and the limits of their offending are determined mostly by men. Their criminal roles are marginalized and their access to new criminal social networks often is determined by romantic relationships with men. Once in these criminal networks, women are not able to move up from small roles the way men do.

Whether females are offending more because of the structural inequalities of society or their historically recent liberation, it remains true that they are outpacing men in their growing rate of incarceration. The US crime problem was for many years the male crime problem but it is rapidly shifting to an equal problem for both men and women. More females are being incarcerated and less on community control and other forms of correctional supervision each year.

THE NATURE OF FEMALE OFFENDING

Female offending tends to be much less violent than male offending. Females are far more likely than men to be arrested and put under correctional supervision for what many would consider to be low level, non-serious offenses. Females often commit crimes out of necessity, engaging in prostitution and drug dealing as a means to make ends meet. These are prominent points that make the nature of offenses committed by females substantively and qualitatively different from male offenses.

Much of the type of crime females commit is based on the opportunities created by our societal structures. Females are responsible for 18.8 percent of all violent crime, but nearly double that, 37.5 percent, in property crimes. The high rate of property crime for which women are responsible may well be related to the types of jobs in which they generally are employed. Women make up the majority of bookkeepers and bank tellers, giving them the opportunity to embezzle funds (often as a means to supplement their lower incomes). But even the embezzlement crimes they commit are of lower seriousness than men. Men often hold higher positions where they have access to larger sums of money and are able to embezzle much more.

There are several explanations for the difference in the male/female ratio in violent offending. Two explanations dominate the discussion: culture/society and biology. The cultural/societal explanation focuses on the tendency in almost all cultures to promote violence as a sign of masculinity. As children, boys are more likely to be involved in aggressive activities such as sports. Wrestling is a sign of boys playing. In most cultures females are involved in less aggressive behavior as children. Playing ‘house’ is promoted; young girls are given toys like dolls and easy bake ovens to acculturate them into their roles as nurturers and to encourage passivity. Individuals internalize these definitions about the appropriateness of violent behavior and react to situations throughout their lives according to this internalization. Culture and society seem to

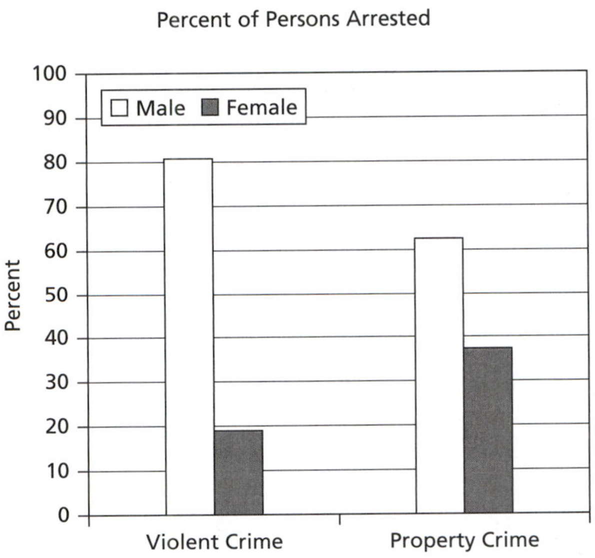

promote violence and aggressive behavior among males while discouraging it among females.

Parents raise and monitor their children. Females are monitored much more closely than males by parents and other informal and formal agencies. The increased monitoring limits the opportunities of females to learn violent behavior and limits their opportunity to respond to events in a violent manner. The gender differences in violent offending are further reinforced by how males and females bond with their peers. Boys are more likely to bond by breaking rules and behaving in an aggressive manner. Girls bond by sharing intimacies. Simply being surrounded by more aggressive peers may result in a greater tendency to engage in violent behavior. Females are more likely to be subject to protective factors like parental controls, while males are more likely to be subject to risk factors like violent/aggressive peers. The differences in risk and protective factors between sexes appear to account for some of the disproportionality in the gender ratio of violent offending.

There is also some evidence that biological differences between males and females may be responsible for the different rates of offending. Females who offend tend to have much higher genetic risk factors for offending than males, meaning that it takes a much higher threshold for women to reach the point of responding to a situation with deviant or violent behavior. Males require a lower genetic threshold and are more likely to respond to trivial events with violence. Researchers also point to the higher levels of testosterone in males. This higher level of testosterone along with its surges at multiple points throughout the life course of males may be responsible for higher levels of deviancy.

Percent of Persons Arrested for Public Order Offenses

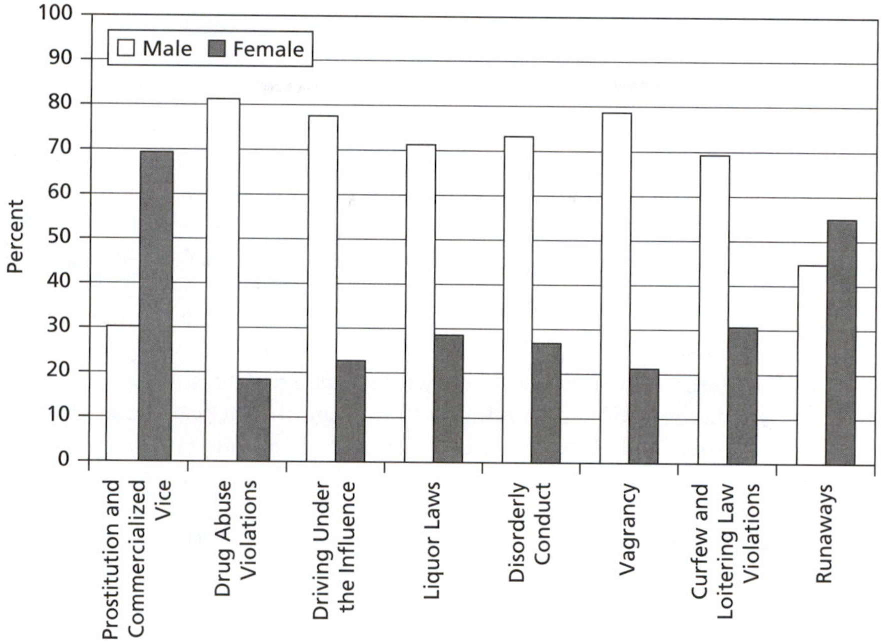

Another explanation for the difference between male and female offending that seems to be supported by a fair deal of anecdotal evidence is the push of females into crime as a result of their romantic relationships with males engaged in crime. Females who may or may not have otherwise engaged in crime do so because of the men they are involved with. The following section provides examples of such anecdotes from the experiences of a warden at a female correctional facility.

FROM A WARDEN'S PERSPECTIVE

I've seen many women in my career enter the criminal justice system after getting involved in crime because of their husband, boyfriend or the father of their child. They prostitute themselves and give the money to their drug addicted boyfriend; they begin using drugs as a result of a relationship; they allow their significant other to abuse their children. It is often impossible to understand. I hear stories from female inmates that make my skin crawl and I think to myself – if only..... if only she had the strength to be independent, if only she could have seen through the deviousness of her husband, if only she had put her children's welfare first.

I recall one case where the female inmate drove the getaway car for her boyfriend during a robbery. They had been involved in drugs together – both addicted to crack and willing to do "whatever" it took to get high. They planned and plotted to rob a convenience store but were high during the event and ended up getting caught. Once they were arrested, the boyfriend, a career criminal who knew the legal process inside and out, turned state's evidence against her. She got 15 years in prison and he, based on his cooperation, was out on probation. The girlfriend, my inmate, continued to profess her love for him, but we all knew she had been used. She would speak highly of him, wait for the daily mail in hopes of a letter, keep his picture next to her bunk. Meanwhile her collect calls to him were declined and her number was blocked. She kept thinking he was going to come and visit her or send her money. He never did. I knew she had been duped and I actually felt sorry for her. She transferred and I never saw her again, but as I recall this story I wonder if she's still waiting for him.

Another female inmate I worked with years ago had a long history of trauma and victimization beginning at about age 3. She had been beaten, molested, burned and virtually tortured as a child by her family members. She was in prison for negligent homicide of her infant child. She had stood by and watched while her boyfriend beat her child to death. When asked in a group session why she didn't respond, she replied "At least he wasn't hitting me." It's hard for us to understand but it was her way of coping with years of trauma, and physical and emotional abuse that had taken its toll on her decision making. She had limited "emotional maturity" – often acting childlike. She spoke in "baby talk" and looked to more mature inmates for guidance. Her IQ was low and her ability to function even in prison was limited. Other inmates berated her and took advantage of her. In the prison subculture inmates have their own hierarchy of "approved" crimes and child molesters, baby killers and other heinous crimes are frowned upon by the general inmate population. She was a simple, battered, torn woman doomed to spend her life in prison living with the knowledge that she played a part in the death of her own child (although her real comprehension of this was limited).

The boyfriend got life in prison, so in some strange way justice was done. We denied their request to write to each other because, as administrators, we felt the relationship was toxic. She didn't understand fully why we prohibited her from contacting him. I believed I was doing what was best for her, but she didn't see it that way.

Many of the women would tell me of their experiences in the sex industry, earning money for their boyfriend or pimp. The men forced the women into prostitution to support their drug habits. Often the sex acts were so degrading and despicable I could barely listen. They engaged in group sex, gang rapes, public sex acts. They made films of the women engaged in sex acts with animals or, even worse, children. The women spoke about feeling trapped into continuing the work. They also talked about the need to be high to carry out some of the sex acts they were being made to perform. I can only speculate, but I imagine the scars from these experiences are deep and the hatred strong.

THE INCAPACITATION OF FEMALES

Incarcerating females is different from incarcerating males. They have unique needs both emotionally and physically, particularly three areas: prison families, sexual victimization, and differential programming.

Prison Families

Male prisoners often struggle for dominance and power in prison, but female prisoners tend to revert to the nurturing passive roles promoted by society. This is not to suggest that there is no violence in female prisons or that dealing with incarcerated females is somehow easier; rather like much of the female experience, incarcerated life is markedly different than it is for male counterparts. For example, family-like structures often are created within female facilities. In these family structures each individual plays a role. The more dominant women take on the father role, others become mothers, and the younger less experienced or developmentally challenged inmates take on the role of the children.

This family life on the inside can even reach the level of extended family membership, with individuals playing the roles of grandparent, aunt or uncle, or even cousin. The construction of this social system provides women with close bonds and emotional relationships. These supportive relationships give the women a support network and help keep each other out of trouble.

Public displays of affection are much more prevalent in female correctional facilities than in male facilities. On one hand, this open and expressive emotionality within women's facilities can create problems for correctional officers and administrators. On the other hand, some correctional agents promote family style behavior as a means of informal social control of the inmates.

FROM A WARDEN'S PERSPECTIVE

When I first heard that female offenders formed "pseudo families" in prison I thought it was an unhealthy idea. I watched as female inmates of all races and ethnic backgrounds hooked up to form a family. There were grandparents (pretending to be both genders), aunties, sisters, mothers, etc. Usually the mother of the clan was the woman who had the most time under her belt. At first I really thought it was odd. I had read about the phenomenon, but I hadn't witnessed it first hand. The more I watched and the more I asked, I found it not necessarily to be a bad thing. Although as a Warden, I wouldn't promote such a concept, the pseudo families had some benefits to the smooth running of the institution.

Women are social beings and what they miss most during their incarceration are their children and their bond with others. These pseudo families provide an opportunity for them to get what many didn't have growing up – unconditional love and support and a family to watch over them. The pseudo families function like a stereotypical American family. Each member has defined roles; Dad is the enforcer and provider. The Pseudo Dad might provide extras from the chow hall or special commissary items for the group. The Mom is the nurturer. She helps the family stay together, solves problems and is the listening ear when things get tough. Mom also encourages the family to get involved in programs and is proud when they accomplish tasks. The siblings, both brothers and sisters, may fight but, they also provide support for each other. I have spoken with many women about these families and, for the most part, they are not sexual in nature and can produce positive results.

Some families do form for more negative reasons like sexual relationships. In these cases, the dominant female (who often acts/looks more manly) plays the husband and offers protection to the family members in exchange for sexual favors. I know some of these pseudo families are fronts for prison gang activity and homosexuality but it should not be hard to differentiate between the two types. If the pseudo family turns out to be gang related, I break them up immediately. Gangs in prisons run drugs, recruit new members, and handle numerous scams at the facility.

Some feel that these relationships are formed as part of the inmates' anti-authority attitude. They know the formation of a family, as well as inmate on inmate sexual contact, is wrong, but continue to do it just to defy the institution's management. The formation of the family and the females' openness about it is a way for them to publicly defy staff. Correctional staff needs to be familiar with the pseudo family structures forming in their facilities. My experience has been that female inmates are very open, so if you work in the field and you get an opportunity, ask them about their prison family. A more comprehensive understanding of these groups will allow correctional administrators to draw from the positives of these groups while combating the negatives at the same time.

Inmate Sexual Victimization

The incapacitation of women creates a dangerous arrangement. Correctional officers are predominantly male, so the environment in female facilities is conducive to sexual misconduct and victimization. As detailed above, many of the women in prison find themselves there as a result of previous victimization by men. This hardship is once again a reality for many of the women incarcerated.

Correctional officers use their power to coerce women into providing sexual favors in return for menial items and privileges. In addition to this coerced consent and sexual bartering, rape is not an uncommon occurrence. Correctional officers and staff rape female inmates with little threat of reprisal. Victims are often seen as liars or the officers claim it was consensual and often face transfer to a male facility as the punishment. It may be that there is not a great deal of public scrutiny because, much like in the other systems of criminal justice, there is a code of silence that limits

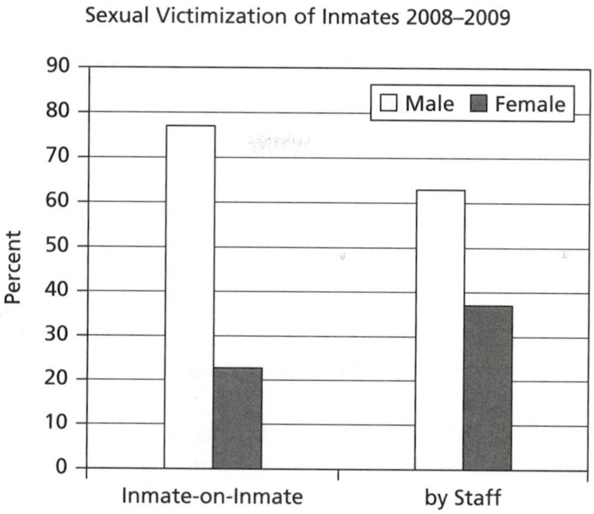

the publication of such events (it should be noted that the reporting of such events is a mandatory requirement of all institutions). Human Rights Watch and Amnesty International have admonished the U.S. government for what appears to be a rampant epidemic in female correctional facilities, but few scholars believe this has had a significant impact. The difficulty for the inmates in substantiating claims provides them with minimal incentive in reporting the events.

Though women constitute only 7 percent of the total incarcerated population (inmates of prisons and jails) they account for 37 percent of inmate sexual victimization complaints against staff. With such a small proportion of the incarcerated population representing such a large number of reported victimizations a serious problem seems apparent. And, sexual victimization in correctional facilities is not limited to staff/inmate victimizations. Inmate on inmate victimization also occurs and again women are overrepresented. Clearly female correctional institutions have a serious problem with protecting their inmates.

FROM A WARDEN'S PERSPECTIVE

The Prison Rape Elimination Act, commonly known as PREA, was established in 2003 by the federal government as an attempt to thwart sexual assault and victimization in prison. The act addresses inmate on inmate sexual violence and also staff misconduct. It also established the first systematic data reporting of prison sexual assault. As the Warden, I personally address sexual activity in prison and remind staff that inmates cannot, by law, consent to sexual activity. Unfortunately, in my career I have seen many staff who nevertheless got involved in inappropriate and sexual relationships with inmates.

Those who work in the field know that inmates will tell. They may not tell today, they might not even tell tomorrow, but when the situation is advantageous to them, they will tell. One long time correctional officer was involved with an inmate over an 18 month period. He was bringing in jewelry, perfume, makeup and hair ties in exchange for sexual favors. The inmate, quite astute, had kept coded documentation which outlined when and where they had these sexual encounters. She also kept the officer's DNA on her garments and swabbed it on the paper in her log book. When he decided the relationship had gone too far, she told. Her evidence collection and documentation was so good it was an open and shut criminal case. He's now doing 15 years for sexual assault and will register as a sex offender for the rest of his life. I felt bad for his family. His children had to go to school after their father's mug shot was shown on the evening news.

Another concern with female inmates is their lack of sexual boundaries. Many have been victims of sexual assault and violence on the outside. Some have worked in the sex industry and have no concept of sexual appropriateness. For example, during shower time many female inmates prance naked in the day room for all to see. Some strip for inmates and officers and inappropriately touch themselves in plain view. None of this behavior is allowed and it is dealt with accordingly, but for a new male officer (often referred to by female inmates as "new cock"), it is a world that can be both shocking and tempting.

I have seen ranking officers, medical professionals, and even a psychiatrist establish inappropriate and sometimes sexual relationships with inmates. They not only lost their jobs, careers, professions and sometimes freedom, but their dignity and integrity as well.

Male prisoners are not immune to sexual activity. Male inmates, however, tend to be secretive about homosexual activity. Some male inmates justify to themselves homosexual behavior thinking that if they are the aggressor they do not consider themselves "gay". Staff and inmates in male prisons also have inappropriate relationships and although I have not seen any data on prevalence, I would guess male and female inmates' sexual activity is equal.

I can't stress enough how important a part of our mission it is to keep inmates safe. This includes keeping them free from the pressures of sexual harassment and keeping them safe from prison rape. I tell staff to think of the inmates as their sister, daughter, or mother. If one of my family members had to do time, they would want them to be in a safe environment, free from staff and inmate sexual predators.

Programming

Programs like automobile repair training that are popular in male correctional facilities may not be as well received in female institutions, so other career training programs may be more appealing. Like male correctional facilities, however, drug treatment and basic education programs are an important aspect of female correctional programming. Several components of successful programming in female facilities include programs that are led by caring female staff, including training that teaches skills that help women with family tasks, and working with peers. Mentoring classes have been well-received and show some empirical promise. Additionally, programs that encourage and develop parenting skills are popular, as many of the women incarcerated are mothers.

FROM A WARDEN'S PERSPECTIVE

You can't simply paint a program pink and call it a specialized female offender program. Unfortunately, all too often, that's what we do. Because female offenders come to prison under a different set of circumstances than their male counterparts, they require gender specific programming in order to succeed.

Women require programming that is gender based, teaches empowerment, educates and assists them in becoming independent and self-confident. Many female offenders have been victims of prior trauma. They need to learn coping skills to handle their past trauma as well as programs that help them understand the totality of the circumstances behind their criminal offending. One program I have been involved with for a decade is ESUBA (abuse spelled backward). ESUBA educates women about abuse and domestic violence. Using a psycho-educational approach, the 24 week, two tiered program empowers women to learn alternate methods of coping with violence. It teaches the inmates the impact of violence on children and the possible impact violence had on their offending behavior. With proven results in trauma symptom reduction, ESUBA has been expanded and is currently being taught to free world women who work in the sex industry.

Programs that teach specific parenting skills to single mothers are also important. I've always said "you can't give what you don't have." Many female offenders are ignorant of basic parenting techniques like time out, or positive reinforcement. A disproportionate percentage of them grow up in a violent home; many female offenders only know how to discipline their children with violence. I used to ask them in group session, "if you hit your child and they still don't comply, what do you do then?" The overwhelming response was "hit them harder." We all know that doesn't work and it often results in injury (both physical and psychological) to the child.

Female offenders need to be equipped with job skills that will enable them to become self sufficient upon release. It is prudent for facilities to check which vocations are most popular in their geographic area and implement programs accordingly.

Lastly, I am a big proponent of art and music in prisons, particularly in female facilities. Women are emotional beings and art and music programs allow them to express themselves in appropriate ways. Every facility I've been at that had an art, music, dance or creative writing program had fewer incidents. It gave the inmates something to work towards (they have to remain disciplinary free to participate). ArtSpring of Florida is a non-profit organization that facilitates art programs behind bars. One of the programs they offer, called Inside Out, is a dance expression program. The inmates "act" out their apology letter to their crime victim, or write about the impact their incarceration has on their children. I have personally seen women be transformed in this program and gain insight into their lives.

As a Warden, I understand that programs in general, and art and music programs specifically, look like "feel good" programs and may offend crime victims and law abiding citizens. That said, we need to remember that almost every inmate has an out date. I would prefer to have inmates released with a better understanding of their circumstances and self-awareness.

Incarcerating Moms

Incarcerating women brings with it the complication of incarcerating mothers. Many of the women that enter correctional facilities are pregnant, new mothers, or the mother of multiple children. The fathers of many of these children are already institutionalized leaving the state with limited options and opportunity for maintaining child/parent relationships. Many states and the federal government have implemented strategies that allow for increased visitation and even housing for babies and young children. Keeping mothers with their children even for short periods of time can improve the otherwise unfortunately limited outcomes and challenges forced upon these children. New and innovative means are being developed as more women, and consequently more mothers, are being incarcerated. While attempts have been made to maintain relationships between mothers and their children, the experience for children of having a mother in prison or jail creates generational strains that affect the future outcomes of these children. The concepts of visitation and generational effects are discussed further.

Visitation and Generational Effects

Several approaches are used to maintain contact between children and their mothers. Some facilities provide training in parenting and childhood education. Many facilities, however, only provide mothers with increased hours of visitation and easier access to children with increased opportunities to directly interact and play. Other facilities have taken more direct approaches by creating separate housing units within facilities where children live with their mothers for the first 3 months after the child is born to as old as up to 3 years and even beyond. Some facilities employ a method of rewarding well-behaved mothers with extended time periods of interaction that can last up to 5 days. These different approaches do not get around the fact that the mother is, in the end, in confinement. The main goal of prisons may always be security and the confinement of inmates, leaving the children of inmates with the stark reality of an absentee parent whose only direct interaction with them takes place in an institutional setting.

The lack or reduction in parental contact can have long lasting effects on the children of incarcerated women. Research is increasing on the effect that incarcerated parents have on the likelihood of their children becoming involved in juvenile delinquency. Initial findings point to increases in juvenile delinquency for children with parents that are incarcerated. So a cycle of institutionalization is perpetuated within these families. This cycle has hit minority and underprivileged populations the hardest. The ability to break the cycle is compounded by the generational poverty of the large number of members in the lower classes of the U.S. that are especially affected by incarceration. The evidence seems to support the fact that children are most affected when the incarcerated parent is their mother. Mothers play a significant role in the emotional development of their children and the absence of the maternal bond at crucial points in this development can, at the very least, exacerbate preexisting tendencies of delinquency. Many of the causes that may have pushed the mother into crime-victimization, poverty, etc.-are also experienced by their children. The incarceration of mothers adds another risk factor thrusting their children in the direction of crime. Though not deterministic in any sense and certainly not without hope, the children of incarcerated parents, especially incarcerated mothers, are faced with an uphill battle and limited opportunities.

CONCLUSION

The rate of female crime appears to be increasing. Over the past decade there has been a steady pattern of growth and currently more females are responsible for crime than at any other period in history. While male crime is on the decline female crime is on the rise. The academic and correctional communities are playing catch-up to try to respond to this unpredicted phenomenon.

Though knowledge is limited, increased access to female offenders and greater interest in creating correctional institutions responsive to their situations are prompting the development of new theories and ideas surrounding women and crime. Researchers and theorists propose theories ranging from the masculinization of women to the effects of the patriarchical power structure limiting women's life chances and forcing them into crime as explanations for this shift. Some blame the empowerment of the women's liberation movement.

Though female crime is increasing the nature of female offending is different than males. Women face a unique experience along their path from offending through incarceration. Their experience, causes, and patterns of offending are different. They have to deal with events that male offenders are not subjected to. Women offenders are often the victims of crimes and find themselves committing crimes as a means to escape. Responding to sexual and other physical abuse seems to be a key reason women are turning to crime. Simply escaping the abuse can be a crime as a youth and running away at young ages often leads to lives of prostitution and drug dealing, crimes for which women are responsible for a large portion of the offenses. While these may not account for all crimes committed by women, it is certainly a unique component of their offending that far fewer of their male counterparts deal with. To the extent that this is the case, legitimate outlets for females to escape such relationships and abusive situations could greatly alleviate some of the growth in female offending. More outreach programs, battered women's shelters, and increased enforcement of domestic abuse cases may be just a few of the approaches that can help prevent female offending.

The incarceration of women also demonstrates a significant issue. The needs of women are not the same as the needs of men. Physically, emotionally, medically, women bring a number of issues that may have otherwise been ignored or neglected in male facilities. With such a small population of female offenders, women have been placed in institutions with programs and facilities that were developed for men. Different programs are needed and have only begun to be implemented. Given the unique pathways into offending, it will be interesting to see the effect different programs have on females.

One of the greatest issues facing women that men do not experience and male facilities do not accommodate is pregnancy and motherhood. A great number of incarcerated women are mothers and the current correctional set up is trying to account for the importance of fostering strong mother/child relationships. Special programs and areas for expectant and new mothers are increasing and the development of specialized parenting classes is becoming essential in female corrections.

Another special challenge facing female corrections is the high rate of sexual victimization of inmates that is occurring. Being admonished by the international community, the U.S. Department of Corrections has paid a great deal of attention to this predicament. The seemingly systemic problem of sexual abuse in female institutions is perhaps the greatest issue facing female corrections today.

DISCUSSION QUESTIONS

1. Discuss prison families and how they are seen from a warden's perspective.
2. Explain gender-oriented theories of offending.
3. What are some reasons female crime is increasing while male crime is declining?
4. Why do women pose a unique challenge for correctional institutions?

SELECTED REFERENCES

Daly, Kathleen. 1998. Gender, Crime, and Criminology. In Michael Tonry ed. *The Handbook of Crime and Punishment*. New York: Oxford University Press.

Miller, Jody and Christopher W. Mullins. 2006. The Status of Feminist Theories in Criminology. In Francis T. Cullen, John Paul Wright, and Kristie R. Blevins eds. *Taking Stock: The Status of Criminological Theory. Advances in Criminological Theory, Vol. 15*. New Brunswick: Transaction Publishers.

U.S. Bureau of Justice Statistics. 2011. National Prisoner Statistics 2009. Washington, D.C.: U.S. Government Printing Office.

U.S. Federal Bureau of Investigation. 2011. *Crime in the United States, 2009: Uniform Crime Reports*. Washington, D.C.: U.S. Government Printing Office.

PART V

Policy Perspectives

The close of the twentieth century saw hopes rise and fall, as research has provided a glimmer of hope for those who believed that the social sciences have the analytical tools to understand crime and to contribute to formation of public policies to deal with it. This research appears to be based on empirical findings and to challenge much of the "conventional wisdom" about crime, criminal behavior, and the administration of justice. There is a new appreciation of the complex dimensions of criminal behavior and of the fact that the law-enforcement function is only one role of the police. The courts are increasingly viewed as organizations composed of small groups, and it is recognized that rehabilitative techniques have had a low success rate—although it can be argued that efforts have never been extensive enough to accurately evaluate their efficacy. In addition, the dominant approach has been that criminal justice is a system.

Research should be one essential variable included in formulating public policies. If government decisions were not influenced by politics, one might be able to show how the findings of social scientists could be directly applied to solving a public problem. Ideally, policies should reflect state-of-the-art research, the best of our expert wisdom. Yet public decisions arise from a complicated confluence of public and legislative recognition of a problem, well-defined and measured solutions in the policy realm, and negotiation in the political arena. A political tug-of-war among interest groups is very apparent in certain policy areas such as gun control, where both sides are organized, have bolstered legal claims allowing them to fight their cause in multiple branches of government, and have substantial public support. In his chapter, "An Overview of Gun Control Policy in the United States," Kleck argues that public opinion and politics on gun control are not reflective of the research that has been conducted. He argues that although the issue of gun control is highly publicized, little attention is paid to the empirical evidence.

NEW RESEARCH AND POLICY PERSPECTIVES

Recently, new problems have been springing up in the criminal justice system, which are leaving more questions than answers. With the media's new fascination on some of these topics, more and more research is being conducted to see how our system should handle these new problems.

WHITE-COLLAR CRIME

The study and interest in white-collar crime amplified following the collapses of WorldCom, Tyco, ENRON, and other major companies wrought with fraud. The saliency of the Bernie Madoff Ponzi scheme has continued the push for understanding and creating policies related to high-profile, high-dollar criminal activity. Most traditional conceptualizations of the causes of crime fall short in explaining why wealthy individuals would commit crimes simply to acquire more wealth. In their chapter, "The Problem of White Collar Crime, and Forestalling Future Epidemics". Grabosky and Shover propose a three-pronged approach to reducing white-collar crime. Through lure reduction, external oversight, and internal oversight and self-restraint, they posit methods of white-collar crime reduction that will carry the United States well into the future.

Historically white-collar criminals have been punished very laxly. They would be sentenced to fines, community service, probation, but rarely prison; however, after some of the notorious scandals, white-collar criminals started receiving harsher sentences. The passing of the Sarbanes–Oxley Act defined new crimes in the corporate world and increased the penalties for some of these white-collar crimes. Although this policy was passed with the intentions of reducing corporate fraud, there is no evidence to support that the reforms mandated by this policy have led to any reduction in corporate fraud. In fact, some studies show that the companies that exercised the strictest controls mandated by the new law actually had higher incidences of fraudulent activity.

BIOSOCIAL PERSPECTIVE

Other areas of increasing policy importance include exploring new ways of increasing the effectiveness of programs. Biology's role in behavior has become an increasingly relevant area of interest in the social sciences. With the work of Kevin Beaver and others the interdependence of biology and society in affecting individual behavior has created interesting policy questions in need of further discussion. He explores some of these issues on the prevention and treatment of criminal behavior in his chapter, "Prevention and Treatment from a Biosocial Perspective." From a biosocial perspective he identifies several areas of interaction between biology and society along with prevention strategies such as educating parents-to-be on the importance of a healthy pregnancy and providing them with adequate prenatal health-care. He also discusses treatment strategies that include using genetics to determine individual eligibility for specific programs.

The biosocial perspective argues that a multitude of different factors lead to crime and antisocial behavior, including genetic factors, neuropsychological factors, environmental factors, and evolutionary factors. This perspective is a departure from the traditional criminological theories, which for the most part overlook the possibility of genetic factors in the possible explanations to crime. Although the biosocial perspective shows promise, it is surrounded by a huge controversy. Many scholars argue that this type of research can lead only to inhumane, oppressive policies. They theorize that biosocial research could lead to a new eugenics movement. Other scholars argue that these types of claims are unfounded and that research is not guided by potential policy implications, but rather by empirical evidence and the pursuit of truth. Despite the debate, the way that biosocial research can inform policy is not known right now, and it might not be known for years; however, emerging evidence is showing that biosocial research may be quite useful in developing programs to prevent crime and delinquency.

SPECIALIZED COURTS

Specialized courts, sometimes referred to as problem-solving courts, have been used to address a number of concerns brought about during modern court reform movements. The common narrative is that specialized courts focusing on drugs, domestic violence, or some other nuanced aspect of crime are highly successful in curing the ills to which they are focused. In her chapter, "Specialized Courts," Mae C. Quinn addresses a number of unmentioned facts pertaining to these courts and offers up some narratives that are not entirely positive.

Many question whether specialized courts are as helpful as they seem. These courts do have benefits, including more efficiency, relieving the pressure of time-consuming cases from the general courts, and instituting special rules. Also, judges in specialized courts tend to have a greater understanding of the issue and are therefore able to give a fairer ruling; however, along with these advantages come disadvantages, such as taking away money and resources from the general court and encouraging special interest groups to take an interest in trying to influence the court's decisions. The more important question though is, do specialized courts lower the rates of recidivism? The empirical research on whether or not specialized courts lower recidivism has shown promising results. Many studies find that the defendants of drug courts, mental health courts, domestic courts, and community courts all have lower rates of recidivism when compared to defendants in general courts. With these promising results, more and more specialized courts are springing up.

COMPSTAT AND COMMUNITY POLICING

Perhaps the most widely adopted reform in policing in the last two decades has been the implementation of Compstat among police departments. In an attempt to mirror the results experienced in New York City, agencies throughout the United States have adopted Compstat-like programs. Weisburd and colleagues explore the implementation and saliency of Compstat throughout U.S. police agencies in their chapter, "The Growth of COMPSTAT."

Compstat is a multilayered approach to the reduction of crime, personnel and resource management, and improvement of quality of life. It includes Geographic Information Systems, which can map crime and locate problems. The introduction of Compstat had many convinced that it would help bring down the crime rate. In fact, this new approach was credited for reducing New York's subway crime by 27 percent and reducing New York's overall crime rate by 60 percent. Although many scholars find Compstat to be successful, others think that its effect on the crime rate has been grossly overestimated, and that it may have had only a small effect on lowering the crime rate. These scholars argue that many other factors occurred at the time that Compstat was introduced, meaning that we cannot be sure Compstat actually affected the crime rate. Alongside the introduction of Compstat came the training and deployment of 5,000 new, better-educated police officers, harsh zero tolerance policies on petty crime, programs that moved hundreds of thousands of citizens from welfare to jobs, the end of the crack epidemic, and many other factors. Also, Compstat may encourage police officers to not report crime to create a false impression of community problems.

With all of the Compstat criticism, many scholars look to community policing for answers. Community policing is the newest form of policing, which emphasizes that the most important role of police officers should be partnering with the community to make neighborhoods safer. Many scholars find that community policing makes the citizens of the community feel safer despite the actual rates of crime. Others argue that actually reducing the crime rate is more important than making citizens feel safe. In their chapter, "Discovering the Impact of Community Policing," Xu and colleagues further expand on community policing, as they discuss the structure of community policing and its impact on crime and disorder.

Now that we have experienced almost 20 years of harsher crime control policies, we ask if we have made a difference. Some will point to the leveling off of the crime rate since the mid-1970s to argue that the tougher policies have worked, but most scholars point to the doubling of the incarcerative population during the past decade as proof that these policies have failed. Walker and Cole argue in their chapter, "Putting Justice Back into Criminal Justice: Notes for a Liberal Criminal Justice Policy," that the policies of the last four decades have not reduced crime, and that more liberal policies would be more likely to reduce crime. Will new research and policies lead to the solution?

WRITING ASSIGNMENTS

1. Should legislators be responsible to public opinion and pass the laws about issues that citizens are concerned about, or should legislators be guided by studies, research, and practice?
2. How might interest groups influence the criminal justice system? Provide more than one example.
3. Describe the new areas of criminal justice research, and how they might affect future criminal justice policies.
4. Newer research is challenging many of the assumptions we had on criminal behavior. Is it appropriate to change our policies if contradictory evidence emerges?

26

Discovering the Impact of Community Policing

Yili Xu, Mora L. Fiedler and Karl H. Flaming

The main purpose of the present study is to demonstrate the structure, mechanisms, and efficacy of community policing and its impact on perceived disorder, crime, quality of life in the community, citizens' fear, and satisfaction with the police. It compares traditional and community policing paradigms on three dimensions: goal, measurement of outcome, and approach to crime. It concludes that community policing has a comprehensive, community-oriented goal, targets both disorder and crime, and emphasizes both organizational and community measures in police evaluation. It also addresses the criticisms of community policing and tests the heatedly debated relationships concerning community policing, disorder, crime, citizens' fear, and collective efficacy. The major findings of the study include (1) Harcourt's falsification of Skogan's findings is invalid because of the methodological flaws, and therefore does not negate the disorder-crime nexus; (2) Sampson and Raudenbush unintentionally demonstrate, through their reciprocal feedback models, that crime and disorder are indirectly related; (3) disorder has strong direct, indirect, and total effects on crime even with collective efficacy being controlled for; (4) contrary to intuition, disorder elicits more fear than crime; (5) community policing reduces crime indirectly; (6) collective efficacy plays a far less significant role in controlling disorder, crime, and fear than community policing; and (7) citizens' fear and perceived life quality are significant predictors of citizen satisfaction with the police.

Source: Yili Xu, Mora L. Fiedler and Karl H. Flaming "Discovering the Impact of Community Policing: The Broken Windows Thesis, Collective Efficacy, and Citizens' Judgment," Journal of Research in Crime and Delinquency, vol. 42 no. 2 147–186.

THE THEORETICAL FRAMEWORK

In both the literature of community policing and the field of law enforcement, there have been heated debates over the philosophy, mechanisms, and efficacy of community policing. Although many believe that community policing has advanced beyond the defining stage, its ability to meet its goals remains largely untested (Sadd and Grinc 1996), and substantial disagreement exists among criminologists, legal scholars, policy makers, and criminal justice practitioners.

Wilson and Kelling (1982), in their classic work, *Broken Windows*, emphasize the prioritization of order maintenance in relation to community policing. They believe that widespread physical and social disorders in a community break down the existing system of informal social controls and the mechanisms regulating social interaction. As a result, crime proliferates and fear overwhelms. Therefore, it is imperative for police agencies to include disorder control as a strategic measure to prevent crime and community decline.

However, some theorists (see Kinsay, Lea, and Young 1986) have argued that the police's proper role is controlling crime and it is on their ability to reduce crime rates that they should be judged. Those incidents, which might be regarded as disturbances but do not involve illegalities, are surely not the areas in which the police should intervene. Some others reject the Wilson-Kelling (1982) theory by casting serious doubt on the connection between disorder (incivility) and crime and by questioning the rationale of policing disorder. Matthews (1992), one of the earlier opponents to the idea of community policing, denies that there is any causal relationship between crime and incivilities or that they are "inextricably" linked because there is only a minimal degree of empirical support for it. Moreover, in the wake of New York City's implementation of the quality-of-life initiative under Mayor Giuliani and commissioner Bratton in the early 1990s and the unprecedented, dramatic drop in crime rates afterwards, more critics have lined up against the ideas of the broken windows theory.

Harcourt's (1998) critique of community policing (the New York style) is launched from two levels. At the empirical level, he rejects a principal study done by Skogan (1990), which is one of the few that have been attempted to provide empirical support for the disorder-crime nexus. At the theoretical level, Harcourt contends that the broken windows theory is based on a simple dichotomy between order and disorder, which does not have a preexistent fixed reality, independent of police order maintenance actions. It is order maintenance policing that creates the category and subjects of the disorderly (Harcourt 1998).

Sampson and Raudenbush's (1997, 1999) work also seriously challenges the key proposition of the broken windows thesis: disorder is linked to crime. The pivotal concept of their framework is collective efficacy, defined as social cohesion among residents combined with shared expectations for the social control of public space. They believe that the relationship between disorder and crime underlying the broken windows theory is spurious, and it is collective efficacy that influences both. The levels of disorder and crime are manifestations of the same explanatory process (Sampson and Raudenbush 1999).

The conflict also exists between community policing as envisioned by academics and theorists and community policing as interpreted and practiced by police organizations (Ziembo-Vogl and Woods 1996). These debates reflect the fundamental differences in goals, assumptions, priorities, scope of responsibilities, and evaluation criteria between the traditional policing and community policing models. The major purposes of the current study are as follows: (1) to demonstrate the structure, mechanisms, and efficacy of community policing by comparing the two policing paradigms and by addressing the major criticisms of the broken windows theory; (2) to provide an empirical test on several key hypotheses that are essential to the community policing paradigm, such as, the effect of community policing on crime, the linkage between disorder and crime, and the relationships between disorder, crime, and citizen fear; (3) to test the effect of collective efficacy on citizen fear and perceived disorder, crime, and the quality of life in the community; and (4) to understand how public opinion of the police is shaped in the dynamic of community policing.

The Difference between the Goals of Traditional Policing and Community Policing: Fighting Crime Versus Enhancing the Life Quality of Citizens

The dominant criminal justice paradigm, derived from the position of President Johnson's Crime Control Commission (President's Commission on Law Enforcement and the Administration of Justice 1967), held that the police were law-enforcement agents, the front end of the criminal justice system, whose purpose was to intercept serious crimes in progress or investigate serious completed crimes and, through arrest, to initiate the processing of criminals by the "criminal justice system" (Kelling and Bratton 1998). Based on this assumption, traditional police departments have long defined their primary mission and overall effectiveness, in terms of their law enforcement tasks, primarily, investigating and arresting criminals. As a result, the guiding principle and measurement of police actions depend mainly on some particular quantities, such as the number of arrests made, crime clearance rates, and so on. An epitome of the situation is that Uniform Crime Reports are undoubtedly the most visible police performance measure (Bayley 1994). However, the danger is that this will lead to policing by and for the numbers and ignoring the real problems and needs of the community. When discussing police accountability, Trojanowicz (1998) asked,

> Is the primary function of the police to fight crime or to maintain the peace? Which is more basic, catching criminals or preventing crimes before they occur? Increasingly, the police have come to recognize that defining the function of the police exclusively in terms of crimes is problematic for several reasons. First, how much crime is there? Much of it is unreported. Secondly, how much can police, by themselves, do to affect the crime rate? And thirdly, is crime the measure that average citizens use to assess the police?

Bayley (1994) also points out that what people most want to know about—safety—is hard to measure and weakly related to what the police do, whereas what the police do is easy to measure but may not make any difference to the public's concerns.

In contrast, community policing takes a more comprehensive approach and embraces the more inclusive concept, the quality of life, as the ultimate goal of policing (Carter and Sapp 1994; Joseph 1994; Kelling and Coles 1996; Skogan 1990; Trojanowicz 1994). The definition of community policing by Trojanowicz (1994) recognizes the need to look beyond the focus of the traditional criminal justice system to find the conditions that generate crime and solutions to eradicate it. When social conditions are factored into the crime-reduction process, we gain a more accurate picture of the cost of crime. Quality of life issues, previously overlooked, are included in calculating the expense of crime. This new way of thinking looks at crime in a holistic view by relating its cost to general social conditions and its reduction to the quality of life in the community. For community policing, fighting crime is not an end by itself, but citizens' quality of life is. Arresting criminals is only a means to the goal. This paradigm shift in policing philosophy requires a change in policing strategy. That is, effective policing should not only cure the symptoms of criminality but also, more importantly, eliminate the causes of the diseases by changing the social conditions that breed crime, generate fear, and deteriorate neighborhoods.

The gist of this new approach is that it in fact expands the focus of traditional policing, rather than abandoning it and integrates the functions of traditional policing into the new paradigm. That is why Trojanowicz (1994) believed there was room for everyone under the tent (Ziembo-Bogl and Woods 1996). This broadened goal is to help communities maintain a safe environment, in which basic institutions (the family, churches, schools, commerce) can operate effectively and thrive (Kelling and Coles 1996). It raises the expectation of policing effort to not only apprehending criminals but also alleviating the fear of citizens and maintaining the quality of life in the community. In this regard, community policing represents a more advanced approach and a higher level of thinking. It has substantially expanded the vision, functionality, and effectiveness of modern policing. Wycoff and Manning (1983) sum up the essence of the new policing accurately; the need to help citizens feel comfortable in their communities, even in the face of whatever crime may exist, is a legitimate and important goal of police agencies.

The Difference in the Measurement of Outcomes Between the Two Policing Models: Crime Statistics Versus Citizens' Fear and the Quality of Life

When policing is directed solely to crime fighting, the most relevant and pragmatic measures of police performance are crime statistics. For example, clearance rates are often the single most important quantified measure of police performance used by police departments, despite being identified as an undependable measure of actual police performance (Greenwood et al. 1977;

Skolnick 1994). The questions are, as Trojanowicz (1998) asks, should those be the only categories that an officer is evaluated on, and are there not more long-term goals and quality of life issues that should be used when evaluating officers? With the traditional evaluation method, the statistics about citizens' fear and their legitimate expectations of safe neighborhoods become irrelevant. The obvious flaw in this system, as Trojanowicz and Bucqueroux (1992) put it, is that the most easily countable items may not be the best indicators of an officer's effectiveness and they may not provide the greatest benefit to the community.

Crime statistics may not be a good measure of police performance even in the context of traditional policing. Several key studies found the ineffectiveness of police actions in controlling crime (Woods and Ziembo-Vogl 1997). In general, these studies did not find covariation between conventional police effort and crime rates. For example, rapid police response led to an arrest in only 3 percent of serious crimes (Kansas City Police Department 1977). When discussing the failure of past policing strategies, Kelling and Coles (1996) point out that the problem today is that the professional crime-fighting model of policing has failed, and to such an extent that some police have all but given up on the idea that they can significantly affect crime. The failure of the traditional policing approach in controlling crime suggests that using crime statistics as the only evaluation criterion is problematic. Trojanowicz (1989) criticizes the conventional evaluation process in terms of its misplaced focus. He contends that communities and neighborhoods are complex social structures. An evaluation system that relies on simplistic assessments, such as tickets issued and arrests made, may measure what requires a fraction of the officer's time and have little to do with what is actually required to do a good job. The underlying point is that the traditional evaluation process fails to involve the community, which provides the necessary external validation of police policy and action. Without the community input, it is hard to define what constitutes good police work, and the performance evaluation is less objective and meaningful as it is solely at the discretion of police agencies.

In the community-policing model, good police work is defined as meeting citizens' needs and expectations, and the bottom line of it is to make people feel safe in their communities. According to Trojanowicz and Bucqueroux (1992), crime is not the measure that average citizens use to assess the police. What citizens are most concerned with and confront daily are their fear and the quality of life in their neighborhoods. Many researchers agree that fear of crime was more prevalent than crime because it reflected not only direct and indirect victimizations but broader conditions of disorder in the community as well (Lewis and Salem 1985; Skogan 1987; Taylor 1997; Taylor and Covington 1993). Empirical studies show a strong support for the argument that disorder constitutes an important source of citizens' fear. Covington and Taylor's (1991) study finds that resident perceptions of incivilities are the strongest predictor of fear; and Perkins and Taylor's (1996) investigation reveals that fear of crime was significantly related to all of the measures of community disorder across all three methods (each with a different ecological measure of disorder). This disorder-fear nexus underlies the importance of disorder control as a means to fear reduction.

In the United States, according to Silverman and Della-Biustina (2001), earnest police attention to fear of crime was first spurred by the 1960s victims' rights movement and criminal justice research, shifting many urban police departments to view the fear of crime as a legitimate police goal. As a result, fear of crime became a prominent issue for the police, and fear reduction was recognized as an important police function. When people have fear they tend to conclude that the police are unwilling or unable to deal with neighborhood problems. This implies that citizens' fear and perceptions of neighborhood conditions may translate directly into residents' evaluations of police performance. Thus, citizens' fear and perceived life quality should be included as the external measures of police effectiveness and accountability, in addition to crime indicators. These measures tie police performance to the feedback of people they serve and make the police accountable to citizens and the community. Impressive crime statistics do not necessarily mean that crime rates are low, people feel safe, police action is effective, or current approach is justified. However, when people have fear walking in their own neighborhoods, clearly, something needs to be done by the police.

The Difference in the Targets of the Two Policing Approaches: Crime Versus Disorder

Traditional policing is incident-oriented. Such an approach does not change the total number of criminals in society at any given time except changing their locations (i.e., moving some of them from the streets to prisons). This practice requires that someone has become a victim before the police act. The police will not take action against disorderly behavior until it has escalated into a criminal act, nor will they address the social conditions that spawn crimes. In this sense, the traditional approach is institutionally indifferent before an individual has turned into a criminal, a crime has been actualized, or someone has been victimized. However, if responding to incidents is all that the police do, the community problems that cause or explain many of these incidents will never be addressed and so the incidents will continue and their number will perhaps increase (Wilson and Kelling 1989).

Aiming at a more effective way to fight crime, community policing emphasizes proactive policing and crime prevention. As Trojanowicz and Bucqueroux (1992) suggest, the best solution for any crime is prevention—dealing with the problem before harm is done. In the long run, crime prevention may actually reduce the number of criminals and lower the social cost of crime. Proactive policing requires eliminating the social conditions of crime, and considers incivilities as a major and immediate condition that breeds crime, while recognizing the functions of "root causes" (poverty, racism, and economic injustices) and normative factors (such as family values). Consequently, its major strategy for dealing with crime is to "fix broken windows."

The order maintenance policy is based on a crucial assumption of the connection between disorder and crime, and efficient policing must target both. Wilson and Kelling (1982) state that at the community level, disorder and crime are usually inextricably linked. Serious street crime flourishes in areas in which disorderly behavior goes unchecked. Kelling (1985) further argues that policing disorder can affect crime control by preventing disorderly behavior from escalating into criminal acts, by encouraging the moral self-defense activities of citizens. Whether malevolent or innocent in intent, disorderly behavior powerfully shapes the quality of urban life and citizens' views of both their own safety and the ability of government to ensure it (Kelling 1987). However, as mentioned previously, the cornerstone of the broken windows thesis—the assumption of the disorder-crime linkage—is facing serious challenges from different perspectives and angles. Now, it comes to a crucial point, where the order maintenance policing would become groundless if we could not answer these challenges. Our response to them focuses on some key criticisms.

Harcourt (1998) concluded, after replicating Skogan's (1990) study, that Skogan's data do not support the claim that reducing disorder deters more serious crime. His evidence is (1) all types of crimes, except for robbery, included in Skogan's study are either not significantly related to disorder or become nonsignificant when neighborhood poverty, stability, and race are held constant. (2) When five Newark neighborhoods are set aside, because of their excessive influence on the statistical findings, the relationship between robbery victimization and disorder disappears (Harcourt 1998).

However, Harcourt's (1989) replication procedure bears several flaws, which make his conclusions questionable. First, when explaining his replication results, Harcourt focused exclusively on the p values and failed to take into consideration the potential impact of the small sample size on them. When a test fails to reject a null hypothesis, people generally tend to conclude that the alternative hypothesis is not supported. However, this is only true when the test commands adequate statistical power. As Harcourt acknowledged, the total neighborhoods included in Skogan's (1990) study is 40 and the estimated effect of disorder on robbery was only based on 30 cases. As is known, a small sample size reduces statistical power and increases the chance of committing Type II error (failure to reject a null hypothesis when it is false). According to Cohen (1988), a widely used rule is that a study should have 80 percent power to be worth conducting. That is, a minimal statistical power of .8 is required before one can consider the argument that the lack of significance may be interpreted as evidence that the alternative hypothesis is false. A nonsignificant result for a study with low power is truly inconclusive (Aron and Aron 2002). Based on our calculation, the statistical power for a regression analysis with 30 cases, 4 independent variables, medium effect size (see Cohen 1988), and $\alpha = .05$ is approximately .3, far below the minimal requirement for a meaningful test. Therefore, Harcourt's (1998) interpretation of his replication results states more than what its power allows. The only certain conclusion that can be drawn from those results is that they are truly inconclusive.

Second, Harcourt (1998) reports that in Skogan's (1990) study, the only significant effect of disorder on robbery disappeared after he had deleted 5 Newark neighborhoods from the data set. Harcourt (1998) justifies the fairness of the deletion by arguing that given the small number of observations, it is especially important to eliminate cases that exert too much influence on the findings. The neighborhoods in Newark are skewing the results. Apparently, the action of "setting aside" five Newark neighborhoods has the same effect as a sample selection. However, the selection is not random. On the contrary, it is very subjective and systematically biased toward eliminating those cases that are most likely to make the disorder-crime nexus significant. The invalidity of such data manipulation can be seen clearly if we imagine that Skogan (1990) deleted from his analysis all the neighborhoods that show the smallest or no correlation between disorder and crime. In addition, the "disappearance" of the effect of disorder on robbery in Harcourt's (1998) replication results could also be the consequence of the further reduction in power. Deleting 5 cases from a 30-neighborhood sample is a 17 percent sample reduction. In such a situation, one should not exclude the possibilities that the nonsignificant coefficient is a result of the further attenuated power and that a Type II error has been committed.

Third, when dealing with missing values, Harcourt (1998) proposed a method of standardizing variables on their means to overcome the inappropriateness of Skogan's (1990) study that averages only the available values to get the index value for a neighborhood. Standardization of variables, however, does not resolve the problem of missing values. The simple truth is that a blank remains a blank no matter what standardization procedure is applied to it. Specifically, there is no way to compute the value of relative weight of disorder for a missing value. A close look at Harcourt's (1998) method reveals that it, too, averages available values for an index value when some variables of the index have missing values. The only difference is that the values it averaged were standardized. Thus, Harcourt's relative weight of disorder index is only relative to those variables that do not have missing values. Consequently, his replication based on the "corrected disorder" still suffers the missing value problem and may not be correct.

Harcourt (1998) also criticizes the broken windows thesis at the theoretical level. He contends that the broken windows theory is based on a recurrent, pervasive, and ubiquitous dichotomy between, for example, order and disorder, law-abiders and criminals, and so on. However, these categories, he believes, do not have a pre-existent fixed reality, independent of police order-maintenance actions. To the contrary, he argues, the category of the disorder is itself a reality produced by the method of policing. Order-maintenance policing helps create the category of the disorderly and, therefore, the subjects of the category, the disorderly people, which in turn reinforces the policing strategy. We feel these arguments are not consistent with the existing knowledge. For example, squeegeeing, turnstile jumping, and public urination had existed long before 1993 when the quality-of-life initiative was launched in New York City. The public's interpretation of these behaviors shows that broad consensus existed among members of all racial and ethnic groups as to what constituted disorderly behavior (Skogan 1990). Recently, according to Associated Press, even Catholic church officials in Italy held a news conference to denounce vagrancy, littering, and public indecency caused by drunks, bums, and lovers that have transformed the areas around their churches into "open toilets" (D'Emilio 2003). The world-wide, independent recognitions of disorderly behaviors and their disturbance to social life, and numerous media's accounts and scholarly discussions of incivilities existing in society prior to the New York Police Department order-maintenance actions reject Harcourt's (1998) assumption that the disorderly is simply created by police's order-disorder dichotomy and its aesthetic of orderliness, cleanliness, and sobriety (Harcourt 1998). The issue is clear, people recognize disorder when they see it, and uniformly want something done about it (Kelling and Coles 1996).

Collective efficacy is the key concept used by Sampson and Raudenbush (1997, 1999) to nullify the connection between disorder and crime. They believe that the relationship between disorder and crime is spurious, and their common source is collective efficacy. Disorder and crime are in fact determined by the same causal structure. It follows that the collective efficacy of residents is a critical means by which urban neighborhoods inhibit the crime and disorder (Sampson and Raudenbush 1997).

First, collective efficacy, as a very important ecological concept, is not totally new to the broken windows theory. In fact, as the bottom line of informal social control, it is implicitly part of the explanatory mechanisms in the theory. According to Sampson and Raudenbush (1997), differential ability of neighborhoods to realize the common values of residents and maintain effective social controls is a major source of neighborhood variation in violence. Socially cohesive neighborhoods will prove the most fertile contexts for the realization of informal social control. Whereas, a key argument of the broken windows thesis asserts that just as an unrepaired window sends a message that no one cares and invites more damage, so unattended disorderly behavior also acts as a signal that no one cares, with the results of more disorderly behavior and serious crime (Kelling and Coles 1994; Wilson and Kelling 1982). "No one cares" seems to be another way to say there is no collective willingness on the part of residents to intervene for the common good, and unrepaired broken windows are a signal or manifestation of dearth of neighborhood social control or collective efficacy. That is, disorder symbolizes the breakdown of both local norms of behavior and formal and informal social controls (Perkins, Meeks, and Taylor 1992; Skogan and Maxfield 1981; Taylor and Shumaker 1990). The breakdown of community control eventually leads to more disorder and crime. It is obvious that the broken windows thesis would face an explanatory gap between disorder and crime, without the elements of informal social control or collective efficacy. In their 1996 book, Kelling and Coles clearly recognized the necessary roles played by citizens in protecting the community. They contend that a logical and inescapable conclusion suggests that if order is to be restored to public space, it will not be without cost. In the current context of limited funds for urban problems, the likely cost will be in terms of different police priorities and a substantially different role for citizens in maintaining public safety.

Second, as Sampson and Raudenbush (1997, 1999) are aware of and the results of their reciprocal feedback models demonstrate, there is a reverse causation of crime on collective efficacy. Skogan (1990) first raised the concern that neighborhood social trust and residents' sense of control are simultaneously undermined by crime, most notable interpersonal crimes of violence. Liska and Warner (1991) found that robbery constrains social interactions in public settings, thereby potentially dampening social cohesion and the emergence of shared expectations among residents for taking action to protect the community. Kelling and Coles (1996) explain explicitly how crime and fear of crime break down social control mechanisms in communities. They expound that fearful citizens will lock themselves behind closed doors, stay off the streets, curtail their normal activities and associations, and abandon their basic civic obligations. As social atomization sets in and citizens withdraw physically, they also withdraw from roles of mutual support with fellow citizens on the streets, thereby relinquishing the social controls they formerly helped to maintain within the community (Kelling and Coles 1996). It follows that crime and fear of crime isolate residents and undermine mutual trust and solidarity among neighbors. When people stop interacting with one another, social cohesion is out of the question and so is shared willingness to engage in informal social control of public space. In general, social atomization works against any collective thinking and action, which are the bottom line of collective efficacy.

The results of Sampson and Raudenbush's (1999) reciprocal feedback models, shown in Table 6 of their article, confirm the reverse influence of crime on collective efficacy. Although the test corroborates the concerns of the above-mentioned researchers, the reverse causation raises a new issue. That is, it indirectly supports the proposition that disorder and crime are related. Figure 1 summarizes the results of Sampson and Raudenbush's reciprocal feedback models with reference to three key relationships between disorder (measured by systematic social observation of disorder), crime (represented by homicide rate), and collective efficacy.

What people need to realize is that once the reverse causation from crime to collective efficacy is confirmed, an indirect causal relationship between

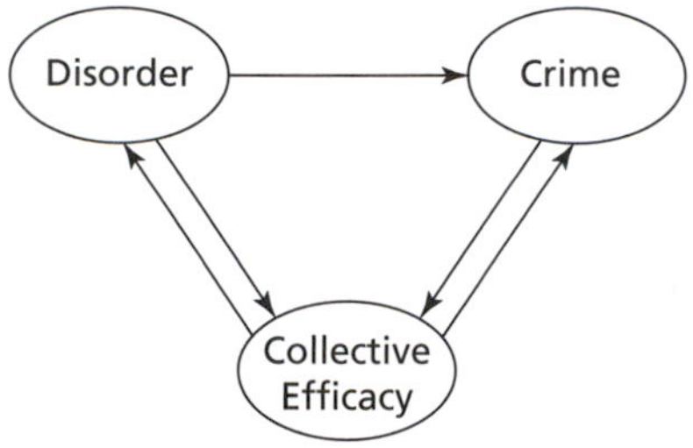

FIGURE 1 A Summary of Implications of Sampson and Raudenbush's (1999) Reciprocal Feedback Models

crime and disorder has been established. The relationship consists of two significant links: one is from crime to collective efficacy (–.06*) and the other from collective efficacy to disorder (–1.69**). It results in a positive relationship between crime and disorder mediated by collective efficacy. Now, a further question is what about the indirect relationship from disorder to crime, which would indirectly support the broken windows thesis? Somehow, Sampson and Raudenbush (1999) did not estimate the path from disorder to collective efficacy (Figure 1). If it were estimated, disorder might have a significant effect on collective efficacy because, according to Sampson and Raudenbush (1999), disorder and crime are manifestations of the same explanatory process, and therefore would be subject to the same causal structure.

In sum, the studies of both Harcourt and Sampson and Raudenbush have not convincingly demonstrated that disorder and crime are not linked. On the contrary, there is a good chance to show that the two are at least indirectly related. Researchers have long suggested that incivilities affect neighborhood crime rates and the fundamental quality and stability of the neighborhood itself (Taylor 2001). Also, even before the order maintenance policing was launched in New York City, many street police officers had long made a connection between disorder and predatory crime. They know that public drunkenness, gambling and prostitution often escalate into fights, robberies, shootings, and fearful citizens (Silverman and Della-Giustina 2001). This suggests that although we should continuously subject the disorder-crime nexus to theoretical debate and empirical test, order maintenance as a policing tactic should not be discouraged by the inconclusive results of criticisms. When discussing the linkage of disorder to crime, Kelling and Bratton (1998) further reinforce the broken windows thesis and state that waiting until serious crimes occur to intervene is too late: dealing with disorderly behavior early would prevent the cycle from accelerating and perpetuating itself.

Hope and Hough's (1988) study, which was designed explicitly to examine the broken-windows thesis, found that the rates of perceived incivilities are more strongly related to levels of fear of crime and neighborhood satisfaction than to the level of victimization itself. This implies that when a policing approach aims at citizens' fear and satisfaction, its outcomes may be more influenced by the levels of disorder control than by crime statistics. Therefore, an important avenue to crime prevention and to enhancement of citizen satisfaction is disorder control. Of course, community policing never claims that order maintenance alone is the sole means of preventing crime. Solving crimes, incarceration, social change, deterrence by other means, police presence and persuasion, citizen vigilance, reduction of opportunities, environmental design, and other factors play a role as well (Kelling and Bratton 1998).

Based on the above discussions and the purpose of the current study, we conceptualized the major theoretical constructs and relationships with reference to the key issues in community policing (see Figure 1). To highlight our primary theoretical focuses, the diagram only shows the key concepts of the structural model, omitting the control variables and measurement models.

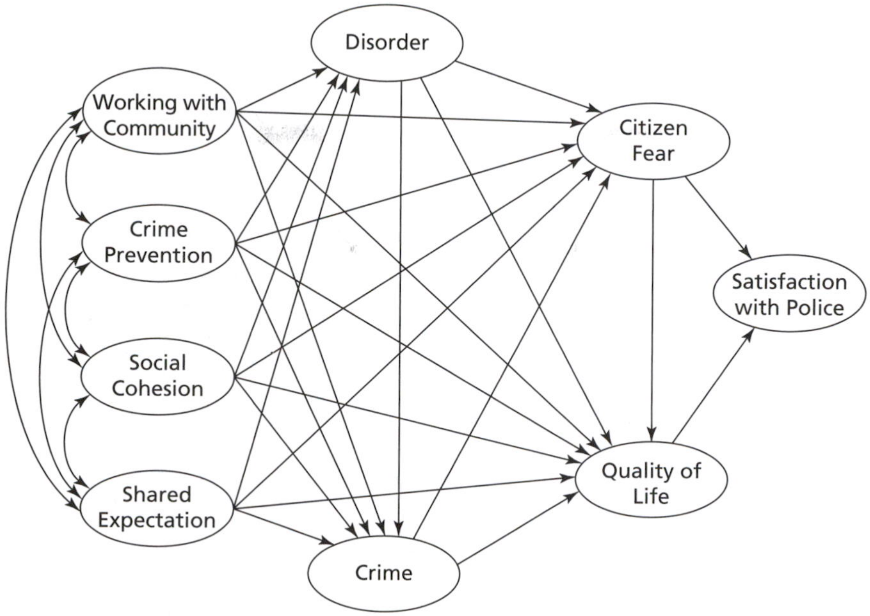

FIGURE 2 A Conceptual Model of the Major Concepts and Relationships to be Tested in this Study

Figure 2 gives a clear presentation of our conceptualization of the issues. In the community policing model, the goal of traditional policing, fighting crime, becomes an integral means to the goal of community policing, whereas fear and life qualities of citizens seem to be irrelevant to the traditional policing paradigm. This situation in turn determines how police work is evaluated in the two models. Another key hypothesized difference is in the target areas of the two systems: traditional policing limits its function only to fighting crime whereas community policing includes both disorder and crime in their service scope.

At the center of our conceptualization are the two key hypotheses: disorder—crime and disorder—fear. The two nexus are internally linked. The linkage is first based on the same origin, disorder, as we assume and the literature has repeatedly demonstrated that disorder leads to both crime and fear. Second, the two are linked because conventional thinking and experience inform us that crime causes fear. The fundamental idea underlying the linkage of the two nexus is that disorder generates fear both directly and indirectly through crime. This line of conceptualization would not be possible without assuming a community policing model. Our goal is to give a comprehensive test of all the key relationships and of the effects of community policing measures (versus collective efficacy measures) on these relationships.

THE DATA AND MODEL

The Data

The data came from The Citizen Survey conducted by the Colorado Springs Police Department in 2001.The purpose of the survey was to get citizen input on issues such as neighborhood disorder, crime, victimization, citizens' fear, perceptions of community environment, and their evaluations of police effectiveness and accountability. The survey was based on a stratified random sampling of noninstitutionalized adults 18 years or older living in the area of Colorado Springs, Colorado. The survey was conducted by telephone, and the response rate was about 60 percent. The data set contained 121 variables and 904 cases.

Measurement Models

Based on the preceding discussions, the goals of the present study, and the availability of the variables in the data set, the current model employs six groups of latent variables (see Appendix A for a complete list of the latent variables and their indicators, including the questions, codings, means, standard deviations, and factor loadings for manifest variables).

The first group represents the concept of community policing and includes two latent variables: respondents' perception of police efforts to work with the community to solve neighborhood problems (Working with Community and Crime Prevention). These two measures, though not exhaustive, represent the essence of community policing (i.e., partnership with the community to solve neighborhood problems and prevent crime). Crime prevention has different meanings for different frameworks. Kelling and Coles (1996; Coles and Kelling 1999) summarize them as follows: The traditional policing paradigm assumes that crime prevention can only be achieved through preventative patrols, deterrence, and incarceration. The "root-causes" proponents would contend that crime prevention requires the elimination or amelioration of these conditions through radical social change. For community policing, order restoration and maintenance are the major tactics for crime prevention. The current study interprets crime prevention of community policing in its broadest sense. It emphasizes the socialization/social learning component in the concept of crime prevention as an important supplement to the order restoration and maintenance tactics.

Socialization/social learning concepts require the police to increase positive stimuli and reinforcement in the community environment, especially, in the lives of youths, by interacting with them on a regular basis, promoting community norms, providing moral guidance, and reinforcing socially acceptable behaviors through activities jointly sponsored by the police and community. This dimension represents a long-term approach to crime prevention, and may reduce the "aggressiveness" of community policing and the conflicts between police actions, the law, and citizens' rights. This emphasis is based on the fact that tomorrow's criminals will come from the population of today's children. Therefore, a logical approach to crime prevention should include prevention that starts with the younger generation and rely more on the power of positive influence, persuasion, and behavioral guidance. The school liaison program or school crime education program are good examples of such an emphasis.

The second group of latent variables is designed to test the theory of collective efficacy. It is of great interest to see what role collective efficacy plays in the process of social control compared to the measures of community policing. Based on Sampson and Raudenbush's definition of collective efficacy, we developed two latent variables: social cohesion and shared expectations.

The third group includes control variables: sex, age, race, and education. Prior research has shown that attitudes toward the police, fear of crime, and perceptions of crime and disorder are related to demographic characteristics of individuals. For example, the literature on fear of crime consistently shows that women and the elderly are highly afraid of crime (Borooah and Carcach 1997; Ferraro 1994; Skogan and Maxfield 1981). As for the effect of education, Figgie (1980) reports that people with the least education, low-income, and so on exhibited the highest rates of formless fear. With regard to racial effect on fear, Perkins and Taylor (1996) found the significant block-level correlation between the two, but it disappeared when other variables were controlled for. Prior research has also addressed the relationship between demographic characteristics and citizens' evaluations of the police. Thomas and Hyman's (1977) study, which included more than 3,000 households in four urban areas, found that citizens with whom the police are statistically more likely to encounter (Black, younger citizens, those who are less affluent, and residents of inner-city areas) are significantly less favorable in their evaluations of the police than are other categories of the population. However, a recent study by Maxson, Hennigan, and Sloane (2003) found that residents' opinion of police performance did not vary by race or ethnicity once other factors (e.g., perceived disorder) were controlled for.

The fourth group of latent variables refers to three target areas of the social control process: citizen perceived disorder, less serious crime, and serious crime. Studies using resident perceptions of incivilities have found more consistent effects than studies based on onsite ratings of physical features (Taylor and Harrell 1996). Perkins and Taylor's (1996) explanation is that it may be because the items (e.g., fear and disorder) were both measured by the same source of data: resident survey. However, very high correlations found, in Taylor's (1996) study, between resident perceptions of, and independently observed, physical disorder suggest that the two should not deviate too much from each other, especially when the former is at aggregated level.

The purpose to differentiate between serious crime and less serious crime is to create, together with disorder, a spectrum of deviant behaviors varying from noncrime nuisance to serious crime, so that we can test whether the community policing measures have differential effects on different levels of deviance. In addition, we can investigate how citizens' fear and perception of the life quality are influenced by the different levels of deviance in neighborhoods.

It should be noted that the factor of disorder is measured in a general term and it conflates physical and social disorders together. When denying the significance of incivilities on the radar screen of police agencies, Matthews (1992) criticizes the Wilson-Kelling thesis as being too generalized or global, meaning it only talks about crime and incivility in general and makes little attempt to investigate them individually. Our response is that general information is as meaningful as specific information on such a research topic. Depending on what level of information is needed, either way of investigation is legitimate. Because the current study primarily focuses on the general relationships among the factors under study, using disorder in general serves the purpose properly. Besides, a global measure of disorder may be a better indicator of the overall social conditions in a community than a measure of a particular disorder. The truth is a neighborhood may not be declining when a particular type of incivility occurs. However, if a community scores high on the global measure of disorders, there is a high probability that its social control mechanisms are eroded, crime rates are high, and residents are exposed to greater fear and vulnerability. In addition, our factor analysis shows the correlation between the two latent constructs, social and physical disorders, is almost .9. On one hand, it indicates that combining the two is statistically acceptable. On the other hand, it may cause the problem of multicollinearity if the two are included in the model as separate factors.

The fifth group contains two latent variables that represent the goals of community policing and citizen input (quality of life, and citizen fear). Due to the availability of suitable variables, we measure quality of life with a single indicator, citizens' evaluation of their neighborhood qualities. The single indicator is assumed to be acceptable in this context because, as far as policing is concerned, the quality of neighborhood environment is the most relevant aspect of the quality of life in the community.

The other latent variable in this group is citizen fear. One argument in the literature is that public fear is caused more by disorder than by serious crime (Skogan and Maxfield 1981). In the current model, citizens' fear, on one hand, is considered as part of the goal of community policing, as it inevitably affects how citizens assess the quality of life in their neighborhoods. On the other hand, citizens' fear together with the perception of the life quality serves as an important criterion, based on which citizens evaluate the police.

The sixth category contains one latent variable: citizen satisfaction with the police (satisfaction with police). By including the factor, we can measure how the fulfillment of the community-policing goals relates to citizen satisfaction with the police. More important, citizens' fear, life quality, and satisfaction, which represent community feedback, provide the necessary external measures of police performance. Information on citizen satisfaction with the police may suggest, to practitioners, how implementation of the community policing strategies and achievement of its goals contribute to citizen satisfactions with police, and how to increase citizen satisfaction by improving police services.

Because the data set came from the citizen survey, all variables used in the model represent citizens' perceived or self-reported information. The unit of analysis is individual residents, as the study is to gauge the interrelations and dynamics in the community social control process through the angle of citizens and investigate how the implementation of community policing influences residents' opinions of the police. A total of 14 latent variables measured by 34 manifest variables are included in the model.

Structural Model

The structural model is specified as follows (see Figure 3 for a complete diagram of the structural and measurement models).

(a). All exogenous variables: two community policing factors, two collective efficacy variables, and four controls, have direct links to the three target area variables: disorder, less serious crime, and serious crime. This is designed to test two theories. First, it is to test the broken windows thesis

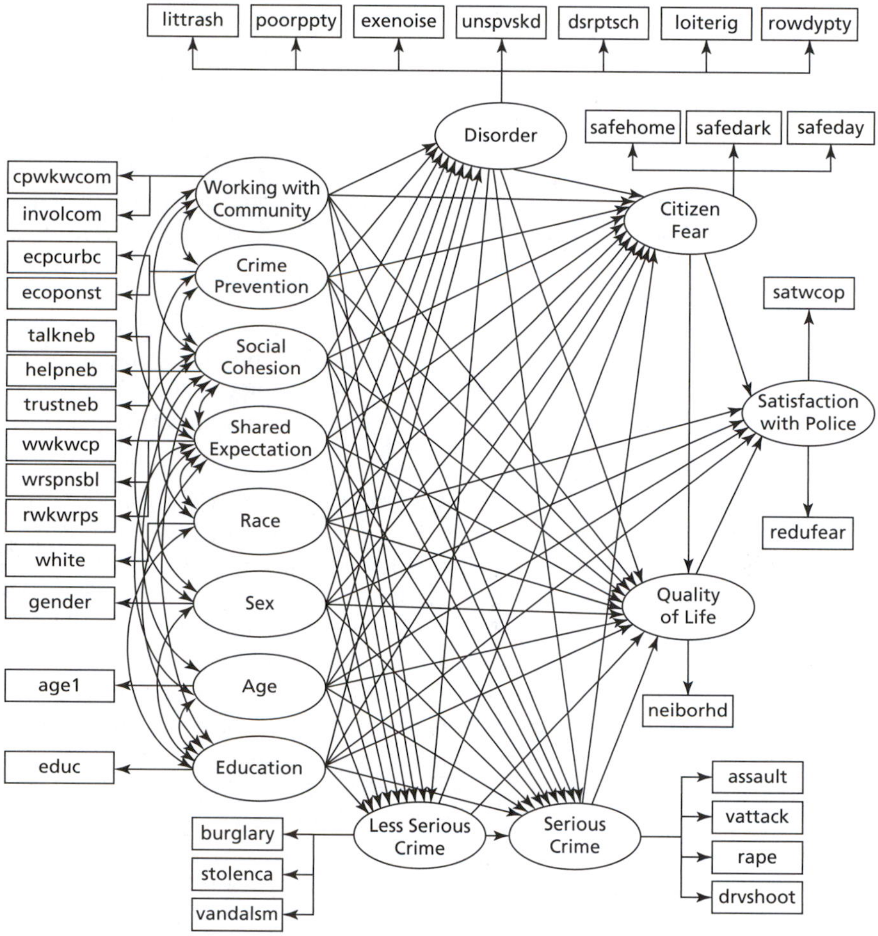

FIGURE 3 The Effects of Community Policing and Collective Efficacy Measures on Disorder, Crime, Citizen Fear, Quality of Life, and Citizen Satisfaction with the Police

and to answer the critical question of whether community policing has a significant effect on crime reduction. There are a total of six direct links from the two community policing factors to the three task variables, and they correspond to six hypotheses. The generic form of the hypotheses can be stated as follows: community policing variable x has a significant effect on reducing the level of the problem referred to by task variable y.

The second objective is to test the theory of collective efficacy. We want to see how it functions, compared to the community-policing measures. Specifically, we want to verify whether the relationship from disorder to crime disappears when collective efficacy is introduced into the model. In addition, by comparing the effects of community policing and collective efficacy side by side, we may get a clear picture of the functions, utilities, and importance of each in the community social control system. Six hypotheses may be derived from this specification. The general form of the hypotheses is: a higher level of collective efficacy represented by social cohesion and shared expectation leads to a lower level of disorder, less serious crime, or serious crime.

(b). The current model stipulates an order among disorder, less serious crime, and serious crime. That is, disorder has a direct link to both less serious crime and serious crime, and less serious crime in turn has a direct link to serious crime. The logic of the order is based on the ideas of crime development and prevention at both individual and community levels. At the individual level, as far as social disorder is concerned, the argument is that no one is born a criminal. Criminal behavior very often starts from disreputable or obstreperous, but noncriminal, behavior, and most of those who have committed serious crime are more likely to have previous records of behavioral problems ranging from minor abnormal behavior to less serious crime. If a person or child's disorderly behavior is corrected in a timely fashion, the chance for it to develop into a full-fledged criminal act may be reduced.

Social psychologists and police officers tend to agree that if a window is broken and left unrepaired, more windows will soon be broken, and "untended" behavior leads to the breakdown of community controls (Wilson and Kelling 1982). When the law enforcement agencies do not want to get involved in controlling incivilities, citing there are no formal laws they can resort to, more individuals would be encouraged, by the lack of the negative reinforcement, to test the limit of disorderly behavior along the spectrum from incivility to crime. Once incivilities are maximized, the social norms governing such behaviors will become ambiguous, and the normative pressures that prevent people from crossing the line will be off. Most important, once reaching the threshold of incivilities, problem youngsters socialized in a disorder saturated environment are very easily slip over to the other end of the spectrum—to commit crime—because society does not, or is unwilling to, set up a checking mechanism to prevent it from happening.

At the community level, urban decay, manifested by devastating disorder and crime, and collapsed moral standards, is the ideal soil for propagation of crime. It alienates people, weakens the informal social control, provides the safe haven for criminals, and makes citizens more vulnerable to crime. In general, deteriorating communities produce more criminals and victims.

The relationships among the three task variables imply three hypotheses: a higher level of disorder is likely to result in a higher level of less serious crime or serious crime, and a higher level of less serious crime is likely to lead to more serious crime. When combining these hypotheses with the hypotheses previously specified, we can derive four more sets of hypotheses about the indirect effects of community policing and collective efficacy on less serious and serious crimes. It is of great interest to test these hypotheses because of the way community policing works. It focuses on crime prevention and targets an immediate source of crime—disorder. Crime prevention in the context of community policing may imply an indirect approach to crime.

(c). Citizen fear is a central concept in this model. It mediates the social reality in the neighborhood and citizen satisfaction with police services. There are three sets of hypotheses with regard to citizens' fear. The first set tests the direct effects of community policing and collective efficacy on citizens' fear. The general statement of the hypotheses about community policing is that a higher level of community-policing effort leads to a lower level of citizens' fear. One of the assumptions of the community-policing movement is that increasing neighborhood and government responsiveness to crime will reduce the fear of crime (McGarrell, Giacomazzi, and Thurman 1997). The generic form of the hypotheses regarding collective efficacy is that a higher level of collective efficacy leads to less fear.

The second set of hypotheses is about the impact of disorder and crimes on citizens' fear. As far as disorder is concerned, extensive research has linked perceptions of physical deterioration and social incivilities with fear of crime and other outcomes relevant to neighborhood viability (Lewis and Maxfield 1980; Skogan 1990). Hope and Hough's (1988) study found that the association between disorder and fear was strong even when other aspects of community life were controlled for. However, other research shows uncertainty about the connection. For example, Miethe (1995) concludes that the empirical evidence on the direct and indirect impact of measures of neighborhood incivilities on individuals' fear of crime is inconclusive.

As for the effect of crime on fear, some researchers found a relationship between victimization (as a measure of crime) and fear (Skogan and Maxfield 1981), yet others found that victimization was either unrelated or only marginally related to fear (Gates and Rohe 1987; Liska, Sanchirico, and Reed 1988). The second set of hypotheses answers two questions. One is whether all the three target area variables have a significant effect on citizens' fear. The other is whether the three task variables generate the same amount of fear. The third set of hypotheses targets the indirect effects of community policing and collective efficacy on citizens' fear.

(d). The quality of life is a key dependent-latent variable, as it represents the ultimate goal of community policing. There are three sets of hypotheses related to it. The first set tests the direct and indirect effects of community policing and collective efficacy on citizens' perceptions of the quality of life. What we hypothesize is that an increased level of community policing or collective efficacy directly or indirectly improves citizens' perceptions of the life quality. The second set of hypotheses investigates the indirect effects of disorder, less serious crime, and serious crime on the life quality of citizens. The assumption is that the more disorder or crime, the lower perceived quality of life. The third set, which consists of one hypothesis, tests how citizens' fear contributes to their perception of the quality of life. The hypothesized relationship is that a higher level of fear leads to a lower perceived quality of life.

(e). Satisfaction with the police is the last endogenous latent variable in the model. It may also be considered as an integrated measure of how well the goals of community policing have been achieved. The corresponding hypotheses are that the less citizens fear, or the higher perceived quality of life, the higher level of citizen satisfaction with the police. In addition, we need to test indirect effects of community policing, collective efficacy, disorder, and crime on citizen satisfaction with the police.

SUMMARY AND FUTURE RESEARCH

The idea of community policing has met constant resistance and criticism since the time it was first put forward. Several authors discussed previously epitomize the forces of the criticism. Matthews' (1992) article, *Replacing "Broken Windows"* criticizes the position that community policing is the solution to social disorder and crime control. Arguing that this approach is based on the erroneous assumption that the physical and moral decay of the community leads to increased criminality, Matthews insists that there is little evidence to support the connection between incivility and crime. Nor is there evidence that community policing actually reduces the crime rates. Harcourt's (1998) study tried to falsify Skogan's (1990) findings that support the disorder-crime nexus, and denied disorder is an independent reality. Obviously, if disorder does not exist, the disorder-crime nexus and the broken windows thesis would be automatically dismissed. Sampson and Raudenbush (1997, 1999) reject the disorder-crime relationship as spurious by introducing the concept of collective efficacy, which they believe is the key for explaining both disorder and crime. The significant accomplishments of this study are two-fold: it has addressed some of the major criticisms and clearly demonstrated the structure, mechanisms, and efficacy of community policing.

First, the current study found Harcourt's (1998) replication of Skogan's (1990) study contains several flaws: (1) ignoring the impact of statistical power on the test results and mistakenly interpreting a possible Type II error as a rejection of alternative hypothesis; (2) selecting/deleting cases based on a subjective, self-serving criterion resulting in a systematic bias and further power attenuation; and (2) implementing a missing value solution that does not solve the missing value problem. All these make Harcourt's (1998) falsification of Skogan's (1990) findings unacceptable. Harcourt's (1998) results do not negate the disorder-crime nexus.

Second, we discovered that even if Sampson and Raudenbush's (1997, 1999) studies aimed at demonstrating the spuriousness of the disorder-crime relationship, they unintentionally showed, through their reciprocal feedback models, that crime and disorder are indirectly related. Although this is not a complete confirmation of the broken windows thesis, it is certainly a reminder that the relationship between disorder and crime may not be dismissed so easily.

Third, the current study provides supportive evidence to the broken windows thesis that the physical and moral decay of the community leads to increased criminality. Because disorder has significant direct, indirect, and total effects on crimes, the connection between incivility and crime is well established in the data. More significantly, these effects were achieved with collective efficacy being controlled for. This may provide an empirical annotation for what it means when Wilson and Kelling (1982) state that disorder and crime are usually *inextricably* linked. The implication is that the physical and moral decay of the community may indeed lead to more crime, and that other things being equal, fixing broken windows may be the best thing the police and community can do to prevent more windows from being broken.

Fourth, the findings of the present study support the conception that community policing is the solution to disorder and crime. Given the current state of the measurement, the cross-sectional data, and the nature of the citizen survey, the key to discover the effects of community policing on crime is to focus on its indirect and total effects. That is, to look at the causal flow from the community-policing measures through the mediating variable, disorder, to the crime factors. These effects may reflect the way proactive policing works and the true pattern of influence of community policing on crime.

Fifth, the findings generally support the conception about the interrelationships among the ultimate goal (the quality of life) and the intermediate goals (citizens' fear, disorder, and crime) of community policing. Citizens' fear is a significant predictor of the perceived quality of life, and both are in turn significantly influenced by disorder (citizens' fear is also significantly predicted by serious crime). An important finding is that, contrary to intuition, disorder is a more important source of fear than serious crime. This underscores the importance of disorder control to fear reduction.

Last, consistent with the new focus of the community-policing philosophy, citizen satisfaction with the police is dependent on the levels of citizens' fear and the perceived quality of life in the community. In addition, both working with community and disorder have a significant indirect effect on satisfaction with the police. These may provide the insight into the basis of public opinion of the police and what the police should do to not only win the war with crime but also win the hearts and minds of citizens.

The current study also has limitations. First, this study deals with issues of social control in communities, and one of the challenges of this type of research is to distinguish individual-level effects from community-level effects.

The reason for this is that what we study may be related to the structural characteristics of ecological units such as face blocks, census tracts, neighborhoods, and so on. Because of many factors such as social inequality, there may be a significant variation from neighborhood to neighborhood in terms of the social, structural, and ecological characteristics. As a result, we may not be able to inform whether the findings are due simply to individual-level traits (e.g., heightened sensitivity to disorder, support for authority) or to actual differences in neighborhood disorder and crime, when multilevel analysis is not employed. However, because our data set was not intended for multilevel analysis, there are no level II variables available. This limitation may have an impact on the interpretation and implication of the results.

Second, community policing is the central concept in this study; however, it may not be adequately measured, due to the availability of variables in the data set. According to the literature, community policing seems to have at least the following characteristics: partnership with community, personalized policing, decentralized place, proactive policing, crime prevention, order restoration and maintenance, problem solving, interagency cooperation, unisolated patrol, permanent beats, and so on. The current study only covered partnership with community and crime prevention (may also implicitly include proactive policing and problem solving), a portion of the content domain of community policing. This may also present a problem for how to accurately interpret the results. For instance, it is hard to know whether an insignificant result reflects the truth or is simply due to the incomplete measurement. This would also work in the other way (i.e., a significant result may not fully confirm a hypothesized relationship).

Third, the external validity of the study needs to be further tested because of the data limitations. (1) Because the data were collected in one metropolitan area in the United States, the results based on them may not be generalizable to the areas, whose demographic, socioeconomic, and ecological structures and characteristics are significantly different from those of Colorado Springs. (2) As typical of social science data, many variables used in the model are Likert-type variables. Ordinal level variables as manifest variables in a structural-equation model tend to bias correlations/covariances toward 0 and generate unreliable standard errors (Rigdon 2003). Therefore, the results should be interpreted with caution, even if our bootstrapping showed certain robustness of the results. (3) The sample size of the data ($n = 710$), though not too small, is at the lower end of what is acceptable. The small sample size may cause larger sample to sample variation and standard errors. As a result, the estimates may not be as stable as what would be with a large sample size.

Finally, the current analysis mainly focuses on the roles of the police and citizens and a limited number of factors, when discussing the mechanisms of social control in the community. However, a more systematic discussion should include a larger context and more relevant parties in the social-control process such as the "Big 6" introduced by Trojanowicz (1994)—the police, citizens, media, politicians, public and private organizations, and business communities. In reality, all parties must contribute to make community policing feasible and fruitful. Without including these or other relevant factors in the model, the effects of community policing may be overestimated. In addition, social, political, and economic processes are also known to have significant impact on the social conditions, disorder, crime rates, and effects of the social control in communities. The present study was not able to incorporate these concurrent social forces and future research may need to control for these processes.

DISCUSSION QUESTIONS

1. Discuss the relationship between disorder and crime.
2. Describe the debate over whether "broken windows" has an impact on crime.
3. How can satisfaction with the police be increased?

REFERENCES

Aron, Arthur and Elaine Aron. 2002. *Statistics for the Behavioral and Social Sciences*. Englewood Cliffs, NJ: Prentice Hall.

Bayley, David H. 1994. *Police for the Future*. New York: Oxford University Press.

Bentler, P. M. and C. Chou. 1987. "Practical Issues in Structural Modeling." *Sociological Methods and Research* 16 (1): 78–128.

Borooah, V. and C. A. Carcach. 1997. "Crime and Fear; Evidence from Australia." *British Journal of Criminology* 37 (4): 635–58.

Browne, M. W. and R. Cudeck. 1993. "Alternative Ways of Assessing Model Fit." Pp. 230–59 in *Testing Structural Equation Models*, edited by K. A. Bollen and J. S. Long. Newbury Park, CA: Sage.

Byrne, Barbara M. 2001. *Structural Equation Modeling with AMOS*. Mahwah, NJ: Lawrence Erlbaum.

Carter, D. and A. Sapp. 1994. "Issues and Perspectives of Law Enforcement Accreditation: A National Study of Police Chiefs." *Journal of Criminal Justice* 22 (3): 195–204.

Cohen, Jacob. 1988. *Statistical Power Analysis for the Behavioral Sciences*. New York: Academic Press.

Coles, Catherine M. and George L. Kelling. 1999, Summer. "Prevention through Community Prosecution." *The Public Interest* 99 (136): 69–85.

Cordner, G. W. 1995. "Community Policing: Elements and Effects." *Police Forum* 5 (3): 1–8.

Covington, J. and Ralph B. Taylor. 1991. "Fear of Crime in Urban Residential Neighborhoods; Implications of Between and Within Neighborhood Sources for Current Models." *Sociological Quarterly* 32 (2): 231–50.

D'Emilio, Frances. 2003, July 31. "Disrespect for Italy's Churches Decried." *Associated Press*, Rocky Mountain News.

Eck, John E. and William Spelman. 1987. "Who Ya Gonna Call? The Police As Problem-Busters." *Crime and Delinquency* 33 (1): 31–52.

Ferraro, K. F. 1994. *Fear of Crime: Interpreting Victimization Risk*. Albany: State University of New York Press.

Figgie, H. 1980. *The Figgie Report on Fear of Crime: America Afraid*. Willoughby, OH: ATO Inc.

Finch J. F., S. G. West, and D. P. MacKinnon. 1997. "Effects of Sample Size and Nonnormality on the Estimation of Mediated Effects in Latent Variable Models." *Structural Equation Modeling* 4 (2): 87–107.

Fulton, R. 1993. "Community Policing on Horseback." *Law Enforcement Technology* 20 (5): 32.

Gates, L. B. and W. M. Rohe. 1987. "Fear and Reactions to Crime: A Revised Model." *Urban Affairs Quarterly* 22:425–53.

Goldstein, H. 1990. *Problem-Oriented Policing*. New York: McGraw-Hill.

Greene, H. 1993. "Community-Oriented Policing in Florida." *American Journal of Police* 12:141–55.

Greenwood, Peter W., Jan M. Chaiken, and Joan Petersilia. 1977. *The Criminal Investigation Process*. Lexington, MA: D.C. Heath and Company.

Harcourt, Bernard E. 1998. "Reflecting on the Subject: A Critique of the Social Influence Conception of Deterrence, the Broken Windows Theory, and Order-Maintenance Policing New York Style." *Michigan Law Review* 97 (2): 2912.

Hope, T. and M. Hough. 1988. "Area Crime and Incivility: A Profile from the British Crime Survey." Pp. 30–47 in *Communities and Crime Reduction*, edited by T. Hope and M. Shaw. London: HMSO.

Hu, L. T. and P. M. Bentler. 1999. Cutoff Criteria for Fit Indices in Covariance Structure Analysis: Conventional Criteria Versus New Alternatives. *Structural Equation Modeling* 6:1–56.

Jöreskog, Karl. G. and Dog Sörbom. 1989. *LISREL 7–A Guide to the Program and Applications*. Chicago, IL: SPSS.

———. 1996. *PRELIS 2: User's Reference Guide*. Chicago, IL: Scientific Software International.

Joseph, T. 1994. "Walking the Minefield of Community-Oriented Policing." *Law Enforcement Bulletin* 63 (9): 8–12.

Kansas City Police Department. 1997. *Kansas City Police Department Response Time Analysis: Vol II Part 1 Crime Analysis*. Kansas City, MO: Author.

Kelling, G. 1985. "Order Maintenance, the Quality of Urban Life, and Police: A Line of Argument." in *Police Leadership in America: Crisis and Opportunity*, edited by W. Geller. New York: Praeger.

———. 1987. "Acquiring a Taste for Order: The Community and Police." *Crime & Delinquency* 33 (1): 90–112.

Kelling, G. and William J. Bratton. 1998. "Declining Crime Rates: Insider Views of The New York City Story." *The Journal of Criminal Law & Criminology* 88 (4): 1217.

Kelling, G. and C. M. Coles. 1994, Summer. "Disorder and the Court." *Public Interest* 94 (116): 57–75.

———. 1996. *Fixing Broken Windows—Restoring Order and Reducing Crime in Our Communities*. New York: Free Press.

Kelling, G., T. Pate, D. Dieckman, and C. E. Brown. 1974. *The Kansas City Preventive Patrol Experiment*. Washington, DC: The Police Foundation.

Kinsay, R., J. Lea, and J. Young. 1986. *Losing the Fight Against Crime*. Oxford, UK: Blackwell.

Leighton, Barry N. 1991. "Visions of Community Policing: Rhetoric and Reality in Canada." *Canadian Journal of Criminology* 33 (3/4): 485–522.

Lewis, D. and M. Maxfield. 1980. "Fear in the Neighborhoods—An Investigation of the Impact of Crime," *Journal of Research in Crime and Delinquency* 172:160–89.

Lewis, D. and G. Salem. 1985. *Fear of Crime: Incivility and the Production of a Social Problem*. New Brunswick, NJ: Transaction.

Liska, Allem and Barbara Warner. 1991. "Functions of Crime: A Paradoxical Process." *American Journal of Sociology* 96:1441–1463.

Liska, A. E., A. Sanchirico, and M. D. Reed. 1988. "Fear of Crime and Constrained Behavior: Specifying and Estimating a Reciprocal Effects Model." *Social Forces* 66:827–37.

Loehlin, John C. 1992. *Latent Variable Models: An Introduction to Factor, Path, and Structural Analysis*. 2d ed. Englewood Cliffs, NJ: Lawrence Erlbaum.

Long, J. S. 1983. *Covariance Structure Models: An Introduction to LISREL*. Beverly Hills, CA: Sage.

Matthews, Roger. 1992. "Replacing 'Broken Windows': Crime, Incivilities and Urban Change." Pp. 19–50 in *Issues in Realist Criminology*, edited by R. Matthews and Jock Young. London: Sage.

Maxson, Cheryl, Karen Hennigan, and David Sloane. 2003, June. "Factors that Influence Public Opinion of the Police." *Research for Practice* 1–12.

McElroy, J. E., C. A. Cosgrove, and S. Sadd. 1993. *Community Policing: The CPOP in New York*. Newbury Park, CA: Sage.

McGarrell, Edmund F., A. L. Giacomazzi, and Q. C. Thurman. 1997. "Neighborhood Disorder, Integration, and the Fear of Crime." *Justice Quarterly* 14 (3): 479–500.

Miethe, T. 1995. "Fear and Withdrawal from Urban Life." *Annals of the American Academy of Political and Social Science* 539:14–27.

Miller, L. and K. Hess. 1994. *Community Policing: Theory & Practice*. St. Paul, MN: West Publishing.

Moore, M., R. Trojanowicz, and G. Kelling. 1989. "Crime and Policing." Pp. 31–54 in *Police Practices in the "90's: Key Management Issues*, edited by J. Fyfe. Washington DC: International City Management Association.

Normandeau, Andre. 1993. "Policing in Montreal: A New Vision." *Canadian Journal of Criminology* 35 (2): 183–86.

Perkins, Douglas D. and Ralph B. Taylor. 1992. "The Physical Environment of Street Blocks and Resident Perceptions of Crime and Disorder; Implications for Theory and Measurement." *Journal of Environmental Psychology* 17:21–34.

———. 1996. "Ecological Assessments of Community Disorder: Their Relationship to Fear of Crime and Theoretical Implications." *American Journal of Community Psychology* 24 (1): 63–108.

President's Commission on Law Enforcement and the Administration of Justice. 1967. *Task Force Report: The Police*. Washington, DC: Government Printing Office.

Rigdon, Edward E. 2003. *Questions and Answers at the Forum of Structural Equation Modeling Network*. Retrieved January 29, 2004, from http://bama.ua.edu/cgi-bin/wa?A0=semnet&X=4CFD0B58F29C76E0C0&Y=xuguolao@yahoo.com

Rosenbaum, D. P. 1988. "Community Crime Prevention: A Review and Synthesis of the Literature." *Justice Quarterly* 5:323–95.

Rosenbaum, D. P. and A. J. Lurigio. 1994. *Fighting Back: Two Sides of Citizen Reactions to Crime*. Pacific Grove, CA: Wadsworth.

Ryan, J. 1994. "Community Policing: Trends, Policies, Programs, and Definitions." In A. Roberts (Ed.), *Critical Issues in Crime & Justice* (Chap. 7). Thousand Oaks, CA: Sage.

Sadd, Susan and Randolph M. Grinc. 1996. "Implementation Challenges in Community Policing: Innovative Neighborhood-Oriented Policing in Eight Cities." in *Research in Brief*. Washington, DC: National Institute of Justice.

Sampson, Robert J. and Stephen W. Raudenbush. 1997. "Neighborhoods and Violent Crime: A Multilevel Study of Collective Efficacy." *Sciences* 277 (5328): 918–25.

———. 1999. "Systematic Social Observation of Public Spaces: A New Look at Disorder in Urban Neighborhoods 1." *The American Journal of Sociology*. 105 (3): 603.

Silverman, Eli B. and Jo-ann Della-Giustina. 2001. "Urban Policing and the Fear of Crime." *Urban Studies* 38 (5–6): 941–57.

Skogan, Wesley. 1987. "The Impact of Victimization on Fear." *Crime and Delinquency* 33:135–54.

———. 1990. *Disorder and Decline: Crime and Decline: Crime and the Spiral of Decay in American Neighborhoods*. New York: Free Press.

Skogan, W. and M. Maxfield. 1981. "Coping with Crime—Individual and Neighborhood Reactions." Volume 124 in *Sage Library of Social Research*. Thousand Oaks, CA: Sage.

Skolnick, Jerome. 1994. *Justice Without Trial: Law Enforcement in a Democratic Society*, 3d ed. New York: John Wiley and Sons.

Taylor, Ralph B. 1997. "Social Order and Disorder of Street Blocks and Neighborhoods: Ecology, Micrioecology, and the Systemic Model of Social Disorganization." *Journal of Research in Crime and Delinquency* 34 (1): 113–56.

———. 2001. *Breaking Away from Broken Windows—Baltimore Neighborhoods and the Nationwide Fight Against Crime, Grime, Fear, and Decline*. Boulder, CO: Westview Press.

Taylor, Ralph B. and J. Covington. 1993. "Community Structural Change and Fear of Crime." *Social Problems* 40:374–96.

Taylor, Ralph B. and Adele V. Harrell. 1996. *Physical Environment and Crime*. Final summary report presented to the National Institute of Justice, Washington, DC.

Taylor, Ralph B. and Sally A. Shumaker. 1990. "Local Crime as a Natural Hazard: Implications for Understanding the Relationship between Disorder and Fear of Crime." *American Journal of Community Psychology* 18 (5): 619–23.

Thomas, C. W. and J. F. Hyman. 1977. "Perceptions of Crime, Fear of Victimization and Public Perceptions of Police Performance." *Journal of Police Science and Administration* 5:305–17.

Trojanowicz, R. 1989. *Preventing Civil Disturbances: A Community Policing Approach*. East Lansing: Michigan State University, National Center for Community Policing.

———. 1994. "The Future of Community Policing." Chapter 15 in *The Challenge of Community Policing: Testing the Promises*, edited by D. Rosenbaum. Thousand Oaks, CA: Sage.

———. 1998. "Police Accountability." A working paper on the principles of police accountability. *Community Policing Pages, 2002–2003 Edition*, vol. 8(1). Retrieved January 29, 2004, from http://www.concentric.net/~dwoods/ourstaff.htm

Trojanowicz, R. and B. Bucqueroux. 1992. *Toward Development of Meaningful and Effective Performance Evaluations*. East Lansing: Michigan State University, National Center for Community Policing.

Weston, J. 1993. "Community Policing: An Approach to Youth Gangs in a Medium-Sized City (Reno Police Department, Nevada, U.S.)." *The Police Chief* 60 (8): 80–5.

Wilson, James Q. and George L. Kelling. 1982. "Broken Windows: The Police and Neighborhood Safety." *The Atlantic Monthly*, 249 (3): 29–38.

———. 1989. "Making Neighborhoods Safe." *The Atlantic Monthly* 263 (2): 46–52.

Woods, DeVere and Joanne Ziembo-Vogl. 1997. "The Mission of Policing: The Lost Imperative." *Community Policing Pages. 2002–2003 Edition* 8(1). Retrieved June 6, 2002, from http://www.concentric.net/~dwoods/mission.htm

Wycoff, M. and P. Manning. 1983. "The Police and Crime Control." Pp. 15–32 in *Evaluating Performance of Criminal Justice Agencies*, edited by G. P. Whitaker and C. D. Phillips. Beverly Hills, CA: Sage.

Wycoff, M.A. and T. N. Oettmeier. 1994. *Evaluating Police Officers Performance.* Washington, DC: National Institute of Justice.

Ziembo-Vogl, J. and D. Woods. 1996. "Defining Community Policing: Practice Versus Paradigm." *Police Studies* 193:33–50.

27

The Problem of White-Collar Crime, and Forestalling Future Epidemics

Peter Grabosky and
Neal Shover

This chapter provides both remarks and concise explanation of recent research and policy proposals related to fraud. Fraud prevention policy options are outlined into three possible categories: decreasing the potential targets, increasing credible external oversight, and increasing effective internal oversight or self-restraint. Throughout the chapter Grabosky and Shover argue that creating these types of policies in not actually difficult, but successfully implementing them is.

Crime-as-choice theory is useful not only for organizing thinking about the causes of white-collar crime epidemics, but also for drawing attention to potentially promising ways of reducing the odds of recurrence. Three target areas for policy initiatives stand out: (1) reducing the supply of lure, (2) increasing prevailing estimates of the credibility of external oversight,

Source: Peter Grabosky and Neal Shover "The Problem of White Collar Crime and Forestalling Future Epidemics" Criminology and Public Policy Vol. 9:3, pp. 641–651.

and (3) increasing the use of effective systems of internal oversight and self-restraint. Effective policies aimed at one or more of these promise to reduce both the supply of white-collar criminal opportunities and the size of the pool of individuals and organizations tempted, if not predisposed, to exploit them.

There is currently a remarkably optimistic consensus in some academic quarters about how to reduce the harm caused by privileged predators. The heart of it lies in the presumed promise of pluralistic, cooperative approaches, and responsive regulation. These assumptions highlight the need for enhanced prevention, more diverse and more effective internal oversight and self-monitoring, and more efficient and effective external oversight. They have gained use throughout a variety of regulatory realms, many since their earliest, albeit embryonic, formulation nearly three decades ago (Braithwaite, 1982). Despite variation on specific points, taken together the policy essays reflect this, now textbook, treatment of white-collar crime control. They make sense theoretically, and we endorse them. We do so not because they have a record of demonstrable success but principally because sole or excessive reliance on state oversight and threat of criminal prosecution is difficult, costly, and uncertain. Still, we are mindful, as others should be, that the onset of the Great Recession occurred during and despite the tight embrace of self-regulation, pluralistic oversight, and notions of self-regulating markets by policy makers and many academicians.

LURE REDUCTION

Reducing the supply of lure is a formidable challenge. An increasing supply inevitably accompanies the complexity of modern life (Shover and Hochstetler, 2006). When coupled with weak oversight, almost every new commodity and government program presents opportunities for criminal exploitation and attracts attention from potential malefactors. Absent credible oversight, every new tax becomes an opportunity for evasion. Every new program of public expenditure is a potential lure for those who would appropriate from it unlawfully. This is no less true of policies implemented with the best of intentions; programs designed to extend opportunities for home ownership to those previously excluded from the residential housing market helped create the subprime mortgage debacle (Collins and Nigro, 2010). The challenge is to enable use of lure for legitimate purposes, while reducing its potential for use as an instrument or target for crime.

Reducing lure, without stifling individual initiative and precluding legitimate opportunities, is complicated. Command economies and socialist systems have tried, but with notable lack of success. These systems, moreover, tend to create substantial black markets and official corruption. Whether the sumptuous levels of executive compensation that prevail in the United States can be significantly reduced, is questionable. So too are the consequences of such policies for individual initiative. If implemented, the effects of such restraint would not see bankers deserting their profession in favor of academic careers.

Some lure can be reduced by technology. Thanks to technological innovation, many of the hazards that regulation exists to mitigate have been significantly reduced, if not eliminated. Some traditional products and practices, alluring but harmful, are no longer attractive. Innovations in paint technology and the development of lead-free petrol have significantly reduced the prevalence of environmental lead. "Greener" products that require fewer raw materials and energy to produce, and which generate less waste, have contributed to a cleaner planet (van Erp and Huisman, 2010). The appeal of midnight dumping is thereby significantly reduced. Satellite imaging can now facilitate more efficient agricultural practice, including water use and the application of agricultural chemicals and fertilizers. Irresponsible or illegal use of these is no longer seen as tempting.

The lure represented by dependent and vulnerable populations has increased in size and importance in the decades since World War II (Shover and Hochstetler, 2006). They include a sizable group of the greedy and gullible. Reducing the supply and vulnerability of these potential victims is challenging, but steps taken in the United States to curb criminal telemarketers suggests it is worthy of attention. Enhancing financial literacy among the general public is a good idea, but gullibility may be deeply engrained in the human behavioral repertoire. It supports a massive global gambling industry. Ponzi schemes likely will remain with us for a while.

INCREASING THE CREDIBILITY OF EXTERNAL OVERSIGHT

Vigilant and determined oversight can provide some protection against the worst excesses of capitalism. Most observers believe that weak oversight was the principal cause of the Great Recession. Certainly, any dissenters have been conspicuously silent. Prudential regulation in Australia, Japan, and Finland shielded those economies from the dislocation experienced in parts of Europe. Enhancing credible oversight might be more achievable than lure reduction as a means of reducing the rate of white-collar crime. A number of institutions—public, private, and non-profit—are in a position to exercise surveillance over financial and other commercial activities. When non-governmental energies can be harnessed in furtherance of public policy, or to the extent that they can operate spontaneously with beneficial effect, this can complement oversight by an overburdened state.

The credibility of external oversight is important not only for would-be offenders, but also for the general public. Belief in the fairness, effectiveness, and equity of a regulatory system is essential to the very legitimacy of a state. Leona Helmsley once stated "We don't pay taxes. Only the little people pay taxes." To the extent that citizens believe that tax is optional for the rich, the tax system, and the state as a whole, can fall into disrepute (Levi, 2010). The weakening of the Greek state as a result of ineffective tax administration became starkly apparent in April 2010.

We live in a world in which symbols matter. In terms of conventional crime, reassuring statistics are less reassuring than visible "blue shirts." The response to sex offenders (especially those who offend against children) in English-speaking democracies tends to be vengeful and unforgiving. The enactment of draconian legislation in the face of public anxiety is a time-honored political strategy, and the imposition of savage sentences serves a similar function. The 150-year sentence imposed on Bernard Madoff might not have restored the financial well-being of his victims, but some of them, and many members of the public, felt better (Pontell and Geis, 2010). The deterrent value of this and similar sentences may be nil, however, and the certainty of detection and response from overseers probably has a more significant effect (Leighton, 2010).

Even a relatively equitable regulatory system can be discredited easily when it is seen to be administered heavy-handedly. When authorities treat those subject to oversight with respect and fairness, the latter may be more inclined to meet their obligations. But a persistent posture of arrogance can be off-putting and can give rise to an "organized culture of resistance" (Bardach and Kagan, 1982). This could find expression in individual, and statistically rare, extreme response. In February 2010, an aggrieved taxpayer flew a light aircraft into a building housing an office of the U.S. Internal Revenue Service in Austin, Texas (Leighton, 2010). V. Braithwaite (2010) observes the importance of discriminating between degrees of non-compliance and the necessity of mobilizing response commensurate with the degree of transgression. Probably the overwhelming majority of oversight personnel do so in any case; it is a characteristically moral and organizational response to managing a volume of work that invariably exceeds resources.

Globalization, as reflected in the rapid movement across national borders of finance, commodities, labor, ideas, and viruses (digital and microbial), poses significant regulatory challenges, as it both creates lure and inhibits development of credible oversight. The "race to the bottom" to find deregulatory havens in developing countries has become a familiar theme. Shipping electronic waste to the third world may rid a wealthy nation of a disposal problem, but in other cases, analogous practices may return to haunt one. Carbon emissions generated in a poor country contribute to climate change for everyone. The global financial system might not be totally integrated, but it is sufficiently tightly coupled that a problem in one nation could reverberate elsewhere. Global financial markets suffered in 2008 in the aftermath of the sub-prime mortgage crisis in the United States. Greek financial woes were felt not only throughout Europe but also across the Atlantic. Institutions of external oversight must be global, as well as local, in scope.

Confidence in the integrity of markets is essential to the stability and growth of financial systems. If too many citizens believe that their money would be safer if kept hidden under a mattress at home than if deposited in a bank or invested in the stock market, the entire economy suffers. Only the most nonchalant of laissez-faire economists would favor a return to the law of the jungle. Most of the rest of us would concur that a degree of criminal enforcement is an essential component of a regulatory system. What is contested is the *context* in which the hard edge of the state is required, and the degree of severity that is appropriate.

INCREASING EFFECTIVE INTERNAL OVERSIGHT AND SELF-RESTRAINT

It will be extremely difficult to engineer cultural change to bring about greater self-restraint (Nguyen and Pontell, 2010). Corporate executives often bring a sense of entitlement to the job (Friedrichs, 2010), and for some people, enough is never enough. The marginal satisfaction to a high flying banker of an additional 2% in bonus on top of $20 million might strike us mere mortals as insignificant, but any baseball player would rather bat .357 than .350. Moreover, incentives matter to most people, and for better or worse, money is a measure of performance. In addition, shareholders generally are happy to acquiesce in lavish rewards to chief executives who are successful. And when times are difficult, it is always tempting to cut corners.

More difficult to measure than personal wealth, but a value that is more important to many, is personal integrity. Despite the old adage that "nice guys finish last," captains of industry often go to great lengths to promote an image of respectability. Philanthropic largesse is one means of cultivating such an image, but ironically, visible largesse tends to vary with personal wealth. Then of course there is the cynical use of philanthropy for insurance against regulatory or law-enforcement authorities. Prominent white-collar offenders often flaunt their generosity, before or after their transgressions. Like Bernie Madoff, some use philanthropy as a means of winning the trust of those who later become victims.

Crime and unethical conduct by corporate personnel typically take place out of public view, behind the respectable facade of their employer, and it can be nearly impossible for outsiders to penetrate this organizational veil. This is one reason why whistleblowers and informants rank among the most important sources of information about corporate crime, illegalities, and unethical conduct (Association of Certified Fraud Examiners, 2010). *Whistleblowers* are employees of legitimate organizations who divulge to outsiders knowledge or suspicions of wrongdoing in the workplace. Recognizing their importance as a source of oversight, van de Bunt (2010) makes encouragement of whistle-blowing a center piece of his proposals for reducing corporate white-collar crime. In the United States, several states and the federal government have enacted legislation providing employment protection and monetary rewards for them. This is meant to spur insiders with knowledge of wrongdoing to come forward and report to authorities and to do so without fear of reprisals.

BEYOND SELF-REGULATION AND PLURALISTIC OVERSIGHT

The absence thus far in most industries and business firms of clear or persuasive evidence of the effectiveness of self-regulation and cooperative approaches to oversight increases the importance of exploring additional policy options grounded in criminological theory (Laufer, 2010). The dominant paradigm of responsive regulation does not preclude innovation and indeed invites continuing reform. Recent history has seen some isolated innovation in regulatory reform, some of which might be replicable. In the aftermath of a bribery scandal that resulted in marketing of tainted products, the former head of the China State Food and Drug Administration, Zheng Xiaoyu, was executed in 2007. Nothing comparable has occurred in any other Western nation.

Perhaps more feasible is public shaming. One recalls that as their companies were failing, chief executives of three major U.S. automobile manufacturers flew to Washington in their corporate jets to ask for federal bailout funds. Although shameless behavior such as this leads one to despair about the prospect of good corporate citizenship, forceful chastisement is still appropriate. The reception that the auto executives received on Capitol Hill was less than warmly welcoming, and their ridicule by the press was entirely fitting. Leighton (2010) suggests that the U.S. Internal Revenue Service publish the names of delinquent taxpayers. There will always be white-collar offenders who are irredeemably shameless, but those captains of industry who depend on a modicum of political and social support for the continued viability of their business ignore public opinion at their peril. And nearly everybody values respect. The potential utility of ridicule as a means of mobilizing public indignation is, in our view, worthy of further attention. We say this despite the fact that refusal to acknowledge the criminality of their conduct is one of the sharpest distinguishing characteristics of white-collar criminals, one reported in studies using a variety of research methodologies (Benson, 1985; Shover and Hunter, 2010).

Outright prohibition of designated products and practices should remain an available option. In other areas of criminology, behaviors that appear at first blush benign, might be prohibited because of their potential for misuse. In Australia, ordinary citizens are effectively prohibited from possessing semi-automatic firearms or oleoresin capsicum spray. One commits a crime by producing data with the intention that it be used in committing a serious computer offense (by creating worms and viruses). Whether certain types of financial instruments could be similarly prohibited is an interesting question. In the United States, Congress currently is debating a potential ban on derivatives trading.

Although there might be no "magic bullet" in the offing, one could take some comfort in the potential for technological developments to enhance regulatory capacity, especially the capacity for credible guardianship and oversight (Gibbs, McGarrell, and Axelrod, 2010). As with computing, the decreasing cost and increasing accessibility of technology make such enhanced guardianship increasingly feasible. Satellite imaging can detect unauthorized land clearing and water storage on individual farms. Digital technology can identify the origin of every pork product produced in the Netherlands, down to the farm where the animal was raised. Automated surveillance methods can identify anomalous patterns of trading on stock markets. The pace of technological change is great and growing. It is safe to assume that applications unforeseen today will increase the capacity of regulatory oversight in years to come.

Ayres and Braithwaite (1992) observed that public interest groups play a central role in some regulatory domains, a role that could easily be enhanced and expanded. They noted that many countries around the world have elected worker safety representatives that complement state inspections. Long before the widespread take-up of digital technology, it was recognized that ordinary citizens are in a position to play a significant role in the regulatory process. In the United States, the Better Business Bureaus (BBBs) grew out of the truth-in-advertising movement in the early 20th century (Pannell, 2002). Comprised of local businesspeople, BBBs scrutinized advertising for deceptive content, gathered evidence, and presented it to local authorities for prosecution.

Consumer boycotts exemplify mass participation in furtherance of oversight reform. Such participation can result in the creation of new regulatory prohibitions in the face of recognized harm, or additional external oversight that complements an existing regulatory regime. Harsh labor practices experienced by California agricultural workers gave rise in the early 1970s to boycotts of lettuce and table grapes. Some amelioration of working conditions followed. The rise of the environmental movement has seen a flowering of grassroots activism, on land and sea. In recent years, the environmental NGO Greenpeace has sent vessels to the Southern Ocean to monitor Japanese whaling. Images of whales being harpooned attract little sympathy for the whaling industry or for the nations that host it.

Private regulatory activity can be autonomous or guided by the state. In the United States, the Surface Mining Control and Regulation Act of 1977 permitted citizens to request an inspection by federal regulatory authorities. In the 1980s, consumer protection authorities in at least one Australian state mobilized volunteers from the consumer movement to keep an eye out for potentially hazardous products on the market. The state can even delegate regulatory power to private interests. In Australia and the United Kingdom, Royal Societies for the Prevention of Cruelty to Animals investigate and prosecute cases of animal cruelty. A former Australian police commissioner once publicly mused that fraud investigation might similarly be undertaken by the private sector.

Technology could enhance not only the capacity of state oversight, but also the power of private parties. We are now well into the information revolution, and the enormous potential for digital technology to enhance the regulatory capacity of ordinary citizens is becoming apparent. More than ever before, private individuals and institutions are in a position to engage in the co-production of regulatory services. Torgler (2010) notes the importance of the media in the regulatory process. In years past it was said that freedom of the press belonged to the person who owned one. Today, thanks to digital technology, individuals around the world can communicate instantaneously, to millions of people, and at negligible cost. Mobile phones can serve as cameras, video recorders, or listening devices and can capture activities that errant companies or government agents would rather not share. The notorious images of prisoner abuse at Abu Ghraib were broadcast around the world in 2006. Investigative reporting is by no means the monopoly of journalists employed by great metropolitan newspapers. Indeed, the economics of the newspaper industry have begun to militate against serious (i.e., expensive) journalism. Instead, individual bloggers and other digital news entrepreneurs have begun to develop an increasing profile (e.g., see slate.com/, wikileaks.org/, and propublica.org/). A ProPublica reporter was awarded a 2010 Pulitzer Prize for Investigative Reporting.

As envisaged by Ayres and Braithwaite (1992), citizens can exercise vigilance over the performance of regulatory agencies, or over the behavior of corporate actors directly. In the West, we already have seen online encouragement of consumer boycotts (boycottnestle.blogspot.com/) and Web sites that monitor particular industries (info.babymilkaction.org/) or companies (untied.com/). The even greater potential of social networking sites, blogs, and related media can be glimpsed in contemporary China. Despite the censorship of Facebook, Twitter, and YouTube by Chinese authorities, alternative media may be seen to flourish in the form of such sites as like QQ Zone, Tianya.cn, and Kaixin001.com (Barboza, 2010). The potential investigative capacity of such media is formidable, although thus far it has been mobilized primarily against low-level corruption and other gross anti-social behavior. The private diary of a mid-level party official in south China was posted on-line, and, unfortunately for him, it contained details of sexual indiscretions and bribes accepted. He was cashiered as a result. In another case, a video clip of unknown provenance depicting a woman killing a kitten was posted on the Web. Public indignation was so great, and cooperation of participants in the network so strong, that the woman was tracked to a small town in a far northeast corner of China. Both she and the camera man were dismissed from their government jobs. In October 2007, a provincial department of forestry announced that it had identified a surviving South China Tiger. Images posted on the Web aroused the suspicions of netizens, and the provincial government later conceded that indeed they had been faked. Thirteen local officials were disciplined (Jin, 2008). If sunlight is the best disinfectant, the potential for vigilance now within the capacity of citizens looms larger and more important than ever before. The potential of technology as an instrument for mobilizing mass indignation against corporate crime may be quite significant.

POLICY ADOPTION AND IMPLEMENTATION

Rothe (2010) is only partly correct that "policy suggestions are difficult to conceptualize and to implement." Development and promulgation of policy proposals is anything but difficult. Seeing proposed policy adopted and implemented faithfully is exceedingly difficult. Conspicuously absent from many of the policy essays included here is discussion of how the proposed policies might be put in place and obstacles to implementation. Snider (2010) is one of the few authors who highlights the critical importance of power relationships in constructing and gaining passage of new rules and oversight. Regulatory space is almost always contested. Proposals for oversight reform, regardless of their intrinsic merit, invariably meet with opposition from someone, somewhere. Not all reforms are costless; those who are asked to the bear increased costs resulting from regulatory initiatives might understandably object. Routinely, proposed oversight initiatives encounter opposition grounded in ideology or political partisanship. More important perhaps, struggles for reform invariably are waged within the political and ideological confines of the political–economic context. Given this fact, fundamental and far reaching policy changes likely will not occur; only proposals for incremental tinkering will be defined as legitimate and potentially workable.

Windows of Opportunity

The strategic environment for reform is changeable, but "to everything there is a season" (Ecclesiastes 3:1–8). Much reform is born of crisis. Acute problems demand solutions. Emergent structural contradictions in the political economy can give rise to problems that cannot be papered over with cosmetic reforms. In these historically opportune circumstances, acute problems can produce mass disaffection and cause citizens to organize and to demand official action. At the very least, crisis conditions can cause a loss of legitimacy and forced acquiescence from those who normally resist oversight. The stock market crash of 1929 and the Great Depression that followed ushered in a degree of government activity that was historically unprecedented. The Federal Deposit Insurance Corporation (FDIC) and the SEC are but two of the institutions created at that time (Schlesinger, 1958). The Watergate cover-up was followed by energetic prosecutorial and legislative oversight activity in defense of public sector integrity (Katz, 1980). The S&L crisis of the 1980s gave rise to the Financial Institutions Reform, Recovery, and Enforcement Act of 1989 (FIRREA). Criminal scandals by Enron and other large corporations helped launch events that culminated in the Sarbanes-Oxley Act of 2002. This legislation mandated new standards of corporate governance and personal responsibility for corporate reporting by high-level executives. By the time this special issue of *Criminology & Public Policy* appears in print, we might know if the window of opportunity opened by the Great Recession was wide enough to allow significant reforms of financial sector oversight.

Scandals and accidents might also create circumstances favorable for reform, as noteworthy historical examples make clear. The death of 146 garment workers in the Triangle Shirtwaist Factory Fire of 1911 not only gave rise to new safety laws, but also inspired the Progressive movement, forerunner to the New Deal, in the United States (von Drehle, 2003). The disastrous Santa Barbara oil spill of 1968 was a powerful catalyst to development of the environmental movement (Molotch, 1970). In April 2010, an explosion in an underground coal mine in West Virginia killed 29 miners, and a few weeks later, a drilled but uncapped undersea well spewed perhaps millions of gallons of oil into the Gulf of Mexico. As this essay is written, the flow of oil has continued uninterrupted for more than five weeks with no end in sight. The long-term impacts of the spill are inestimable. Mine explosions and oil spills, particularly when there is reason to believe that lax oversight contributed to their occurrence, are opportunities that do not come along every day.

Opportunities, however, are only as good as those who would exploit them. The skillful policy entrepreneur might succeed, where the inept would fail. In addition, the relational distance between policy entrepreneurs and sources of potential resistance might be highly significant in explaining the success or failure of reform initiatives (Black, 1993). Consider Richard Nixon, conservative president of the United States. The Nixon Administration saw the creation of the Environmental Protection Agency (EPA) and the Occupational Health and Safety Administration (OSHA).

Social Movements

In the absence of acute crisis, public consciousness about a given harm and support for regulatory reform may grow slowly together with calls for remediation. In some cases this public consciousness can be boosted by a landmark publication. Among the earlier manifestations of risk identification and information was the classic novel, *The Jungle* (1906), by the author and journalist Upton Sinclair. The book led to the enactment of The Meat Inspection Act and the Pure Food and Drug Act.

A half century later, the nature writer Rachel Carson published *Silent Spring* (1962), which led not only to the strengthening of pesticide regulation in the United States, but also to the growth of the environmental movement more generally. Three years after publication of Carson's book, Ralph Nader published *Unsafe at Any Speed* (1965), a critique of automobile safety in the United States. Nader's book contributed to the enactment of the 1966 National Traffic and Motor Vehicle Safety Act, which established the National Highway Traffic Safety Administration. Reforms that emerge almost effortlessly from changing public consciousness and spontaneous calls for action are the exception. More common are reforms that owe their adoption to organized and sustained movements (Snider, 2010).

Voluntary/Private Actions

Trust is the foundation of responsive regulation. And like successful perpetrators of fraud, corporate officials are skilled at creating belief in others that they merit trust. When subjected to external scrutiny and criticism for criminal or illegal conduct, they unfailingly attribute the problems to a few "bad apples." The vast majority of officers and firms are said to be honest and honorable and can be trusted to behave in a socially responsible fashion. Likewise they can be trusted to implement effective internal controls, to detect and respond to rule breaking, and to report the incidents to state agencies.

For corporate officials, however, trust is treated not as something which continually must be earned in day to day actions but instead as an entitlement. There are countless actions they could take to demonstrate that trust is merited. One is changes in policies of corporate governance. *Corporate governance* refers to a variegated mix of structural and procedural changes put in place by business firms to reduce the likelihood of financial loss to shareholders or investors caused by distracted, incompetent, or overly self-interested managers. Exemplary initiatives include change in the composition of boards of directors, revamped compensation schemes for managers, and more robust internal monitoring systems (Denis and McConnell, 2003). But the importance of compliance with externally required standards of conduct and performance is almost entirely absent from corporate governance codes; the emphasis instead is limited almost entirely to the importance of honesty in internal dealings. Revisions to code of ethics and internal governance documents that emphasize the obligation to obey the law would send a clear signal to those skeptical of the integrity of respectability of corporate actors. They also might promote self-restraint.

Another way of demonstrating that corporate actors can be trusted to behave responsibly is by spending funds for research on serious non-compliance and crime. Historically, empirical research into these matters has been funded almost entirely by state and other non-corporate sources. Research supported by corporate interests by contrast has focused narrowly on economic misconduct that victimizes business firms (Bussmann and Werle, 2006). If trust and compliance with oversight are priority concerns, business could demonstrate this by committing resources to support research into illegal actions that harm outsiders and the general public. The costs to victims of their experience at the hands of corporate criminals is a topic pregnant with potential symbolic messages of trust and responsibility. Research into a wider and less self-centered range of topics would send a powerful signal of commitment and might lead to more effective internal oversight and self-restraint. Trust in corporate officials could be enhanced also by reforming their approach to and treatment of whistleblowers.

Far from the venues in which celebration of self-regulation takes place, corporations engage relentlessly in attacks on countless aspects of oversight of their activities. In legislatures, regulatory fora and appellate courts, they work to expand their self-interested notions of fair and reasonable oversight (Michaels and Monforton, 2005). As they support efforts to weaken the capacity of regulatory agencies to monitor and sanction their misconduct, for example, they press for relief from civil suits on grounds that they have received certificates of compliance from regulators (Harris and Berenson, 2008). These efforts do little to promote and much to undermine trust. The results of a mail survey of compliance with requirements of trade practices legislation by 999 large Australian businesses showed "that implementation is overwhelmingly partial and possibly symbolic. Most businesses have implemented some, but far from all, of the compliance system elements considered by the [government], practitioners and scholars to be necessary for effective compliance management" (Parker and Nielsen, 2006: 482). It is noteworthy that corporate actors apparently have made little effort to fund studies of the implementation and efficacy of "trust-and-hope" oversight. It is difficult to credit their good will when they seem disinclined to commit resources to identifying best practices of internal oversight. The electronics industry Citizenship Coalition noted by van Erp and Huisman (2010) might be an exception.

Discussions of how to devise and gain adoption of policies that limit lure, reduce the ranks of those who are predisposed or tempted to exploit it, and increase the credibility of oversight can be overly technocratic in focus and neglect larger constraints and obstacles. The dominant political economy, its structural integrity, operating premises, and power relationships severely constrain consideration and adoption of policy options. Prominent among these constraints is the perceived need to avoid any actions that would jeopardize business confidence and the stability of the markets. They can cause advocates to lose sight of the fact that the fight against corporate crime is linked inextricably to the fight for social justice. It is a fight in which wealth, access to policy makers, and other resources generally are determinative. But populist social movements can make a difference. Crises, scandals, and accidents will continue to occur, giving rise to episodic disaffection and attempts at reform. The odds of success will be affected significantly by political–economic conditions. Reform is harder to resist and more likely to succeed during economic boom times when profits are up. Future attempts to limit the harm caused by white-collar crime likely will mirror the past, and whether or not the Great Recession will inspire organized and unrelenting demands for change in the practice of governments and the choices made by industry remains to be seen. The contributors to this special issue have shown what form these might take.

DISCUSSION QUESTIONS

1. What is white-collar crime?
2. Discuss precautions that can be taken to prevent becoming a victim of white-collar crime.
3. What is identity theft and why is it one of the fastest-growing white-collar crimes?
4. Discuss how to devise and gain adoption of policies that limit, lure, and reduce the ranks of those who are predisposed or tempted to exploit it.

REFERENCES

Association of Certified Fraud Examiners. 2010. *2008 Report to the Nation on Occupational Fraud and Abuse.* Austin, TX: Association of Certified Fraud Examiners. Retrieved May 10, 2010 from acfe.com/resources/publications.asp?copy=rttnhttp://www.acfe.com/documents/2006-rttn.pdf.

Ayres, Ian and John Braithwaite. 1992. *Responsive Regulation.* Cambridge, UK: Cambridge University Press.

Barboza, David. 2010. For Chinese, web is the way to entertainment. *New York Times,* April 18. Retrieved April 19, 2010 from nytimes.com/2010/04/19/technology/19chinaweb. html?hp.

Bardach, Eugene and Robert A. Kagan. 1982. *Going by the Book: The Problem of Regulatory Unreasonableness.* Philadelphia: Temple University Press.

Benson, Michael L. 1985. Denying the guilty mind: Accounting for involvement in a white-collar crime. *Criminology*, 23: 589–599.

Black, Donald. 1993. *The Social Structure of Right and Wrong.* San Diego: Academic Press.

Black, William K. 2010. Echo epidemics: Control frauds generate "white-collar street crime" waves. *Criminology & Public Policy.*

Braithwaite, John. 1982. Enforced self-regulation: A new strategy for corporate crime control. *Michigan Law Review*, 80: 1466–1507.

__________. 2010. Diagnostics of white-collar crime prevention. *Criminology & Public Policy.*

Braithwaite, Valerie. 2010. Criminal prosecution within responsive regulatory practice. *Criminology & Public Policy.*

Bunt, Henk van de. 2010. Walls of secrecy and silence: The Madoff case and cartels in the construction industry. *Criminology & Public Policy.*

Bussmann, Kai-D. and Markus M. Werle. 2006. Addressing crime in companies: First findings from a global survey of economic crime. *British Journal of Criminology*, 46: 1128–1144.

Callahan, David. 2004. *The Cheating Culture.* New York: Harcourt.

Caro, Robert A. 2002. *Master of the Senate.* New York: Alfred A. Knopf.

Carson, Rachel. 1962. *Silent Spring.* New York: Houghton Mifflin.

Clinard, Marshall B. and Peter C. Yeager. 1980. *Corporate Crime.* New York: Free Press.

Collins, M. Cary and Peter J. Nigro. 2010. Mortgage origination fraud: The missing links. *Criminology & Public Policy.*

Denis, Diane K. 2001. Twenty-five years of corporate governance research . . . and counting. *Review of Financial Economics*, 10: 191–212.

Denis, Diane K. and John J. McConnell. 2003. *International Corporate Governance.* European Corporate Governance Institute. Retrieved May 13, 2010 from papers.ssrn. com/sol3/papers.cfm?abstract_id=320121.

Downey, Tom. 2010. China's cyberposse. *New York Times*, March 3. Retrieved May 13, 2010 from nytimes.com/2010/03/07/magazine/07Human-t.html?emc=eta1.

Erp, Judith van and Wim Huisman. 2010. Smart regulation and enforcement of illegal disposal of electronic waste. *Criminology & Public Policy.*

Frankel, Tamar. 2006. *Trust and Honesty: America's Business Culture at a Crossroad.* New York: Oxford University Press.

Friedrichs, David O. 2010. Mortgage origination fraud and the global economic crisis: Incremental versus transformative policy initiatives. *Criminology & Public Policy.*

Gibbs, Carole, Edmund F. McGarrell, and Mark Axelrod. 2010. Transnational white-collar crime and risk: Lessons for the global trade in electronic waste. *Criminology & Public Policy.*

Harris, Gardiner and Alex Berenson. 2008. Drug makers near old goal: A legal shield. *New York Times*, April 6. Retrieved May 13, 2010 from nytimes.com/2008/04/06/washington/06patch.html?hp.

Jin, Liwen. 2008. *Chinese Online BBS Sphere: What BBS Has Brought to China.* MA Thesis, Massachusetts Institute of Technology.

Karstedt, Susanne and Stephen Farrell. 2006. The moral economy of everyday crime: Markets, consumers, and citizens. *British Journal of Criminology*, 46: 1011–1136.

Katz, Jack. 1980. The social movement against white-collar crime. In (Egon Bittner and Sheldon Messinger, eds.), *Criminology Review Yearbook*, vol. II. Beverly Hills, CA: Sage.

Laufer, William S. 2010. Secrecy, silence, and corporate crime reforms. *Criminology & Public Policy*.

Leighton, Paul. 2010. Fairness matters—more than deterrence: Class bias and the limits of deterrence. *Criminology & Public Policy*.

Levi, Michael. 2010. Serious tax fraud and noncompliance: A review of evidence on the differential impact of criminal and noncriminal proceedings. *Criminology & Public Policy*.

Michaels, David and Celeste Monforton. 2005. Scientific evidence in the regulatory system: Manufacturing uncertainty and the demise of the formal regulatory system. *Journal of Law & Policy*, 13:17–41.

Minkes, John. 2010. Silent or invisible? Governments and corporate financial crimes. *Criminology & Public Policy*.

Molotch, Harvey. 1970. Oil in Santa Barbara and power in America. *Sociological Inquiry*, 40: 131–144.

Nader, Ralph. 1965. *Unsafe at Any Speed: The Designed-in Dangers of the American Automobile*. New York: Grossman.

Nguyen, Tomson H. and Henry N. Pontell. 2010. Mortgage origination fraud and the global economic crisis: A criminological analysis. *Criminology & Public Policy*.

Pannell K.E. 2002. *Origins of the Better Business Bureau: A Private Regulatory Institution in the Progressive Era*. Unpublished manuscript, DePauw University. Retrieved August 11, 2009 from cs.indiana.edu~yonliu/econdesk/pannell.pdf.

Parker, Christine E. and Vibeke Lehmann Nielsen. 2006. Do businesses take compliance systems seriously? An empirical study of the implementation of trade practices compliance systems in Australia. *Melbourne University Law Review*, 30: 441–494.

Pontell, Henry N. and Gilbert Geis. 2010. How to effectively get crooks like Bernie Madoff in Dutch. *Criminology & Public Policy*.

Reichman, Nancy. 2010. Getting our attention. *Criminology & Public Policy*.

Rothe, Dawn L. 2010. Global E-waste trade: The need for formal regulation and accountability beyond the organization. *Criminology & Public Policy*.

Schlesinger, Arthur M. Jr. 1958. *The Coming of the New Deal*. Boston: Houghton Mifflin.

Shover, Neal and Andy Hochstetler. 2006. *Choosing White-Collar Crime*. New York: Cambridge University Press.

Shover, Neal and Ben W. Hunter. 2010. Blue-collar, white-collar: Crimes and mistakes. In (Wim Bernasco, ed.), *Offenders on Offending: Learning about Crime from Criminals*. Collompton, UK: Willan.

Sinclair, Upton. 1906. *The Jungle*. New York: Doubleday, Jabber, and Company.

Snider, Laureen. 2010. Framing e-waste regulation: The obfuscating role of power. *Criminology & Public Policy*.

Torgler, Benno. 2010. Serious tax noncompliance. *Criminology & Public Policy*.

von Drehle, David. 2003. *Triangle: The Fire that Changed America*. New York: Atlantic Monthly Press.

28

Prevention and Treatment from a Biosocial Perspective

Kevin Beaver

Biosocial criminology is an emerging perspective that has gained traction in the past few years. Unfortunately, even though more and more students are becoming interested in learning about the genetic, biological, and neurological foundations to antisocial behaviors, most criminology programs do not offer classes in biosocial criminology. As a result, most undergraduate and graduate criminology students earn their degrees with very little, if any, exposure to the biosocial correlates to crime and delinquency. The purpose of this chapter is to provide those who are interested in biosocial criminology a concise introduction to this perspective.

INTRODUCTION

One of the main criticisms leveled against the biosocial perspective is that it does not provide any guidance on how to prevent antisocial behaviors or how to rehabilitate criminals. According to this line of reasoning, criminal behavior is controlled by genes, and since genes are immutable, then criminal behavior is not preventable nor is it treatable. Some biosocial opponents even go so far as to argue that biosocial

Source: Pages 203–215 of Biosocial Psychology: A Primer by Kevin M. Beaver.

criminology can only lead to "lock-them-up-and-throw-away-the-key" crime control policies, where criminals are identified through genetic testing and then incarcerated for the remainder of their life. Criminals, in other words, are "born bad" and thus are impervious to prevention and treatment strategies.

The critics who set forth this argument (or some variant thereof) are engaging in pure rhetoric. No biosocial criminologist believes that genes are the end-all-be-all to antisocial phenotypes. In fact, biosocial criminologists draw attention to the complexity of human behavior and argue that a confluence of genetic, biological, and environmental factors produce antisocial behaviors. Most importantly, all of these factors work *interactively* and are *co-dependent* on each other. What this means is that the effects of genetic factors are dependent on the presence of environmental factors and vice versa. This has particular relevance to prevention and treatment strategies because genes do not have to be physically altered in order to alter their effects; *genetic effects can be altered by altering the environment*. It is also narrow thinking to assume that biosocial criminologists always examine genetic factors. This simply is not the case. There are a number of different environmental factors that may exert an effect on the development of antisocial phenotypes, independent of genotype. Many of these environments, such as prenatal exposure to cigarette smoke, can be eliminated without having to worry about genotype.

The goal of the current chapter is to provide a rough sketch of how the biosocial perspective can be used in the prevention and treatment of antisocial behaviors. In so doing, this chapter will be divided into two halves. The first half will be devoted to exploring how biosocial research can inform crime prevention strategies. Emphasis will be placed on altering environmental factors. The second half of the chapter will examine how biosocial research can inform strategies designed to rehabilitate criminals.

BIOSOCIAL PREVENTION STRATEGIES

Before moving into a discussion of biosocial prevention strategies, it is essential to make the distinction between prevention programs and treatment programs. Prevention programs are designed to impede antisocial behaviors from ever surfacing, while treatment programs (sometimes referred to as rehabilitation programs) are designed to reduce future criminal involvement among criminals. Although both of these programs can be effective at reducing criminal involvement, the general consensus is that prevention programs are better able to reduce crime than are treatment programs. To see why this is the case, let's take a quick look at when antisocial phenotypes begin to emerge and how they relate to later life involvement in crime and delinquency.

Generally speaking, behavioral problems begin to emerge during childhood or even earlier. For the most part, childhood antisocial behavior is just a phase and by the time most children enter into school, their behavior improves markedly. But for a small group of children—especially those who are the "worst of the worst"—their antisocial behavior persists.[1] What this means is that these children will eventually grow into adolescents who engage in acts of serious violence and, as adults, they will become hardened criminals, wracking up long rap sheets, accruing multiple arrests, and spending a considerable amount of time incarcerated.[2] Because the majority of adult criminals have long histories of antisocial conduct, usually dating back to childhood, it is common to hear that the best predictor of future misbehavior is past misbehavior. In academic terms, this means that antisocial behavior is highly stable across the life course, where the way someone acts as a child is a harbinger of how they will act as an adult. The most effective prevention programs thus must be implemented in childhood (or earlier) in order to prevent antisocial behaviors from emerging.

To quell the emergence of antisocial phenotypes, prevention programs are frequently based on what is known as the "risk factor prevention paradigm."[3] To understand this paradigm, it is first necessary to introduce what is meant by a risk factor.[4] A risk factor is any factor that when present increases the odds of displaying antisocial phenotypes. Associating with delinquent peers is a risk factor for delinquency because if an adolescent is exposed to antisocial friends then they are more likely to become delinquent than if they had not been exposed to antisocial friends. Some risk factors, such as delinquent peers and low levels of self-control, have strong effects on delinquency and thus are potent risk factors, while others, such as poverty and low socioeconomic status, have small effects on antisocial behaviors and thus are weak risk factors.[5] Risk factors that are associated with crime, delinquency, or some other antisocial outcome are often referred to as criminogenic risk factors or crime-producing risk factors.

Not all criminogenic risk factors are *causes* of antisocial phenotypes; some are only correlates.[6] To understand this, think back to the discussion of spurious associations where we discussed the interrelationships among ice cream sales, temperature, and violent crime. Remember that although ice cream sales and violent crime were positively correlated, this correlation disappeared after taking into account temperature. If we use this example again, we could identify ice cream sales as a criminogenic risk factor for violent crime. Of course you would not identify ice cream sales as a *causal* criminogenic risk factor, but it is a risk factor nonetheless. When using the risk factor approach in the prevention of crime, the goal is to identify causal criminogenic risk factors, not risk factors that are spuriously related to crime. Although it is impossible to establish causality, it is not impossible to establish spuriousness. Prevention programs should focus on those risk factors that have not yet been found to be spurious.

There are, in general, two main types of risk factors: static risk factors and dynamic risk factors. Static risk factors are those risk factors that cannot be changed. Gender is an example of a static risk factor because although being a male is a potent criminogenic risk factor it cannot be altered. Dynamic risk factors, in contrast, are those risk factors that can be changed. Associating with delinquent peers is an example of a dynamic risk factor because a youth's peer group can be changed (e.g., they could shed their delinquent peers and begin to associate with prosocial friends). When working from a biosocial perspective, the distinction between static risk factors and dynamic risk factors often becomes muddied. For example, is a genetic polymorphism that confers an increased risk to aggression a static risk factor or a dynamic risk factor? On the one hand, it is a static risk factor because it is not possible to physically alter the gene. But, on the other hand, it is a dynamic risk factor because the effects of many genetic polymorphisms are contingent on the presence of certain environments; changing the environment will change the effect of the gene. So when considering whether a gene is a static risk factor or a dynamic risk factor it is imperative to examine how the effect of the particular gene waxes and wanes in response to environmental conditions.

In addition, some biosocial risk factors are dynamic risk factors at one point in time, but become static risk factors at another point in time. Consider, for instance, prenatal exposure to cigarette smoke. Prenatal exposure to cigarette smoke is a dynamic risk factor prior to or during pregnancy. Why?—because it is possible to alter whether a pregnant mother smokes cigarettes. After birth, however, prenatal exposure to cigarette smoke changes from a dynamic risk factor into a static risk factor. Why?—because it is impossible to undo any harmful effects that exposure to cigarette smoke had on the developing fetus. Time, therefore, matters when considering whether some biosocial risk factors are dynamic or static.

Risk factors work probabilistically. What this means is that the presence of a criminogenic risk factor *increases the likelihood* of antisocial behavior; however, not all people who have a particular criminogenic risk factor will become antisocial and some people without a particular criminogenic risk factor will become antisocial. Let's explore this in a little greater detail. Suppose that we could assign probabilities to each risk factor, such that the probability equaled the odds of criminal involvement. Pretend that one risk factor, let's call it risk factor X, had a probability of .20, while another risk factor, risk factor Z, had a probability of .10. If we ignored all of the other risk factors, and looked just at X and Z, we could determine the probability that someone would become a criminal. For example, the probability of someone becoming a criminal if they had risk factor X would be .20, while the probability of becoming a criminal for someone with risk factor Z would be .10. These risk factors clearly increase the probability of becoming a criminal, but they do not determine with 100 percent accuracy who will and who will not become an offender.

Given that criminogenic risk factors are associated with the development of antisocial phenotypes, the key to preventing crime is to suppress these risk factors from emerging or, if they have already emerged, eliminate them before they can have an effect. To do so, prevention (and treatment) efforts are most interested in identifying causal criminogenic risk factors that are potent and dynamic. Potent risk factors are targeted because they are the risk factors that have the strongest effects. Presumably this means that if potent risk factors are eliminated, then the odds of future antisocial behavior will also drop. If we return to the previous example with risk factors X and Z, we can see that it would make more sense to target risk factor X instead of risk factor Z. Why?—because if risk factor X is successfully eliminated, then the odds of antisocial behavior should decrease by .20, while successfully eliminating risk factor Z would only decrease the odds of antisocial behavior by .10.

Dynamic risk factors are targeted because they can be altered. It would not make any sense to focus on static risk factors (no matter how potent they are) because they cannot be changed. For example, pretend that having blue eyes was a potent risk factor for criminal involvement. While this surely would be important information to know, it would not be particularly relevant when trying to prevent crime because it is not a modifiable risk factor. The effectiveness of prevention programs hinges on the ability to identify potent dynamic risk factors.

Prevention efforts often target families that are at-risk for having children who will become involved in crime and delinquency. These at-risk families can be identified using a variety of different methods, but typically risk factors are used. For example, children born into families that are poor, that are headed by a single mother, and that are located in disadvantaged neighborhoods would be considered at-risk for delinquency. Other risk factors beyond those just listed could also be used to identify at-risk children. Once these at-risk families have been selected, then prevention programs can be employed to prevent the emergence of criminogenic risk factors (e.g., helping women to quit smoking prior to becoming pregnant) or to eliminate the existing criminogenic risk factors (e.g., informing parents about the dangers of abuse and neglect). For prevention programs to be effective, they must successfully change or modify potent dynamic risk factors.

The most difficult task is figuring out which risk factors to target and how to alter them. Part of the reason that some prevention programs have not been very successful is because they focus on changing the wrong risk factors. For example, sociological criminologists often point to negative parental socialization as a criminogenic risk factor that prevention programs should target.[7] According to this logic, children are molded into behaving or misbehaving depending on how they are socialized by their parents. Contrary to popular belief, parental socialization is not a strong criminogenic risk factor. Consequently prevention programs that focus narrowly on altering the way a parent parents most likely will not be very successful at reducing antisocial behaviors. This is exactly what research has revealed.

For example, in a large-scale study, Harriet Hiscock and colleagues implemented a randomized experiment to determine whether decreasing harsh parenting would reduce childhood behavioral problems.[8] To do so, they split the sample into two groups: an experimental group that received the parent-training program and a control group that did not. Prior to the parenting intervention, the two groups were identical in terms of the child's behavioral problems and parent's harsh parenting—in other words, there were not any preexisting differences between the two groups. After the parent-training class, the parents from the experimental group were significantly less likely to use harsh discipline in comparison with parents from the control group—initial evidence that the program worked. There was a catch, however: the behavioral problems for the children from the two groups remained identical. In other words, although parenting improved for the experimental group, this improvement did not correspond with an improvement in the child's behavior.

This study highlights the fact that effective prevention programs must be successful in identifying potent criminogenic risk factors. If the wrong risk factors are targeted (e.g., parental socialization), then the odds of future criminal involvement will be unaffected. There are certainly hundreds of risk factors that can be used by prevention programs, but the ones that appear to be among the most salient are biosocial risk factors. Of all the biosocial risk factors, those that adversely affect brain development, such as prenatal risk factors, perinatal risk factors, and risk factors in infancy and childhood, appear to be the most applicable to early life crime prevention strategies. Presented below are three main ways that these biosocial risk factors can be targeted by prevention programs.

1. Prevention programs should educate parents-to-be, especially mothers-to-be, on the importance of a healthy pregnancy.

One of the keys to reducing antisocial behavior is promoting healthy fetal brain development. Too often, however, normal fetal brain development is compromised—either knowingly or unknowingly—by the actions of the mother. Pregnant mothers who smoke, consume alcohol, or use other types of drugs may cause irreversible damage to their unborn child. Although it may seem like common knowledge that these substances may adversely affect the fetus, not all women are aware of the effects that these drugs have on the developing fetus. There is some evidence to indicate, however, that educating women about the deleterious effects that these substances have on the fetus may actually reduce rates of use.[9] This is why prevention programs need to educate expectant mothers on the dangers of using tobacco, alcohol, and illegal drugs during pregnancy.

Fathers can also be a major culprit in exposing the fetus to toxins. To see how this could be the case, consider that research has shown that pregnant mothers who are exposed to second-hand smoke have offspring who are at-risk for behavioral problems.[10] A major source of exposure to second-hand smoke for pregnant mothers is their spouse or significant other. As a result fathers also need to be educated by prevention programs on how their behaviors can place the developing fetus in jeopardy.

2. Prevention programs should provide parents with adequate prenatal healthcare.

Although educating parents-to-be about the importance of a healthy pregnancy is vitally important to fetal development, it is not a substitute for prenatal healthcare coverage. Routine checkups can be used to provide information to mothers about their pregnancy, including what to do (e.g., eat properly) and what not to do (e.g., consume alcohol). Regular doctor visits are also needed in order to monitor the pregnancy, including both the mother and the fetus. Many problems that arise during pregnancy (e.g., gestational diabetes) do not pose a threat to the fetus as long as they are tracked closely by a doctor. This is especially true near the end of pregnancy, where the fetus is monitored to ensure it is not in distress and to ensure it is delivered within a normal time frame. Unfortunately, not all pregnant women have access to healthcare, a problem that disproportionately affects single, unmarried women living in poverty. Prevention programs should thus provide free prenatal healthcare coverage to those families that cannot afford it.

3. Prevention programs should offer free post-birth classes that are designed to inform new parents about early childhood development.

Many parents are woefully ignorant about early childhood development, including how early-life experiences, such as abuse, may lead to later life behavioral problems. There is often a misconception that if the child is too young to remember the event (e.g., abuse) they will not be affected by it. This is not true; abuse, neglect, and trauma very early in the life course (even before the formation of memories) can have lasting effects by interrupting brain development. Likewise, parents often lack a full appreciation of the important role that nutrition has on brain development and even behavioral problems later in life. Prevention programs should thus educate parents about early childhood development, especially about how the brain can be affected by early-life experiences. This information would likely prove useful in fostering healthy brain development and preventing behavioral problems.

The Nursing-Family Partnership: A model biosocial prevention program. One prevention program that follows many of the recommendations set forth above is the Nursing-Family Partnership (NFP) developed by David Olds. The NFP was developed to improve the developmental outcomes of children born into high-risk families, where high-risk families were defined as pregnant teens who were unmarried and who were of low socioeconomic status. (Children born to mothers with these characteristics are at high-risk for a range of maladaptive outcomes, including antisocial phenotypes.) Once identified, the pregnant women were randomly assigned to either an experimental group where they received the NFP or to a control group where they received "comparison" services.

Women who were enrolled in the NFP were provided with a range of different services that began before the birth of their child. As Olds explains:

> During pregnancy, the nurses helped women complete 24-hour diet histories on a regular basis and plot weight gains at every visit; they assessed the women's cigarette smoking and use of alcohol and illegal drugs and facilitated a reduction in the use of these substances through behavioral change strategies. They taught women the signs and symptoms of pregnancy complications, encouraged women to inform the office-based staff about those complications, and facilitated compliance with treatment. They gave particular attention to urinary tract infections, sexually transmitted diseases, and hypertensive disorders of pregnancy (conditions associated with poor birth outcomes). They coordinated care with physicians and nurses in the office and measured blood pressure when needed.[11]

The NFP thus targets many of the prenatal and perinatal environments (e.g., prenatal exposure to cigarette smoke, diet/nutrition, and birth complications) as having some of the strongest effects on brain development and antisocial phenotypes. But, the NFP did not end here; the nursing visits continued from birth until the child was about two years old. During these visits, parents were educated about how to care for their child, how to understand their child, the importance of parent-child interactions, the consequences of abuse and neglect, and other skills needed to promote healthy development. Overall, then, the NFP focused resources on two time periods: pregnancy and the first two years of life. Olds summarized the NFP in the following way:

> The Nurse-Family Partnership (NFP) is different from most mental-health, substance-abuse, and crime-prevention interventions tested to date in that it focuses on improving *neuro-developmental, cognitive*, and behavioral functioning of the child by improving prenatal health, reducing child abuse and neglect, and enhancing family functioning and economic self-sufficiency in the *first two years of the child's life*. These early alterations in biology, behavior, and family context are expected to shift the life-course trajectories of children living in highly disadvantaged families and neighborhoods away from psychopathology, substance use disorders, and risky sexual behaviors. *Part of the program effect is now thought to be accomplished by moderating environmental risks that interact with genetic variations to increase the risk for poor child health and development.*[12] [emphasis added]

So the NFP targets many of the criminogenic risk factors that biosocial criminologists point to as particularly salient, but the real pressing question is whether the NFP was effective? Be your own judge. In comparison with the control group, women who participated in the NFP smoked fewer cigarettes while pregnant, had better prenatal diets, and had fewer kidney infections during pregnancy.[13] After birth, NFP women, in comparison with the control group, were less likely to abuse and neglect their children.[14] Clearly, the criminogenic risk factors targeted by the NFP were successfully altered, but did modifying these risk factors result in a concomitant decrease in offspring antisocial phenotypes? Without a doubt. Children from the NFP, when compared to children from the control group, were less likely to run away from home, had fewer arrests, had fewer convictions, had fewer sexual partners, smoked fewer cigarettes, consumed less alcohol, and had fewer alcohol- or drug-related behavioral problems.[15] These substantial reductions in antisocial behavior—reductions that are rare among crime prevention programs—are testimony to the fact that biosocial criminology has the potential to guide the development of successful crime prevention programs.

BIOSOCIAL TREATMENT STRATEGIES

Although prevention programs that are implemented very early in life are the most effective way to prevent antisocial phenotypes, there are numerous obstacles with using such programs. For example, it is not possible to identify all at-risk families; some at-risk families may decline to participate in the program; and there may not be programs available in certain areas. Even among children who participate in these programs, a substantial number will still develop into adolescent delinquents or adult criminals. As a result, treatment programs are needed to help rehabilitate offenders into law-abiding citizens. Unfortunately recidivism rates are extremely high—even among offenders who successfully complete rehabilitation programs. But, there are at least four ways that the findings from biosocial criminological research can be used to improve the success rates of treatment programs.

1. Treatment programs should assess each offender's genetic risk to determine their eligibility in the program.

Not all offenders are equally likely to benefit from participating in a rehabilitation program. What is particularly interesting to learn is that treatment programs are the most effective for high-risk offenders, not low-risk offenders.[16] In fact, there is even some empirical research showing that low-risk offenders who complete treatment programs have higher recidivism rates when compared to low-risk offenders who did not participate in such programs.[17] As a result, many of the leading rehabilitation scholars advocate assessing each offender's risk level.[18] This is typically accomplished by using some type of actuarial tool that measures antisocial personality traits, antisocial cognitions, and other criminogenic risk factors (but not biosocial criminogenic risk factors). If the assessment indicates that the offender is high-risk, then they are funneled into a rehabilitation program, while offenders who are not high-risk are not placed into treatment programs. Again, it is important to reiterate that treatment programs are most effective at reducing recidivism among high-risk offenders.

Although risk assessment has become commonplace among rehabilitation programs, there is virtually no discussion of assessing offenders based on their genetic risk. Even though critics of biosocial criminology would argue that genetic testing is unconstitutional, dangerous, and evil, it should be pointed out that it is quite possible that treatment programs would be most beneficial to offenders with high genetic risk, not low genetic risk. In other words, genetic testing could be used as a way of delineating those who are the most likely to benefit from the program versus those who are the least likely to benefit from the program. That is precisely what the current risk assessments are designed to do, but instead of looking at genetic polymorphisms, they look at other criminogenic risk factors.

No study has explored the possibility that genetic risk may be related to success rates for criminals. There is, however, one study that examined the association among parenting skills training courses, cortisol levels (remember, cortisol is secreted in response to stressful situations), and DRD4 in a sample of children with externalizing behavioral problems.[19] The results of the study indicated that the parent-training class was associated with decreased levels of cortisol for children with high genetic risk (as measured by the 7R allele of DRD4), but not for children with low genetic risk. This single study, while only suggestive, provides empirical evidence that genetic risk level may be an important factor in determining the effectiveness of rehabilitation programs.

Given the potential importance of this topic, future clinicians should begin to entertain the possibility of assessing genetic risk prior to shuffling offenders into treatment programs.

2. Treatment programs should consider the possibility that genetic factors moderate the effectiveness of the program.

It is widely recognized that individual-level characteristics are highly influential in structuring how offenders respond to treatment programs. Characteristics, such as age, gender, IQ and even some biological factors, such as neurocognitive skills[20], may moderate the effectiveness of the rehabilitation program. To illustrate, males may be less likely than females to recidivate after completing treatment program A, while females may be less likely than males to recidivate after completing treatment program B. What this means is that in order to achieve the highest rates of success, rehabilitation programs need to be individually tailored to the offenders' characteristics.

Although a host of individual-level characteristics have been identified as potentially moderating program effectiveness, genetic factors have, once again, been overlooked. This is a serious oversight because genetic factors often interact with or condition the effects of environmental factors. This has direct application to rehabilitation programs because the program's effectiveness may depend on genotype. For example, people with one particular genotype may respond well to a particular treatment, but people with a different genotype may respond better to a different treatment. By taking into account genotype, rehabilitation programs can be individually tailored to each person giving them the highest chance of success (i.e., non-recidivism).

The importance of genotype to treatment response, while not investigated by criminologists, has been recognized in other fields of study. The medical community, in particular, has long recognized the possibility that genes may be implicated in how people respond to drugs. Known as pharmacogenomics, this field of study has shown that certain drugs are effective for people with particular genotypes, while these same drugs are ineffective or produce harmful side effects for people with different genotypes.[21] There is no reason why rehabilitation programs could not engage in this same practice, a view originally pointed out by the renowned scholar Richard Tremblay when he stated:

> Drug companies are developing a new research field which has been labeled 'pharmacogenomics.' Its aim is to create the knowledge which will enable the creation of pharmaceutical products meant to match the genetic makeup of an individual. It is easy to imagine that we can do the same with psychosocial interventions: match the intervention to the genetic profile of the client.[22]

Although rehabilitation programs have yet to use genotype as a way to construct personalized rehabilitation programs, the NFP program is taking this possibility seriously. According to David Olds: "We are beginning to conduct genotyping of the mothers and children in our samples in order to understand more precisely those groups who benefit from the intervention, and those who do not, and why."[23] Hopefully other programs will follow the lead of Olds' NFP and begin to genotype their clients. If this becomes standard practice, then the effectiveness of rehabilitation programs will likely increase.

3. Treatment programs should use brain-imaging techniques to monitor each offender's progress through the program.

A wide range of treatment modalities have been employed in attempts to rehabilitate criminals. Some of these modalities, such as those involving acupuncture, have bordered on the ridiculous and have not, in any way, shape, or form, been effective at curbing recidivism. Others, such as those that emphasize interpersonal skills, have been relatively successful at reducing recidivism. But overall, the most effective treatment programs are those that use cognitive behavioral therapy. Very briefly, cognitive behavioral therapy focuses on changing what offenders think and how offenders think. To do so, cognitive behavioral programs are grounded in social learning theories, where change is encouraged by modeling prosocial cognitions, practicing these newly-acquired cognitive skills, and being rewarded for using them correctly. Programs that use cognitive behavioral therapy have been found to reduce recidivism by as much as 50 percent.[24]

Why are cognitive behavioral programs so effective at reducing recidivism? To answer this question, remember that some criminals have brain abnormalities, where certain regions of their brains (e.g., the prefrontal cortex, the amygdala, etc.) function differently than non-criminals. That is particularly important because cognitive behavioral programs have been found to alter brain activity in clinical samples. For example, Kimberly Goldapple and her colleagues examined the association between brain functioning and cognitive behavioral therapy in a sample of depressed patients.[25] This team of researchers used neuroimaging techniques to determine whether the cognitive behavioral program changed brain activity in the sample. The results indicated that cognitive behavioral therapy was associated with changes in the limbic system and the frontal cortex. Similar findings were reported in another study that examined the association between cognitive behavioral therapy and brain functioning in a sample of patients with posttraumatic stress disorder.[26] In this research, the application of cognitive behavioral therapy reduced activity levels in the amygdala. The results of these studies, along with others[27], indicate that the most effective treatment programs are the ones that alter brain functioning.

These findings point to the likelihood that cognitive behavioral programs are effective at reducing recidivism because they change brain functioning. Unfortunately no study has ever tested this possibility on samples of criminals and so it remains to be seen whether cognitive behavioral programs alter brain functioning in offenders. To the extent that they do, then it would be possible to monitor progress through rehabilitation programs by examining brain functioning. Prior to release, offenders could be subjected to brain scans to determine whether they are ready to be released. If the brain scan reveals appropriate changes to the brain, then they would be released; if not, they would have to remain in the program for an extended period of time. By using neuroimaging techniques, practitioners would be provided with an empirically based and objective way to determine whether the offender has been rehabilitated.

4. Treatment programs should begin to take seriously the possibility that epigenetic therapies may be a powerful way to reduce antisocial behaviors.

There is growing recognition that diseases and disorders, such as cancer, that are strongly influenced by genetic factors may be treated with epigenetic drugs (sometimes referred to as pharmacoepigenetics).[28] Recall that epigenetic modifications refer to alterations in gene activity (e.g., genes being switched "on" or "off") without alterations to the DNA. To see how knowledge about epigenetics can be used to treat disorders, pretend that a particular gene, say gene C, is a cause of a particular disorder, say disorder D. Let's also pretend that gene C is the only cause of disorder D, meaning that persons with gene C will always develop disorder D. Now let's suppose that a certain drug could be used to "silence" or "turn off" gene C via epigenetic modifications. In theory, it would be possible to erase disorder D through epigenetic changes that result from taking epigenetic drugs.

All of this may sound a bit like science fiction, but it's not. Researchers are beginning to identify certain drugs that affect epigenetic processes, and these drugs are potentially important in the treatment of certain diseases, especially cancer. Although it is much too early to determine how effective these drugs are in the fight against cancer, initial results indicate high levels of success.[29]

So epigenetic drugs may be useful when treating disorders and diseases, but would they have any application to preventing crime or rehabilitating criminals? The short answer is that we do not know; there is not any research conducted on humans that has examined whether epigenetic drugs could change antisocial behaviors. There are two main reasons why it makes logical sense to think that epigenetic drugs could be used as a way to reduce antisocial phenotypes. First, it is known that genetic factors account for at least 50 percent of the variance in antisocial phenotypes. In addition, a number of genetic polymorphisms have been identified that are associated with delinquent and criminal involvement. Thus, if it was possible to somehow "silence" these genes, then it would stand to reason that criminal involvement should decrease. Of course, the human genome and the human epigenome are much too complex to predict in advance how epigenetic drugs may work on criminals, but it is a line of inquiry that needs to be explored.

The second reason to suspect that epigenetic drugs may be effective at crime and delinquency is because these phenotypes are influenced, in part, by early abuse, neglect, and maltreatment. These criminogenic environments likely exert part of their influence by producing epigenetic modifications. To illustrate let's look at a study conducted by Ian Weaver and colleagues where they examined maternal nurturing among rats.[30] The rats that were nurtured by their mothers were relatively calm and passive, while the rats that were not nurtured by their mothers were anxious and not adaptive. The differences between these two groups of rats were tied to differences in epigenetics, where rats that were nurtured had different epigenetic patterns when compared to rats that were not nurtured by their mothers. One of the more fascinating aspects of this study was that if the rats that were not nurtured were administered a drug, their epigenetic patterns were reversed and resembled the epigenetic patterns of the nurtured rats. What's more is that after the epigenetic patterns had been reversed by the drug, the rat pups' behavior changed; no longer were they anxious, but they were more passive and docile just like the rat pups that were nurtured their mothers. This study hints at the possibility that epigenetic drugs may be able to erase—at least partially—the deleterious effects of certain adverse environments.

Given that the study of epigenetics and how it relates to human phenotypes remains in its infancy, much of what is known about epigenetic therapies remains pure speculation. Even so, the possibility that epigenetic drugs could potentially be used to treat criminals should be taken seriously by criminologists and clinicians alike.

SUMMARY

This chapter explored the various ways that biosocial criminological research could be used to prevent the emergence of antisocial phenotypes and to rehabilitate criminal offenders. It was shown that prevention and rehabilitation programs based on biosocial research offer new and refreshing ways to increase the effectiveness of such programs. Most importantly, especially to opponents of biosocial criminology, is that the prevention of crime and the treatment of criminals need not be oppressive, punitive, or unnecessarily harsh. This should go a long way in assuaging the concerns that sociological criminologists have in studying the biosocial underpinnings to antisocial behaviors.

DISCUSSION QUESTIONS

1. Describe David Olds's Nurse-Family Partnership. Identify the main reasons that it is so effective at reducing antisocial behaviors.
2. Describe how the biosocial perspective could be used to develop an effective prevention program.
3. Describe how the biosocial perspective could be used to develop an effective rehabilitation program.
4. Suppose someone was arguing that biosocial criminology could only lead to oppressive and inhumane crime-control policies. How would you explain to this critic that his or her view is unfounded?
5. Discuss why it is important to target biological, genetic, and environmental criminogenic risk factors when attempting to reduce criminal involvement.

ENDNOTES

1. Beaver, K.M., & Wright, J.P. (2007). The stability of low self-control from kindergarten through first grade. *Journal of Crime and Justice, 30*, 63-86; Loeber, R. (1982). The stability of antisocial and delinquent child behavior: A review. *Child Development, 53*, 1431–1446; Nagin, D., & Paternoster, R. (2000). Population heterogeneity and state dependence: State of the evidence and directions for future research. *Journal of Quantitative Criminology, 16*, 117–144; Olweus, D. (1979). Stability of aggressive reaction patterns in males: A review. *Psychological Bulletin, 86*, 852–875.

2. DeLisi, M. (2005). *Career criminals in society*. Thousand Oaks, CA: Sage.

3. Farrington, D.P. (2000). Explaining and preventing crime: The globalization of knowledge—the American Society of Criminology 1999 Presidential Address. *Criminology, 38*, 1–24.

4. I will not discuss protective factors here. For a discussion of protective factors see Farrington (2000).

5. Andrews, D.A., & Bonta, J. (2003). *The psychology of criminal conduct, 3rd edition*. Cincinnati, OH: Anderson.

6. Kazdin, A.E., Kraemer, H.C., Kessler, R.C., Kupfer, D.J., & Offord, D.R. (1997). Contributions of risk-factor research to developmental psychopathology. *Clinical Psychology Review, 17*, 375–406.

7. Lykken, D.T. (2000). The causes and costs of crime and a controversial cure. *Journal of Personality, 68*, 559–605.

8. Hiscock, H., Bayer, J.K., Price, A., Ukoumunne, O.C., Rogers, S., & Wake, M. (2008). Universal parenting programme to prevent early childhood behavioural problems: Cluster randomised trial. *British Medical Journal, 336*, 318–321.

9. Fang, W.L., Goldstein, A.O., Butzen, A.Y., Hartsock, S.A. et al. (2004). Smoking cessation in pregnancy: A review of postpartum relapse prevention strategies. *Journal of the American Board of Family Medicine, 17*, 264–275; Gebauer, C., Kwo, C.Y., Haynes, E.F., & Wewers, M.E. (1998). A nurse-managed smoking cessation intervention during pregnancy. *Journal of Obstetric, Gynecologic, and Neonatal Nursing, 27*, 47–53.

10. Gatzke-Kopp, L.M., & Beauchaine, T.P. (2007). Direct and passive prenatal nicotine exposure and the development of externalizing psychopathology. *Child Psychiatry and Human Development, 38*, 255–269.

11. Olds, D.L. (2007). Preventing crime with prenatal and infancy support of parents: The Nurse-Family Partnership. *Victims and Offenders, 2*, 205–225, pp. 212–213.

12. Olds, D.L. (2007). Preventing crime with prenatal and infancy support of parents: The Nurse-Family Partnership. *Victims and Offenders, 2*, 205–225. pp. 212–213, p. 206.

13. Olds, D.L., Henderson, C.R., Kitzman, H.J., Eckenrode, J.J., Cole, R.E., & Tatelbaum, R.C. (1999). Prenatal and infancy home visitations by nurses: Recent findings. *The Future of Children, 9*, 44–65.

14. Eckenrode, J., Ganzel, B., Henderson, C.R., Smith, E., Olds, D.L., Powers, J., Cole, R., Kitzman, H., & Sidora, K. (2000). Preventing child abuse and neglect with a program of nurse home visitation: The limiting effects of domestic violence. *Journal of the American Medical Association, 284*, 1385–1391.

15. Olds, D., Henderson, C.R., Cole, R., Eckenrode, J., Kitzman, H., Luckey, D., Pettitt, L., Sidora, K., Morris, P., & Powers, J. (1998). Long-term effects of nurse home visitation on children's criminal and antisocial behavior: 15-year follow-up of a randomized controlled trial. *Journal of the American Medical Association, 280*, 1238–1244.

16. Andrews, D.A., Zinger, I., Hoge, R.D., Bonta, J., Gendreau P., & Cullen, F.T. (1990). Does correctional treatment work? A clinically relevant and psychologically informed meta-analysis. *Criminology, 28*, 369–404.

17. Lowenkamp, C.T., & Latessa, E.J. (2005). Increasing the effectiveness of correctional programming through the risk principle: Identifying offenders for residential placement. *Criminology and Public Policy, 4*, 263–290.

18. Andrews, D.A., Zinger, I., Hoge, R.D., Bonta, J., Gendreau P., & Cullen, F.T. (1990). Does correctional treatment work? A clinically relevant and psychologically informed meta-analysis. *Criminology, 28*, 369–404.

19. Bakermans-Kranenburg, M.J., van IJzendoorn, M.H., Mesman, J., Alink, L.R.A., & Juffer, F. (2008). Effects of an attachment-based intervention on daily cortisol moderated by dopamine D4: A randomized control trial on 1- to 3-year-olds screened for externalizing behavior. *Development and Psychopathology, 20*, 805–820.

20. Fishbein, D.H., Hyde, C., Coe, B., & Paschall, M.J. (2004). Neurocognitive and physiological prerequisites for prevention of adolescent drug abuse. *The Journal of Primary Prevention, 24*, 471–495; Fishbein, D.H., Hyde, C., Eldreth, D., Paschall, M.J., Hubal, R., Das, A., Tarter, R., Ialongo, N., Hubbard, S., & Yung, B. (2006). Neurocognitive skills moderate urban male adolescents' responses to preventive intervention materials. *Drug and Alcohol Dependence, 82*, 47–60.

21. Evans, W., & Relling, M.V. (1999). Pharmacogenomics: Translating functional genomics into rational therapeutics. *Science, 286*, 487–491; March, R. (2000). Pharmacogenomics: The genomics of drug response. *Yeast, 17*, 16–21.

22. Tremblay, R.E. (2005). Towards an epigenetic approach to experimental criminology: The 2004 Joan McCord Prize Lecture. *Journal of Experimental Criminology, 1, 397–415*, p. 407.

23. Olds, D.L. (2007). Preventing crime with prenatal and infancy support of parents: The Nurse-Family Partnership. *Victims and Offenders, 2*, 205–225. pp. 212–213, p. 210.

24. Landenberger, N.A., & Lipsey, M.W. (2005). The positive effects of cognitive-behavioral programs for offenders: A meta-analysis of factors associated with effective treatment. *Journal of Experimental Criminology, 1*, 451–476.

25. Goldapple, K., Segal, Z., Garson, C., Lau, M., Bieling, P., Kennedy, S., & Mayberg, H. (2004). Modulation of cortical-limbic pathways in major depression: Treatment-specific effects of cognitive behavior therapy. *Archives of General Psychiatry, 61*, 34–41.

26. Felmingham, K., Kemp, A., Williams, L., Das, P., Hughes, G., Peduto, A., & Bryant, R. (2007). Changes in anterior cingulated and amygdala after cognitive behavior therapy of posttraumatic stress disorder. *Psychological Science, 18*, 127–129.

27. Brody, A.L., Saxena, S., Stoessel, P., Gillies, L.A., Fairbans, L.A. et al. (2001). Regional brain metabolic changes in patients with major depression treated with either paroxetine or interpersonal therapy: Preliminary findings. *Archives of General Psychiatry, 58*, 631–640; Martin, S.D., Martin, E., Rai, S.S., Richardson, M.A., & Royall, R. (2001). Brain blood flow changes in depressed patients treated with interpersonal psychotherapy or venlafaxine hydrochloride. *Archives of General Psychiatry, 58*, 641–648.

28. Peedicayil, J. (2006). Epigenetic therapy – A new development in pharmacology. *Indian Journal of Medical Research, 123*, 17–24; Yoo, C.B., Cheng, J.C., & Jones, P.A. (2004). Zebularine: A new drug for epigenetic therapy. *Biochemical Society Transactions, 32*, 910–912.

29. Garcia-Manero, G., Kantarjian, H.M., Sanchez-Gonzalez, B., Yang, H. et al. (2006). Phase 1/2 study of the combination of 5-aza-2'-deoxycytidine with valproic acid in patients with leukemia. *Blood, 108*,

3271–3279; Issa, J.-P.J., Garcia-Manero, G., Giles, F.J., Mannari, R., Thomas, D. et al. (2004). Phase 1 study of low-dose prolonged exposure to schedules of the hypomethylating agent 5-aza-2'-deoxycytidine (decitabine) in hematopoietic malignancies. *Blood, 103*, 1635–1640.

30. Weaver, I.C.G., Cervoni, N., Champagne, F.A., D'Alessio, A.C., Sharma, S., Seckl, J.R., Dymov, S., Szyf, M., & Meaney, M.J. (2004). Epigenetic programming in maternal behavior. *Nature Neuroscience,* 7, 847–854.

29

An Overview of Gun Control Policy in the United States

Gary Kleck

With nearly one-half of all households owning firearms, the gun control issue has never been more significant. In this chapter Kleck summarizes the literature on guns, violence and gun control, as well as reporting new research. Some of the topics addressed are the tradition of gun ownership, guns and violence, gun control policies, both on the state and federal level, gun control and criminals, and the future of gun control policies.

On June 26, 2008 a divided Supreme Court handed down its decision in District of Columbia v. Heller, declaring that the Second Amendment to the Constitution recognizes an individual right to keep and bear arms, and rejecting the notion that the right pertained only to arms possession in connection with militia service. The decision was unclear as to exactly what gun control measures would thereby be impermissible, beyond absolute prohibitions of home handgun possession for self-defense. Two years later, the Court further declared, in McDonald v. Chicago, that this right restricted what state and local governments, as well as the federal government, could do in the way of gun control (*New York Times*, 6-27-08, p. A1; 6-29-10, p. A1). Spokespersons for gun control advocacy groups deplored the decisions, the Violence Policy Center even declaring that "people will die because of this [McDonald] decision," and castigating "the wrong-headed notion that more guns make us safer" (PRNewswire 2010). Representatives of gun rights groups

Source: "An Overview of Gun Control Policy in the United States" by Gary Kleck. Reprinted with permission from the author.

like the National Rifle Association applauded the decisions as long overdue recognitions of fundamental rights, asserting that the decisions helped advance the safety of law-abiding citizens who keep and bear guns for self-defense.

Although the Court was largely silent as to what kinds of gun controls would not pass constitutional muster, it did make it clear that governments could not impose an absolute prohibition of the keeping of handguns in the home for purposes of self-defense. A right to keep guns for protection, however, would be of little significance if doing so did not in fact confer some defensive benefit or if few people enjoyed such benefits. There is a substantial body of scholarly research that bears on these sorts of factual issues, and many others that underlie heated American debate over guns. This chapter summarizes that body of knowledge.

THE TRADITION OF GUN OWNERSHIP IN THE UNITED STATES

In contrast to most other nations, gun ownership has always been widespread in the United States. An average of about 46 percent of US households reported owning guns in surveys in recent decades and, taking into account some gun owners' reluctance to report their gun ownership to surveyors, the true share could easily be 5–10 percentage points higher. Firearms ownership may well have been even higher in the past, when the nation was more rural, and hunting and other shooting sports were more widely pursued (Kleck 1997, Chapter 3). Lindgren and Heather (2002) estimated, based on probate court records from 1774, that 52% of male "wealthholders" (persons who had any property that needed to be allocated to heirs after their death) in the 13 colonies owned guns at the time of their death, a figure considerably higher than the percent of elderly males who reported personally owning guns in the 1990s.

By international standards, the share of US households with guns is extraordinarily high. The nearest known competitor is Switzerland, where about a third of households have guns, mainly due to military service requirements (Killias 1990). By 2011, there were probably over 320 million guns in private hands in the United States, about 36 percent of them handguns. The size of the US gun stock increased enormously from the 1960s through 2010, especially the handgun stock, though the share of US households with guns showed little change. One obvious policy implication of this huge existing stock is that an enormous supply of guns would remain available, to criminals and noncriminals alike, even if all further manufacture and importation of guns ceased immediately (Kleck 1997, Chapter 3). In contrast, only a few hundred thousand guns are used to commit violent crimes each year. Thus, the supply available greatly exceeds criminal demand.

Perhaps what is most striking about the patterns of gun ownership in the US is that ownership is generally highest in those groups where violence is lowest. Although both gun ownership and violence are more frequent among males and Southerners, gun ownership is also higher among whites than among blacks, higher among middle-aged people than among young people, higher among married than unmarried people, higher among richer people than poor, and higher in rural areas and small towns than urban areas - patterns that are all the reverse of the ways that violent criminal behavior is distributed (Kleck 1997, Chapter 3).

Most owners of guns in general, and long guns in particular, own them primarily for recreational reasons unrelated to crime, but about half of handgun owners, and some long gun owners as well, own guns mainly for protection against crime. Most American gun ownership is culturally patterned, linked with a rural hunting subculture. The culture is transmitted across generations, with gun owners being socialized from childhood by their parents into gun ownership and use. Thus, much gun ownership results from membership in subcultural groupings and the acceptance of norms and values favorable to gun ownership and use.

Discussing the conflicts among Americans over gun control, Bruce-Briggs (1976, p. 61) contrasted "two alternative views of what America is and ought to be," views that sociologists would identify as elements of two distinct subcultures:

> "On the one side are those who take bourgeois Europe as a model of a civilized society: a society just, equitable, and democratic; but well ordered, with the lines of responsibility and authority clearly drawn, and with decisions made rationally and correctly by intelligent men for the entire nation. On the other side are persons whose model is that of the independent frontiersman who takes care of himself and his family with no interference from the state. They are "conservative" in the sense that they cling to America's unique pre-modern tradition – a nonfeudal society with a sort of medieval liberty writ large for everyman."

In the gun-hunting subculture of rural and small town America, a boy's introduction to guns and hunting is an important rite of passage to manhood. Stinchcombe and his associates (1980) portrayed much gun ownership as resulting from membership in a rural hunting culture originating in the early settlement of the American frontier. They argued that the culture is found today primarily in rural areas and small towns and among ethnic and religious groups whose ancestors came to the United States early in its pre-industrial history. Persons with a family tradition of hunting, and an exposure, especially in the South and West, to regional values and norms encouraging hunting are more likely to own guns. Recreational gun owners are likely to have parents who owned guns, to have obtained their first gun at an early age, and to have been trained in gun use, suggesting socialization into a sporting gun culture (Lizotte and Bordua 1980).

In contrast, among persons who own guns for protection, there is no evidence of socialization into a gun-owning subculture. Protective gun owners commonly obtain their first guns as adults, without training in gun use, and without any family background in gun ownership. Defensive handgun owners are more likely to be disconnected from any gun subcultural roots, and their gun ownership is less likely to be accompanied by association with other gun owners in connection with gun-related activities or by training in the safe handling of guns. Defensive ownership is more likely to be an individualistic response to life circumstances perceived as dangerous (Lizotte and Bordua 1980).

The evidence supports a simple explanation of the unusually high level of gun ownership in America. Most of the guns in America are rifles and shotguns, and most of these are owned for hunting and for other shooting sports common among hunters. Unlike European nations with a feudal past, the US has had both widespread ownership of farmland and millions of acres of public lands available for hunting. Rather than being limited to a small land-owning aristocracy, hunting has been accessible to most ordinary Americans. Having the income and leisure to take advantage of these resources, millions of Americans have hunted for recreation, long after it ceased to be essential to survival for any but an impoverished few. Rather than high gun ownership being the result of a lack of strict gun control laws, widespread gun ownership predated the modern (largely post-1910) push for controls over firearms, and the huge mass of gun-owning voters later discouraged the enactment of stricter gun laws.

Beginning in the mid-1960s, however, concerns about crime began to drive up handgun acquisition. Crime rates rose rapidly in the period 1964-1974, then leveled off, showed short-term fluctuations through 1992, then steadily declined through 2000. While some Americans responded to rising crime rates by calling for stricter gun controls, others responded by acquiring guns, mostly handguns, for self-protection. As a result, the stock of guns owned, especially handguns, increased rapidly in the 1970s and 1980s, and more slowly in later decades.

THE USE OF GUNS IN VIOLENCE

It is well known that guns are used in many violent crimes in the US. There were as many as 350,000 violent crimes committed in the US in 2009 by offenders armed with guns, though not all of these involved the perpetrators actually using the guns, as distinct from merely possessing them during the incident. About 24 percent of robberies and five percent of assaults were committed by gun-armed offenders in 2008 (U.S. Bureau of Justice Statistics 2011, Table 66). Two thirds of homicides in 2009 were committed with guns, or about 10,227 gun homicides (U.S. Federal Bureau of Investigation 2011).

It is not so widely known that large numbers of crime victims in America also use guns in self-defense, usually against criminals without guns. Based on sixteen national telephone surveys of probability samples of the adult US population, the best available evidence indicates that guns are used by victims in self-protection considerably more often than crimes are committed by offenders using guns. For example, victims used guns defensively about 2.0–2.5 million times in 1993, compared to fewer than 600,000 violent crimes committed by offenders with guns (Kleck and Gertz 1995).

Defensive gun use is effective in preventing injury to the victim and property loss. Research based on interviews with large nationally representative samples of crime victims consistently indicates that those who use guns during crime incidents are less likely to be injured or lose property than those who either adopt other resistance strategies or do not resist at all. These effects are usually produced without shooting the gun or wounding a criminal – only 24 percent of gun defenders even fired the gun (including warning shots), only 16 percent tried to shoot the perpetrator, and at most 8 percent wounded the offender (evidence summarized in Kleck and Kates 2001, Chapter 7).

There is also evidence indicating that some criminals may be deterred from making some criminal attempts in the first place by the prospect of victim gun use against them. Criminals interviewed in prison indicate that they have refrained from committing crimes because they believed a potential victim might have a gun, and crime rates have dropped substantially after highly publicized instances of prospective victims arming themselves or being trained in gun use, or victims using guns against criminals. Evidence also indicates that US burglars are careful to avoid residences where the victims are home because they fear being shot. In one period, 43 percent of British residential burglaries were committed while victims were home, but only 9 percent of residential burglaries in the US were committed under such circumstances (research summarized in Kleck and Kates 2001, Chapter 7). In sum, many criminals use guns to commit violence and other crimes, but many victims also use guns to avoid injury and property loss. Thus, there are both harms from gun use by criminals and benefits from gun ownership and use by victims.

The research on gun use by victims is very consistent - it reduces the likelihood of harm. The best established effect of gun use by aggressors, on the other hand, is a 'lethality effect' – if an aggressor attacks and wounds a victim, the victim is more likely (probably about three to four times more likely) to die if the wound was inflicted with a gunshot than if it was inflicted with a knife, the weapon most likely to be used by a lethally minded attacker if a gun were not available (Kleck 1997, Chapter 7).

On the other hand, it is not so widely known that when criminal aggressors possess guns in a crime incident, they are substantially *less* likely to attack and injure their victims in the first place. At least nineteen studies have found that offenders possessing guns are less likely to injure their victims than offenders with other weapons or no weapons. The explanation appears to be that possession of a lethal weapon enables aggressors to intimidate victims without actually attacking them, in crimes where the offender's goal is not to kill the victim. Since a killing cannot occur if a wound is not inflicted, this is a fatality-reducing effect of aggressor gun possession. Thus, even gun possession by aggressors has some inadvertently violence-reducing effects, along with the violence-increasing 'lethality effect.' Nevertheless, the net effect of offender gun possession is that it increases the likelihood that a violent crime will result in the death of the victim.

Because gun possession among largely noncriminal prospective victims has beneficial effects, and gun possession among criminals has a mixture of both harmful and inadvertently beneficial effects, it is not at all obvious what the net effect of overall gun ownership levels on violence rates is likely to be. Research on crime rates in macro-level units like cities and states has produced distinctly mixed results on this issue, and most of the research is seriously flawed. In particular, most studies fail to properly model the possibility of a two-way relationship between violence rates and gun ownership rates, making it impossible to interpret the meaning of a positive association between the two (i.e. higher violence rates are found where there are higher gun levels). While more guns may lead to more crime, higher crime rates might also motivate more people to acquire guns for self-protection. The more sophisticated studies, which addressed this possible reciprocal causation, mostly have found that higher crime rates cause higher gun ownership levels, but that general gun ownership levels have no net effect on rates of violence and crime, including homicide. This finding does not preclude the possibility that gun ownership among criminals and other high-risk subsets of the population increases violence rates, but does suggest that any such effects are counterbalanced by violence-reducing effects of guns in the hands of crime victims and prospective victims.

GUN CONTROL IN AMERICA

The US is unusual in having a constitution that limits what the national government may do in restricting gun ownership. The meaning of the Second Amendment to the US constitution continues to be debated but the Supreme Court has ruled that the provision does recognize an individual right to keep and bear arms, including guns, and that the right restricts what gun controls state or local governments, as well as the federal government, may impose. The court made it clear that governments may not ban home handgun possession for defense, but otherwise left it largely open what other controls might be acceptable. For example, it is not clear whether restrictive licensing systems like that existing in New York City, which are arguably as restrictive as outright bans, could be considered constitutional.

Even before the Heller and McDonald decisions, most Americans believed that they have a right to own guns, and opposed gun controls that would interfere with that right. The huge body of evidence on American public opinion concerning gun control can easily be summarized: most Americans are willing to support a wide array of moderate regulatory controls aimed at keeping guns away from criminals, juveniles, and other higher-risk groups, but oppose gun bans or other controls that would preclude them from legally acquiring or owning guns. As a result, there is a huge number, and bewildering variety, of gun control laws in the US, but almost none (excepting those of New York City) seriously restrict noncriminal adult citizens' access to guns.

FEDERAL LAW

Under the federal system of government in the US, criminal laws are made at both the national and state level, as well as the local level. The vast majority of criminal laws, including gun control laws, are made at the state level. Federal gun laws are both less numerous than state laws and less restrictive than the laws prevailing in most states. Complicating things still further, local governments in some states are allowed to make some gun laws, and the strictest controls of all in the US are those enacted by municipal governments (the information on gun laws in this section is derived from US Bureau of Justice Statistics 1996; Brady Campaign to Prevent Gun Violence 2011; National Rifle Association 2011).

Under federal law, all persons in the regular business of selling guns must have a federal firearms dealer's license. Anyone purchasing a gun of any kind from a licensed dealer must pass a background check for a criminal conviction and other disqualifying attributes. It is unlawful for a convicted felon to purchase a gun or for a dealer to sell a gun to a felon. It is unlawful for any convicted felon to possess a gun of any kind, regardless of how it was obtained. It is unlawful, everywhere in the US, for a juvenile to possess a handgun, and unlawful to sell guns to juveniles.

Although all licensed dealers must record the identity of each gun buyer and the particulars of the gun transferred, there is no national registry of guns or gun owners, since records of active dealers are not centralized in federal government hands. There is also no federally mandated permit required for purchasing guns, nor any license required to own guns, though such controls are common at the state level. Thus, it is deliberate national policy that there be no national registry of guns or gun owners that could be used to facilitate the mass confiscation of guns. Perhaps most consequential of all limitations in federal gun law, firearms transfers between private persons, i.e. nonlicensees, are not subject to any background check under federal law.

STATE LAW

Each of the fifty states has a different array of gun laws. Some states have controls stricter than the average level prevailing among democracies outside the US (United Nations 1997, pp. 11–17), while others have only very limited controls. No state bans the private possession of guns, or of handguns, though a few states ban the purchase or possession of certain models of semi-automatic firearms loosely labeled "assault weapons" – guns that fire just one shot at a time but that look like, or were adapted from, military guns that could fire like machineguns. Almost all of the states forbid possession or purchase of handguns by convicted felons and juveniles, and most also do so with respect to other higher risk categories of persons, such as mentally ill persons and illicit drug users.

Fourteen states require a permit to purchase a handgun, and six of these also require a permit to buy a long gun. Although 25 of the states require that records of gun sales be reported to state or local authorities, only five have state-mandated handgun registration systems, and only two states register long guns other than "assault weapons." Although registration was once justified as a way to identify the perpetrators of individual crimes, the current rationale is that a record system that allows tracing the history of crime guns can help identify gun trafficking operations.

Nine states require a minimum waiting period of anywhere from one to fourteen days before buyers may take delivery of handguns they have purchased; six of these states also mandate waiting periods for long guns. The rationale for waiting periods has also changed. When it was thought that significant numbers of murderers acquired guns in the heat of passion to kill their victims, it was argued that the waiting period served as a "cooling-off" period during which the murderous impulse could fade. When it was found that virtually no killers acquired guns at the last minute from the licensed dealers likely to observe the waiting period, the rationale changed to the advantages of being able to conduct background checks that were more thorough than just the "instant" computer check mandated by federal law.

There are also diverse laws governing the concealed carrying of firearms in public places. In 40 states, covering most of the nation's population, adult residents without a criminal record may get a permit allowing concealed carrying if they pass a background check and complete a course in firearms safety and the law pertaining to self-defense and firearms. In two states (Illinois and Wisconsin), concealed carrying by civilians is completely forbidden, while in the remaining eight states and D.C. permits are technically available at the discretion of authorities but in practice are rarely granted, making these states effectively identical to those banning carrying.

GUN CONTROL LAWS AND THE SUPPLY OF GUNS TO CRIMINALS

Much U.S. gun law is concerned with regulating the sale and purchase of guns for the purpose of keeping them away from criminals. These regulations mostly cover transactions involving licensed gun dealers (U.S. Bureau of Alcohol, Tobacco and Firearms 1980). The limitation of this regulatory focus is that many guns are acquired through private, largely unregulated, channels. Even among members of the general, mostly noncriminal, population, about a third of guns were acquired by their present owners from private parties (DM1 1979, p. 71; Cook and Ludwig 1997, p. 25). Although nominally regulated in some jurisdictions, these transactions are largely invisible to legal authorities under existing law, and are even more common routes to gun possession among criminals. The best work on the ways that criminals get guns was done by Wright and Rossi (1986), who surveyed over 1,800 imprisoned felons in

10 states about their guns. Among 943 felon handgun owners, 44 percent had acquired their most recently acquired handgun through a purchase, usually from a source other than a dealer, 32 percent had stolen the gun, 9 percent rented or borrowed it, 8 percent each obtained it in trade or as a gift. Only 16 percent of the total had obtained their handgun by a purchase from a conventional retail dealer (p. 185).

On the other hand, black market dealers were also unimportant as sources of guns – only 2.9 percent of the felons mentioned a "black market source" and only 4.7 percent got the gun from a "fence" (dealer in stolen goods). While many criminals, such as residential burglars, occasionally sell guns they have stolen, large-scale illicit gun trafficking organizations are rare, and are responsible for only a tiny share of the guns acquired by American criminals. Thus, while many criminals get their guns from unlicensed sources, they rarely get them from black market dealers regularly engaged in the business of selling illegal guns. Most of the felons' guns were obtained outside of licensed, easily regulated channels, yet not from persons in the business of illegal gun selling.

The federal agency charged with enforcing the federal gun laws, the Bureau of Alcohol, Tobacco and Firearms (BATF), devotes a significant share of its resources to suppressing illicit gun trafficking activity. BATF has been the primary source of information used to support the claim that organized gun trafficking is a significant source of criminal guns, yet their own data indicate that each year they catch fewer than 15 traffickers who illegally sold more than 250 guns, and that the average number of guns trafficked per trafficking case was just 33 in fiscal year 1997 (U.S. BATF 1998, p. 17; 2000, p. 24). The "illicit gun dealers" that come to law enforcement attention turn out to be numerous, but with each "dealer" handling so few guns that arresting them could have little or no impact on the availability of guns to criminals. Criminals do occasionally sell guns for profit, but this is mostly a low-volume activity done as a by-product of other criminal activities, such as burglary, drug-dealing or trafficking in stolen property. The gun "traffickers" caught by BATF in Fiscal Year 1997 accounted for only 51,540 known guns (U.S. BATF 1998, p. 17), many of which were not sold to criminals, since gun traffickers almost never sell exclusively to prohibited persons (Vizzard 2000, p. 31). Even if half of these guns ended up in criminal hands, they would claim only about one percent of the estimated two million-plus guns acquired annually by criminals (Kleck 2009). Further, there is no reason to believe that the handful of criminals who do get guns as a result of trafficking activity could not simply turn to other sources if trafficked guns were not available. Consequently, organized gun trafficking appears to be of little significance in supplying guns to criminals.

As a result of the enormous numbers of guns owned by Americans, there are at least 600,000 guns stolen in a typical year in the US, so at any one time there are millions of stolen guns circulating among criminals. The volume of gun theft is so large that, even if one could completely eliminate all voluntary transfers of guns to criminals, including either lawful or unlawful transfers, involving either licensed dealers or private citizens, and even if police could confiscate all firearms from all criminals each year, a single year's worth of gun theft alone would be more than sufficient to rearm all gun criminals and supply the entire set of guns needed to commit the current number of gun crimes (about 340,000 in 2008) (Kleck 2009; U.S. Bureau of Justice Statistics 2011). As a result, large-scale gun trafficking (as distinct from burglars occasionally selling guns they have stolen) is largely superfluous to supplying criminals with guns in most areas.

These estimates imply serious limits on the results that can be realistically expected from controls applied only to voluntary (non-theft) transfers such as gun sales. One cannot substantially reduce the flow of water through a sieve by blocking just a few of the holes, especially if one cannot block the largest holes. Since burglary and other forms of theft are already illegal and severely punished, the gun theft figures imply that, to have any further impact, gun controls must decrease possession and use of firearms by the small high-risk subset of owners most likely to use guns for criminal purposes, above and beyond efforts to prevent them from acquiring guns in the first place.

For example, carry laws are intended to reduce unlicensed possession of guns in public places, without necessarily preventing anyone from acquiring a gun or keeping it in their home. Likewise, bans on possession of guns by convicted criminals could deter some criminals from possessing guns anywhere, without directly blocking their initial acquisition. Similarly, laws enhancing penalties for committing violent crimes if they are committed with firearms could conceivably reduce the *use* of guns in crimes without preventing any criminals from acquiring guns in the first place.

THE IMPACT OF GUN LAWS ON VIOLENCE

The enormous number and variety of gun controls, and the huge variation in strictness of controls across different states and cities makes the US a natural laboratory for evaluating the impact of gun control laws. In nations where a single set of laws prevail everywhere, the only practical way of assessing any given control's impact on violence rates is to make crude comparisons of national violence rates before and after introduction of the new measure. Unfortunately, there is very little longitudinal data available on other factors that influence violence rates, making it impossible to control for any significant number of other determinants of violence rates and thereby isolate the impact of national gun controls, or state or local measures for that matter. As a result, longitudinal evaluations of legal impact are of limited value (Britt, Kleck and Bordua 1996). On the other hand, because far more data are available describing multiple areas at a given point in time such as a Census year, cross-sectional studies of many different legal jurisdictions, with explicit controls for confounding factors, give considerably more power to separate the impact of a given gun law from the effects of other factors.

One review of the results and weaknesses of 39 U.S. studies of the impact of gun control laws on crime rates indicated that most of the studies found no impact of gun laws on violence rates. Of the 16 studies providing at least mixed support for a gun law impact, 12 were unacceptable univariate time series case studies, usually of a single law in a single nonrandomly selected area, and three of these were evaluations of the same law (Kleck 1997, pp. 357–359, 378–379). A more recent review likewise concluded that there was no firm basis to believe that existing gun control laws reduce violence (Centers for Disease Control 2007).

The most sophisticated and comprehensive evaluation of gun law impact was done by Kleck and Patterson (1993). It is unique in simultaneously evaluating the impact of 19 major types of gun control, on rates of homicide, robbery, aggravated assault, rape, suicide, and fatal gun accidents, separately examining gun and nongun violence (e.g. gun homicide vs. nongun homicide), as well as assessing the impact of gun laws on gun ownership levels. They controlled for dozens of possible confounding factors and gun ownership levels, assessed both state and city controls, and used multiple sources of information on gun laws.

Regarding whether gun laws reduce gun ownership levels, none of the 19 common types of gun laws showed consistent evidence of reducing gun ownership. Only two of the regulations, requiring a license to possess guns, and prohibiting possession by mentally ill persons, showed even mixed support for an impact. Of course, for many gun regulations, such as carry controls or add-on penalties, these findings are not surprising, since the laws were not intended to reduce gun ownership.

Some gun controls may operate to restrict ownership only among "high-risk" groups such as criminals or alcoholics. However, the results also indicated that most state and local controls fail to reduce gun use in acts of violence, undercutting the idea that gun ownership was reduced even in the limited subsets of the population that commit violent crimes. One reasonable explanation for this failure would be the huge size of the U.S. gun stock – with over 300 million guns in private hands, it is hard to deny guns to anyone who truly wants one.

As to the impact of gun laws on violence rates, the findings generally indicated that gun controls common in the US appear to exert no significant negative effect on total violence rates. Of 102 tests of the direct effects of 19 different major types of gun law on six different categories of crime and violence, only three tests unambiguously supported the gun law efficacy hypothesis, while 15 others provided ambiguous support.

Favorites of the American public and gun control advocacy groups, such as waiting periods and gun registration, clearly do not reduce violence rates to any measurable degree. Neither the Kleck-Patterson research nor other research has ever indicated that these controls reduce any form of violence. On the other hand, the gun control strategy most favored by the gun owner groups, mandatory add-on penalties for committing crimes with a gun (aka "sentence enhancements"), also is ineffective.

Why do so many varieties of gun control laws appear to have no impact on many of the types of violence that frequently involve guns? Several possible explanations suggest themselves. First, gun laws intended to have their effects by reducing gun ownership levels, either in the general population or, more usually, within various high-risk subsets, may fail simply because they do not achieve their proximate goal of reducing gun ownership. Second, given that the best research indicates that general gun ownership levels do not have a net positive effect on crime and violence, even if gun laws did reduce general gun ownership, this reduction would have no net negative impact on total violence rates. On the other hand, laws that reduced gun availability among criminals in particular, without disarming noncriminal victims, might reduce violence. Unfortunately no research has managed to distinguish gun availability among criminals from that among noncriminals.

Many US gun laws regulate only handguns, or regulate handguns more stringently than the more numerous long guns such as rifles or shotguns. This permits the substitution of the less regulated long guns for the more heavily regulated handguns. This common feature of U.S. gun laws can have the undesirable effect of encouraging some prospective criminals to substitute the more lethal long guns. The implication for the homicide rate is that the harmful effects of long gun substitution by some criminals could either cancel out or even outweigh the beneficial effects of denying handguns to other criminals, and produce a net increase in homicide. This is why regulating only handguns is a dubious policy (Kleck 1997, Chapter 4).

It has been argued that local or state controls fail because guns from jurisdictions with weaker controls 'leak' into those with stricter controls. This argument is misleading with regard to any kind of possession ban, since the illegality and risks of possessing firearms in a restrictive jurisdiction are unaffected by the presence or absence of controls in surrounding areas - only controls over acquisition of guns are affected by interjurisdictional leakage. With respect to controls over acquisition, advocates have argued that federal measures are necessary to avoid the leakage problem (e.g., Newton and Zimring 1969). Research on the relatively weak federal regulations existing prior to the Brady Act generally found these controls to be ineffective in reducing crime (Zimring 1975; Magaddino and Medoff 1984), and an early (perhaps premature) evaluation of the 1994 Brady Act likewise found no impact on homicide rates (Ludwig and Cook 2000).

Most case studies of changes in gun law are studies of increases in gun control restrictiveness. However, there is as much to be learned about the efficacy of gun controls from decreases in strictness as there is from increases. Between 1986 and 2010, 32 states amended their gun laws to make it easier for noncriminal adult residents to get permits allowing them to carry concealed firearms in public places. Critics of these laws feared that the increase in legally authorized gun carriers would result in increased acts of violence involving permit holders. These fears were not realized. For example, statewide data on permit revocations in Florida indicated that only about eight persons a year had their carry permits revoked due to a gun crime conviction, compared to 194,356 people holding permits on September 30, 1995 (Kleck 1997, pp. 367–72).

The first sophisticated study of the impact of these laws was a pooled cross-sections time-series study conducted by John Lott and David Mustard (1996), who analyzed all 3,000 counties in the nation for which requisite data were available and studied every shall issue carry law passed between 1977 and 1992. Their results indicated that violence rates, including gun homicide rates, declined after these laws went into effect, and declined more than in the states that liberalized carry laws than in those that did not. Many attempts to replicate these findings, however, failed to do so, instead generally finding nonsignificant negative associations between crime rates and passage of the laws. Making it easier to get carry permits did not increase crime rates, but also probably did not reduce them either (Kovandzic and Moody 2003).

Lott and Mustard believed that the laws caused substantial reductions in violence rates by deterring prospective criminals afraid of encountering an armed victim. This would be surprising in light of how modest the intervention was. The 1.3 percent of the population in places like Florida who obtained permits would represent at best only a slight increase in the share of potential crime victims who carry guns in public places, given that about 10 percent of Americans at least occasionally carried guns in public places for self-protection even before these laws were passed (Kleck 1997, p. 212). And if those who got permits were merely legitimating what they were already doing before the new laws, it would mean there was no increase at all in total (with or without permits) carrying rates or in actual risks to criminals. Thus, changes in carry laws may not have increased criminals' perceptions of risk from armed victims. On the other hand, contrary to what critics expected, making it easier for noncriminals to get carry permits did not increase crime.

Some have sought to assess gun law impact through cross-national comparisons of violence rates. Typically, pairs of nations are compared, but are arbitrarily selected so as to prove whatever point the analyst wishes, or many nations are compared and any observed differences in violence are arbitrarily attributed to differences in gun control strictness. The most common paired comparison is made between the US and Great Britain (GB). The latter does indeed have both stricter gun laws and less homicide than the US, and the residents of GB rarely kill one another with guns. However, there is little reason to believe that gun controls play any role in the lower British total homicide rates. Conclusions to the contrary typically rely on static comparisons of the two nations in fairly recent years. These comparisons overlook one crucial fact: GB had far less violence than the United States long before the former had strict gun laws. Causation cannot run backward in time, so controls implemented after 1920 could not have produced the low homicide rates already prevailing in GB prior to 1920.

Before 1920, gun control was at least as lenient in GB as in the US – there were few significant controls on any common gun type. The Library of Congress referred to the pre-1903 period in GB as 'the era of unrestricted [gun] ownership' (p. 75), while noting for the 1903–1920 period that although a license was required to obtain a gun, 'licenses were available on demand' (US Library of Congress 1981, pp. 75–6). Since 1920, British controls have been made progressively stricter, first in response to the Russian revolution and political unrest at home, and only later were promoted as crime-control measures (p. 76; Kopel 1992, pp. 70–4).

In 1919 the homicide rate for England and Wales was 0.8 per 100,000 (Archer and Gartner 1984). It has been estimated that the homicide rate for the entire United States was 9.5 in 1919 (Kleck 1991, p. 393), 11.9 times as large as the British rate. By 1983-1986, the homicide rate for England and Wales was 0.67, and the rate in the United States was 7.59 (Killias 1990, p. 171) – 11.3 times as high as the English rate. Thus, after more than 60 years of increasingly stringent gun regulation, GB's homicide rates relative to the US had actually gotten worse.

SELECTED RECENT TRENDS AND POSSIBLE FUTURE DEVELOPMENTS

The most significant federal gun legislation passed since 1968 is the Brady Handgun Violence Prevention Act, or Brady Act, which become effective on 28 February 1994. It provided for a waiting period of five working days between purchase and delivery of a handgun, during which a background check on the prospective buyer had to be performed. The law applied only to purchases from federally licensed dealers, initially covered only handguns, and operated only in the 26 states that did not already have similar background checks in effect under state laws (U.S. Congressional Research Service 1994). The background checks were thereby extended to about 39 percent of the US population not already covered by state checks. The waiting period requirement, emphasized heavily by the press during debate over the measure, was only a temporary provision, in effect only until November 29, 1998, after which a national 'instant record check' system was in place, capable of performing computerized checks of criminal history files that could be accomplished in a few minutes at the point of purchase. At that time the waiting period was dropped, while the background checks were extended to cover rifles and shotguns as well as handguns. The law prohibited law enforcement agencies from retaining records of the gun purchases or conveying information about them to anyone other than those carrying out the checks (United States Code 922(s)(6)(B)), thereby preventing the establishment of a national registry of gun owners.

The principal shortcoming of the law is that it does not cover nondealer transactions, which probably account for the majority of transfers of guns to criminals (Wright and Rossi 1986, p. 183; U.S. Bureau of Justice Statistics 2001, p. 6). Nevertheless, many attempts by criminals to buy guns from dealers were denied as a result of the law. It is, however, impossible to tell from denials how many criminals were actually prevented from getting handguns, since it is unknown how many of those blocked from buying firearms in gun stores simply acquired them instead from unlicensed sellers, from licensed dealers by using phony identification documents to avoid being identified as a disqualified person, or by using a "straw purchaser" without disqualifying attributes to make the purchase on their behalf, or by theft. None of this, however, contradicts the assertion that the law may reduce violence, since there may well be some persons who will commit serious acts of violence in the future but who would not be sufficiently motivated and able to make use of these evasion strategies. Since the Brady law only blocked future gun acquisitions, without taking guns away from anyone who already had them, its effects, if any, will become evident only gradually in the future.

At the state level, one of the most important and highly publicized developments in the past fifteen years was the widespread passage of "right to carry" or "shall issue" laws promoted by gun owner organizations, especially the National Rifle Association (NRA). These laws made it easier for noncriminals to get permits to carry concealed weapons in public. These have already been discussed. Arguably of even greater significance, but largely unheralded, was the passing of 'state preemption' laws, which now exist in 47 of the 50 states (in four of these states as a result of judicial rulings rather than new legislation). These laws forbid local governments from passing their own gun controls – the state government "preempts" the field of gun control for itself. The significance of these measures is that, while most political struggles over gun control involved just a single kind of control in a single jurisdiction, these laws forbade the passing of almost any kind of gun control in future, while also eliminating many local controls implemented in the past, and did so for thousands of local jurisdictions. This was even more significant given that the strictest gun laws in the US have been passed at the local level.

The strictness and character of gun law in America reflects the broad patterns of public opinion. Most Americans oppose bans on ownership of major categories of guns, but support a wide variety of moderate regulatory measures aimed at keeping guns away from criminals. Some moderate controls that have been proposed, however, have not been voted into law, despite majority support, due to the efforts of gun owner organizations, the most prominent of which is the NRA. Their success in recent decades is largely due to the fact that support for moderate control measures is widespread but weak, while opposition, concentrated among gun owners, is narrower but intense. As a result, opponents of stricter controls have been more effectively mobilized by the gun owner organizations to take politically significant actions such as contacting their elected representatives, casting their votes based largely on a candidate's stand on the gun issue, and making contributions to pro-gun candidates and organizations (Kleck 1997, Chapter 10; Vizzard 2000).

In this political context, it is not surprising that much proposed gun control legislation is weak and unlikely to influence rates of crime or violence. For legislators faced with many voters who would be mildly disappointed if they voted "no" on new gun controls, and a smaller number who would be intensely hostile if they voted "yes," the politically prudent compromise has been to pass weak "feel-good" measures unlikely to have any measurable impact on crime yet also unlikely to seriously anger gun owners. The most likely future trend is more of the same-symbolic, minor changes in gun laws, touted as major advances by supporters and decried as disasters by opponents.

Another possible future trend, however, is increased federalization of the criminal law in the gun control area, paralleling trends in other areas of law. Traditionally, Congress has had little to do with the criminal laws prevailing in America, most of which were enacted at the state level. Congress was supposed to address issues that were inherently national in character, such as national defense and commerce with other nations, and crime was regarded as a state and local matter. As crime became a political issue beginning in the 1960s, and "tough-on-crime" stances became popular political positions in the 1970s and 1980s, many Congressmen saw potential political rewards in adopting similar positions. Indicative of its merely symbolic, rather than substantive, significance, federal criminal laws passed in the 1980s and 1990s often duplicated state laws, merely adding federal penalties on top of existing state penalties, and thus were of little substantive significance regarding crime control, outside of the area of drug control. A federal ban on gun possession among juveniles (already forbidden by almost all states) was a prime example of such a duplicative measure in the area of gun control.

The impact of the Supreme Court's Heller and McDonald decisions remains to be seen. It could be argued that by taking handgun bans off the table, the Supreme Court took away the NRA's most potent argument against moderate controls – that they might, via a slippery slope, lead to gun prohibition. Such an interpretation of these decisions may be premature. While Heller forbade total bans on home handgun possession for self-defense, neither Heller nor McDonald forbids near approximations of handgun bans, such as restrictive licensing laws of the sort that operate in New York City. The rulings do not even preclude complete bans on the acquisition or possession of common types of rifles and shotguns, and certainly do not forbid bans on "assault weapons," even if very broadly defined. Likewise, nothing in the rulings forbids banning possession of guns outside the home. Whether highly restrictive gun laws are enacted in the foreseeable future is more likely to be determined by the balance of political power between pro- and anti-control forces than by the narrow dictates of Heller and McDonald.

DISCUSSION QUESTIONS

1. What recent court cases have been decided on the right to keep and bear arms and what were the rulings?
2. Discuss defensive gun use.
3. Discuss the differences in state and federal gun laws.
4. Why might the federal government create new gun control laws?

REFERENCES

Archer, Dane, and Rosemary Gartner. 1984. *Violence and Crime in Cross-National Perspective*. New Haven: Yale University Press.

Brady Campaign to Prevent Gun Violence. 2011. Information available at Brady website at http://www.bradycampaign.org/stategunlaws/ .

Britt, Chester, III, Gary Kleck, and David J. Bordua. 1996a. "A reassessment of the D.C. gun law: some cautionary notes on the use of interrupted time series designs for policy impact assessment." *Law & Society Review* 30:361–380.

Bruce-Briggs, Barry. 1976. "The great American gun war." *The Public Interest* 45:37–62.

Cook, Philip J., and Jens Ludwig. 1997. *Guns in America*. Summary Report. Washington, D.C.: Police Foundation.

DMI (Decision-Making-Information). 1979. *Attitudes of the American Electorate Toward Gun Control*. Santa Ana, Calif.: Decision-Making-Information.

Killias, Martin. 1990. "Gun ownership and violent crime: the Swiss experience in international perspective." *Security Journal* 1:169–174.

Kleck, Gary. 1991. *Point Blank: Guns and Violence in America*. N.Y.: Aldine de Gruyter.

Kleck, Gary. 1997. *Targeting Guns: Firearms and their Control*. N.Y.: Aldine de Gruyter.

Kleck, Gary. 2009. "The myth of big-time gun trafficking and overinterpretation of gun tracing data." *UCLA Law Review* 56:1233–1294.

Kleck, Gary, and Marc Gertz. 1995. "Armed resistance to crime: the prevalence and nature of self-defense with a gun." *Journal of Criminal Law and Criminology* 86:150–187.

Kleck, Gary, and Don B. Kates. 2001. *Armed: New Perspectives on Gun Control*. Buffalo, NY: Prometheus.

Kleck, Gary, and E. Britt Patterson. 1993. "The impact of gun control and gun ownership levels on violence rates." *Journal of Quantitative Criminology* 9:249–288.

Kopel, David. 1992. *The Samurai, the Mountie, and the Cowboy*. Buffalo, N.Y.: Prometheus.

Lindgren, James, and Justin Lee Heather. 2002. "Counting guns in early America." *William and Mary Law Review* 43(5):1777–1842.

Lizotte, Alan J., and David J. Bordua. 1980. "Firearms ownership for sport and protection: two divergent models." *American Sociological Review* 45:229–44.

Lott, John, and David B. M. Mustard. 1997. "Crime, deterrence and right-to-carry concealed handguns." *Journal of Legal Studies* 26:1–68.

Ludwig, Jens, and Philip J. Cook. 2000. "Homicide and suicide rates associated with implementation of the Brady Handgun Violence Prevention Act." *Journal of the American Medical Association* 284(5):585–591.

Magaddino, Joseph P., and Marshall H. Medoff. 1984. "An empirical analysis of federal and state firearm control laws." Pp. 225–58 in *Firearms and Violence: Issues of Public Policy*, edited by Don B. Kates, Jr. Cambridge, Mass.: Ballinger.

National Rifle Association. 2011. Information available at NRA website at http://www.nraila.org/GunLaws/ .

Newton, George D., and Franklin Zimring. 1969. *Firearms and Violence in American Life*. A Staff Report to the National Commission on the Causes and prevention of Violence. Washington, D.C.: U.S. Government Printing Office.

PRNewswire. 2010. Statement of Kristen Rand, Violence Policy Center Legislative Director, June 28, 2010. NY: PR Newswire Association LLC.

Stinchcombe, Arthur, Rebecca Adams, Carol A. Heimer, Kim Lane, Scheppele, Tom W. Smith, D. Garth Taylor. 1980. *Crime and Punishment — Changing Attitudes in America*. San Francisco: Jossey-Bass.

United Nations. 1997. Draft - *United Nations International Study on Firearm Regulation*. Vienna: Crime Prevention and Criminal Justice Division, United Nations Office at Vienna.

U.S. Bureau of Alcohol, Tobacco and Firearms. 1980. *State Laws and Published Ordinances, Firearms – 1980*. Washington, D.C.: Department of the Treasury.

U.S. Bureau of Alcohol, Tobacco and Firearms. 1998. *ATF Annual Report, 1997*. Washington, D.C.: Department of the Treasury.

U.S. Bureau of Alcohol, Tobacco and Firearms. 2000. *Following the Gun*. Washington, D.C.: Department of the Treasury.

U.S. Bureau of Justice Statistics. 1996. *Survey of State Procedures Related to Firearm Sales*. Washington, D.C.: Department of Justice.

U.S. Bureau of Justice Statistics. 2001. *Firearm Use by Offenders*. Washington, D.C.: U.S. Government Printing Office.

U.S. Bureau of Justice Statistics. 2011. *Criminal Victimization in the United States, 2008*. U.S. Department of Justice. Available online at http://bjs.ojp.usdoj.gov/content/pub/pdf/cvus08.pdf

U.S. Congressional Research Service. 1994. "Brady Handgun Violence Prevention Act." CRS Report for Congress number 94–14 GOV, dated January 6, 1994. Washington, D.C.: Library of Congress.

U.S. Federal Bureau of Investigation. 2011. *Crime in the United States, 2009: Uniform Crime Reports*. Washington, D.C.: U.S. Government Printing Office. Available online at http://www.fbi.gov/about-us/cjis/ucr/ucr#cius.

U.S. Library of Congress. 1981. *Gun Control Laws in Foreign Countries*. Law Library. Washington, D.C.: U.S. Government Printing Office.

Vizzard, William J. 2000. *Shots in the Dark: The Policy, Politics, and Symbolism of Gun Control*. Lanham, MD: Rowman & Littlefield.

Wright, James D., and Peter H. Rossi. 1986. *Armed and Considered Dangerous: A Survey of Felons And Their Firearms*. New York: Aldine de Gruyter.

Zimring, Franklin E. 1975. "Firearms and federal law: the Gun Control Act of 1968." *Journal of Legal Studies* 4:133–98.

30

Specialized Courts

Mae C. Quinn

In this chapter Quinn discusses the creation and implementation of "problem solving courts," such as drug court, mental health courts, and family court. These courts tend to be seen as quite successful in reducing social ills like addiction or recidivism. However, Quinn argues in this chapter that the success, which has been assigned to these courts, is misleading and only tells one part of the story.

INTRODUCTION

There is a chasm between the rhetoric about and the reality of modern court reform movements. It is a deeply troubling divide. This chapter is not concerned with innovations within the family court system. Rather, it examines modern criminal justice reforms. It focuses on the claims of the contemporary "problem-solving court" movement—a movement that has resulted in the development of thousands of specialized criminal courts across the country over the last two decades.

Problem-solving courts, which focus on social concerns like addiction, domestic violence, mental health issues, and prostitution, purport to be a great success. Their proponents assert that such courts cure addiction, address inti-

Source: Mae C. Quinn, "The Modern Problem-Solving Court Movement," Washington University Journal of Law and Policy. Reprinted by permission of the author and the Washington University Journal of Law and Policy.

mate violence, prevent recidivism, reduce costs, and even save lives. But this success story—the seemingly linear and dominant narrative offered primarily by proponents of problem-solving courts—is misleading. The near-singular tale of triumph told by modern court reformers obscures alternative experiences within, and contrary opinions about, these contemporary institutions. It also fails to acknowledge another important story—that is, the checkered history of criminal court experimentation in this country.

We need to mine and carefully consider these currently submerged accounts in order to fully appreciate both the promises and the significant perils of contemporary criminal court reform efforts. This chapter is intended to help in that endeavor by urging more meaningful discussions about judicial experiments. It is a project that focuses on the largely untold present and the forgotten past of such institutions, with a view toward helping shape criminal courts and justice in the future.

I. COURT REFORM'S DOMINANT DISCOURSE: THE MODERN SUCCESS STORY

The problem-solving court movement, many proclaim, began in this country with the founding of the Miami Drug Treatment Court in 1989. When that court opened two decades ago, it was viewed as groundbreaking in its attempt to remedy a social problem through informal criminal court processes. Developed by the criminal justice community as an alternative to incarceration for qualifying defendants, the Miami Drug Court sought to address the underlying issue that brought narcotics offenders into the system—addiction—as opposed to the specific crime charged.

In the Miami Drug Court, the judge changed from passive arbiter to active participant in helping defendants reach sobriety by rewarding success but sanctioning setbacks with jail terms and other penalties. Prosecutors and defense attorneys changed their roles, too, shedding their adversarial posture to become part of the treatment court "team." This model was and is depicted as a success.

Today, twenty years after the Miami Court opened its doors, over 2,300 drug treatment courts are operating across the country and more are on their way. The purportedly "innovative" methods utilized in the Miami Drug Court—concern for remedying a particularized social problem, active judicial involvement through defendant-monitoring and sanctioning, and informal courtroom processes—have been adopted and applied in other problem-solving court settings. Jurisdictions have created everything from domestic violence courts, to community courts, to mental health courts, to gun courts, to smoking courts for juveniles. It would appear that for nearly every problem in our society, there exists a specialty court within the criminal justice system that is trying to "solve" it.

Yet, proponents of the modern problem-solving court movement continue to call for even more specialized institutions, along with broader acceptance of their nontraditional approach to criminal case processing. Toward this end, many judges broadcast the work of their courts by publicizing drug court graduations and asking those honored to share success stories publically.

Newspapers and the Internet are filled with accounts of how problem-solving courts "saved" these individuals.

More systemically, the Conference of Chief Judges, which represents judges from the high courts of every state, has established a "national agenda" to encourage further implementation of problem-solving court programs. The agenda calls for each jurisdiction to develop a particularized "state plan to expand the use of the principles and methods of problem-solving courts." It also calls for judges to reach beyond the courthouse walls and press law schools to "include the principles and methods of problem-solving courts in their curricula" in order to train lawyers to embrace problem-solving court techniques. Related think tanks and policy shops similarly have dominated the airwaves through white papers, websites, and press accounts—urging us to take the problem-solving court experiment "to scale."

II. SUBTEXT AND "OTHER" STORIES OF THE PROBLEM-SOLVING COURT MOVEMENT

The seemingly singular story told about problem-solving courts portrays them as benevolent and exciting alternatives to the traditional case-processing model. It is difficult not to get swept up in the promise offered by those telling this tale. However, other accounts also must be considered. For a more robust understanding, dissenting voices and those who question such assurances also must be heard.

Questions remain about the efficacy and propriety of problem-solving courts. It is not at all clear that specialized courts offer a superior alternative to the traditional case-processing model in preventing recidivism or that they resolve the underlying social problems they are created to address. In addition, there has been insufficient study of the real economic costs of such courts, or the extent to which defendants' legal rights and our system of justice may be undermined by the informal procedures that such institutions use.

As an initial matter, few are aware of the reasons the Miami Drug Court was established. Although reportedly focused on the problems of defendants, it was established largely to address a set of more utilitarian concerns for the system. Miami faced both staggering narcotics-based caseloads for prosecutors and jail overcrowding as a result of the 1980s "drug war." Indeed, at the time it established the "first" drug court, Miami-Dade County was under court order to reduce its enormous jail population. It had to try something new.

Other self-serving reasons may encourage replication of the drug court model, including substantial financial support offered by the federal government to those willing to establish such institutions. These reasons call into question the purportedly pure motives behind the "therapy" being provided by our courts. The various and sometimes disparate goals and incentives underlying specialty courts must be more transparent if we are to understand the real story of these venues. This subtext may affect public perceptions and support, as well as the way outcomes are interpreted. This is a particularly important consideration when proponents of the problem-solving court movement claim part of the drive to create such venues is to increase public trust in courts.

The perspectives of the criminal defense bar also were largely missing from initial narratives about these courts. Nearly a decade ago, I was one of the first defense lawyers in the United States to write about my experience practicing in a drug court. I argued that the teamwork approach urged in such institutions could thwart defense attorneys' ethical obligation to zealously defend their clients and undermine defendants' rights to due process of law.

Since that time, more defense attorneys—individually and on an institutional level—have raised similar concerns. Over the past two years the National Association of Criminal Defense Attorneys ("NACDL") convened a task force to examine potential issues raised by problem-solving courts. It held public hearings across the country to hear testimony from defenders and others based on their experiences within the courts. Just this month it issued its report summarizing its findings, which include many of the concerns I have raised previously.

In addition, the Maryland State Office of the Public Defender recently filed a lawsuit challenging the very existence of Maryland's Drug Treatment Court. In the suit, defenders argued that the Circuit Court for Baltimore City lacked fundamental jurisdiction to create a drug court for felony charges, and that the court's sanctioning practices violated constitutional double jeopardy principles.

Carefully vetted and well-crafted accounts of reformers also overlook the stories of the thousands of defendants who "fail out" of problem-solving courts. These defendants often are sent to prison for faltering in their treatment efforts—sometimes for longer periods than they would have served had they forgone the problem-solving court option. They are not invited to speak to high school classes or community groups. What becomes of these individuals—and their views on problem-solving courts, or the legal system in general—is largely missing from the conversation.

Also absent is a full accounting of these failures. Indeed, although reformers have declared their success, questions remain about the efficacy of purported problem-solving institutions. Recent estimates suggest that between one-third and one-half of all drug treatment court defendants fail out of treatment. Thus, for a large percentage of defendants, the drug court model does not serve as an alternative to incarceration. Despite the nearly 300 million federal dollars spent on these nontraditional experiments, drug court defendants still are largely serving traditional prison sentences. Because drug court sentences often are longer than ordinary drug sentences, it is hard to see how drug courts save money in the long run.

In fact, in April 2002 the General Accounting Office ("GAO") warned that the returns were not all in on drug treatment courts and that more thorough study was needed. In a lengthy and detailed report, the GAO admonished the Department of Justice for not sufficiently managing the collection and use of operational and outcome data from federally funded drug court programs. It found that the Department fell short of its stated objectives of completing meaningful and comprehensive impact evaluations for such courts.

In 2005, the GAO reviewed the 117 drug court evaluations—many federally funded—that had been conducted between 1997 and 2004. Of those studies, the GAO considered only twenty-seven methodologically sound for purposes of assessing recidivism and other success factors. The methodologically sound studies showed "fewer incidents of rearrests or reconvictions and a longer time until rearrest or reconviction than comparison group members"; however, there was not conclusive evidence to tie the reduction in recidivism to any particular drug court component or feature, such as judicial involvement or graduated sanctioning. Moreover, the GAO determined that "[e]vidence about the effectiveness of drug court programs in reducing participants' substance abuse"—the very problem drug courts are supposed to solve—"is limited and mixed."

Most recently, the Sentencing Project, an independent non-profit organization interested in criminal justice reforms, issued a report reviewing available research on the effectiveness of drug treatment courts. That April 2009 study expressed a number of concerns about drug court proponents' claims and identified various areas where more research was needed. For instance, the study indicated that although "it is generally accepted that drug courts effectively reduce rearrest rates relative to simple probation or incarceration, there is some reason to be cautious when interpreting these results." It also explained that "[s]ome studies show little or no impact from drug court participation and it can be difficult to specify which components of the program or the research design may be contributing to these results."

As I have argued elsewhere, the problem-solving court movement has oversold its innovations in other ways, too. Even less impressive than drug courts are the batterer intervention programs touted by many domestic violence court advocates as a revolutionary approach to abuse between intimates. The data demonstrate that such programs are ineffectual as a method of treatment—they simply do not work to deter violence. At best, they keep track of alleged batterers for at least the period of time they are in the mandated classes.

And victims' voices have been drowned out, too, by the dominant discourse surrounding domestic violence court practices. Women purportedly protected by the courts' no-drop and mandatory prosecution policies frequently oppose this black-and-white approach to intimate violence. Studies suggest that the courts' practices can even put women's lives at risk. Women's problems frequently are exacerbated rather than solved by a lack of financial and other support from their incarcerated partners.

III. THE FORGOTTEN HISTORY OF UNITED STATES

Criminal Court Reform

More fundamentally, specialized, problem-oriented criminal courts simply are not new or innovative. Despite claims by today's innovators that they are engaged in a series of firsts, the creation of specialized, problem-oriented courts is an old concept. Experiments with problem-oriented courts originated in this country about a century ago. The checkered history of criminal court reform is conspicuously absent from current conversations about problem-solving courts.

Innovators who came long before today's reformers made similar attempts to engage in social engineering through criminal court reform. Judge Anna Moscowitz Kross, a Russian immigrant who came to the United States at the end of the 1800s, was one of the first women to graduate from New York University School of Law in 1910, one of the first women to practice law in New York, and one of the state's first woman judges. Kross spent the entirety of her legal career trying to reform the criminal justice system in ways that closely parallel the efforts of today's problem-solving court movement.

Kross's innovations took many forms. She established a number of specialized criminal courts that looked very much like what we are seeing today. She engaged in court reform work while she was a judge in New York City's Magistrates' Court, which is where low-level, non-felony cases were prosecuted in New York City until the 1960s. In this way, I argue that Kross was responsible for New York's "original" problem-solving court movement—a movement that largely has been forgotten by today's legal community. Looking back at Kross's early attempts at innovation is instructive given the similarities between alleged problem-solving then and now. Many of these parallels suggest that we may be returning to institutions and practices that grew out of paternalistic Progressive Era concerns, and that were subsequently discarded as less than ideal in a modern system of criminal justice.

For instance, in 1936 Kross established the Wayward Minors' Court for Girls to deal with young women accused of violating the law. In much the same way that specialty courts are funded by the Department of Justice today, the Wayward Minors' Court began with the support and backing of the federal Works Progress Administration ("WPA"). The court dealt predominantly with women between the ages of sixteen and twenty-one who were charged with acts of prostitution and other "sexual misconduct" under the Wayward Minors' Act.

Too old for New York's Children's Court, these young women otherwise would have been processed with adult female defendants in the Women's Court; however, Kross thought it was appropriate to divert and adjust their cases more informally. The Wayward Minors' Court for Girls began by holding sessions "one day each week, at a different location" from the Women's Court. The experimental venue aimed to help young women rather than punish them, employing less "legalistic" court processes which usually included *pro se* representation throughout treatment.

In a booklet Kross wrote to describe and promote the court, she expressed concerns about preexisting formal and technical adjudication processes for young women alleged to be sexual delinquents. She believed that some young women needed court intervention, even if there was not sufficient evidence to convict them. Accordingly, the Wayward Minors' Court sought to "minimize the strictly legalistic character of the court as a tribunal" while using "individualized and socialized techniques and procedures" to provide assistance to the wayward young women before it.

For instance, at a first appearance in the adult Women's Court, the magistrate decided whether sufficient information existed for a formal complaint; if so, the defendant was arraigned and formal trial held. If sufficient grounds for a complaint did not exist, the court simply dismissed the case. By contrast, in the Wayward Minors' Part:

> Upon the first appearance of the girl complete Intake information is presented to the presiding Magistrate. The summary of the Intake Interview sets forth not only the immediate complaint but also the real problems involved, whether they be economic, vocational, family i[n]compatibility or any other reason. . . . At the first appearance . . . the complaint is formally read to the girl and she is advised of her legal rights. The Judge explains to her that this formal procedure is observed to cover all necessary legal requirements. However, this is the only *formal procedure* observed at this stage.

From that point forward, as in many of today's problem-oriented courts, formal courtroom processes were jettisoned. Instead, the court engaged in therapeutic interventions based upon the individual needs and problems of the accused. Because the Probation Department did not have sufficient resources to adequately investigate these issues on a pretrial basis, and in fact was legally precluded from doing so, Kross created her own "cooperating agency" to do this work. Her organization—the Magistrates' Court Social Services Bureau—was comprised mostly of volunteers whom Kross personally recruited to assist in her experiment.

The Wayward Minors' Court magistrate also determined at arraignment whether the accused "shall be returned home pending investigation or detained elsewhere; and . . . [whether] provision for physical and mental examinations" was necessary. Notably, institutional detention was considered "remand by consent" and seen by the court's workers as an important criminal procedure "innovation." Although there had been no formal adjudication or finding of guilt at this stage, the young women were held at residential facilities like the Florence Crittenton League or the House of Good Shepherd for between one and four weeks so that a more thorough social work investigation could be completed.

In her 1941 evaluation and review of the courts, Dorris Clarke, a liaison officer in the Wayward Minors' Court, noted:

> This [initial detention], of course, raised numerous questions as to the legality of detaining a person beyond the statutory period of seventy-two hours, *without hearing*. Questions were also raised as to whether a minor could "consent" to such deprivation of liberty; or whether a parent, who was a complainant against her daughter, could "consent" to such detention.

Given the court's problem-solving orientation, however, Clarke believed the potentially illegal processes were generally defensible:

> Actually, no harm was done to any of these girls and all were glad to consent to such shelter—and, as a matter of fact, many, on the adjourned date, requested to be returned to the institution. The question of the legality of the procedure, however, continued to disturb those of us concerned with the proper functioning of this court.

To protect against legal challenges, the court ultimately modified its procedures. Thereafter, the magistrate was required to complete a form at the time of remand indicating that the defendant was "arraigned and advised of [her] rights, [and] has consented to necessary shelter, examination, and care at your institution pending further disposition of the charges at the Wayward Minors' Court."

Before the defendant's next court appearance, the investigating agent presented the gathered information to the presiding judge, usually Kross. This information included further facts underlying the complaint; a full social history of the accused; and additional mental and physical health data, including details about the woman's sexual history. With this information, the court established an individualized treatment plan and adjourned the matter for further informal supervision. "Further supervision" frequently involved venereal disease testing and treatment, still without any formal finding of guilt.

While under the court's supervision, the defendant repeatedly returned to court for conferences so the judge could maintain "personal contact in each case . . . until rehabilitation [was] assured." Not unlike practices in today's drug courts, the judge conferenced the matter with court staff and other supervisory agents prior to each court appearance to learn about the defendant's progress. If necessary, "changes of plans [would be] recommended" and defendants might be "remanded during long adjournments, for treatment at a hospital, or for correction and training at a private or public institution."

This method of handling the case "on the basis of preadjudicated, unofficial, probationary supervision," as with the first remand and adjournment, was "predicated on the implied consent of the defendant." Kross conceded that this consent generally was extracted from the defendant using "moral suasion," and that the court "accomplish[ed] its object[ives] by a resort to expedients, contemplated in [its] inception, but not clearly authorized" by law. One such "expedient," Kross explained, was for "the Magistrate to sign a commitment [order] to the House of Detention, at the time of arraignment to be used if the contingency" arose.

In the end, defendants who were "recalcitrant" or appeared to have "no prospect of an adjustment pursuant to the plans suggested," could be brought to trial, adjudicated wayward minors, and immediately sentenced to an institution. Those who demonstrated that "desired results were underway," would have their cases dismissed, but would continue to be monitored informally by Kross's volunteers.

Like today's court reform advocates, Kross was a vocal spokesperson for her experiments. She made sure her courts received media attention for their unusual socio-legal approach—sometimes writing news articles herself—while she pressed for their replication across the country. As early as the first year of its operation, Kross announced her hope that the Wayward Minors' Court would "serve as a model for an impetus to the establishment of similar Courts elsewhere . . . ." Similar to today's reformers, she attempted to maintain records and statistics to share with others interested in replicating her experimental venue, claiming they demonstrated the success of her "scientific" approach. In this way, Kross became well-known for her "improvisation" and "zeal."

Despite Kross's strong advocacy and personal public relations campaign, her criminal court experiments were largely criticized and ultimately abandoned. Kross's use of volunteers and outsiders to run her courts brought them—and her—under tremendous scrutiny. For her alleged personal overreaching and privatization of the judicial system, Kross herself became the center of a Department of Investigation probe.

During the 1950s, a study by various legal and social work experts indicated that Kross's approach to dealing with social issues through criminal courts was too fragmented. It resulted in more confusion for litigants than help. Similarly, running a variety of individualized, specialized courts—each with its own special social focus—was costly. Indeed, Kross's programs were so costly that they never expanded in the way she envisioned, despite her own rigorous fundraising campaigns.

Moreover, while social work intervention might be helpful for children and families in distress, critics believed this was best accomplished outside of the criminal court system. Important commentators like Paul Tappan argued further that the court's treatment methods were not sufficiently effective or scientific, but rather were reflective of the personal morality and biases of those involved in their creation. When New York's courts were reorganized in the 1960s, the kind of therapeutic intervention common in the Wayward Minors' Court was found to be best suited for the civil family court setting. The Magistrates' Court system was completely abolished in 1962.

Indeed, this criticism and dismantling of Kross's problem-solving courts occurred as legal protections for accused persons were being expanded to include the set of rights well-accepted in today's criminal justice system. For instance, during this same time period, the Supreme Court decided *Gideon v. Wainwright*, ensuring the right to counsel for indigent criminal defendants in certain cases. The Supreme Court also recognized individual privacy and the right to silence as core values. During this period, civil rights lawyers and the criminal defense bar became more organized and were widely recognized as an important force. Kross's efforts to engage in social engineering through criminal courts were seen by many, including Tappan, as inconsistent with these emerging conceptions of individual civil rights and liberties.

Kross's story has been largely left out of the accounts of contemporary reformers who claim that they have established the first problem-solving courts. But like experimental courts such as the Wayward Minors' Part from decades ago, today's problem-oriented venues utilize informal procedures and the coercive power of the court to try to change the way people live their lives. By adopting a carrot and stick approach in an attempt to "save" people, we again are engaging in social engineering through the criminal courts. In so doing, we are returning to anachronistic practices that grew out of the Progressive Era's paternalistic concern for sexually active young women that many, even at the time, argued were deeply troubling. Now, however, we are applying these practices to autonomous adults.

CONCLUSION

As we embark on another new era and presidential administration, it is a good time to pause and take stock of our nation's efforts to solve its problems through criminal courts. To be clear, this chapter is not written to squelch innovation. Indeed, it calls for innovation in the ways that we innovate.

Policymakers should consider all voices—agnostics, critics, as well as those from days gone by—as they work to improve courts. The missing accounts discussed in this chapter suggest that we should stop pouring money into problem-solving courts to simply encourage further experimentation. And true success in specialized courts should be measured not only by improved outcomes, but also by proven compliance with legal standards. New state courts, like new medications, should not receive federal support or approval without proper study, testing, and vetting, as well as delivery of promised results.

Perhaps in each jurisdiction one model problem-solving court could be created and carefully monitored over a substantial period of time with federal financing, not just by the court's planners and proponents, but by a truly cross-cutting panel of both legal and social-science experts. The court's legal practices and therapeutic or other outcomes could be assessed to ensure that the institution complies with existing standards of law and delivers meaningful services that do, in fact, work to solve problems. If necessary, courtroom processes and treatment modes could be modified over time to ensure that particularized best practices are developed and delivered. Further federal funding for replication of these institutions would not be provided until optimum features were established for a given jurisdiction, defendant population, and the like.

Future attempts to solve this country's problems should not be driven solely by the criminal court reformers who have dominated the conversation to date. It is healthy to hope. But if we wish to avoid repeating history's criminal justice mistakes, better informed, more balanced, and truly thoughtful discourse about problem-solving courts must inform our decisions.

DISCUSSION QUESTIONS

1. What is drug court?
2. Discuss the pros and cons of drug court.
3. Do participants of a drug court have a lower rate of becoming repeat offenders as opposed to those who forego this type of program?
4. Examine past and previous problems with drug courts and discuss how these problems could be fixed.

31

The Growth of COMPSTAT

David Weisburd, Stephen D. Mastrofski, Rosann Greenspan, and James J. Willis

Compstat has been recognized as a major innovation in American policing. Police Departments around the country have adopted Compstat or one of its variations. Compstat refers to a strategic control system developed to gather and disseminate information on the police department's crime problems and to track efforts to deal with them. Compstat addresses the problem of inadequate information and seems most utilized in a data-saturated environment. Compstat reports serve as the database for commanders to demonstrate their understanding of the crime problems in their areas and discuss future strategies with other law enforcement officials. Departments that adopt a Compstat model have a strong desire to reduce serious crime and increase management control over field operations. The goals of policing are more prominent in the departments that adopt Compstat models than in those that chose not to utilize a Compstat model.

INTRODUCTION

Introduced as recently as 1994 by then commissioner William Bratton of the New York City Police Department, Compstat has already been recognized as a major innovation in American policing. In the few years since its appearance, police departments around the country have begun to adopt Compstat or variations of it (Law Enforcement News 1997; Maas 1998; McDonald 1998). The program has received national publicity, including awards from Harvard University and former Vice President Al Gore, and has been credited by its originators and proponents with impressive reductions in crime and improvements in neighborhood quality of life (Bratton 1999; Gurwitt 1998; Remnick 1997; Silverman, 1996).

Despite the national attention that has been paid to Compstat, to date there has been little systematic analysis of Compstat programs in policing. In fact, most of what we know comes from those involved in its implementation (Sparrow et al. 1990; Moore 1995). With support from the National Institute of Justice, the Police Foundation has tried to further our knowledge of Compstat by undertaking a national study of the program (Weisburd et al. 2001; Weisburd et al. 2003). Drawing on a representative survey of American police departments, this report examines the diffusion of Compstat and factors associated with its implementation.

THE EMERGENCE OF COMPSTAT

The particulars of Compstat's origins have been detailed elsewhere (Bratton 1998; Kelling and Coles 1996; Maple 1999; Silverman 1999; McDonald et al. 2001). The impetus behind Compstat was New York City's police commissioner William Bratton and his efforts to make a huge organization, legendary for its resistance to change (Sayre and Kaufman 1960), responsive to his leadership—a leadership that had clearly staked out crime reduction and improving the quality of life in the neighborhoods of New York City as its top priorities (Bratton 1999). Based on his belief in principles of strategic leadership (Bratton 1998; Silverman 1999) and his own experiences with the Boston Police Department and the New York City Transit Police, Bratton and his lieutenants set out to disprove skeptics who claimed that the police can do little about crime and disorder.

At the outset, Bratton and his administration's analysis of the NYPD's problems revealed several deficiencies that have long been identified as forms of bureaucratic dysfunction (Merton 1940). First, the organization lacked a sense of the importance of its fundamental crime control mission. Second, because the NYPD was not setting high enough expectations about what its officers could do and accomplish, a lot less was getting done than was possible. Third, too many police managers had become moribund and were content to continue doing things the way they had always been done rather than exploring new theories and studies for promising strategies to reduce crime and improve the quality of life in neighborhoods. Fourth, the department was beset with archaic, unproductive organizational structures that did more to promote red tape and turf battles than to facilitate teamwork to use scarce resources effectively. As a result, operational commanders were "handcuffed" by headquarters and lacked authority to customize crime control to their precincts' individual needs. Finally, the department was "flying blind". It lacked timely, accurate information about crime and public safety problems as they were emerging; had little capacity to identify crime patterns; and had difficulty tracking how its own resources were being used. Since middle managers were not in the habit of monitoring these processes, they served as a weak link in the chain of internal accountability between top brass and street-level, police employees.

Bratton used a "textbook" approach to deal with these problems, following the major prescriptions offered by organizational development experts to accomplish organizational change (Beer 1980). He brought in outsiders to obtain a candid diagnosis of the organization's strengths and weaknesses. He incorporated both top-down and bottom-up processes to implement change (Silverman 1996). He sought and obtained early indicators of the success of the change efforts and sought ways to reinforce the individual efforts of his precinct commanders and the rank-and-file by using both incentives and disincentives (Bratton 1996).

Strictly speaking, Compstat refers to a "strategic control system" developed to gather and disseminate information on the NYPD's crime problems and to track efforts to deal with them. As such, it addresses the problem of inadequate information described above and, in this sense, it is a structure intended to serve the implementation of the NYPD's crime-control and quality-of-life strategies (Office of Management Analysis and Planning n.d.: 1). At the same time, Compstat has become shorthand for the full range of strategic, problem-solving activities in the NYPD. These elements of the department's Compstat approach are most visible in the twice-weekly Compstat "Crime-Control Strategy Meetings," where precinct commanders appear before several of the department's top brass to report on crime problems in their precincts and what they are doing about them.

This occurs in a data-saturated environment in which Compstat reports play a central role. Precinct crime statistics and other information about a precinct and its problems are projected onto overhead screens, and commanders respond to queries about what they are doing to deal with those problems. Crime data that were once three to six months late are now available to precinct commanders on a weekly basis for the preceding week. The report includes weekly, monthly, and annual tallies of crime complaints, arrests, summonses, shooting incidents and victims, organized by precinct, borough, and citywide. In addition, electronic pin maps are generated to show how crimes and police activities cluster geographically. Hour-of-the-day analyses and "crime spike" analyses are also carried out. The reports also profile the background of the precinct commander, as well as other features of the precinct under his or her command, such as demographic data, workload data, and various activities.

Compstat reports serve as the database for commanders to demonstrate their understanding of the crime problems in their areas and discuss future strategies with the top brass and other commanders present. Cross-unit coordination is planned if necessary and all of the plans are thoroughly documented. When the precinct is reselected for participation in a Compstat meeting, the commander must demonstrate that he or she has followed up on these strategies. Sometimes commanders bring subordinates with them so that they can report on their efforts and receive recognition. The press and other outside agencies are sometimes invited to attend these sessions with as many as 200 people in attendance, thus providing "great theater" and developing a greater public awareness of how the department is being managed (Bratton 1998, 296).

There are indicators that police leaders around the nation are interested in and willing to explore Compstat but we do not know how widely Compstat models have diffused across the United States or what types of departments are most likely to develop Compstat programs. Why are American police departments adopting the Compstat model? Below we present answers to these questions based on our national survey of police agencies.

RESEARCH METHODS

We sent our survey to all American police agencies with over 100 sworn police officers and to a sample of 100 agencies with between 50 and 100 sworn officers (see Weisburd et al. 2001). The full universe of larger departments was sampled because we believed that Compstat programs are most appealing to such departments and thus most likely to be implemented in them. We thought it important, nevertheless, to assess whether smaller agencies are also beginning to develop Compstat-like programs. It would have been prohibitively costly to survey all smaller agencies, but our random sample of agencies with 50-99 officers allows us to assess whether Compstat programs are also influencing smaller departments. We decided not to sample from among departments with fewer than 50 full-time, sworn officers because we thought it reasonable to assume that such police agencies lack the resources and organizational complexity to implement Compstat.

At the time of our sample selection in 1999, the most complete, current listing of American police agencies was the 1996 Directory Survey of Law Enforcement Agencies conducted by the U.S. Bureau of the Census and the U.S. Bureau of Justice Statistics (BJS) which gave us both the file and its documentation (Bureau of Justice Statistics 1998). According to the directory, there were 515 agencies with 100 or more sworn officers, and 698 agencies with 50-99 officers. We sent the survey instrument by mail to all of the 515 largest agencies and a random sample of 100 agencies with between 50 and 99 officers. This mailing included a letter asking the chief to complete (or to delegate to a person who could reflect his/her views) the part of the survey relevant to overall departmental policy and someone familiar with technology to complete those sections of the survey. We assured the departments of complete confidentiality and included a survey instrument with a unique identification number affixed and a stamped, addressed, return envelope. We followed up with a series of phone calls as well as a second and third mailing. The first mailing occurred on August 18, 1999, and the final surveys were received in January of 2000. The overall response rate of 86 percent achieved using this method was very high for a mail survey (see Table 1).

Table 1 Response Rate for the Sample

Department Size	Received/Total	Percent
Small (50–99 Sworn)	85/100	85
Large (100 + Sworn)	445/515	86.4
Total	530/615	86.2

Table 2 Department Response Rate by Region

Region	Received/Total	Percent
Northeast	119/146	81.5
North Central	102/122	83.6
South	192/215	89.3
West	117/132	88.6

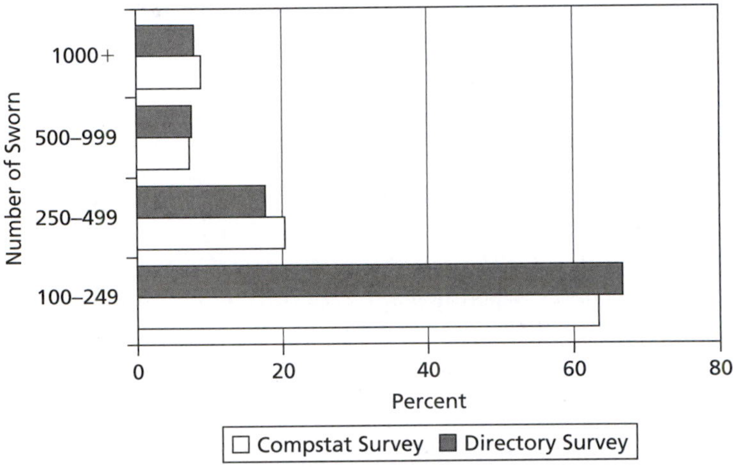

FIGURE 1 Percent of Departments of a Certain Size in the Sample as Contrasted with the BJS Directory Survey

We found no systematic reasons for non-response by selected departments. We received about the same proportion of responses from larger departments as from smaller ones (see Table 1). Moreover, there are relatively small differences in our response rate across regions (see Table 2), though departments in the South and West were somewhat more likely to return the survey. When we compare the distribution of our sample in terms of size of department to the BJS Directory Survey in 2000 we find that our sample is representative of the population of police agencies in the United States (see Figure 1).

HOW WIDELY HAS COMPSTAT BEEN ADOPTED AND WHAT TYPES OF DEPARTMENTS ARE IMPLEMENTING COMPSTAT?

Our first concern is simply whether Compstat models have been adopted widely across American police agencies. This has been the impression of commentators but has not been backed up with hard evidence. Our study suggests that Compstat has in fact diffused widely across the landscape of American policing (see Table 3). A third of departments with 100 or more sworn officers

Table 3 Has Your Department Implemented a Compstat-Like Program?

Department Size	Percent Yes	Percent No, But Planning	Percent No
Small (50–99 Sworn)	11.0	29.3	59.8
Large (100 + Sworn)	32.6	25.6	41.8

Due to rounding, rows may not add to 100.

in our study responded "yes" when asked whether they had "implemented a Compstat-like program." An additional quarter of the large departments in our survey claimed to be "planning" a Compstat-like program. As we expected, departments in our small department sample were much less likely to have implemented a Compstat model. Only nine departments or 11 percent of the departments with between 50 and 99 sworn officers had done so. However, almost 30 percent claimed to be planning to implement a Compstat program. Because the number of departments in our sample with between 50 and 99 sworn officers that have implemented a Compstat model is small, unless otherwise noted in the tables below, we examine characteristics of Compstat in the large department sample only.

We also asked departments when their Compstat program was implemented. As would be expected, the large growth in implementation of Compstat programs occurs after New York's program had begun to gain wide-scale publicity (see Figure 2). Compstat implementation was greatest in 1998. The downward trend in 1999 may be an artifact of our study, since some departments who responded quickly to our survey may have implemented a Compstat program later in that year.

Interestingly, eighteen departments in our large agency sample report implementation before 1994, the year the NYPD introduced Compstat. How could departments claim to have implemented a Compstat-like program before New York City coined the term? It appears that in such cases, departments believed that they had implemented the essential elements of Compstat even before New York City's model had become prominent. This

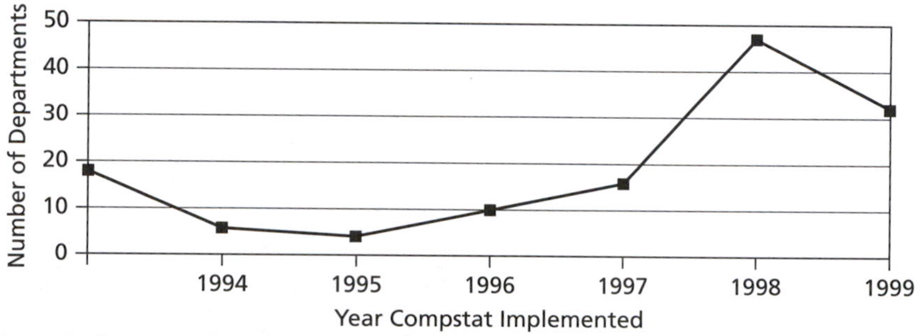

Figure 2 The Year of Compstat Implementation

is illustrated in Table 4 which reports the percentage of departments that claimed to have implemented specific features "associated with Compstat and similar programs" at least six years before the survey, a time that predates the creation of Compstat in New York City. Twenty-six percent of departments said that they "set specific objectives in terms that can be precisely measured" or that they held "regularly scheduled meetings with district commanders to review progress toward objectives." Thirty percent report using data to "assess progress towards objectives" before 1994.

Our survey shows that larger American police agencies claim to have adopted Compstat at a high rate and very rapidly. How does this compare with the adoption of other social or technological innovations? In recent years, there has been growing interest in the analysis of innovation which has been found to have a fairly consistent form called the "s" curve of innovation (Rogers, 1995). The "s" curve is developed by measuring the cumulative adoption of an innovation over time. In Figure 3, the innovation adoption curve for Compstat-like programs in police agencies with over 100 sworn officers is presented.

Table 4 Was This Feature (of Compstat) Implemented Six or More Years Ago?

Survey Item	Percent Yes
Set specific objectives in terms that can be precisely measured	26.0
Hold regularly scheduled meetings with district commanders to review progress toward objectives	26.3
Hold middle managers responsible for understanding crime patterns and initiating plans to deal with them	22.7
Give middle managers control over more resources to accomplish objectives	23.1
Use data to assess progress toward objectives	30.2
Develop, modify, or discard problem-solving strategies based on what the data show	24.8

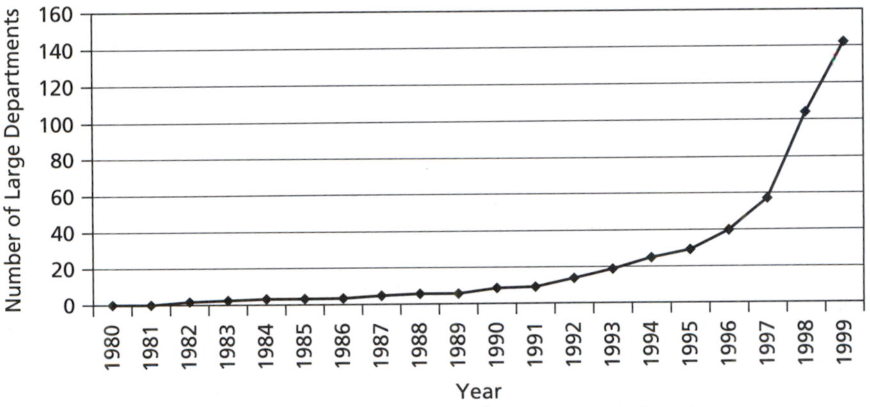

FIGURE 3 Observed Compstat Cumulative Adoption Curve Based on Survey

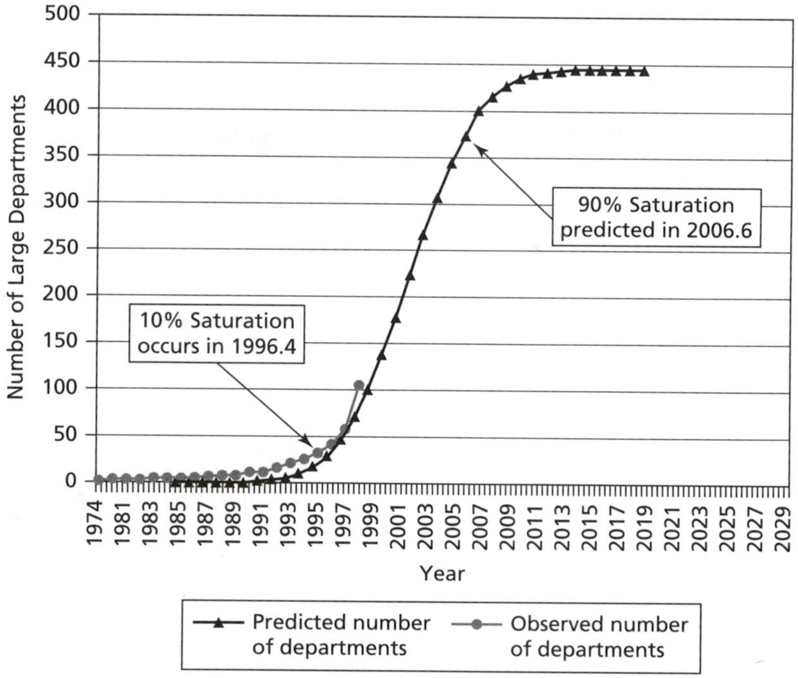

FIGURE 4 The Extrapolated Cumulative Adoption Curve for Compstat-like

Can we argue from this that the diffusion of Compstat-like programs suggests a rapid rate of innovation? Arnulf Grübler (1991) provides a yardstick. He analyzes two samples of technologies, including such areas as energy, transport, communication, agriculture, military technologies, as well as some social changes such as literacy, in the United States for which data on diffusion of innovation were available. He constructs a measure, delta t, which is the time period it takes for an innovation to go from 10 percent to 90 percent of its saturation or highest level of adoption. He finds that between 13 and 25 percent of different types of technology progress from 10 percent to 90 percent of their saturation level within fifteen years. Another 25 to 30 percent of his samples reached this saturation level in thirty years.

Calculation of the delta t precisely for a Compstat-like program is not possible before the saturation process is complete. However, we can estimate the cumulative adoption curve using the data available from our survey. Rogers (1995, 257) notes that the adoption of an innovation generally "follows a normal bell-shaped curve" when plotted over time as a frequency distribution. In Figure 4, we develop a cumulative adoption curve based on this assumption extrapolating from our observed data. Based on this distribution and allowing saturation to include all police departments in our sample, we estimate a 90 percent saturation level between 2006 and 2007. As a 10 percent saturation using the observed data was defined as occurring between

1996 and 1997, our estimate of delta t is about ten years. Accordingly, if the adoption of Compstat-like programs were to follow the growth patterns observed in our data, Compstat would rank among the most quickly diffused forms of innovation.

THE ROLE OF THE NEW YORK POLICE DEPARTMENT IN THE DIFFUSION OF COMPSTAT-LIKE PROGRAMS

While a number of departments claim to have implemented elements of Compstat before New York formally introduced this model, the influence of the New York Police Department and its centrality in the diffusion of Compstat models is reflected in the large number of police agencies that came to New York to learn about Compstat (see Figure 5). An overwhelming number of departments who observed a Compstat meeting or department did so at the NYPD. While departments that have implemented Compstat-like programs have also visited Los Angeles, New Orleans, or Broward County, Florida, all places that have well publicized Compstat programs, New York is clearly the site where most police agencies go to learn about this innovation.

The profound influence of New York City's promotion of Compstat becomes even more apparent when considering the level of familiarity the surveyed departments claim to have with New York City's Compstat program. Table 5 shows that fully 40 percent of the smallest agencies that had not implemented a Compstat-like program considered themselves very or somewhat familiar with the NYPD's program. The percentage of the non-Compstat departments claiming familiarity increases with each size category, reaching 90 percent for the largest departments. A similar pattern (albeit at higher levels) is shown for Compstat departments.

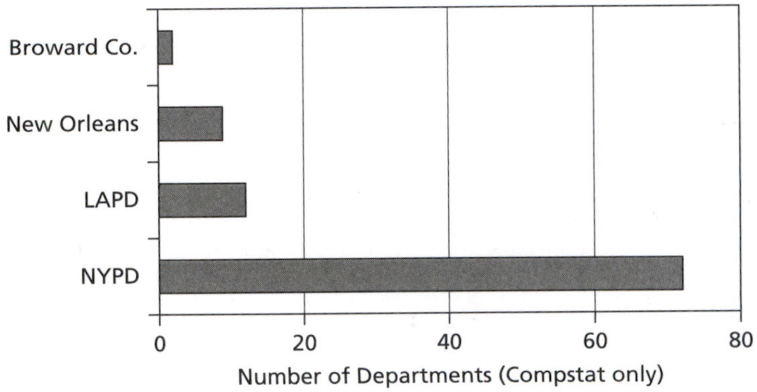

FIGURE 5 Where Compstat Departments Observed a Compstat Meeting

Table 5 Familiarity with the NYPD's Compstat by Department Size (Small Agency Sample Included)

	Percent Very or Somewhat Familiar with New York City's Compstat Program	
Number of Sworn	Compstat-like program not implemented	Compstat-like program implemented
50-99	40.3	71.4
100-299	55.7	73.2
300-499	66.7	100.0
>500	90.3	97.6

CHARACTERISTICS OF COMPSTAT DEPARTMENTS

The relationship between department size and the implementation of Compstat is not restricted to a broad comparison between the largest and smallest departments (as was illustrated in Table 1). As Figure 6 illustrates, there is a direct linear relationship between Compstat programs and department size across our sample. Almost 60 percent of departments with 500 or more sworn officers claim to have implemented a Compstat-like program. Forty-four percent of departments with between 300 and 499 sworn officers, and 31 percent of departments with between 200 and 299 sworn, say that they have established a Compstat-like program. This relationship between department size and implementation of a Compstat-like program is strong and statistically significant ($p < .001$).

We also find a statistically significant relationship of $p < .05$ between geographic region and implementation of Compstat-like programs (see Figure 7), though the relationship is not as strong as that of size of department. Over 40 percent of the departments with over 100 sworn officers in the South have implemented Compstat. This can be contrasted with the Northeast where only

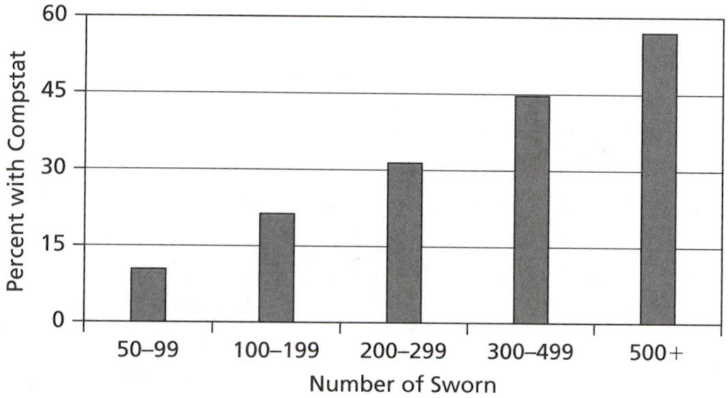

FIGURE 6 Implementation of Compstat and Department Size (Small Agency Sample Included)

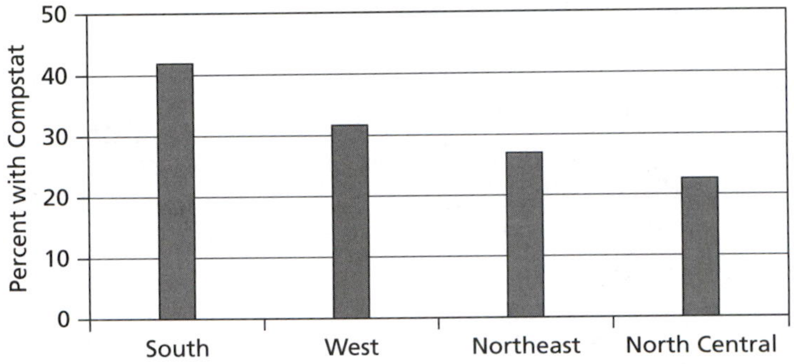

FIGURE 7 Compstat Departments by Region

26 percent of departments claim that they have implemented a Compstat-like program. We think that this distribution reflects a more general phenomenon in American policing over the last decade. While innovation, as in the case of Compstat, may begin in older police agencies in the East or Central regions of the country, police agencies in the South and West are, on average, more willing or perhaps more able to adopt those innovations.

MOTIVATIONS FOR ADOPTING COMPSTAT

While the survey did not ask respondents to indicate directly the motivations or priorities that led to the implementation of Compstat, it affords an opportunity to observe patterns from which we might infer such motivations. Respondents were asked to rank the top five goals that the chief executive pursued in the previous twelve months, selecting from a list of nineteen. We assigned a score of five to the top goal identified by each respondent, a four to the second ranking goal and so on, giving all unranked goals a score of zero. Because we wanted to examine priorities of departments close to when they implemented a Compstat program we excluded all departments that had implemented Compstat before 1998. We compare these departments with those that stated in the survey that they had not implemented a Compstat-like program and they were not planning to do so.

The average ranking for the nineteen goals was .78 for the large department sample. Only four of the nineteen items showed a statistically significant difference ($p < .05$) between the two groups of departments (see Table 6). Accordingly, there is a good deal of consensus in these police agencies regarding the priority goals for policing. However, departments that had recently implemented Compstat tended to rank the reduction of serious crime and increasing management control over field operations substantially higher than departments that were not planning implementation of Compstat. Departments that were not planning to implement a Compstat-like program

Table 6 Comparing Top Goals of Compstat Departments (pre-1998 implementation) with Departments Not Planning to Implement Compstat: Statistically Significant Differences

	Average Rank of Goal	
	Compstat-like program implemented after 1997 (n=79)	Not planning implementation (n=178)
Reduce serious crime	3.32	2.26
Increase police managers' control over field operations	.91	.44
Improve officers' policing skills	.46	.96
Improve employee morale	.28	.68

tended to score much higher than departments that claimed to recently have adopted Compstat on the ranks they assigned to improving officer policing skills and employee morale.

Departments that had recently implemented Compstat gave the reduction of serious crime a priority ranking 1.5 (3.32/2.26) times that of departments not planning to implement Compstat, and increasing management control a ranking of 2.1 (.91/.44) times that of such departments. Similarly, though in reverse, departments not planning to implement Compstat gave priority rankings to improving police officer skills that were on average 2.1 (.96/.46) times those of agencies that had claimed to have recently implemented a Compstat-like program, and priority rankings for improving employee morale that were on average 2.4 (.68/.28) times those of such agencies. This pattern is consistent with the interpretation that the dominant motivations for implementing Compstat are to secure management control over field operations that will reduce serious crime. At the same time, focus on improving skills and morale of street level officers—which, for example, have been high priorities in many community-policing programs—are relatively lower priorities for recently implemented Compstat departments.

CONCLUSIONS

Our study confirms what many police observers have noted: that Compstat has literally burst onto the American police scene. Our survey took place a few years after the development of Compstat in New York City, but it shows that police agencies throughout the United States have begun to adopt Compstat-like programs. We also find that the adoption of Compstat-like programs in police agencies follows a process of diffusion of innovation that is rapid as compared with innovations in other social and technological areas.

Our study also suggests that Compstat is being differentially implemented in police agencies. Not surprisingly, larger police agencies are more likely to adopt Compstat-like programs. We suspect that this is due to the relevance of Compstat for reinforcing management control in larger police agencies, where hierarchical control tends to be more problematic. Whatever the cause, there is a direct linear relationship in our study between the adoption of Compstat-like programs and the size of a police agency. We also find that agencies in the South and West of the country have been more likely to adopt Compstat-like programs, suggesting in our view the more general level of innovation found in agencies in these parts of the country.

The specific motivations for adopting Compstat vary across police agencies, but we found that the model of Compstat that has been touted in New York City has strongly influenced its adoption elsewhere in the country. Moreover, our study shows that the adoption of Compstat is strongly related to a department's expressed desire to reduce serious crime and increase management control over field operations. These goals for policing are much more prominent in agencies that have adopted Compstat than those that have not. At the same time, we found that agencies that had adopted Compstat programs are much less likely to focus on improving skills and morale of street-level officers. This suggests that Compstat may represent not only a new movement in police efforts to develop effective crime-control strategies, but also a departure from the priorities of "bubble-up" community-policing programs that rely on initiative from street-level officers.

DISCUSSION QUESTIONS

1. Who created COMPSTAT and why was it created?
2. How has COMPSTAT changed since 1994 and have these changes produced effective information to police departments?
3. Why do you see COMPSTAT in the larger police departments verses the smaller police departments.
4. Why is COMPSTAT rapidly spreading across the United States?

REFERENCES

Beer, Michael 1980. *Organizational Change and Development: A Systems View.* Santa Monica, CA: Goodyear Publishing Company.

Bratton, William J. 1999. Great Expectations: How Higher Expectations for Police Departments Can Lead to a Decrease in Crime. In *Measuring What Matters: Proceedings from the Policing Research Institute Meetings*, ed. Robert H. Langworthy, 11-26. Washington, DC: National Institute of Justice.

Bratton, William J. 1998. *Turnaround: How America's Top Cop Reversed the Crime Epidemic.* New York: Random House.

Bratton, William J. 1996. Cutting Crime and Restoring Order: What America Can Learn from New York's Finest.

Heritage Foundation Policy and Research Analysis, lecture no. 573, http://www.heritage.org/Research/Crime/HL573.cfm.

Grubler, Arnulf. 1991. Diffusion and Long-Term Patterns and Discontinuities. *Technological Forecasting and Social Change* 39: 159-180.

Gurwitt, Rob. 1998. The Comeback of the Cops. *Governing* (January): 14-19.

Kelling, George L., and William J. Bratton. 1998. Declining Crime Rates: Insiders' Views of the New York City Story. *Journal of Criminal Law and Criminology* 88: 1217-1232.

Kelling, George L., and Catherine M. Coles. 1996. *Fixing Broken Windows: Restoring Order and Reducing Crime in Our Communities*. New York: Free Press.

Law Enforcement News. 1997. NYC's Compstat Continues to Win Admirers. October 13.

Maas, Peter. 1998. What We're Learning from New York City. *Parade*, May 10.

Maple, Jack. 1999. *The Crime Fighter: Putting the Bad Guys Out of Business*. New York: Doubleday.

McDonald, Phyllis Parshall, Sheldon Greenberg, and William J. Bratton. 2001. *Managing Police Operations: Implementing the NYPD Crime Control Model Using COMPSTAT*. Belmont, CA: Wadsworth Publishing Co.

McDonald, Phyllis Parshall. 1998. *The New York City crime control model: A guide to implementation*. Unpublished manuscript. Washington, DC.

Merton, Robert K. 1940. Bureaucratic Structure and Personality. *Social Forces* 18:560-568.

Moore, Mark H. 1995. *Creating Public Value: Strategic Management in Government*. Cambridge, MA: Harvard University Press.

Office of Management Analysis and Planning. n.d. *The Compstat Process*. New York: New York City Police Department.

Remnick, David. 1997. The Crime Buster. *The New Yorker*, February 24 and March 3.

Rogers, Everett M. 1995. *Diffusion of Innovations*. New York: Free Press.

Sayre, Wallace Stanley, and Herbert Kaufman. 1960. *Governing New York City: Politics in the Metropolis*. New York: Russell Sage Foundation.

Silverman, Eli B. 1999. *NYPD Battles Crime: Innovative Strategies in Policing*. Boston: Northeastern University Press.

Silverman, Eli B. 1996. Mapping Change: How the New York City Police Department Re-engineered Itself to Drive Down Crime. *Law Enforcement News*, December.

Sparrow, Malcolm K., Mark H. Moore, and David B. Kennedy. 1990. *Beyond 911: A New Era for Policing*. New York: Basic Books.

U.S. Department of Justice, Bureau of Justice Statistics. 1998. *Census of State and Local Law Enforcement Agencies*, 1996, http://www.ojp.usdoj.gov/bjs/abstract/csllea96.htm.

Weisburd, David, Stephen Mastrofski, Ann Marie McNally and Rosann Greenspan. 2001. *Compstat and Organizational Change: Findings from a National Survey*. Report submitted to the National Institute of Justice by the Police Foundation.

Weisburd, David, Stephen Mastrofski, Ann Marie McNally, Rosann Greenspan, and James Willis. 2003. Reforming to Preserve: Compstat and Strategic Problem Solving in American Policing. *Criminology and Public Policy* 2 (3): 421-456.

32

Putting Justice Back into Criminal Justice

Notes for a Liberal Criminal Justice Policy

Samuel Walker
George F. Cole

Almost forty years ago the President's Commission on Law Enforcement and Administration of Justice recommended crime policies that attacked the causes of crime, that rehabilitated offenders, and that upheld civil rights. Many of these ideas have been criticized by conservatives as not effectively dealing with crime control. Samuel Walker and George Cole argue that the policies of the past four decades have not reduced crime and that liberal policies are more likely to achieve justice.

INTRODUCTION

The principal thrust of criminal justice policy for the last forty years has been the effort to enhance crime control: to arrest, prosecute, convict, and punish more offenders—or at least those who are guilty of serious crimes. There has

Source: "Putting Justice Back into Criminal Justice: Notes for a Liberal Criminal Justice Policy" by Samuel Walker and George F. Cole. Reprinted with permission from the authors.

been an increase in the number of actions that are criminalized; the War on Drugs serves as a prime example. That effort, which should be seen as a vast social experiment, has failed. We do not control crime any more effectively now than we did before, and have strained our correctional system well beyond its capacity. The time has come for a new direction in criminal justice policy. It is time to focus less on the tool of the law and reintroduce justice back into criminal justice.

The conservative domination of criminal justice policy is the result of several forces. Persistently high crime rates have produced deep public frustration about crime and about efficacy of the criminal justice system, and the perceived leniency of judges. Fear of crime, moreover, is inextricably bound up with issues of race—as evidenced by the Willie Horton issue in the 1988 presidential election. The 1990s gave us the debate over disparate punishments for powder versus crack cocaine, and in the twenty-first century we are still grappling with racial profiling and police brutality, as evidenced by the beating of Abner Louima (1997), the killing of Amadou Diallo (1999), and the Cincinnati riots in 2001. Evidence of the conservative mood on crime policy is everywhere. The philosophy of rehabilitation has been abandoned in favor of a new interest in punishment, retribution, incapacitation, and deterrence. But beyond punishing a broader range of crimes for a longer time, we are also turning to forms of punishment that are particularly liberty invasive—detaining people past their sentence if they are still designated as dangerous, or requiring compulsory medication for sex offenders if they are "potentially" violent. There has been particular interest in identifying and punishing the so-called career criminal or high-rate offender.[1] In its zeal to combat drugs, Congress and state legislatures have imposed long mandatory minimum sentences for drug offenders. The number of people incarcerated has skyrocketed 300 percent.[2] And, since the death penalty was reinstituted in 1977, more than eight hundred and twenty five individuals have been executed and by 2003 more than thirty-seven hundred were on death rows.[3]

The Supreme Court has followed the popular mood as expressed in national elections. On crime policy issues the Court has a razor-thin conservative majority. Unlike the Warren court in the 1960s, the Court today is willing to side with the asserted claims of law-enforcement officials. It has sanctioned drunk driving checkpoints, a public safety exception to the *Miranda* warning, and a good faith exception to the exclusionary rule, has dramatically limited the use of habeas corpus as an avenue of relief for convicted offenders, has allowed the use of pretextual traffic stops by police officers, and has held schools liable for student-on-student harassment.

This, at any rate, is the conventional wisdom about national crime policy over the past forty years. Upon closer inspection, however, the matter is a lot more complex. Change in the criminal justice system has not been completely dominated by a conservative agenda. There have been a number of very important changes that reflect the traditional liberal values of due process and equal protection. A surprising number of reforms have in fact achieved their stated goals.[4] These successes form the building blocks for a new direction in national criminal justice policy.

TWO DEADLY MYTHS ABOUT CRIMINAL JUSTICE POLICY

Creating a liberal criminal justice policy has to begin by demolishing two prevalent myths about national crime policy.

The first is that liberal reforms don't work. While many reforms reflecting liberal social values did prove to be failures, others have succeeded and represent significant improvements in criminal justice policy. The second myth is that conservative "get-tough" crime-fighting policies do work. There is no evidence to support this belief. We can view the past forty years as a vast social experiment in which conservative crime policies have been tried and found wanting.

THE FOUNDATIONS OF A LIBERAL CRIMINAL JUSTICE POLICY

A liberal criminal justice policy begins with a renewed commitment to the traditional liberal values of fairness and equality. These values are embodied in the constitutional principles of due process, equal protection of the law, and protection against cruel and unusual punishment. In many, but not always all, cases, liberal values are consistent with civil libertarian principles. The criminal justice system has two basic goals: to control crime and ensure justice. The time has come to put a renewed emphasis on justice for people who are the victims of discrimination at the hands of the system.

A renewed commitment to a national policy based on liberal values does not mean that every proposal cloaked in the garb of justice and fairness is a good idea. Good intentions alone do not make for good crime policy. Some of the well-intentioned reforms of the 1960s did fail. And we now see that the noble goals inherent in determinate sentencing have resulted in net-widening, particularly for those already disenfranchised. Nor does a commitment to liberal values mean that criminal behavior is excused. Wrongdoing should be punished. There is nothing inconsistent between liberal values and punishing those people found guilty of a serious crime. Liberal values, however, do require that use of the most serious penalties be carefully limited and tailored to the crime involved.

The second key element in a liberal criminal justice policy is a sober appreciation of the limits of the criminal justice system. We should not ask it to do things it cannot do. Criminal justice officials need to learn how to "just say no." When the public and elected officials ask it to do things that are beyond its power, responsible officials have a professional and social obligation to explain why they cannot. Already, for example, some police chiefs have been willing to publicly say that more arrests will not solve the nation's drug problem. The evidence on the limits of some of the more popular crime control programs is explored in detail later in this essay.[5]

The third element of a liberal approach to crime would be to direct public attention to the social problems that underlie criminal behavior. This point flows inexorably from a recognition of the limits of the criminal process. The problems the criminal justice system is asked to handle (murder, robbery) are the end product of larger forces, which in turn are influenced by social policies related to employment, housing, race relations, transportation, social welfare, and so on.

The limits of the criminal justice system are best symbolized by the police officer called for the third time to a domestic disturbance. The people involved have a lot of problems: unemployment, alcohol abuse, psychological problems, and so on. The officer cannot solve those problems. At best, he or she can do a professional job of resolving the immediate dispute. Policies based on liberal values should attempt to enhance that professionalism. But the ultimate solution to this particular domestic incident lies elsewhere, outside the justice system.

The Myth of Liberal Failure

The conservative mood that began in the mid-1970s and reached its peak with the election of Ronald Reagan as president in 1980 was based in part on a reaction against liberal social programs of the 1960s. According to the conventional wisdom, those policies failed. With respect to criminal justice policy, that indictment is partly true. But it is also true that we know many liberal reforms in criminal justice were tempered in the compromises that are characteristic of the legislative process. Our large-scale omnibus crime bills of the 1990s illustrate how difficult it is to maintain the integrity or spirit of the research idea or philosophy. The task of policy analysis at the moment is to sort out the failures and the successes.

The proper point of reference for this analysis is the 1967 report of the president's crime commission, *The Challenge of Crime in a Free Society*.[6] The commission's recommendations had two broad thrusts. The first was that more money needed to be spent on criminal justice. The administration of justice would be substantially improved by hiring more police, raising their salaries, subsidizing their education, expanding their training, developing more sophisticated communications technology, expanding pretrial services for arrestees, creating more community-based treatment programs for convicted offenders, funding research, and so on. This approach was consistent with liberal social policy generally: investing in programs to deal with social problems (for example, the so-called War on Poverty). Furthermore, the commission recommended that the federal government undertake, for the first time, comprehensive assistance to state and local criminal justice agencies.

In many respects, this goal was achieved. Spending on criminal justice did increase substantially. The federal government did initiate a comprehensive program of financial assistance. Whether or not all this spending improved the administration of justice, however, is another question altogether. Much of the increase in spending has been a result of inflation and rising crime rates. It is not clear that the spending has improved either the crime control effectiveness of the system or the quality of justice.

The second general element of the crime commission's recommendations was a general belief in rehabilitation. This consisted of several different parts. The first was the optimistic belief that criminal offenders would be rehabilitated (or corrected, or treated, or resocialized) into productive law-abiding lives. The second element was the belief that this could be more effectively achieved in a community-based setting. There was a strong anti-institutional current in the commission's recommendations. Diversion was better than prosecution; probation was better than imprisonment; parole was better than long imprisonment.

It is the commitment to rehabilitation that has been the target of the strongest reaction over the past twenty years. The concept of rehabilitation fell into disrepute and is, today, the object of much derision. The reaction against rehabilitation was summed up by Robert Martinson's survey of correctional treatment programs. Asking the basic question, "What works?" he found that few programs could persuasively demonstrate their effectiveness.[7] Although he did find that some programs were more effective than alternatives, the public translated his findings into the conclusion that "nothing works."

The idea that nothing works has, on occasion, been inflated into a general indictment of criminal justice reform, particularly reforms reflecting liberal values. Some analysts argue that well-intentioned reforms backfire and aggravate the problem they set out to correct.[8] Other analysts argue that reforms are simply negated by the informal resistance of criminal justice officials.[9]

The most extreme versions of the nothing-works argument arise from the literature on correctional programs. Martinson's report seemed to indict all rehabilitation programs. One widely cited example of failure is the so-called "net-widening" phenomenon. Some evaluations indicated that programs designed to divert offenders from the criminal justice system actually brought more people under some form of official control.

With respect to the issue of rehabilitation, the critics have a good point. Few correctional treatment programs have persuasively demonstrated that a convicted offender is less likely to recidivate because he or she received a particular kind of "treatment" as opposed to a conventional form of punishment or treatment. Thus, the prisoner who participated in group therapy sessions is no less likely to recidivate than the offender who did his time in prison and was released at the same time; intensive parole supervision is no more successful than normal supervision. The list could be extended.

The Hidden Successes of Criminal Justice Reform

Not all of the crime commission's recommendations failed, however. A number of them have had considerable vitality and are responsible for significant improvements in the administration of justice. Nearly all are consistent with liberal values. The most important of these goals are (1) the control of discretion, (2) the reduction of official misconduct, and (3) equal employment opportunity. In addition, there is a new goal, (4) community renewal, which is an indirect result of the crime commission's work.

Controlling Discretion

Perhaps the most important recommendation made by the crime commission was one that did not receive much attention at the time: the control of discretion by criminal justice officials. In fact, it is largely hidden in the commission's report, buried among innumerable other recommendations. It was most explicit with respect to the police, where the commission recommended that "police departments should develop and enunciate policies that give police personnel specific guidance for the common situations requiring exercise of police discretion."[10] It also recommended that departments develop "a comprehensive regulation" on officer use of firearms.[11] With respect to plea bargaining, the commission recommended the "establishment of explicit policies for the dismissal or informal disposition" of cases,[12] along with a written record for guilty pleas (pp. 337–338). Correctional agencies, meanwhile, were advised to adopt "explicit standards and administrative procedures" for decisions affecting prisoners.[13]

The commission's recommendations were part of a broader recognition of the phenomenon of discretion. The pioneering field research by the American Bar Foundation has identified discretion as one of the key elements of a new paradigm of the administration of justice. This paradigm was embodied in the now-famous flowchart of the criminal justice system. It not only provided a graphic representation of the "system" but also focused attention on the many decision points in the system.

In the intervening years, the control of discretion has become one of the central issues in criminal justice policy. Every decision point in the system has been subject to new controls. The police department SOP (Standard Operating Procedure) manual has become a large document and the principal instrument of contemporary police management. Bail decisions have been subject to controls by several different types of bail reform. Prosecutors' decisions to charge and to accept guilty pleas have been subject to both legislative and administrative controls. Sentencing, through mandatory provisions and sentencing guidelines have been instituted to limit discretion. Prisoners' rights litigation produced an intricate network of controls over correctional decisions, particularly disciplinary actions against inmates.

There are several notable examples of positive gains resulting from new controls over discretion. Restrictive deadly force policies have reduced the number of citizens shot and killed by the police. This has been accomplished without endangering police officers or contributing to an increase in the crime rate. Even more important, Lawrence W. Sherman's and Ellen G. Cohn's data indicates that the limits on shootings have reduced the racial disparity in persons shot and killed, from about 6:1 to 3:1.[14] Given the urgent nature of the race issue in American society, this reduction in police shootings is extremely important.

There are also new police department policies attempting to control officer discretion with respect to domestic violence and high-speed pursuits. It is still too early, however, to say whether these policies have had a significant effect on routine police practices.

Other attempts at discretion control have also produced some modest gains. The bail reform movement of the 1960s, which sought to guide bail-setting decision of judges, did reduce the number of pretrial detainees in many cities, thereby reducing discrimination against defendants because of their economic status. Some analysts, however, suggest that this reduction might have occurred even without the benefit of "reform." There is also some evidence that administrative controls over plea negotiations, in the form of written standards about dismissals and charge reductions, have resulted in greater consistency in case disposition.

The results of attempting to control judicial sentencing discretion through sentencing guidelines are even more dramatic. The greatest success appears to have occurred in Minnesota, where formal guidelines have significantly limited the use of imprisonment and have reduced, although not eliminated, racial and economic disparities in sentencing.[15] Minnesota has the second lowest imprisonment rate in the entire country (Maine is slightly lower). Moreover, it maintained a very low rate through the 1980s and 1990s while other states were drastically increasing their prison populations. As will be discussed below, limiting the use of imprisonment yields additional benefits in terms of maintaining humane conditions within prisons.

These successes represent building blocks for a more comprehensive effort to control discretion. One of the principal items on the agenda of a liberal criminal justice policy should be to continue the effort to control discretion for the purpose of reducing and eliminating racial and economic injustice. Formal controls over discretionary decision making should be extended to those decision points that remain free of controls. The most important of all is the arrest decision. Apart from the new policies on domestic violence, the decision of the police officer to take a suspect into custody is unregulated. A second extremely important area involves the complex relationship between the various decisions that constitute plea bargaining and sentencing.

Reducing Official Misconduct

A second major goal should be the elimination or reduction of official misconduct. The control of discretion is one means of achieving this goal, although there are several other means as well.

In the 1960s the most important attacks on official misconduct came through Supreme Court decisions. The exclusionary rule (*Mapp v. Ohio*) was essentially an attempt to eliminate illegal searches and seizures. The *Miranda* warning was an attempt to eliminate or reduce coercive interrogations. The *Gault* decision imposed some minimal standards of due process in juvenile court proceedings. The many prisoners' rights decisions have reduced some of the more barbaric practices in prisons.

One of the most important corollary effects of these Supreme Court decisions was a transformation of the working environment of policing. A study of narcotics detectives in Chicago found that court decisions had forced significant improvements in training and supervision. At the same time, a new generation of officers had come to accept the principles underlying court decisions protecting individual rights. Many stated that formal, externally imposed limits on police powers were a necessary means of controlling police conduct.[16]

Another important area of police misconduct involves the unjustified use of physical force and abusive language directed at citizens. The crime commission recommended that police departments create a formal process for handling citizen complaints. As a part of that, it also recommended that every department have a separate internal-affairs unit. To a large extent these recommendations have been fulfilled. Formal complaint procedures are now standard items in virtually all big-city departments. Despite this progress, the problem of police misconduct continues—as the killing of Amadou Diallo by New York City officers, the indictment of forty-three officers in Cleveland for cocaine dealing, and corruption of Los Angeles officers assigned to the Ramparts area clearly indicate. However, the number of fatal shootings is down since the 1970s, and grotesque incidents of physical brutality are rare rather than common events. Most observers believe that with the exception of certain departments, police behavior has in fact improved in most cities and counties over the past thirty years.[17]

Public attention has now focused on the effectiveness of police disciplinary procedures. The belief that they are inadequate has led to the creation of some form of civilian oversight procedures in about 80 percent of the police departments in the fifty largest cities.[18]

One of the most important consequences of the 1991 beating of Rodney King in Los Angeles has been the new focus on the phenomenon of the "problem-prone" officer. Investigations in Los Angeles, Kansas City, Boston, Houston, and elsewhere have consistently found that a small percentage of officers are involved in a disproportionate number of citizen complaints.[19]

The U.S. Civil Rights Commission identified this problem in 1981 and recommended that police departments create "early-warning systems" to identify these officers and take appropriate remedial steps.[20] Apparently, no department followed this recommendation. In the wake of the Rodney King incident, however, several police departments have begun to address the problem. A liberal criminal justice program would emphasize the reduction of police misconduct through the development of "early-warning" procedures in all police departments.

A major part of a liberal criminal justice program would be to continue the movement to instill respect for legal principles in criminal justice agencies and to encourage the growth of self-regulation. One form of self-regulation is accreditation. Litigation against police misconduct led to the creation of the Commission on Accreditation for Law Enforcement Agencies, which by 1998 accredited more than 460 agencies. Administrative rule making—controls over deadly force, handling of domestic violence, and high-speed pursuits—may be the most promising avenue for controlling police behavior in the immediate future.

Another significant area of official misconduct involves the abuse of prison inmates: physical brutality, prolonged sentences to solitary confinement, absence of due process in disciplinary procedures, and the violation of other individual rights such as access to reading material, visits, mail, and so forth. The crime commission called for "explicit standards and administrative procedures" regarding decisions affecting prisoners, but it did not give the matter a great deal of attention.[21] The commission's report was published before the modern prisoners' rights movement began. Since then, litigation based on constitutional principles has created a vast body of prisoners' rights, including physical facilities, services and programs, and the rights and privileges of inmates.

This litigation has had a far-reaching impact on American prisons. Many of the grossest abuses have been eliminated. Formal disciplinary procedures have been established. Also, litigation stimulated the correctional accreditation movement, which has resulted in the development of minimum standards for institutions. As is the case with the police, these developments represent a step in the direction of self-regulation and a transformation of the working environment of institutions. This is an important and overdue development that a liberal criminal justice program would continue to foster.

Many of the gains of the prisoners' rights movement began to be eroded in the 1980s, however. The dramatic increase in prison populations resulted in severe overcrowding, which, in turn, aggravated tensions among inmates, overloaded prison programs, and made routine supervision and discipline far more difficult.

The key to maintaining humane conditions in prisons—and in the process reducing both misconduct by officials and violence by inmates—is to limit the use of imprisonment. The state of Minnesota has shown that this can be done. The use of sentencing guidelines to control judicial discretion is a viable technique for limiting imprisonment. By limiting prison populations, states will be able to maintain humane conditions inside prisons within the constraints of limited state budgets.

Providing Equal Employment Opportunity

The crime commission also recommended the hiring of more racial minorities and women in policing. The commission produced devastating data on the under representation of African-Americans (then referred to as Negroes) in big-city police departments. In 1967 they represented 38 percent of the population of Atlanta but only 9.3 percent of the police force; 23 percent of the population of Oakland but only 2.3 percent of the police; 29 percent of the population of Detroit but only 3.9 percent of the police force.[22] Significantly, the employment of Hispanic Americans was not even mentioned.

In the intervening years, there has been considerable progress in minority employment. A study of the nation's 62 local police departments serving a population of 250,000 or more found that from 1990 to 2000 the percentage of African American officers rose to 20 percent of the force, Hispanic rose to 14 percent, and Asian/Pacific Islanders/Native Americans to 3.2 percent. The fact that minority officers constitute 38 percent of these departments represents a dramatic change in staff composition. In some departments the percentage of minority officers on the force equals the percentage of minorities in the community.[23]

Increased racial-minority employment has furthered several important goals. Most important, it represents a commitment to the principle of equality. In the process it has created real employment opportunities for thousands of people of color. It also has some positive impact on police–community relations. A more diverse police force does not appear to be an all-white occupying army. Diversity also alters the police subculture such that, today, national organizations representing African-American officers offer a different point of view on such issues as civilian review and police brutality. Together with the growing number of female officers, minority officers have shattered the once-homogeneous police subculture.

At the same time, however, increased minority employment has not fulfilled all the objectives of reformers. The impact on police–community relations is indirect at best. Studies of police behavior have found no significant differences between white and black officers. Thus, minority employment does not automatically translate into improved police work.

With respect to women in policing, there has been a revolution in social policy since the mid-1960s. At that time, women represented an estimated 1 percent of all sworn officers and were relegated to second-class status in police work: excluded from patrol work and restricted to juvenile, clerical, or other peripheral tasks. In some departments they were barred from promotion to the highest ranks as a matter of official policy. *The Task Force Report* (but not the main report) delicately raised the question of recruiting more women officers and assigning them to patrol duty.[24]

Following the crime commission's recommendation, the Police Foundation conducted an experiment on women on patrol in 1973. This was followed by similar experiments. Evaluations of these experiments reached consistent conclusions: despite minor differences, women officers performed just as well as male officers in routine patrol duty. The formal barriers to female recruitment quickly fell, in large part because of federal civil rights laws. The presence of women in policing increased to about 10 percent of all sworn officers by 1997. Informal barriers to employment, however, have remained.[25]

As has been the case with racial-minority employment, the addition of female officers has enhanced the principle of equality, provided real job opportunities for many women, and diversified the police subculture. At the same time, the addition of female officers has not fulfilled all reform expectations. The performance of female officers is essentially the same as male officers; thus, they are not fundamentally better able to mediate disputes. This notion rested on an inverse sexist stereotype of women as more verbal and nurturing than men.

There has also been progress in terms of the employment of women in other parts of the criminal justice system. The enrollment of women in law schools has increased substantially, and more women are securing jobs as prosecutors and defense attorneys, as well as election and appointment as judges. Women are also being employed as correctional officers in male institutions.

The increase in racial-minority and female employment in criminal justice represents a good beginning. But it is only a beginning. In every occupation category, both groups remain underrepresented. The studies of employment in policing all conclude that affirmative action plans have been critical to increased racial-minority and female employment. In 2003 the Supreme Court approved affirmative action for colleges and universities and the decision may be applied to criminal justice employment practices. A liberal criminal justice program would reaffirm the commitment to equal employment opportunity in all aspects of the criminal justice system.

Stimulating Community Renewal

Another important goal of a liberal criminal justice program is community renewal. Specifically, this refers to programs that criminal justice agencies might undertake to help communities resist the downward spiral of deterioration. This goal rests on the recognition that the criminal justice system cannot, by itself, control crime. It is a last-resort mechanism that comes into play only when all other instruments of social control have failed.

Some of the most creative thinking in policing over the past two decades argues that the police might play a vital role in community renewal. This idea has been given the label "community policing." The essence of community policing is that the police should de-emphasize traditional crime fighting in favor of attention to long-range problem solving and attention to small signs of disorder in the community.

Community policing is an indirect result of the crime commission's work. First, the commission's *Task Force Report: The Police* was the first full statement of the idea that the police have a diverse and complex role, with only a small part of their work being devoted to crime fighting.[26] This point was reinforced by the field studies of policing sponsored by the commission.[27] Subsequent studies found that increased patrol presence did not reduce crime[28] and that faster response time did not result in more arrests. All of this research demolished the "crime fighter" image of the police role.

Drawing upon this accumulated research, first Herman Goldstein and then James Q. Wilson and George Kelling sketched out new models of policing. Wilson and Kelling argued that the capacity of the police to control crimes was very limited and that, instead, they should concentrate on the less serious problems of disorder (which they identified by the metaphor of "broken windows").[29] This was designed to accomplish two things. First, it would enhance feelings of community safety. Second, it would help to arrest the process of community deterioration at an early stage and, thus, help prevent neighborhoods from sinking into serious crime. Wilson and Kelling's "Broken Windows" article was enormously influential and, more than anything else, launched the community policing movement.

Herman Goldstein, meanwhile, had already developed the concept of "problem-oriented policing."[30] He argued that the police should disaggregate the different aspects of their role and develop strategies to address particular ones. Problem-oriented policing is really a planning process. It does not tell the police what to do; it tells them only how to approach their mission in a different fashion. Community policing, at least as defined by Wilson and Kelling, did have a specific content. By de-emphasizing crime fighting, however, both approaches involved a very different conception of the police role.

In *Fixing Broken Windows*, a book written in response to the Wilson and Kelling article, George L. Kelling and Catherine Coles call for strategies to restore order and reduce crime in public spaces.[31] They point to many American cities where the police are paying greater attention to "quality-of-life crimes"—by arresting subway fare-beaters, rousting loiterers and panhandlers from parks, and aggressively dealing with those obstructing sidewalks, harassing, and soliciting. By handling these "little crimes," they argue that the police not only reduce disorder and fear but their actions help to stem deterioration of the community.

By the 1990s, community policing and problem-oriented policing had, together, become a national movement. Many, if not most, police departments claimed to be engaged in one or the other. Community policing received a major boost with the 1994 Violent Crime Control Act, which provided $8 billion to hire 100,000 additional police officers. The program is administered by the Office of Community Oriented Police Services (COPS), which requires that departments develop a community policing plan in order to receive the federal funds for additional officers.[32]

The jury is still out on community policing. There is the danger that it will be destroyed by its own early success. It has quickly become a fad, in some cases nothing more than a rhetorical phrase with no content. As was the case with team policing thirty years ago, many departments are jumping on the bandwagon with no planning. In some instances, community policing has become a trendy label for putting more police on the streets in response to community fears about crime. Even under the best of circumstances—assuming careful planning, training, and supervision—there are serious limits to what community policing could accomplish in the way of community renewal. The key word here is *renewal*. Taking Wilson and Kelling at their word, the police might be able to help communities resist the downward spiral of deterioration. That, however, assumes the existence of a viable community. Yet in the most crime-ridden neighborhoods today, no such community exists. One of the main characteristics of economically devastated neighborhoods is the absence of the institutions and informal networks that make up a "community." Indeed, one could argue that drug gangs thrive because they fill that void, providing identity, protection, work, and income. In this respect, community policing has been oversold.

Nonetheless, community policing represents a bold concept of the police role. It recognizes that the police cannot, by themselves, control crime, but that they might be able to help communities renew themselves and resist the forces that lead to high levels of crime.

The blunt fact is that the police cannot create a community where one does not exist. No amount of creative community policing can hope to overcome the devastating effect of massive unemployment and declining job opportunities—the conditions that affect today's inner cities. The real solution to the crime problem lies outside the realm of criminal justice policy: in the realm of economic policy and job creation. This conclusion is not based on liberal sentimentality about the "roots" of crime; it reflects a sober assessment of what the criminal justice system can and cannot do.

THE FAILURE OF TOUGH CRIME CONTROL

For the past forty years, national criminal justice policy has been dominated by a conservative "get tough with crime" approach. This represents a far longer period than the heyday of 1960s liberalism. We can now look back and evaluate it as we would any other social experiment.

Contrary to public opinion and the claims of politicians, rates for many crimes have dropped since the early 1980s. The National Crime Victimization Surveys have shown that the greatest declines are in property crimes, but crimes of violence have also dropped, especially since 1993.[33] These declines, however, can be attributed largely to demographic changes, particularly the aging of the baby boom generation, fewer users of crack cocaine, and the positive economic climate of the 1990s. There is little evidence that the "tough on crime policies" have had much impact on the crime problem.[34]

What is evident is that the conservative experiment has been costly. Operating the criminal justice system costs taxpayers more than $100 billion a year. A major portion of these resources could be diverted to the underlying causes of criminal behavior—poor housing, unemployment, and racial injustice. Another price of the tough crime control policies has been an erosion of civil rights and liberties—especially for racial and ethnic minorities. Tough incarceration policies have devastated poor communities. With large numbers of young males in prison, families live in poverty, and children grow up without guidance from their fathers and older brothers.

It is now the conventional wisdom, even among conservatives, that traditional police crime control efforts will not reduce crime. Adding more patrol officers, increasing response time, and adding more detectives will not produce either fewer crimes or more arrests. The evidence is also overwhelming on the long-standing controversy over the exclusionary rule. Studies have convincingly found that the rule affects a tiny percentage of criminal cases at best.

With respect to bail, the federal government and many states have adopted some form of preventive detention that is designed to allow judges to deny bail to allegedly dangerous offenders. The Supreme Court upheld the federal law in 1987. The impact of preventive detention on crime has been negligible. Prior studies indicated that serious crime by persons on pretrial release was confined to a small percentage of defendants and that it was impossible to identify exactly which ones they were. Evaluations of the federal preventive detention law have found little change in the total percentage of defendants being held before trial. Judges have always practiced a covert form of preventive detention. The new procedures have yielded no gain.[35]

With respect to the disposition of criminal cases, studies have persuasively demonstrated that plea bargaining is not a loophole by which dangerous people beat the system. Persons who have committed a serious crime against a stranger, who have a prior criminal record, and against whom there is solid evidence are charged with the top offense, convicted of that offense, and sentenced to prison. "Career criminal" prosecution programs have produced no net gain in the imprisonment of dangerous criminals because those people were being treated fairly harshly under normal conditions.[36]

With respect to sentencing, there has been an enormous increase in imprisonment. The prison population more than tripled between 1980 and 2000. With more than two million behind bars, the size of the United States prison population is now the world's largest. This growth has largely resulted from changes to sentencing statutes that emphasize retribution and incapacitation through policies or mandatory minimums, "three strikes," "truth in sentencing," and restrictions on parole release. Community corrections, initially conceptualized as an alternative to incarceration, are now being used to extend sentences. Split sentences are not replacing lengthy sentences, they are being used in addition to them.

Trends with respect to drug offenses dramatize the failure of the conservative experiment even further. In every state and the federal system, the most dramatic change has been the increase in the number of incarcerated drug offenders. Yet there is no evidence that this has curbed the drug problem through either incapacitation or deterrence. In fact, the problem of drug gangs and gang-related violence worsened in the early 1990s—after more than fifteen years of increasing use of imprisonment. The much-publicized idea of selective incapacitation had no effect on policy, in large part because normal prosecution and sentencing were already highly selective.

Nor has the revival of the death penalty had any discernible effect on crime. The sudden upsurge in murders in the early 1990s, almost all of them related to inner-city drug gang activity, occurred after a yearly average of more than twenty people were executed in the mid-1980s. Only at the end of the century were a few politicians, such as Governor George Ryan of Illinois, willing to raise questions about the possibility that innocent people have been executed.

In short, the conservative criminal justice program of "getting tough" with crime has failed in all of its manifestations.

CONCLUSION

A sound criminal justice policy begins with a sober respect for the limits of what can be accomplished through the criminal justice system.

The first principle is that criminal justice agencies—police, courts, prisons—cannot make significant changes in the level of criminal behavior. This is where much of the liberal thinking of the 1960s went wrong. It assumed that the right kind of programs—diversion of minor offenders, community-based treatment programs, and the like—would affect the lives of offenders: resocializing them into law-abiding lives. There is no reason to believe that today. By the same token, it should be noted that many of the popular conservative crime control programs of the past thirty years assume an ability to change people's behavior. To cite one example: the concept of deterrence assumes that by raising the cost of crime, potential offenders will choose not to offend. Altering criminal justice programs, in short, has little effect on criminal behavior.

The crime commission also assumed that pouring more money into the justice system—for more personnel, better equipment, better training, more research—would enhance the crime control capacity of the system. There is no support for that assumption either.

This is not to say that many of the crime commission's proposals were entirely wrong. More money, resources, and research may not reduce crime but it can help to improve the *quality* of justice. And that is an important goal. By the same token, community-based programs for convicted offenders may not rehabilitate them, but they may well be cheaper and more humane forms of punishment. By 2002 and 2003, financial stresses have forced a member of states to consider ways to reduce their prison populations and the attendant costs.

If our capacity to affect the behavior of criminals and potential criminals is very limited, we can control the behavior of criminal justice officials. The evidence indicates that we can control their discretion, we can reduce misconduct, and we can eliminate employment discrimination. These goals, which reflect the liberal values of fairness and equality, are the proper goals of a national criminal justice policy.

DISCUSSION QUESTIONS

1. Describe the key elements of a liberal criminal justice policy.
2. Explain the recommendation of the control of discretion, and discuss whether or not this recommendation has been successful.
3. Discuss the ways in which the criminal justice system has tried to reduce official misconduct.
4. What are some of the benefits associated with increased hiring of racial minorities and women in the criminal justice system?
5. How could community policing help with the goal of community renewal?
6. Describe how the conservative "get tough with crime" policies have failed.

NOTES

1. Alfred Blumstein et al., *Criminal Careers and "Career Criminals"* (Washington, D.C.: National Academy Press, 1986).

2. U.S. Department of Justice, Bureau of Justice Statistics, *Bulletin* (April, 2003).

3. NAACP Legal Defense and Educational Fund, *Death Row USA* (Winter, 2003).

4. A full discussion of these developments is in Samuel Walker, *Taming the System: The Control of Discretion in Criminal Justice, 1950–1990* (New York: Oxford University Press, 1993).

5. The limits of the "get-tough" approach are examined in Samuel Walker, *Sense and Nonsense about Crime and Drugs: A Policy Guide*, 5th ed. (Belmont, Calif.: Wadsworth, 2001).

6. U.S. President's Commission on Law Enforcement and Administration of Justice, *The Challenge of Crime in a Free Society* (Washington, D.C.: Government Printing Office, 1967).

7. Robert Martinson, "What Works? Questions and Answers about Prison Reform," *Public Interest* 35 (Spring, 1974): 22–54.

8. Eugene Doleschal, "The Dangers of Criminal Justice Reform," *Criminal Justice Abstracts* 14 (March, 1982): 133–152.

9. Malcolm Feeley, *Court Reform on Trial* (New York: Basic Books, 1983).

10. President's Commission, *The Challenge of Crime*, p. 104.

11. Ibid., p. 119.

12. Ibid., p. 134.

13. Ibid., pp. 181–182.

14. Lawrence W. Sherman and Ellen G. Cohn, *Citizens Killed by Big City Police, 1970–1984* (Washington, D.C.: Crime Control Institute, 1986).

15. Terance D. Miethe and Charles A. Moore, "Socioeconomic Disparities under Determinate Sentencing Systems: A Comparison of Preguideline and Postguideline Practices in Minnesota," *Criminology* 23 (May, 1985): 337–363. Minnesota Sentencing Guidelines Commission, *Guidelines and Commentary*, rev. ed. (St. Paul: August, 1981).

16. "The Exclusionary Rule and Deterrence: An Empirical Study of Chicago Narcotics Officers," *University of Chicago Law Review* 54 (1987): 1016–1069.

17. Samuel Walker, *Police Accountability: The Role of Citizen Oversight* (Belmont, Calif.: Wadsworth, 2001), p. 45.

18. Ibid., p. 40.

19. Ibid., p. 110.

20. Samuel Walker, *The Police in America*, 3d ed. (New York: McGraw-Hill, 1999), p. 285.

21. President's Commission, *The Challenge of Crime*, pp. 181–182.

22. President's Commission, *Task Force Report: The Police* (Washington, D.C.: Government Printing Office, 1967), p. 168.

23. Brian A. Reaves and Andrew L. Goldberg, *Local Police Departments, 1997*. (Washington, D.C.: Bureau of Justice Statistics, U.S. Government Printing Office, 2000).

24. President's Commission, *Task Force Report: The Police*, (Washington, D.C.: Government Printing Office, 1967), p. 168.

25. U.S. Department of Justice, Bureau of Justice Statistics, *Fiscal Year 1996: At a Glance* (Washington, D.C.: Government Printing Office, 1996), p. 25.

26. President's Commission, *Task Force Report: The Police*.

27. Albert Reiss, *The Police and the Public* (New Haven, Conn.: Yale University Press, 1971).

28. George Kelling et al., *The Kansas City Preventive Patrol Experiment* (Washington, D.C.: The Police Foundation, 1974).

29. James Q. Wilson and George L. Kelling, "Broken Windows: The Police and Neighborhood Safety," *Atlantic Monthly* 249 (March, 1982): 29–38.

30. Herman Goldstein, "Improving Policing: A Problem-Oriented Approach," *Crime and Delinquency* 25 (1979): 236–258; Herman Goldstein, *Problem-Oriented Policing* (New York: McGraw-Hill, 1990).

31. George L. Kelling and Catherine M. Coles, *Fixing Broken Windows: Restoring and Reducing Crime in our Communities* (New York: Free Press, 1996).

32. U.S. Office of Community Oriented Policing Services, *COPS Office Report* (Washington, D.C.: Government Printing Office, 1997).

33. U.S. Department of Justice, Bureau of Justice Statistics, *National Crime Victimization Survey* (August, 2000).

34. *The Crime Drop in America*, ed. Alfred Blumstein and Joel Wallman (New York: Cambridge University Press, 2000).

35. Lynn Zimmer, "Proactive Policing against Street-Level Drug Trafficking," *American Journal of Police IX* (1990, No. 1), 43–74.

36. Eleanor Chelimsky and Judith H. Dahmann, *National Evaluation of the Career Criminal Program: Final Report* (McLean, Va.: Mitre Corp., 1979).

Index

C

H

I

N

O

P

X

Y

Z